Priorities for Britain's modern railway

Britain's fastest domestic trains, the Hitachi Class 395s, Nos 395001 and 395002 on test near Charing on 31 August 2008. Patrick Seale

HSBC Rail is pleased once again to support The Modern Railway, which I hope you will find provides a useful guide to Britain's railway industry.

The long-lasting assets that make up our railway system require long-term investment and in-service care, and HSBC Rail is pleased to be playing its part in the introduction of new train fleets, including Britain's fastest-ever domestic trains, and modern new rolling stock for one of the most intensive urban networks, in Scotland. Also at the top of the agenda is the importance of making sure that our train fleets are as efficient and reliable as possible, giving good value for money, and meeting high environmental standards.

By the end of 2009, the fleet of 29 Hitachi 140mph trains will be running domestic services on High Speed 1 between London and Kent. HSBC Rail took delivery of the first train in August 2007, the first tangible sign of an investment worth some £260million, and an intensive programme of tests and trials quickly got under way. In trials on HS1 these Class 395 trains have reached speeds in excess of 150mph, over 10mph above the maximum in normal service. In a year, 32,000 miles of running were completed.

Hitachi has used friction stir welding in building the Class 395s - this strengthens the area around the joints to maintain the properties and strength of the aluminium, and also allows the body to be constructed to the least weight possible, though meeting British safety standards does increase the mass of the trains compared with Japanese.

As well as improving the quality of life for thousands of commuters, I believe the high-speed service will be a shot in the arm for the local economy in Kent and east London.

HSBC Rail is also delighted to be backing a fleet of new electric trains for Scotland in a £200million partnership with Transport Scotland, First ScotRail and Siemens. The biggest electric train order in Scotland for a decade, the 130 new vehicles will add capacity to the network, enabling current electrification plans to go ahead while creating jobs to operate and maintain the new fleet.

Getting the best from our existing train fleets has been a particular and long-term focus for HSBC Rail. As well as the high-speed trains, HSBC Rail's partnership with Hitachi includes the programme to re-equip our Class 465 Kent suburban fleet with a new Hitachi traction package, which is estimated to bring a 16 to 20% saving in power consumption and an improvement in 'miles per casualty' (MPC) reliability figures from 12,000 to 20,000.

Another approach is the Train Automatic Performance Analysis System – TAPAS. This condition-monitoring system has helped drive up the reliability of Southern's Class 455 fleet from 7,000 to 18,000 MPC. A partnership between HSBC Rail, Southern, and software solutions company Tessella, it analyses - off the train - all the data captured in the train's 'black box' data recorder, working from the reality of 'in service' measurement collected over long periods, using sophisticated analysis modules.

Southern's focus on good depot maintenance performance is greatly helped when staff can go straight to the problems, rather than first having to identify the faults. This has resulted in the previously undreamt-of achievement of only four 'no defect found' reports in 18 months.

Another of HSBC Rail's long term commitments is in supporting the continued performance and reliability of the East Coast InterCity route's Class 91 locomotives, in collaboration with the train operator - and also now with Wabtec Rail. A major contract signed in 2007 with Wabtec made Doncaster the home for heavy maintenance and overhaul of the Class 91. The Class 91 locomotives, refurbished and re-equipped to improve reliability, are now consistently achieving about 48,000 MPC, with the InterCity 225 fleet achieving around 22,000 MPC: this makes it the best performing intercity fleet.

There are many other programmes of work that I could mention. Assets such as wheelsets have become 40% more expensive in 2008 alone. So we are developing strategies, in collaboration with ATOC and the train operating companies, which include all aspects of improving wheelset management in order to treat these precious assets appropriately. First TransPennine's Class 185 diesel multiple-units have been modified to increase their fuel efficiency. And the industry is looking closely at how train driving techniques can cut fuel and power costs, and - further ahead - at how 'green' benefits can be designed into new rolling stock.

With the majority of our fleet electric-powered, HSBC Rail also has a special interest in plans for further electrification, which will make clear the future value of investment in both electric and diesel trains. Whatever the challenges, we look forward to working in partnership within the rail industry to help deliver services that satisfy the most important people in our business, the railways' customers.

Chris Moss
HSBC Rail's head of engineering services

Photo: Alstom

Photo: Network Rail

127 Chinese built wagons for Europe: CSRE Ltd
128 English, Welsh & Scottish Railway
130 First GBRf
131 Direct Rail Services
132 Freightliner

134 Freight, haulage and rolling stock providers: Fastline Freight, Riviera Trains, Cotswold Rail, West Coast Railway, Cargo D

INNOVATIONS
140 Regen revolution cuts energy costs and emissions: Technical Review by Roger Ford

143 Atkins Rail: Innovation: beating the resource crunch

144 Earls Court to host next Railtex show
- The Railway Industry Innovation Awards
- Golden Spanners focus on reliable trains
- The Fourth Friday Club
- Innovation file

KEY PROJECTS AND CONSULTANTS

150 - Key projects
- Thameslink programme
- Crossrail
- London 2012 - The Olympics
- Scotland

- West Coast route modernisation
- King's Cross redevelopment
- Heathrow Airtrack
- Intercity Express Programme

154 Consultant files – supporting rail developments

INFRASTRUCTURE MAINTENANCE AND RENEWAL
158 Network Rail's investment and availability challenges
- The main infrastructure contractors

SIGNALLING AND CONTROL
166 Westinghouse Rail Systems
168 Signalling and Control: Plans for implementing ERTMS shape scope of signalling renewals

LIGHT RAIL AND METRO
174 Light Rail and Metro - sector developments spotlighted, systems reviewed

182 Transport for London
- London Underground
- London Overground

INTO EUROPE
188 Halcrow's growth focus
190 Into Europe - Ken Harris reviews significant European rail developments

The Modern Railway

Editor:	Ken Cordner
Production Editor:	David Lane
Contributors:	Roger Ford
	John Glover
	Chris Shilling
	Ken Harris
	Tony Miles
	Chris Cheek
Advertisement Manager:	Chris Shilling
Advertising Production:	Jenny Bell
	Xania Mansell
Graphic Design:	Matt Chapman
Project Manager:	David Lane
Publishing Manager:	Paul Appleton
Chairman:	David Allan

The Modern Railway is published by:
Ian Allan Publishing Limited,
Hersham, Surrey KT12 4RG

The Modern Railway is supported by:
- The Institution of Railway Operators
- RFG Rail Freight Group
- The Railway Forum
- Railway Industry Association
- RSA Railway Study Association

Printing:
Ian Allan Printing Limited,
Hersham, Surrey KT12 4RG

Purchasing additional copies of The Modern Railway: Please contact our Mail order department by calling 01932 266622 or by email at subs@ianallanpublishing.co.uk
Corporate and bulk purchase discounts are available on request.

Thank you!
We are very grateful to the many individuals from businesses in all sectors of the railway who have kindly provided help in compiling The Modern Railway.
Information contained in The Modern Railway was believed correct at the time of going to press in November 2008. We would be glad to receive corrections and updates which will be published with the June issue of *Modern Railways* magazine.
Please contact Chris Shilling on 01778 421550 or by email at chris@shillingmedia.co.uk with your updated details.

© Ian Allan Publishing Ltd 2008
All rights reserved. No part of this publication may be reproduced or transmitted in any form by any means, electronic or mechanical, including photocopying, recording or by any information storage and retrieval system, without prior permission in writing from the copyright owner. Multiple copying of the contents of the publication without prior written approval is not permitted.

Cover photos: National Express, Paul Bigland, Tony Miles, Alstom and Brian Morrison
ISBN 978-0-7110-3375-7

Foreword

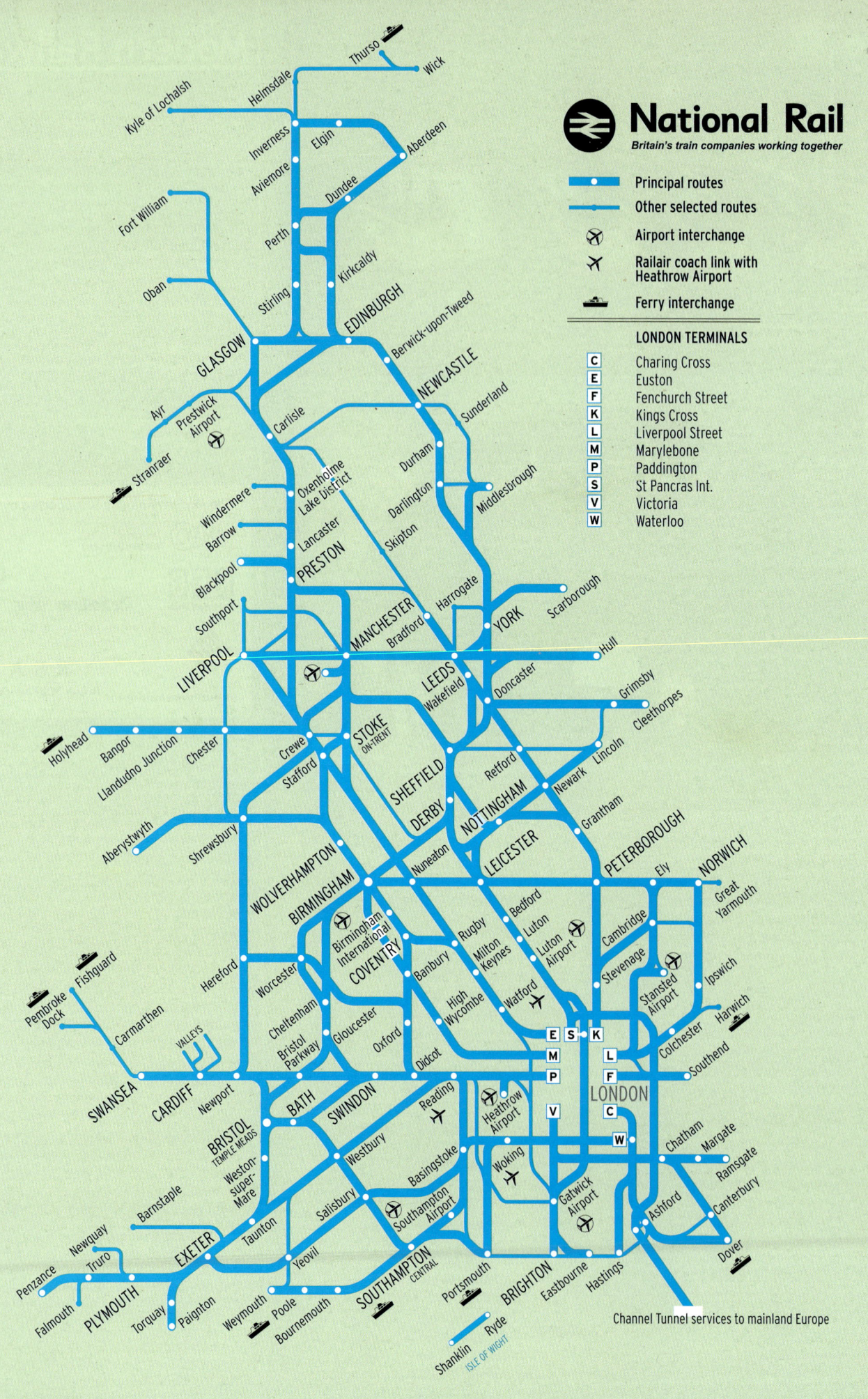

National Rail
Britain's train companies working together

- Principal routes
- Other selected routes
- ✈ Airport interchange
- ✈ Railair coach link with Heathrow Airport
- ⛴ Ferry interchange

LONDON TERMINALS

C	Charing Cross
E	Euston
F	Fenchurch Street
K	Kings Cross
L	Liverpool Street
M	Marylebone
P	Paddington
S	St Pancras Int.
V	Victoria
W	Waterloo

Channel Tunnel services to mainland Europe

© ATOC 2007. All rights reserved. MT/IP 12/07 - A

Setting the Agenda

In association with

ALSTOM

- securing improvements
- understanding the needs of rail passengers
- influencing decisions
- empowering rail passengers

www.passengerfocus.org.uk

0870 336 6000
contact@passengerfocus.org.uk

Passengerfocus
putting rail passengers first

A symbol of confidence - the striking concept design by Foreign Office Architects for the £600million Gateway project to transform Birmingham New Street station.

Meeting the industry's challenges

Britain's railway industry moves into 2009 in a much more healthy condition than most other sectors, despite the financial sector problems and the resulting effects on the economy. Further growth in passenger and freight traffic is forecast, although the rate of growth may slow, and the rail sector is undertaking some very large spending programmes, already at historically high levels, with a high level of government commitment. National infrastructure and London network expenditure on maintenance, renewals and enhancements is running at around £8bn per year and continuing to rise, as well as orders anticipated for some 3,500-5,500 vehicles for the national railway.

But delivering the programmes with the required efficiency gains will require a major joint effort by all parts of the industry. One of the key messages that we have been emphasising is that the supply side of the industry is fundamental to the economics of the railway. However, few supply side challenges are those of the suppliers alone; most are shared with clients. Similarly, most challenges to clients depend on suppliers for resolution, so the answer has to be joint action. Without it, success will not be achieved.

RIA has been working closely with Network Rail, ATOC and others in addressing some of the key issues. We have identified key changes needed to process, technology and culture to allow more efficient and cost-effective delivery, frequently by doing things differently. We need to encourage investment in plant, training and business infrastructure to deliver larger programmes at lower cost. We need to encourage innovation, and to identify where waste is occurring and remove it. Above all we need to build supplier confidence through clarity, consistency and delivery of demand forecasts and policies at reasonable levels of baseload.

Effective planning is also fundamental, as the many major programmes have extensive interdependencies. For example, projects on the Great Western main line in the next few years are likely to include the Intercity Express Programme, ERTMS, Reading remodelling, Crossrail and electrification. Bringing these together will be a major cross-industry challenge.

And we are not alone. We face competition for resources from projects in many other sectors, not least the Olympics, as well as from a huge number of major railway projects across the world. The availability of skilled staff is one of the greatest challenges facing us. In a recent RIA survey, some 80% of members reported their businesses as currently affected by a skills shortage, with labour availability being the leading or one of the leading constraints on output across virtually all sectors. There is an obvious concern that this could increase costs, and there are a number of initiatives seeking to address this, including Network Rail's graduate and apprentice facilities; Project Brunel, seeking to identify skills gaps throughout the industry; and the proposed National Rail Engineering Skills Academy.

The task is substantial. Much needs to be done, but the process is underway. Suppliers have a key role to play, and are contributing strongly already.

Jeremy Candfield
Director General
Railway Industry Association

The prime candidate for further electrification is the Great Western main line. One of the present diesel High Speed Trains forms the 10.30 from Bristol Temple Meads to London Paddington on 29 August 2008, headed by power car No 43188. The location is Reading. Tony Miles

Transport Secretary launches strategy study

Railway electrification and new railways are included in the remit of a programme of work announced by the Secretary of State for Transport, Geoff Hoon. He said he wants to ensure that the best use is made of national transport networks and to accelerate the process of identifying where future expansion is needed.

Our national transport networks are essential for people going about their day to day lives, said Mr Hoon: 'In order to stimulate Britain's economic growth and support our position as a leading world economy it is essential that we make the right long-term investments in our transport infrastructure today and that we plan for future growth, in a way which is consistent with reducing greenhouse gas emissions overall.

'The work will build on the recommendations by Sir Rod Eddington and the Government's October 2007 response, "Towards a Sustainable Transport System"'.

The Minister of State, Lord Adonis, is chairing a National Networks Strategy Group, with senior partners from the Highways Agency, Network Rail, HM Treasury and other government departments as required. The group is focusing on two issues: first, how to make best use of the existing key networks, for example, by the selective extension of rail electrification, or the wider implementation of hard shoulder running on motorways to provide additional capacity for motorists and to give them greater reliability and choice.

Alongside this, the study will focus on longer term solutions for the strategic corridors. This will include consideration of wholly new rail lines, including high speed rail. Mr Hoon said, 'We are committed to developing a modern sustainable rail system that supports economic growth, including housing development, and the climate change agenda. New lines have great potential and it is important that we start now to plan for future growth.

'However, it is crucial that the case for such investment is underpinned by robust evidence on long-term demand projections and a clear understanding of the capacity of the existing networks, and takes full account of relevant geographical, technical and environmental considerations. The National Networks Strategy Group will build on the work on new lines being undertaken by Network Rail.'

Lord Adonis has indicated that he expects the study to produce, in the first half of 2009, a plan for rail electrification and possibly long-term capacity improvements.

New ministerial team
Heading the new Department for Transport ministerial team appointed in autumn 2008, Rt Hon Geoff Hoon MP, Secretary of State for Transport, has been MP for Ashfield since 1992. He was previously Chief Whip and Parliamentary Secretary to the Treasury and has held a number of Cabinet positions, including Secretary of State for Defence and Leader of the House of Commons.

Lord Andrew Adonis, Minister of State for Transport, was previously Parliamentary Under Secretary of State for Schools and Learners at the Department for Children, Schools and Families. Prior to this he worked as adviser to Prime Minister, Tony Blair, on education and public services and as Head of the No 10 Policy Unit, joining in 1998 after a career as an academic and journalist.

His responsibilities include national networks (strategic road network and rail), Crossrail, environment and climate change, cleaner fuels and vehicles.

Paul Clark MP, Parliamentary Under Secretary of State for Transport, has responsibility for city and regional networks including light rail and Transport & Works Act orders.

Jim Fitzpatrick MP, Parliamentary Under Secretary of State, has responsibilities including transport in London.

The Institution of Railway Operators

GLASGOW CALEDONIAN UNIVERSITY

Professional Qualifications

- **Bachelor of Science Degree**
- **Diploma in Higher Education**
- **Certificate Course**

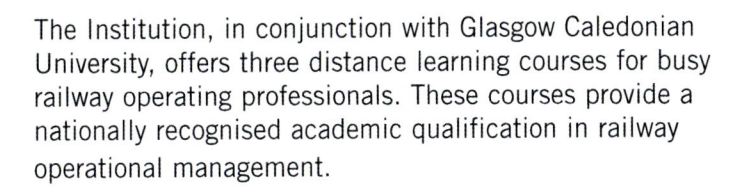

The Institution, in conjunction with Glasgow Caledonian University, offers three distance learning courses for busy railway operating professionals. These courses provide a nationally recognised academic qualification in railway operational management.

If you want to improve your industry knowledge and enhance your career prospects, look up our courses at: **http://www.railwayoperators.org/pages/education.html**

If you have questions about the course availability and application processes, consult the FAQs on the website or email Mike Hill: **education@railwayoperators.org**

Diploma modules
Personal and professional development; railway operating principles; customer service; managing people; train planning and performance management; safety law and management; railway business organisation and an end of course project.

Degree modules
Personal and professional development; managing passenger and freight operations; train planning and performance management; safety law and management; train movement control systems; emergency planning, mishap management and investigation; railway engineering; railway economics and an end of course project.

Certificate course
Personal and professional development, background to railway operations, basic railway operations, effective learning, information and communication skills and an end of course project.

The Institution of Railway Operators

PO Box 128, Burgess Hill, West Sussex RH15 0UZ, United Kingdom
Tel: 01444 248931 - Fax: 01444 246392 - Email: admin@railwayoperators.org - Website: www.railwayoperators.org

Setting the Agenda

2009 – entering unknown territory

In an economic downturn, the railway industry needs the confidence to justify major long term spending, writes Roger Ford, Industry & Technology Editor of Modern Railways magazine

After 12 years of uninterrupted economic growth since privatisation, the railway industry is facing its first recession. The downturn could not have come at a worse time, with the High Level Output Specification (HLOS) and the associated Statement of Funds Available (SoFA) for England and Wales based on sustained annual passenger revenue growth of 8% over the five years of Control Period 4 (CP4), which starts on 1 April 2009.

While the total cash available to the railway increases during CP4, government subsidy remains effectively constant, according to the SoFA published in July 2007.

If subsidy is to remain constant, as the government intended, the farepayer's contribution to the overall cost of the railway will have to increase from half to two-thirds of the total income. In other words, ticket sales will have to provide a greater proportion of a larger sum.

Meeting this aspiration will mean annual farebox revenue rising from around £5.6billion in 2007-08 to £8 billion in 2013/14 (Chart 1). This growth will be generated, in part, by train operators being allowed to increase regulated fares by one percent above inflation (RPI+1%), except for Southeastern which is allowed RPI+3%. Unregulated fares will also have to rise above inflation.

Growth

When the HLOS was published, the government believed that the industry was in 'the most stable position in 50 years'. This was because 'growth is delivering significantly enhanced revenues while industry cost control continues to improve'. As we go to press, just over 18 months on, the financial position is changing fast, but predicting the effects of the economic situation on the railway is almost impossible.

Forecast revenue growth – England & Wales (£million)

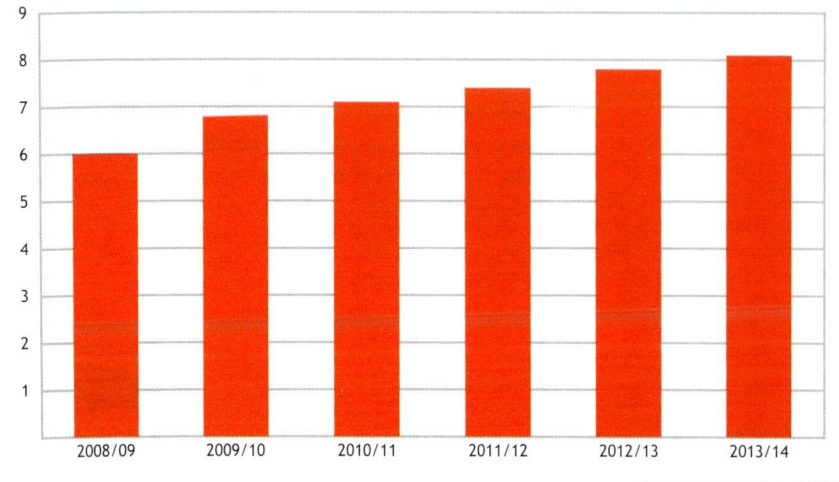

Source: DfT Rail and ORR

How will inter-city traffic hold up in an economic downturn? Bird's eye view of a High Speed Train, in the new National Express East Coast livery, on the Forth Bridge approaches. National Express

The Institution of Railway Operators

GLASGOW CALEDONIAN UNIVERSITY

Professional Qualifications

- Bachelor of Science Degree
- Diploma in Higher Education
- Certificate Course

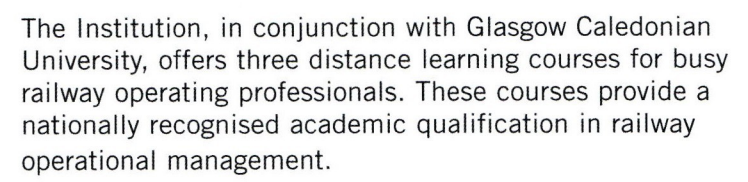

The Institution, in conjunction with Glasgow Caledonian University, offers three distance learning courses for busy railway operating professionals. These courses provide a nationally recognised academic qualification in railway operational management.

If you want to improve your industry knowledge and enhance your career prospects, look up our courses at:
http://www.railwayoperators.org/pages/education.html

If you have questions about the course availability and application processes, consult the FAQs on the website or email Mike Hill: **education@railwayoperators.org**

Diploma modules
Personal and professional development; railway operating principles; customer service; managing people; train planning and performance management; safety law and management; railway business organisation and an end of course project.

Degree modules
Personal and professional development; managing passenger and freight operations; train planning and performance management; safety law and management; train movement control systems; emergency planning, mishap management and investigation; railway engineering; railway economics and an end of course project.

Certificate course
Personal and professional development, background to railway operations, basic railway operations, effective learning, information and communication skills and an end of course project.

The Institution of Railway Operators

PO Box 128, Burgess Hill, West Sussex RH15 0UZ, United Kingdom
Tel: 01444 248931 - Fax: 01444 246392 - Email: admin@railwayoperators.org - Website: www.railwayoperators.org

Setting the Agenda

2009 – entering unknown territory

In an economic downturn, the railway industry needs the confidence to justify major long term spending, writes Roger Ford, Industry & Technology Editor of Modern Railways magazine

After 12 years of uninterrupted economic growth since privatisation, the railway industry is facing its first recession. The downturn could not have come at a worse time, with the High Level Output Specification (HLOS) and the associated Statement of Funds Available (SoFA) for England and Wales based on sustained annual passenger revenue growth of 8% over the five years of Control Period 4 (CP4), which starts on 1 April 2009.

While the total cash available to the railway increases during CP4, government subsidy remains effectively constant, according to the SoFA published in July 2007.

If subsidy is to remain constant, as the government intended, the farepayer's contribution to the overall cost of the railway will have to increase from half to two-thirds of the total income. In other words, ticket sales will have to provide a greater proportion of a larger sum.

Meeting this aspiration will mean annual farebox revenue rising from around £5.6 billion in 2007-08 to £8 billion in 2013/14 (Chart 1). This growth will be generated, in part, by train operators being allowed to increase regulated fares by one percent above inflation (RPI+1%), except for Southeastern which is allowed RPI+3%. Unregulated fares will also have to rise above inflation.

Growth

When the HLOS was published, the government believed that the industry was in 'the most stable position in 50 years'. This was because 'growth is delivering significantly enhanced revenues while industry cost control continues to improve'. As we go to press, just over 18 months on, the financial position is changing fast, but predicting the effects of the economic situation on the railway is almost impossible.

Forecast revenue growth – England & Wales (£million)

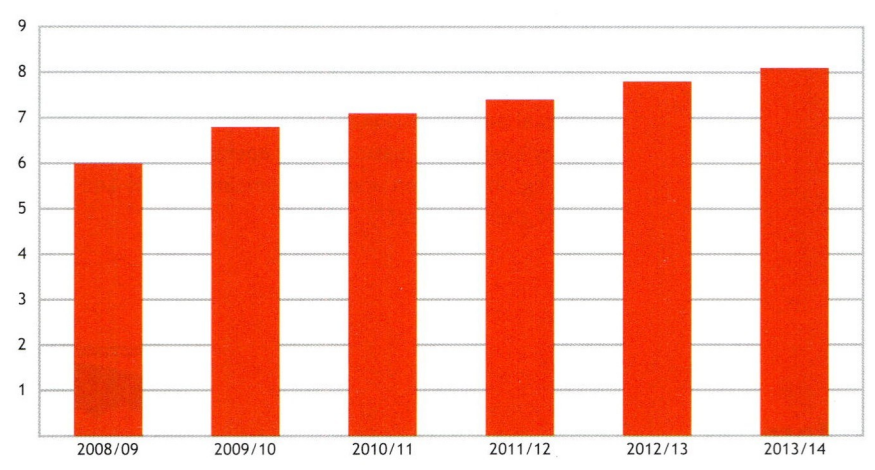

Year	£million
2008/09	6.0
2009/10	6.8
2010/11	7.1
2011/12	7.4
2012/13	7.8
2013/14	8.1

Source: DfT Rail and ORR

How will inter-city traffic hold up in an economic downturn? Bird's eye view of a High Speed Train, in the new National Express East Coast livery, on the Forth Bridge approaches. National Express

In association with ALSTOM

Table 1 - ORR determination of Network Rail's revenue requirement - Great Britain

£m (2006-07 prices)	2009-10	2010-11	2011-12	2012-13	2013-14	Total	SBP update*	Shortfall	Shortfall %
Network Rail's Gross revenue requirement									
Draft Determination	5267	5304	5334	5320	5314	26539	29119	2580	8.9%
Final Determination	5301	5349	5381	5357	5340	26728	29119	2391	8.2%

* Network Rail's Strategic Business Plan (SBP) contained the company's proposals for CP4 and the funding required

Historically, inter-city and London commuter services were the first British Rail sectors to feel the effects of a recession. The graph of ridership in Network Southeast tracked central-London employment with little lag.

In 2008, despite the economic situation deteriorating throughout the year, the transport groups which own the passenger franchises have been reporting buoyant revenues, to the point where the 'cap and collar' system was generating payments to the Department for Transport (DfT).

'Cap and collar' is the term for a revenue risk sharing mechanism in recent franchise agreements. If revenue is ahead of predictions in the franchise plan, the surplus is shared with DfT Rail. But if revenue falls behind forecast, DfT Rail provides additional support.

However, this revenue support function, intended to protect train operators against long term changes, does not come into effect until after year four of the franchise. Then, if revenue falls below 98% of target, DfT Rail makes up 50% of the shortfall, while support increases to 80% if revenue falls to 94% or further below target.

In the case of the eight franchises let since 2006, with revenue profiles reflecting expectations of continuous growth, cap and collar support will not become available until April 2010 at the earliest (Southeastern, First Capital Connect, First Great Western); and 2012 in the case of the four let at the end of 2007 (London Midland, East Midlands Trains, CrossCountry and National Express East Coast).

This is the first unknown. Has the historical link between the economy and ridership been broken by external factors, such as the rising cost of motoring and road congestion?

Franchise owners are reporting continued growth for the 12 months to autumn 2008, although some interim results have been suggesting that the rate of growth is slowing. Brian Souter, Chief Executive of Stagecoach Group, has suggested that this time round, the effect of the recession will be to drive car users onto public transport.

First indications have been that the abrupt change from growth to declining revenue experienced by British Rail's inter-city traffic at the end of the late-1980s boom is being replaced by a softer transition. If this is indeed the case, it will emerge during 2009.

Network Rail

Complementing rising revenue in DfT Rail's financial planning is a reduction in railway costs. According to the Office of Rail Regulation, the railway specified in the HLOS is affordable within the SoFA. However, this assumes that Network Rail can maintain, renew and enhance the infrastructure required to deliver the HLOS with the income ORR thinks it needs.

This is the second unknown. ORR believes that Network Rail has scope for substantial efficiencies in CP4 and has based its final determination, published in October 2008, on overall efficiency savings of 21%. This is two thirds of the 35% efficiency gap which ORR claims exists between Network Rail and the most efficient European railways.

ORR concedes that it will take time to introduce the new methods of working and other changes necessary to catch up, and so is allowing Network Rail two Control Periods to close the gap by 2019. Broken down, the overall 21% is made up of 16.4% improvement on operational expenditure, 18% on maintenance and a massive 23.8% on renewals.

Network Rail has been highly critical of ORR's 'efficiency gap'. Responding in September 2008 to ORR's Draft Determination of its funding for CP4, Network Rail said: 'Our clear view is that the overall package proposed in the draft determinations is currently unreasonable and unrealistic. This situation arises because every element of the package is, on its own, extremely challenging, since ORR makes optimistic or aggressive assumptions across all parts of the business. Taken together the scale of the challenge is simply too great'.

On 30 October 2008, ORR published its Final Determination (Table 1) which showed that ORR is sticking to its guns. It should be noted that the main differences between draft and final determinations are an additional £432million for maintenance, partly offset by a reduction of £212million

Setting the Agenda

Table 2 - Affordability of HLOS - England & Wales

£m (2006-07 prices)		2009-10	2010-11	2011-12	2012-13	2013-14	Total
SoFA		2,888	2,700	2,706	2,567	2,444	13,302
Less base franchise support payments		-1288	-1036	-727	-501	-220	-3,772
Less incremental franchise support payments*		-208	-224	-262	-256	-253	-1,199
Add back franchise payments to Network Rail (as assumed in the SoFA)		2,864	2,880	2,888	2,891	2,895	14,418
Funds available for Network Rail		4,256	4,320	4,605	4,703	4,866	22,749
Less Network Rail net revenue requirement to deliver the HLOS	Draft	4,248	4,296	4,318	4,318	4,312	21,492
	Final	4,343	4,400	4,402	4,382	4,364	21,890
Surplus/deficit(-)	Draft	8	24	286	385	554	1,257
	Final	-87	-80	203	321	502	859

for Schedule 4 and Schedule 8 income. These Schedules cover disruption and performance, reflecting the harder line being taken on improving the Public Performance Measure (of punctuality) and reducing disruption.

Network Rail had until 5 February 2009 to object to the final determination. This is clearly the biggest unknown in an uncertain year.

If Network Rail decides that it cannot work within the funding proposed, the company will ask the ORR to refer the final determination to the Competition Commission for review. Such a review would take up to a year and could decide that ORR had been too generous.

During this year, Network Rail would have to live with the funding allowed in the determination for 2009-10. And even if the commission upheld the referral, there is no guarantee that the government would make more money available.

Under the Periodic Review process, the 2005 Railways Act is clear that the government specifies the railway it wants (the HLOS) and how much it is prepared to pay for it (the SoFA). If ORR decides that there is enough money in the SoFA to pay for the HLOS, it can ask for more funding. If the government rejects this request, then it is down to ORR to determine the necessary cuts in the HLOS.

ORR's calculation show that, provided Network Rail can meet the efficiency targets, the SoFA will pay for the HLOS – just. Table 2 shows how the affordability is worked out for England and Wales, and identifies the changes from the draft determination. Note that the headroom has fallen to under £1billion and that in the first two years there is now a deficit.

Overall, ORR has allowed Network Rail an additional £475million. Meanwhile, Network Rail has also agreed to reductions in civil engineering expenditure and the deferment of some enhancement schemes in the Strategic Business Plan (SBP) which together take £805million off the SBP total.

Efficiency

Together, these changes reduce the shortfall to £1.3billion. ORR has also re-profiled the efficiency savings over the five years, while keeping the total the same.

As a result, Network Rail has to achieve smaller efficiency gains in the first two years in exchange for larger savings over the remaining years of CP4. In other words ORR has given more time for efficiency methods and equipment in return for high efficiency gains when they are in place.

Whether these concessions will be enough to persuade Network Rail to accept the final determination remained to be seen. But given the risks outlined above, a challenge had probably become less likely.

Rolling stock

But the impact of the recession on revenues and arguments over Network Rail's funding for the new control period are not the only uncertainties facing the industry in 2009. In rolling stock (as described in the opening article in our Finance & Leasing section), the final recommendations of a Competition Commission report hang over the rolling stock companies, while massive uncertainty surrounds the 1,300 additional vehicles in the High Level Output Specification.

Compounding this uncertainty is the radical change in policy on electrification. 'Towards a sustainable railway', the White Paper published in July 2007, was opposed to further electrification, arguing that biofuels and hydrogen fuel cells would make self propelled trains more attractive in 10-15 years.

Within nine months, this policy had been reversed, and a rolling programme of electrification starting in Control Period 5 (2014-2019) is now high on the government's agenda. This has major implications for traction and rolling stock policy, in particular the Intercity Express Programme and diesel multiple-unit replacement.

Compounding this uncertainty is the implementation of the European Train Control System (ETCS) in the UK. There are strong arguments for combining ETCS with electrification since it would eliminate signal-sighting issues when electrification masts are planted next to the tracks.

New trains, electrification and ETCS come together on the Great Western main line. There is a strong business case for electrification, resignalling will fall due in the next decade and the diesel High Speed Train fleet will need replacement by 2025, followed shortly after by the diesel multiple-units on the Paddington commuter services.

While all these related issues come to a head in Control Period 5, decisions will have to be taken in 2009-10 if the new policy is to be reflected in the next HLOS, which will be published in 2012.

Starting in 2009, the railway industry will have to persuade government that it has the competence, and confidence, to justify major long term spending decisions made against a background of economic crisis and a wide range of uncertainties – not least energy and the environment.

Table 3 - Affordability of HLOS - Scotland

£m (2006-07 prices)	2009-10	2010-11	2011-12	2012-13	2013-14	Total
SoFA	759	826	676	668	673	3,600
Less base franchise support payments	-317	-330	-325	-333	-340	-1,635
Less incremental franchise support payments	-4	-11	-34	-27	-27	-103
Plus assumed (in the SoFA) franchise payments to Network Rail	150	150	150	150	150	750
Funds available for Network Rail	588	645	467	458	456	2,612
Less Network Rail revenue requirement to deliver the HLOS	505	513	514	511	506	2,549
Surplus/deficit(-)	83	132	-47	-53	-50	64

Christiane von Kalben,
Key Account Manager, Voith Turbo Scharfenberg

Moving the trains of the world.
This moves us.

Voith Turbo is a specialist for drive and cooling systems, control technology and Scharfenberg couplers. There is hardly a freight or passenger train that does not operate with our products, components and systems – up to complete locomotives or vehicle front ends. Be it higher speeds, more comfort, reduced fuel consumption or fewer emissions: with our wealth of experience we solve any task, however complex and challenging it may be, and offer you outstanding service – on the rails of the world.

www.voithturbo.com

Voith Turbo

VOITH
Engineered reliability.

Setting the Agenda

Across the Industry

A Virgin Trains Pendolino passes through Rugby station, now remodelled for extra capacity as part of the West Coast Route Modernisation. Orders have also now been placed to lengthen Pendolino trains and add some additional trains to the fleet. Network Rail

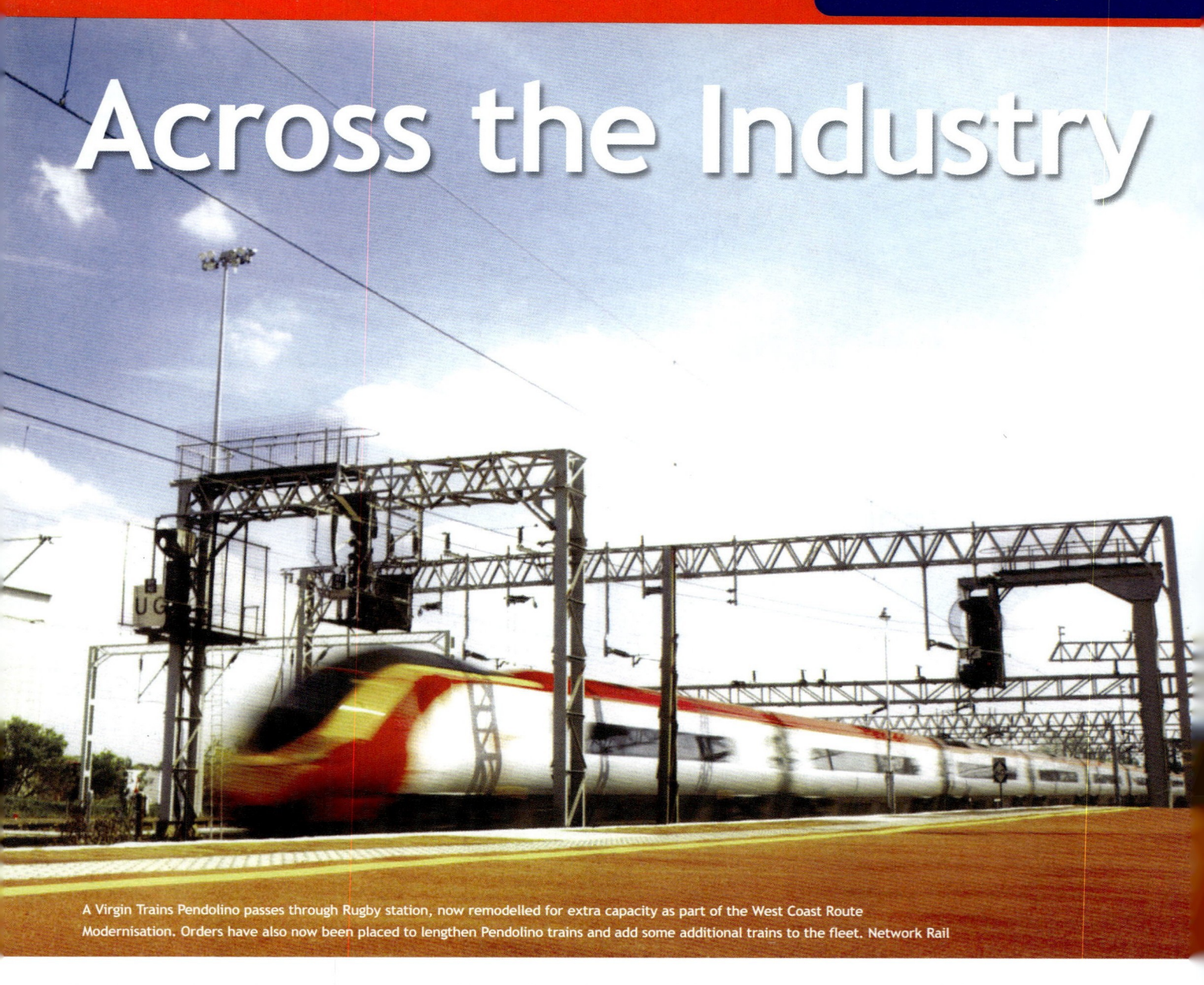

Department for Transport

The government sees its role in the running of the railways as providing strategic direction, and procuring rail services and projects that only it can specify - with responsibility for day-to-day delivery of railway services resting with the industry.

The Department for Transport's (DfT's) Rail Group combines the Department's overarching strategic and financial responsibilities for the railways with many of the functions carried out before 2005 by the Strategic Rail Authority (SRA).

The government specifies what it wants to buy from the railway (in terms of safety, performance and capacity) in a five-year High Level Output Statement, accompanied by a 'statement of funds available' (SOFA) and a long-term rail strategy.

DfT is responsible for specifying and letting contracts to train operating companies to run franchised passenger services in England and intercity services to and from Scotland and Wales, and it works with partners to deliver major projects.

The Rail Group also works with Transport Scotland and the Welsh Assembly Government which have devolved rail responsibilities, and with a wide range of local and regional bodies such as regional assemblies, regional development agencies, Transport for London, and Passenger Transport Executives for major urban areas. The group also is responsible for alignment between UK and EU rail strategies and standards, such as interoperability and the European Rail Traffic Management System.

The DfT created a new Rail & National Networks group in April 2007, aiming to take a strategic, cross-modal approach. This followed the study by Sir Rod Eddington on Transport and the Economy which recommended reforms in the planning, funding and delivery of transport to maximise sustainable returns from investment, as well as recognising the need to improve environmental performance.

The new group took in the DfT Rail group, and teams dealing with the Highways Agency's operations and projects for the strategic roads network. It is also responsible for implementation of planning reforms for major transport infrastructure projects.

The Rail Strategy & Stakeholder Relations directorate is responsible for franchise specification, national rail strategy, network management and rail freight, stakeholder liaison and international issues. The Rail Projects Directorate takes the lead in projects such as West Coast main line modernisation, Channel Tunnel Rail Link (High Speed 1), the Thameslink programme, and station accessibility.

Other DfT Groups deal with city and regional networks, including the city-regions' Passenger Transport Executives; and international networks and the environment.

Transport Scotland

Since 1 April 2006, the devolved Scottish government has had powers covering most transport issues. Scottish Ministers have responsibility for the franchising of ScotRail services, specifying and funding the output of Network Rail in Scotland, and awarding grants to encourage transfer of freight from road to rail and water. Safety and the licensing of railway operators remains reserved for Westminster.

Transport Scotland is the National Transport Agency, the tasks of which include the specifying and funding of the rail network, overseeing safe and efficient running, and delivering major infrastructure projects. The Chief Executive is Malcolm Reed.

Transport Wales

The Welsh Assembly Government has powers to fund transport infrastructure enhancements, develop new passenger rail services, and fund rail freight improvements through grants.

Responsibility for the Wales & Borders rail franchise was transferred to the Welsh Assembly from 1 April 2006. The Assembly Government has the power to specify services and regulated fares, and is responsible for the franchise's financial performance and for enhancements. Subsidy was £142.2m in 2007-08. Other revenue support is given to rail links such as Cardiff-Holyhead, and capital spending allocated, such as for the new Ebbw Vale rail link. The Assembly Government's Transport Wales organisation is headed by the Director of Transport and Strategic Regeneration, James Price.

Passenger Transport Executives

The six Passenger Transport Executives (PTEs) cover the areas of West Midlands (Centro), Greater Manchester, Merseyside (Merseytravel), Tyne & Wear (Nexus), South Yorkshire and West Yorkshire (Metro). A seventh PTE, Strathclyde, was disbanded in 2006.

These are statutory bodies, responsible for setting out policy and expenditure plans for public transport. The Passenger Transport Authorities (PTAs) are political and funding bodies to which the PTEs are responsible.

PTE powers have been limited by the Railways Act 2005, under which they co-sign the Department for Transport's franchise agreement with train operators, but need to secure the agreement of the DfT for any additional services which they might want, to be funded by themselves. PTEs also contract for bus services which the private sector does not provide commercially, and provide local transport information.

PTEG, the Passenger Transport Executive Group, is a non-statutory body bringing together and promoting PTE interests; Transport for London is an associate member.

The Local Transport Bill for England, which had reached a late stage of the Parliamentary process in late 2008, proposed an enhanced duty for PTEs to produce an Integrated Transport Strategy for the conurbation. There would also be scope for reallocating and varying duties of the PTA/Es and Metropolitan District Councils. The Bill allows new PTAs to be considered for England, if the Secretary of State thinks this will improve the exercise of statutory transport functions and the effectiveness and efficiency of transport in the area concerned. Boundary changes will also be possible. The new bodies will be known as Integrated Transport Authorities (ITAs).

In England, Regional Development Agencies have the role of fostering regional economic development and regeneration within the context of sustainability. Local proposals for transport and other infrastructure need to have regard for their strategies.

Network Rail

Network Rail (NR) owns, operates, maintains and develops the main rail network in Great Britain, including tracks, signalling, structures and level crossings. It also owns and operates 17 of the larger stations; others are mostly owned by NR but operated by franchised passenger train operators.

NR is a company limited by guarantee, operating as a commercial business, but with members in place of shareholders. The members are drawn from the rail industry and the general public and do not have any financial or economic interest in the company. NR is accountable to the Office of Rail Regulation (ORR).

A 'heartening' continuation in NR's improvement of its stewardship of the rail network is reported in ORR's annual assessment for 2007-08. Four years into the current control period (2004-09), ORR said NR was on course to achieve the targets set in the access charges review of 2003 (ACR2003), with the exception of efficiency.

Safety performance was overshadowed by the death of two track workers during the year. No passengers were killed in train accidents. Although the risks from level crossings were judged to be well managed, there was an increase in cases of level crossing misuse.

Train punctuality improved, with a reduction of 15% in the number of trains arriving late and a 10% reduction in delay attributed to NR.

Senior personnel

Department for Transport

DfT Rail & National Networks Group:
Director General
Mike Mitchell
Director of Rail Service Delivery
Gary Backler
Director of Rail Projects
Graham Dalton
Director, Group Finance and Business Planning
Chris Hall
Director Rail Strategy and Stakeholder Relations
Bob Linnard
Director, Rail Technical and Professional
Tony Mercado
DfT Director of Procurement
Jack Paine

Rail freight grants
Divisional Manager, Logistics Policy
Stephen Fidler
Accessibility - Head of Mobility & Inclusion Unit
Miranda Carter

In 2007-08, in comparison with ACR2003 targets, NR marginally overspent on controllable operating, maintenance and non-WCRM (West Coast Route Modernisation) renewals expenditure (OMR) by £34million (0.8%). Network Rail deferred £324million of spending on non-WCRM renewals relative to its 2007-08 budget.

Over the first four years of the period, NR outperformed on controllable operating and maintenance expenditure by £350million, but underperformed on renewals expenditure,

Passengers board a Heathrow Connect service at Southall. Airport company BAA has pledged financial support for the extension of the new cross-London railway, Crossrail, to Heathrow airport, taking over from this Heathrow-London Paddington service. ATOC

Setting the Agenda

An Arriva Trains Wales Class-150 train passes Radyr weir. The Welsh Assembly Government is responsible for the Wales & Borders rail franchise's financial performance and for enhancements. Arriva Trains Wales

driven particularly by significant overspend on track.

Overall, the condition of the network improved during 2007-08. Generally, infrastructure assets performed more reliably and caused less delay.

In October 2008, ORR published its determination of Network Rail's outputs and its funding from access charges and other sources for control period 4 (CP4, April 2009 to March 2014). It sets out significant improvements in train reliability, network capacity and safety, and ORR has determined that the revenue NR requires to deliver these outputs is £26.7bn.

The enhancement programme is the largest on the network for decades, says ORR, including additional capacity for over 20% more passenger journeys. Key output requirements are:

- Improved reliability and less disruption - 20% reduction in late or cancelled trains; punctuality increasing to at least 93% (southeast England) or 92% (elsewhere); at least 25% reduction in delays to freight trains caused by Network Rail; reductions of over a third in disruption to passenger services caused by engineering work and no worsening of the position for freight (includes introducing NR's 'seven-day railway' concept on priority routes).
- Improvements in safety - 3% reduction in the risk of death or injury to passengers and rail workers from accidents on the railway.
- Maintaining and improving station condition.

Key enhancement schemes will be:
- linking King's Cross commuter services to the Thameslink route and increasing its capacity throughout (including the bottleneck at London Bridge);
- rebuilding Reading station to remove a bottleneck;
- rebuilding Birmingham New Street station;
- capacity improvements in Cardiff;
- providing capacity relief to the East Coast main line;
- improving line speeds on the Midland main line;
- the new Glasgow Airport rail link;
- completing the new Airdrie-Bathgate line;
- extensions to more than 500 platforms for longer trains; and
- improvements under a strategic freight network initiative.

ORR also considers that Network Rail can achieve significantly more efficiency improvement than it included in its plans for CP4.

Office of Rail Regulation

The Office of Rail Regulation (ORR) is an independent statutory body led by a Board. It was established in 2004 under the Railways & Transport Safety Act 2003, in place of an individual regulator, responsible for regulating the national rail network operator (Network Rail). From April 2006, ORR became a combined safety and economic regulator, with the transfer of safety regulation for the 'operational railway' from the Health & Safety Executive (HSE).

Passenger train operating companies (TOCs) are granted franchises by the Department for Transport, and apply to ORR for licences to operate. ORR also licences freight train operators. TOCs and Network Rail undertake track and station access agreements, requiring ORR approval. ORR also monitors the rolling stock leasing company code of practice. The Secretary of State for Transport makes appointments to the ORR board.

ORR's Health and Safety Strategy for the railways sets out an overall aim to contribute to, and regulate, an environment in which health and safety can be continuously improved. The rail industry is expected to continuously examine its behaviour and management systems to identify and implement reasonably practicable improvements. ORR believes that good health and safety performance contributes to good business performance.

ORR says its health and safety enforcement policy incorporates the principles of proportionality, consistency, targeted

---

Senior personnel

Network Rail

Chairman
Sir Ian McAllister

Chief Executive
Iain Coucher

Group infrastructure director
Peter Henderson

Director, operations and customer service
Robin Gisby

Director, infrastructure investment
Simon Kirby

Director, planning and regulation
Paul Plummer

Sir Ian McAllister is to step down from the board in 2009.

About to enter the 'new' 1894 Standedge tunnel, Siemens-built Class 185 No 185103 forms a First TransPennine Express on 16 February 2008. Paul Bigland

Setting the Agenda

enforcement action, transparency and accountability, and mimics the policy established by the Health & Safety Executive for other industries so that enforcement across industrial sectors is approached in a consistent manner.

The Periodic Review 2008 (PR2008) of NR's outputs and charges is taking place between 2006 and 2009. Government (the Secretary of State for England & Wales, and Scottish Ministers) has specified what it wants the industry to deliver and how much it is prepared to pay, and ORR has assessed output and expenditure implications for Network Rail, and for access charges.

Association of Train Operating Companies
The Association of Train Operating Companies (ATOC) is the voice of the passenger rail industry. Set up in 1994, it fulfils this role both as a trade association and as a group of 'schemes' which act as the operational engine room of the passenger railway, and guarantee the continued benefits of a national network.

These schemes provide key support services for passengers, including National Rail Enquiries, Rail Settlement Plan, which allocates fares revenue to the train operators, the marketing of National Rail products and services such as railcards and the National Conditions of Carriage, and licensing of the network of travel agents selling rail services to the public.

ATOC's trade association role includes representing train companies to the government, Office of Rail Regulation, the media and other opinion formers on transport policy issues and interpreting government and rail industry policy and planning initiatives for its members.

ATOC is a membership-based organisation made up of the franchised train operating companies, plus Eurostar and Rail Express Systems. Associate members include Grand Central, Heathrow Express, Hull Trains and Wrexham & Shropshire.

Its work is undertaken through four limited companies:
- ATOC Limited, through which it provides most of its services, employs the association's staff and acts as agent for many of the schemes.
- Rail Settlement Plan Limited, which manages the ticket revenue collection, allocation and settlement process.
- National Rail Enquiries Limited, which oversees the call centre services and the National Rail website www.nationalrail.co.uk and the voice recognition service called TrainTracker.
- Rail Staff Travel Limited, which manages travel arrangements for thousands of rail industry employees.

ATOC acts as the facilitator for many joint activities and as guarantor of 'network benefits' for passengers on behalf of train operators, which enables them to comply with their franchise agreements and operating licences. These benefits include the maintenance of 'through-ticketing' across all train operators and arrangements with Transport for London, settlement of ticket revenues between operators; the administration and marketing of railcard products - Young Persons, Family, Senior and Disabled Persons Railcards - through advertising, public relations and direct mail. ATOC is also responsible for the licensing of travel agents, international rail travel products such as the BritRail and Inter-Rail passes, and rail staff travel arrangements.

Outside these core statutory areas, ATOC works in many ways to improve the planning, operation, delivery and marketing of rail services. These include:
- Making the purchase of rail tickets easier through the use of the internet, telesales, travel agencies, station booking offices, self-service vending machines and the roll-out of the ticket-on-departure 'fast ticket' machines.
- Helping to drive forward industry initiatives such as fares simplification, integrated transport, rolling stock strategy, network capacity, engineering training, rail safety research and fleet reliability.
- Industry planning: working with ATOC's members, the Department for Transport and Network Rail in developing plans to increase capacity and develop new rail services on the network.
- Looking to the future: exploring new ways of retailing and marketing rail by exploiting the latest mobile phone and smart card technology and developing new methods of ticketing such as print at home and mobile phone ticketing.
- Providing a 'voice' for the passenger railway: through its Chairman, Chief Executive and Communications department, ATOC promotes and explains the role of train operators to a wide range

---

Senior personnel

Office of Rail Regulation

Chairman
Chris Bolt

Chief Executive
Bill Emery

Director of Access, Planning and Performance
Michael Lee

Director, Railway Safety
Ian Prosser

Director of Rail Policy
Michael Beswick

Rail-bus interchange on Merseyrail – a passenger rail franchise unique in the UK, as the franchising role has been delegated by Parliament to the Passenger Transport Executive, Merseytravel. PTEG / Merseytravel

of stakeholders including the media, politicians, local and regional government, transport pressure groups and trade bodies.

ATOC continues to invest in improvements to passenger information through the National Rail website - including its Journey Planner, 'print your own' pocket timetables, simplified fares information and award-winning Live Departure Boards. The National Rail Enquiries telephone service is Britain's most called telephone number with more than 1.4million calls per month, while the website, www.nationalrail.co.uk attracts nearly 10million hits per month. National Rail Enquiries is also diversifying the range of information sources for passengers reflecting ever-changing technology by making journey information available by mobile phone, WAP and SMS.

In addition, National Rail Enquiries has continually upgraded the automated telephone service TrainTracker which handles almost 400,000 calls per month and now provides fares information. It also enhanced the TrainTracker Text service further to provide live departure and arrival times direct to mobiles via SMS text message.

ATOC led the introduction of a simpler fares structure across the National Rail network during 2008. The changes were first trailed in the government's railway White Paper in July 2007, which incorporated proposals made by ATOC and has resulted in reducing the number of ticket types to three for single and return journeys: Advance; Off-peak; Anytime.

Rail Settlement Plan continues its work with TOCs and stakeholders to deliver the necessary standards, systems and services which enable new retail and ticketing initiatives to be offered, including smartcard, and barcode and mobile services.

The future size, use and shape of the railway is now being examined through the development of Route Utilisation Studies (RUS), a process led by Network Rail. ATOC's Rail Planning Support Team co-ordinates TOC input.

In addition, the team has been given the role of recommending small scale investments and enhancements in order to cope with projected growth. The team has also contributed to the government's Regional Planning Assessments – providing 'best practice' input into local assessments of regional transport needs and to major projects such as the planned introduction of ERTMS and the impact of Crossrail. Much work has been focused on the development of the Network Rail's Strategic Business Plan for Control Period 4, future electrification strategy, and the case for a substantial enhancement of the rolling stock fleet. ATOC also expects to play an important role in the government's new lines strategy evaluation.

Recent developments at ATOC include:
- Mike Alexander took up the role of ATOC's Executive Chairman in March 2008, and in April 2008 Michael Roberts started as Chief Executive following the retirement of George Muir as Director General.
- ATOC's The Billion Passenger Railway, published in April 2008, provided continued proof that Britain was still one of Europe's fastest growing railways. In 2007, 30.1billion passenger miles were generated, up from 28.1billion miles in 2006, resulting in the highest number of passengers travelling on Britain's railways in peacetime. In total 1.232billion passengers travelled on Britain's railways in 2007. 2008 has also been another year of passenger growth despite volatile economic circumstances.
- ATOC has produced a 20 point programme to help TOCs to improve their Energy Efficiency and curb CO_2 emissions.
- ATOC gave evidence to the Public Accounts Committee on Reducing Rail Delays, and to the Transport Select Committee on the 30 Year Strategy for Railways, Ticketing, the Local transport Bill and the Blue Badge Parking scheme. ATOC also spoke for train operators at the All Party Railways Group Meeting in October.
- In London, ATOC continues to work with its members and Transport for London on the roll-out of smartcard ticketing such as Oyster across the capital's travelcard zones.
- Working with the Olympic Delivery Authority (ODA), ATOC continues to be actively involved in planning transport links for the 2012 London Olympics on behalf of its members.

Passenger Focus

The mission of Passenger Focus is 'to get the best deal for Britain's rail passengers'. With a strong emphasis on evidence-based campaigning and research, it aims to influence decisions that affect passengers, and work with the rail industry, other passenger groups and governments to secure improvements to services.

The Railways Act 2005 abolished the regional Rail Passengers Committees and the former national Rail Passengers Council and Passenger Focus was created to represent the views of all rail passengers across Great Britain.

Passenger Focus is structured as an executive non-departmental public body, sponsored by the Department for Transport. The Scottish Executive, Welsh Assembly Government and the Greater London Authority are each able to appoint a member to the board. The remaining appointments are made by the Secretary of State for Transport. The organisation's independence is guaranteed by an act of Parliament.

Passenger Focus runs its central functions from offices in London and Manchester. In addition 12 Passenger Link Managers based in different locations across Great Britain liaise with individual train operating companies.

Asking passengers about their experiences on train journeys and what they need and expect from their railways is a stated principle for Passenger Focus. The watchdog is committed to a research-based approach, and to act on what passengers have said they want.

www.passengerfocus.org.uk

Chairman Colin Foxall
Chief Executive Anthony Smith

British Transport Police

The specialist police service for Britain's railways, British Transport Police provides a service to rail operators, staff and passengers throughout England, Wales and Scotland, as well as the London Underground, Docklands Light Railway, Glasgow Subway, Midland Metro light railway, Croydon Tramlink and Eurostar.

Working closely with the rail industry and local police forces, BTP is a national police service divided into seven areas, covering 10,000 miles of track and more than 3,000 railway stations and depots. It has over 2,700 Police Officers, supported by more than 250 Special Constables, 200 Police Community Support Officers (PCSOs) and 1,200 police staff.

www.btp.police.uk

Chief Constable Ian Johnston

Senior personnel

ATOC

Chairman
Mike Alexander
Chief Executive
Michael Roberts
Director of Policy & Regulation
Alec McTavish
Director of Communications
Edward Funnell
Chief Executive, National Rail Enquiries
Chris Scoggins
Chief Executive, Rail Settlement Plan
Steve Howes
Commercial Director
David Mapp

Setting the Agenda

Transport preparations are under way for the London 2012 Olympic and Paralympic games, centred on Stratford, east London. Freightliner's No 86605 waits at Stratford's Platform 10a with a Daventry-Felixstowe train as National Express East Anglia's No 321359 passes through the station on Platform 10 on 19 March 2008. A new loop east of the station will allow freight services to wait there when Platform 10a is refurbished for passenger use. John Sully

Rail Accident Investigation Branch

The Rail Accident Investigation Branch (RAIB) is the independent railway accident investigation organisation for the UK, operational from October 2005.

The RAIB says the purpose of its investigations is to improve the safety of railways, and to prevent further accidents - achieving this by identifying the causes of accidents and other aspects that made the outcome worse.

Its investigations are entirely independent and are focused solely on safety improvement, says RAIB: not on apportioning blame or liability, nor enforcing law or carrying out prosecutions.

The RAIB makes recommendations addressed to ORR which has the role of National Safety Authority. ORR considers the recommendations and passes them on to dutyholders who are required to consider and act on them.
www.raib.gov.uk
Chief Inspector   Carolyn Griffiths

Rail Safety & Standards Board

The Rail Safety and Standards Board (RSSB) was established in April 2003, and has the primary objective of leading and facilitating the railway industry's work to achieve continuous improvement in health and safety performance, and thus facilitating reduction of risk to passengers, employees and the affected public.

The Department for Transport in September 2008 announced the allocation of an additional £15million for a new strategic research programme to be managed by RSSB. The new programme will help achieve long term goals set out in the DfT's Rail Technical Strategy, and support the rail industry and its stakeholders in the delivery of 'step changes' over the next 30 years.

The Sustainable Rail Programme, a future-looking cross-industry initiative on sustainable development, is facilitated by RSSB, and led by executive / director-level representatives from across the industry.

RSSB is a not-for-profit company owned by major industry stakeholders.
www.rssb.co.uk
Chief Executive   Len Porter

The Railway Forum

The Railway Forum is an industry-wide body promoting the growth of a safe, efficient and affordable railway in the UK, and represents the majority of the industry - including operating companies, rolling stock leasing companies, infrastructure providers, equipment suppliers, Network Rail and Transport for London. The Passenger Transport Executive Group is an associate, and the Railway Industry Association and ATOC are members.

The Railway Forum's roles are principally to act as a lobby group and think tank for the industry. In addition, it runs events including the annual Railway Industry Innovation Awards (jointly with Modern Railways magazine), an annual conference, and seminars on such topics as future power technologies and high-speed railways.

The Railway Forum campaigns on the development of high speed rail, on the basis of benefits not only in terms of journey time reduction, but also capacity enhancement and economic regeneration - with the potential to reduce the economic disparity between London and the rest of the country, as well as reducing the demand for domestic aviation. The Railway Forum also believes that there is a case for further electrification beyond the 39% of the network presently electrified, and has worked with member companies to press the case to the Department for Transport for this to be part of the long term planning strategy for the railway industry, to bring operational and environmental benefits.
www.railwayforum.com
Director General   Paul Martin

Railway Industry Association

The Railway Industry Association is the trade association for UK-based suppliers of equipment and services to the rail industry worldwide. It has around 140 member companies across the whole range of railway supply, including many skills and resources previously part of the national railway but which now operate in the private sector. RIA is an active member of UNIFE, the trade association for the European railway supply industry, and of the Confederation of British Industry.

RIA members cover all aspects of railways, including rolling stock and infrastructure manufacturing, component supply, maintenance, and design, as well as consultancy, training, project management and safety.

RIA provides its members with extensive services, including technical, commercial and political information; representation to government, Network Rail and others; providing opportunities for dialogue and networking; and export promotional activity.
www.riagb.org.uk
Director General   Jeremy Candfield

AGV
REVOLUTIONIZING VERY HIGH SPEED TRAINS

The AGV is the only interoperable train designed to carry passengers at 360 km/h in comfort and total safety. The AGV's articulated architecture, distributed power, modularity and sleek profile have all benefited from Alstom Transport's leading-edge technologies. The AGV is environmentally-friendly*, thus contributing to sustainable mobility.

* Compared with the competition, the AGV uses 15% less energy to generate 18% more power.

www.transport.alstom.com

We are shaping the future | **ALSTOM**

Setting the Agenda

Diesel passenger train fleets have been stretched to the limit - often by patronage growth - with most off-lease trains snapped up by the new train operating franchises that began in late 2007. A London Midland Class-153 single unit is seen under refurbishment by Wabtec at Eastleigh. London Midland

The Institution of Railway Operators

The Institution of Railway Operators, was formed in 2000 and aims to be the industry's custodian of best practice in operational management. It offers educational programmes and networking opportunities for railway operators at all levels and experience.

In conjunction with Glasgow Caledonian University (GCU), the insitution has created two distance-learning courses in professional studies relating to railway operational management.

The undergraduate courses offer a Bachelor of Science Degree and a Diploma in Higher Education in professional studies relating to railway operational management. The degree course was a first for railway operators.

The courses are aimed at giving successful students a transferable academic qualification as well as improving their industry knowledge, and so boosting career prospects.

The courses are divided into modules and include day study events. Diploma modules include personal and professional development; railway operating principles; customer service; managing people; train planning and performance management; safety law and management; railway business organisation and an end of course project.

Degree modules also include managing passenger and freight operations; train movement control systems; emergency planning, mishap management and investigation; railway engineering; railway economics and an end of course project.

A Foundation Course, launched in 2008, will assist students to qualify for entry to the Diploma Course if they have not previously experienced higher education at this level.

In addition to access to education programmes in the theory and practice of railway operations, membership of the institution offers individual professional development planning and the opportunity to gain experience; conferences, exhibitions, meetings, seminars, lectures and classes; a network of industry professionals committed to mutual learning and personal development; and forum for discussion and the exchange of information.

The Institution's longer-term aspirations are to seek chartered status and to develop an honours degree.
www.railwayoperators.org

Permanent Way Institution

The PWI promotes and encourages the acquisition and exchange of technical and general knowledge about the design, construction and maintenance of every type of railed track.

The PWI organises local meetings in all its geographically-based Sections, as well as technical conferences and visits. Its textbooks have been the industry standard works of reference for over half a century and members receive a widely consulted journal.
www.permanentwayinstitution.com

Railway Civil Engineers Association

The RCEA is an associated society of the Institution of Civil Engineers for professional engineers who involved in the development, design, construction, or maintenance of infrastructure for railway operations. It exists to foster continuing professional development and the exchange of knowledge and experience.
www.ice.org.uk/knowledge/knowledge_rcea.asp

Institution of Railway Signal Engineers

The IRSE is the professional institution for railway signalling, telecommunications and allied professions and is active in the UK, Europe and worldwide. It aims to advance, for the public benefit, the science and practice of signalling and telecommunications engineering within the industry and to maintain high standards of knowledge of the profession amongst the membership.
www.irse.org
Chief Executive & Secretary   Colin Porter

Railway Engineers Forum

The Railway Engineers Forum (REF) is an informal liaison grouping of the Professional Engineering Institutions' rail interest sections. These are the Institution of Mechanical Engineers (IMechE) Railway Division; the Institution of Engineering & Technology (IET); the Institution of Railway Signal Engineers (IRSE); the Permanent Way Institution (PWI); the Railway Civil Engineers Association (RCEA) of the Institution of Civil Engineers (ICE); the Chartered Institute of Logistics and Transport (CILT); and the Institution of Railway Operators (IRO). The REF organises multi-disciplinary conferences and produces statements on topical railway subjects.
Reports are posted at *www.irse.org*

The Railway Study Association

The Railway Study Association provides a cross industry focal point to drive personal and professional development in the railway environment. This development is achieved through the promotion, discussion and demonstration of the issues facing the industry today, making the RSA an effective forum to gain a broad understanding of all aspects of the rail industry.

The association offers a co-ordinated programme of lectures, seminars and site visits, annual conventions and international visits, and informal networking. The RSA gives access to members to keynote speakers who are delivering and driving improvement in today's railways.

Members come from a broad spectrum of the railway industry, typically from passenger and freight operations, network provision and regulatory bodies, as well as many students and those preparing for a career in the industry.

The RSA attracts corporate members from a broad spectrum of the railway profession. These range from Network Rail with 32,000 employees to consultancies with 100 or less.

In association with ALSTOM

The President introduces the year's theme at an address and reception in London in October. This is followed by monthly meetings in both London and Birmingham, when senior managers from within and outside the industry speak on subjects of topical interest. The President for 2008-09 is Jim Steer, a Director of the Steer Davies Gleeve consultancy, and Director of Greengauge 21, which aims to research and develop the concept of a high speed rail network.

Day or half-day visits to see transport and industrial installations are arranged, as well as an annual Convention in a major city, arranged with the local railway or transport administration. At an Annual Dinner in London, members and their guests can meet informally, and hear from the President and a guest speaker.

The annual subscription to the Railway Study Association includes copies of Modern Railways magazine, the House Journal of the Association, which publishes papers and reports and highlights forthcoming Association events.
www.railwaystudyassociation.org

Derby & Derbyshire Rail Forum

Derby & Derbyshire Rail Forum was formed in 1993 to promote the area as a world class centre of rail excellence, with its cluster of rail engineering, design, manufacture and consultancy companies.

DDRF's approach involves inward and outward trade missions, establishing successful networking opportunities, attending trade exhibitions, facilitating topical workshops and seminars, assisting the preparation and development of tenders, and providing a collective voice for the area in promoting the area's rail industry to a global market. DDRF has around 100 members and holds quarterly networking meetings and annual conference.

DDRF has dedicated local support from the City and County Councils, the East Midlands Development Agency, UK Trade & Investment and other industry groups.

This support helps DDRF members locate and access new markets and promote international expansion. It also helps bring new organisations to the region, to continue the growth and reputation of the region's rail industry.

Membership of DDRF is not restricted to technology and manufacturing companies. Finance, legal and other support organisations are also members.
www.derbyrailforum.org.uk

The Association of Community Rail Partnerships (ACoRP)

ACoRP is a federation of over 60 community rail partnerships and rail promotion groups, focused on practical initiatives to develop a better, more sustainable local railway. Improved station facilities, better train services and improved integration with other forms of transport are central to the work of ACoRP and its members.

The government's Community Rail Development Strategy provides a framework for partnerships to improve the effectiveness of local railways in meeting social, environmental and economic objectives.

Community rail partnerships are a bridge between the railway and local communities. They are about positive development, bringing together a wide range of interests along the rail corridor. Some partnerships have been instrumental in achieving spectacular increases in use of rail through innovative marketing, improved services and better station facilities.

Their work includes improving bus links to stations, developing walking and cycling routes, bringing station buildings back to life, art and education projects and organising special events which promote the railway.
www.acorp.uk.com

The privatised rail industry

Until 1994, the nationalised British Railways Board (BRB) operated what became known as a vertically integrated railway - provision of infrastructure, ownership of trains and operation of services were all functions of the Board.

Under the Railways Act 1993, these and other functions were split. The ownership of the track went to a new infrastructure company, Railtrack, subsequently privatised. All operators paid Railtrack for the use of the track, signalling and electrification systems.

Passenger train operation was split into what initially were 26 separate franchises, using the BR business sector organisation as a basis. They were the subject of competitive bidding and mostly for a seven year term. Franchise awards took into account bidders' additional service and investment commitments, and whether that company required a subsidy or would make payments to the government over the franchise term.

The passenger stations were owned by Railtrack, but apart from the major stations, stations were run by the train operating companies (TOCs).

The passenger rolling stock became the property of three rolling stock companies (ROSCOs), which then leased the stock to the TOCs - because relatively short franchises contrast with rolling stock assets with a life of around 30 years.

The freight companies were also privatised, taking on the existing locomotives and those wagons not privately owned by customers.

Franchising was carried out by the Office of Passenger Rail Franchising (OPRAF) and various aspects of the industry including licensing were overseen by the independent Rail Regulator, plus the Health & Safety Executive.

The Association of Train Operating Companies (ATOC) was created to manage passenger railway affairs such as running the National Rail Enquiry Service and settling accounts between companies.

The last franchises were let very shortly before the 1997 General Election, which brought a change in government from Conservative to Labour. Labour said it wished to improve overall direction and planning in the industry, and created the Strategic Rail Authority (SRA) in 2001. But other problems afflicted the industry, in particular the inability of some franchisees to make the financial returns they had expected, plus the level and quality of investment by Railtrack. A series of high profile rail accidents in which infrastructure shortcomings were identified led to the eventual downfall of that company.

Rising traffic levels and operation of many more trains, whether to add to capacity, to compete for revenue, or to fill the timetable to prevent new competition, led to performance problems. These became chronic after the severe operational restrictions hastily put in place following the Hatfield derailment of 2001. This led in turn to huge political and media criticism of the industry.

Over time, many of the franchises were acquired by groups active in the bus industry, notably Arriva, First Group, Go-Ahead, National Express and Stagecoach.

The cost of the railway to the public purse rose fast, with high profile problems as the projected costs of the West Coast Route Modernisation. When the Rail Regulator made his ruling at the end of 2003 on the much increased level of access charges needed to fund Network Rail (as Railtrack's successor) to provide the infrastructure for 2004-09, this proved too much for the government. It would in effect be a charge to be funded by government, since the TOCs were protected by an indemnity clause in their contracts.

The result was the Railways Act 2005. This abolished the SRA with most of its functions (including strategy, finance and the awarding of franchises) subsumed into an enlarged Department for Transport. The safety policy, regulation and enforcement functions were transferred to a new Office of Rail Regulation (ORR), while the government set out what Network Rail was expected to deliver for the public money it received in a High Level Output Statement (HLOS) plus a Statement of Funds Available (SoFA). The access charges review process was amended, and there was a transfer of powers and budgets to Scotland, Wales and London.

Today, TOC franchises commonly run for seven years, extendable if performance is satisfactory. Franchise conditions are not identical, but in general specify frequency levels and carrying capacity to be provided, punctuality and reliability standards, and control on some fares levels. The TOCs also commit themselves to a financial regime, in recent cases typically requiring progressively less subsidy or paying an increasing premium. They may also undertake specific enhancements.

Setting the Agenda

railalliance

Active new business forum

The Rail Alliance is an active business forum where members can network, collaborate, innovate and thrive in order to maintain and grow the prosperity and sustainability of their business. Membership spans all aspects of the railway and supporting industries, with suppliers and customers, both public and private sector.

The Rail Alliance's website provides links to other support organisations, on-line advice and tools, information on member companies and organisations and a comprehensive database of products, services and expertise, alongside news and industry opportunities. The Alliance believes that developing the current and future skills and knowledge base is going to be vitally important for the industry, and it has set out a wide-ranging programme of networking opportunities, seminars and also a variety of educational and development events. A railway orientated MBA programme is being developed with Worcester University Business School.

The Alliance is also engaged with a number of other education providers regarding a training and education package, to be focused on keeping companies in touch with market opportunities at home and abroad, aware of new legislation/compliance requirements and maximising training/development opportunities; all with a real commitment to making sure the sector retains its people and attracts the next generation of engineers and rail professionals.

At a time when it believes the major customers in the railway industry, such as Network Rail, are looking to reduce their supplier base in terms of interfaces rather than capabilities, the Rail Alliance says it is absolutely vital that companies look to new and innovative ways of ensuring that the goods and services they are offering are not neglected. The Alliance sees this as core territory and it has been putting a great deal of emphasis on creating dynamic, collaborative networks which will enable the many to continue to trade with the few. It believes that to be effective in this new procurement era, companies will have to concentrate on ensuring their compliance with a wide range of accreditation requirements, learn from the best practice of others and other industries, and above all to concentrate on adding value to both their products and others whilst driving costs and waste down.

Rail Alliance membership spans all aspects of the railway and supporting industries, with suppliers and customers, both public and private sector. A range of industry suppliers are now involved in London Underground improvement works. Metronet

Capability database

The Rail Alliance Members Capability Database has been conceived as a central tool in procurement, connecting buyers with sellers, as well as enabling individual member companies to find synergistic businesses to create a consortium for large tender opportunities - essential in supply-chain matchmaking. It is a centrally maintained and fully searchable database of rail sector related businesses, including thousands of specialised manufacturing, service, consultancy and product specific companies. It is an innovation gateway where rail buyers and procurement professionals can quickly find suppliers with the relevant skills. Members get increased visibility of their company to government and private sector procurement professionals. Special features will enable buyers to find not only individual firms but consortia capable of delivering entire systems.

The Rail Alliance initiative was 'brought to life' by Advantage West Midlands in partnership with the West Midlands Manufacturing Advisory Service (MAS-WM). The West Midlands enjoys a significant concentration of high value adding engineering, design and integrated supply companies that have developed considerable expertise since the privatisation of the UK rail industry.

The West Midlands has been very successful in promoting and developing its rail business through a wide variety of programmes that have seen many tangible benefits, including the UK's first IRIS-accredited company, a number of very successful technology transfer projects and significant export contracts being won by Midlands-based companies through their involvement with UK Trade & Investment.

The Rail Alliance actively works with other trade associations to complement their established activities, rather than covering the same ground. At its heart is the belief that new business can be created by opening up the synergies amongst its members and the programme of events supported by the interactive website facilitates this.
www.railalliance.co.uk
www.advantagewm.co.uk/working-with-us/business-clusters/rail.aspx

Left: Major customers in the railway industry, such as Network Rail, are changing their relationships with their supplier base. Leeds station has been the focus of major improvement work, and more capacity enhancement is proposed in the latest regional Route Utilisation Strategy. Network Rail

Finance & Leasing

In association with

angel Trains

Finance & Leasing

Uncertainty overshadows new trains market

Roger Ford, Modern Railways' Industry & Technology Editor, analyses plans for new passenger train fleets

Despite the commitment to 1,300 additional vehicles in the Department for Transport's High Level Output Specification (HLOS), and the current procurement exercises for the Intercity Express Programme (IEP) and the new Thameslink fleet, manufacturers and leasing companies have been far from clear on what passenger traction and rolling stock will be delivered in the new five-year Control Period 4 (CP4) which starts on 1 April 2009.

As the Competition Commission pointed out in August 2008, in the provisional findings of its investigation into train leasing, new rolling stock is already difficult to justify and implement within the current policy of short franchises for train operating companies. A number of external factors, such as the global financial crisis and energy policy, mean that both the timescale for delivery and the form of traction are uncertain in many cases.

While the rolling stock leasing companies (ROSCOs) were largely absolved from the Department for Transport's (DfT's) claims of excess profits in the Competition Commission's provisional findings, the DFT challenged the Commission in the strongest terms to think again. The DfT Rail division's response generated further uncertainty by calling for the rentals of follow-on orders for new trains to be capped, in addition to those of the ex-British Rail fleets which were the subject of the original complaint.

With the ROSCOs already finding it difficult to justify investment from their owning banks, the threat of price capping is unlikely to encourage investment. The final report of the Competition Commission's investigation of the leasing market was due to be published in January 2009. Even if, as expected, it continues to exonerate the ROSCOs from making excess profits, the owning banks are likely to view rolling stock investment as vulnerable to government intervention.

Although the Competition Commission highlighted the obstacles that face new rolling stock leasing companies entering the established UK market, there were signs, before the world economic crisis, that a new breed of 'finance only' ROSCOs was starting to emerge. Such companies would outsource control of maintenance to manufacturers or third party depots.

In the UK, Transport for London is to lease its fleet of Bombardier Electrostar electric multiple-units (EMUs) from a new company, QW Rail Leasing Ltd, a joint venture of National Australia Bank and Sumitomo Mitsui Banking. In July 2008, HSH Nordbank and KfW IPEX Bank announced the formation of Railpool, which is intended to explore opportunities in the European passenger and freight rolling stock leasing market.

Above: Among the first routes due to see new Intercity Express Programme trains is the East Coast main line. On 21 July 2008 the fully re-liveried 08.40 National Express East Coast express from Leeds to King's Cross, led by Class 43 HST powercar No 43306, overhauls the 10.23 First Capital Connect local service from Welwyn Garden City to Moorgate, formed by Class 313/0 No 313038, at Harringay. Brian Morrison

Rolling Stock Plan

Delivery of the 1,300 net additional vehicles in the DfT Rolling Stock Plan (RSP) is linked to cascades initiated by new builds. This complex process can only be implemented through variations to existing franchise agreements. For example, the provision of additional EMUs to First Capital Connect (FCC) for Key Output Zero (KO Zero) of the Thameslink programme (the phase of work beginning in March 2009) required changes to three franchise agreements – FCC, Southern and SouthEastern - to be signed off simultaneously.

Confusing the analysis is the presentation of the 1,300 'Net Additional Vehicles' in the DfT Rail's Rolling Stock Plan (RSP - Table 1). This Table lists the additional vehicles each train operating company (TOC) will have gained by the end of Control Period 4 (CP4) in 2014.

It should be noted that this is not a list of new vehicles. In some cases, the additional vehicles listed will be cascaded from another TOC, having been released by the delivery of new trains which will not necessarily appear in the table.

For example, the 188 net additional vehicles for National Express East Anglia are made up of 120 new EMU vehicles plus 17 four-car Class 321 EMUs to be cascaded from London Midland. The Class 321s were to be released by the new Desiro Class 350/2 units being delivered to LM from late 2008.

However, continuing ridership growth means that since Table 1 was published, LM planned to retain seven Class 321 units. Thus NXEA may need to increase its new build to 148 vehicles to cover the shortfall.

DfT had also introduced some double counting. Initially, the 1,300 vehicles in the RSP and the 1,100 vehicles under the Thameslink new build were considered to be separate. However in the updated RSP (Table 1), 126 vehicles in the new Thameslink fleet were allocated to FCC, effectively reducing the 1,300 to 1,174. When a mis-stated quantity for TransPennine Express is taken into account ('42' apparently mis-keyed for '24') the actual total becomes 1,156. Manufacturers and ROSCOs expect the final total to be lower.

DfT Rail's table also excluded the substantial London Overground orders from the nominal 1,300. Table 2 shows the latest estimate, at the time of going to press, for new train orders based on analysis of the RSP, drawn from my Modern Railways magazine feature, 'Informed Sources'. This estimate does not include the Intercity Express Programme, or the EMUs for Thameslink and Crossrail.

Intercity Express Programme

At the time of going to press, it was predicted that a preferred bidder for the Intercity Express Programme (IEP) would be selected by the end of 2008. However the DfT Rail procurement team appeared reluctant to take into account two external factors which have emerged since the project was launched – the global financial crisis, and the growing support for a rolling programme of railway electrification.

Against the background of its dispute with the ROSCOs, DfT Rail decided to adopt a new procurement model for IEP, based on a 30-year train service provision contract. This would be provided by a consortium of companies - including finance, manufacture and maintenance partners. The contract period had to be cut back to 20 years to avoid the deal appearing on the government's books.

Two consortia had submitted bids - the Express Rail Alliance (ERA) (made up of Bombardier, Siemens, Babcock & Brown, and Angel Trains) and Agility Trains (with Hitachi Europe joined by John Laing Projects & Development, and Barclays Private Equity). DfT Rail officials have claimed that both bids are within budget and fully compliant with the specification.

What seems more likely is that the consortia are trading off concessions on the basis of realistic, but non-compliant technical offers. But even without the worldwide financial crisis, funding IEP is likely to be difficult and expensive because of the uncertainty over electrification.

Table 1 - Net additional vehicles in the DfT Rolling Stock Plan (RSP)

RSP phase	Train operating company / scheme	Net vehicles
1	National Express East Anglia	188
1	TransPennine Express	42*
1	First Capital Connect (Batch 1)	61
1	London Midland (Batch 1)	16
2	First Great Western	52
2	c2c	40
2	South West Trains	105
2	London Midland (Batch 2)	51
3	Northern Rail	182
3	First Capital Connect (Batch 2)	24
3	London Midland (Batch 3)	26
3	Arriva Cross Country	6
3	East Midlands Trains	3
Other	First Capital Connect (KO1)	44
Other	First Capital Connect (KO2)	126
Other	South Central	106
Other	South Eastern	110
Other	Chiltern	12
Other	Virgin West Coast	106
	Total	**1300**

Table 1 - Notes
KO1 and KO2 - 'key output' phases of work on the Thameslink Programme of route redevelopment.
* This figure should have been 24 (DfT error).

Source: DfT Rail, July 2008.

Creation of 10-car Class 450 trains for South West Trains' Windsor line services, by adding additional vehicles to existing trains, is one of the elements of the DfT rolling stock plan. A pair of Class 450 EMUs stands at London Waterloo. Tony Miles

Finance & Leasing

Table 2 – Analysis of '1,300 vehicles' for Control Period 4, 2009-2014

Present train operating company	Power	Maker	class	trains	formation (cars)	vehicles	Delivery
Intercity							
(F) Virgin West Coast	EMU	Alstom	390	4	11	44	2011
(F) Virgin WC (lengthening)	EMU	Alstom	390	31	2	62	2012
Virgin WC (lengthening option)	EMU	Alstom	390	21	2	42*(A)	2012
IEP (pre series)	EMU				Various	90*(A)	2013
London & Southeast							
National Express East Anglia	EMU	(Siemens) (L)		37(b)	4	148	2010
First Great Western (to be confirmed)	DMU						
(F) Southeastern (HS1 Domestic)	EMU	Hitachi	395	29	6	174*(A)	2009
Southeastern	EMU	(Bombardier) (L)				110	
(F) TfL - London Overground	EMU	Bombardier	378	24	3	72*(A)	2008-2009(May)
(F) TfL - London Overground	EMU	Bombardier	378	20	4	80*(A)	2008-2009(May)
(F) TfL - London Overground	EMU	Bombardier	378			36*(A)	2009-2010 (May)
(F) TfL - London Overground	EMU	Bombardier	378	7	4	28*(A)	2009-2010 (May)
(F) TfL - London Overground	DMU	Bombardier	172	8	2	16*(A)	2009 (Q4)
(F) Chiltern Railways	DMU	Bombardier	172	4	2	8	2010 (Q3)
Chiltern Railways	DMU	(Bombardier) (L)	172			12	
(F) Southern (d)	EMU	Bombardier	377	12	4	48	2009
(F) Southern (e)	EMU	Bombardier	377	11	4	44	2009
Southern	EMU	(Bombardier) (L)				154	
South West Trains (f)	EMU	(Siemens) (L)	450			33	2010
South West Trains	EMU	(Siemens) (L)	450	18	4	72	
Regional							
TransPennine Express (g)	DMU	Siemens	185			24	
(F) London Midland	EMU	Siemens	350/2	37	4	148	2010 (July)
(F) London Midland	DMU	Bombardier	172	27	2/3*	69	2010 (July)
London Midland	DMU	(Bombardier) (L)	172			26	
London Midland (h)	EMU	(Siemens) (L)		4	4	16	
Northern (j)	DMU					125	
Northern	EMU	(Siemens) (L)		25	3	75	
(F) ScotRail	EMU	Siemens		38	3/4	130 *(A)	2010 (Dec)
Total in RSP						**1218**	

Table 2 - Notes
*(A) - vehicles not in RSP's '1,300 vehicles' and excluded from total.
L) - manufacturer shown in brackets could logically win a repeat order.
(d) - transferred to FCC for Thameslink Key Output Zero.
(e) - allows transfer of Class 377 units for Thameslink Key Output Zero.
(g) - in DfT table, figure of 42 shown in error. TPE seeking 24 vehicles to lengthen Class 185 fleet.
(h) - additional to Class 323 cascade to meet 66 net additional vehicles in RSP.
(j) - actual quantity depends on size of Class 150 cascade from London Overground and London Midland.

F) - firm orders placed.
(b) - assumes London Midland retains seven x Class 321.
(f) - single vehicles to provide 10 car Windsor Line trains.

Source - Modern Railways 'Informed Sources' analysis

IEP was conceived originally as a replacement for the diesel InterCity125 High Speed Train (HST) and was then known as HST2. The largest HST fleet is operated by First Great Western, and the Great Western main line is now likely to be electrified within the next 15 years, making new diesel trains redundant at half life.

This clearly affects residual value, which would be reflected in high lease rentals. In addition, few observers believe that - even without electrification - diesel traction will be viable over the full 30-year book life of a new diesel power car.

Leasing experts consider that the risk of early displacement, plus the rising price of oil, or both, will make the diesel IEP unfundable. At the time of writing, procurement of the diesel and hybrid (diesel plus electric) versions of IEP is going ahead, but this position is unlikely to be sustainable.

Fortunately, the existing HST fleet is capable of further life extension in addition to the recent re-engineering of power cars. A 40 year working life would take the fleet through to 2025. This would maintain services until the GWML is electrified.

Diesel multiple-units
Concerns over the long term viability of diesel traction are already manifest in the current rundown of the diesel multiple-unit (DMU) market. Bombardier will continue to take Turbostar orders while the continuity of production can be sustained, but the company estimates that the remaining UK market totals only 100-200 vehicles at most. Siemens will not bid for further DMUs because it does not have a Turbostar equivalent. It is unlikely that another other manufacturer would go through the long and expensive acceptance process to enter a shrinking niche market.

With an uncertain service life, residual value for new DMUs is poor. Already Porterbrook is telling operators that it is unlikely to fund further expansion of its Turbostar fleet except for small numbers in particular circumstances.

In addition to residual value issues, DMUs are becoming increasingly expensive. A Bombardier

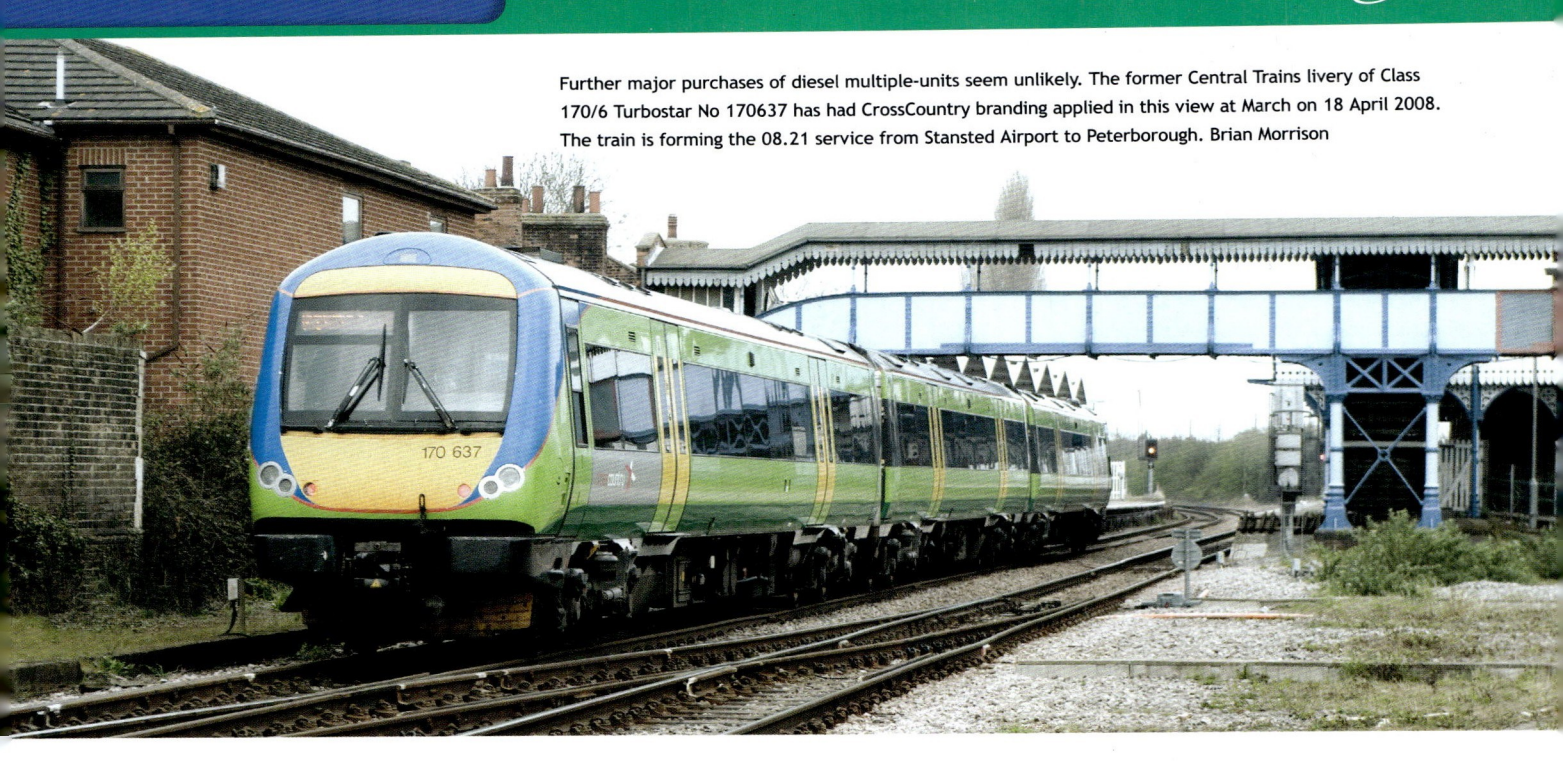

Further major purchases of diesel multiple-units seem unlikely. The former Central Trains livery of Class 170/6 Turbostar No 170637 has had CrossCountry branding applied in this view at March on 18 April 2008. The train is forming the 08.21 service from Stansted Airport to Peterborough. Brian Morrison

Turbostar now costs 20-30% more than the equivalent Electrostar. In the current financial crisis, funders will direct the limited investment available to electric multiple-units, where you can acquire more vehicles with strong residual values for the limited funding available.

There is also the long term future of the 1,500 ex-British Rail DMU vehicles to be considered. These will start to fall due for replacement from 2015 onwards. One estimate expects around half to be displaced by a rolling programme of electrification.

To maintain services on the remaining unelectrified network, life extension and re-engineering is likely to provide the answer for the foreseeable future. This will allow time for alternative sources of traction energy for self-propelled trains to emerge.

Table 3 - Passenger train orders since privatisation

Original customer	Manufacturer	Type	No of vehicles	Delivery	Funder
Anglia Railways	Bombardier	Class 170 DMUs	32	2000	P
Arriva Tr Nthn	Siemens/CAF	16x4-car Class 333 EMUs	64	2000-04	A
c2c	Bombardier	74x4-car Electrostar EMUs	296	1999-2001	P,A
Central Trains[a]	Bombardier	23x2-car, 10x3-car Class 170 DMUs	76	2000-04	P
Central/Silverlink	Siemens	30x4-car Class 350/1 (West Coast route)	120	2004-05	A
Chiltern Railways	Bombardier	Class 168 DMUs	67	1998-2005	P, H
Connex	Bombardier	Electrostar EMUs	618	2000-05	H
Connex / Southern	Bombardier	28x3-car, 154x4-car Electrostar EMUs	700	2002-05	P
First N Western	Alstom	16x3-car, 11x2-car Class 175 DMUs	70	2000	A
Gatwick Express	Alstom	8x8-car Juniper EMUs	64	1999	P
First Great Eastern	Siemens	21x4-car Desiro EMUs	84	2002	A
First Great Western	Alstom	14x5-car Class 180 DMUs	70	2000-01	A
Heathrow Connect	Siemens	5x5-car Class 360/2 EMUs	25	2005-06	T
Heathrow Express	CAF/Siemens	9x4-car, 5x5-car EMUs	61	1998-2002	T
Hull Trains	Bombardier	4x3-car Class 170 DMUs	12	2004	P
Hull Trains	Bombardier	4x4-car Class 222 DMUs	28	2005	H
Midland Mainline	Bombardier	17x2-car, 10x1-car Class 170 DMUs		2000-04	P
Midland Mainline	Bombardier	16x4-car, 7x9-car Class 222 DEMUs	127	2004-05	H
ScotRail	Alstom	40x3-car Class 334 Juniper EMUs	120	1999-2000	H
ScotRail	Bombardier	55x3-car Class 170 Turbostar DMUs	165	1999-2005	P, H
Southern	Bombardier	Class 170 DMUs	42	2003-04	P
South West Trains	Siemens	127 x 4-car Class 450 Desiro EMUs	508	2002-07	A
South West Trains	Bombardier	9x2-car Class 170 DMUs	18	2000-02	A
South West Trains	Siemens	45x5-car Class 444 Desiro EMUs	225	2002-05	A
TransPennine	Siemens	51x3-car Class 185 Desiro DMUs	153	2005-06	H
Virgin CrossCountry	Bombardier	40x5-car, 4x4-car tilting DEMUs	216	2001-03	V
Virgin CrossCountry	Bombardier	34x4-car non-tilting DEMUs	136	2000-02	V
Virgin West Coast	Alstom	53x9-car Pendolino trains	477	2001-05	A

Table 3 - Notes

[a]	Plus 1x2-car and 2x3-car originally ordered by Porterbrook for spot hire	A	Angel Trains
V	Halifax Bank of Scotland and Royal Bank of Scotland.	P	Porterbrook
T	Owned by Heathrow Express.	H	HSBC Rail

Finance & Leasing

angel Trains

Increased UK commitment

Leading rolling stock provider, Angel Trains, was acquired from the Royal Bank of Scotland in August 2008 by a consortium of investors advised by Babcock & Brown. Angel Trains International was simultaneously sold to another consortium, and the two companies are now entirely separate.

Rob Verrion has been appointed CEO of the UK business, Angel Trains Ltd. Rob was previously Chief Operating Officer and director of Transco plc where he was responsible for the safety, operations and financial results of the UK gas distribution business.

The owning consortium of Angel Trains Ltd includes the Babcock & Brown European Infrastructure Fund, Babcock & Brown Public Partnerships, AMP Capital Investors, and Public Sector Pension Investment Board, with funds advised by Access Capital Advisers; while Babcock & Brown advised the consortium, structured the transaction and arranged long-term financing.

As an operating lessor, Angel Trains leases a diverse range of rolling stock, including regional, commuter and high speed passenger trains, and freight locomotives, to train operators. It also offers financing and project management for the procurement of new rolling stock, as well as management of heavy maintenance, refurbishment and modifications throughout the whole life of rolling stock assets.

Angel Trains provides about 4,100 passenger train vehicles and 280 freight locomotives to passenger and freight operators in the UK. Angel Trains' customers include 18 of the 20 train operating companies, including significant fleets with South West Trains and Virgin West Coast.

Angel Trains is part of Express Rail Alliance (ERA), a consortium which is bidding for the Intercity Express Programme to design, build, maintain and finance the UK's next generation of high-speed trains. The consortium also comprises Bombardier and Siemens - both with strong track records in delivery and whole life service of long-distance train contracts in the UK - and Babcock & Brown, with its expertise in the structuring and delivery of PFI and PPP type procurement projects.

IEP is one of the largest PPP projects in the world, and ERA says it has put forward to the Department for Transport a proposal that is deliverable, not only in terms of manufacturing and services but also from a financial point of view.

A significant increase in Angel Trains' commitments to the UK rail industry took place in October 2008, when it signed contracts with Alstom for the supply of new Pendolino rolling stock and a 10-year maintenance regime worth a total of £1.5billion. Angel Trains already owns 52 Pendolino tilting train sets on the West Coast main line, in service with Virgin Trains.

The new rolling stock contract includes four new 11-car Pendolino trains and the lengthening by two cars each of 31 of the existing trains. The additional rolling stock (106 vehicles) will create a total of 7,420 extra seats on the fleet. There is an option to extend the remaining 21 existing trains at a future date.

The contract approved by the Department for Transport includes a full service provision for the Pendolino fleet and will extend Alstom's current contract by ten years, beginning on 1 April 2012, the date on which the contract with private operator Virgin

Impression of an Express Rail Alliance high speed train proposed for the Intercity Express Programme. Bombardier / Siemens / Express Rail Alliance

Angel Trains' large fleet of Siemens Desiro electric multiple-units for South West Trains includes Class 450 (as seen here on the left in a 12-car formation) and the long-distance Class 444 (right). The location is Clapham Junction. Tony Miles

Investing in trains

Leasing trains and locomotives across the UK

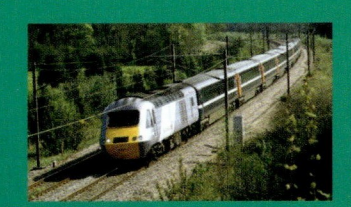

High speed trains
Regional passenger trains
Freight locomotives

www.angeltrains.co.uk

angel Trains

Finance & Leasing

Senior personnel

Chief Executive Officer
Rob Verrion

Re-powering of most High Speed Trains with MTU engines followed a trial financed and led by Angel Trains in collaboration with Brush Traction and First Great Western, two of whose HSTs are seen at Reading. Network Rail

Trains expires. The new trains and the lengthened train sets will all be in service by December 2012. The introduction of the new vehicles will be overseen by Angel Trains with support from Virgin Rail Projects Limited.

Angel Trains placed a major order in January 2008 for Bombardier Transportation's next generation 'Green Trains' for London Overground Rail Operations Limited (LOROL) and Chiltern Railways. The contract, worth approximately £33million, is for eight 2-car next generation Class 172 diesel multiple units for use on the London Overground network and four 2-car units for Chiltern Railways. This vehicle is one of the lightest and greenest modern DMUs available, meeting the latest legislation in emissions and improving the passenger experience.

Angel Trains' milestone investments in the UK have included Desiros for the South West Trains network (approx £0.65billion); over £0.7billion investment in the original fleet of Alstom Pendolino high-speed tilting trains for Virgin on the West Coast main line; and 280 diesel freight locomotives for English, Welsh & Scottish Railway, a capital investment of £0.33billion.

Angel Trains largest refurbishment project, valued at nearly £75million, has been on its fleet of HSTs, including re-powering 49 power cars. The launch of the re-powered fleet was the result of a trial financed and led by Angel Trains, with the integration of the trial engines undertaken by Brush Traction, and the project developed in conjunction with First Great Western. This has now resulted in 49 of Angel Trains' HST power cars having Paxman Valenta engines replaced, by Brush Traction, with new MTU 16V4000R41 engines and Voith Turbo cooling systems. 26 of the power cars are on lease to First Great Western and 23 to National Express East Coast. First Great Western is also committed to fitting MTU engines to the remainder of its fleet, totalling 117.

Other major refurbishment programmes have included the Merseyrail fleet of electric multiple units, including refurbished interiors and engineering modifications; and Chiltern Railways' fleet, including interior re-fitting, air-conditioning retrofit and reliability enhancements.

Over the past 10 years, Angel Trains has invested nearly £3billion in new trains and refurbishment programmes in the UK.

In October 2008, Angel Trains signed contracts with Alstom for the supply of additional Pendolino trains, lengthening of trains, and a 10-year maintenance regime. Pendolino No 390003 arrives at Birmingham International on 6 August 2007, forming the 11.05 service from Wolverhampton to Euston. In the opposite platform is a Class 220 Voyager on a Bournemouth-Edinburgh service. Brian Morrison

In association with **angel** Trains

HSBC

Financing new trains for High Speed 1 and Scotland

HSBC Rail (UK) Limited provides a comprehensive range of services including asset finance and related services for the changing needs of the railway industry.

The latest new fleet financed by HSBC Rail is of electric multiple-units for ScotRail, valued at over £185m. Government agency Transport Scotland will fund the contract with Siemens and HSBC to provide 130 new vehicles from December 2010 – adding 9,000 seats to the Scottish network. The deal is also expected to lead to 134 new jobs being created to operate and maintain the new fleet and expanded depot facilities.

Providing extra capacity in Ayrshire and Inverclyde, the new trains will also allow the release of rolling stock to operate on other key routes such as Airdrie-Bathgate, and will also run new passenger services on the forthcoming Glasgow Airport Rail Link. The trains will be fully air-conditioned and spacious, with full disabled access, provision for cyclists and luggage, as well as CCTV and power sockets for laptops.

Major fleets owned by HSBC Rail include National Express East Coast's electric trains of Class 91 locomotives and Mk4 coaches; First TransPennine Express's Class 185 Desiro diesel multiple-units; Southeastern's fleet of Class 375 and 376 Electrostars; the East Midlands Trains Class-222 'Meridian' trains built by Bombardier; 65 of Freightliner's Class 66s; 27 First GBRf Class 66s; and 12 Class-168/170 'Turbostar' diesel multiple-units.

The company's portfolio of rolling stock acquired since privatisation also includes wagons for Freightliner and First GBRf, and Class 66 locomotives for a number of continental European freight operators. HSBC Rail's Class 66 fleet in the UK totals 92 locomotives. Matisa tamping machines for Grant Rail have also been funded.

A major contract with Wabtec Rail continues a long term commitment on heavy maintenance and overhaul for the East Coast inter-city route's Class 91 locomotives, whose performance and reliability have been improved in a major programme of refurbishment and re-equipment in collaboration with the train operator. The Mk4 coaches hauled by the Class 91s have also recently been undergoing heavy overhaul, following a £30m interior refurbishment over two years, funded by HSBC Rail.

After the arrival in the UK in mid 2007 of the first Hitachi-built Class 395 train for domestic services on High Speed 1, a testing programme has progressed well on both High Speed 1 and Network Rail routes, with the trains fulfilling all expectations.

The trains' new depot at Ashford, developed by HSBC Rail in conjunction with its Depco partners, was opened in October 2007. The project, with an overall value of £87million, includes new depot facilities at Ramsgate as well as Ashford, to support the new Hitachi rolling stock as well as existing fleets.

Hitachi traction will also be introduced to the Southeastern network with the replacement of the existing traction system on the HSBC Rail-owned 'Networker' Class 465/0 and 465/1 electric multiple-unit fleets. Starting in 2009, a highly reliable new traction system designed, built and maintained by Hitachi Rail will be fitted, under a contract signed in 2007.

The 51-train fleet of First TransPennine Express Class-185 Desiro diesel multiple-units was equipped during 2008 for full EcoMode operation. The latest upgrade allows the train to run automatically on two engines out of three where full power is not required, depending on factors such as speed requirements, gradients and station calls, and is expected to bring reduction in fuel consumption to 11% annually. Only one engine remains in use during idling at stations.

During 2008, the overhaul of 114 Class-321 electric multiple-units owned by HSBC Rail, and currently operated by London Midland and National Express East Anglia, got under way.

Senior personnel

Chief Operating Officer
Mary Kenny

Head of Commercial Finance
Simon Purves

Head of Relationship Development
Stephen Timothy

Head of Projects and Procurement
Richard Carrington

Head of Asset Management
John Reddyhoff

Head of Engineering
Chris Moss

Head of Business Standards
Clive Thomas

The programme is expected to run until mid 2011, with trains moved from depots in Ilford and Northampton to Wabtec's Doncaster works for overhaul and repainting plus refurbishment work.

A reliability improvement modification programme on Southern's Class 455 electric multiple-unit fleet has been complemented by a highly successful condition-based maintenance and fault diagnostic system, TAPAS, developed jointly by HSBC Rail, Southern and Tessella, which has been deployed in operation on the Class 455s since 2007.

Other recent work programmes have included bogie overhaul for the Class 465 Networkers by Wabtec at Doncaster, and a corrosion rectification programme on these trains, completed at Stewart's Lane by Serco.

Refurbishment of National Express East Anglia Class 315 electric multiple-units was carried out by Bombardier, with overhauls of First Capital Connect and Silverlink Class 313 electric multiple-units by Railcare at Wolverton. Refurbishment of First ScotRail Class 318 trains was also completed, by Brush Barclay.

During 2008 a programme of fitting Passenger Load Determination equipment to National Express East Anglia's Class 321s and 315s was completed successfully.

Fresh East Midlands Trains livery on Class 222 Meridian No 222019, arriving at Wellingborough as the 14.00 service from London St Pancras to Derby on 2 September 2008. Brian Morrison

Finance & Leasing

Mainstay of the Porterbrook new EMU fleet - the Electrostar. A London Victoria to Littlehampton service restarts from the Clapham Junction stop, formed of Class 377/3 Electrostars Nos 377326 and 377308. Brian Morrison

PORTERBROOK

Expanding and optimising the fleet

Since Porterbrook's creation, it has invested heavily in the UK rail market and currently leases almost 6,000 vehicles: locomotives, coaches, and wagons, to UK train operating companies and freight companies.

Porterbrook's expenditure on new rail vehicles totals some £1.9billion, with significant sums also having been invested in the refurbishment of the fleet which was transferred during the privatisation process. This important contribution has resulted in over 1,700 new passenger and 1,500 new freight vehicles being ordered for the UK market. The next few years will see Porterbrook's continued investment in new rolling stock to ease the capacity constraints on the network. Orders have already been placed for a number of vehicles as a result of the DfT's High Level Output Specification (HLOS). Specifically, Porterbrook has placed orders for the following vehicles:

- 148 Class-350/2 Desiro vehicles which are to be leased to London Midland.
- 69 Class-172 Turbostar vehicles, these are also to be leased to London Midland.
- 48 Class-377 Electrostar vehicles, initially for New Southern Railway but which will now be sub-leased to First Capital Connect.
- 2 Class-139 (Parry People Mover) vehicles for dedicated use by London Midland on the Stourbridge branch.

Fleet performance is a key consideration within the business and in light of this Porterbrook says it was delighted to be in the position to acquire a fleet of Desiro EMUs. This is a new product range for Porterbrook, but with the impressive performance of the existing Desiro fleet there is a great deal of confidence that the vehicles will be a success when they are introduced.

The mainstay of the Porterbrook new EMU fleet is the Electrostar. This fleet provided a significant contribution to the Mk1-rolling-stock replacement project in the south and now achieves performance levels significantly better than the vehicles that were replaced, despite the understandable apprehension which existed during the replacement period. This is an achievement that should not go unnoticed, Porterbrook believes.

In developing the portfolio, Porterbrook has invested in some new technology. While the Turbostar classification is not new, the Class 172 fleet is significantly different from those which have gone before. These vehicles will be delivered with a new drive train arrangement, new bogies, and gangways fitted on driving vehicles. These changes bring risk to the project and Porterbrook is working with London Midland and manufacturer Bombardier in an effort to reduce the likelihood of these problems crystallising during the project.

While new trains often steal the headlines, the existing Porterbrook fleet, both passenger and freight rolling stock, is the lifeblood of the business. The optimisation of the fleet is based on Reliability, Availability, Maintainability and Safety (RAMS) - characteristics which Porterbrook points out it places at the heart of the business. Whether the relationship with the train operator is based on a 'Dry Lease' (operator conducts all maintenance activities) or a 'Soggy Lease' (Porterbrook takes responsibility for heavy maintenance arrangements), a consistent interface is maintained. The approach allows fleet management actions to be correctly aligned and for the short and long term perspective on the fleet to be given adequate consideration.

Pursuing this strategy, Porterbrook has conducted and facilitated vehicle refurbishment and reliability programmes. The most extensive project in this regard was the South West Trains Class-455 electric multiple-unit refurbishment. Essentially the programme brought a number of elements together - vehicle overhaul, passenger enhancement and reliability improvements - in a most effective and collaborative manner. These types of activities are essential, believes Porterbrook, if the industry is to maximise its economic performance as the demand for the services which it offers continues to grow.

Fundamentally, Porterbrook's aim in the coming years is to not only continue with its investment in new trains for the UK rail industry, but to also further improve the RAMS characteristics and passenger environment of its existing fleet by working closely with the train operators and suppliers to identify opportunities.

Porterbrook told The Modern Railway that as the industry continues to advance, there is still much to do, and as ever Porterbrook will strive to be at the forefront of UK rolling stock procurement and development.

The purchase of Porterbrook Leasing from Abbey National was agreed in October 2008 by a consortium including Antin Infrastructure Partners (the BNP Paribas sponsored infrastructure fund), Deutsche Bank and Lloyds TSB, subject to regulatory approvals.

Senior personnel

Managing Director
Paul Francis

HSBC

In association with **angel** Trains

DeltaRail

- Design and Project Management of Rolling Stock Refurbishment and Enhancement
- Dynamic Signalling & Signalling Control
- Operational Planning and Real Time Railway Management
- Infrastructure Support Services and Systems
- Rolling Stock Maintenance Solutions

See www.deltarail.com for further information
or contact Adam Perry +44 (0)870 190 1526

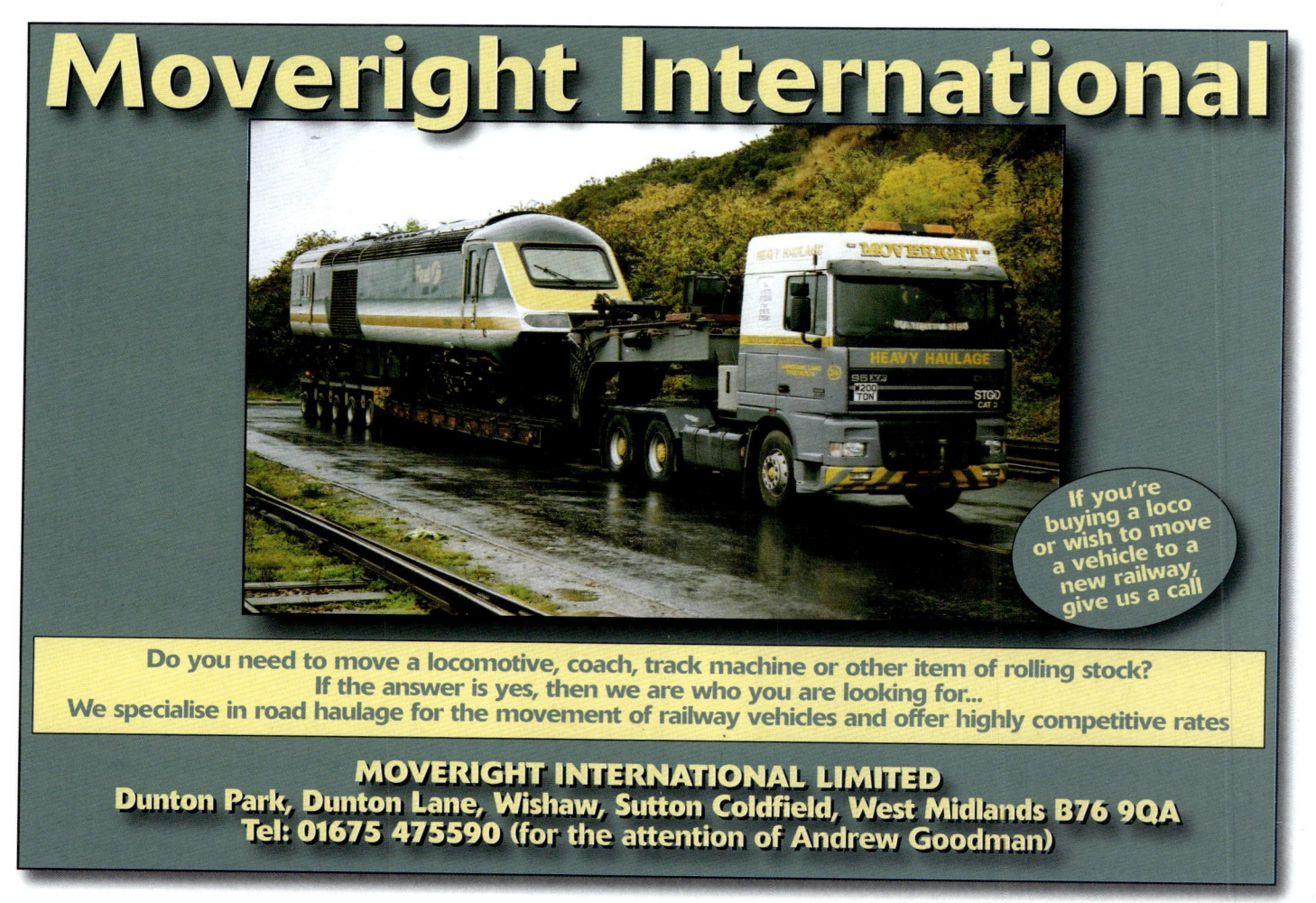

Moveright International

If you're buying a loco or wish to move a vehicle to a new railway, give us a call

Do you need to move a locomotive, coach, track machine or other item of rolling stock?
If the answer is yes, then we are who you are looking for...
We specialise in road haulage for the movement of railway vehicles and offer highly competitive rates

MOVERIGHT INTERNATIONAL LIMITED
Dunton Park, Dunton Lane, Wishaw, Sutton Coldfield, West Midlands B76 9QA
Tel: 01675 475590 (for the attention of Andrew Goodman)

HSBC

CSRE

RESCO EUROPE

CSRE & RESCO Europe - your one stop shop for freight wagon supply

Wagons supplied
Leasing arranged
TSI Certification & Authorisation managed
Maintenance provided

We offer a new concept in the provision of freight wagon supply, taking responsibility and ownership of the entire process of freight wagon supply.

This enables operators and logistics providers to focus on their core businesses without additional hassle whilst at the same time ensuring that their fleets grow cost-effectively, reliably and safely.

CSRE Limited
Address: Unit 3, Dyrham, SN14 8DY
Tel: +44-1279-778999 / +44-7973-450026
E-Mail: enquiry@csre.co.uk
Web: www.csre.co.uk

RESCO Europe Limited
Address: Suite 3D, Belper, DE56 1YD
Tel: +44-1773-828666 / +44-7971-329653
E-mail: enquiry@rescoeurope.co.uk
Web: www.rescoeurope.co.uk

Train Fleet Maintenance & Manufacture

In association with

SIEMENS

Train Fleet Maintenance/Manufacture

The bogie drop at Siemens Northam (Southampton) depot, serving the South West Trains fleet. Tony Miles

SIEMENS

2008 marked ten years since Siemens gained a first foothold in the UK main line market, with the entry into service of the Siemens/CAF Class 332 electric multiple-units (EMUs) with Heathrow Express. A second significant step came five years ago, with the deliveries of the first Desiro EMUs to First Great Eastern (now National Express East Anglia). The Desiro is undoubtedly a successful product with AC, DC and diesel variants all at the top of the reliability tables.

The announcement that Siemens will be supplying 38 new Class 380 Desiro EMUs to ScotRail, in a mixture of three and four-car formations, means that, by the end of 2010, a total of 354 Desiro trains will be in service on Britain's railways. The diesel variant, the First TransPennine Express Class 185, has become the most reliable DMU in the country and is also saving around 2million litres of fuel a year, following the introduction of the Eco Mode – this shuts down an engine on each set when operating on less demanding parts of the network, and allows drivers to coast for significant distances when power is not required.

The DfT's commitment to add more capacity across the railway in the UK, along with a confirmation that electrification is back on the agenda, means that Siemens is already working on proposals for further orders. The next generation of electric units, derived from the successful Desiro design, is being specifically targeted at inner suburban applications such as Thameslink and Northern Rail.

As well as highlighting the excellent performance of the Desiro family, Siemens is keen to point to the environmental credentials of the trains themselves. The Desiro units are almost 98% recyclable and, while the industry is just getting to grips with the challenge of handling regenerative braking on DC lines, the DC sets were built with regenerative capability - and the regenerative braking on the AC fleet is significantly reducing energy consumption.

For Siemens, however, success is measured not just by the delivery of a well designed and tested product, but by ensuring that the 600-strong, hand-picked, service team which manages the trains shares the vision of the train operating companies (TOCs), their immediate customers, and has the right maintenance philosophy and organisation in place. A major innovation has been to organise the various train fleets into product groups rather than a more traditional division by TOCs or other geographical lines. So the Class 332/333 sets form one group, the AC Desiro Classes 350 and 360 form another, and the DC Classes 444 and 450 form a third group, while the Class 185 DMUs stand alone.

This organisation ensures resilience, in that lessons learned on one fleet are shared with others of the same type and there is no holding back of information that might see one TOC benefit at the expense of another. The practical benefit of this is that after over 100million miles of operation, Classes 450, 444, 350 and the National Express East Anglia Class 360 are now in the exclusive 30,000 miles per casualty (MAA) club. The award of three Silver Spanners in consecutive years, in the informal competition devised by Modern Railways' Roger Ford, is helping the trains to gain the 'out of the box' reliability recognition. The knowledge gained through the product group management organisation enabled Siemens to gain permission to switch the exam periodicity on the London Midland Class 350s from every 8,000 miles to every 16,000 miles from March 2008. This clearly has financial implications and is thought to have played a key part in the successful bid for the ScotRail EMU order. This periodicity has now also been applied to the SWT Desiro fleet.

Clean and well presented trains also play an important part in encouraging people to use the railways, and so every time a Siemens train comes onto a depot it is washed. Ensuring that this is also environmentally friendly is the aim

100 million miles and still going strong

The award winning Siemens Desiro UK fleet has reached a landmark in passenger service. These trains operate fast connections to London's Heathrow airport and regional services to cities, towns and villages across the UK. With excellent track records for on time delivery and with regenerative braking to recycle energy, the Siemens Desiro offers a reliable, sustainable and trusted mode of transport.
Complete mobility.

www.siemens.com/mobility

SIEMENS

Train Fleet Maintenance/Manufacture

of the latest equipment which recycles 75% of the water used and works down to minus 5°C.

Purpose-built depots

In all, ten depots are involved in servicing Siemens trains, but most of the maintenance of the various fleets takes place in the company's own purpose-built depots, aiming it to deliver on a 'passion for reliability' from facilities designed for the 21st century. The new buildings at Ardwick in Manchester, Northam in Southampton, Kings Heath in Northampton, and York all conform to the latest building regulations and employ equipment developed by Siemens Building Technologies after many years of research and development.

The use of appropriate materials means that the depots require a lot less heating to achieve their ambient temperature and lose less of the energy that is put into them. Lighting levels inside the depots are adjusted in accordance with ambient 'lux levels' outside via sensors in the ceilings, whilst plenty of skylights mean that on a good day the ambient lighting can be turned down automatically as natural light takes over. The depots all have eco-friendly waste management systems and ensure proper waste segregation and the recycling of materials where possible. Siemens is proud that its safety team is known as 'SQE Engineers', standing for Safety, Quality and Environment, ensuring that all aspects are treated equally. Siemens is also proud to be the only maintenance organisation to have been 'Recognised for Excellence' by the British Quality Foundation.

Whilst the word 'partnership' is sometimes over-used on the railways, Siemens suggests that it is the bedrock of the success of the improved performance of the railways, as one senior manager points out: 'The level that the railways are performing at now is being achieved through partnership and co-operation rather than through contractual clout and leverage.'

The strong link between manufacturer and TOC also means as far as passengers are concerned there should be no divide between the train manufacturers and their maintenance teams and the TOCs themselves. As Siemens explains: 'If you go to some meetings you can't tell who is from the TOCs and who is from Siemens. You just see a group of people who want to provide the best service they can. We've consciously recruited people from TOCs as part of our team.' Managers from Siemens are encouraged to travel regularly on their trains and to join in 'meet the managers' sessions alongside TOC managers, even if it means that they end up answering passenger questions about timetables!

This level of partnership has also ensured that the service teams on the depots understand exactly why the TOCs don't just need every diagram to be covered, but want every train to be clean and well presented with all onboard facilities working and able to run to the end of the diagram without an intervention. Ensuring that the trains look attractive to passengers and continue to deliver a 'new train' feel even after many years in service is taken seriously and even damage to exterior paintwork or vinyls is rectified as quickly as any interior defects.

Underpinning all of this is the fact that delivering new trains, on time, which are comfortable and safe, which run 'out of the box', brings in praise from existing passengers and wins new ones to rail.

The first of the latest order of Class 350/2 for London Midland, No 350234 is rolled out at Siemens' Wildenrath test facility in Germany on 8 October 2008. Ken Brunt

Siemens UK train fleets

Existing

Class 332	4/5-car EMUs - Heathrow Express (14 trains)
Class 333	4-car EMUs - Northern Rail (16 trains)
Class 350/1	4-car Desiro EMUs - London Midland (30 trains)
Class 350/2	4-car Desiro EMUs - London Midland (37 trains)
Class 360/1	4-car Desiro EMUs - National Express East Anglia (21 trains)
Class 360/2	5-car Desiro EMUs - Heathrow Connect (5 trains)
Class 444	5-car Desiro EMUs - South West Trains (45 trains)
Class 450	4-car Desiro EMUs - South West Trains (127 trains)
Class 185	3-car Desiro DMUs - First TransPennine Express (51 trains)

On order

Class 380	3/4-car Desiro EMUs - First ScotRail (38 trains)

Senior personnel

Managing Director, Rolling Stock
Steve Scrimshaw

Director Rolling Stock Sales
David Wilson

Director Rolling Stock Service
Steve White

Onboard for total reliability

Saft MATRICS MRX nickel-cadmium (Ni-Cd) batteries have logged millions of track miles on UK EMU trains. Impressively, six years after the first of the new specialized rail batteries entered service on the passenger network they continue to provide a consistently high level of performance and reliability. And, in contrast to lead-acid batteries that would have already needed replacing, they will be good for at least nine more years.

Thanks to this outstanding track record, a growing number of OEMs and operators are making the switch to MATRICS MRX batteries for new projects. Their decisions are based on the TCO (total cost of ownership) analysis that shows Ni-Cd batteries to be the most cost-effective option over the whole life of the train due to their reliability, long service life and extended maintenance intervals.

Saving space and weight

Saft MATRICS MRX batteries are tailor made to deliver maximum performance and reliability and low TCO in rail applications. They provide the low maintenance and long service life benefits of sintered/PBE technology within a slim, light-weight block battery package, housed in a flame retardant polypropylene case, which shows a major size and volume advantage compared with conventional batteries. The MATRICS MRX design is also extremely reliable and does not suffer from the unpredictable failure which can affect some batteries, even in extreme temperatures ranging from -30°C to +70°C.

Extended service intervals

For operators, the extended service intervals offered by the Saft batteries can be a vital factor. MATRICS MRX battery top-ups are only needed at 12 month intervals. What is more, the integrated filling system means that all the cells can be filled from one central point – a simple operation that can take just 10 minutes.

Saft. Expert in battery systems for key railway projects

- Complete battery system solutions
- Extremely long life – mature and reliable Ni-Cd technology
- Low maintenance, low total cost of ownership
- Saft recycles, globally

www.saftbatteries.com

Train Fleet Maintenance/Manufacture

47 of these eight-car trains are being produced for the London Underground Victoria Line by Bombardier. Bombardier

BOMBARDIER

Significant new train contracts

Bombardier plays a leading role in the manufacturing, refurbishment and maintenance of rolling stock in Great Britain and is the only remaining train builder in the country. Bombardier Transportation has production facilities in Derby and Plymouth, and 24 maintenance, refurbishment and overhaul centres across the UK. Bombardier currently maintains approximately 2,500 vehicles in Great Britain.

Bombardier's rail transportation products are in operation in all major British regions, in the full range of rail services - intercity, urban and suburban, metros and light rail systems. Across the south of Britain, Bombardier's Electrostar electric multiple-units are high in the reliability tables for new generation EMUs, with the star performers the Class 357 Electrostars operated by c2c. Electrostar trains are also successful on Southeastern and Southern, where they help to bring thousands of commuters to and from London daily.

Bombardier has won significant new contracts from Transport for London for Electrostar trains for London Overground, a total of 216 vehicles, plus an associated train services agreement. These new units will be operated on the East London Line and North London Railways and will enter passenger service during 2009 and 2010.

Further orders of Electrostars for Southern were also awarded in 2007-08, to increase the overall fleet and ease pressure on the busy First Capital Connect Thameslink route.

The revamped CrossCountry and West Coast networks run Bombardier non-tilting Voyager and tilting Super Voyager diesel electric multiple-units (DEMUs). Bombardier DEMUs are also in daily passenger service with UK operator, East Midlands Trains, and Bombardier's Turbostar diesel multiple-units are in service with many operators, helping to connect towns and cities across Britain. The 'greener' new generation Turbostar has been ordered by Porterbrook Leasing for Govia's London Midland

55 new-generation Bombardier built Docklands Light Railway cars are being delivered. Nos 106, 105 and 104 were previewed at West India Quay station on 13 March 2008. Brian Morrison

Senior personnel

Chief Country Representative UK
Colin S. Walton

franchise and by Angel Trains for Transport for London, and Chiltern, with over 90 cars ordered to date. These Turbostars are lighter and offer reduced CO2 emissions, improved fuel consumption and are over 90% recyclable.

Traffic congestion in Croydon has been significantly reduced through the use of Bombardier FLEXITY Swift light rail vehicles on Transport for London's Tramlink system, and the Nottingham Express Transit system now benefits from Bombardier INCENTRO low-floor trams. 55 new-generation Bombardier built Docklands Light Railway cars will also be delivered through until 2009, joining the current Bombardier-manufactured fleet of 94 automatically driven vehicles.

Bombardier is a participant in the renewal of the London Underground network, as the supplier of 1,778 metro cars, to be built at Bombardier's production site at Derby. Bombardier is also responsible for the introduction of new signalling systems, project management and fleet maintenance.

Bombardier's Services Division provides a wide range of services support from full fleet maintenance through refurbishment to technical support and spares supply agreements. The CrossCountry and West Coast fleet of Bombardier-built DEMUs are fully maintained at a purpose-built facility, Central Rivers, and a number of overnight outstation depots. Bombardier is also giving a new lease of life to many ageing fleets across the UK and has a specialist refurbishment centre based a Derby, which has handled the contract from First Great Western to refurbish 405 High Speed Train trailer cars.

Bombardier's UK Derby site is also housing the first Orbita Knowledge Control Centre. Orbita is a leading edge predictive maintenance capability which helps operators to increase fleet utilisation, improve reliability and availability, reduce in-service failures and improve the passengers' overall journey experience.

Bombardier has joined forces with Siemens, Angel Trains and international investment and advisory firm, Babcock & Brown, in the Express Rail Alliance, bidding to win the Intercity Express Programme (IEP) which is planned to introduce a new generation of long distance trains by 2014.

Bombardier is also active in rail signalling systems through its Rail Control Solutions Division, which has its global manufacturing base in Plymouth. Bombardier's RCS Division is a leader in the field of automatic train protection (the European Rail Traffic Management System, ERTMS), integrated control systems (Interflo and Citiflo), computer and relay based interlocking systems and complete life cycle support.

The first London Overground Class 378 Electrostar electric multiple-unit to be built, No 378001, at work on the test track at Bombardier's Litchurch Lane Works, Derby, on 16 September 2008. The full fleet will number 54 four-car trains of two types, DC-only for the East London Railway and dual-voltage for the North London Railway group of lines, which includes London Euston-Watford Junction, Stratford to Richmond, and Willesden Junction to Clapham Junction. Eight new-generation two-car Turbostar diesel multiple-units have also been ordered for London Overground. Brian Morrison

Interior of London Overground Class 378 Electrostar. Brian Morrison

The Class 357 Electrostars operated by c2c are star reliability performers. Class 357/0 Electrostar No 357005 (left) arrives at Grays on 7 January 2008, forming the 11.20 service from London Fenchurch Street to Southend Central. Arriving in the opposite direction No 357004 forms the 11.20 from Southend Central to Fenchurch Street. Brian Morrison

Train Fleet Maintenance/Manufacture

The first orders have been secured for the AGV, seen here undergoing dynamic tests. Alstom / F. Christophorides

ALSTOM

Long term revenue projects and new generation trains for the UK boost Alstom

Alstom Group, serving the worldwide power generation and rail transport markets, continued its strong commercial and operational performance through FY 2007/08, achieving record results, with orders of 23.5billion Euro and sales of 16.9bn Euro.

During 2008, Alstom consolidated its leadership in the high-speed sectors of its Transport business by securing sales of its advanced AGV train to NTV, the private Italian operator. The AGV will run at 360km/h, the fastest train in commercial service.

Alstom wholly funded the development of the AGV prototype, the first very-high-speed train to combine distributed power and the articulated bodyshell, which was unveiled in February 2008.

In the UK, the latest Pendolino contracts will contribute significantly to current order book, and mark a return to form for the UK business, with the 1.8bn Euro deal for new cars and a 10-year extension to the current maintenance contract to 2022.

Alstom will deliver four new 11-car trainsets and extend 31 of the trains in the current fleet to 11 cars, providing a total of 7,420 extra seats on the West Coast main line for operation when the new franchise begins in 2012. All Alstom's Traincare centres will be adapted to accommodate the longer trains, with a new facility being built at the Liverpool site which will integrate the new vehicles.

The step up in maintenance is not new to Alstom – it is providing an extra trainset every day for the December 2008 timetable, which also requires the trains to be more extensively used.

Alstom employs 2000 people in its UK Transport business. The majority of these are employed on the long-term maintenance projects held by Alstom, such as the West Coast main line Pendolino, Northern and

Alstom has long-term maintenance responsibility for its trains on two London Underground lines – this is the Northern Line's Morden depot. Alstom / P. Bigland

In association with **SIEMENS**

Senior personnel

Managing Director, Alstom Transport UK and Ireland - Paul Robinson

Jubilee lines of the London Underground, and Northern and Arriva Train Wales fleets.

Today Alstom is looking to grow the business, in accordance with its strategy of profitable growth, focusing on selectivity in order intake. Where it is possible to capitalise on existing, successful products, Alstom offers these for the opportunities in the UK that require them, such as an enhanced Jubilee Line train proposed for the Piccadilly fleet renewal, Citadis trams, and also tram-trains based on successful vehicles running in Germany and the Netherlands.

Alstom is also developing a new generation EMU for the UK from one of its generic platforms, adapting it to UK specifications and incorporating technological advances.

The company's platforming strategy, developed in answer to market evolution towards standard products, enables it to maximise the benefit of shared development costs. The necessary customisation is made possible through modular design combined with specific developments.

Apart from new rolling stock and experience in maintenance, Alstom also brings to the market a pedigree in turnkey projects, enabling it to provide new depots and infrastructure, from a catalogue including the Lausanne metro in Switzerland and the Singapore Circle Line.

Train Tracer

The innovative Train Tracer tool converts raw train fault data into business information that drives Alstom Transport's maintenance activity and also provides reports to the operator and infrastructure provider. This integrated, regimented business process allows the business to plan repairs for today's failures tonight.

Alstom believes this is a pioneering approach to train fault data recovery, analysis and exploitation - already implemented for the West Coast main line project, it has accelerated fleet management and reliability growth.

An automated back office function automatically recovers train operation and fault data from trains, and distributes it throughout the project and across the organisation using internet protocols that support home working and Inter-Enterprise exchange. Routine tasks are propelled through a service-orientated framework for action to be taken.

Automated, structured analysis of live fault data is available at all workstations. Value is added to the raw train data through correlation with other business data, and critical events are delivered as 'pop ups' on users' screens.

Live fleet-view 'dashboard' screens, presenting 'Faults In Today's service', indicate where today's problems are. Value is added by a live connection to the business' Service Order System, hosted in a SAP application, helping to optimise the response to problems.

Exception reports monitor the bigger picture and highlight fault trends that may not be visible on a daily basis.

Faults on the infrastructure can also be identified using geo-spatial analysis from measurements taken on the train, with information presented in mapping format.

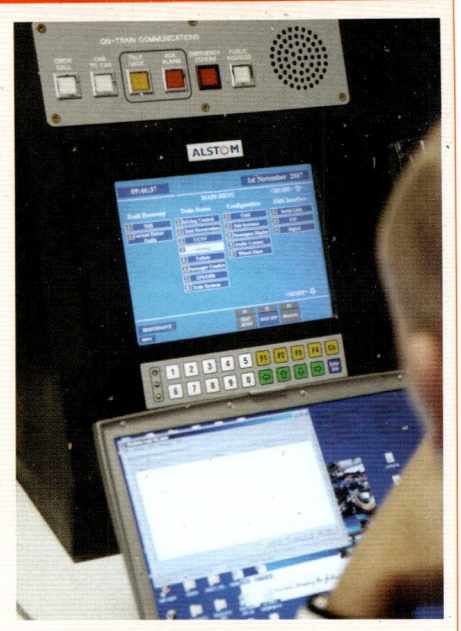

Train Tracer makes automated, structured analysis of live fault data available at all workstations. Alstom/TOMA/C. Sasso

Pendolino trains at Manchester Traincare centre. A major order was placed in late 2008 for new Pendolino cars, and a 10-year extension to the current maintenance contract. Alstom/TOMA/C. Sasso

HSBC

Train Fleet Maintenance/Manufacture

KNORR-BREMSE

Total Operational Support from *rail*services

Issues such as deregulation, heightening customer demands and new technologies are combining to bring dramatic changes for rail operators in the 21st Century.

Dramatic changes

Increased ridership and the growth of incentivised regimes, often with heavy penalties for delays and particularly in-service failure, is now highlighting further attention on areas such as securing customer satisfaction and revenue optimisation.

These pressures and the resultant challenges, force operators and manufacturers alike to maximise their levels of in-service availability. This is particularly relevant with regards to new braking and other train systems, many of which now employ sophisticated electronic control systems.

The increasingly demanding climate within the industry makes it essential for train operators to remain totally focused on running a railway safely, efficiently and profitably. To enable rail operators and train builders to meet these demands and keep trains running, specialist support is needed.

New levels of support

Knorr-Bremse understands the new environment and appreciates the resultant pressures faced by rail operators and train builders, says Business Development Manager, Ian Palmer. 'Knorr-Bremse has the resources and expertise to counter this pressure and has taken the step of actually restructuring its business to deliver new levels of service and maintenance support to customers. The result is *rail*services.'

*rail*services is not simply a brand or a short term initiative but is a dedicated service and maintenance business division within the Knorr-Bremse Rail Group. High demand components are now available on all Knorr-Bremse brands, even at short notice. Knorr-Bremse production schedules for replacement parts and original manufacture have been organised separately to avoid any delays caused by potentially conflicting priorities.

By using *rail*services, customers can be confident that the company that designed, developed, tested, installed and commissioned the original system can fully support that system over its entire operational life.

In addition, by using *rail*services the integrity and quality that went into the creation of the original Knorr-Bremse system is maintained in terms of performance, reliability and safety, says Ian Palmer. Further, this quality is fully warranted by Knorr-Bremse, who can still hold responsibility for the design integrity and systems assurance, providing further value added support for the customer.

The type of support available from *rail*services ranges from fleet service contracts, project specific overhauls, modernisation, refurbishment, systems and servicing training as well as original parts provision; *rail*services provides comprehensive but flexible support. Obsolescence management, increasingly important with the widespread use of sophisticated electronics and mechatronics, is also available through *rail*services.

Knorr-Bremse understands that speed of turn around is essential to ensure that trains stay in operational service, Ian Palmer explains. 'Skilled Knorr-Bremse *rail*services personnel, using extensive in-house resources, including specialist equipment and software, ensure that turn around times are minimised. It only takes some five working days, for example, to overhaul the complete braking system of a London Underground Central Line eight car train.'

The ability to deliver

The *rail*services status is allocated only to those locations within the global Knorr-Bremse Rail Group who can demonstrate that they have the ability to deliver total service support combined with fast turn around times.

In the UK and Ireland, rail operators can access *rail*services from Knorr-Bremse Rail Systems (UK) Limited (KBRS) who are based in Melksham, Wiltshire.

Microelettrica Scientifica brake resistor undergoing a complete railservices rebuild.

Knorr-Bremse Rail Systems (UK) Limited moved to a new, purpose built facility in March 2005. The move saw over £10million of investment by the company in both a new building and new equipment to fully support the operational promises of its *rail*services status. This new resource, with a staff of over 300, is, the company claims, probably the best of its type in the industry. New, state-of-the-art equipment in dedicated areas such as; strip and clean, vibration test, environmental chamber, full brake system test, electronics and software development, compressor test, platform screen system test and the paint shop, means that *rail*services can cope, whatever the demand, says Ian Palmer.

'The natural choice for maintenance support on all Knorr-Bremse Rail Group brands in the UK and Ireland - including Frensistemi, IFE, Merak, Microelettrica, Westinghouse Brakes, and Westinghouse Platform Screen Doors - is *rail*services.'

Contact

Business Development Manager
Ian Palmer
www.knorr-bremse.co.uk

Production hall at Knorr-Bremse Rail Systems (UK).

In association with **SIEMENS**

CAF

CAF - Construcciones y Auxiliar de Ferrocarriles, SA - has been selected to deliver Edinburgh's tram vehicles, and has built several fleets of electric multiple-units and diesel multiple-units for railway operators in the UK and Ireland.

The company's products range from complete transportation systems for urban, suburban and long-distance routes and turnkey solutions, to custom-made parts and components. With several manufacturing plants in Spain, CAF has the capability and experience to manufacture using steel, aluminium or stainless steel. CAF also offers maintenance, upgrading and overhaul of vehicles and components.

For the Edinburgh Tram project, CAF is responsible for the design, production, testing and delivery of 27 tram units, with delivery of the first tram in April 2010, and passenger service due to begin in July 2011. A structural warranty for up to 30 years is provided. At over 40m long, Edinburgh's fully accessible trams will be the biggest in the UK, carrying 250 passengers, and have been designed to give a timeless and attractive appearance. Each tram will be made up of seven articulated carbodies resting on four bogies, and will feature an access height of 300mm above the rail. CAF has also recently supplied trams to Seville's new tram system.

CAF's diesel multiple-unit for Northern Ireland. CAF

CAF provided the 14 electric multiple-unit trains for Heathrow Express, in conjunction with Siemens, and 16 trains based on that design were also supplied for the Airedale and Wharfedale lines between Leeds, Bradford Forster Square, Ilkley and Skipton.

The company has also put into service a fleet of 23 diesel multiple-units for Northern Ireland Railways, in three-car units. CAF's Class 2900 diesel multiple-units for Iarnród Éireann (IE - Irish Rail) are formed of four cars, all powered. The most recent order supplied to IE was for 67 Mk4 intercity carriages, including driving cars.

In a major research project, AVI-2015, CAF is heading a consortium of six companies to develop technologies to optimise high-speed interoperability between tracks with different signalling systems, power supplies and gauges. Major reduction in train weight, energy consumption and certification time are key aims.

CAF's latest high-speed trains developed for Spanish Railways, RENFE, have bogies that can change from 1435mm standard gauge to 1664mm Spanish gauge without stopping, at up to 40km/h. In service since 2005, other complex features include dual signalling, radio and electrification systems. They have a 275km/h design speed, and are operating at up to 250km/h.

In 2007 CAF made a profit before taxation of almost 98million euros, an increase of 130% on 2006. Turnover in 2007 amounted to 874million euros, a 9% increase on the figure for the previous year.

LUCCHINI UK

Part of **LUCCHINI RS** GROUP

Ashburton Road West
Wheel Forge Way
Trafford Park
Manchester M17 1EH
Tel: +44 (0) 161 886 0300
m.wood@lucchini.co.uk

Key Projects

New Wheelsets for:
- Hitachi "CTRL"
- BT "Electrostar"
- BT Trains for London

Wheelset Overhaul:
- Unipart Rail
- Alstom "Virgin Pendolino"
- Siemens "Desiro"
- GE Rail Systems

Wheel & Axle Supply:
- Alstom Transport
- Irish Rail
- Metronet Rail

We Supply:
- Monobloc wheels
- Machined Axles
- New Wheelsets

Services Offered:
- Wheelset heavy overhaul
- Wheel reprofiling
- Gearbox overhaul
- Bearing overhaul
- Mobile NDT
- Design & validation

As Agent for Ascometal & other Lucchini plants:
- Rolled carbon, alloy & stainless bars
- Steel rails
- Forgings & castings

HSBC

Train Fleet Maintenance/Manufacture

Hitachi Class 395 No 395002 departs from Ashford on 3 July 2008, on a test run. Stabled alongside is Southeastern's Class 375/6 Electrostar No 375613. Patrick Seale

HITACHI

New high speed trains to enter service in 2009

Hitachi won its first order in the UK rolling stock market in 2004, when it was selected to supply the fleet of 29 high-speed trains to be introduced in December 2009 on domestic services using the Channel Tunnel Rail Link, High Speed 1.

The company submitted its tender in June 2008 for the Intercity Express Programme (IEP), through Agility Trains Ltd - a consortium of Hitachi (Japan) Ltd, Barclays Private Equity and John Laing Projects and Developments.

Hitachi said it was confident that its bid would deliver on the Department for Transport's key objectives and its offering would deliver significant environmental benefits, with the energy consumption lower than existing rolling stock.

Alistair Dormer, General Manager, Hitachi Rail Group, London, said: 'We are delighted to submit our tender for the IEP, offering British rail passengers the best of Japanese design combined with high speed UK rail expertise. The Hitachi Super Express Train design has been developed using proven technology from the latest Japanese Shinkansen "bullet train" and the 140mph Hitachi class 395 trains for CTRL which are on schedule to enter service in Kent in 2009'.

The new six-car trains for High Speed 1 have been dubbed Olympic Javelins in the context of the rapid service that they will provide between London, Kent and Stratford for the London 2012 Olympic and Paralympic games. Longer term, the trains will be used for services not only over High Speed 1, but also onto local lines in Kent, and operated by the Southeastern passenger rail franchise.

Hitachi Europe Ltd's new Ashford train maintenance facility was unveiled along with the first Class 395 train in October 2007. The depot includes a five track maintenance shed, with a double road bogie and equipment drop pit, and a heavy inspection road. It also includes carriage washing plants, a waste removal facility, a 25kV test track and a tandem wheel lathe. The depot was built by the Depco consortium, including HSBC Rail, Fitzpatrick Contractors, RPS Burks Green, EMCOR UK, GrantRail, Mace and Norton Rose.

A further three trains joined the first Class 395, manufactured in Kasado, Japan, for a rigorous testing programme on High Speed 1 and on the Kent network. The remaining 25 trains will be delivered in 2009.

The £250million contract for an original total of 28 Class-395 trains was signed in June 2005 with the former Strategic Rail Authority, as the award of the Southeastern passenger rail franchise to Govia had not yet taken place. A 29th train, valued at an extra £8.5m, was announced in July 2006, to allow a service to Dover, after Network Rail confirmed that it will fund the improvements needed to Shakespeare tunnel, near Dover. HSBC Rail (UK) is financier of the trains.

Each train consists of six coaches and will have the ability to rapidly couple for 12-coach trains. Hitachi will also maintain the new trains, initially for the duration of the new franchise.

The Southeastern network is seeing another application of Hitachi traction with the replacement of the existing traction system on the HSBC Rail-owned 'Networker' Class 465/0 and 465/1 electric multiple-unit fleets, starting in 2009.

In late 2006, Hitachi and its partners Porterbrook Leasing, Network Rail and Brush Traction concluded trials of Europe's first hybrid high-speed train. The test train's new hybrid traction system (consisting of a battery-assisted diesel-electric traction drive) was installed in an existing High Speed Train power car, with the equipment fitted into the front power car and a modified trailer car. The test vehicles began service trials in November 2007 on Network Rail's New Measurement Train, with a conventional power car at the other end of the train.

The hybrid design allows the train to move off using battery power alone, with power from the diesel engine blended in from 30km/hr. The traction motors act as generators and charge the batteries during braking - about 80% of the regenerated braking energy is expected to be recovered.

For space reasons, the bank of 48 lithium ion battery modules (1 kWh each) was fitted in the coach next to the power car - both vehicles were made available by Porterbrook, with modification undertaken by Brush Traction.

Experience with running in the New Measurement Train saw fuel savings ranging from 12% on long runs with few stops, to 20% on routes involving frequent braking.

Senior personnel

General Manager - Alistair Dormer

Passenger Train Operators

In association with

railservices
from KNORR-BREMSE

Passenger Operators

Train operating companies - index

Company	Owning group	Franchise start date	end date	Page no
First Great Western	First	4/2006	4/2016	p59
First Capital Connect	First	4/2006	4/2015	p60
First ScotRail	First	10/2004	10/2014	p62
First Trans-Pennine Express	First/Keolis	2/2004	1/2017	p63
*First Hull Trains	First/Renaissance	-	-	p64
Southern	Govia	5/2003	9/2009	p66
Southeastern	Govia	4/2006	3/2014	p67
London Midland	Govia	11/2007	9/2015	p69
National Express East Coast	National Express	12/2007	3/2015	p72
National Express East Anglia	National Express	4/2004	3/2014	p74
c2c	National Express	5/1996	5/2011	p75
Arriva Trains Wales	Arriva	12/2003	10/2018	p77
Cross Country	Arriva	11/2007	3/2016	p78
Northern Rail	SercoNed	12/2004	9/2013	p80
*Merseyrail (a)	SercoNed	7/2003	7/2028	p81
South West Trains	Stagecoach	2/2007	2/2017	p83
East Midlands Trains	Stagecoach	11/2007	3/2015	p84
Virgin Trains	Virgin/Stagecoach	3/1997	3/2012	p86
Chiltern Railways	DB Regio	2/2002	12/2021	p88
*Wrexham & Shropshire	DB Regio/Renaissance	-	-	p90
*Grand Central	-	-	-	p91
*Heathrow Express	BAA	-	-	p94
*Eurostar	London & Continental	-	-	p92
*Eurotunnel	-	-	-	p93
*London Overground Concession (b)	LOROL (MTR and DB Regio)	11/2007	11/2014	p185

Notes:
* Not franchised by national authorities
(a) concession agreement with Merseytravel
(b) concession agreement with Transport for London.

As a result of franchise and fleet changes in recent years, all Class 175 'Coradia' diesel multiple-units are now in Arriva Trains Wales' fleet. Class 175/0 No 175006 'Brondyffryn Trust' arrives at Crewe on 17 October 2008, forming the 10.34 service from Manchester Piccadilly to Milford Haven. Brian Morrison

Paddington station concourse at night. 3rd October 2008. Paul Bigland

Passenger operator finances

Chris Cheek of consultant TAS reviews the financial performance of the train operating companies

After a year of financial and economic uncertainty, the remarkable thing about the UK's public transport operations in 2008 has been the resilience of their patronage and revenue levels in the face of a downturn in retail activity, and falling employment levels.

There is certainly both anecdotal and statistical evidence that suggests a market shift towards both bus and rail travel by motorists. There appear to be two motives: to achieve a reduction in spending on petrol, and to make a change in travel habits for some journeys in order to make at least a gesture towards reducing carbon emissions.

At the same time, though, transport operators have faced very significant increases in operating costs – particularly fuel. Rises in electricity and diesel prices have been particularly strong, whilst rising commodity prices have affected the cost of other raw materials. However, the cooling of the economy did seem to be resulting in a slowdown in labour cost inflation.

The latest accounts for the train operators cover the year 2006/07, a period when these trends were just beginning to make their presence felt. But the increases in costs – coupled with further changes in track access charge levels as part of the settlement of the 2003 interim review or railway financing – can clearly be seen in double digit increases in both turnover (reflecting increased grant as well as revenue growth) and operating costs.

The analysis undertaken by consultant TAS in its latest 'Rail Industry Monitor' publication shows turnover for all train operating companies (TOCs) rising by 13.1% to £7,676m, whilst operating profits totalled £287m (previous year: £241m on £6,787m), to give an operating margin of 3.7% (previous year: 3.5%). This marks a recovery after two years of reductions, which (at least in part) reflected changes to industry structures. These included the movement away from cost-plus contracts in some of the regional businesses and changes in track access charges. Though TOCs are protected against the cash outlay, the relative movement of subsidy and cost levels does affect overall margins.

Operating costs reached a total of £7,388m, 12.9% above the 2005/06 total of £6,547m. This reflects the increases in fuel and power costs which began to take effect during the year.

The analysis suggests that trends have not been uniform across the industry – with some sharp contrasts between sectors, and between different operators. The analysis reports on 22 companies with financial year ends between 31 December 2006 and 1 July 2007.

InterCity operators saw total turnover rise by 11.5% to £2,595.1m, whilst operating costs rose by 10.9% to £2,534.7m. The resulting operating profit of £60.4m was more than 40% up on the £43m achieved in 2005/06, and was achieved at a margin of 2.3% (2005/06: 1.8%, 2004/05: 3.1%).

In London and the South East, turnover by the companies grew by 12.9% to £3,109m. Operating costs rose by 12.1% to £2,961m. The resulting operating profit of £148.1m compared with £113.4m in the previous year, at a margin of 4.8% (2005/06: 4.1%, 2004/05: 4.8%).

The regional franchises show a slippage in profit levels, as the last of the 'cost plus'

Passenger Operators

contracts came to an end. Turnover rose by 15.6% to £1,971.5m, outstripped by cost increases of 16.7%. Operating profits were 6.6% down at £78.4m (last year £84.4m), at a margin of 4.0% (4.9%).

Looking at individual TOCs, the most profitable individual company in 2006/07 was TransPennine Express, the rapidly growing operator run by a joint venture between FirstGroup and Keolis, which returned an operating margin of 10.3%.

Next came South West Trains, which achieved 8.1% during the last few months (May-February) of its second three-year franchise. Third came another franchise heading towards a new competition – the South Central operator New Southern Railway (trading as 'Southern') on 6.7%.

The worst performing TOC was Midland Mainline, with an operating loss of 6.1%. Other loss makers included Chiltern (3.9%), c2c Rail (1.4%), Island Line (0.7%) and Gatwick Express (0.2%).

In the summaries below, figures are extracted from accounts lodged at Companies House. Practice concerning the declaration and calculation of different cost and revenue items varies between train operators. This occasionally makes interpretation and reconciliation difficult: major issues are noted in the brief commentaries.

InterCity operators

First Great Western
This was the first full year of the new franchise, which incorporates the old Thames Trains commuter services and the Wessex Trains regional routes as well as the high speed Great Western services. The comparative figures illustrate the scale of the change in the business, which almost doubled its turnover following the change.

Period to:	31 Mar 07 £000	31 Mar 06 £000
Turnover	701,478	396,840
Operating Costs:	664,598	372,247
Operating Profit:	36,880	24,593
Operating Margin:	5.3%	6.2%
Turnover per Employee	£157,494	£148,075
Track Access	218,442	76,958
Rolling stock lease	63,072	50,900
Revenue Grant	97,400	0

Gatwick Express
This franchise ceased in June 2008 and the Victoria-Gatwick service passed to Southern. During the year in question, Gatwick Express reduced its operating losses substantially, and made a small pre-tax profit. This resulted from strong revenue growth at around three times the prevailing rate of inflation, which outstripped the rise in operating costs to deliver the sharply reduced operating loss.

Period to:	31 Dec 06 £000	31 Dec 05 £000
Turnover	62,519	56,169
Operating Costs:	62,650	59,520
Operating Profit:	(131)	(3,351)
Operating Margin:	-0.2%	-6.0%
Turnover per Employee	£215,583	£167,170
Rolling stock lease	5,934	6,096
Track Access	14,212	10,251

Midland Mainline
The company recorded operating and pre-tax losses during the year, as revenue growth failed to keep pace with rising operating costs - particularly arising from increases in rolling stock leasing costs.

Period to:	31 Dec 06 £000	31 Dec 05 £000
Turnover	186,944	184,065
Operating Costs:	198,320	178,827
Operating Profit:	(11,376)	5,238
Operating Margin:	-6.1%	2.8%
Turnover per Employee	£171,666	£165,824
Track Access	52,365	14,050
Rolling stock lease	30,574	26,079

GNER
The company traded profitably during the year, but concluded that it would not be able to meet its franchise obligations under the new agreement which commenced in March 2005. Consequently, a new agreement was reached with the Department for Transport in December 2006 under which the financial risks were assumed by the Department until a new franchise could be let. This was achieved in November 2007, when this company ceased to trade, and the franchise passed to National Express Group.

Period to:	06 Jan 07 £000	07 Jan 06 £000
Turnover	531,615	477,690
Operating Costs:	508,268	470,447
Operating Profit:	23,347	7,243
Operating Margin:	4.4%	1.5%
Turnover per Employee	£184,653	£155,853
Track Access	139,805	86,135
Rolling stock lease	62,207	69,511

Virgin Cross Country
This was the last full year of Virgin's franchise, before the remapping and hand-over to Arriva in November 2007. The company saw profits dip sharply during the year as revenue growth failed to keep pace with cost increases.

Period to:	03 Mar 07 £000	04 Mar 06 £000
Turnover	470,942	411,792
Operating Costs:	470,046	406,355
Operating Profit:	896	5,437
Operating Margin:	0.2%	1.3%
Turnover per Employee	£280,323	£242,373
Rolling stock lease	122,879	117,177
Track Access	166,963	117,371
Revenue Grant	181,492	150,786

Virgin West Coast
The company returned to profit during the year, which saw Virgin resume responsibility for revenue risk after the signing of a revised franchise agreement. In return, Virgin receives a revised subsidy profile through to the original franchise end date of 2012. This took effect on 9 December 2006.

Strong revenue growth and higher subsidies contributed to the turnover increase, which significantly exceeded the rise in operating costs.

Period to:	03 Mar 07 £000	04 Mar 06 £000
Turnover	641,642	558,239

The best performers in 2005/06 - and the worst

No	Company	Operating margin	Pre tax margin
1	First TransPennine	10.3%	11.4%
2	South West Trains [a]	8.1%	9.8%
3	Southern	6.7%	7.9%
4	South West Trains [b]	5.9%	7.7%
5	Merseyrail Electrics	5.8%	6.3%
6	Silverlink	5.6%	6.9%
7	First Capital Connect	5.3%	6.5%
8	First Great Western	5.3%	6.0%
9	GNER	4.4%	4.4%
10	Southeastern	3.8%	4.9%
11	Central Trains	3.7%	4.3%
12	Northern Rail	3.5%	4.4%
13	Arriva Trains Wales	2.7%	3.5%
14	First ScotRail	2.3%	3.3%
15	Virgin West Coast	1.7%	2.6%
16	NEX East Anglia	1.6%	2.6%
17	Cross Country	0.2%	0.6%
18	Gatwick Express	(0.2%)	0.8%
19	Island Line [a]	(0.7%)	3.5%
20	c2c Rail	(1.4%)	(1.0%)
21	Chiltern	(3.9%)	(5.2%)
22	Midland Mainline	(6.1%)	(4.4%)

[a] until February 2007
[b] from February 2007

Operating Costs:	630,818	574,060
Operating Profit:	10,824	(15,821)
Operating Margin:	1.7%	-2.8%
Turnover per Employee	£237,206	£202,481
Rolling stock lease	161,666	161,268
Track Access	210,247	158,832
Revenue Grant	83,718	68,163

London and the South East Operators

First Capital Connect
This was the first year of the new franchise, which combines the old Thameslink cross-London service with the Great Northern routes operating from King's Cross and Moorgate to Hertford, Welwyn, Stevenage, Peterborough and Cambridge – services that will also use the Thameslink tunnels when upgrade works are complete in 2014. The franchise traded profitably as well as paying a premium to the government.

Period to:	31 Mar 07
	£000
Turnover	361,198
Operating Costs:	342,134
Operating Profit:	19,064
Operating Margin:	5.3 %
Turnover per Employee	£178,988
Rolling stock lease	30,109
Track Access	104,316

Southern
The Govia-group company improved its profits by more than 50% on the back of strong revenue growth, though with continuing above-inflation cost increases. Revenue grew by more than over 14%, though it is not immediately clear whether this is due to the efforts of the company or the taxpayer, since no separate declaration of passenger revenue and subsidy payments has been made.

Period to:	30 Jun 07	01 Jul 06
	£000	£000
Turnover	538,774	474,767
Operating Costs:	502,655	451,772
Operating Profit:	36,119	22,995
Operating Margin:	6.7 %	4.8 %
Turnover per Employee	£150,328	£132,432
Rail contracts	213,943	179,804

Southeastern
This was the first year of the new South Eastern franchise, after its three years of direct state operation. The new operator, Govia, has a different accounting period, so the results cover a 65-week period.

Period to:	30 Jun 07	31 Mar 06
	£000	£000
Turnover	686,805	465,294
Operating Costs:	660,636	470,845
Operating Profit:	26,169	(5,551)
Operating Margin:	3.8%	-1.2%
Turnover per Employee	£178,067	£119,644
Track Access	0	101,979
Rail contracts	245,303	0
Revenue Grant (est.)	165,500	82,509

National Express East Anglia
The company improved its performance during the year, recording the first profits since the franchise started in April 2004. Revenue growth was strong, and more than double the prevailing rate of inflation. It was also double the level of cost increases, so driving the company into the black.

Period to:	31 Dec 06	31 Dec 05
	£000	£000
Turnover	454,329	411,065
Operating Costs:	447,097	423,366
Operating Profit:	7,232	(12,301)
Operating Margin:	1.6%	-3.0%
Turnover per Employee	£147,318	£133,897
Track Access	99,173	53,569
Rolling stock lease	96,815	92,495

c2c Rail
The company continued to post operating and pre-tax losses, albeit much reduced during the year from previous levels. Strong growth in revenue outstripped rising operating costs to produce the reduced operating loss. This was further assisted by increased net interest earnings. The disappointing commercial performance came in spite of good service quality.

Period to:	31 Dec 06	31 Dec 05
	£000	£000
Turnover	106,628	93,294
Operating Costs:	108,107	95,699
Operating Profit:	(1,479)	(2,405)
Operating Margin:	-1.4%	-2.6%
Turnover per Employee	£177,123	£152,941
Track Access	21,445	11,031
Rolling stock lease	22,526	21,801
Revenue Grant	16,114	9,079

Passengers come and go on Merseyrail's busy city-centre underground route. Merseytravel/PTEG

Passenger Operators

Revenue protection is a key issue for train operating companies, including here at Cardiff Central. Arriva

Silverlink

Cash profits rose, but margins fell, as turnover and costs rose by roughly one-third in this, the last full year of the franchise in this form. The company split in two in November 2007, passing to the new London Midland and London Overground operators. Cost increases of one-third outstripped the revenue increase, producing a slightly higher cash profit, but lower margins.

Period to:	31 Dec 06	31 Dec 05
	£000	£000
Turnover	233,257	177,688
Operating Costs:	220,113	164,755
Operating Profit:	13,144	12,933
Operating Margin:	5.6%	7.3%
Turnover per Employee	£190,881	£145,408
Rolling stock lease	28,414	23,067
Track Access	66,364	51,037
Revenue Grant	84,945	49,937

Chiltern

The company recorded a loss during the year as it continued to suffer the after-effects of the line closure in the summer of 2005, due to a tunnel collapse.. Whilst there was a healthy increase in turnover - and particularly a strong recovery in passenger revenue - operating cost increases were even more substantial.

Period to:	06 Jan 07	07 Jan 06
	£000	£000
Turnover	110,009	98,907
Operating Costs:	114,249	91,666
Operating Profit:	(4,240)	7,241
Operating Margin:	-3.9%	7.3%
Turnover per Employee	£154,507	£131,700
Rolling stock lease	14,210	12,772
Track Access	30,250	17,176
Revenue Grant	20,056	13,923

Island Line

The franchise ended on 4 February 2007 and was merged with South West Trains into a new company, Stagecoach South Western Trains; thus, the more recent set of figures covers 40 weeks only. The company recorded a small trading loss during its few months. On an estimated annualised basis, revenue was 19% ahead, whilst operating costs rose by 30%.

Period to:	04 Feb 07	29 Apr 06
	£000	£000
Turnover	3,611	3,942
Operating Costs:	3,636	3,639
Operating Profit:	(25)	303
Operating Margin:	-0.7%	7.7%
Turnover per Employee	£92,590	£101,077
Rolling stock lease	93	121
Revenue Grant	2,600	2,703

South West Trains

On 4 February 2007, Stagecoach's original South West Trains franchise and Island Line were taken over by a new company, Stagecoach South Western Trains. These figures for the original South West Trains therefore only cover 40 weeks. On an estimated annualised basis, turnover rose by 13% whilst costs were 14.2% higher.

Period to:	04 Feb 07	30 Apr 06
	£000	£000
Turnover	592,158	683,475
Operating Costs:	544,235	622,206
Operating Profit:	47,923	61,269
Operating Margin:	8.1%	9.0%
Turnover per Employee	£116,087	£128,958
Rolling stock lease	78,677	102,128
Track Access	148,590	102,367
Revenue Grant	147,009	124,116

Regional franchises

Arriva Trains Wales

Profits fell slightly during the year as increases in subsidy and passenger revenue did not match the rise in operating costs, though the slippage was offset by high net interest earnings, and particularly increased pension finance credits. Wales' Assembly Government oversees the franchise.

Period to:	31 Dec 06	31 Dec 05
	£000	£000
Turnover	252,897	238,309
Operating Costs:	246,007	230,812
Operating Profit:	6,890	7,497
Operating Margin:	2.7%	3.1%
Turnover per Employee	£122,172	£129,095
Track Access	66,285	64,113
Rolling stock lease	35,523	34,452
Revenue Grant	142,031	136,264

First ScotRail
The company achieved a substantial increase in cash profits during the year, albeit at only slightly improved margins. There was a strong increase in revenue which outstripped rising costs to produce the cash profit improvement, which was further assisted by increased net interest earnings.

Period to:	31 Mar 07	31 Mar 06
	£000	£000
Turnover	494,347	404,681
Operating Costs:	482,947	395,798
Operating Profit:	11,400	8,883
Operating Margin:	2.3%	2.2%
Turnover per Employee	£120,191	£102,972
Rail contracts	215,464	143,548
Revenue Grant	270,794	201,590

First TransPennine
The company increased its profits in cash terms during the year, but traded at slightly lower margins. The franchise saw the addition of the Blackpool-Manchester Airport services in June 2006 and completed the introduction of its new fleet of Class 185 trains. Increases in both revenue and subsidy payments were overtaken by higher operating costs during the year - though the company remains one of the most profitable train operators.

Period to:	31 Mar 07	31 Mar 06
	£000	£000
Turnover	210,877	184,852
Operating Costs:	189,218	165,018
Operating Profit:	21,659	19,834
Operating Margin:	10.3%	10.7%
Turnover per Employee	£209,828	£189,982
Track Access	66,802	60,952
Rolling stock lease	41,816	24,138
Revenue Grant	112,233	95,450

Central Trains
The company traded profitably in what was the final full year of the franchise prior to the remapping of November 2007. However, though cash profits were higher, margins were virtually unchanged as increased costs matched revenue growth. The profits were insufficient to offset £26.7m worth of accumulated losses from earlier years.

Period to:	31 Dec 06	31 Dec 05
	£000	£000
Turnover	383,446	315,935
Operating Costs:	369,392	303,994
Operating Profit:	14,054	11,941
Operating Margin:	3.7%	3.8%
Turnover per Employee	£158,777	£130,282
Track Access	107,361	65,242
Rolling stock lease	62,335	45,914
Revenue Grant	231,006	176,169

Merseyrail Electrics
The company earned higher profits in cash terms but traded at very slightly lower margins during the year. Turnover rise by 17% during the year, but costs rose by a marginally higher percentage.

Period to:	06 Jan 07	07 Jan 06
	£000	£000
Turnover	109,845	93,866
Operating Costs:	103,437	88,352
Operating Profit:	6,408	5,514
Operating Margin:	5.8%	5.9%
Turnover per Employee	£94,776	£83,215
Track Access	18,689	10,886
Rolling stock lease	11,494	11,299

Northern Rail
The company saw profits fall sharply. Despite strong revenue growth, which rose at over three times the prevailing rate of inflation, operating cost increases more than wiped this out, driving the operating profits down.

Period to:	06 Jan 07	07 Jan 06
	£000	£000
Turnover	520,117	468,354
Operating Costs:	501,704	437,606
Operating Profit:	18,413	30,748
Operating Margin:	3.5%	6.6%
Turnover per Employee	£113,439	£102,350
Track Access	123,875	78,056
Rolling stock lease	32,805	33,355
Revenue Grant	337,747	297,110

Non-franchised operators

Hull Trains
The company experienced very strong revenue growth during the year, which helped the business to more than double its profits. Passenger volumes were 30% up, and the company has now recouped its set up costs and early losses.

Period to:	31 Mar 07	31 Mar 06
	£000	£000
Turnover	18,012	13,601
Operating Costs:	14,923	12,326
Operating Profit:	3,089	1,275
Operating Margin:	17.1%	9.4%
Turnover per Employee	£207,034	£186,315

Eurostar UK
The company recorded increased losses during the year, as revenue growth failed to keep pace with rising operating costs. This was of course ahead of the opening of High Speed 1 and the move to St Pancras in November 2007, which has resulted in very strong revenue and patronage growth.

Period to:	31 Dec 06	31 Dec 05
	£000	£000
Turnover	234,300	220,900
Operating Costs:	362,700	329,100
Operating Profit:	(128,400)	(108,200)
Operating Margin:	-54.8 %	-49.0 %
Turnover per Employee	£176,165	£166,969
Track Access	41,900	40,800

London & Continental
Revenue growth outstripped rising costs for Eurostar's parent and High Speed 1's developer, to result in reduced operating and pre-tax losses during the year.

Period to:	31 Dec 06	31 Dec 05
	£000	£000
Turnover	273,900	235,500
Operating Costs:	353,800	313,700
Operating Profit:	(79,900)	(78,200)
Operating Margin:	-29.2%	-33.2%
Turnover per Employee	£177,511	£158,693

More details of the 'Rail Industry Monitor' project can be found on the TAS website at www.tas.uk.net

---

A portrait of TAS
TAS was founded in 1989, and operates two businesses: the Preston-based consultancy company, The TAS Partnership Limited, and its publishing arm, TAS Publications & Events, based in the Yorkshire Dales.

The TAS Partnership now employs some 25 full-time staff, plus a network of associates and has a turnover in excess of £1.4m. Clients include central and local government, as well as a wide range of operators, including all the major groups.

TAS works exclusively in public passenger transport, and has expertise and experience in bus, community transport, light rail and conventional rail.

TAS Publications produces a range of reports on the market and financial performance of public transport operations, including the major annual Rail Industry Monitor and Bus Industry Monitor reports, published since 1991.

For further details, visit www.tas.uk.net.

Passenger operator articles
In the following pages, statistics for train operating companies are drawn from data published by the Office of Rail Regulation and the companies.

Punctuality figures are the Public Performance Measure annual average for 2007-08 - for long distance operators, the percentage of trains arriving within ten minutes of planned arrival time at final destination; and for London & South East operators and regional operators, the percentage arriving within 5min of planned arrival time.

Passenger Train Operators

First Group Rail Franchises
Simplified Diagram

- First ScotRail
- Hull Trains
- First Great Western
- First TransPennine Express
- First Capital Connect

First Group

First Group's UK passenger operations embrace the franchises for Greater Western and Thameslink/Great Northern (branded as First Great Western and First Capital Connect, both commencing in April 2006); ScotRail, and (in conjunction with Keolis) TransPennine Express. First also operates Hull Trains, the non-franchised open access operator in which it has an 80% share, resulting from the purchase of GB Railways in 2003. First also provides rail freight services through First GB Railfreight. First UK Rail has 13,000 employees. The group also runs the Croydon Tramlink network.

First is responsible for running almost a quarter of the UK passenger rail network and carrying almost 275million train passengers a year (year to 31 March 2008).

Group revenue increased by 26.9% over 2006-07 to £4,707.6m in 2007-08 (year to 31 March). Adjusted operating profit rose to £360.1m, an increase of 38.9%. The Group operating margin increased to 7.6% (2007: 7.0%). First's other major operations are in UK Bus and North America. In 2007 it won a contract, in partnership with Danish State Railways, to run train services in the Oresund region, in both Denmark and Sweden, from 2009 until 2015. During 2007-08, First Group joined the FTSE 100 index in the UK.

Revenue in the UK Rail division increased by 6.2% in 2007-08 to £1,937.0m (2006-07: £1,824.1m) and operating profit increased by 10.3% to £120.0m (2007: £108.8m). The train operating companies delivered passenger volume and revenue growth of 6.9% and 10.8% respectively. The group said its main growth drivers in UK Rail were improved performance and quality, revenue protection measures and an overall appetite for rail travel.

First Great Western

7 year franchise from 1 April 2006
Possible three year extension

The new Greater Western franchise, branded as First Great Western, began operation on 1 April 2006 for seven years with a possible three-year extension. Operating services out of London Paddington, across the South and West of England and South Wales, it combines previous Great Western inter-city, London and Thames area and West Country regional franchises, bringing together more than 4,000 staff. First committed to pay the DfT a premium of £1.13billion during the franchise.

First says it has been working hard to improve performance and customer service at the franchise, which had fallen short of its own standards and the expectations of passengers.

£29m was committed by First in early 2008, as part of a remedial action plan agreed with the Department for Transport, for a substantial package of passenger benefits to improve punctuality, improve customer service and reduce overcrowding. More drivers, guards and technicians were recruited to improve reliability; station information systems were being upgraded; and more trains were hired to increase seating capacity on some of the busiest services, including the Cardiff-Portsmouth route; an enhanced training programme was introduced; and the London and Thames Valley fleet was to benefit from a more comprehensive interior refurbishment than previously planned.

A number of new management appointments were made, including a new, dedicated Performance Director and team. New route directors were recruited for Intercity, London & Thames Valley, and the West Country to concentrate on improving performance in the geographically diverse franchise.

On winning the franchise, First Group committed itself to a £200m investment programme on First Great Western, with ten additional diesel High Speed Trains (HSTs) and infrastructure improvements. Upgrading of the majority of the Reading-London relief lines to 90mph, completed by mid-2008, was aimed at creating greater capacity, reliability and improved journey times for commuters.

Significant improvements in performance were achieved in 2008, with new timetable introduced in December 2007 credited with helping to improve punctuality and increase seating capacity on the busiest parts of the network.

First Great Western's 12.07 from London Paddington to Plymouth passes through Starcross on 25 May 2008, led by Class 43 power car No 43005, with No 43187 on the rear. Brian Morrison

Passenger Train Operators

The entire HST fleet has now been completely overhauled with revamped interiors and more seats in its 405 carriages and new more reliable, environmentally friendly engines in its 117 power cars. The new engines have improved operating performance, doubled reliability (the power cars reaching 33,000 miles per casualty by mid 2008), cut carbon emissions by 64% and smoke emissions by 42%.

The contract for refurbishment of the HST coaches was awarded to Bombardier. The project, valued at £63m, covered 405 carriages, and increased the number of seats by more than 10% with a higher density seating layout in Standard class. In late 2008, First Great Western was planning to retain a small counter-service area instead of the trolley service previously envisaged on some HSTs.

The power cars were refurbished with new engines from MTU, cooler groups from Voith, and new electronic controls, all being installed by Brush Traction.

12 of the HST power cars and 42 trailer cars added to the fleet are owned outright by First Group, and ten additional power cars have been leased from Porterbrook. Three of the original 14 Class-180 'Adelante' 125mph diesel multiple-units which entered service in 2002 are expected to remain with FGW until mid 2009, by when an additional HST transferred from National Express East Coast is due to enter service after refurbishment.

The refresh of the West Country regional train fleet is due for completion early in 2009, aiming to provide a more comfortable and cleaner on-board environment, with a range of technical improvements to make the trains more reliable.

Close working has continued with Network Rail to tackle significant railway infrastructure challenges. A number of initiatives have been designed to improve performance.

First had been a shareholder in Great Western Holdings, formed by former British Rail management and employees, which won the original Great Western InterCity franchise in 1996. First later bought the whole company, which also won the North Western Trains franchise (now split to form parts of the Northern, Wales & Borders, and TransPennine Express franchises).

Heathrow Connect, a stopping service between Paddington and Heathrow Airport using Class 360 electric multiple-units built by Siemens, is a joint venture between First Great Western and BAA plc, complementing the non-stop Heathrow Express service.

First Great Western has three major depots: Old Oak Common, London; Laira, Plymouth; and St Philips Marsh, Bristol; with other depots at Penzance, Landore (Swansea) and Exeter. The Bristol depot has been re-equipped with new, state-of-the-art, maintenance facilities for local trains.

For London & Thames Valley services, First Great Western has 36 Class-165 Networker Turbo diesel multiple-units (DMUs) and 21 Class-166 Networker Express Turbos.

For West Country regional services, there are five 2-car and ten 3-car Class-158 Express DMUs; 15 Class-153 single car diesel trains; 25 Class-150 Sprinter DMUs (five temporarily sub-hired from Arriva Trains Wales); eight Class-143 Pacer railbus trains, and (on hire from Northern until 2010) seven Class-142 Pacers. A refurbishment programme (£4m on interiors, £7m on technical improvements) is being carried out - the contractors are Wabtec (Classes 143, 153 and 158), and Pullman Rail (Class 150/2).

A £2million refurbishment contract for First Great Western's 17 sleeper carriages was carried out by Railcare. Four Class 57 diesel locomotives are mainly used on the London-Penzance overnight sleeper trains.

First Great Western
Key statistics 2007/08

Punctuality (0-10 minutes):	89.6 %
Passenger journeys (millions):	80.9
Passenger kilometres (millions):	4,985.9
Timetabled train kilometres (millions):	44.8
Route kilometres operated:	2129
Number of stations operated:	211
Subsidy per passenger kilometre (pence):	-0.09
Staff Employed as at 31/03/2007:	4,454

Senior personnel

Chief Operating Officer
Andrew Haines (left)
Engineering Director
Andy Mellors
Trains Director
Kevin Gale
Commercial Director
Tom Stables
Customer Services Director
James Burt
Performance Director
Mark Hopwood
Projects Director
Matthew Golton
Route Director, High Speed Services
Tom Joyner
Route Director, West
Malcolm Drury
Route Director, London & Thames Valley
Ian Smith

First Capital Connect

Six year franchise from 1 April 2006
Possible extension to nine years

First Capital Connect has two groups of routes: Thameslink runs from Brighton and Gatwick Airport through London to Luton and Bedford, with a London loop line via Wimbledon and Sutton, while Great Northern runs from London King's Cross and Moorgate to Welwyn, Hertford, Stevenage, Peterborough, Cambridge and King's Lynn.

Thameslink and Great Northern were previously operated by separate companies, and will be linked at King's Cross by the Thameslink Programme, on which work is now underway. This will provide major capacity improvements for the cross-London core of the Thameslink route. Major service changes to assist with construction work will be introduced in March 2009.

The First Capital Connect franchise is to run for up to nine years, depending upon performance targets and implementation of the Thameslink Programme. The franchise has a performance-related break clause after four years, and is extendable, at the DfT's discretion, to a total of between six and nine years.

First was expected to pay £808million in premium payments to the government if the franchise term ran to the full nine years. £55m worth of improvements, the majority in the first three years of the franchise term, were pledged to improve service to customers.

Demand has steadily increased on all FCC routes, and the company says this has been particularly strong on the Great Northern services from Cambridge and Peterborough due to good punctuality.

An increase in capacity is planned from May 2009, with five additional Class 321 four-car trains acquired from London Midland. These are to run on the Peterborough route, allowing Class 365s to be switched to the Cambridge route to lengthen four trains to 12 carriages instead of eight, giving 15% capacity increase. FCC said it was working with the Department for Transport to seek a further five extra trains by December 2009.

Also from May 2009, the timetable is being recast to make best use of track capacity on the East Coast main line. A programme of platform lengthening and power supply upgrading was under way on the Cambridge route.

The start of the Thameslink Improvement Project will see 23 new dual-voltage 4-car Class-377 Electrostar trains introduced on the Thameslink route from March 2009. They will be sub-leased by Southern to FCC: most of them will be deployed between Bedford, London and Brighton, with some on services between

Southeastern territory and the Thameslink route. The final eight Class 319s used by Southern should also be transferred to FCC by March 2009.

These changes will give FCC 86 four-car units, enough for 8-car trains on all but six peak Thameslink services - bringing an additional 1,150 seats in the morning peak and 2,080 seats in the evening peak on FCC services, according to the DfT.

Southeastern's Blackfriars-terminating services will be extended to north London via the Thameslink route, using Class 319 trains, along with three peak-period trains operated by 8-car Class 377s, going beyond Blackfriars to Bedford / St Albans. The Class 319s and 377s will be sub-hired from FCC to Southeastern while running on Southeastern's network.

The number of trains running through central London on the Thameslink route will increase from eight to 15 per hour during peak hours from March 2009, said the DfT - essentially combining the existing terminating services at Blackfriars (from the south) and Moorgate (from FCC's Thameslink route). FCC's Moorgate-Farringdon branch will close in March 2009 to allow extension of platforms at Farringdon.

In June 2006, FCC introduced restrictions on the use of off-peak ticket types in the evenings between 16.30 and 19.01. FCC said the changes were introduced to help the company deal with severe overcrowding on northbound evening peak services out of London, prioritising seats for season or full fare ticket holders.

A new station was completed on the Thameslink route in 2007 to serve the new High Speed 1 / Channel Tunnel Rail Link terminal at St Pancras International. The sub-surface structure to house the station was constructed below Midland Road, next to St Pancras, during an eight-month closure of the route from September 2004.

A new performance and training academy, and simulator centre, valued at £1.2million, was opened by FCC in August 2008. It will be used to teach the new drivers required for the Thameslink Programme and help support the company's existing team of 700 drivers. It includes a Class 319 train simulator replicating the train on the Bedford to Brighton route, and a Class 365 train simulator as seen on the Great Northern route.

FirstGroup in 2008 announced a trial of 'Train Energy Management Systems' (TEMS) which could reduce energy consumption by up to 13% on its electric multiple-unit (EMU) fleets. Scheduled to last a minimum of two years from Spring 2008, the trials involve 15 EMUs from First Capital Connect and ten from First ScotRail. The cost of the purchase and management of the TEMS - supplied by FAR Systems SpA - will be around £500,000.

The TEMS work like a railway energy meter to determine energy used by trains when stabled on depot or during station layover, and also monitor the energy usage of driving the train, which can help to develop eco-friendly driving styles.

First Capital Connect
Key statistics 2007/08

Punctuality (0-5 minutes):	90.6 %
Passenger journeys (millions):	96.4
Passenger kilometres (millions):	3,212.3
Timetabled train kilometres (millions):	23.9
Route Kilometres Operated:	495
Number of Stations operated:	79
Subsidy per passenger kilometre (pence):	-2.26
Staff Employed as at 31/03/2007:	2,018

Prior to the March 2009 changes, FCC's Thameslink route has a fleet of 78 Class-319 dual-voltage electric multiple-units, owned by Porterbrook - trains change over at Farringdon between the 750V DC third rail electrification used on the former Southern Region and the 25kV AC overhead system used north of Farringdon. The total includes 12 trains sub-leased from train operator Southern, with eight more to be transferred by March 2009.

Maintenance of FCC's Class 319 trains, previously undertaken at Southern's Selhurst depot, has been transferred to FCC's own depots. The main depot is at Hornsey in north London on the Great Northern route, where heavy maintenance of all FCC trains is carried out, and depot re-equipment is taking place. Another £13m maintenance depot, at Bedford Cauldwell Walk, was opened to service trains when they could not easily reach Selhurst during the closure of the Thameslink route at St Pancras in 2004-05. It is the main maintenance base for Class 319. Cricklewood depot in London was reopened in 2006 for stabling, light maintenance and cleaning of Thameslink trains.

Senior personnel

Managing Director
Elaine Holt (left)
Commercial Director
Hugh Clancy
Customer Services Director
Karen Boswell
Engineering Director
Andy Cope

Class 319s are undergoing a £27million programme of major overhaul and refurbishment.

Great Northern inner suburban services are run by a fleet of 41 Class-313 electric multiple-units leased from HSBC, and FCC was to be responsible for their heavy maintenance from 2008. Angel-owned Class 317 (12 trains) and HSBC-owned Class-365 EMUs (40 trains) form longer distance trains. A £2.7m refurbishment programme for Great Northern trains began with the '365s', continuing with Classes 313 and 317.

First Capital Connect's No 319425 on the 13.25 Bedford-Brighton crosses Blackfriars bridge on 4 July 2007. Part of the expanded station to be built under the Thameslink Programme will be supported by the old piers to the right. Tony Miles

Passenger Train Operators

The first train in the new ScotRail livery, No 170434, at Glasgow Queen Street on 22 September 2008. Bill Wilson

ScotRail

10 year franchise to November 2014

First ScotRail operates passenger services within Scotland, as well as the cross-border Caledonian Sleeper service to London.

The Scottish Government in April 2008 extended First ScotRail's franchise by three years to November 2014. The extension activated a provision in the original agreement and created an investment fund of more than £70million, for control by Transport Scotland, to further improve Scotland's railway. This has been achieved by converting future estimated revenue share payments. The fund can be used for additional train services, to improve journey times, connections and quality of services which will bring direct passenger benefits. It is additional to the £40m First pledged to invest on winning the franchise.

By extending the contract, the government said it was providing continuity for ongoing improvement and development of rail services.

In September 2008, the 25th anniversary of the ScotRail identity was marked by the unveiling of a new livery for trains and stations, incorporating Scotland's flag, the Saltire. It is intended to deliver savings by providing a consistent brand which will not change with a new franchise operator.

In April 2004, the Scottish Government took on full funding responsibility for the rail franchise, in 2008 costing around £281million per year in subsidy. The contract was valued at around £2.5billon for the 10-year franchise, with annual payments varying as they are linked to performance. This is monitored by a Service Quality Incentive Regime (SQUIRE), focusing on 20 areas of station quality and 16 areas of train quality.

The first set of full annual results, published in July 2008, showed 'consistent high performance' in areas including clearing station graffiti, ticket collection and train cleanliness. Areas where there was 'room for improvement' included toilets, litter and contamination, and station fault records. Performance overall has improved, resulting in a significant drop in total penalties.

On 1 January 2006, the new Executive Agency, Transport Scotland, assumed responsibility for the majority of rail powers in Scotland, and also for infrastructure projects, working in conjunction with regional transport partnerships. (The Strathclyde Partnership for Transport took over roles and functions of the Strathclyde Passenger Transport Authority and Executive. Rail functions were transferred to Transport Scotland.)

Network Rail and First ScotRail are both parties to a Local Output Commitment agreement. Targets are set to monitor performance in terms of delay, cancellations, and the quality of the network. The measurement is of minutes of delay attributable to Network Rail. Failure to meet targets result in compensation payments by Network Rail.

Since 2004, delays for which First ScotRail is responsible have been reduced by 50% compared with a commitment of 2% per annum. A record public performance measure score of 93.8% was achieved in March 2008. The number of passengers has grown by 20% since 2004, attributed to good performance and marketing.

The opening of the Stirling-Alloa line in May 2008 connected Clackmannanshire to the passenger rail network for the first time in 40 years, with an hourly Alloa-Glasgow service.

Two other significant extensions under way are the Glasgow Airport Rail Link, and a third route between Edinburgh and Glasgow created by reopening the Airdrie-Bathgate line, with electrification throughout.

In July 2008, a new 130-vehicle fleet of electric multiple-units was announced under a contract with Siemens and HSBC, valued at over £200m.

The trains - 22 three-car and 16 four-car sets of Class 380 funded by Transport Scotland - are to be used from December 2010 to increase capacity on Ayrshire routes, releasing other trains for the new Airdrie-Bathgate services, and augmenting the fleet for the expected 2012 opening of the Glasgow Airport Rail Link. The air-conditioned trains will be formed of 23-metre long vehicles.

The new Borders rail link south from Edinburgh to Tweedbank, which in mid 2008 the government decided to proceed with, is expected to be worked by diesel trains released from the Bathgate line.

The government's High Level Output Statement in 2007 listed projects that it wants the industry to prepare. These include electrification of the main Edinburgh-Glasgow line; infill electrification for the Paisley Canal, Whifflet, Cumbernauld, Maryhill, Stirling/Dunblane, and Alloa routes; and further electrification later, including to East Kilbride and Barrhead/Kilmarnock.

A new timetable from December 2008 improves Edinburgh-Fife-Perth and Aberdeen services to offer greater capacity and shorter journey times. It also improves Far North, Kyle of Lochalsh and Aberdeen-Inverurie services. Extra peak services in Fife are provided by newly-hired locomotive hauled trains.

An improved, half-hourly service between Glasgow and Kilmarnock is planned for December 2009 after Network Rail completes works to improve line capacity.

The diesel multiple-unit train fleet is made up by Class 156 (48 trains) and Class 158 (40 trains plus 7 on temporary hire from Northern), and - acquired post-privatisation - a total of 59 Class-170 Turbostar sets, including four previously used by Hull Trains.

The 25 Inverness-based Class 158s are being refurbished at a cost of £9million at Railcare, Springburn, and the 20 Class-156s working outside Strathclyde are receiving similar treatment at a cost of £2.7million, both funded by Transport Scotland.

First ScotRail
Key statistics 2007/08

Punctuality (0-5 minutes):	90.6 %
Passenger journeys (millions):	81.3
Passenger kilometres (millions):	2,503.8
Timetabled train kilometres (millions):	38.7
Route Kilometres operated:	3,032
Number of Stations operated:	341
Subsidy per passenger kilometre (pence):	11.4*
Staff Employed as at 31/03/2007:	4,113

* 2006/07 figure

Strathclyde's '156s' have already been refurbished.

The Strathclyde electrified network is served by electric multiple-units of Classes 314 (16 trains), 318 (21 trains), 320 (22 trains) and 334 (40 trains), and the Edinburgh-North Berwick line is operated by five Class 322 units.

The Class 322s saw a £3m refurbishment programme in 2006-07, carried out by Hunslet-Barclay in Kilmarnock, also responsible for the recent refurbishment of Class-318 trains.

First ScotRail is participating in the trial of Train Energy Management Systems, as mentioned in the section on First Capital Connect.

In February 2007, a £6m extension to Haymarket depot in Edinburgh was opened, providing the opportunity for more trains to be maintained more quickly.

Senior personnel

Managing Director: Mary Grant (left)
Deputy MD and Operations & Safety Director: Steve Montgomery
Engineering Director: Kenny Scott
Finance Director: Kenny McPhail
Commercial Director: Peter Williams

Caledonian Sleeper services are hauled by EWS locomotives, and Class 90 electric locomotives used for the main haul between London and Glasgow/Edinburgh are finished in First Group livery.

Eight year franchise from 1 February 2004
Possible five-year extension

First TransPennine Express is a joint operation by First Group (55%) and Keolis. It is made up of inter-urban services previously operated by the First North Western and Arriva Trains Northern franchises, whose remaining services were combined in the Northern Rail franchise.

A total of over £635million in subsidy will be paid over the initial eight-year franchise period, with private sector funds of over £260m being injected - the bulk of this (£250million) is represented by a fleet of 51 new three-car, 100mph 'Desiro' trains built by Siemens and leased from HSBC Rail.

A new £28m traincare depot at Ardwick, Manchester opened in 2006 to service the new trains and is designed to deliver optimum train performance and standards of cleanliness. Smaller stabling and lighter maintenance depots have been built at York and Cleethorpes.

Since the franchise began, passenger journeys have increased from 13.5million to over 20m a year, and the continuing growth in patronage has led to discussions on lengthening Class 185 trains. The Department for Transport's rolling stock plan of 2008 included 24 extra vehicles.

Since December 2007, the First TransPennine Express network has included the Manchester to Glasgow and Edinburgh services, previously run by the Cross Country franchise. The new services were anticipated to contribute an additional £10m of revenue per annum. First TransPennine Express's network had previously expanded, with the transfer from Northern Rail of Manchester Airport-Blackpool North services in June 2006. The Glasgow and Edinburgh services, run with Class 185 trains, are extended to start from Manchester Airport, with three trains on weekdays to Glasgow and four to Edinburgh. From December 2008, there are two extra Monday-Friday trains to Edinburgh.

The first of nine two-car Class 170 Turbostar sets to be fully refurbished by Transys Projects for use by First TransPennine Express entered service in September 2007 - eight trains transferring from South West Trains and one from Central Trains. A £2million refurbishment programme aimed at giving the trains a similar feel to the new Class 185s. Maintenance of the

First TransPennine
Key statistics 2007/08

Punctuality (0-10 minutes):	91.7 %
Passenger journeys (millions):	20.6
Passenger kilometres (millions):	1,069.5
Timetabled train kilometres (millions):	14.4
Route kilometres operated:	1251
Number of stations operated:	30
Subsidy per passenger kilometre (pence):	9.82
Staff employed as at 31/03/2007:	1,005

Senior personnel

Managing Director Vernon Barker (left)
Customer Service Director Edith Rogers
Commercial Director Leo Goodwin
Engineering Director Nick Donovan

'170s' is carried out by Bombardier Transportation at Crofton, near Wakefield.

With the Class 185 fleet complete, the Class 175 units previously used on the Manchester Airport to Barrow/Windermere trains were switched from 2007 to services of Arriva Trains Wales.

First TransPennine Express has continued a £12million station improvement programme,

Passenger Train Operators

First TransPennine's No 185149, at the restored Grange-over-Sands station, forms the 12.22 Barrow-in-Furness to Manchester Airport on 29 April 2008. Tony Miles

including refurbishment of waiting areas and customer and staff facilities, with digital help points from Cityspace providing real-time train information, a local taxi finder, station maps, and local weather news. Additional funding from the Department for Transport is providing accessibility improvements such as automatic doors, disabled facilities and ticket counters at stations.

'Eco Mode' - an environmental improvement initiative developed by First TransPennine Express and Siemens Transportation Systems has cut the fuel consumption of the Class 185 by 7% and reduced engine running time by 80min per vehicle per day, saving over 1.8m litres of fuel per year.

It has been developed through train control modifications, selective engine use, evaluation of route-by-route fuel consumption rates and analysis of driving techniques - all with the overall objective of reducing CO_2 emissions.

One of the key features is reduced engine idling time, by automatically shutting engines down when trains are stationary and through using just two of the three engines on selected routes. 'Eco-driving' guidelines to optimise coasting - developed following comprehensive modelling of train performance over the geography of the core route and consultation with drivers ñ have been introduced. The goal is to increase the fuel savings to at least 2.5million litres per year.

First TransPennine Express has achieved certification to the ISO 14001 environmental performance standard. It is the first train operating company outside London to achieve this certification for all sections of the business.

Since 2006-07, TransPennine Express has been classified as a 'long distance' operator for the Public Performance Measure (punctuality is measured as within 0-10min of planned arrival time at final destination).

First Hull Trains

Non-franchised intercity train company

First Hull Trains, the non-franchised (ëopen accessí) intercity train company operating between London King's Cross and Hull, was formed in 2000 and passenger numbers have grown by 20% year-on-year since. It carries approximately 700,000 passengers each year.

Seven weekday return services are now operated - with the seventh introduced in December 2006 - and new 125mph trains were introduced in Summer 2005.

Five services run each way on Saturday and Sunday. The fastest weekday schedule between Hull and London is 2hr 32min (as at late 2008).

In June 2002 the company was awarded 10-year rights by the Rail Regulator, providing security of access at least until May 2010. An application for rights to be extended until 2018 was made to the Office of Rail Regulation (ORR) in 2008.

First Hull Trains is 80% owned by First Group, following the buyout of its previous parent company, GB Railways. The original promoter of Hull Trains, Renaissance Trains, set up by two former British Rail managers, John Nelson and Michael Jones, owns the remaining 20%.

In 2007, First Hull Trains outlined expansion plans, with possible further investment in rolling stock to meet 'ever increasing demand'. In 2008, the company sought Office of Rail Regulation (ORR) approval for four trains a day between Harrogate and London King's Cross via York. It was anticipated that, if granted

Senior personnel

Managing Director: Mark Leving
Sales and Marketing Manager: David Townend
Operations and Standards Manager: Ian Dunn
Finance Manager: Glenn McLeish-Longthorn

regulatory approval, a separate company, Harrogate Trains Limited - also backed by First Group and Renaissance Trains - could begin operating in the summer of 2009. Another new service, from King's Cross to Lincoln and Cleethorpes (via Peterborough and Sleaford), is proposed, but the likelihood of major engineering work on the Peterborough-Sleaford-Lincoln line meant that this was not being pursued so urgently.

Investment of some £36million saw the new fleet of Class 222 'Pioneer' trains come into use in 2005. The four Pioneers, built and maintained by Bombardier, leased from HSBC, are second-generation diesel-electric multiple units, developed from the concept used initially for the Cross Country franchise's Voyagers. The four-car 125mph trains replaced 100mph Class-170 Turbostar diesel multiple-units and accommodate 183 passengers on each train. They are named after key figures that have helped to shape the modern history of Hull. After the trains' introduction, First Class seating capacity was increased from 22 to 33 seats.

Serious damage was caused to two vehicles of one of the Pioneer trains in an accident at Bombardier's Crofton depot in January 2007. Reconstruction was expected to take until mid 2009. Two Class 180 Adelante trains, formerly used by First Great Western, went into service in April 2008, initially to provide maintenance cover for the Pioneers. The five-car Class 180s offer around 40% additional capacity. Class 180s were expected to replace the Pioneer fleet. Agreement had been reached to lease a total of four Class 180s, with three more a possibility - this is likely to be related to plans for additional services. Plans for a full internal refit of the Class 180s were being developed.

Class 222/1 Pioneer No 222104 'Sir Terry Farrell' passes Alexandra Palace on 21 July 2008, forming the 09.48 First Hull Trains service from King's Cross to Hull. Brian Morrison

Passenger Train Operators

Govia

Govia, responsible for nearly 30% of all rail passenger journeys in the UK, is a joint venture between the Go-Ahead Group and Keolis. Go-Ahead is the 65% majority partner and employs a total of 27,500 people in three different sectors in the UK - rail, bus and aviation. Keolis operates trains, buses and metros in Europe and Canada and is jointly owned by AXA Private Equity and the Caisse dépôt et placement du Québec (52%), French Railways (SNCF) (45.5%) and Keolis managers (2.5%).

Rail has been a key element of Go-Ahead's transport strategy since privatisation, and initially the southeast of England was seen as a key area as opportunities existed for integration with the group's bus activities.

Go-Ahead operated the Thames Trains franchise from October 1996 to April 2004 and, following the establishment of Govia, the Thameslink franchise from March 1997 to April 2006.

Govia in 2001 took over the South Central franchise, which it subsequently rebranded as Southern. On 22 June 2008 Southern took over operation of the Gatwick Express service as part of the process of creating the new South Central franchise, which will run for five years and ten months from 20 September 2009. Govia is one of four shortlisted bidders for the new franchise.

Govia was awarded the Integrated Kent franchise, now branded as Southeastern, in 2006, and in November 2007 began operating the new West Midlands franchise under the name London Midland.

SOUTHERN

6 year 4 month franchise from May 2003

Southern has a complement of 3,700 staff and operates around 2,000 trains every day. The company operates a mix of suburban commuter and main line routes between London and the Southeast coast, providing train services through South London, Surrey and Sussex, and to parts of Kent and Hampshire.

While the franchise started in May 2003, Govia took over operations from previous franchisee Connex from August 2001.

The franchise will run until 30 September 2009, three months earlier than previously stated, to ensure the new franchisee is in place to implement major changes to the south London timetable in December 2009, including provision for the East London Line extension.

Since the start of the franchise, Southern has consistently improved its operating performance both in terms of punctuality and reliability, ticket buying facilities, car parking, security on stations and on trains, the cleanliness of its rolling stock and the helpfulness of staff. This has contributed significantly in the achievement of the best ever customer satisfaction scores in recent National Passenger Surveys. A programme of station refurbishment, along with improved signage and a substantial safety improvement programme, have helped passengers to feel more secure while travelling on Southern. By the autumn of 2008, 102 of the company's 162 managed stations had achieved Secure Station accreditation. All of Southern's fleet of 276 trains are fully covered by CCTV, and an integrated operations control and CCTV control centre at Croydon receives live feeds from cameras at 70 Southern stations in south London and in the Sussex coast area.

The flagship route of the franchise, the Brighton main line, has been the subject of a route utilisation strategy. Following consideration of its findings, the Gatwick Express service, while retaining its existing identity and market positioning, was transferred to a seamless operation with Southern in June 2008. From 14 December 2008, new peak-period Gatwick Express services are scheduled between Brighton, Gatwick Airport and London Victoria, using pairs of Class 442 electric multiple-units. The 17 sets transferred to Southern were undergoing extensive refurbishment, including new internal layouts, before entering service with Southern. From December 2008, six services worked by Class 442 sets will start from Brighton in the morning peak, and six services will be extended to Brighton in the evening peak.

This, along with other significant changes to the timetable - such as faster, more frequent services to London from Brighton and an increase in services on the Redhill corridor - means that a 10.7% increase in seating capacity (almost 2,000 seats) will be provided on the Brighton main line in the weekday morning peak.

Running non-stop through Mitcham Eastfields' staggered platforms on the station's official opening day of 10 July 2008, Southern's Class 455/8s Nos 455828 and 455831 form the 11.23 service from Sutton to London Victoria.
Brian Morrison

In association with **rail**services from KNORR-BREMSE

Southern
Key statistics 2007/08

Punctuality (0-5 minutes):	89.9%
Passenger journeys (millions):	144.5
Passenger kilometres (millions):	3,421.9
Timetabled train kilometres (millions):	28.1
Route kilometres operated:	666
Number of stations operated:	161
Subsidy per passenger kilometre (pence):	1.92
Staff employed as at 30/06/2007	3,584

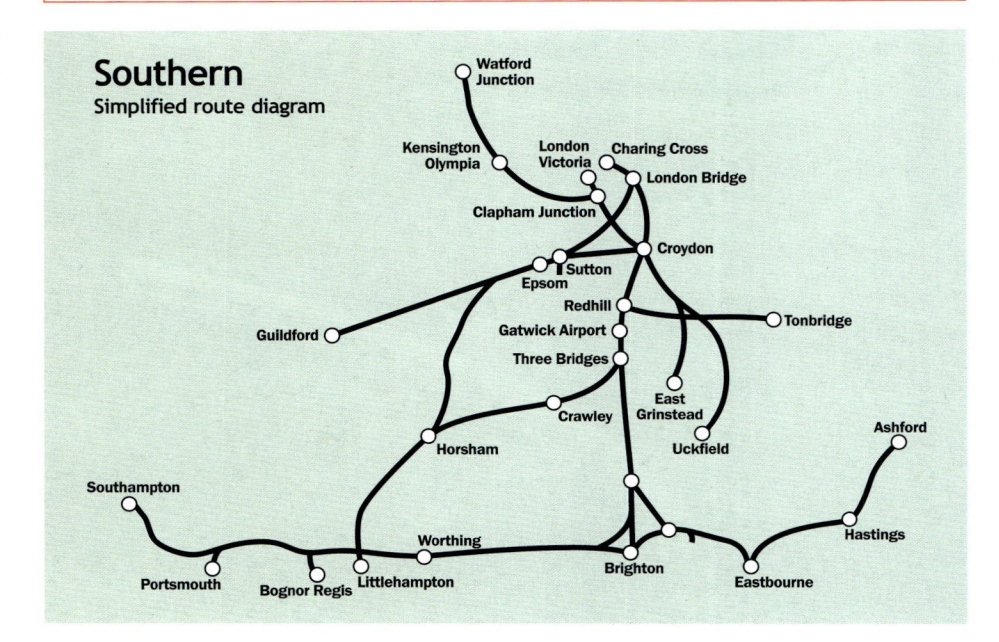

Senior personnel

Managing Director
Chris Burchell
Finance Director
Bob Mayne
Engineering Director
Gerry McFadden
Operations Director
Andy Byford
Commercial Director
Alex Foulds

Southern
Simplified route diagram

As part of the Thameslink Programme, Southern is planning to transfer the last eight of its fleet of Class 319 trains to First Capital Connect (FCC) by March 2009. Also, as part of the programme, Southern will sub-lease 21 new 4-car dual voltage Class 377 trains to FCC. This will enable sufficient rolling stock to become available to deliver key stages of the programme.

All of Southern's routes are electrified at 750V DC except for the sections from Oxted to Uckfield and Ashford to Hastings, which are worked by its fleet of Class 171 Turbostar diesel units. In 2008, Southern and sister train operating company Southeastern were the first train operators in the country to introduce third rail regenerative braking, involving their Electrostar trains. It is estimated that trains from Southern and Southeastern fleets will return enough electricity to the national grid to power approximately 6,000 homes.

As part of the creation of the new South Central franchise, Southern took over the operation of all trains between Redhill and Tonbridge in December 2008.

Gatwick Express services depart every 15 minutes from dedicated platforms at London's Victoria station. Passengers can check their flight details on information screens at Victoria which show airline logos, the flight number, flight destination, departure time and departure terminal. The platform at Gatwick Airport is conveniently positioned next to the south terminal.

Gatwick Express offers both Express class and First class travel and is designed to take the hassle out of transferring to and from the airport, with the air traveller in mind. Accommodation in Express class is stylish, modern and air-conditioned with a range of drinks, snacks and light refreshments served at the seat. First class interiors are designed to provide a spacious environment for customers and also include large, comfortable, reclining seats with tables for laptops or magazines, as well as complimentary copies of the Times and the Evening Standard, and at-seat refreshment service.

The DfT will pay Govia a subsidy of £103.6m from 1 January 2008 to 19 September 2009 for running the Southern franchise (figure nominal, with inflation).

Southern's rolling stock is mainly leased from Porterbrook with some units belonging to HSBC. The fleet of 1,105 vehicles operates over 17.5million miles per year.

Class	vehicles per train	trains
319	4	8
455	4	46
456	2	24
460	8	8
377 Electrostar	3	28
377 Electrostar	4	154
171 Turbostar	4	6
171 Turbostar	2	10
442	5	17

Gatwick Express
Key statistics 2007/08
(Franchise merged with Southern, June 2008)

Punctuality (0-10 minutes):	92.2%
Passenger journeys (millions):	5.1
Passenger kilometres (millions):	219.5
Timetabled train kilometres (millions):	2.4
Route kilometres operated:	43
Number of stations operated:	0
Subsidy per passenger kilometre (pence):	-9.66
Staff employed as at 31/12/2006	290

southeastern

6-year franchise from 1 April 2006 with possible two-year extension

The Southeastern franchise serves Kent, southeast London and part of East Sussex and will introduce high-speed domestic services on the Channel Tunnel Rail Link (HS1) from December 2009. The franchise runs for six years, until 31 March 2012, with an automatic two-year extension if performance targets are met.

Commitments include a £17.6million programme to install high quality CCTV on the entire train fleet, introduce passenger load weighing equipment onboard trains to help tackle crowding, make improvements to passenger information systems and enhance station security. The franchise agreement commits Southeastern to lift the number of trains arriving within 5min of scheduled time

Passenger Train Operators

Southeastern's Class 376 No 376004 rounds the curve from Cannon Street to Borough Market Junction on 30 November 2007, forming the 10.49 'roundabout' service, returning to Cannon Street via Sidcup and Woolwich Arsenal. Brian Morrison

from 89.2% in 2008 to 93.74% in 2014, and by October 2008 Southeastern had made significant progress by lifting performance to 90.7%.

At franchise award, the DfT said the total subsidy will be £585m over eight years, with fares to be increased at 3% above inflation for five years from 2007 'to ensure there is a fair balance in cost between the taxpayer and the farepayer'.

New early morning and evening services were introduced in 2006 aimed at easing demand around the peak periods, and further improvements were delivered in December 2007 as the company worked to improve both capacity and punctuality. The December 2008 timetable change sees the transfer of all Tonbridge-Redhill services to become part of the Southern franchise, following consideration of proposals outlined in the Brighton-main-line route utilisation study.

2009 will see big changes in the Southeastern timetable, with the start of high-speed services over the HS1 route in December. Before this, on 2 March 2009, through running is to start over the Thameslink route, when the terminal platforms at Blackfriars are taken out of use as part of the Thameslink improvement project. The First Capital Connect (FCC)-served Moorgate branch will close at the same time.

From March, Southeastern services which previously terminated at Blackfriars and FCC's Moorgate services will, in effect, be combined to offer through services along the Thameslink corridor, running north of Blackfriars to Kentish Town, St Albans, Luton or Bedford.

The Thameslink routes will be worked by

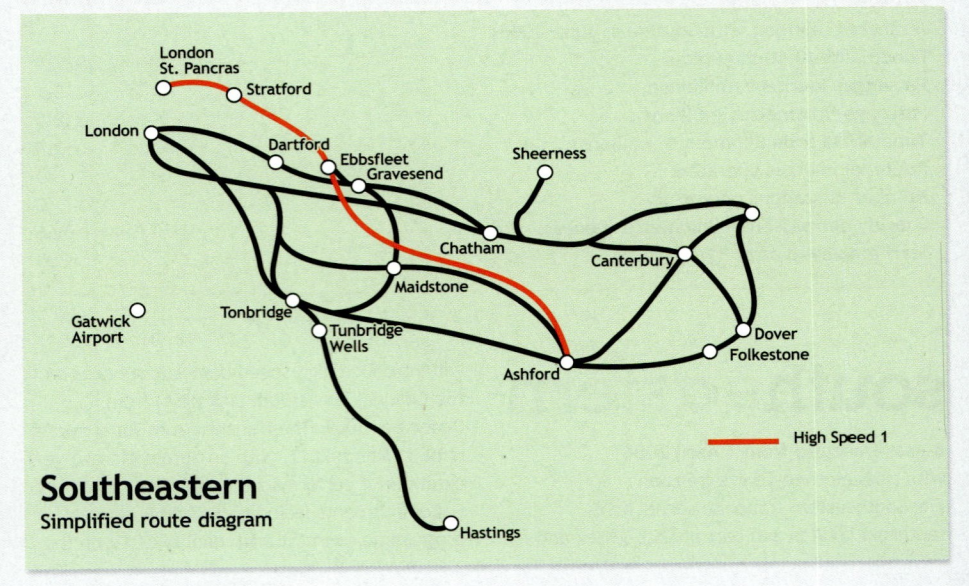

Southeastern
Simplified route diagram

Southeastern

Key statistics 2007/08

Punctuality (0-5 minutes):	90.6%
Passenger journeys (millions):	154.5
Passenger kilometres (millions):	3,844.2
Timetabled train kilometres (millions):	28.8
Route kilometres operated:	779
Number of stations operated:	182
Subsidy per passenger kilometre (pence):	2.14
Staff employed as at 30/06/2007:	3,857

Senior personnel

Managing Director
Charles Horton
Finance Director
Wilma Allan
Engineering Director
Wayne Jenner
Operations Director
Mike Hodson
Commercial Director
Vince Lucas

dual voltage Class 319 and Class 377 stock sub-leased to Southeastern. This additional rolling stock will enable several Southeastern trains to be lengthened and a small number of additional early morning inner-suburban Metro services to Cannon Street to be introduced. During the morning peak, 12 six-coach trains will be strengthened to eight coaches and 13 eight-coach trains will be strengthened to ten coaches. During the evening peak, 12 six-coach trains will be increased to eight coaches and nine eight-coach trains to ten coaches. These improvements will offer over 4,000 extra seats during the morning peak and over 3,500 extra seats during the evening peak.

On the long-distance routes, some trains will be lengthened from four to eight coaches while a number of minor timetable adjustments will be made as calling patterns are amended, or as paths north and south of London are linked together.

The new high-speed services will serve three new stations: Ebbsfleet, Stratford and St Pancras. To operate these trains, Hitachi is supplying 29 Class-395 six-car EMUs, designed for both HS1 and conventional railway lines, the first of which arrived for testing on 23 August 2007, followed by three more sets. Construction was then paused for a programme of testing and evaluation on the High Speed 1 line between Ashford and St Pancras, and on the Kent network. The remaining 25 trains will be assembled and delivered in 2009. The high-speed services will bring greatly improved journey times to parts of Kent, for example the London to Ashford journey will be reduced from about 83 minutes to 37min. The new trains will also operate the 'Javelin' shuttle service to the 2012 London Olympic and Paralympic games' main location at Stratford, east London.

An entirely new timetable will also be introduced across the Southeastern network in December 2009, including metro and main line services.

Southeastern runs a completely electric train fleet, with units leased from HSBC Rail and Angel Trains - Class 375 Electrostars (total of 112 trains); Class 376 Electrostars (36); Class 465 Networkers (147); and Class 466 Networkers (43).

Maintenance is carried out at Slade Green near Dartford (Networkers) and Ramsgate (main-line trains), with smaller depots for maintenance and cleaning at Ashford, Grove Park and Gillingham. A new Hitachi depot at Ashford will maintain the 29 Class 395 six-car high-speed trains.

london midland

7 year 10 month franchise from November 2007

The London Midland franchise began on 11 November 2007, combining the previous Silverlink County franchise and the major part of the Central Trains franchise. London Midland operates train services under two sub-brands. London Midland City caters for the West Midlands cities and the region and gives full prominence to Centro's Network West Midlands brand. London Midland Express services run on the longer distance routes connecting London, the Midlands and the Northwest. The company manages 149 stations and expects over 45million journeys to have been taken on its trains in the year 2008-09.

December 2008 is the date for introduction of a radical new timetable which includes new direct London Midland services between Birmingham and London, an increase in the number of services between Liverpool and Birmingham (which will see a doubling of frequency at key times), and many other improvements on London Midland's West Midlands routes. Perhaps most significant, however, is the new service between London Euston and Crewe via the Trent Valley route. This will bring a significant improvement in service frequency to many stations and the restoration of rail services to others which have not seen trains for several years - a by-product of major route engineering work. It will include the reopening of Stone station, which was extensively restored in 2003 but which has had to wait a further five years for trains to call at its refurbished platform. Between Stafford and Crewe these trains will travel via Stoke-on-Trent and then through Kidsgrove and Alsager along the route which was electrified in 2003.

Highlights of the franchise include the introduction of 37 new four-car Siemens-built Class-350/2 Desiro EMUs, entering service from December 2008, and 12 two-car and 15 three-car Class 172 Bombardier Turbostar DMUs which will arrive in 2010. These will replace the existing Class 321 EMUs and Class 150 DMUs which will be transferred to other operators as part of the DfT rolling stock strategy.

The Class 350/2 sets include Standard class seating in 3+2 arrangement, offering additional seating capacity. These sets will be concentrated on the Northampton to London Euston corridor, allowing the Class 350/1 sets, with 2+2 seating throughout, to be deployed on longer distance services between Euston and Crewe and on Birmingham to Liverpool trains.

During its first year, London Midland achieved several key milestones including the refurbishing and re-branding of its Class 153, 170, 323 and 350 fleets which will be retained throughout the franchise. The company has also introduced new uniforms and achieved 'Investors in People' accreditation two years

Senior personnel

Managing Director
Steve Banaghan (left)
Finance Director
Julian Edwards
Engineering Director
John Barlass
Operations Director
Andy Thomas
Commercial Director
Alex Hynes

London Midland

Key statistics 2007/08

Punctuality (0-5 minutes):	88.0 %
Passenger journeys (millions):	20.1
Passenger kilometres (millions):	591.5
Timetabled train kilometres (millions):	7.0
Route kilometres operated:	867.4
Number of stations operated:	149
Subsidy per passenger kilometre (pence):	7.56

Figures cover November 2007-March 2008 only

Passenger Train Operators

ahead of schedule. Fortnightly 'Meet the Manager' sessions have been set up across the network and new timetables, aimed at being easier to read and more informative, have been issued. Improvements to stations and car parks are underway, and the company is aiming to gain Secure Station accreditation at 73 stations by the end of the franchise.

Automatic ticket gates have been installed at five stations in Birmingham and three 'model' stations have been refurbished in a project that will set the standards for the refurbishment programme at all 149 stations the company operates, improving signage, facilities and security.

This programme has also seen the construction of a new multi-storey car park at Tring, the installation of new cycle parking, shelters and CCTV at Leighton Buzzard, a new waiting room, baby change and toilet facilities at Nuneaton and the renovation of St Albans Abbey station.

During the franchise, London Midland will be investing £300million in new trains, improvements at stations, information to passengers, security and the introduction of Smartcard ticket technology.

The Department for Transport at franchise award in 2007 put total subsidy at £1,127m over the franchise period (net present value).

The 14.24 London Midland service from Euston to Northampton passes Carpenders Park on 11 August 2008, formed of Class 350 Desiro No 350122. Brian Morrison

RAILTEX 2009

9th International Exhibition of Railway Equipment Systems and Services

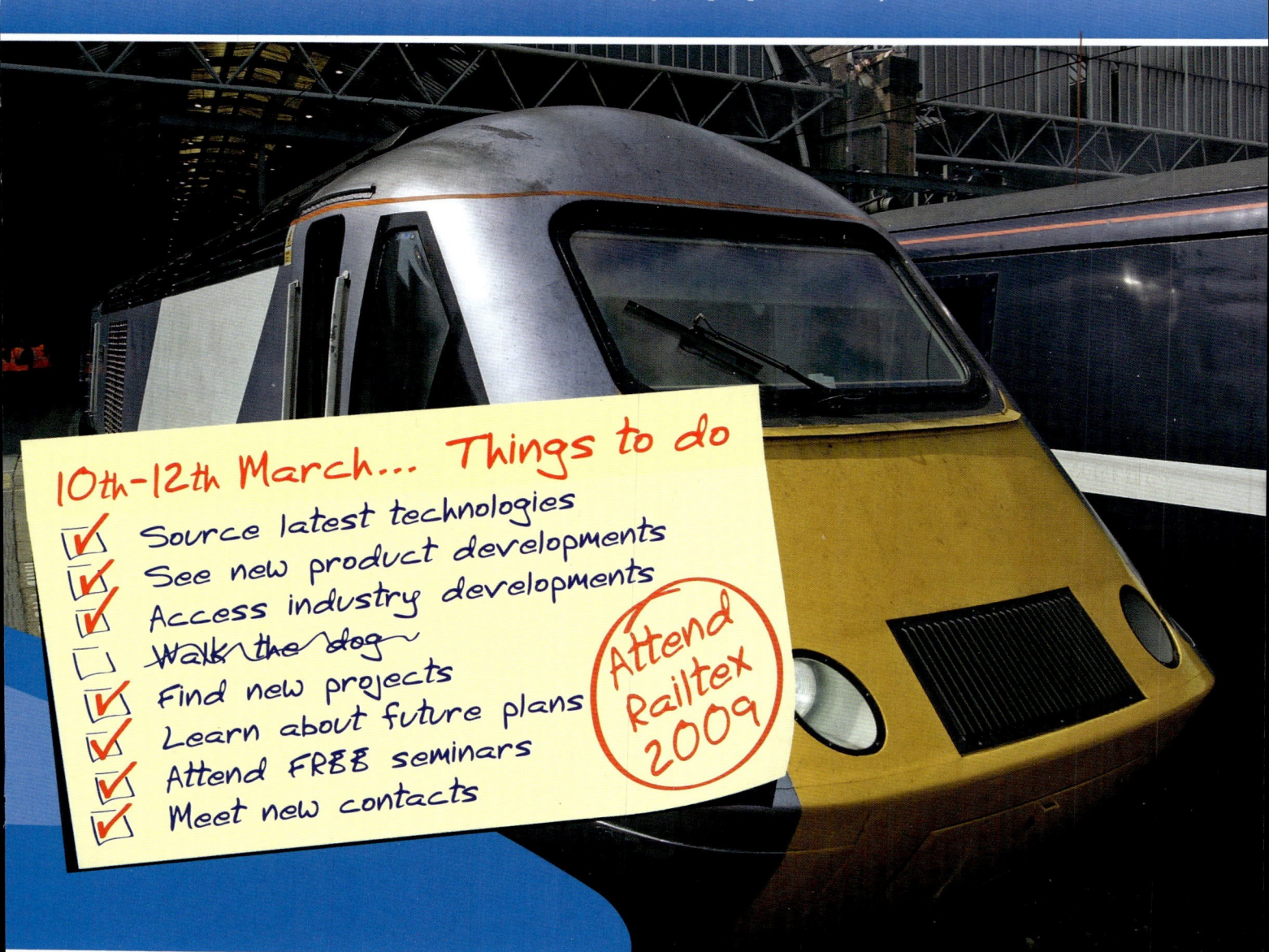

10th-12th March... Things to do
- ☑ Source latest technologies
- ☑ See new product developments
- ☑ Access industry developments
- ☐ ~~Walk the dog~~
- ☑ Find new projects
- ☑ Learn about future plans
- ☑ Attend FREE seminars
- ☑ Meet new contacts

Attend Railtex 2009

10 - 12 March 2009

Earls Court, London, UK

Register now for free entry

at www.railtex.co.uk
or pay £15 on the day

Tel: +44 (0)1727 814400 Email: railtex@mackbrooks.co.uk www.railtex.co.uk

Supporting Organisations

Official Media Partner

Crossrail | esmerk a Sanoma company | Network Rail | RAILNEWS | RFG Rail Freight Group | Railway Industry Association | the rail engineer | Railway Gazette INTERNATIONAL

Passenger Train Operators

National Express

National Express has been a significant player in the UK's railways since the start of privatisation.

The group has run some of the best performing franchises in each of the long distance, commuter and regional service groups.

In 1996 National Express was awarded the Gatwick Express and Midland Mainline franchises, which were amongst the first to be let. It followed this in 1997 by winning the North London Railways (renamed Silverlink), ScotRail and Central Trains franchises and in September 2000 acquired Prism Rail, which added London commuter companies, WAGN and c2c, to its portfolio, as well as Wales & West and Valley Lines. WAGN, c2c and Silverlink were managed as 'LondonLines', resulting in cost savings, while maintaining the identity of the individual companies.

In subsequent rounds, National Express has seen several franchises transfer to other operators while winning others in some fiercely fought contests.

In January 2004 the group was awarded the new Greater Anglia franchise. Initially branded as 'one', it was renamed National Express East Anglia (NXEA) in 2008. In August 2007 National Express was awarded the InterCity East Coast franchise.

Former National Express franchises were:
- ScotRail (1997 to 2004), the first company to deliver e-ticket services.
- Wales & Borders and Wessex - The Wales & West franchise was transferred from Prism Rail to National Express in 2000. Following remapping by the SRA to create a new Wales & Borders franchise, the West Country service group was separated in October 2001 as Wessex Trains. In April 2006, Wessex became part of the Greater Western franchise.
- WAGN - West Anglia and Great Northern, another ex-Prism franchise, was split in 2004, with Great Northern services remaining as a separate franchise until 2006, when they became part of the new Thameslink/Great Northern franchise, now trading as First Capital Connect. West Anglia and Stansted Express services became part of the Greater Anglia franchise in 2004.
- Central Trains - initially awarded as a seven-year franchise in March 1997, but extended amid proposals to remap a number of franchises, its services were transferred to the East Midlands, West Midlands (London Midland) and Cross Country franchises in 2007. Shrewsbury to Aberystwyth and Pwllheli services became part of the Wales & Borders franchise in 2001.
- Midland Mainline - awarded as a ten year franchise from April 1996, extended to April 2008 and then cut back to 11 November 2007 to fit with franchise remapping. A score of 97.9% punctuality was achieved during March 2006, breaking the industry record for a long-distance operator since the introduction of the Public Performance Measure in 1998.
- Silverlink - 1997 to 2007. Through the second half of the franchise the company managed to deliver a consistently good performance despite extensive disruption cause by the West Coast main line upgrade programme. The County service group was transferred to the new London Midland franchise and the Metro service group became part of the new London Overground concession.
- Gatwick Express - initially awarded as a 15-year franchise to National Express from April 1996, the service become part of the Southern franchise in June 2008 after National Express agreed terms for an early end of the franchise. National Express has been shortlisted as one of the four companies which have been invited to submit bids for the new franchise.

National Express's third quarter results for 2008 indicated revenue growth of 11% on National Express East Coast and 6% on National Express East Anglia, resulting in 9% across the whole rail portfolio, on a like for like basis.

national express East Coast

New franchise from December 2007

The InterCity East Coast franchise was awarded to National Express in August 2007, the new franchise runs from 9 December 2007 to 31 March 2015, with the last 17 months dependent on meeting performance targets.

The East Coast franchise covers the arterial North-South route which links London with Scotland via Peterborough, Leeds, Doncaster, York, Newcastle, Edinburgh, Aberdeen and Inverness. Currently National Express East Coast (NXEC) operates 136 services each weekday, manages 12 stations, calls at 52, and employs just over 3,000 staff. The franchise plans include £48million of investment, in people, trains, technology and stations.

At the launch of the franchise NXEC announced plans to introduce a new two-hourly service between Lincoln and London King's Cross via Retford, and a new London-York service at two-hourly intervals calling at intermediate stations from December 2010. Together these services would increase the number of weekday trains from 136 to 161.

In June 2008, NXEC submitted revised proposals to the Office of Rail Regulation for 25 new direct services to and from London, creating at least 7,000 extra seats per day, from December 2009. These plans, which are subject to regulatory approval, include: a new service every two hours to/from Lincoln, additionally serving Market Rasen, Grimsby and Cleethorpes once a day; an extra service every two hours between Harrogate, Pannal, Horsforth, Leeds, Garforth and London; and an extra service every hour direct from Bradford Forster Square to Leeds and London which would be created by extending some Leeds services. The plans also include a new even interval timetable from London, reducing journey times and creating more capacity in what NXEC believes would amount to the biggest improvement to the East Coast timetable since electrification in 1991.

To enable the additional services, the original plan was to use Class 90 electric locomotives leased from EWS with Mk3 coaches, but the requirement for 125mph rolling stock, and the need for more trains to operate on non-electrified routes, has seen NXEC consider Class 180 'Adelante' trains (ex-First Great Western) instead. The new services would enable some stops to be removed from longer-distance trains to Leeds and Edinburgh, with journey times reduced to 2hr for London-Leeds and 1hr 45min London-York.

NXEC is also looking to cut average journey times between London and Edinburgh, so that several services in each direction would take less than 4hr 20min. At the same time the company will be working to deliver a 2% reduction in fuel consumption per passenger km over the franchise term.

The new franchise aims to deliver a Public Performance Measure score of 90.1% by

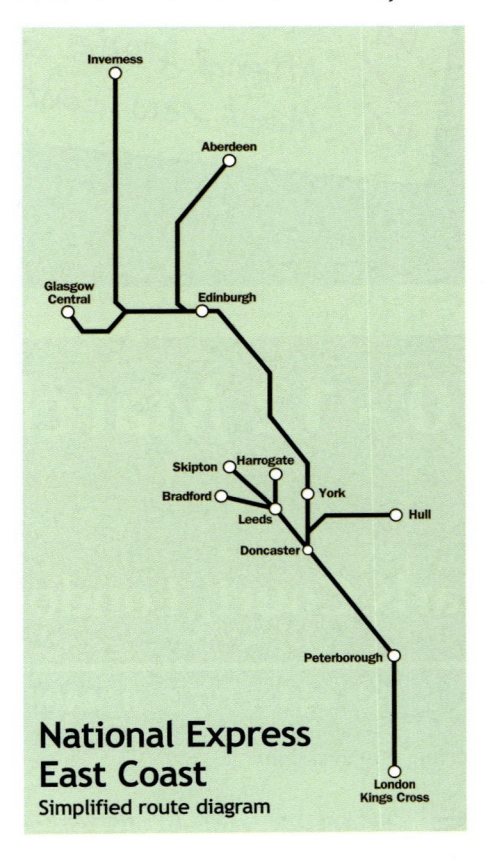

National Express East Coast
Simplified route diagram

A High Speed Train in new National Express livery crosses the Forth bridge. National Express

January 2010, and in July 2008 the TOC appointed three route performance managers to drive punctuality improvements. In the four weeks to 11 October 2008, NXEC delivered a PPM score of 91.1%. At that point, performance on a Moving Annual Average basis had risen from 81.7% at the start of the franchise to 85.5%, placing National Express on track to achieve its target by January 2010.

The new franchise saw a commitment to provide a free Wi-Fi service to all passengers, and usage tripled over the first month of the franchise as this was implemented. NXEC has also introduced a free Wi-Fi zone covering much of York station.

The company has also launched a redesigned website and is working to provide a 'one-stop-shop' for entire journeys, where specific seats can be reserved online; and an offer to provide a refund if a seat is not available to customers who have pre-booked tickets and a seat reservation.

NXEC announced that it would be seeking to build on the reputation for good catering on East Coast services, with an updated offering available to First and Standard Class passengers through at-seat service. In May 2008 the company introduced afternoon tea as one of the highlights of a new food and drink range. The new restaurant menu was based on advice from catering experts Eugene McCoy and Marcus Bennett. In August 2008, NXEC started trials of a weekend bistro service, offering gastropub-style menus on selected trains, to establish the demand for a more substantial hot and cold catering selection at the weekend.

In September 2008, NXEC announced a new reward programme for regular travellers, offering benefits including free First Class travel vouchers, food and drink offers and access to First Class lounges.

As well as installing CCTV on all trains, NXEC is locating an extra 80 cameras on stations to improve security, and a £7.4million station upgrade programme will provide improved facilities including waiting rooms, electronic real-time information points and electronic information 'totem poles'. Electronic 'posters' at stations will provide real-time information on train performance, incidents and future engineering works. £8million will be spent on station gating schemes and £2million will be spent on providing up to 33% more car parking spaces during the franchise term.

NXEC has made a commitment to develop the use of mobile phones to deliver real time travel information and for making car park payments, alongside print-at-home ticketing.

NX East Coast*
Key statistics

Punctuality (0-10 minutes):	83.6%*
Passenger journeys (millions):	17.6
Passenger kilometres (millions):	4,301.9
Timetabled train kilometres (millions):	18.8
Route kilometres operated:	1473
Number of stations operated:	12
Subsidy per passenger kilometre (pence):	-0.31
Staff employed as at 06/01/2007:	2,879

* Punctuality is 2007-08 figure, other figures for 2006-07.
  Franchise operator changed in December 2007.

Senior personnel

Managing Director
David Franks (left)
Production Director (acting)
Adrian Caltieri
Finance Director
Tom Fielden
Sales and Marketing Director
Rachel Dawson
Engineering Director (acting)
Tony Brown

Passenger Train Operators

The introduction of Smartcard technology will make buying tickets simpler, while a new ticketing system was promised to match demand to capacity, supported by a simplified fares structure to give customers the best possible fares.

During 2009 NXEC planned to continue with the £45million rebuild of all 13 HST diesel trains in its fleet, add 250 extra car parking spaces, and introduce automatic ticket barrier gates at eight stations, plus manual barriers at Peterborough and Doncaster.

The current train fleet is comprised of 31 Class-91 electric locomotives which power 30 rakes of Mk4 coaches, and there are 13 diesel HST sets. Following major overhauls, a six-fold improvement has been achieved in the reliability of the Class 91 fleet and a two-fold improvement for the HST power cars over four years.

The fleet operates from three depots: Bounds Green in north London, Craigentinny near Edinburgh and Clayhills, Aberdeen. Trains are also serviced at Neville Hill, Leeds; Heaton, Newcastle; and Polmadie, near Glasgow.

national express East Anglia

7-year franchise from 1 April 2004
Possible three-year extension

The Greater Anglia franchise was the first to be awarded under plans drawn up by the SRA to reduce the number of UK franchises and to move towards a single operator out of most London termini. The franchise brought together the services provided by Anglia, Great Eastern, West Anglia and Stansted Express, which all served London Liverpool Street, into one operation. It was awarded to National Express in a seven year deal from April 2004, which extends automatically by a further three years if the company achieves performance and service quality targets.

Originally trading under the name 'one', the franchise was re-branded National Express East Anglia (NXEA) in February 2008 as part of the integration and re-branding of National Express subsidiaries. NXEA is committed to improve timetables, to give better connections to key locations and to invest over £11 million in station improvements.

Performance continued to improve on a Moving Annual Average basis, from 88.64% in September 2007 to 90.4% in September 2008. A second Joint Performance Improvement Plan with Network Rail, which was launched in summer 2008, aims to improve annual performance to over 91% in 2009.

The company has completed the replacement and refurbishment of the entire fleet of trains which work on the Norwich to London inter-city route with Mk3 coaches and Class 90 locomotives. NXEA has also completed the £60m refresh and upgrade programme on the 484 vehicles in its Class 315 and 317 electric multiple-unit fleets and has invested an additional £4m in on-board CCTV and passenger information systems, meaning that all 636 vehicles in the Class 315, 321 and 360 fleets are now fitted with on-board CCTV equipment. The interior refurbishment of the Class 156 diesel multiple-units has been achieved through an innovative partnership scheme, and refurbishment of NXEA's 77 Class-321s began during 2008. Since the start of 2007, all 21 Class-360 EMUs have been operating with activated regenerative braking.

During 2008, NXEA launched 'Making Travel Safer' schemes on the Clacton line and Metro routes, completed the £250,000 upgrade of the London Liverpool Street ticket office and opened a new carriage stabling and light maintenance facility at Orient Way in East London, which has facilitated the release of the former Thornton Fields site for Olympic development.

In 2009, NXEA is to complete the £2m Manningtree station car park extension, which will provide 150 additional spaces, and continue with the installation of automatic ticket barriers at more stations, including Harlow Town, Ipswich, Norwich and Romford. Refurbishment of Bury St Edmunds ticket office hall is to begin, with provision of additional car parking spaces. Work will continue to enhance ticket offices and car parks at a number of other locations. Since the Customer Service Academy (CSA) opened at Stratford in 2006, each employee has, on average, visited it on six occasions for training or development. £1.2m has been invested in two state-of-the-art train driving simulators, also based at the CAS, and all drivers have been trained in energy efficient driving.

The company has continued to be praised for its work to develop and promote rural 'community' railways, receiving a large

The 11.30 NXEA express from London Liverpool Street to Norwich is headed past the Docklands Light Railway station of Pudding Mill Lane on 1 July 2008 by driving van trailer No 82107, with Class 90 No 90008 at the rear. To the left, Class 315s Nos 315828 and 315841, carrying 'interim' white stripe livery, form the 11.32 from Liverpool Street to Shenfield. Brian Morrison

In association with **rail**services from KNORR-BREMSE

National Express East Anglia
Key statistics 2007/08

Punctuality (0-5 minutes):	90.0%
Passenger journeys (millions):	111.9
Passenger kilometres (millions):	3,946.0
Timetabled train kilometres (millions):	31.4
Route kilometres operated:	1,611
Number of stations operated:	167
Subsidy per passenger kilometre (pence):	-1.46
Staff employed as at 31/12/2006:	3,084

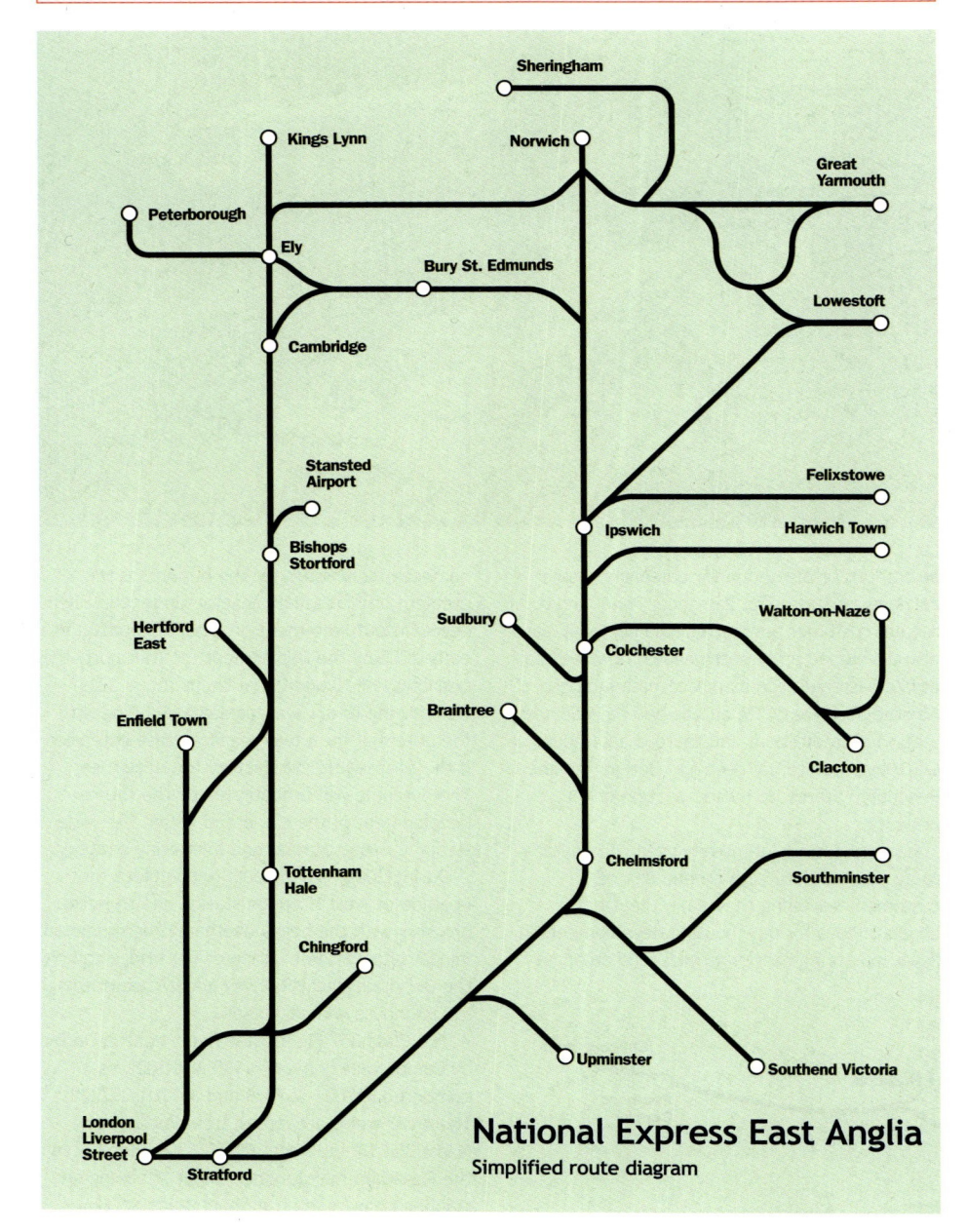

Senior personnel

Managing Director
Andrew Chivers (left)
Operations and Planning Director
Mark Phillips
Finance Director
Adam Golton
Sales and Marketing Director
David Lewis
Engineering Director
John Ratcliffe
Human Resources Director
Mike Goddard
Projects Director
Theo Steel
Change Director
Denise Lennox
Head of Safety and Environment
Andy Sanders
Head of Corporate Affairs
Jonathan Denby

National Express East Anglia
Simplified route diagram

number of awards for both its Community Rail initiatives and for customer service since the franchise started. Norwich-London on-train catering was expected to change for 2009, with buffet and at-seat service provided.

The NXEA fleet is leased from Angel Trains, HSBC and Porterbrook and is based at two main depots, Ilford and Norwich, with cleaning and stabling at a number of other locations.

Its fleet of 219 four-car EMUs, based at Ilford, is made up of: 61 Class-315s, 60 Class-317s, 77 Class-321s and 21 Class-360s.

The DMU fleet is made up of: five single-car Class-153s, nine Class-156s, four two-car Class-170s and eight three-car Class-170s.

The locomotive-hauled fleet is comprised of 15 Class-90 locomotives and 15 Mk3 Driving Van Trailers along with 14 rakes of Mk3 coaches, from a fleet of 119 vehicles which includes nine restaurant cars, six buffet cars, 28 First Open coaches (14 with disabled toilets) and 76 Standard Class coaches.

NXEA also hires three Class 08 shunters and Class 47 diesel locomotives for 'Thunderbird' rescue duties and to power the Norwich-Great Yarmouth legs of the high season London-Great Yarmouth services, as well as additional trains for special events such as the Lowestoft Airshow.

c2c

15-year franchise from May 1996

The franchise for the London, Tilbury & Southend (LTS) route, which operates out of London's Fenchurch Street station and serves major population centres in south Essex, was initially awarded to Prism Rail in May 1996 in a 15-year agreement. In September 2000, financial problems at other Prism franchises brought the opportunity for National Express to take over Prism, adding c2c to its rail portfolio while agreeing to honour all investment commitments made by Prism.

In July 2002 the company name was changed to c2c, as part of a £400million investment programme to completely rejuvenate the route, which included a £300million fleet of 74 new trains and improvements to stations and other customer facilities. According to past company statements, 'c2c' did not stand for anything specific, but it could indicate 'coast to capital' or 'commitment to customers'.

c2c has continued to deliver industry-leading levels of performance in 2008 with a moving annual average punctuality figure of over 94.8%. Underpinning this has been the excellent reliability of its Class 357 Electrostar fleet, based at East Ham depot, which has attained an impressive annual 'miles per casualty' rate of over 56,000 - the best in the country. This has helped support very good National Passenger

Passenger Train Operators

c2c's Class 357/0 Electrostars Nos 357005 and 357018 pass Leigh Bay and approach Chalkwell on a warm and sunny 11 October 2008, forming the 11.30 service from Fenchurch Street to Shoeburyness. Brian Morrison

Survey results with c2c achieving a score of 89% in spring 2008.

Between March and June 2007 the company switched its entire fleet of 74 trains to regenerative braking, which saw a saving in energy consumption of up to 20%. In October 2007, c2c signed an agreement with E.ON to use renewably generated electricity sources - such as wind farms and hydro power - at all stations, maintenance facilities and offices.

All c2c stations are staffed and gated, and all relevant stations and train services are already part of the London Oyster 'Pay As You Go' network. Other recent enhancements have included a free text alert about service alterations or disruption for passengers, quiet carriages, a successful Passenger Panel and a regular customer newsletter. The company has also developed an initiative which now sees 25% of c2c passengers on its direct mail database. All stations have CCTV, all but two have Secure Station accreditation, and there is a 24-hour CCTV live monitoring centre at Barking for the Fenchurch Street-Upminster section of the network.

c2c is the most intensively used commuter route into London, with around 85% of customers travelling to work in the City of London. Plans for new housing developments in Essex may bring further growth, and among a number of key issues for the business is the problem of increasing capacity. Under the High Level Output Statement process, announced in early 2008 by the Department for Transport, the possibility of 10 additional trains (Class 321s) transferring to c2c was highlighted, along with the potential for a two-year franchise extension if the terms were satisfactory for all parties. The outcome will probably shape the future development of the c2c brand within the wider National Express brand and marketing strategy.

During 2009, c2c expects to complete the upgrade of West Horndon station and to make progress with the heavy overhaul programme on its train fleet. Construction of the bridge to link the Docklands Light Railway and c2c platforms at Limehouse will also begin.

The Class 357 Electrostar fleet, built in Derby by Bombardier between 1999 and 2002, is numbered 357001-357046 and 357201-357228. The 4-car trains are leased from Porterbrook (Class 357/0) and Angel (357/2). Supplementing the East Ham maintenance depot, cleaning and stabling is carried out at Shoeburyness.

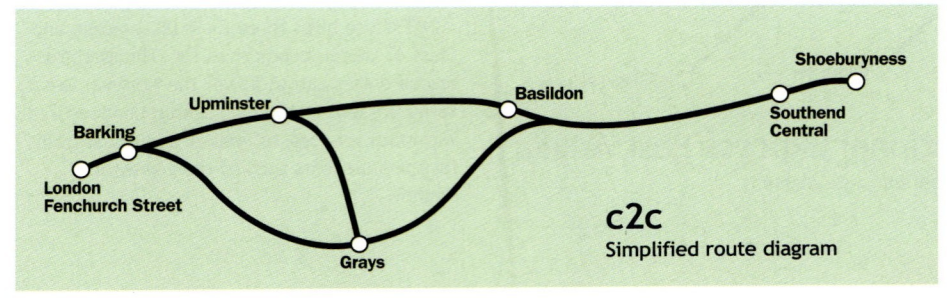

c2c Simplified route diagram

c2c
Key statistics 2007/08

Punctuality (0-5 minutes):	94.5%
Passenger journeys (millions):	31.9
Passenger kilometres (millions):	916.8
Timetabled train kilometres (millions):	6.4
Route kilometres operated:	129
Number of stations operated:	24
Subsidy per passenger kilometre (pence):	1.21
Staff employed as at 31/12/2007:	570

Senior personnel

Managing Director
Julian Drury (left)
Head of Operations
Kevin Frazer
Finance Director
Richard Bowley
Head of Marketing
Alan Bray
Engineering Director
Steve Rees

In association with **rail services** from KNORR-BREMSE

Arriva

Carrying more than one billion passenger journeys a year on buses, trains, and water buses, Arriva has the vision of being recognised as the leading transport services provider in Europe. It is active in transport networks of 10 countries, with 40,000 employees (including a share of associate companies).

In 2007, after absorbing significant costs from tendering of three rail franchises, the UK Trains division operating profit reduced to £7.5million (2006: £12.3m). Revenue increased 27%, to £322.4m (2006: £253.9m), following the inclusion of the new CrossCountry franchise from 11 November 2007.

ARRIVA Trains Wales / Trenau Arriva Cymru

15 year franchise from December 2003

Arriva's 15-year Wales & Borders franchise, operated as Arriva Trains Wales/Trenau Arriva Cymru, commenced on 7 December 2003. It includes national, regional and local routes within Wales; through services to Birmingham, Manchester and Gloucester; and the 'Borders' route via Hereford and Shrewsbury.

From 1 April 2006 the Welsh Assembly Government (WAG) took responsibility for the franchise, with subsidy transferred from the Department for Transport (DfT). The WAG also gained powers to fund rail improvements. Responsibility for the rail network remains with Network Rail, funded by the DfT, which also funds some ATW services in England.

Arriva Trains Wales' operating profit was £9.4m in the year to 31 December 2007, an increase of 36%, with operating costs down by 2.8%. Passenger revenue grew by 15% to almost £75m and revenue grant was over £148m.

The average journey length is 17.4 miles, reflecting the mix of urban rail network in south Wales and business orientated travel in north Wales and north-west England.

New direct services from Aberystwyth to Birmingham International, and Holyhead to Birmingham International via Wrexham, were notable changes in the December 2008 timetable, with improved services for Llandudno, and an hourly Sunday service for Cardiff-Manchester. A new locomotive-hauled train between Holyhead and Cardiff, with Premier class service, was also scheduled, with a half-hourly service from Merthyr to Cardiff expected to start in May 2009, after completion of infrastructure improvements.

Passenger services between Cardiff and Ebbw Vale were restored in February 2008. The £30million project upgraded 18 miles of freight railway, and was led by Blaenau Gwent in partnership with Caerphilly and Newport councils, the WAG, Network Rail and Arriva.

The Ebbw Valley service carried over 250,000 passengers in its first six months, twice as many as forecast in 2002 planning work. Four-car trains are provided on Saturdays and public holidays.

The WAG has announced investment of up to £2.6m to install a new connection at Gaer Junction, Newport and provide signalling improvements between there and Park Junction - an essential prerequisite for a passenger rail service between Ebbw Vale and Newport and part of the wider resignalling project at Newport. A joint WAG / Network Rail project will also see a £22million revamp for Newport station in time for the 2010 Ryder Cup.

Development of proposals to improve the rail network of Cardiff and the Valleys got under way after WAG and DfT funding was announced in June 2008. Significant improvements to Cardiff Central and Queen Street stations and the Cogan Junction area (near Barry) are among the proposals.

Improvements announced in 2007 included a £13million package for the Aberystwyth-Shrewsbury line (£8million from the WAG, £5million from Network Rail), with new or improved passing loops and flood prevention measures - plus funds to continue providing four vehicles on nearly all Machynlleth-Birmingham trains.

A £13.2million project to extend station platforms, aimed at bringing six-car trains to the Rhymney and Treherbert lines, was funded by the WAG with the aid of European Structural Funds, and involves a partnership with Network Rail, ATW and the South East Wales Transport Alliance of local authorities (SEWTA). The £18.8million scheme to improve the Merthyr service to half-hourly was also announced in 2007, and a £4.3million scheme to reopen Llanharan station, east of Bridgend, was completed in 2008.

ATW began a new service in June 2005 over the reopened Vale of Glamorgan line (Cardiff-Barry-Bridgend). Restoring the line cost £17million, funded by the WAG.

In December 2005, a new 'standard pattern' timetable added 950 services a week to the network, with more seats on peak services. Services to southwest England were transferred

Arriva Trains Wales' Class 142 Pacer No 142082 departs from Ninian Park, Cardiff, forming a local service from Coryton to Radyr. Brian Morrison

Passenger Train Operators

Arriva Trains Wales

Key statistics 2007/08

Punctuality (0-5 minutes):	92.4 %
Passenger journeys (millions):	23.9
Passenger kilometres (millions):	953.3
Timetabled train kilometres (millions):	23.7
Route kilometres operated:	1671
Number of stations operated:	244
Subsidy per passenger kilometre (pence):	2.00
Staff employed as at 31/12/2007:	2,048

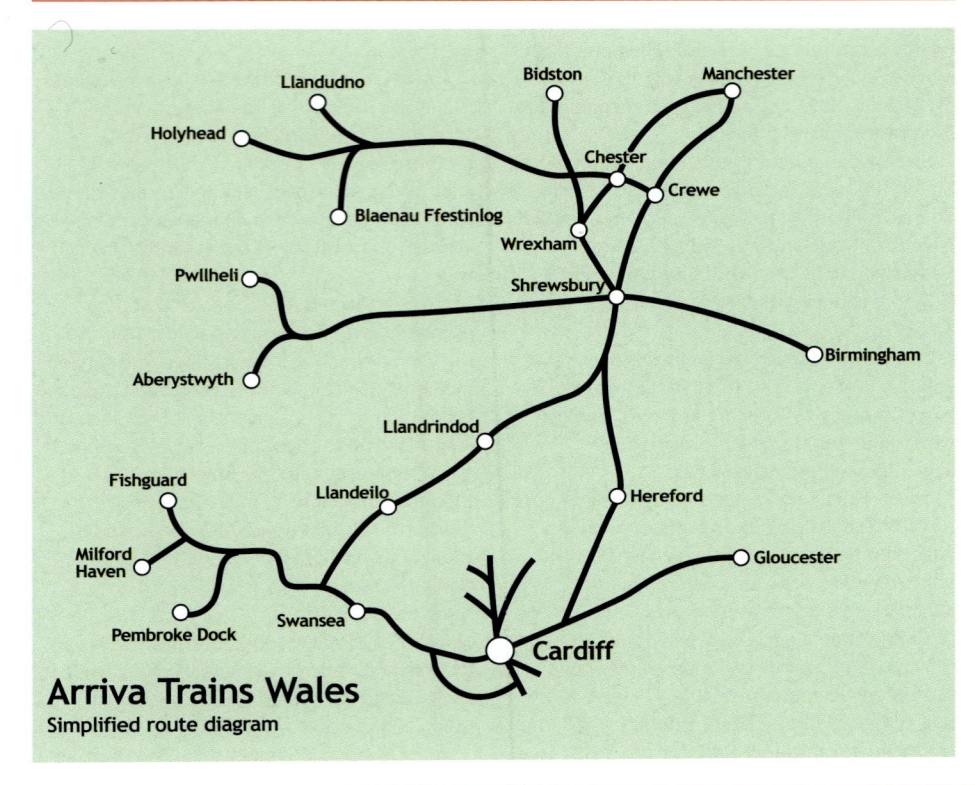

Senior personnel

Managing Director
Tim Bell (left)
Operations and Safety Director
Peter Leppard
Customer Services Director
Ian Bullock
Commercial Director
Mike Bagshaw
Finance Director
Amanda Furlong
Fleet Director
Jon Veitch

Arriva Trains Wales
Simplified route diagram

to Wessex Trains (now First Great Western). A two-hourly Holyhead-Cardiff service was introduced.

For long-distance services, ATW uses Class 158 diesel multiple-units (24 trains) and Class 175 'Coradias' (27 trains). A fleet of 30 Class-142 and 143 Pacer railbuses is mainly used in the Cardiff area, and a refurbished Class 121 railcar works a Cardiff Bay shuttle. There are also 30 Class-150s and 8 single-car Class-153s in the fleet.

A new £3million purpose-built train care facility at Machynlleth was officially opened in August 2007, to service ATW's entire fleet of Class 158 trains. The new depot was additional to original franchise commitments. The majority of the ATW fleet is based at Cardiff Canton depot, and has been refurbished in recent years. The Class 175s are maintained at the Chester depot of their manufacturer, Alstom's, maintenance arm.

crosscountry

Franchise from November 2007 to March 2016

Arriva's CrossCountry franchise runs from 11 November 2007 to 31 March 2016, with the last two years and five months conditional upon achieving agreed performance targets.

With Birmingham at its core, the new CrossCountry network stretches from Aberdeen to Penzance and from Stansted to Cardiff, covering around 1,500 route miles and serving more than 100 stations. CrossCountry provides fast services to the major English cities including Newcastle, Leeds, Sheffield, Manchester, Nottingham, Bristol and Southampton, as well as the capitals of Wales and Scotland. It also provides direct links to the airports at Birmingham, Southampton and Stansted.

The new CrossCountry timetable from December 2008 is based on consultation led by the Department for Transport during the lead up to refranchising. The stated aim is to offer a simplified service which makes better use of limited capacity at Birmingham New Street, and to provide more consistent journey patterns throughout the day.

Highlights of the new timetable include regular half-hourly services on key sections of the network including Birmingham to Bristol, Reading, Manchester, Sheffield and Leicester; hourly direct services between Bristol and Manchester; hourly through services for Plymouth-Edinburgh (via Leeds), Reading-Newcastle (via Doncaster), Bournemouth-Manchester, Cardiff-Nottingham, and Birmingham-Stansted Airport. Services to Brighton are withdrawn but a single return train between Newcastle and Guildford via Reading is retained.

Journey times are improved on some services to the Northeast of England and additional trains are operating to Stansted Airport in the evenings.

The busy Birmingham New Street station is not ideal for changing trains, and the company is working to help passengers use alternative changing points wherever possible. With almost half of all journeys on its network requiring a change of train, CrossCountry is also investing £1million in additional ticket machines and information screens at key stations. Improvements in ticketing and reservation booking are being introduced; a new internet retailing service will guide passengers towards the cheapest fares and best interchange options, while innovative technology will enable train seating plans to be updated in real time during journeys so that vacant reserved seats can be reallocated to other passengers, and low fares can be obtained closer to the time of travel. At-seat catering is available to passengers in First and Standard class on all trains, and hot food is available on many trains for First class passengers. Wi-Fi access will be provided on High Speed Trains and Voyagers, free in First class.

CrossCountry operates a fleet of 34 Class-220 four-car Voyagers and 23 Class-221 Super Voyager trains (22 five-car and one four-car), 29 Class-170 Turbostar diesel multiple-units (16 3-car, 13 2-car) and five 8-coach HST sets. All CrossCountry trains offer First and Standard Class accommodation. The five HST sets are being fully refurbished - including fitment of MTU engines in the ten power cars and the refurbishment of 40 trailers. This work includes fitting new seating and tables, carpets, curtains, refreshed toilet facilities, enhanced lighting and power sockets throughout, along with the creation

CrossCountry-liveried Class 220 No 220011 passes through Southall on 30 August 2008, forming the 07.54 train from Manchester Piccadilly to Brighton. Brian Morrison

of significantly more space for luggage. A number of these trailers are being converted from locomotive-hauled Mk3 stock.

The first rake was released from Wabtec at Doncaster in September 2008, and included the first ever 'Trailer Composite Catering' vehicle. These vehicles, replacing buffet cars, are equipped with a combination oven and boiler and a base for the catering trolleys. The HSTs will provide an average of 550 seats and will operate on the main Northeast-Southwest route between Edinburgh and Plymouth, releasing Voyagers to strengthen services on other routes. The HST programme will contribute to a 35% increase in capacity on principal routes in the evening peaks by June 2009.

The Voyagers are also being refreshed and reconfigured internally and, with the removal of the shop, will provide 202 seats per 4-car unit and 264 seats per 5-car, with additional storage space for luggage. Isolation of the tilt system on the Class 221 sets has helped a significant improvement in miles per casualty figures. Reliverying of the CrossCountry Voyager and SuperVoyager fleet was completed in October 2008.

The Class 170 Turbostars are being refreshed at Transys Projects' depot in Clacton-on-Sea, with repainting by Axiom Rail at Toton depot and Marcroft, Stoke-on-Trent. Seats are being re-upholstered, new carpets fitted and at-seat power points installed in the two-plus-one seating of the new First class accommodation. Work is due to be completed by June 2009. The trains, which operate on the Cardiff-Nottingham, Birmingham-Nottingham, Birmingham-Stansted Airport and Birmingham-Leicester routes, will provide 120 seats in the 2-car and up to 200 in the 3-car units.

Passenger revenue for the six months to 30 June 2008 was estimated to be up 10.3% on the equivalent services in 2007.

Cross Country
Simplified route diagram

CrossCountry
Key statistics 2007/08

Punctuality (0-10 minutes):	81.6 %
Passenger journeys (millions):	11.4
Passenger kilometres (millions):	1,136.6
Timetabled train kilometres (millions):	50.2
Route kilometres operated:	2662
Number of stations operated:	0
Subsidy per passenger kilometre (pence):	3.87

Figures cover Nov 2007-Mar 2008 only

Senior personnel

Managing Director
Andy Cooper (left)
Commercial Director
David Watkin
Finance Director
Richard Harrison
Customer Service Director
Jeremy Higgins
Production Director
Sarah Kendall
Head of Operational and Community Safety
Sean Forster

Passenger Train Operators

Serco and NedRailways

A partnership of Serco and NedRailways holds two UK passenger rail franchises, Northern Rail and Merseyrail. Serco Group works in a diverse range of public service roles around the world. In 2007, transport revenues grew by 4.7%% to £655m, accounting for 23% of group revenue. NedRailways is a wholly owned subsidiary of Netherlands Railways (NS), the major passenger operator in the Netherlands.

Serco operates, maintains and supports the Docklands Light Railway in London under a new seven-year franchise agreement signed in March 2006. It may be extended for a further two years and is valued at around £400m over the extended period. Serco is also to operate and maintain the first two lines of the new Dubai Metro, a contract valued at around £500m over 12.5 years.

Serco Rail Technologies specialises in the design, development, and provision of measurement and assessment solutions for the rail industry.

NedRailways draws on the wide range of expertise and experience available within the Netherlands' national railways. Besides fleet maintenance and operational planning and timetabling, NS develops and operates station hubs and retail facilities.

Northern's No 156479 enters Liverpool Lime Street on 7 October 2008, after negotiating the dramatic cutting and tunnel approach from Edge Hill. Tony Miles

northern

6 year 9 month franchise from 12 December 2004. Possible two-year extension

Serco-NedRailways' Northern Rail franchise runs local and regional train services for the northwest and northeast of England, Yorkshire, and Humberside.

The franchise was made up from the former North Western and North East franchises, with major inter-urban services transferred to TransPennine Express.

The franchise has contractual targets to reduce cancellations and delays by over 15% in the first five years; a new incentive/penalty regime on maintenance of stations and trains; and more local focus on performance, with monitoring and enforcement based on five sub-regions. The projected subsidy was £2434.6million (2004 prices) for 8 years 9 months, including a possible two-year extension, conditional on performance.

Northern Rail stretches over 1,675 miles of route, about 20% of Britain's rail network, serving 519 stations and managing 471. 2,500 services are run each weekday, the most of any franchised train operating company. Many services sponsored by five of the metropolitan Passenger Transport Executives are Northern's responsibility. Greater Manchester, Merseyside, South Yorkshire, Tyne & Wear, and West Yorkshire PTEs were signatories to the franchise agreement, though under new legislation, this will not be repeated in future.

As part of a two-year trial of tram-trains, Northern is to operate five new vehicles on the Sheffield-Barnsley-Huddersfield line from 2010, and in October 2008 issued an Invitation to Tender to build and maintain a minimum of five vehicles.

Service changes from December 2008 include a new hourly limited-stop train between Leeds and Nottingham via Wakefield Kirkgate, Barnsley, Sheffield, Chesterfield and Alfreton; and an accelerated service as part of a revised pattern between Leeds, Bradford Interchange and Manchester Victoria. A series of changes in the Manchester area was required to fit in with more frequent Virgin West Coast services.

Northern has successfully attracted more than £60m of external investment to help improve trains and stations, and passenger numbers rose by nearly a quarter to 80million a year over the first three years of the franchise. The number of trains on time increased from 83% to nearly 89%.

A joint programme with Network Rail strives to deliver improved punctuality. Challenges have come from cable theft, freak weather, leaf fall and even network congestion from freight traffic.

Northern is tightening up on revenue protection, with automatic gates for Manchester Oxford Road, Leeds and Blackpool North, and additional revenue protection staff.

Additional Class-158 trains were leased from Angel Trains in 2007, but some Class 142 railbuses went on loan to First Great Western. In an innovative partnership with Yorkshire Forward and Northern Rail in 2006, Metro (West Yorkshire PTE) backed a £20m package to finance six Class 158 trains.

Northern operates a diverse fleet of diesel multiple-units: 91 Class-142 or 144 Pacer railbus trains, 40 Class-150 Sprinter trains, 53 Class-155/156 Super Sprinters, 46 Class-158 Express diesel multiple-units, and 18 single car Class-153 diesel units. There are three Class-321 electric multiple-units and 16 Class-333s operated in West Yorkshire, and 17 Class-323 electric multiple-units used mainly in Greater Manchester. Northern was also planning to lease

Northern

Key statistics 2007/08

Punctuality (0-5 minutes):	88.5 %
Passenger journeys (millions):	78.9
Passenger kilometres (millions):	1,831.9
Timetabled train kilometres (millions):	48.2
Route kilometres operated:	2696
Number of stations operated:	471
Subsidy per passenger kilometre (pence):	6.51
Staff employed as at 06/01/2007:	4,585

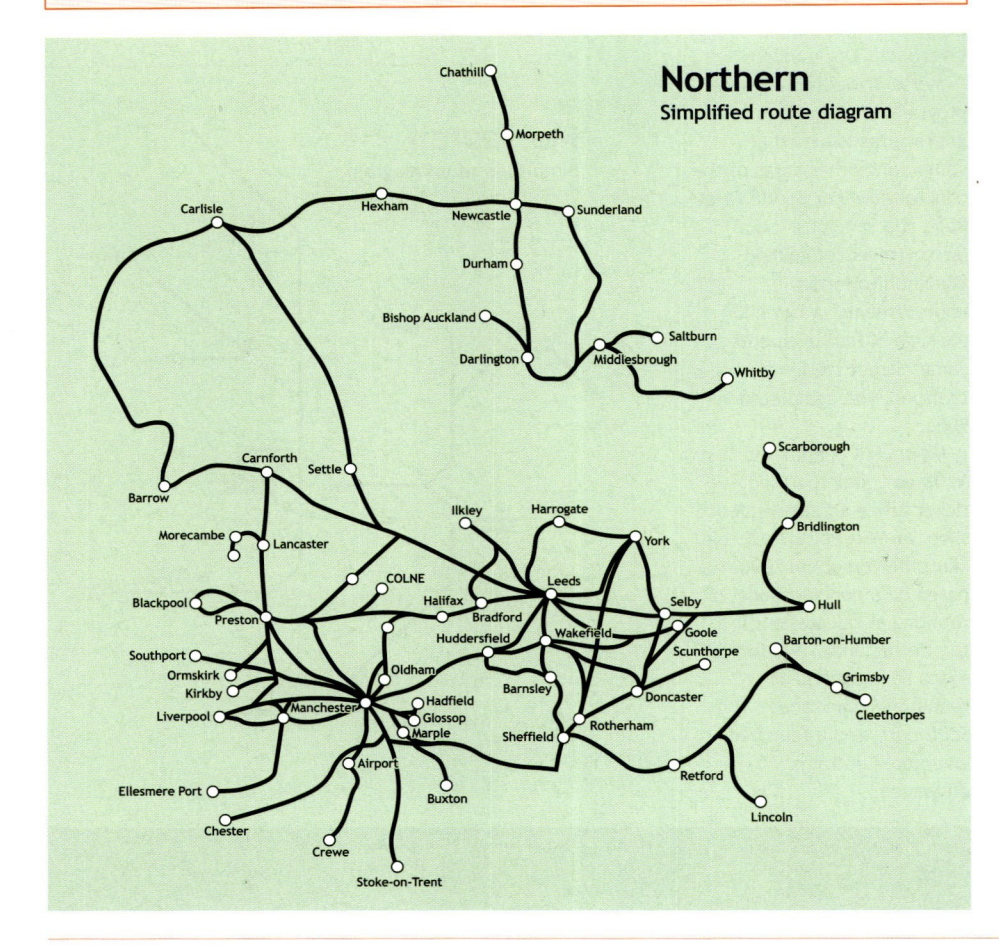

Senior personnel

Managing Director
Heidi Mottram
Finance Director and Deputy MD
Ian Bevan
Commercial Director
Jo North
Engineering Director
Ruud Haket
Performance and Planning Director
Rob Warnes
Safety and Assurance Director
Gary Stewart
Area Director, East
Steve Butcher
Area Director, West
Jamie Ross
Area Director, North
Iryna Terlecky

Northern — Simplified route diagram

a number of Class 180 Adelante trains in the short term.

The main maintenance depots are at Newcastle (Heaton), Manchester (Newton Heath), and Leeds (Neville Hill). Concentrating maintenance of each type of train at particular depots has helped to improve reliability (Class 150 and most of Class 142 and 156 at Newton Heath; the North East fleet of Classes 142 and 156 at Heaton; and Classes 144, 153, 155, 158 and EMUs at Neville Hill.) Alstom's West Coast Traincare maintains the Class 323s at Manchester.

Most heavy maintenance is now carried out in house, releasing funds for improvements. Refurbishment of Class 153 and 158 trains was nearing completion in 2008, with Class 150 to follow, and repainting of trains has been accelerated. Seven Class 158s are on hire to First ScotRail.

Merseyrail

25-year concession from 20 July 2003

The Merseyrail franchise is run under a concession agreement with Merseytravel, the Merseyside Public Transport Executive, by Merseyrail Electrics (2002) Ltd, a 50/50 Joint Venture company between Serco and NedRailways. It covers a self-contained network of electrified railway, and trains and stations are in Merseytravel livery, to present the network as a seamless team.

Merseyrail is unique in the UK as the franchising role has been delegated by Parliament to Merseytravel. The length of the concession is also unique - 25 years from 20 July 2003 with regular review dates. The contract has a total value of £3.6 billion.

The 75-mile network, electrified at 750V DC, third-rail, is one of the most heavily used outside London, with 780 trains daily (Monday to Friday). A clockface, regular interval timetable generally provides 15-minute train frequencies, increasing to 5-minute on city centre sections. The Merseyrail electric lines feed in from Southport, Ormskirk, the Wirral, and Chester into underground sections serving Liverpool city centre - 6.5 miles in tunnel with five underground stations.

Passenger traffic has been increasing sharply in recent years - approximately 100,000 passenger journeys are made per weekday, or 35million per annum. Nearly 50% of passengers are daily users. Punctuality levels are consistently good, with a best ever PPM score recorded in mid 2008, and overall satisfaction ratings are also high.

As part of a campaign to celebrate and play a part in Liverpool's status as European Capital of Culture in 2008, Merseyrail named one of its trains 'Capital of Culture', and four trains were wrapped in a special Capital of Culture livery.

Merseyrail services are operated by a total of 59 trains of Class 507 and Class 508, built in 1978-79. The fleet is maintained and stabled at Kirkdale and Birkenhead North depots. All trains have undergone major refurbishment in partnership with Angel Trains and Merseytravel in a £34.2million project, bringing improved reliability. A wheel lathe costing £2m and a new wash plant were installed at Kirkdale depot in 2006.

Replacement of the rolling stock, whose lease expires in 2014, is under consideration by Merseytravel, along with electrification and integration into Merseyrail of the Bidston-Wrexham, Kirkby-Wigan and Ormskirk-Preston lines.

In July 2008, another six Merseyrail stations were awarded Secure Station status, bringing Merseyrail Electrics closer to becoming the first fully 'secure' rail network in the country, with more than 95% of stations accredited.

A penalty fare scheme is operated to reduce the number of passengers travelling

Passenger Train Operators

Merseyrail

Key statistics 2007/08

Punctuality (0-5 minutes):	94.7 %
Passenger journeys (millions):	29.2
Passenger kilometres (millions):	341.8
Timetabled train kilometres (millions):	6.0
Route kilometres operated:	121
Number of stations operated:	66
Staff employed as at 06/01/2007:	1,159

Senior personnel

Managing Director
Bart Schmeink
Operations Director
Andy Heath
Engineering Director
Kevin Thomas
Finance and Commercial Director
Peter Morton
Concession Development Director
Rudi Boersma

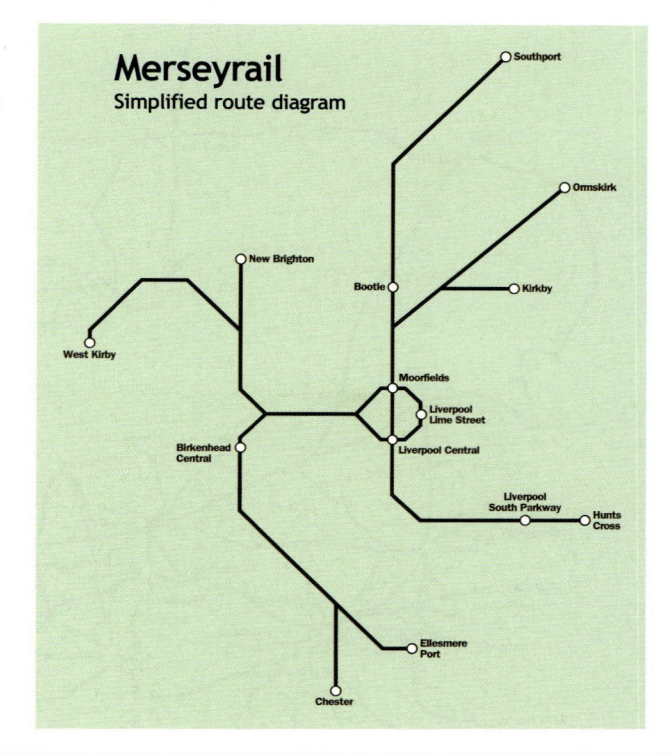

without a ticket, CCTV systems are installed in all cars of the refurbished trains and automatic ticket gates are in operation at the major stations. All stations within Merseyside are staffed for virtually the whole traffic day, and the number of security guards on stations and trains has been increased, particularly at night, to deter anti-social behaviour. In 2007 Merseyrail launched a campaign to actively target passengers committing offences under the railway byelaws, including putting their feet on seats in trains, and prosecute if appropriate.

Merseytravel has extended its sponsorship of six Police Community Support Officers to patrol the Merseyrail network until 2012.

The Passenger Transport Authority is keen for the local rail system is to play a role in stimulating the regional economy. In 2006, a £32million new station at Liverpool South Parkway was opened at the intersection of the Merseyrail electric and Liverpool-Crewe routes. It has a bus shuttle to Liverpool John Lennon Airport, acts as a hub for local bus routes, and offers park-and-ride opportunities, as well as opening up improved commuter access to many areas by a change of trains. A new station at Brunswick has supported the economic regeneration of Liverpool's Docklands.

Merseytravel has a programme of station improvements aimed at stimulating other areas of the conurbation. For Bootle Oriel Road and Sandhills, Merseytravel committed £8million towards improvements. A £2million package of improvements to James Street station in Liverpool was completed in 2008.

Merseyrail opened the first 'M to go', an integrated ticket office and convenience shop, at Moorfields station in central Liverpool in 2006, based on a popular model of retailing at rail stations in the Netherlands. Two further shops have opened at Hamilton Square and Southport, and a fourth at Liverpool Central is envisaged.

Merseyrail
Simplified route diagram

Commuters wait at Hunts Cross as their morning Merseyrail train to Liverpool arrives. Tony Miles

In association with **rail**services *from KNORR-BREMSE*

Stagecoach Group

Stagecoach Group has extensive bus and rail operations in the UK and North America, employing around 30,000 people. It has run the South West Trains franchise since it was first awarded in 1996. The group's new East Midlands franchise began in November 2007, and it also has a 49% shareholding in Virgin Rail Group, which operates the West Coast intercity rail franchise.

In light rail, Stagecoach Supertram serves the Sheffield network covering 29km, on a 27-year concession until 2024. In July 2007, Stagecoach took over operation and maintenance of Manchester Metrolink - including infrastructure - under a 10-year contract with Greater Manchester Passenger Transport Executive, making Stagecoach Britain's biggest tram operator.

Revenue from UK Rail subsidiaries for the year ended 30 April 2008 was up by 36.1% to £777.8m, reflecting strong organic revenue growth and the first contributions from East Midlands Trains and Manchester Metrolink.

Like-for-like revenue was up by 13.6% to £649.3m (2007: £571.5m). Operating profit was £59.1m (2007: £58.8m), giving an operating margin of 7.6% (2007: 10.3%), the operating margin of the new South West Trains franchise being below that of the former one. Absolute operating profit for the UK Rail division increased with the first contribution from East Midlands Trains.

SOUTH WEST TRAINS

10-year franchise from February 2007

Stagecoach Group's South West Trains and Island Line (Isle of Wight) franchises were merged from 4 February 2007 under a new franchise.

An approximate 20% increase in peak capacity was announced, with maximum length trains on almost all peak services. As well as £40m on revenue protection and security measures at stations, £19m was pledged for introduction of smartcard ticketing.

From December 2008 an additional peak-period service from Basingstoke to Waterloo was to be formed of Class 159 diesel units, with a 10 coach service introduced from Salisbury to Waterloo in the morning peak.

A second Waterloo-Weymouth train per hour was introduced from December 2007, replacing Poole area stopping services. Two Bristol-Waterloo trains per day and a regular service for Chandlers Ford were retained under the new franchise, and an improved, hourly Waterloo-Exeter service was planned after infrastructure improvements, expected by December 2009. South West Trains services west of Exeter (to Plymouth/Paignton) would then end.

Stagecoach promised investment to keep Island Line rolling stock - six ex-London Underground trains dating from 1938 - in service. The trains were transferred to Stagecoach ownership in March 2007 by HSBC Rail.

A new 'standard pattern' timetable was introduced in December 2004, and together with a South West Trains / Network Rail integrated control centre, is credited with helping performance figures improve to among the best in London and the South East. A best ever figure of 95% punctuality (Public Performance Measure) was recorded for the four weeks to 13 September 2008. Passenger volumes were up 5.7% in the year to 30 April 2008.

The megatrain.com website, offering budget seats on off-peak services, was launched on South West Trains in November 2005, and has been extended to cover East Midlands Trains.

Stagecoach's new 10-year franchise is worth more than £530million in annual revenues, it said, and is to generate £1,191million (Net Present Value) in premium payments to the Department for Transport (DfT).

In May 2007, South West Trains introduced a new off-peak fare structure for travel into London. Customers travelling between 09.30 and 12.00 saw fares increase by up to 20%, while those travelling later or at weekends saw a rise averaging 3%. SWT said the new fares were necessary both to enable it to meet franchise commitments and to attempt to tackle the 'second peak' of passengers just after the morning peak.

The electric multiple-unit fleet has 45 Class-444 five-car Siemens Desiro trains and

One of the Desiro electric multiple-units rearranged to provide greater passenger capacity. Class 450/5 Desiro No 450570 calls at Virginia Water on 11 April 2008, forming the 12.03 Weybridge-Waterloo service. Brian Morrison

Passenger Train Operators

Key statistics 2007/08
South West Trains

Punctuality (0-5 minutes):	92.3 %
Passenger journeys (millions):	187.8
Passenger kilometres (millions):	5,185.1
Timetabled train kilometres (millions):	40.7
Route kilometres operated:	870
Number of stations operated:	185
Subsidy per passenger kilometre (pence):	0.2
Staff employed as at 30/04/2007:	5,093

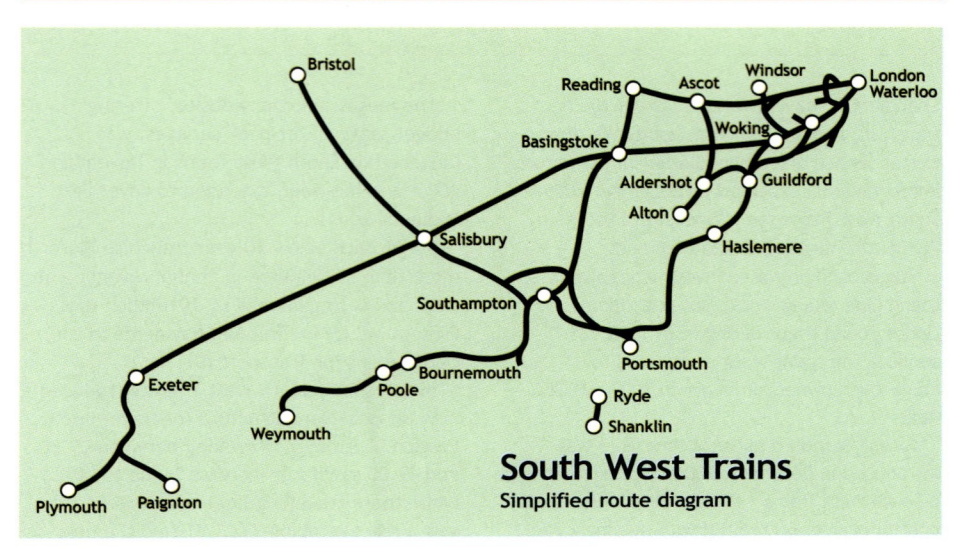

Senior personnel

Chairman
Ian Dobbs
Managing Director
Stewart Palmer (left)
Operations Director
Jan Chaudry
Engineering Director
Mac Mackintosh
Customer Service Director
Ian Johnston

South West Trains
Simplified route diagram

127 Class-450 four-car Desiros – 28 of them recently converted to higher-capacity specification. There are also 30 Alstom-built Class-458 trains, and the pre-privatisation Class 455 (91 trains) whose £67m refurbishment, with a revised internal layout, was completed in early 2008. Two Class 421 slam-door trains are used on the Lymington branch.

The diesel multiple-unit fleet, used on the non-electrified routes from Southampton and Basingstoke to Salisbury and beyond, has undergone major refurbishment by Wabtec. There are 30 three-car Class 159s and 11 two-car Class 158s. Some of the '158s' were on hire during 2008 to East Midlands Trains.

EAST MIDLANDS TRAINS

Seven year, four month franchise from 11 November 2007

The new East Midlands franchise was won by Stagecoach subsidiary East Midlands Trains, which began operations on 11 November 2007 and is due to continue until 1 April 2015. The franchise is a combination of the previous Midland main line intercity franchise with the eastern section of Central Trains.

The Department for Transport said the franchise will deliver increased capacity, better performance and the introduction of smartcard technology by 2010, but it has the right to terminate the franchise after six years if performance targets are not met. Over the full franchise period, a premium of £133m (net present value) will be paid to the DfT. Stagecoach said the new franchise is worth £235m in annual total revenues.

Innovations in the December 2008 timetable change include an extra hourly Kettering-London service (removing the need to split/join trains at Leicester), extending to the reopened Corby station.

Other features include:
■ a new daily service between London St Pancras and Lincoln;
■ 9% increase in peak capacity into and out of St Pancras;
■ Matlock-Derby service increased to hourly and extended to Nottingham;
■ journey times between Sheffield, Derby and London reduced;
■ additional early morning train from Derby to cater for demand.

An additional High Speed Train was planned from June 2012 to increase capacity in time for the Olympic and Paralympic Games.

Stagecoach was expected to increase unregulated fares by an average of RPI+3.4% per annum. A significant increase in capacity was promised, with more than 850 extra main line peak seats into and out of London and an increase of nearly 10,000 off-peak seats per weekday.

It is hoped to develop a business case for new trains on the busy Liverpool-Nottingham route, with infrastructure improvements to speed up journeys. Meanwhile, the new Nottingham-Sheffield-Leeds service run by Northern from December 2008 should alleviate crowding on the Nottingham-Sheffield section. The number of Liverpool-Nottingham trains operated with four vehicles is planned to increase from seven to 15 per day from December 2011.

The Robin Hood Line service, from Nottingham to Worksop via Mansfield, was to run on Sundays for the first time from December 2008. Nottinghamshire County Council will fund the service until May 2011, but if it is as well used as expected, it is hoped the Department for Transport will then fund it on a permanent basis.

Other franchise plans included improvement the public performance measure (PPM) to 90.4% from 83.6% by focusing on poorer performing regional services and trains. A figure of 90.9% was achieved for a four-week period ending in September 2008. A performance improvement programme has included an initiative to improve train punctuality, which has included issuing radio-controlled watches and new whistles to all staff; a new joint control centre, shared with Network Rail, to improve communication on day-to-day operation; performance drives and improved service recovery arrangements on several different routes; introduction of an internal 'delay hotline'; and improved processes, including better contingency plans and a new performance management system.

For the period from 11 November 2007 to 30 April 2008, the revenue of East Midlands Trains was 9.5% higher than a year earlier, compared to the equivalent former businesses.

A £26.5m fleet interior and performance improvement programme, including decor, seats, on-train CCTV and technical modifications is under way, with significant investment at Derby (Etches Park), designated EMT's centre of train maintenance operations. Neville Hill depot, Leeds, continues to carry out work on High Speed Trains. Repainting of the fleet began in 2008, and a full refurbishment of Class 158 trains, contracted to Delta Rail, began. Buffet cars have been retained on High Speed Trains after consultation, contrary to original plans for the new franchise.

The Bombardier-built Meridian trains, introduced from 2004, are allocated to the hourly Sheffield services (off peak) from December 2008 with faster journey times.

During 2008, all remaining Paxman Valenta-engined High Speed Train power cars were being

East Midlands Trains
Key statistics 2007/08
Punctuality (0-5 minutes):	85.2 %
Passenger journeys (millions):	15.3
Passenger kilometres (millions):	1,597.9
Timetabled train kilometres (millions):	10.1
Route kilometres operated:	1567.5
Number of stations operated:	88
Subsidy per passenger kilometre (pence):	1.41

(Figures cover November 2007-March 2008 only)

Senior personnel
Managing Director
Tim Shoveller (left)
Customer Service Director
Jake Kelly
Commercial Director
David Horne
Human Resources Director
Margaret Kay
Operations Director
Mark Steward
Finance Director
Richard Bodicoat
Engineering Director
Tony Wrighton
Safety and Environment Director
David Maxwell

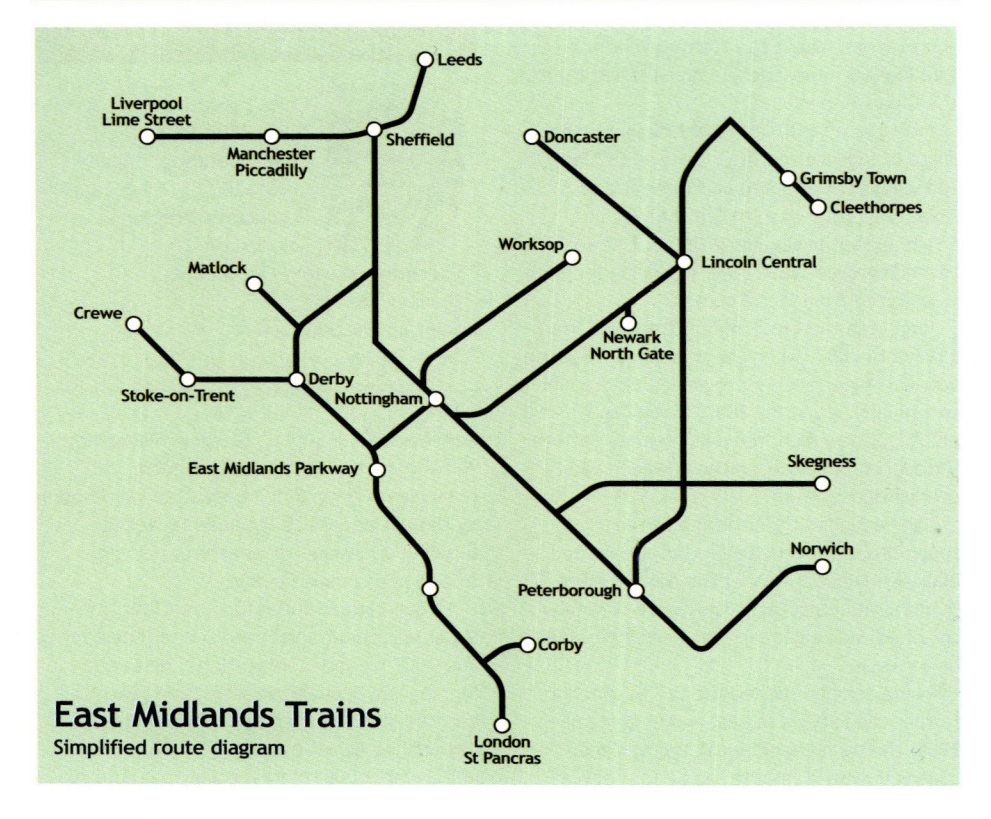

East Midlands Trains
Simplified route diagram

fitted with Paxman VP185 engines, and EMT is also standardising on a Brush Traction cooler group on these trains.

EMT is working with Bombardier to modify the Class 222s' train management system to allow easier shutdown of engines at turnarounds and possible en-route coasting. Further environmental improvements were being sought from better fuel monitoring and management, as well as the introduction of eco-driving to driver training programmes.

East Midlands Trains' 11 HSTs are formed from a pool of 25 power cars and 94 trailers. An additional power car, formerly used for the Porterbrook/Hitachi hybrid traction trials, was also joining the fleet in late 2008. The Class 222 Meridian fleet was being reorganised in 2008 to form six 7-car and seventeen 5-car sets, and additional 4-car Class 222s were expected to be transferred from Hull Trains. Regional and local services are operated by 17 Class-153, 11 Class-156 and 25 Class-158 diesel multiple-units.

A locomotive-hauled train hired by East Midlands Trains was used to help cater for holiday peak demand between Nottingham and Skegness in summer 2008, and use of a hired loco-hauled train elsewhere was also predicted while new maintenance facilities at Derby were being completed.

In fresh Stagecoach / East Midlands Trains livery, Class 43 HST power car No 43058 is seen in Neville Hill depot, Leeds on 30 April 2008. Brian Morrison

Passenger Train Operators

Virgin Trains

**West Coast franchise -
15 years from March 1997**

Virgin Rail Group (VRG) - a joint venture between Virgin Group (51%) and Stagecoach Group (49%) - runs the West Coast intercity franchise under the Virgin Trains banner. The main train fleet is of 52 Alstom-built Pendolino electric tilting trains.

The franchise began in March 1997, and new terms were agreed with the Department for Transport (DfT) in December 2006, replacing an agreement put in place in 2002. This followed the collapse of Railtrack, and delays and a reduced scope for the West Coast Route Modernisation project that was linked to the franchise. The new terms see VRG receiving an average of £259m per year until March 2012 - mainly to contribute to Network Rail track access charges, which rose to more than £400million a year as the cost of the route modernisation reached £8.6billion.

The 2007 agreement provided for the 'VHF' (very high frequency) recast of services from December 2008, with nine Virgin trains per hour from Euston in off-peak periods, and 11 in the peak. The nine off-peak services are three to the West Midlands (two to Birmingham New Street, one to Wolverhampton); three to Manchester (two via Stoke, one via Crewe); one to Liverpool; one to Chester or North Wales; and for most of the day, one to Glasgow. The number of trains on Sundays almost doubles. 47 of the 52 Pendolino trains will be needed in service every weekday, rather than 46.

Virgin also operates an hourly Birmingham-Scotland service, taken over from the CrossCountry franchise at the end of 2007, and has proposed a London-Wrexham service via Chester.

A few of the VHF changes were postponed until early 2009 because Network Rail had yet to fully complete route modernisation. During rescheduled work at the south end of the route, Virgin has run an alternative Birmingham International-London service via the Chiltern line.

In the year to 30 April 2008, Stagecoach's share of VRG's profit after tax was £32.2m (previous year, £18.9m) and the share of operating profit was £41.9m (£12.4m plus £5.4m exceptional gains in 2007). Like-for-like revenue growth was 11.2%, excluding services transferred from CrossCountry.

Virgin ran the CrossCountry franchise from 1997 until 2007, when the remapped franchise was won by Arriva. Passenger journeys doubled to 24million a year by 2007, though an ambitious new high frequency service pattern introduced in 2002 hit difficulties and was reorganised.

The Pendolino trains have a nominal top speed of 225km/h (140mph) but are limited to 200km/h (125mph) under the revised route modernisation package. They were originally specified with eight cars but were increased to nine cars.

Rising demand has led the DfT to sanction further capacity increases, and in September 2008, the train lessor, Angel Trains, signed contracts with Alstom to supply four new 11-car Pendolino trains, two extra cars for 31 existing trains, and a 10-year maintenance regime, worth a total of £1.5billion. There is an option to extend the remaining 21 trains. Commissioning will take place at Alstom's Traincare Centre at Edge Hill, Liverpool which will accommodate a new depot. Network Rail was to spend £15m at Edge Hill, part of a package to upgrade five centres, including Manchester (Longsight), Glasgow (Polmadie), Wolverhampton (Oxley), and London (Wembley). Virgin Rail Projects Ltd was chosen by the DfT as Service Provider, to support DfT throughout design, manufacture, delivery, testing and commissioning.

13 five-car and three four-car Class 221 Super Voyagers transferred to West Coast in late 2007 to work London-North Wales and Birmingham-Scotland services, and also services diverted from electrified routes. A further five '221s' transfer from CrossCountry in December 2008. Virgin is not to create six-car '221s' as previously planned, but sets were being reorganised with the 'shop' vehicle given First Class-style seating and placed next to the First Class vehicle.

Since the Grayrigg accident in February 2007, caused by faulty points, the Pendolino fleet was reduced from 53 to 52 sets and a hired locomotive hauled train was expected to continue in use in 2009.

West Coast
Key statistics 2007/08

Punctuality (0-10 minutes):	86.2%
Passenger journeys (millions):	21.8
Passenger kilometres (millions):	4,213.5
Timetabled train kilometres (millions):	23.4
Route kilometres operated:	1172
Number of stations operated:	17
Subsidy per passenger kilometre (pence):	3.84
Staff employed as at 03/03/2007:	2,705

Senior personnel

Chief Executive
Tony Collins (left)
Chief Operating Officer
Chris Gibb
Production Director
Ross Spicer
Executive Director, Commercial
Graham Leech
Sales and Marketing Director
Sarah Copley

During West Coast route modernisation work, Virgin has run services between Euston and Birmingham International via the Chiltern line. The 11.03 from Euston is seen near Saunderton, south of Princes Risborough, on 5 July 2008, formed of Class 221 Voyagers Nos 221104 and 22108. Brian Morrison

rail alliance

Discover the fastest growing rail network in Europe

Free, impartial and confidential business development advice and support.

Access to a database of over 1000 companies.

The opportunity to network and take part in a wide range of events held regularly throughout the year. Most of which will be free to members.

Belonging to an organisation that will represent your interests no matter how large or small your company is. We will influence key decision makers and lobby through a network of strategic alliances with existing trade associations and public bodies.

An education, training and management development program that is unique

Participation in a comprehensive international program, and benefiting from a wide range of support activities to promote international trading.

Access to a wide variety of membership benefits including discounted web-site design and hosting packages, promotional DVD development, discounts at major shows and events

Being in the company of like minded and progressive businesses

Why not?

For further information contact: Rhona Clarke
The Control Tower, Long Marston Storage, Campden Road, Long Marston
Stratford on Avon CV37 8QR
Telephone: 01789 720026

info@railalliance.co.uk www.railalliance.co.uk

Passenger Train Operators

Chiltern Railways

20 year (maximum) franchise from February 2002

Holding a maximum 20-year franchise until 2022, Chiltern Railways is part of DB Regio AG, the division of Deutsche Bahn (DB - German Railways) responsible for operating regional and local services.

DB's acquisition of Laing Rail – the owners of Chiltern Railways, and joint owners of London Overground Rail Operations and Wrexham, Shropshire & Marylebone Railway - was confirmed in March 2008, and marked DB's entry into the UK passenger rail market. An order for four new two-car Class 172 diesel multiple-units from Bombardier, financed by Angel Trains, was announced alongside the change of ownership.

The London Rail concession for the London Overground network was awarded in 2007 to a joint venture of Laing Rail with Hong Kong's MTR. Laing in 2006 joined Renaissance Trains in the Wrexham, Shropshire & Marylebone Railway project. Laing Rail's former parent group, John Laing, has a continued involvement in the rail industry through rail infrastructure and facilities management businesses.

Chiltern has announced plans for a Transport & Works Act application for works to enable an Oxford to London Marylebone service via Bicester. The approximately £200million scheme involves upgrading and doubling of the Oxford-Bicester line, a new quarter-mile link to the Chiltern line at Bicester; and a new station at a park & ride site north of Oxford.

Trains would run half hourly, taking 66min from Oxford to Marylebone. Birmingham-London services would also benefit from line-speed improvements. Additional trains (not covered by the £200million figure) would be required, and the service could be running by 2012.

Aylesbury Vale Parkway, a new station 3km north of Aylesbury, set to open in late 2008, is designed to serve housing development and a park-and-ride scheme. A 20 year, £13million concession was jointly funded by the government's Community Infrastructure Fund, Buckinghamshire County Council and John Laing. Chiltern and Laing were responsible for Warwick Parkway, the first non-Railtrack station delivered on the UK rail network, in 2000.

In 2002 Chiltern extended operations north of Birmingham, to Kidderminster, and in 2004 took over services between Stratford-upon-Avon and London.

The 20-year franchise awarded by the former Strategic Rail Authority from 2002 was subject to delivery of investment. Chiltern committed to £371million of improvements, including additional and refurbished trains and station improvements - and the £80million Project Evergreen 2. This Design, Build, Finance and Transfer project, completed in 2006, created new station capacity, signalling and line enhancements. It enables 20 trains per peak hour to use Marylebone, which gained two additional platforms. The company said its long franchise was a key factor in attracting finance. A new £20million Wembley depot was completed in 2005. Project Evergreen Phase 1 had already doubled single track between Aynho Junction (near Banbury) and Princes Risborough.

Ticketing by mobile phone was introduced by Chiltern in January 2007. Passengers receive their 'ticket' as a barcode sent to their mobile phone which is checked with special scanners.

Since 1996, Chiltern has more than doubled in size its fleet of diesel multiple-units. The Bombardier-built Class 168 'Clubman' fleet, for longer distance services, has 10 x 4-car and nine x 3-car units, which saw a £6million makeover in 2007/08. There are 28 x 2-car and 11 x 3-car Class 165 'Turbo' trains, refurbished in a £17million programme. A refurbished Class-121 single-car diesel is used on Aylesbury-Princes Risborough shuttles. Chiltern's main maintenance depot is at Aylesbury. All seats on Chiltern services are Standard class.

Major disruption was caused by the collapse of an artificial tunnel being built over the railway for a Tesco store at Gerrards Cross in 2005. In 2007, Chiltern recorded a net profit of £8.1m after recieving £18m compensation from Tesco. Turnover was up 12% at £123.4m.

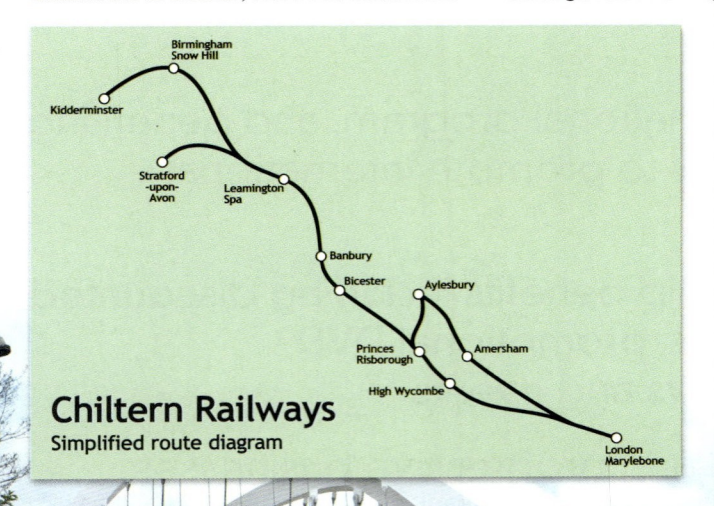

Key statistics 2007/08
Chiltern Railways

Punctuality (0-5 minutes):	95.0 %
Passenger journeys (millions):	16.8
Passenger kilometres (millions):	897.1
Timetabled train kilometres (millions):	9.3
Route kilometres operated:	336
Number of stations operated:	27
Subsidy per passenger kilometre (pence):	1.38
Staff employed as at 05/01/2008:	725

Senior personnel

Chairman
Adrian Shooter (left)
Operations Director
Richard MacLennan
Engineering Director
Tim Sayer

Chiltern Railways — Simplified route diagram

Class 168 'Clubman' No 168109 passes through Wembley Stadium station at speed on 27 April 2008, forming the 06.30 Chiltern service from Kidderminster to Marylebone. Brian Morrison

RAIL
It's the way forward

Punctuality much improved

Simpler fares

Better information

More new trains coming

More reliable infrastructure

ATOC
Association of Train Operating Companies

Passenger Train Operators

Class 67 No 67014 'Thomas Telford' powers the 07.25 Wrexham & Shropshire service from Wrexham to Marylebone at Princes Risborough on 23 October 2008. Nearest the camera is newly-introduced Class 82/3 DVT No 82303. Brian Morrison

wrexham & shropshire

Renaissance Trains and DB Regio joint venture

Wrexham & Shropshire operates open-access passenger services between Wrexham and London Marylebone. Services began on 28 April 2008 and have been well received by a wide range of passengers and stakeholders.

The Wrexham, Shropshire & Marylebone Railway (WSMR) joint venture was set up by Renaissance Trains (originator and still a shareholder of Hull Trains) and Laing Rail (parent of Chiltern Railways, whose route WSMR uses at the London end). In 2008, DB Regio, a subsidiary of German state railway operator Deutsche Bahn, took over Laing Rail and its interest in the joint venture, which trades as Wrexham & Shropshire. The company aims to set a new standard for rail travel that provides a viable alternative to the car for both business and leisure travellers. Modern, comfortable trains with excellent facilities are central to that aim.

As well as serving Wrexham, the trains have restored a direct link to the capital for Shrewsbury, Telford and a number of intermediate stations. Initially the track access agreement runs for seven years, allowing five services each way on weekdays, four on Saturdays and three on Sundays. The redrafting of the timetable from December 2008 has created improved paths which will see average journey times between Wrexham and London cut to around four hours.

From the outset the company has been keen to support the local economy. A local team of staff was recruited for the start-up, with over 50 new jobs created. Train servicing is carried out at a new facility constructed at Wrexham General station and the on-board menu uses locally sourced food wherever possible.

After a period of operation with two locomotives, trains were being formed of three Mk3 coaches and a driving van trailer (DVT) powered by a Class 67 locomotive. The coaches and DVTs are owned by DB Regio UK and leased to WSMR; the locomotives are hired in from EWS, also a DB company.

Initially coaches were hired from Cargo-D while WSMR's own fleet of Mk3 vehicles, purchased from Porterbrook, was refurbished by EWS company Axiom Rail at Stoke-on-Trent. Wi-Fi internet access, power sockets at seats, and space for luggage, bicycles, and pushchairs are all part of the formula. A total of £5.5million has been invested in the refurbishment, £0.5m for access and facilities for disabled people.

Modifications enable the DVT to control the Class 67 locomotive via a 27-way cable, using the multiple-working function fitted to all General Motors-derived locomotives operating in the UK. The DVTs are also being fitted with a sanding device for increased safety, the first time such a modification has been made to these vehicles. They retain the ability to work in push-pull mode with electric locomotives. The only change to the locomotives has been to fit a fire extinguisher system that can be remotely triggered from the DVT.

The first refurbished DVT entered service in October 2008 and the first rake of WSMR's own Mk3 coaches in November 2008.

Wrexham & Shropshire was carrying over 4,500 passengers each week by late 2008, and since its launch the Wrexham-London rail travel market has grown by 32% year on year (although around 4% of this can be attributed to population growth and economic factors). Shrewsbury and Telford have been the top two stations in terms of passenger numbers, but higher than expected numbers have been seen from Wrexham and Gobowen.

Wrexham & Shropshire has a total of four complete trains, using 12 Mk3 coaches, four Mk3 DVTs and four dedicated locomotives in company livery. DB Regio UK owns sufficient vehicles to form a fifth train and extend all trains to four coaches. The purchase of 12 DVTs gives sufficient spares for future projects.

Senior personnel

Managing Director
Andy Hamilton (left)
Commercial Manager
Richard Harper
Operations Manager
Mark Edlington
Customer Services Manager
Diane Davidson
Finance Manager
Andy Deacon

Grand Central Railway

New open access group seeks expansion

Grand Central Railway's new train services from Sunderland/Hartlepool to London were launched in December 2007, introducing a second open-access train operator to the East Coast main line, after a protracted series of administrative and engineering challenges.

Services were at first restricted, as only one complete High Speed Train was available from a fleet being refurbished for Grand Central (GC). With further power cars and coaches delivered, the full service was introduced in March 2008. Major component problems led to a reduced service from May 2008, but following overhauls, all services were restored from July 2008.

The way had been cleared for Grand Central to launch its services in July 2006 after a Judicial Review. This was brought by the franchised East Coast intercity train operating company, Great North Eastern Railway, against the Office of Rail Regulation's decision to approve track access rights for GC's trains.

In March 2006, the Office of Rail Regulation (ORR) approved three of the four daily London-Sunderland return services applied for. ORR did not consider there was sufficient capacity to accommodate GC's proposed services to Bradford without significant changes to many existing services.

The major shareholder in Grand Central was Fraser Eagle Group, supplier of transport services to the UK rail industry, including bus replacement services. In March 2007, ownership changed, when a new funding package was secured by a new investment team led by Giles Fearnley and Bob Howells, founder directors of Prism Rail plc, with Giles Fearnley becoming GC Chairman. (Prism was a train operating group, sold to National Express in September 2000.)

The new team enabled Grand Central to press ahead with refurbishment of three High Speed Trains (HSTs) purchased from Porterbrook Leasing, each with six passenger vehicles, while six spare vehicles were also acquired. Because of a shortage of HST trailer vehicles, former locomotive hauled vehicles were converted. DML at Plymouth (power cars) and Marcroft Engineering/EWS Engineering Support Group (passenger vehicles) were contracted to carry out the refurbishment. Due to performance problems, GC took the step of sending most of the power cars to Brush Traction during late Spring 2008 to (successfully) improve reliability of major components.

Northern Rail maintains Grand Central's trains at Heaton depot in Newcastle and provides three Riding Inspectors to check on the health of trains en route.

Sunderland, Hartlepool, Eaglescliffe and Thirsk gained direct trains to London for the first time in many years from Grand Central's service, as well as direct links to York and connectional opportunities beyond.

Grand Central believes passengers should not be penalised for last minute decisions to travel, and offers a simple fare structure, with no penalty for purchasing tickets on the train.

Grand Central and associate company, Grand Union, have long had plans for a number of other new services, and in 2008 applications were placed for a direct service between Bradford and London King's Cross via Halifax and Pontefract, and for a route linking Bradford, Huddersfield and London Euston. Grand Central also applied for an additional daily train between London and Sunderland. Because of the protracted consideration by the ORR of competing applications for new East Coast main line services, Grand Union later temporarily shelved its Bradford-Huddersfield-Euston proposals.

Senior personnel

Chairman
Giles Fearnley
Managing Director
Tom Clift (left)
Marketing Manager
Roger Wheatley
Fleet Engineer
Neil Heaton
Operations Director
Sean English
Finance Director
David Lowrie

Three more possible services to King's Cross that have been under development are from Cleethorpes (via Grimsby and Scunthorpe); Scarborough; and Huddersfield (via Wakefield Kirkgate, Rotherham, Sheffield, Worksop and Retford). A Bradford-Doncaster service, calling at Brighouse, Wakefield Kirkgate and Pontefract is another aspiration.

In addition, Grand Union entered into discussions in 2007 with the Welsh Assembly Government about provision of extra services between north, mid and south Wales leading to the paths being allocated to Grand Union, though Arriva Trains Wales was given the go-ahead for this service in October 2008.

A new rolling stock company, Sovereign Trains, is a sister company which leases the HSTs to GC. Proposals have been published for future new 140mph diesel trains for GC from CSR Ziyang of China, similar in concept to the HST, with 23-metre-long steel-built coaches and 15-metre long power cars.

A range of other Chinese-built traction, rolling stock and components is also marketed for Europe by CSRE Limited, a further sister company, including a diesel multiple-unit and diesel locomotives, as well as an electric high-speed train and freight locomotives and wagons.

Grand Central's 08.55 Sunday service from King's Cross to Sunderland passes Harringay on 10 August 2008, led by Class 43 powercar No 43080, with No 43065 on the rear. Brian Morrison

Passenger Train Operators

Eurostar's new London Engineering Centre at Temple Mills on 24 June 2008, showing Eurostar trains – and one of the bicycles used by staff inside the quarter-mile-long building. Brian Morrison

Strong growth on international service

Eurostar, the high-speed train service between Britain, France and Belgium via the Channel Tunnel, experienced strong growth after the opening in 2007 of High Speed 1, the Channel Tunnel Rail Link.

The service was launched in 1994 by French and Belgian state railways, and a British Rail subsidiary which was sold in 1996 to London & Continental Railways (LCR), the government's chosen Channel Tunnel Rail Link development group. In 1998, LCR awarded a contract to manage Eurostar UK Ltd, until 2010, to InterCapital and Regional Rail, a consortium of National Express (40% shareholding), French Railways (35%), Belgian Railways (15%) and British Airways (10% shareholding - a 'sleeping' partner).

A unified Eurostar Group structure was established in 1999, and though a proposed merger of French, Belgian and British interests did not go ahead, Eurostar did further consolidate the management team.

Eurostar services transferred to London St Pancras International from Waterloo International on 14 November 2007, with the opening of High Speed 1. Journey times were cut by at least 20min, with non-stop times of London-Paris in 2hr 15min, London-Brussels in 1hr 51min and London-Lille in 1hr 20min. Eurostar also serves a new station at Ebbsfleet International in north Kent, and (less frequently than before) the longer established Ashford International in east Kent. A start date for Eurostar services to call at Stratford International, east London, which will be at the heart of the 2012 London Olympic and Paralympic games, has not been set.

The number of weekday services on the London-Paris route increased from 15 to 17 by February 2008, with 10 weekday services to Brussels. A service of up to 20 trains on Fridays from London to Paris and 19 trains from Paris was introduced from 11 July 2008. A daily train also runs to Disneyland Resort Paris, and a second ran four days a week in the 2008 summer school holidays.

An 18th service in each direction on the Paris route (Monday-Thursday) was planned from September 2008, and an 11th (Monday-Friday) on the Brussels route was planned from December - but the Channel Tunnel fire on 9 September 2008 meant that a reduced Eurostar service, with journey times about 20min longer than normal, was expected to run for several months until it was possible to restore full access to both Channel Tunnel running tunnels.

On 4 September 2007, a record Paris-London journey time of 2hr 3min was set by a special Eurostar arriving at the new St Pancras, 10 weeks before the transfer of normal services. On 20 September, the first train from Brussels to St Pancras set another record, taking 1hr 43min to cover the 232 mile (373km) distance.

Under its Tread Lightly initiative, Eurostar has set a target of reducing carbon dioxide emissions by 25% per passenger journey by 2012, and will offset emissions that it cannot eliminate at its own expense.

In July 2007, Eurostar UK joined German, French, Belgian, Netherlands, Austrian and Swiss companies in Railteam, an alliance aiming to give travellers seamless high-speed train travel across international borders.

In 2007, Eurostar passenger numbers rose to 8.26million – up 5.1% on the previous year. Ticket sales rose by 15.5% to £599million.

In the first six months of 2008, sales were up 13.6% to £295.7million and traveller numbers by 4.8% to 3.91million. Train punctuality stood at 92.6%. Because of economic factors, the rate of growth was expected to slow in the second half of the year. An all-time monthly high of 900,000 passengers was recorded in July 2008 -16.8% up on 2007.

Eurostar operates a fleet of 27 trains - each 400 metres long, weighing 750 tonnes and carrying 750 passengers in 18 carriages. Three more 'Three Capitals' trains are used only on French domestic services. Six of the seven 14-car trains built for aborted UK regional services have been leased to SNCF, also for use on services within France.

Senior personnel

Chairman
Guillaume Pepy
Chief Executive Officer
Richard Brown (left)
Commercial Director
Nicholas Mercer
Customer Service Director
Marc Noaro
Chief Operating Officer
Nicolas Petrovic

Cars are loaded onto a Eurotunnel car shuttle train. Eurotunnel

EUROTUNNEL

Revenue hit by tunnel fire

Eurotunnel holds a concession agreement to operate the Channel Tunnel until 2086, signed in 1986 by its precursors with the French and British governments.

The Channel 'Tunnel', opened in 1994, is actually made up of twin railway tunnels and a service tunnel. Terminals, at Folkestone, Kent and Coquelles, in the Nord Pas-de-Calais, provide car, coach and lorry access to shuttle trains. International passenger and freight trains also run through the tunnel.

A plan to reduce Eurotunel's £6.2billion debt was implemented in 2007, simplifying a 'project finance' structure, which Eurotunnel said kept it under the administrative control of creditors. A successful exchange tender offer was carried through by a new Groupe Eurotunnel SA for shares in the original UK and French companies.

In 2007, revenues improved for the third consecutive year: up 6% compared to 2006, at 775million Euro, with growth in the cross-Channel market and in Eurotunnel's share of lorry traffic. Eurotunnel said its pricing policy had increased average yields.

Up until the end of November 2006, 'railways' revenues from international passenger and freight trains were protected by the Minimum Usage Charge (MUC), a slice of revenue originally guaranteed by the UK and France via their state railways, and representing 94million Euro in 2006 (restated at average 2007 exchange rate). Disregarding the MUC in 2006, railways revenue grew by 3% in 2007, with a 5% increase in Eurostar passengers, but decreased rail freight tonnage (down 23%).

Eurotunnel trading profit in 2007 was 277million Euro compared to 321million Euro in 2006 - a 22% improvement if the MUC is excluded.

After a serious fire on a lorry shuttle on 11 September 2008, one section of Eurotunnel's north running tunnel remained closed after 29 September. Eurotunnel approved contracts to renovate the damaged section, with a target of complete reopening in mid February 2009, at a budget expected to be under 60million Euro.

With capacity restrictions after the fire, revenues for the third quarter of 2008 were down by 6%. Without the impact of these restrictions, estimated at 22million Euro in September (excluding insurance cover), Eurotunnel believed revenues would have increased by about 5%.

Despite the effect of the fire, for the first nine months of 2008, revenues improved by 5% at a constant exchange rate compared to 2007.

The end of the MUC jeopardised the continuation of through freight traffic, and the UK Department for Transport agreed that the government-owned residuary company, British Railways Board, should go on paying part of Eurotunnel's operating charges under the terms of the Channel Tunnel Rail Usage Contract.

Eurotunnel announced in October 2007 that it was cutting tolls for freight trains and would charge by train rather than by tonnage, after discussions with rail companies and government. This would cut the average toll to £3,000 a train compared with £5,300.

But with a decline of 7% in the number of trains over the first nine months of 2008, Eurotunnel said rail freight had still not shown signs of growth.

Eurotunnel's international rail freight subsidiary, Europorte 2, began operations in November 2007, and is now responsible for French Railways freight train haulage between the Dollands Moor (UK) and Frethun (France) rail freight yards, as well as ground operations for Frethun. In the short term, Europorte 2 aimed to develop as a local operator, collaborating with existing operators on low or medium density traffic; and serving port and private infrastructure. Eurotunnel has acquired eleven Class 92 locomotives equipped to work in the tunnel (seven from Eurostar UK and four from French Railways), and authorised to work on the entire British rail network.

A strategic agreement between Eurotunnel and the Port of Dunkerque is aimed at forwarding containers unloaded at Dunkerque to the UK; local freight train operation; and pooling of technical knowledge.

Eurotunnel's shuttle rolling stock includes 58 electric locomotives, nine passenger shuttles for cars and coaches, and 16 lorry shuttles. Each 800-metre long shuttle has two locomotives, one at each end.

The locomotives have three bogies, each with two motorised axles, giving excellent adhesion between wheel and rail. There are seven 7MW locomotives, and 20 of the initial 5.6MW locomotive fleet have been upgraded to 7MW, making it possible for freight shuttles to have a capacity of 12.6MW or even 14MW, to maintain crossing times with a heavier load of lorries.

Eurotunnel has been preparing to deploy two major building blocks of ERTMS (the European Rail Traffic Management System). GSM-R (Global System for Mobiles - Railways), the international standard for wireless communications specifically for railway operations, was planned to be applied progressively up to 2012. ETCS (European Train Control System) equipment has also been under evaluation.

Senior personnel

Chairman and Chief Executive
Jacques Gounon (left)
Chief Operating Officer
Jean-Pierre Trotignon
Director of Operations
Pascal Sainson
Commercial Director
Jo Willacy

Passenger Train Operators

The 13.40 Heathrow Express from Paddington arrives at the new Heathrow Terminal 5's Platform 4 on 3 April 2008, led by Class 332 No 332012. Brian Morrison

Heathrow express

Terminal 5 extension opened in 2008

Heathrow Express, which celebrated its tenth anniversary in 2008, is a private train operating company wholly owned by airports company BAA, and is not part of the franchised national railway. Its infrastructure within Heathrow Airport was built and is owned by BAA, which has a long-term strategy to increase public transport use for journeys to the airport. The full service to Terminals 1 to 4 was opened in June 1998, and an extension to Heathrow's new Terminal 5, using a new pair of 1.8km-long tunnels, opened in March 2008.

The new Terminal 5 station is the size of six football pitches and has six platform faces – two for Heathrow Express, two for the Piccadilly Underground line, and two in reserve for the proposed Airtrack rail link to Staines and the Waterloo-Reading line. Heathrow Express operates the station, including despatch of London Underground trains.

Heathrow Express uses the Great Western main line from Paddington, reaching the airport on a branch line tunnelling for more than four miles (6.5km). Journey time from London Paddington to Heathrow Central (Terminals 1,2,3) station is 15min, with trains departing every 15min. Heathrow Express's Class 332 electric trains, owned (under a leaseback arrangement) by BAA, were built by Siemens in partnership with CAF of Spain, the first of the UK's Siemens train fleets.

The trains have a news and entertainment TV service on board, but there are quiet zones with no TV. A Wi-Fi HotSpot service provided by T-Mobile and Nomad Digital was introduced on all Heathrow Express trains in 2007, enabling internet and e-mail access throughout the entire journey, including tunnels.

From May 2008, Heathrow Express made it possible for customers to print a ticket at home or the office or display a barcode 'ticket' on a mobile phone. Full single fares (late 2008) are £16.50 Express Class, £26.00 First Class.

Heathrow Connect is a complementary service to Heathrow Express, introduced in June 2005. Using new Class 360/2 trains built by Siemens and owned by Heathrow Express, it runs half-hourly between Paddington and Heathrow (journey time 26min to Terminals 1,2,3), calling at Ealing Broadway, West Ealing, Southall, Hanwell and Hayes & Harlington. It represents a £35million investment by BAA, in partnership with FirstGroup.

The Heathrow Connect service aims to improve access to the airport for London residents (including via the Ealing Broadway Underground interchange), Thames Valley residents and airport workers. In November 2006, fares were significantly reduced to target price-sensitive and local London markets.

Heathrow Express serves Terminals 1, 2, 3 and the new branch line to Terminal 5 (journey time 21min between Terminal 5 and central London). Heathrow Connect serves Terminals 1, 2, 3 and the Terminal 4 branch, also providing a shuttle service to give four trains per hour between Terminals 1, 2, 3 and Terminal 4.

For the calendar year 2007, the number of passengers using Heathrow Express was put at 5.1million, with 300,000 using Heathrow Connect.

An overall satisfaction rate of 96% in the independent National Passenger Satisfaction Survey was achieved by Heathrow Express in 2007 - the highest score in the survey's eight-year history.

Siemens carries out train maintenance, with reliability standards specified in the contract. The total value of the original train order, including a 10-year maintenance element, was about £70million. A new, 19-year maintenance contract valued at £70million was awarded in 2005, covering both Heathrow Connect and Heathrow Express trains. A purpose-built depot is at Old Oak Common, near Paddington.

The 14 Class-332 trains run in pairs, making up eight or nine-car trains. (Five additional carriages, valued at £6million, were later ordered to increase five trains to five-car length.) Distance travelled by the Class 332 trains between major overhauls has been extended from the originally expected 450,000 miles to an impressive one million miles, by a project team including Delta Rail as well as Heathrow Express and Siemens. This is expected to deliver a cost saving of over £35million through the life of the fleet. The overhaul project (a £7million investment by Heathrow Express) saw significant reliability improvement work added to a normal railway specification. Train interior refurbishment has been carried out under a £2million programme.

The Great Western main line is fitted with Automatic Train Protection, and Heathrow Express was the first service in Britain to have the system in full use.

Heathrow Express and Heathrow Connect together contributed £80million to Heathrow's revenue and £21million to its operating profit for the year 2007.

Senior personnel

Managing Director
Brian Raven (left)
Head of Service Proposition
Steve Chambers
Business Lead, Engineering
Gareth Vest
Sales and Marketing Director
Kyle Haughton

Directory
The UK Rail Industry in Your Hands

In association with

railalliance

Directory

Welcome to the 2009 Modern Railway Directory - a fully revised collection of almost 1,500 businesses involved in the operation of the UK Rail Industry. Company details are of course constantly changing. This essential guide includes hundreds of amended entries and around 100 new entries since our last update, including for the first time, railtour operators. To keep the information as fresh as possible we update the information TWICE per year. Look out of our summer update supplement issued FREE with the June issue of *Modern Railways* Magazine.

As always we'd like to extend a huge thank you to the many marketing and administrative staff who have contacted us with revisions. If your business is not currently featured please let us know and we will include your details in the next update. Don't forget we'll include your address and contact details including email and website details totally free of charge. For extra prominence we offer 'Deluxe' listings - these are the colour advertisements which can be seen dotted throughout the guide.

How to use this guide

If you're using *The Modern Railway* for the first time we hope you find your way around easily. We present the full list in a straightforward A-Z format, with coloured icons denoting the appropriate business discipline. For clarity the number of categories is restricted to just 10. These are given broad labels allowing closely allied areas of the business to be consolidated under a single banner. Thus 'Consulting' for example will include Consultants, but also Law firms, Economists, Project Management, Industry Reporting etc.

The full key is shown below.

How to get your business listed.
If your business is a current supplier to the UK Rail Industry simply contact us for an entry form, telephone your details to me, Chris Shilling on 01778 421550 or email *chris@shillingmedia.co.uk*

KEY TO SYMBOLS

TRAIN OPERATORS
Passenger and Freight Train Operators, TOC Owning Groups, Railway, Metro and Tramway Operators, Rail Tour Operators, Passenger Transport Authorities/Executives.

ROLLING STOCK MANUFACTURE, SUPPLY AND DELIVERY
Locomotive, Carriage and Wagon Manufacture, Locomotive, Wagon and Coaching Stock Hire, Chartering, Rolling Stock Leasing Companies, Heavy Haulage, Replacement Buses and Vehicle Hire.

CIVILS, PLANT & EQUIPMENT
Civil Engineering, Construction, Projected Developments, Buildings & Building Refurbishment, Plant, Tools, Architects, Surveying, Welding, Clothing & Boots, Chemicals and Lubricants.

INFRASTRUCTURE
Infrastructure Maintenance and Renewal, Workshop Equipment, Carriage Washing, Weighing & Lifting, Fencing & Security, Lighting (except rolling stock), Platforms, Cable Management, Power Supply, Freight Terminals, Car Parking, Cleaning, Grafitti Removal, Pest Control Ticketing, CCTV, Test Facilities, Fares and Collection.

ROLLING STOCK MAINTENANCE/PARTS
Locomotive, Carriage and Wagon Maintenance, Component supply, Lighting and Cabling, Decals and Transfers, De-Icing, Sanding, Upholstery, Disposal, Textiles and Carpeting.

CONSULTING
Consultants, Legal Services, Economists, Industry Reporting, Insurance, Accreditation & Compliance, Verification & Validation, Assessment, Test & Development, Systems & Software, IT Services, Data Management, Financial Services Port Authorities, Solutions and Turnkey Providers, Project Management.

SIGNAL & TELECOMMUNICATION
S&T Installation and Equipment, Wireless Technology and Datacoms.

PERSONNEL SERVICES & TRAINING
Recruitment and Training Companies/Consultancies, Personnel Supply.

INDUSTRY BODIES
Trade Associations, Alliances and Authorities, Advisory Boards, Government Departments, Customer Organisations, Accident Investigators, Campaigning Organisations, Passenger Watchdogs, Trade Unions, Development Agencies.

MISCELLANEOUS
Conferences & Exhibitions, Catering, Medical services, Property, Journey Planning, In-Train Entertainment, Photography, Video & Film Production.

We hope you'll enjoy this launch issue, and find this directory a real benefit in finding your way around the UK rail industry. That said, if you have any suggestions to help us make this Directory even better, please don't hesitate to contact us. CHRIS SHILLING, November 2008

3D Laser Mapping
1a Church St, Bingham,
Nottingham NG13 8AL
T: 0870 442 9400
F: 0870 121 4605
E: info@3dlasermapping.com
W: www.3dlasermapping.com

3M CPPD
Standard Way, Northallerton,
N.Yorks DL6 2XA
T: 01609 780170
F: 01609 777905
E: copon@ewood.com
W: www.copon.co.uk

3M United Kingdom PLC
3M Centre, Cain Rd, Bracknell,
Berks RG12 8HT
T: 01344 857939
F: 01344 857829
E: aanderson@mmm.com
W: www.3m.co.uk/railsolutions

A1 Secured
Unit 4, 113 Albion Drive,
London E8 4LT
T: 020 3228 1301
E: chris@a1secured.com
W: www.a1secured.com

Aardvark Site Investigations Ltd
Unit 7-14, Smallford Works,
Smallford Lane, St Albans,
Herts AL4 0SA
T: 01727 827375
F: 01727 828098
E: info@aardvarksi.com
W: www.aardvarksi.com

Abacus Lighting Ltd
Oddicroft lane, Sutton in Ashfield,
Notts NG17 5FT
T: 01623 511111
F: 01623 552113
E: sales@abacuslighting.com
W: www.abacuslighting.com

ABA Surveying
Lansbury Est., Lower Guildford St,
Knaphill, Woking, Surrey
GU21 2EP
T: 01483 797111
F: 01483 797211
W: www.abasurveying.co.uk

Abbeydale Training Ltd
26 Stonewood Grove,
Sheffield S10 5SS
T: 0114 230 4400
E: abbeydale.training@btconnect.com
W: www.abbeydaletraining.co.uk

Abbey Pynford Plc
Second Floor, Hille House, 132 St
Albans Rd, Watford WD24 4AQ
T: 0870 085 8400
F: 0870 085 8401
E: info@abbeypynford.co.uk
W: www.abbeypynford.co.uk

ABB Ltd
Daresbury Park, Daresbury,
Warrington WA4 4BT
T: 01925 741111
F: 01925 741212
E: karen.wilds@gb.abb.com
W: www.abb.com/railway

Abbott Risk Consulting Ltd
11 Albyn Place,
Edinburgh EH2 4NG
T: 0131 220 0164
F: 0131 220 2926
E: gareth.topham@consultarc.com
W: www.consultarc.com

AB Connectors Ltd
Abercynon, Mountain Ash, Rhondda
Cynon Taff CF45 4SF
T: 01443 740331
F: 01443 741676
E: sales@ttabconnectors.com
W: www.ttabconnectors.com

ABET Ltd
70 Roding Rd, London Ind. Park,
London E6 4LS
T: 020 7473 6910
F: 020 7476 6935
E: sales@abet.ltd.uk
W: www.abetuk.com

AB Hoses & Fittings Ltd
Units 6-7, Warwick St Ind Est.,
Chesterfield, Derbys S40 2TT
T: 01246 208831
F: 01246 209302
E: info@abhoses.com
W: www.abhoses.com

ABM Precon
Ollerton Rd, Tuxford, Newark,
Notts NG22 0PQ
T: 01777 872233
F: 01777 872772
E: precast@abmeurope.com
W: www.abmprecon.co.uk

Abracs Ltd
Glaisdale Rd, Northminster
Business Park, Upper Poppleton,
York YO26 6QT
T: 01904 789997
F: 01904 789996
E: abracs@abracs.com
W: www.abracs.com

ABS
See EQE International

Abtus Ltd
Falconer Rd, Haverhill,
Suffolk CB9 7XU
T: 01440 702938
F: 01440 702961
E: chris.welsh@abtus.com
W: www.abtus.com

Accolade Associates
63 Elgar Drove, Shefford,
Beds SG17 5RZ
T: 01462 709854
F: 01462 709854
E: mike@accoladeassociates.com
W: www.accoladeassociates.com

Acetech Personnel Ltd
Pembroke House, Pegasus Bus.
Park, Castle Donnington, Derby
DE74 2TZ
T: 01509 676962
F: 01509 676867
E: simon.terry@acetech.co.uk
W: www.acetech.co.uk

Achilles Information Ltd
30 Park Gate, Milton Park,
Abingdon, Oxon OX14 4SH
T: 01235 861118
F: 01235 838156
E: enquiries@achilles.com
W: www.achilles.com

ACIC International Ltd
14 Blacknest Business Park,
Blacknest,
Nr Alton Hants GU34 4PX
T: 01420 23930
F: 01420 23921
E: sales@acic.co.uk
W: www.acic.co.uk

ACM Composite Bearings Ltd
Derwent Way, Wath West Ind Est,
Rotherham, S Yorks S63 6EX
T: 01709 874951
F: 01709 878818
E: sales@acmbearings.co.uk
W: www.acmbearings.co.uk

Acumen Design Associates Ltd
1 Sekforde St, Clerkenwell,
London EC1R 0BE
T: 020 7107 2900
F: 020 7107 2901
E: info@acumen-da.com
W: www.acumen-da.com

ACoRP
Association of Community Rail Partnerships

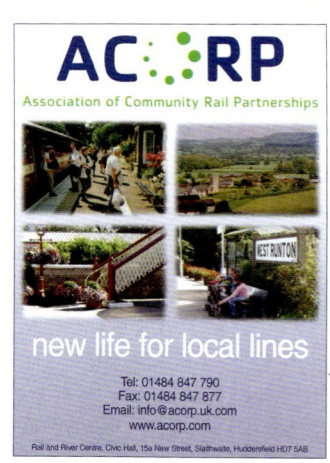

new life for local lines

Tel: 01484 847 790
Fax: 01484 847 877
Email: info@acorp.uk.com
www.acorp.uk.com

Rail and River Centre, Civic Hall, 15a New Street, Slaithwaite, Huddersfield HD7 5AB

Adaptaflex
Station Rd, Coleshill,
Birmingham B46 1HT
T: 01675 468222
F: 01675 464276
E: sales@adaptaflex.com
W: www.adaptaflex.com

Adien Ltd
Armstrong House, Hayfield Lane,
Finningley Estate, Doncaster
DN9 3GA
T: 01302 802200
F: 01302 802201
E: info@adien.com
W: www.adien.com

ADR Recruitment
Suite 12, Intech House, 34-35 Cam
Centre, Hitchin, Herts SG4 0TW
T: 01462 440722
F: 01462 442005
E: uk@adr-recruitment.com
W: www.adr-recruitment.com

ADT Fire & Security
Security House, The Summit,
Hanworth Rd, Sunbury on Thames
TW16 5DB
T: 01932 743229
F: 01932 743047
E: scotter@tycoint.com
W: www.tycoint.com

Advanced Human Resources
Warnford Court, 29 Throgmorton
St, London EC2N 2AT
T: 020 7847 8883
E: info@advancedhumanresources.com
W: www.advancedhumanresources.com

Advantage Technical Consulting
Eastgate House, Dogflud Way,
Farnham, Surrey GU9 7UD
T: 01252 899606
F: 01252 899699
E: enquiries@advantage-business.co.uk
W: www.advantage-business.co.uk

Advante Strategic Site Services
4th Floor, Phoenix House,
Christopher Martin Rd, Basildon
SS14 3HG
T: 01268 280500
F: 01268 293454
E: sales@advante.co.uk
W: www.advante.co.uk

Advenza Freight
Westgate House, The Island,
Gloucester GL1 2RU
T: 01453 899260
F: 01452 414455
F: 01452 419922
E: office@advenza.com
W: www.advenza.com

AEG
Power Solutions
Peregrine Road, Hainault, Essex IG6 3XJ

• Signal and Telecommunication Power
• Infrastructure Renewal/Maintenance
• Loco/Rolling Stock Chargers & Batteries

Through our AEG and Harmer & Simmons brands we supply the world's railways with AC UPS, DC Telecom and Axle counter power, on-board Inverters, Chargers and Batteries.

Telephone: +44 (0)208 498 1177
Fax: +44 (0)208 500 9365

hs.sales@aegps.com - www.aegps.com

AEG Power Supply Systems
Peregrine Rd, Hainault,
Essex IG6 3XJ
T: 020 8498 1177
F: 020 8500 9365
E: hs.sales@aegp.com
W: www.aegp.com

Aegis Engineering Services
Unit 19 Queens Sq. Bus. Park,
Honley, Huddersfield HD9 6QZ
T: 01484 667 077
F: 01484 667 045
E: info@aegisengineering.co.uk
W: www.aegisengineering.co.uk

Aerco Ltd
16-17, Lawson Hunt Ind. Park,
Broadbridge Heath, Horsham,
W. Sussex RH12 3JR
T: 01403 260206
F: 01403 259760
E: kray@aerco.co.uk
W: www.aerco.co.uk

Aerial Facilities Ltd
Aerial House, Asheridge Rd,
Chesham, Bucks HP5 2QD
T: 01494 777000
F: 01494 777002
E: sales@aerial.co.uk
W: www.aerialfacilities.com

Aerosystems International
Alvington, Yeovil,
Somerset
BA22 8UZ
T: 01935 443000
F: 01935 443111
E: nicky.donovan@aeroint.com
W: www.aeroint.com

AGD Equipment Ltd
Avonbrook House, Masons Rd,
Stratford upon Avon, Warks
CV37 9LQ
T: 01789 292227
F: 01789 268350
E: info@agd-equipment.co.uk
W: www.agd-equipment.co.uk

Aggregate Industries UK Ltd
Bardon Hill, Coalville,
Leics LE67 1TL
T: 01530 510066
F: 01530 510123
E: corporatecommunivations@aggregate.com
W: www.aggregate-uk.com

Ainscough
Bradley Hall, Bradley Lane,
Standish, Lancs WN6 0XQ
T: 01257 473423
F: 01257 473286
E: heavy.cranes@ainscough.co.uk
W: www.ainscough.co.uk

Airdrie Bathgate Rail Link
Network Rail, Buchanan House, 58
Port Dundas Rd, Glasgow G4 0LQ
T: 0141 555 4108
E: info@airdriebathgateraillink.co.uk
W: www.airdriebathgateraillink.co.uk

Air International (UK) Ltd
Unit 21, Rising Sun Ind. Est.,
Blaina, Abertillery,
Blaenau Gwent NP3 3JW
T: 01332 576820
F: 01495 292990
E: pmoon@airinter.com
W: www.airtecinternational.co.uk

Airquick (Newark) Ltd
Brunel Business Park, Jessop Close,
Newark, Notts NG24 2A
T: 01636 640480
F: 01636 701216
E: info@airquick.co.uk
W: www.airquick.co.uk

Airscrew Ltd
See Ametek

Airtec International Ltd
40, Couper St, Glasgow G4 0DL
T: 0141 552 5591
F: 0141 552 5064
E: enquiries@airtecintl.com
W: www.airtecinternational.co.uk

ALA Rail Services
T: 01639 885435
F: 01639 899842
E: sales@ala-rail.com
W: www.ala-rail.com

Alan Dick UK Ltd
The Barlands, London Rd,
Cheltenham GL52 6UT
T: 01242 518500
F: 01242 510191
E: john.oliver@alandick.com
W: www.alandick.com

Albatros UK
Unit 9, Garamonde Drive,
Clarendon Ind Park, Wymbush,
Milton Keynes MK8 8DF
T: 01908 305740
F: 01908 577839
E: info@albatros-uk.co.uk
W: www.albatross-uk.co.uk

Alcad
1st Floor, Unit 5, Astra Centre,
Edinburgh Way, Harlow,
Essex CM20 2BN
T: 01279 772555
F: 01279 420696
E: carter.sarah@alcad.com
W: www.alcad.com

Alcatel-Lucent UK & Ireland
Voyager Place, Maidenhead,
Berks SL6 2PJ
T: 01628 428200
F: 01628 423785
E: bill.f.brown@alcatel.co.uk
W: www.alcatel-lucent.co.uk

Alert Safety Technologies
Nasmyth Buildings, Nasmyth Ave,
East Kilbride, Glasgow G75 0QR
T: 01355 272828
F: 01355 272788
E: sales@alertsafety.net
W: www.alertsafety.net

Alfred Mc Alpine Plc
Exchange House, Kelburn House,
Kelburn Court, Leacroft Rd,
Birchwood Warrington WA3 6SY
T: 01925 658075
W: www.alfredmcalpineplc.com

ALH Rail Coatings
Station Rd, Birch Vale,
High Peak Derbys SK22 1BR
T: 01663 748045
F: 01663 746605
E: help@dowhyperlast.com
W: www.hyperlast.com

All Clothing & Protection Ltd
Unit 5, 4 Lulworth Business Centre,
Nutwood Way, Totton,
Southampton SO40 3WW
T: 023 8042 8003
F: 023 8086 9333
E: sales@allclothing.co.uk
W: www.allclothing.co.uk

Allelys Heavy Haulage
The Slough, Studley,
Warks B80 7EN
T: 01527 857621
F: 01527 857623
E: robert@allelys.co.uk
W: www.allelys.co.uk

Allen & Douglas
Compton Park, Wildmere Road,
Banbury, Oxon OX16 3EZ
T: 01255 228441
F: 01255 278972
E: sales@aandd.co.uk
W: www.andd.co.uk

Alltype Fencing Specialists Ltd
Ye Wentes Wayes, High Rd,
Langdan Hills, Essex SS16 6HY
T: 01268 545192
F: 01268 545260
E: alltypefencing@btinternet.com
W: www.alltypefencing.com

Alpha Adhesives & Sealants
Llewellyn Close, Sandy Lane Ind.
Est., Stourport-on-Severn, Worcs
DY13 9RH
T: 01299 828626
F: 01299 828666
E: help@dowhyperlast.com
W: www.alpha-adhesives.com

In association with **railalliance**

ATKINS

We plan, design and enable transport solutions.

Through an extensive network of offices, Atkins applies global expertise to local markets.

Birmingham	0121 483 5000
Cardiff	02920 485 159
Crewe	01270 509 961
Crewe (TIC)	01270 533 338
Croydon	020 8663 5000
Daventry	01327 313010
Derby	01332 225 522
London	020 7121 2000
Glasgow	0141 220 2000
Manchester	0161 245 3400
Orpington	01689 885 263
Plymouth	01752 697 700
Swindon	01793 538 000
Vauxhall	020 7121 2100
Warrington	01925 238 000
York	01904 678 100

www.atkinsglobal.com/railandmetro
www.atkinsglobal.com
rail@atkinsglobal.com

Plan Design Enable

HSBC

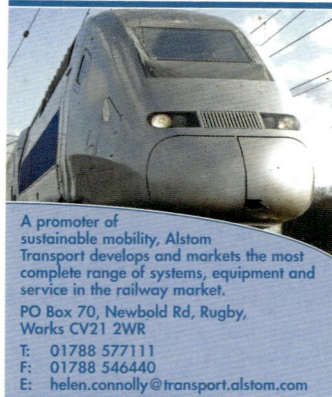

A promoter of sustainable mobility, Alstom Transport develops and markets the most complete range of systems, equipment and service in the railway market.

PO Box 70, Newbold Rd, Rugby, Works CV21 2WR

T: 01788 577111
F: 01788 546440
E: helen.connolly@transport.alstom.com

www.transport.alstom.com ALSTOM

Alstom Transport
PO Box 70, Newbold Rd,
Rugby, Warks CV21 2WR
T: 01788 577111
F: 01788 546440
E: helen.connolly@transport.alstom.com
W: www.transport.alstom.com

Aluminium Special Projects Ltd (ASP Group)
Unit 39, Second Ave, The Pensnett Estate, Kingswinford, W.Midlands DY6 7UW
T: 01384 291900
F: 01384 400344
E: david@aspgroup.co.uk
W: www.aspgroup.co.uk

Alvey & Towers
The Springboard Centre, Mantle Lane, Coalville, Leics LE67 3DW
T: 01530 450011
F: 01530 450011
E: office@alveyandtowers.com
W: www.alveyandtowers.com

Amalgamated Construction Ltd (AMCO)
Whaley Rd, Barugh, Barnsley, S.Yorks S75 1HT
T: 01226 243413
F: 01226 320202
E: enquiries@amco-construction.co.uk
W: www.amco-construction.co.uk

Amber Composites
94 Station Rd, Langley Mill, Nottingham NG16 4BP
T: 01773 530899
F: 01773 768687
E: sales@ambercomposites.co.uk
W: www.ambercomposites.co.uk

Ameron UK Ltd
Bankside, Hull HU5 1SQ
T: 01482 341441
F: 01482 348350
E: sales.uk@ameron-bv.com
W: www.ameron.co.uk

Ametek Airscrew
111 Windmill Rd, Sunbury-on-Thames TW16 7EF
T: 01932 765822
F: 01932 761098
E: mail.airscrew@ametek.co.uk
W: www.ametek aerodefense.com.co.uk

Amey
The Sherard Building, Edmund Halley Rd, Oxford OX4 4DQ
T: 01865 713100
F: 01865 713357
E: ais@amey.co.uk
W: www.amey.co.uk

Amicus
General Secretary, 35 King St, Covent Garden, London WC2E 8JG
T: 0845 8504242
W: www.amicustheunion.org

AMOT
Western Way, Bury St Edmunds, Suffolk IP33 3SZ
T: 01284 762222
F: 01284 760256
E: info@amot.com
W: www.amot.com

Amphenol Ltd
Thanet Way, Whitstable, Kent CT5 3JF
T: 01227 773200
F: 01227 276571
E: pninfo@amphenol.co.uk
W: www.amphenol.co.uk

AMPL Ltd (Alfred McAlpine Plant Ltd.)
Prospect House, Deva Ind. Park, Factory Rd, Sandycroft, Deeside CH5 2QJ
T: 01244 527600
F: 01244 527601
W: www.ampl.co.uk

Amtrain (Midlands) Ltd
PO Box 1869, Walsall, West Midlands WS2 9YD
T: 01922 610607
F: 01922 648518
E: info@amtrain.co.uk
W: www.amtrain.co.uk

AMT Sybex Ltd
The Spirella Building, Bridge Rd, Letchworth Garden City, Herts SG6 4ET
T: 01462 476400
F: 01462 476401
E: info@amt-sybex.com
W: www.amt-sybex.com

Anders Elite Ltd
Dashwood House, 69, Old Broad St, London EC2M 1NQ
T: 020 7256 5555
F: 020 7256 9898
E: rail@anderselite.com
W: www.anderselite.com

Anderson Young UK Ltd
40 New Rd, Ascot, Berks SL5 8QQ
T: 0845 241 2727
F: 01344 890888
E: shellycg@andyoung.co.uk
W: www.andyoung.co.uk

Anderton Concrete Products Ltd
Anderton Wharf, Soot Hill, Anderton, Northwich, Cheshire CW9 6AA
T: 01606 79436
F: 01606 871590
E: sales@andertonconcrete.co.uk
W: www.andertonconcrete.co.uk

Andrew Muirhead & Son Ltd
273-289 Dunn St, Glasgow G40 3EA
T: 0141 554 3724
F: 0141 554 3724
E: james.long@muirhead.co.uk
W: www.muirhead.co.uk

Angel Trains leases trains and locomotives across the UK

Angel Trains Limited, Portland House, Bressenden Place, London, SW1E 5BH

Tel: +44 (0)20 7592 0500
Fax: +44 (0)20 7592 0520
Email: uk@angeltrains.co.uk
www.angeltrains.co.uk

angel Trains

Angel Trains Limited
Portland House, Bressenden Place, London SW1E 5BH
T: 020 7592 0500
F: 020 7592 0520
E: uk@angeltrains.co.uk
W: www.angeltrains.co.uk

Anixter Adhesives
3 Edmund St, Sheffield S2 4EB
T: 0114 275 5884
F: 0114 275 7169
E: enquiries@anixteradhesives.com
W: www.infast.com

Anixter (UK) Ltd
Unit A, The Beacons, Warrington Rd, Risley, Warrington WA3 6GB
T: 0870 242 2822
F: 01925 848006
E: railsales@anixter.com
W: www.anixter.com

Ansaldo STS
Bravington House, Bravington Walk, London N1 9AF
T: 020 7841 6897
F: 020 7841 6851
E: dcollins@ansaldo-signal.co.uk
W: www.ansaldo-signal.com

Ansec
Ansec Business Park, Burma Rd, Blidworth, Notts NG21 0RT
T: 01623 491422
F: 01623 798958
E: mail@ansecuk.com
W: www.ansecuk.com

Antagrade Electrical Ltd
Victoria Building, Lewin St, Middlewich, Cheshire CW10 9AT
T: 01606 833299
F: 01606 836959
E: enquiries@antagrade.co.uk
W: www.antagrade.co.uk

Antal International Network
170 Lanark Rd West, Currie, Edinburgh EH14 5NY
T: 0870 428 1745
F: 0870 428 1745
E: edinburgh@antal.com
W: www.antal.com

Antislip Antiwear Treads Int.
11 Swinborne Drive, Springwood Ind. Est, Braintree, Essex, CM7 2YP
T: 01376 346248
F: 01376 348480
E: mgeorge@aati.co.uk
W: www.aati.co.uk

APB Group Ltd
Ryandra House, Ryandra Business Park, Cheadle, Stoke-on-Trent ST10 1SR
T: 01538 755377
F: 01538 755010
E: apbgroup@aol.com

APD Communications Ltd
Newlands Centre, Inglemire Lane, Hull HU6 7TQ
T: 01482 808300
F: 01482 803901
E: info@apdcomms.com
W: www.apdcomms.com

Aperio Ltd
See Fugro Aperio

Apex Cables Ltd
St Johns Rd, Meadowfield Ind Est, Durham DH7 8RJ
T: 0191 378 7908
F: 0191 378 7809
E: apex@apexcables.co.uk
W: www.apexcables.co.uk

A Plant
See Ashtead

Appleyards Consulting
72, Brighton Rd, Horsham, West Sussex RH13 5BU
T: 08705 275201
F: 08705 143047
E: mail@appleyards.co.uk
W: www.appleyards.co.uk

Applied Inspection Ltd
Bridge House, Bond St, Burton upon Trent DE14 3RZ
T: 01283 515163
F: 01283 539729
E: feedback@appliedinspection.co.uk
W: www.appliedinspection.co.uk

Application Solutions (Safety & Security) Ltd
Unit 17, Cliffe Ind. Est, Lewes, E Sussex BN8 6JL
T: 01273 405411
F: 01273 405415
E: contactus@asl-control.co.uk
W: www.asl-control.co.uk

Aqua Fabrications Ltd
Belmont House, Garnett Place, Skelmersdale, Lancs WN8 9UB
T: 01695 51933
F: 01695 51891
E: salesaquafab.co.uk
W: www.aquafab.co.uk

Aquarius Railroad Technologies Ltd
Old Slenningford Farm, Mickley, Ripon, N Yorks HG4 3JB
T: 01765 635021
F: 01765 635022
E: enquiries@railrover.com
W: www.railrover.com

Arbil Lifting Gear
Providence St, Lye, Stourbridge, West Midlands DY9 8HS
T: 01384 424006
F: 01384 892803
E: info@arbil.co.uk
W: www.arbil.co.uk

Archer Signs & Panels Ltd
Unit 6 Daniels Way, Hucknall, Nottingham NG15 7LL
T: 0115 927 3100
F: 0115 976 1110
E: brian@archersigns.co.uk
W: www.archersigns.co.uk

Aries Power Solutions Ltd
Oaklands, Flordon Rd, Creeting St Mary, Ipswich IP6 8NH
T: 01449 720842
F: 01449 722846
E: john@ariesgen.co.uk
W: www.generating-sets.co.uk

ARM Engineering
Langstone Technology Park, Langstone Rd, Havant, Hants PO9 1SA
T: 02392 228228
F: 02392 228229
E: rail@arm.co.uk
W: www.arm.co.uk

Arriva Trains Wales
St Mary's House, 47 Penarth Rd, Cardiff CF10 5DJ
T: 0845 606 1660
W: www.arrivatrainswales

Arriva Cross Country
3rd Floor, 85 Smallbrook Queensway, Birmingham B5 4HA
T: 0870 010 0084
F: 0121 654 7603
E: info@crosscountrytrains.co.uk
W: www.crosscountrytrains.co.uk

Arrow Cleaning & Hygeine Solutions
Rawdon Rd, Moira, Swadlincote, Derbys DE12 6DA
T: 01283 221044
F: 01283 225731
E: sales@arrowchem.com
W: www.arrowchem.com

Arrowvale Electronics
Arrow Business Park, Shawbank Rd, Lakeside, Redditch, Worcs B98 8YN
T: 01527 514151
F: 01527 514321
E: sales@arrowvale.co.uk
W: www.arrowvale.co.uk

Arthur D Little Ltd
Unit 300, Science Park, Milton Rd, Cambridge CB4 0XL
T: 0870 336 6700
F: 0870 336 6701
E: enquiries.uk@adlittle.com
W: www.adl.com

Arthur D Little

We support top rail industry teams worldwide providing Independent Safety Assessment (ISA), strategic safety management advise, risk assessment and safety training leading to a more sustainable rail industry.

Address: 300 Science Park, Milton Road, Cambridge CB4 0XL

Tel: +44-(0)870-336-6700
Fax: +44(0)870-336-6701

Contact: enquiries.uk@adlittle.com

Website: www.adl.com

Arthur Flury AG
CH-4543 Deitingen, Switzerland
T: 0041 32613 3366
F: 0041 32613 3368
E: info@aflury.ch
W: www.aflury.ch

Arup
The Arup Campus, Blythe Gate, Blythe Valley Park, Solihull, West Midlands B90 8AE
T: 0121 213 3412
F: 0121 213 3001
E: rail@arup.com
W: www.arup.com/rail

Ashley Group
704 London Rd, North Cheam, Sutton, Surrey SM3 9BY
T: 020 8644 4416
F: 020 8644 4417
E: colin@ashleygroup.co.uk
W: www.ashleygroup.co.uk

Ashtead Plant Hire Co Ltd (APlant)
102 Dalton Ave, Birchwood Park, Birchwood, Warrington WA3 6YE
T: 0870 050 0797
F: 01925 281005
E: enquiries@aplant.com
W: www.aplant.com

Ashurst
Broadwalk House, 5 Appold St, London EC2A 2HA
T: 020 7859 1897
F: 020 7638 1112
E: raymond.beven@ashurst.com
W: www.ashurst.com

ASL Contracts
4, Regent Court, South Way, Andover, Hants SP10 5NX
T: 01264 335564
F: 01264 336590
E: sales@aslcontracts.co.uk
W: www.aslcontracts.co.uk

ASLEF
9 Arkwright Rd, Hampstead, London NW3 6AB
T: 020 7317 8600
F: 020 7794 6406
E: info@aslef.org.uk
W: www.aslef.org.uk

Aspin Foundations Ltd
The Freight Yard, Hemel Station, London Rd, Hemel Hempstead, Herts HP3 9BE
T: 01442 236507
F: 01442 239096
E: barry.mcmahon@aspingroup.com
W: www.aspingroup.com

Aspire Rail Consultants
Unit 15b, Crewe Hall Enterprise Park, Weston Lane, Crewe CW1 6UA
T: 01270 254176
F: 01270 253267
E: bob@aspirerailconsultants.co.uk

Associated British Ports
150 Holborn, London EC1N 2LR
T: 0207 430 1177
F: 020 7430 1384
E: pr@abports.co.uk
W: www.abports.co.uk

Associated Rewinds (Ireland) Ltd
Tallaght Business Park, Whitestown, Dublin 24, Ireland
T: 00353 1 452 0033
F: 00353 1 452 0476
E: sales@associatedrewinds.com
W: www.associatedrewinds.com

Associated Train Crew Union
PO Box 647, S72 8XU
T: 01226 716417
E: admin@atcu.org.uk
W: www.atcu.org.uk

Association of Community Rail Partnerships (ACORP)
Rail & River Centre, Canal Side, Civic Hall, 15a New St, Slaithwaite, Huddersfield
T: 01484 847790
F: 01484 847877
E: office@acorp.uk.com
W: www.acorp.uk.com

Association of Train Operating Companies (ATOC)
3rd Floor, 40 Bernard St, London WC1N 1BY
T: 020 7841 8000
F: 020 7841 8263
E: enquiry@atoc.org
W: www.atoc.org

Association for Project Management
150 West Wycombe Rd, High Wycombe, Bucks HP12 3AE
T: 01494 460246
F: 01494 528937
E: info@apm.org.uk
W: www.apm.org.uk

ASTE Rail UK Ltd
Unit 4, Fen End, Astwick Rd, Stotfold, Beds SG5 4BA
T: 0870 770 4567
F: 0870 770 4568
E: general@aste-rail.co.uk
W: www.aste-rail.co.uk

Astrac Training Solutions Ltd
PO Box 10224, West Mersea, Colchester CO5 8XG
T: 0845 634 1829
F: 020 8082 5451
E: admin@astrac-training.ltd.uk
W: www.astrac-training.ltd.uk

ATOC represents train operating companies to government and other opinion formers on transport policy issues and manages joint activities such as revenue allocation and settlement, National Rail Enquiries and marketing of railcards.

Association of Train Operating Companies, 3rd Floor, 40 Bernard Street, London WC1N 1BY

020 7841 8020

www.atoc-comms.org

Train Operators Working Together ATOC

AST Recruitment Ltd
22a, HighSt, Aldridge, Walsall, West Midlands WS9 8NE
T: 01922 743600
F: 01922 744690
E: ian.perry@astr.co.uk
W: www.astrecruitment.co.uk

ATA Rail
Catalis Rail Training, Derby Conference Centre, London Rd, Derby DE24 8UX
T: 01332 752792
F: 01332 752756
E: recruitment@ata-rail.co.uk
W: www.ata-group.co.uk

Atkins
Euston Tower, 286 Euston Road, London NW1 3AT
T: 020 7121 2000
F: 020 7121 2111
E: rail@atkinsglobal.com
W: www.atkinsglobal.com

Atlantic Design Transportation Limited
Branch Hill Mews, Branch Hill, London NW3 7LT
T: 020 7435 1777
F: 020 7435 0050
E: enq@atlanticdesign.uk.com
W: www.atlanticdesign.uk.com

Atlantis International Ltd
18 Weldon Rd, Loughborough LE11 5RA
T: 01509 233770
F: 01509 210542
E: sales@atlantisint.co.uk
W: www.atlantisinternational.co.uk

Atlas Copco Compressors Ltd
Swallowdale Lane, Hemel Hempstead HP2 7HA
T: 01442 261201
F: 01442 234791
E: gba.info@uk.atlascopco.com
W: www.atlascopco.co.uk

Atlas Copco Tools Ltd
Swallowdale Lane, Hemel Hempstead, Herts HP2 7HA
T: 01442 261202
F: 01442 214705
E: paul.booth@uk.atlascopco.com
W: www.atlascopco.com

Atlas Rail Components Ltd
Altas Works, Nelson St, Carlisle, Cumbria CA2 5NB
T: 01228 529522
F: 01228 529530
E: rpotter@atlasrail.co.uk
W: www.atlasrail.co.uk

ATOS Origin
4 Triton Square, Regents Place, London NW1 3HG
T: 020 7830 4447
F: 020 7 830 4445
E: findout.more@atosorigin.com
W: www.atosorigin.com

AUS Ltd
1 Dearne Park Ind Est, Park Mill Way, Clayton West, Huddersfield HD8 9XJ
T: 01484 860575
F: 01484 860576
E: sales@aus.co.uk
W: www.aus.co.uk

HSBC

Austin Reynolds Signs
Augustine House, Gogmore Lane, Chertsey, Surrey KT16 9AP
T: 01932 568888
F: 01932 566600
E: sales@austinreynolds.co.uk
W: www.austinreynolds.com

Autoclenz Holdings Plc
Stanhope Rd, Swadlincote, Derbys DE11 9BE
T: 08707 510410
F: 01283 552272
E: sales@autoclenz.co.uk
W: www.autoclenz.co.uk

Autodrain
Wakefield Rd, Rothwell Haigh, Leeds LS26 0SB
T: 0113 288 0022
F: 0113 288 0999
E: mark@autodrain.net
W: www.autodrain.net

Autoglym PSV
Letchworth Garden City, Herts SG6 1LU
T: 01462 677766
F: 01462 686565
E: npro@autoglym.com
W: www.autoglym.com

AVE Rail Products
See Compin UK

Avoidatrench Ltd
Brookes lane, Middlewich, Cheshire CW10 0JQ
T: 01606 831600
F: 01606 831260
W: www.pochins.plc.uk/avoidatrench

Avondale Environmental Services Ltd
Fort Horsted, Primrose Close, Chatham, Kent ME4 6HZ
T: 01634 823207
F: 01634 844485
E: info@avondaleuk.com
W: www.avondaleuk.com

Axiom Rail
Lakeside Business Park, Carolina Way, Doncaster DN4 5PN
T: 0870 140 5000
F: 0870 140 5009
E: sales@axiomrail.com
W: www.axiomrail.com

Axion Technologies
Lokesvej 7-9, 3400 Hilleroed, Denmark
T: 0045 721 93500
F: 0045 721 93501
E: info@axiontech.dk
W: www.axiontech.dk

Axminster Carpets Ltd
Woodmead Rd, Axminster, Devon EX13 5PQ
T: 01297 630686
F: 01297 35241
E: sales@axminster-carpets.co.uk
W: www.axminster-carpets.co.uk

Axon Bywater
Axon Centre, Egham, Surrey TW20 9QB
T: 01784 480936
F: 01784 480946
E: training@axonbywatertraining.co.uk
W: www.axonbywater.com

Aztec Chemicals
Gateway, Crewe CW1 6YY
T: 01270 655500
F: 01270 655501
E: info@aztecchemicals.com
W: www.aztecchemicals.com

Babcock Rail
Kintail House, 3 Lister Way, Hamilton International, Blantyre G72 0FT
T: 01698 203005
F: 01698 203006
E: enquiries@babcockrail.co.uk
W: www.babcock.co.uk

Alfred Bagnall & Sons (North)
6, Manor Lane, Shipley, West Yorks BD18 3RD
T: 01274 714800
F: 01274 530171
E: info@bagnalls.co.uk
W: www.bagnalls.co.uk

Bailey Rail
Forder Way, Hampton, Peterborough PE7 8GX
T: 01733 425700
F: 01733 425701
E: andy.holt@baileyrail.co.uk
W: www.baileyrail.co.uk

Bakerail Services
4 Green Lane, Hail Weston, St Neots, Cambs PE19 5JZ
T: 01480 471349
F: 01480 218044
E: info@bakerailservices.co.uk
W: www.bakerailservices.co.uk

Baldwin & Francis Ltd
President Park, President Way, Sheffield S4 7UR
T: 0114 286 6000
F: 0114 286 6059
E: cmarr@baldwinandfrancis.com
W: www.baldwinandfrancis.com

Balfour Beatty Rail
130 Wilton Rd, London SW1V 1LQ
T: 020 7216 6800
F: 020 7216 6950
E: info@bbrail.com
W: www.bbrail.com

Balfour Kilpatrick Ltd
Lumina Building, 40 Aislie Rd, Hillington Park, Glasgow G52 4RU
T: 0141 880 2001
F: 0141 880 2201
E: enquiry@balfourkilpatrick.com
W: www.balfourkilpatrick.com

Ballast Tools (UK) Ltd
Unit 4, Gloucester House, County Park Business Centre, Shrivenham Rd, Swindon SN1 2NR
T: 01793 697800
F: 01793 527029
E: sales@btukltd.com
W: www.btukltd.com

BAM Nuttall
See Edmund Nuttall

Bance
Cockrow Hill House, St Mary's Rd, Surbiton, Surrey KT6 5HE
T: 020 8398 7141
F: 020 8398 4765
E: admin@bance.com
W: www.bance.com

Bank of Scotland Corporate
155 Bishopsgate, London EC2M 3YB
T: 020 7012 8001
F: 020 7012 9455
E: katherineward@bankofscotland.co.uk
W: www.bankofscotland.co.uk/corporate

Barclays
1 Churchill Place, London E14 5HP
T: 0207 116 5214
F: 020 7116 7653
E: rob.riddleston@barclayscorporate.com
W: www.barclays.co.uk/logistics_transport

Bardon Aggregates
See Aggregate Industries

Barhale
Barhale House, Bescot Cres., Walsall WS1 4NN
T: 01922 726731
F: 01922 726795
E: info@barhale.co.uk
W: www.barhale.co.uk

Barker Ross Recruitment
7 Faraday Court, Conduit St, Leicester LE2 0JN
T: 0800 0288 693
F: 0116 2550 811
E: people@barkerross.co.uk
W: www.barkerross.co.uk

Powerful, user friendly chemical solutions combatting seasonal related problems on the rail network.

Basic Solutions Ltd,
Helios 47,
Leeds.
LS25 2DY

Tel: 0113 385 3855
Fax: 0113 385 3854

info@basic-solutions.co.uk
www.basic-solutions.co.uk

Basic SOLUTIONS

Basic Solutions Ltd
Helios 47, Leeds LS25 2DY
T: 0113 385 3855
F: 0113 385 3854
E: info@basic-solutions.co.uk
W: www.basic-solutions.co.uk

H S Bassett
Coronet Way, Enterprise Park, Morriston, Swansea SA6 8RH
T: 01792 790022
F: 01792 790033
E: info@hsbassett.co.uk
W: www.hsbassett.co.uk

BATT Cables
The Belfry, Fraser Rd, Erith, Kent DA8 1QH
T: 01322 441166
F: 01322 440492
E: battindustrial.sales@batt.co.uk
W: www.batt.co.uk

BBT Rail
14 Buckingham Palace Rd, London SW1W 0QP
T: 020 7828 1555
F: 020 7282 1941
W: www.bbt.co.uk

BCL Rail Services
Ardmore Construction, BCL House, Cody Business Centre, 11a South Cres., London E16 4SR
T: 020 7474 5335
F: 020 7511 5020
E: info@ardmoregroup.co.uk
W: www.ardmoregroup.co.uk

BCM Glass Reinforced Concrete
Unit 22, Civic Industrial Park, Whitchurch, Shropshire SY13 1TT
T: 01948 665321
F: 01948 666381
E: info@bcmgrc.com
W: www.bcmgrc.com/railhome

Beakbane Bellows Ltd
Stourport Rd, Kidderminster, Worcs DY11 7QT
T: 01562 820561
F: 01562 820560
E: amd@beakbane.co.uk
W: www.beakbane.co.uk

Bechtel Ltd
Bechtel House, 245 Hammersmith Rd, Hammersmith, London W6 3DP
T: 020 8846 5111
F: 020 8846 4938
E: jgreen2@bechtel.com
W: www.bechtel.com

Becorit GmbH
PO Box 189, Holmes Chapel Cheshire CW4 7FB
T: 07866 424869
F: 01270 269000
E: becorit@btinternet.com
W: www.becorit.de

Beejay Rail Ltd
79 Charles St, Springburn, Glasgow G21 2PS
T: 0141 553 1133
F: 0141 552 5333
E: info@beejayrewinds.com
W: www.beejayrewinds.com

A Belco Engineering
Jubilee Ind. Est., Ashington, Northumberland NE63 8UG
T: 01670 813275
F: 01670 851141
E: sales@a-belco.co.uk
W: www.a-belco.co.uk

Bell & Webster Concrete Ltd
Alma Park Rd, Grantham, Lincs NG31 9SE
T: 01476 562277
E: bellandwebster@eleco.com
W: www.eleco.com/bellandwebster

Benchmark Technologies Ltd
Unit 307, Springvale Ind Est, Cwmbran, NP44 5BR

Bender UK Ltd
Low Mill Business Park, Ulverston, Cumbria LA12 9EE
T: 01229 480123
F: 01229 480345
E: info@bender.org.uk
W: www.bender.org.uk

Bentley Systems UK
Monarch House, Waterford Way, Wokingham, Berks RG40 2AR
T: 0118 977 7550
F: 0118 977 7556
W: www.bentley.com

Bestchart Ltd
6A, Mays Yard, Down Rd, Horndean, Waterlooville, Hants PO8 0YP
T: 02392 597707
F: 02392 591700
E: info@bestchart.co.uk
W: www.bestchart.co.uk

Best Impressions
15 Starfield Rd, London W12 9SN
T: 020 8740 6443
F: 020 8740 9134
E: talk2us@best-impressions.co.uk
W: www.best-impressions.co.uk

Beta Cable Management Systems Ltd
Nothway Lane, Newtown Trading Est, Tewkesbury GL20 8JG
T: 01684 274274
F: 01684 276266
E: sales@betacable.com
W: www.betacable.com

Bewator Ltd
Brecon House, Llantarnam Park, Cwmbran NP44 3AB
T: 0871 386 0800
F: 0871 386 0888
E: sales@bewator.co.uk
W: www.bewator.com

Bex Railstaff Services
Waterloo Training Centre, Newnham Terrace, London SE1 7DR
T: 020 7902 3681
F: 020 7902 3683
E: rtt@bexplc.com
W: www.bexplc.com

Bideem Rail
Bideem Maintenance, Jubilee House, Jubilee way, Avonmouth, Bristol BS11 9HU
T: 0117 916 3800
F: 0117 916 3801
W: www.bideem.co.uk

Bierrum International Ltd
Bierrum House, High St, Houghton Regis, Dunstable, Beds LU5 5BJ
T: 01582 845745
F: 01582 845746
E: solutions@bierrum.co.uk
W: www.bierrum.co.uk

Bingham Rail
Barrow Rd, Wincobank, Sheffield S9 1JZ
T: 0870 774 5422
F: 0870 774 5423
E: info@trainwash.co.uk
W: www.trainwash.co.uk

Bircham Dyson Bell LLP
50 Broadway, London SW1H 0BL
T: 020 7227 7076
F: 020 7233 1351
E: robbieowen@bdb-law.co.uk
W: www.bdb-law.co.uk

Birse Rail Ltd
15th Floor, Lyndon House, 58-62, Hagley Rd, Edgbaston, Birmingham B16 8PE
T: 0121 456 4200
F: 0121 456 3880
E: lisa.maidment@birse.co.uk
W: www.birserail.co.uk

Blackpool Transport Services
Rigby Rd, Blackpool, Lancs FY1 5DD
T: 01253 473001
F: 01253 473101
E: jean.cox@blackpooltransport.com
W: www.blackpooltransport.com

Blue I UK Ltd
4 Chater Court, Halifax Drive, Market Deeping, Peterborough PE6 8AH
T: 01778 349000
E: info@blueuk.co.uk
W: www.blueuk.com

BMAC Ltd
Units 13-14, Shepley Ind. Est., South Shepley Road, Audenshaw, Manchester M34 5PW
T: 0161 337 3070
F: 0161 336 5691
E: enquiries@bmac.ltd.uk
W: www.bmac.ltd.uk

BMT Rail Ltd
12 Little Park Farm Rd, Fareham, Hants PO15 7JE
T: 01489 553200
F: 01489 553101
E: bob.smith@bmtrail.com
W: www.bmtrail.com

BNV UK Ltd
The Nova Building, Herschel St, Slough SL1 1XS
T: 01753 728754
F: 01753 728755
E: info@bnvconsultants.com
W: www.bnvconsultants.com

BOC
Customer Service Centre, Priestley Rd, Worsley, Manchester M28 2UT
T: 0800 111 333
F: 0800 111 555
E: custserv@boc.com
W: www.bocindustrial.co.uk

Boddingtons Electrical Ltd
Unit 10, Chelmsford Rd Ind. Est., Great Dunmow, Essex
T: 01371 876496
F: 01371 876438
E: info@boddingtons-electrical.com
W: www.boddingtons-electrical.com

Bodycote Materials Testing
Bodycote International Plc, Halley Rd, Macclesfield, Cheshire SK10 2SG
T: 01625 505300
F: 01625 505313
E: info@bodycote.com
W: www.bodycote.com

Bodyguard Workwear Ltd
33 Rea St, Digbeth, Birmingham B5 6HT
T: 0121 622 4444
F: 0121 622 4004
E: sales@bodyguardworkwear.co.uk
W: www.bodyguardworkwear.co.uk

BOMBARDIER

Bombardier is a world-leading manufacturer of innovative transportation solutions, from commercial aircraft and business jets to rail transportation equipment, systems and services.

Litchurch Lane,
Derby, DE24 8AD

T: 01332 344 666
F: 01332 289 271

www.bombardier.com

Bombardier Transportation UK Ltd
Litchurch Lane, Derby DE24 8AD
T: 01332 344666
F: 01332 289271
W: www.bombardier.com

Bonar Floors Ltd
High Holborn Rd, Ripley, Derbys DE5 3NT
T: 01773 740615
F: 01773 744142
E: telemarketing@bonarfloors.com
W: www.uk.bonarfloors.com

Bond Insurance Services
Salisbury House, 81 High St, Potters Bar, Herts EN6 5AS
T: 01707 291200
F: 01707 291202
W: www.bond-insurance.co.uk

C F Booth Ltd
Armer St, Rotherham, S.Yorks S60 1AF
T: 01709 559198
F: 01709 561859
E: info@cfbooth.com
W: www.cfbooth.com

Boston Phoenix Ltd
228 Nantwich Rd, Crewe CW2 6BP
T: 01270 588305
E: bostonphoenix@aol.com

Bovis Lend Lease
142 Northolt Rd, Harrow Middx HA2 0EE
T: 020 8271 8000
F: 020 8271 8188
E: andrew.bond@eu.bovislendlease.com
W: www.bovislendlease.com

Boxwood Ltd
15 Old Bailey London EC4M 7EF
T: 020 7170 7240
F: 020 7170 7241
E: info@boxwoodgroup.com
W: www.boxwoodgroup.com

Bradgate Containers
Leicester Rd, Shepshed, Leics LE12 9EG
T: 01509 508678
F: 01509 504224
E: sales@bradgate.co.uk
W: www.bradgate.co.uk

The Bradley Group
Russell St, Heywood, Lancs OL10 1NU
T: 01706 360353
E: jbs@johnbradleygroup.co.uk
W: www.johnbradleygroup.co.uk

Branch Line Society
37 Osberton Place, Hunters Bar, Sheffield S11 8XL
T: 0114 275 2303
E: info@branchline.org.uk
W: www.branchline.org.uk

Brand-Rex Ltd
Speciality Cabling Solutions, West Bridgewater St, Leigh, Lancs WN7 4HB
T: 01942 265500
F: 01942 265576
E: speciality@brand-rex.com
W: www.brand-rex.com

BRB (Residuary) Ltd
Whittles House, 14 Pentonville Rd, London SW1H 0EU
T: 020 7904 5079
W: www.brb.gov.uk

Brecknell, Willis & Co Ltd
PO Box 10, Tapstone Rd, Chard, Somerset TA20 2DE
T: 01460 64941
F: 01460 66122
E: enquiries@brecknell-willis.co.uk
W: www.brecknell-willis.co.uk

Bridgen Holdings Ltd
Bridgen House, 10-16 Byron Rd, Wealdstone, Harrow HA3 7ST
T: 020 8427 0339
F: 020 8424 0604
E: info@bridgen.com
W: www.bridgen.com

Bridgezone
22 Lower Town, Sampford Peverill, Tiverton, Devon EX16 7BT
T: 01884 822899
W: www.bridgezoneltd.co.uk

Bridgeway Consulting Ltd
Bridgeway House, Beeston Business Park, Technology Dr. Beeston, Nottingham NG9 1LA
T: 0115 919 1111
F: 0115 919 1112
E: stockdalen@bridgeway-consulting.co.uk
W: www.bridgeway-consulting.co.uk

Bright Bond (BAC Group)
Stafford Park 11, Telford, Shropshire TF3 3AY
T: 01952 206524
F: 01952 290325
E: brightbond@bacgroup.com
W: www.brightbond.com

British American Railway Services (BARS)
Unit 1, Greens Ind Park, Calder Vale Rd, Wakefield, west Yorks WF1 5PH
T: 01924 234440
E: mike.fairburn@rmslocotec.com

British Geological Survey
Kingsley Dunham Centre, Keyworth, Nottingham NG12 5GG
T: 0115 936 3100
F: 0115 936 3200
E: enquiries@bgs.ac.uk
W: www.bgs.ac.uk

British Springs
See GME Springs

British Transport Police (BTP)
25 Camden Rd, London NW1 9LW
T: 020 7830 8854
F: 020 7830 8944
E: simon.lubin@btp.pnn.police.uk
W: www.btp.police.uk

Brixworth Engineering Co Ltd
Cracton Rd, Brixworth, Northampton NN6 9BW
T: 01604 880338
F: 01604 880252
E: sales@benco.co.uk
W: www.benco.co.uk

Brockhouse Forgings Ltd
Howard St, West Bromwich, West Midlands B70 0SN
T: 0121 556 1241
F: 0121 502 3076
W: www.brockhouse.co.uk

Broadland Rail
7 York Rd, Woking, Surrey GU22 7XH
T: 01483 725999
E: info@broadlandrail.com
W: www.broadlandrail.com

BRP Ltd
Central Buildings, Parkfield Rd, Rugby, Warks CV21 1QJ
T: 01788 559300
F: 01738 559333
E: reception@brprugby.co.uk
W: www.bannerrail.co.uk

Brush Barclay
Caledonia Works, West Longlands St, Kilmarnock KA1 2QD
T: 01563 523573
F: 01563 541076
E: sales@brushtraction.com
W: www.brushtraction.com

Directory

Brush Traction
PO Box 17, Loughborough,
Leics LE11 1HS
T: 01509 617000
F: 01509 617001
E: sales@brushtraction.com
W: www.brushtraction.com

BTMU Capital Corporation
Floor 28, 30 St Mary Ave,
London EC3A 8BF
T: 020 7015 0030
F: 020 7015 0001
E: nbennett@btmucapital.com
W: www.btmucapital.com

C Buchanan
See Colin Buchanan

Buckhickman Inone
Siskin Parkway East, Middlemarch
Business Park, Coventry CV3 4FJ
T: 02476 306444
F: 02476 514214
E: enquiries@buckhickmaninone.com
W: www.bhinone.com

Buckingham Group Contracting Ltd
Silverstone Rd, Stowe,
Bucks MK18 5LJ
T: 01280 823355
E: mail@buckinghamgroup.co.uk
W: www.buckinghamgroup.co.uk

Buildbase
Gemini One, 5520 Oxford Business
Park, Cowley. Oxford OX4 2LL
T: 01865 871700
E: tony.newcombe@buildbase.co.uk

Bupa Wellness
Bupa House, 15-19 Bloomsbury
Way, London WC1A 2BA
T: 020 7800 6458
E: akehursd@bupa.com
W: www.bupawellness.co.uk

Bureau Veritas Weeks
Tower Bridge Court,
224-226 Tower Bridge Rd,
London SE1 2TX
T: 020 7550 8900
F: 020 7403 1590
E: transport.logistics@bureauveritas.com
W: www.bureauveritas.com

Burgess Rail Ltd
Bulwark St, Dover, Kent CT17 9TZ
T: 01304 245450
F: 01304 208803
E: info@burgessrail.co.uk
W: www.theburgessgroup.co.uk

Burges Salmon LLP
Narrow Quay House, Narrow Quay,
Bristol BS1 4AH
T: 0117 939 2000
F: 0117 902 4400
E: email@burges-salmon.com
W: www.burges-salmon.com

Burns Carlton Plc
Simpson House, Windsor Court,
Clarence Drive, Harrogate
HG1 2PE
T: 01423 792000
F: 01423 792001
E: admin@burnscarlton.com
W: www.burnscarlton.com

Butler & Young (BYL) Ltd
Unit 3-4 Jansel House, Hitchin
Road, Luton LU2 7XH
T: 01582 404 113
F: 01582 483 420
E: debbie.clark@byl.co.uk
W: www.byl.co.uk

Butterley Engineering
Ripley, Derbys DE5 3BQ
T: 01773 573573
F: 01773 749898
E: mail@butterleyengineering.com
W: www.butterleyengineering.com

M Buttkereit Ltd
Unit 2, Britannia Rd,
Sale, Cheshire M33 2AA
T: 0161 969 5418
F: 0161 969 5419
E: sales@buttkereit.co.uk
W: www.buttkereit.co.uk

C2C
10th Floor, 207 Old St, London
EC1V 9NR
T: 020 7324 8044
E: custrel@c2crail.co.uk
W: www.c2c-online.co.uk

C3S Projects
Canal Mills, Elland Bridge,
Elland, Halifax HX5 0SQ
T: 01422 313800
E: info@c3s.com
W: www.c3s.com

C4 Industries Ltd
Unit 3-5, Yardley Rd, Knowsley Ind
Park, Kirkby, Liverpool L33 7SS
T: 0151 548 7900
F: 0151 548 7184
E: paul.lighton@c4-industries.com
W: www.c4-industries.com

Cablecraft Ltd
Cablecraft House, Unit 3, Circle
Business Centre, Blackburn Rd,
Houghton Regis, Beds LU5 5DD
T: 01582 606033
F: 01582 606063
E: sales@cablecraft-rail.co.uk
W: www.cablecraft-rail.co.uk

Cabletec ICS Ltd
Sunnyside Rd,
Weston Super Mare BS23 3PZ
T: 01934 424900
F: 01934 636632
E: sales@cabletec.com
W: www.cabletec.com

CAF
See Construcciones

Calco
Lawrence House, 9 Woodside
Green, London SE25 5EY
T: 020 8655 1600
F: 020 8655 1588
E: careers@calco.co.uk
W: www.calco.co.uk

Caledonian Heritage Tours
11 Mavis Bank, Newburgh, Ellon,
Aberdeenshire AB41 6FB
T: 01358 789513
E: info@caledonian-heritage-tours.co.uk
W: www.caledonian-heritage-tours.co.uk

Calmet Laboratory Services
Hampton House, 1 Vicarage Rd,
Hampton Wick, Kingston upon
Thames KT1 4EB
T: 0845 658 0770
F: 020 8614 8048
E: sales@lazgill.co.uk
W: www.calmet.co.uk

Camira Fabrics Ltd
Hopton Mills, Mirfield,
West Yorks WF14 8HE
T: 01924 490591
F: 01924 495605
E: info@camirafabrics.com
W: www.camirafabrics.com

Campaign for Better Transport
12-18 Hoxton St, London N1 6NG
T: 020 7613 0743
F: 020 7613 5280
E: info@bettertransport.org.uk
W: www.bettertransport.org.uk

CAN
Smeckley Wood Close, Chesterfield
Trading Est., Chesterfield S40 3JW
T: 01246 261111
F: 01246 261626
E: info@can.ltd.uk
W: www.can.ltd.uk

C & S Equipment Ltd
9d Wingbury Court, Leighton Rd,
Wingrave HP22 4LW
T: 01296 688500
F: 020 3070 0050
E: info@candsequipment.co.uk
W: www.candsequip,ment.co.uk

Cannon Datacom Ltd
13 Queensway, Stem Lane,
New Milton, Hants BH25 5NU
T: 01425 638148
F: 01425 629178
E: sales@cannontech.co.uk
W: www.cannontech.co.uk

Capita Architecture
90-98 Goswell Rd,
London EC1V 7DF
T: 020 7251 6004
F: 020 7251 6744
E: mervyn.franklin@capita.co.uk
W: www.capitaarchitecture.co.uk

Capita Symonds
24-30 Holborn, London EC1N 2LX
T: 020 7870 9300
F: 020 7870 9399
E: steve.twigg@capita.co.uk
W: www.capitasymonds.co.uk

Capital Project Consultancy Ltd (CPC)
130 Fenchurch St,
London EC3M 5DJ
T: 020 7015 8500
F: 020 7015 8502
E: tim.barber@cpcltd.com
W: www.cpcltd.com

Capital Safety Group Northern
Unit 7, Christleton Court, Manor
Park, Runcorn, Cheshire WA7 1ST
T: 01928 571324
F: 01928 571325
E: csgne@csgne.co.uk
W: www.uclsafetysystems.com

Captec Ltd
11 Brunel Way, Segensworth,
Fareham, Hants PO15 5TX
T: 01489 866066
F: 01489 866088
E: sales@captec.co.uk
W: www.captec.co.uk

Cardev International
See Ecolube

Cargo D
32 Sydney Rd, Haywards Heath,
West Sussex RH16 1QA
T: 01444 450011
F: 01444 450011
E: dirk.ottermans@cargo-d.co.uk
W: www.cargo-d.co.uk

Carillion Rail
24 Birch St, Wolverhampton
WV1 4HY
T: 01902 422431
F: 01902 316165
E: railenquiries@carillionplc.com
W: www.carillionrail.com

Carlbro Group
Grove House, Mansion Gate Drive,
Leeds LS7 4DN
T: 0113 262 0000
F: 0113 262 0737
E: enquiries@carlbro.co.uk
W: www.carlbro.co.uk

Carlton Technologies Ltd
Unit 1, Dunston Place, Dunston Rd,
Chesterfield S41 8NL
T: 01246 455300
F: 01246 455899
E: sales@carltontech.co.uk
W: www.carltontech.co.uk

Carson Industries Ltd
IDA Industrial Est., Racecourse Rd,
Roscommon, Ireland
T: 00353 9066 25922
F: 00353 9066 25921
E: sales@carsoneurope.com
W: www.carsoneurope.com
W: www.multiduc.com

Catalis
The Derby Conference Centre,
London Rd,
Derby DE24 8UX
T: 0845 880 8108
F: 0870 890 0027
E: hotline@catalis.co.uk
W: www.catalis.com

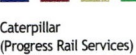

Caterpillar (Progress Rail Services)
Eastfield, Peterborough PE1 5NA
T: 01733 583000
E: mcdonald_michael@cat.com
W: www.progressrail.com

CBISS
11 Ark Royal Way,
Lairdside Technology Park,
Birkenhead CH41 9HT
T: 0151 666 8300
F: 0151 666 8329
E: sales@cbiss.com
W: www.cbiss.com

CB Rail
Level 7, Bishopsgate Exchange, 155
Bishopsgate,
London EC2M 3YB
T: 020 7203 7300
E: info@cbrail.com
W: www.cbrail.com

CCD Design and Ergonomics
95 Southwark St, London SE1 0HX
T: 0207 593 2900
F: 020 7593 2909
E: rachel.bredin@ccd.org.uk
W: www.ccd.org.uk

CCL Rail Training
North Wing, The Quadrangle,
Crewe Hall, Weston Rd,
Crewe CW1 6UB
T: 01270 252400
E: info@ccltraining.com
W: www.ccltraining.com

CDL Group (Collinson Dutton)
19 Berkeley St, London W1J 8ED
T: 0207 290 5770
F: 020 7290 5771
E: cdl@cdlgroup.co.uk
W: www.cdlgroup.co.uk

CDS Rail Ltd
1570, Parkway, Solent Business
Park, Portsmouth PO15 7AG
T: 01489 571771
F: 01489 571555
E: sales@cdsrail.com
W: www.cdsrail.com

Celtic Promotions
PO Box 165, LL29 0BY
E: celtictours@live.co.uk
W: www.freewebs.com/celticpromotions

Cembre Ltd
Dunton Park, Kingsbury Rd,
Curdworth, Sutton Coldfield
B76 9EB
T: 01675 470440
F: 01675 470220
E: sales@cembre.co.uk
W: www.cembre.com

Cemex Rail Products
Aston Church Rd, Washwood
Heath, Saltley, Birmingham
B8 1QF
T: 0121 327 0844
F: 0121 327 7545
E: sleepers@cemex.com
W: www.cemex.co.uk

Centinal Group
The Brookworks, 174 Bromyard Rd,
St Johns, Worcester WR2 5EE
T: 01905 748569
F: 01905 420700
E: les@mfhydraulics.co.uk
W: www.mfhydraulics.co.uk

Centro
Customer Relations,
16 Summer Lane,
Birmingham B1
9 3SD
T: 0121 200 2787
W: www.centro.org.uk

Charcon
See Aggregate Industries

The Chartered Institute of Logistics and Transport (UK)
CILT(UK) is committed to supporting professionals in the rail industry to achieve your career aspirations. To find out how, call 01536 740104, email membership@ciltuk.org.uk or visit our website at: www.ciltuk.org.uk
CILT RAIL

The Chartered Institute of Logistics and Transport (UK) (CILT)
Logistics and Transport Centre,
Earlstrees Court, Earlstrees Rd,
Corby NN17 4AX
T: 01536 740100
F: 01536 740101
E: enquiry@ciltuk.org.uk
W: www.cilt.org.uk

Charter Security Plc
Cambridge House, Cambridge Rd,
Barking, Essex IG11 8NR
T: 020 7507 7717
E: info@charter-security.co.uk
W: www.charter-security.co.uk

Chela Ltd
78 Bilton Way, Enfield,
Middx EN3 7LW
T: 020 8805 2150
F: 020 8443 1868
E: tony.philippou@chela.co.uk
W: www.chela.co.uk

Chester le Track Ltd
See the Trainline

Chieftain Trailers Ltd
207 Coalisland Rd, Dungannon,
Co Tyrone BT71 4DP
T: 028 8774 7531
F: 028 8774 7530
E: sales@chieftaintrailers.com
W: www.chieftaintrailers.com

Chiltern Railways
2nd Floor, Western House,
Rickfords Hill, Aylesbury, Bucks
T: 08456 005165
F: 01296 332126
E: marketing@chilternrailways.co.uk
W: www.chilternrailways.co.uk

Chloride Power Protection
George Curl Way, Southampton
SO18 2RY
T: 02380 610311
E: industrial.sales@chloridepower.com
W: www.chloridepower.com

Chubb Electronic Security Systems Ltd
Shadsworth Rd,
Blackburn BB1 2PR
T: 01254 688583
F: 01254 688781
E: transport@iess.co.uk
W: www.iess.co.uk

Cintec International Ltd
Cintec House, 11 Gold Tops,
Newport, S.Wales NP20 4PH
T: 01633 246614
F: 01633 246110
E: johnbrooks@cintec.co.uk
W: www.cintec.co.uk

CIRAS
Floor 3, Shropshire House,
179 Tottenham Court Rd,
London W1T 7NZ
T: 020 7580 0217
F: 020 7637 4066
E: support@ciras.org.uk
W: www.ciras.org.uk

CITI
Lovat Bank, Silver St, Newport
Pagnell, Bucks MK16 0EJ
T: 01908 283600
F: 01908 283601
E: bdu@citi.co.uk
W: www.citi.co.uk

Cityspace Ltd
Astley House, 33 Notting Hill Gate,
London W11 3QJ
T: 020 7313 8400
F: 020 7313 8401
E: enquiries@cityspace.com
W: www.cityspace.com

Civils Select
16 Posting House, Station Road,
Tring, Herts HP23 5QS
T: 01442 890 900
E: kevin.clancy@civilsselect.co.uk
W: www.civilsselect.co.uk

CJ Associates Ltd
26 Upper Brook St,
London W1K 7QE
T: 020 7529 4900
F: 020 7529 4929
E: nharrison@cjassociates.co.uk
W: www.cjassociates.co.uk

Clara
42 Farnborough Ave, South
Croydon CR2 8HP
T: 020 8657 5673
E: dh@clara.net
W: www.uk.clara.net

R.S. Clare & Co Ltd
8-14, Stanhope St, Liverpool
T: 0151 709 2902
F: 0151 709 0518
E: bill.sutton2@btopenworld.com
W: www.rsclare.com

Class 40 Preservation Society
25 Westholme Close,
Crewe CW2 6UW
T: 075000 40145
E: railtours@cfps.co.uk
W: www.cfps.co.uk

Cleartrack
Salcey-EVL Ltd
The Old Woodyard, Forest Rd,
Hanslope, Milton Keynes MK19 7DE
T: 01908 516250
E: info@cleartrack.co.uk
W: www.cleartrack.co.uk

Clemtech Rail
9 The Spinney, Parklands Business
Pk, Forest Rd, Denmead,
Waterlooville, Hants PO7 6AR
T: 0870 757 2855
F: 0870 757 2856
E: rail@clemtech.co.uk
W: www.clemtech.co.uk

Cleveland Bridge Uk
PO Box 27, Yarm Rd,
Darlington DL1 4DE
T: 01325 381188
F: 01325 382320
E: bob.forrest@clevelandbridge.com
W: www.clevelandbridge.com

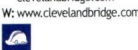

Clyde Materials Handling Ltd
Carolina Court, Riverside,
Doncaster DN4 5RA
T: 01302 321313
F: 01302 554400
E: solutions@clydematerials.co.uk
W: www.clydematerials.co.uk

CMCR Ltd
Nevis Suite, Glenbervie Bus.
Centre, Larbert FK5 4RB
T: 01324 682200
F: 01324 682201
E: info@cmcr.biz
W: www.cmcr.biz

CMS Cameron McKenna
Mitre House, 160 Aldersgate St,
Londoin EC1A 4DD
T: 020 7367 2113
F: 020 7367 2000
E: jonathan.beckitt@cms-cmck.com
W: www.law-now.com

Co Channel Electronics
Victoria Rd, Avonmouth,
Bristol BS11 9DB
T: 0117 982 0578
F: 0117 982 6166
E: sales@co-channel.co.uk
W: www.co-channel.co.uk

COE Ltd
Photon House, Percy St,
Leeds LS12 1EG
T: 0113 230 8800
F: 0113 279 9229
E: sales@coe.co.uk
W: www.coe.co.uk

Coffey Geotechnics
Bretby Business Park, Ashby Rd,
Burton upon Trent DE15 0YL
T: 01283 553270
F: 01283 553273
W: www.coffey.com

CO_AS Rail
Dacre House, 19 Dacre Street,
London SW1H 0DQ
T: 020 7593 5353
F: 020 7593 5343
E: enquiries.colasrail.co.uk
W: www.colasrail.co.uk

Colin Buchanan
10 Eastbourne Terrace,
London W2 6LG
T: 020 7353 1511
F: 020 7053 1301
E: hugh.chaplain@cbuchanan.co.uk
W: www.cbuchanan.co.uk

Collis Engineering Ltd
Salcombe Rd, Meadow Lane Ind.
Est.,Alfreton, Derbys DE55 7RG
T: 01773 833255
F: 01773 520693
E: sales@colis.co.uk
W: www.collis.co.uk

Compass Group
Rivermead, Oxford Rd, Denham,
Uxbridge UB9 4BF
T: 01895 554554
F: 01895 554555
W: www.compass-group.co.uk

Compass Tours
46 Hallville Rd, Liverpool L18 0HR
T: 0151 722 1147
E: compasstours@ycos.co.uk
W: www.compasstoursbyrail.co.uk

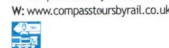

Competence Assurance Solutions Ltd
221 St John St, Clerkenwell,
London EC1V 4LY
T: 020 7688 2840
F: 020 7688 2829
E: info@casolutions.co.uk
W: www.casolutions.co.uk

Complete Drain Clearance
49 Weeping Cross,
Stafford ST17 0DG
T: 01785 665909
F: 01785 664944

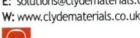

Compin UK
Derby Carriage Works,
Litchurch Lane, Derby DE24 8AD
T: 01332 257500
F: 01332 371950
E: admin@averail.co.uk
W: www.averail.co.uk

Complus Teltronic
Park House, Cambridge Rd,
Harlow, Essex CM20 2EU
T: 01279 457510
F: 01279 445453
E: sales@complus.co.uk
W: www.compluselectronic.co.uk

Comtech Europe
Abbey House, 25 Clarendon Rd,
redhill, Surrey RH1 1QZ
T: 01737 852152
F: 01737 852101
E: office@comtech-europe.com
W: www.comtech-europe.com

Conductix Ltd (Insul 8)
1 Michigan Ave, Salford M50 2GY
T: 0161 848 0161
F: 0161 873 7017
E: info@conductix.co.uk
W: www.conductix.co.uk

Confederation of Passenger Transport UK
Drury House, 34-43 Russell St,
London WC2B 5HA
T: 020 7240 3131
F: 020 7240 6565
E: admin@cpt-uk.org
W: www.cpt-uk.org

HSBC

In association with railalliance

Consillia Ltd
The Old Iron Warehouse, The Wharf, Shardlow, Derby DE72 2GH
T: 01332 799705
F: 01332 799209
E: sales@consillia.com
W: www.consillia.com

Construcciones y Auxiliar de Ferrocarriles SA (CAF)
Jose Miguel Iturrioz St.26, 20200 Beasain, Spain
T: 0034 943 880100
F: 0034 943 881420
E: caf@caf.net
W: www.caf.net

Containerlift
PO Box 582, Great Dunmow, Essex CM6 3QX
T: 0800 174 546
F: 0800 174 547
E: joostbaker@containerlift.co.uk
W: www.containerlift.com

Continental Contitech
Chestnut Field House, Chestnut Field, Rugby, Warks CV21 2PA
T: 01788 571482
F: 01788 542245
W: www.contitech.co.uk

Cook Rail
See William Cook

Cooper and Turner Ltd
Templeborough Works, Sheffield Rd, Sheffield S9 1RS
T: 0114 256 0057
F: 0114 244 5529
E: sales@cooperandturner.co.uk
W: www.cooperandturner.com

Cooper B-Line
Walrow Ind. Est, Highbridge, Somerset TA9 4AQ
T: 01278 783371
F: 01278 789037
E: sales@cooperbline.co.uk
W: www.cooperbline.co.uk

Copon E Wood Ltd
See 3m PPD

Coronet Rail Ltd
Castor Rd, Sheffield S9 2TL
T: 0114 256 2225
F: 0114 261 7826
E: info@coronetrail.co.uk
W: www.coronetrail.co.uk

Corporate College
Derby College, Prince Charles Ave, Deby DE22 4LR
T: 01332 520145
E: training@derby-college.ac.uk
W: www.corporatecollege.co.uk

Correl Rail Ltd
Gee House, Holborn Hill, Birmingham B7 5PA
T: 0121 326 9900
F: 0121 328 5343
E: paul.craper@correl-rail.co.uk
W: www.correl-rail.co.uk

CORUS COGIFER
Manufacturers of all types of Switch and Crossing systems and ancillary components for the Heavy Rail, High Speed and Light Rail markets
Hebden Road, Scunthorpe, North Lincs. DN15 8XX
T: 01724 862131
F: 01724 295243
info@coruscogifer.com
www.coruscogifer.com

Corus Cogifer
Hebden Rd, Scunthorpe, North Lincs DN15 8XX
T: 01724 862131
F: 01724 295243
E: info@coruscogifer.com
W: www.coruscogifer.com

Corus Rail Infrastructure Services
PO Box 298, York YO1 6YH
T: 01904 454600
F: 01904 454601
E: rail@corusgroup.com
W: www.muchmorethanrail.com

Corus Northern Engineering Services
PO Box 1, Brigg Rd, Scunthorpe, N.Lincs DN16 1BP
T: 01642 498041
F: 01642 404726
E: info-cnes@corusgroup.com
W: www.corusnes.com

Corys T.E.S.S
74 Rue des Martyrs, 38027 Grenoble, France
T: 0033 476 288200
F: 0033 476 288211
E: coryscom@corys.com
W: www.corys.com

Cosalt Ltd
Banner House, Greg St, Reddish, Stockport SK5 7BT
T: 0161 429 1100
F: 0161 429 1103
E: graham.robinson@cosalt.com
W: www.cosalt.com

Costain Ltd - Rail Sector
Costain House, Nicholsons Walk, Maidenhead, Berks SL6 1LN
T: 01628 842444
F: 01628 842362
E: ken.stewart@costain.com
W: www.costain.com

Cotswold Rail Engineering Ltd
Westgate House, Westgate St, Gloucester GL1 2RU
T: 01453 899260
F: 01453 899261
E: info@cotswoldrail.com
W: www.cotswoldrail.co.uk

Cowans Sheldon
The Clarke Chapman Group Ltd, PO Box 9, Saltmeadows Rd, Gateshead NE8 1SW
T: 0191 477 2271
F: 0191 477 1009
E: martin.howell@clarkechapman.co.uk
W: www.cowanssheldon.co.uk

Coyle Personnel Plc
First Floor, 66-68 College Rd, Harrow, Middx HA1 1BE
T: 0208 861 3000
E: roger@coyles.co.uk
W: www.coylerail.co.uk

CP Fims Solutia (UK) Ltd
13 Acorn Business Centre, Northarbour Rd, Cosham PO6 3TH
T: 02392 219112
F: 02392 219102
E: michelle.testar@llumar.eu.com
W: www.llumar.eu.com

C P Plus Ltd
10 Flask walk, Camden, London NW3 1HE
T: 020 7431 4001
F: 020 7435 3280
E: info@cp-plus.co.uk
W: www.cp-plus.co.uk

Craig & Derricott Ltd
Hall Lane, Walsall Wood, Walsall WS9 9DP
T: 01543 375541
F: 01543 452610
E: sales@craigandderricott.com
W: www.craigandderricott.com

Creactive Design
22 New St, Leamington, Warks CV31 1HP
T: 01926 833113
F: 01926 832788
E: info@creactive-design.co.uk
W: www.creactive-design.co.uk

Critical Project Resourcing Ltd
6 Blighs Rd, Blighs Meadow, Sevenoaks, Kent TN13 1DA
T: 01732 455300
F: 01732 458447
E: rail@cpresourcing.co.uk
W: www.cpresourcing.co.uk

Cross Coutry Trains
See Arriva

Cross London Rail Links (Crossrail)
6th Floor, Portland House, Bressenden Place, London SW1E 5BH
T: 0845 602 3813
F: 020 3023 9101
E: helpdesk@crossrail.co.uk
W: www.crossrail.co.uk

WH Crossley Ltd
Unit 27, Newby Rd Ind. Est., Hazel Grove, Stockport SK7 5DJ
T: 0161 480 2461
F: 0161 474 7360
E: david.greenwood@whcrossley.co.uk
W: www.sheetmetalworks.co.uk

Cross Services Group
Cross House, Portland Centre, Sutton Rd, St Helens WA9 3DR
T: 01744 25254
F: 01744 26072
E: talk2@crossgroup.co.uk
W: www.crossgroup.co.uk

Crouch Waterfall & Partners
Solly's Mill, Mill Lane, Godalming, Surrey GU7 1EY
T: 01483 425314
F: 01483 425814
E: office@cwp.co.uk
W: www.cwp.co.uk

Crowd Dynamics Ltd
The Mill House, Staveley Mill Yard, Staveley, Kendal, Cumbria LA8 9LS
T: 01539 822950
F: 01539 822951
E: david@crowddynamics.com
W: www.crowddynamics.com

CSE International Ltd
Glanford House, Bellwin Drive, Flixborough, N.Lincs DN15 8SN
T: 01724 862169
F: 01724 846256
E: info@cse-international.com
W: www.cse-international.com

CSRE
European representative of several Chinese rolling stock manufacturers, with combined capability to produce 350 locomotives, 10,000 freight wagons and 650 passenger vehicles (DMU/EMU/ coaches) per annum.
David Shipley, Managing Director
Unit 3, Lower Ledge Farm, Dyrham, Nr. Chippenham, SN14 8DY
Tel: +44-1279-778999
Fax: +44-1279-778084
david.shipley@csre.co.uk
www.csre.co.uk

CSRE Ltd
Unit 3, Lower Ledge Farm, Dyrham, Bristol SN14 8DY
T: 01279 778999
F: 01279 778084
E: david.shipley@csre.co.uk
W: www.csre.co.uk

CTS Rail Services
The Maltings, Greg St, Burwell, Cambridge CB5 0HB
T: 01638 743596
F: 01638 744136
E: sales@ctsrailservices.co.uk
W: www.ctsrailservices.co.uk

Cubic Transportation Systems
AFC House, Honeycrock Lane, Salfords, Redhill, Surrey RH1 5LA
T: 01737 782200
F: 01737 789759
E: jennifer.newell@cubic.com
W: www.cubic.com/cts

Cummins
Yarm Rd, Darlington DL1 4PW
T: 01327 886464
F: 0870 241 3180
E: cabo.customerassistance@cummins.com
W: www.everytime.cummins.com

Cyril Sweett
2nd Floor, 45 Summer Row, Birmingham B1 3JJ
T: 020 7061 9000
F: 020 7430 0603
E: ken.davis@cyrilsweett.com
W: www.cyrilsweett.com

Dailys UK Ltd
Suite 5 Portside House, Lower Mersey Street, Ellesmere Port, Cheshire CH65 2AL
T: 0151 357 3309
F: 0151 356 9316
E: support@dailys.co.uk
W: www.ledlines.co.uk

Dalkia Rail
5 Limeharbour Court, Limeharbour, London E14 9RH
T: 020 7001 7000
F: 020 7001 7273
E: pos.kamintgi@dalkia.co.uk
W: www.dalkia.co.uk

Dallmeier Electronic UK Ltd
Dallmeier House, 3 Beaufort Trade Park, Pucklechurch, Bristol BS16 9QH
T: 0117 303 9303
F: 0117 303 9302
E: dallmeieruk@dallmeier-electronic.com
W: www.dallmeier-electronic.com

D&D Rail Ltd
Time House, Time Square, Basildon, Essex SS14 1DJ
T: 01268 520000
F: 01268 520011
E: info@ddrail.com
W: www.ddrail.com

Dartford Composites Ltd
Unit 1, Ness Rd, Erith, Kent DA8 2LD
T: 01322 350097
F: 01322 359438
E: sales@dartford composites.co.uk
W: www.dartford composites.co.uk

Data Display UK Ltd
3 The Meadows, Waterberry Drive, Waterlooville, Hants PO7 7XX
T: 023 9224 7500
F: 023 9224 7519
E: sales@datadisplayuk.com
W: www.dtadisplayuk.com

Data Systems & Solutions
SIN D-7, Sinfin Lane, Derby DE24 8BJ
T: 01332 771700
F: 01332 763180
E: info@ds-s.com
W: www.ds-s.com

david brice consultancy ltd
Independent consultancy actively engaged worldwide in rail planning, operations and management. Specialising in UK, European and International Freight, Intermodal and Combined Operations.
11 Sebastian Ave, Shenfield, Brentwood, Essex CM15 8PN
T: 01277 221422 F: 01277 263614
davidpbrice@aol.com
www.bricerail.co.uk

David Brice Consultancy
11 Sebastian Ave, Shenfield, Brentwood, Essex CM15 8PN
T: 01277 221422
F: 01277 263614
E: davidpbrice@aol.com
W: www.bricerail.co.uk

David Simmonds Consulting
Suite 14, Millers Yard, Mill Lane, Cambridge CB2 1RQ
T: 01223 316098
F: 01223 313893
E: dsc@davidsimmonds.com
W: www.davidsimmonds.com

WH Davis Ltd
Langwith Rd, Langwith Junction, Mansfield, Notts NG20 9SA
T: 01623 741600
F: 01623 744474
E: mac.burge@whdavis.co.uk
W: www.whdavis.co.uk

Davis Pneumatic Systems Ltd
Huxley Close, Newnham Ind Est, Plympton, Plymouth PL7 4BQ
T: 01752 336421
F: 01752 345828
E: sales@davispneumatic.co.uk
W: www.davispneumatic.co.uk

DBK Technitherm Ltd
Unit 11, Llantrisant Business Park, Llantrisant CF72 8LF
T: 01443 237927
F: 01443237867
E: dcourt@dbkt.co.uk
W: www.dbktechnitherm.ltd.uk

DCA Design International
19, Church St, Warwick CV34 4AB
T: 01926 499461
F: 01926 401134
E: transport@dca-design.com
W: www.dcatransport.co.uk

Dean & Dyball Rail Ltd
Unit 8, Viewpoint Office Village, Babbage Rd, Stevenage SG1 2EQ
T: 01438 765360
F: 01438 765361
E: gemmawatts@deandyball.co.uk
W: www.deandyball.co.uk

Dedicated Micros
1200 Unit, Daresbury Park, Daresbury, Warrington WA4 4HS
T: 0845 600 9500
F: 0845 600 9504
E: customerservices@dmicros.com
W: www.dedicatedmicros.com/uk

DEG Signal Ltd
Aspect House, Crusader Park, Warminster, Wilts BA12 8BT
T: 01985 212020
F: 01985 2120053
E: sarah.hill@degsignal.co.uk
W: www.degsignal.co.uk

Delimon Denco Lubrication (London Office)
2nd Floor, Business Innovation Centre, Innova Park, Electric Ave, Enfield EN3 7XU
T: 01992 782410
F: 01992 782425
E: harry.hastwell@delimon.co.uk
W: www.delimon.co.uk

Delta Rail Group Ltd
Hudson House, 2 Hudson Way, Pride Park, Derby DE24 8HS
T: 0870 190 1000
F: 0870 190 1008
E: enquiries@deltarail.com
W: www.deltarail.com

Deltix Transport Consulting
7 Merchiston Mews, Edinburgh EH10 5AL
T: 0131 221 9019
E: david@deltix.co.uk
W: www.deltix.co.uk

DeltaRail

Leading suppliers of advanced railway technology and solutions; combining hardware, software and specialist consultancy to improve business performance for our customers across the entire railway.
Hudson House
2 Hudson Way
Pride Park
Derby
DE24 8HS
Tel: 0870 190 1000
Fax: 0870 190 1008
e-mail: enquiries@deltarail.com
website: www.deltarail.com

Deltone Training Consultants
Ground Floor, 42-48 High Rd, South Woodford, London E18 2QL
T: 020 8532 2208
F: 020 8532 2206
E: sales@deltonetraining.com
W: www.deltonetraining.com

Demco
Heyford Close, Aldermans Green Ind. Est., Coventry CV2 2QB
T: 02476 602323
F: 02476 602116
E: info@mgs.co.uk
W: www.demco.co.uk

Denton Wilde Sapte
One Fleet Place, London EC4M 7WS
T: 020 7242 1212
F: 020 7246 7777
E: info@dentonwildesapte.com
W: www.dentonwildesapte.com

Department for Transport
Great Minster House, 76 Marsham St, London SW1P 4DR
T: 020 7944 5409
F: 020 7944 2158
E: fax9643@dft.gsi.gov.uk
W: www.dft.gov.uk

Derby & Derbyshire Rail Forum
Commerce House, 2 Victoria Way Pride Park, Derby DE24 8AN
T: 01332 851297
F: 01332 851283
E: debbie.cook@dncc.co.uk
W: www.derbyrailforum.org.uk

Derby Engineering Unit Ltd
Units 3,4 & 5, Stockbrook St, Derby DE22 3WR
T: 01332 206766
F: 01332 206767
E: sales@derby engineeringunit.co.uk
W: www.derby engineeringunit.co.uk

The Deritend Group Ltd
Cyprus St, off Upper Villiers St, Wolverhampton WV2 4PA
T: 01902 392315
F: 01902 390186
E: sales@deritend.co.uk
W: www.deritend.co.uk

Design & Projects Int. Ltd
2 Manor Farm, Flexford Rd, North Baddesley, Hants SO52 9FD
T: 02380 277910
F: 02380 277920
E: colin.brooks@designandprojects.com
W: www.railwaymaintenance.com

Design Triangle Ltd
The Maltings, Burwell, Cambridge CB25 0HB
T: 01638 743070
F: 01638 743493
E: mail@designtriangle.co.uk
W: www.designtriangle.com

Deuta-Werke GmbH
Paffrather Str 140, 51465 Bergisch, Gladbach, Germany
T: 0049 2202 958 139
E: support@deuta.de
W: www.deuta.de

Develop
Derby Training Centre, Ascot Drive, Derby DE24 8GW
T: 01332 253500
F: 01332 834699
E: terry.whitley@develop-solutions.co.uk
W: www.develop-solutions.co.uk

Devol Engineering Ltd
Clarence St, Greenock, Strathclyde PA15 1LR
T: 01475 883274
F: 01475 787873
E: elspeth.halley@devol.com
W: www.devol.com

Dewalt
210, Bath Rd, Slough SL1 3YD
T: 01753 567055
F: 01753 521312
W: www.dewalt.co.uk

Dewhurst Plc
Melbourne Works, Inverness Rd, Hounslow, Middx TW3 3LT
T: 020 8607 7300
F: 020 8572 5986
E: railsales@dewhurst.co.uk
W: www.dewhurst.co.uk

Dext-online Ltd
Buckham Hill, Uckfield E.Sussex TN22 5XZ
T: 07711 123784
E: info@dext-online.net
W: www.dext-online.net

Difuria
Wood Lane, Beckingham, Doncaster DN10 4NR
T: 01427 848712
F: 01427 848056
W: www.difuria.co.uk

The Direct Group
Unit 1, Churnet Court, Churnetside Business Park, Harrison Way, Cheddleton, Staffs ST13 7EF
T: 01538 360555
F: 01538 369100
E: dpl@direct-group.co.uk
W: www.direct-group.co.uk

Direct Link North
56 Beverley Gardens, Wembley, Middx HA9 9QZ
T: 020 8908 0638
F: keith.gerry@virgin.net
W: www.directlinknorth.com

Direct Link North
The Direct Link North - Britain's affordable High Speed Railway for the 21st Century
56 Beverley Gardens, Wembley, Middlesex HA9 9QZ
T: 020 8908 0638
E: keith.gerry@virgin.net
W: www.directlinknorth.com

Direct Rail Services (DRS)
Kingmoor Depot, Etterby Rd, Carlisle CA3 9NZ
T: 01228 406600
F: 01228 406601
E: enquiries@drsl.co.uk
W: www.directrailservices.com

Discovery Drilling Ltd
32 West Station Yard, Maldon, Essex CM9 6TS
T: 01621 851300
F: 01621 851305
E: enquiries@discoverydrilling.co.uk
W: www.discoverydrilling.co.uk

DLA Piper UK LLP
Princes Exchange, Princes Square, Leeds LS1 4BY
T: 0113 369 2468
F: 0113 369 2999
E: neil.mclean@dlapiper.com
W: www.dlapiper.com

DML Group
Devonport Royal Dockyard, Plymouth, Devon PL1 4SG
T: 01752 605665
F: 01752 326193
E: john.small@devonport.co.uk
W: www.dmlgroup.co.uk

DMS Technologies
Belbin's Business Park, Cupernham Lane, Romsey, Hants SO51 7JF
T: 01794 525463
F: 01794 525450
E: info@dmstech.co.uk
W: www.dmstech.co.uk

DNH WW Ltd
31 Clarke Rd, Mount Farm, Bletchley, Milton Keynes MK1 1LG
T: 01908 275000
F: 01908 275100
E: dnh@dnh.co.uk
W: www.dnh.co.uk

DNV (Det Norske Veritas)
Highbank House, Exchange St, Stockport SK3 0ET
T: 0161 477 3818
F: 0161 477 3819
E: david.salmon@dnv.com
W: www.dnv.com

Docmate Services Ltd
15 Millside rd, Peterculter, Aberdeen AB14 0WE
T: 01224 732780
E: cknowles@docmates.co.uk
W: www.docmates.co.uk

Docklands Light Railway
Castor Lane, Poplar, London E14 0DX
T: 0207 363 9898
F: 020 7363 9708
E: enquire@tfl.gov.uk
W: www.dlr.co.uk

Dold Industries Ltd
11 Hamberts Rd, Blackall Ind Est, South Woodham Ferrers, Essex CM3 5UW
T: 01245 324432
F: 01245 325570
E: admin@dold.co.uk
W: www.dold.co.uk

Domnick Hunter Industrial Operations
Dukesway, Team Valley Trading Est., Gateshead, Tyne & Wear NE11 0PZ
T: 0191 402 9000
F: 0191 482 6296
E: dhindsales@parker.com
W: www.domnickhunter.com

Donaldson Associates
Eastfield, Church St, Uttoxeter, Staffs ST14 8AA
T: 01889 563680
F: 01889 562586
E: tunnels@donaldson associates.com
W: www.donaldsonassociates.com

The UK's leading designer and supplier of LED signalling to Network Rail
DORMAN
Rufford Rd, Crossens, Southport PR9 8LA
T: 01704 220911
F: 01704 232221
E: info@dorman.co.uk
W: www.dorman.co.uk

Dorman
Rufford Rd, Crossens, Southport PR9 8LA
T: 01704 220911
F: 01704 232221
E: info@dorman.co.uk
W: www.dorman.co.uk

Dorman Varitext
5 Stephenson Court, Skippers Lane Ind Est, Middlesbrough TS6 6UT
T: 01642 461222
F: 01642 461567
E: info@dormanvaritext.com
W: www.dormanvaritext.com

Donyal Engineering Ltd
Hobsin Ind Est, Burnopfield, Newcastle upon Tyne NE16 6EA
T: 01207 270909
F: 01207 270333
E: mike@donyal.co.uk
W: www.donyal.co.uk

DP Consulting
Unit 4, Tygan House, The Broadway, Cheam, Surrey
T: 0845 094 2380
F: 0700 341 8557
E: info@dpconsulting.org.uk
W: www.dpconsulting.org.uk

DPSS Cabling Services Ltd
Unit 16, Chiltern Business Village, Arundel Rd, Uxbridge UB2 2SN
T: 01895 251010
F: 01895 813133
E: adam.moss@dpsscabling.co.uk
W: www.dpsscabling.co.uk

DRail
Brookside, Padmoor Lane, Upton, Gainsborough, Lincs DN21 5NH
T: 01427 839520
F: 01427 839520
E: drail@btinternet.com

Drum Cussac
8 Hill St, St Helier, Jersey JE4 9XB
T: 0870 429 6944
E: risk@drum-cussac.com
W: www.drum-cussac.com

Durapipe
Walsall Rd, Norton Canes, Cannock, Staffs WS11 9NS
T: 01543 279909
E: enquiries@durapipe.co.uk
W: www.durapipe.co.uk

Dyer & Butler Ltd
Mead House, Station Rd, Nursling, Southampton SO16 0AH
T: 02380 742222
F: 02380 742200
E: enquiries@dyerandbutler.co.uk
W: www.dyerandbutler.co.uk

Dyer Engineering Ltd
Solution House, Unit 3, Morrison & Busty North Ind Est, Annfield Plain, Stanley, Co Durham DH9 7RU
T: 01207 234315
F: 01207 282834
E: sales@dyer-engineering.ltd.uk
W: www.dyer-engineering.ltd.uk

Dynex Semiconductor Ltd
Doddington Rd, Lincoln LN6 3LF
T: 01522 500500
F: 01522 500020
E: power_solutions@dynexsemi.com
W: www.dynexsemi.com

Dywidag-Systems International Ltd
Northfield Rd, Southam, Warks CV47 0FG
T: 01926 813980
F: 01926 813817
E: sales@dywidag.co.uk
W: www.dywidag-systems.co.uk

EAO Ltd
Highland House, Albert Drive, Burgess Hill RH15 9TN
T: 01444 236000
F: 01444 236641
E: sales.euk@eao.com
W: www.eao.com

E A Technology
Capenhurst Technology Park, Capenhurst, Chester CH1 6ES
T: 0151 339 4181
F: 0151 347 2404
E: john.hartford@eatechnology.com
W: www.eatechnology.com

Eagle Pest Control Services UK Ltd
1 King Alfred Way, Cheltenham GL52 6QP
T: 01242 696969
F: 01242 696970
E: sales.eagle@mitie.co.uk
W: www.epest.demon.co.uk

East Lancashire Railway
Bolton St Station, Bury BL9 0EY
T: 0161 764 7790
F: 0161 763 4408
E: andy.coward@east-lancs-rly.co.uk
W: www.east-lancs-railway.co.uk

East Midlands Development Agency
Apex Court, City Link, Nottingham NG2 4LA
T: 0115 988 8533
F: 0115 853 3666
E: ericb@emd.org.uk
W: www.ukrailcentre.com

East Midlands Trains
Midland House, Nelson St, Derby DE1 2SA
T: 01332 262010
F: 01332 262011
E: getintouch@eastmidlandstrains.co.uk
W: www.eastmidlandstrains.co.uk

Ecolube
Cardev International Ltd, Ripon Way, Harrogate HG1 2AU
T: 01423 817200
F: 01423 817400
E: admin@ecolube.co.uk
W: www.ecolube.co.uk

ECT Group
See British American Railway Services

Eden Brown
222 Bishopsgate, London EC2M 4QD
T: 020 7422 7300
F: 0845 434 9573
E: london@edenbrown.com
W: www.edenbrown.com

Eden Business Analysis Ltd
23 Station Rd, Upper Poppleton, York YO26 6PX
T: 01904 780781
F: 01904 780785
E: neil@edenba.co.uk
W: www.edenba.co.uk

EDF Energy
49 Southwark Bridge Rd, London SE1 9HH
T: 020 7089 0000
F: 020 7089 0299
E: bob.lane@edfenergy.com
W: www.edfenergy.com

Edilon (Sedra International bv)
32 Lydiard Way, Trowbridge, Wilts BA14 0UJ
T: 01225 763416
F: 01225 763619
E: b.vennell@edilonsedra.com
W: www.edilonsedra.com

Edgar Allen
See Balfour Beatty

Edmund Nuttall Ltd
St James House, Knoll Rd, Camberley, Surrey GU15 3XW
T: 01276 63484
F: 01276 66060
E: info@bamnuttall.co.uk
W: www.bamnuttall.co.uk

EFD Corporate
Blackhill Drive, Wolverton Mill, Milton Keynes MK12 5TS
T: 08451 285174
E: enquiries@efd-corporate.com
W: www.efd-corporate.com

EFS (Eye for Solutions) Ltd
RailCare House, Mariner, Lichfield Rd Ind Est, Tamworth, Staffs B79 7UL
T: 01827 302928
F: 07500 794056
E: lynn.holmes@eyeforsolutions-uk.com
W: www.eyeforsolutions-uk.com

Elan
Park Row House, 19-20 Park Row, Leeds LS1 5JF
T: 0113 201 0333
F: 0113 201 0303
E: info@elanit.co.uk
W: www.elanit.co.uk

Elan Public Transport Consultancy
Room 202, Dunston Innovation Centre, Dunston Rd, Chesterfield S41 8NG
T: 0845 123 5733
F: 01246 267989
E: office@elanptc.com
W: www.elanptc.com

Eland Cables
120 Highgate Studios, 53-79 Highgate Rd, London NW5 1TL
T: 020 7241 8787
F: 020 7241 8700
E: sales@eland.co.uk
W: www.eland.co.uk

Eldapoint Ltd
Manufacturing Division
Eldapoint Ltd manufacture Re-Locatable Equipment Buildings (REB's) built to the "BR1615D" Specification. We are an ISO 9001:2000 accredited company and Link-up approved.
Charleywood Road, Kirkby Industrial Estate, Kirkby, Merseyside, L33 7SG
Tel: 0151 548 9838
Fax: 0151 546 4120
paul.wyatt@eldapoint.co.uk
www.eldapoint.co.uk

Eldapoint Ltd
Charleywood Rd, Kirkby Ind. Est., Kirkby, Merseyside L33 7SG
T: 0151 548 9838
F: 0151 546 4120
E: paul.wyatt@eldapoint.co.uk
W: www.eldapoint.co.uk

Electro Motive
9301 W.55th St, LaGrange, Illinois 60525, USA
T: 001 800 255 5355
F: 001 708 387 6626
E: scott.garman@emdiesels.com
W: www.emdiesels.com

Ellis Fairbank Plc
10th Floor, Portland House, Bressenden Place, London SW1E 5BH
T: 0845 094 6001
F: 0845 011 0883
E: jim.newsom@ellisfairbank.com
W: www.ellisfairbank.com

Eltek Valere UK Ltd
Eltek House, Maxted Rd, Hemel Hempstead, Herts HP2 7DX
T: 01442 219355
F: 01442 245894
E: uksales@eltekvalere.com
W: www.eltekvalere.com

EMEG Electrical Ltd
Unit 3, Dunston Place, Whittington Moor, Chesterfield, Derbys S41 8XA
T: 01246 268678
F: 01246 268679
E: enq@emeg.co.uk
W: www.emeg.co.uk

Emergi-Lite Safety Systems
Thomas & Betts Ltd, Bruntcliffe Lane, Morley, Leeds LS27 9LL
T: 0113 281 0600
F: 0113 281 0601
E: emergi-lite-sales@tnb.com
W: www.tnb.com

Emerson Crane Hire
Emerson House, Freshwater House, Dagenham, Essex RM8 1RX
T: 020 8548 3900
F: 020 8548 3999
E: liam@emersoncranes.co.uk
W: www.emersoncranes.co.uk

Enerpac
Bentley Rd South, Darlaston, West Midlands WS10 8LQ
T: 0121 505 0787
F: 0121 505 0799
E: info@enerpac.com
W: www.enerpac.com

Enersys Ltd
Rake Lane, Clifton Junction, Swinton, Manchester M27 8LR
T: 0161 794 4611
F: 0161 727 3809
W: robert.marshall@uk.enersys.com
W: www.enersysinc.com

Engcon UK Ltd
Unit 4a, The Hen House, Oldwich Lane West, Chadwick End, Solihull B93 0BJ
T: 01564 785161
F: 01564 785181
E: caroline.sigge@engcon.com
W: www.engcon.se

Engineering Support Group
31 Brunel Parkway, Off Locomotive Way, Pride Park, Derby DE24 8HR
T: 0870 140 7630
F: 01332 297313
E: celia.freer@esg-railconsultancy.co.uk
W: www.esg-railconsultancy.co.uk

Ennstone Concrete Ltd
Doseley, Telford, Shropshire TF4 3BX
T: 01952 630300
F: 01952 501537
E: trevor.beddow@ennstoneproducts.co.uk
W: www.ennstone.co.uk

Enotrac (UK) Ltd
Times House, Throwley Way, Sutton, Surrey SM1 4AF
T: 020 8770 3501
F: 020 8770 3502
E: info@enotrac.co.uk
W: www.enotrac.com

Entec UK Ltd
Atlantic House, Imperial Way, Reading RG2 0TP
T: 01189 036686
F: 01189 036261
E: whitr@entecuk.co.uk
W: www.entecuk.com

Entech Technical Solutions Ltd
4th Floor, York House, Empire Way, Wembley, Middx HA9 0PA
T: 020 8900 9390
F: 020 8900 9490
E: saul@entechts.co.uk
W: www.entechts.co.uk

Environmental Management Solutions Group Holdings Ltd (EMS)
Global House, Geddings Rd, Hoddesden, Herts EN11 0NT
T: 01992 535445
F: 01992 456435
E: charmaine.paraskevas@emsgroup.org
W: www.emsgroup.org

Environment Hygeine Services (EHS)
32 Clay Hill, Enfield EN2 9AA
T: 020 8367 7350
E: info@pigeonglide.com
W: www.pigeonglide.com

Envirotech
See LH Group Services

EPC Global
PO Box 1413, First Floor, Broadway Chambers, Hammersmith Broadway, London W6 7PW
T: 020 8600 1600
F: 020 8741 2001
E: firstname.lastname@epcglobal.com
W: www.epcglobal.com

EQE International (ABS Consulting)
EQE House, The Beacons, Warrington RD, Birchwood, Warrington WA3 6WJ
T: 01925 287300
E: enquiriesuk@absconsulting.com
W: www.eqe.co.uk

ERA Technology
Cleeve Rd, Leatherhead, Surrey KT22 7SA
T: 01372 367030
F: 01372 367102
E: rail@era.co.uk
W: www.era.co.uk

Ergonomics & Safety Research Institute (ESRI)
Holywell Building, Holywell Way, Loughborough, Leics LE11 3UZ
T: 01509 226900
F: 01509 226960
E: esri@lboro.ac.uk
W: www.lboro.ac.uk

ERM Ltd
8 Cavendish Square, London W1G 0ER
T: 020 7465 7200
F: 020 7465 7272
E: karen.ray@erm.com
W: www.erm.com

Ernst & Young LLP
Transaction Advisory Services
1 More London Place, London SE1 2AF
T: 020 7951 2000
F: 020 7951 3167
E: droth@uk.ey.com
W: www.ey.com/uk

ESAB (UK) Ltd
Hanover House, Queensgate, Britannia Rd, Waltham Cross EN8 7TF
T: 01992 768515
F: 01992 788053
E: info@esab.co.uk
W: www.esab.co.uk

Esmerk
Thames Tower, Station Rd, Reading RG1 1LX
T: 0118 956 5820
F: 0118 956 5850
E: response@esmerk.com
W: www.esmerk.com

ESR Technology Ltd
410 Birchwood Park, Warrington, Cheshire WA3 6FW
T: 01925 843400
F: 01925 843500
E: info@esrtechnology.com
W: www.esrtechnology.com

Essempy
1 Phoebe Lane, Church End, Wavendon, Bucks MK17 8LR
T: 01908 585979
F: 01908 585979
E: diana.price@essempy.co.uk
W: www.essempy.co.uk

ESS Rail
3rd Floor, Regal House, 70 London Rd, Twickenham TW1 3QS
T: 0845 245 3000
F: 0845 245 3061
E: john.lynch@essrail.com
W: www.esslimited.com

ETS Cable Components
Units 4/5, Red Lion Business Park, Red Lion Rd, Tolworth KT6 7QD
T: 020 8405 6789
F: 020 8405 6790
E: sales@etscc.co.uk
W: www.etscc.co.uk

Eurailscout GB Ltd
Unit 2, Kimberley Court, Kimberley Rd, Queens Park, London NW6 7SL
T: 020 7372 2973
F: 020 7372 5444
E: info@eurailscout.com
W: www.eurailscout.com

Euro Cargo Rail SAS
Immeuble la Palacio, 25-29 Place de la Madelaine, 75008 Paris France
T: 0033 977 400 000
F: 0033 977 400 200
E: info@eurocargorail.com
W: www.eurocargorail.com

Eurochemi
Kingsbury Park, Midland Rd, Swadlincote, Derbys DE11 0AN
T: 01283 222111
F: 01283 550177
E: info@hkw.co.uk
W: www.eurochemi.co.uk

Eurocom Ltd
1 Glyn St, Vauxhall, London SE11 5HT
T: 020 7820 8344
E: comms@eurocomltd.co.uk
W: www.eurocomltd.co.uk

Eurolog Ltd
Orlando House, 3 High St, Teddington TW11 8NP
T: 020 8977 4407
F: 020 8977 3714
E: info@eurolog.co.uk
W: www.eurolog.co.uk

HSBC

European Friction Industries Ltd (EFI)
6/7 Bonville Rd, Brislington, Bristol BS4 5NZ
T: 0117 977 7859
E: rail@efiltd.co.uk
W: www.efiltd.co.uk

European Track Safety Services Group
Dallam Court, Dallam Lane, Warrington WA2 9QY
T: 01925 425934
F: 01925 425936
E: info@tracksafety.net
W: www.tracksafety.net

Europe Rail Consultancy Ltd
North Court, Hassocks, West Sussex BN6 8JS
T: 01273 845583
E: chris.dugdale@europerailconsultancy.com

Eurostar Group
Times House, Bravingtons Walk, Regent Quarter, London N1 9AW
E: press.office@eurostar.co.uk
W: www.eurostar.com

Eurotech Ltd
3 Clifton Court, Cambridge CB1 7BN
T: 01223 403410
F: 01223 410457
E: sales@eurotech-ltd.co.uk
W: www.eurotech-ltd.co.uk

Eurotunnel
The Channel Tunnel Group Ltd, UK Terminal, Ashford Rd, Folkestone, Kent CT18 8XX
T: 01303 282222
F: 01303 850360
E: info@eurotunnel.com
W: www.eurotunnel.com

Eve Trakway
Bramley Vale, Chesterfield, Derbys S44 5GA
T: 01246 858600
F: 08700 737373
E: mail@evetrakway.co.uk
W: www.evetrakway.co.uk

Evergrip Ltd
Unit 4, Flaxley Rd, Selby YO8 4BG
T: 01757 212744
F: 01757 212749
E: sales@evergrip.com
W: www.evergrip.com

EWS
Lakeside Business Park, Carolina Way, Doncaster DN4 5PN
T: 0870 140 5000
E: communications.press@ews-railway.co.uk
W: www.ews-railway.co.uk

Excalibur Screwbolt Ltd
Gate 3, Newhall Nursery, Lower Rd, Hockley, Essex SS5 5JU
T: 01702 206962
F: 01702 207918
E: info@screwbolt.com
W: www.excaliburscrewbolts.com

Excel Passenger Logistics
Airways House, Stansted Airport, Essex CM24 1RY
T: 01279 681800
F: 01279 682268
E: mail@excelpl.co.uk
W: www.excelpl.co.uk

Exide Technologies Network Power
P.O. Box 1, Salford Road, Over Hulton, Bolton, BL5 1DD
T: 01204 661462
F: 01204 661479
E: cmpsales@eu.exide.com
W: www.industrialenergy.exide.com

Expamet Security Products
PO Box 14, Longhill Ind. Est. (North), Hartlepool TS25 1PR
T: 01429 867366
F: 01429 867355
E: fencing@exmesh.co.uk
W: www.expandedmetalfencing.com

Express Electrical
37 Cable Depot Rd, Riverside Ind Est, Clydebank G81 1UY
T: 0141 941 3689
F: 0141 952 8155
E: sales@expresselectrical.co.uk
W: www.expresselectrical.co.uk

Express Medicals Ltd
8, City Business Centre, Lower Rd, London SE16 2XB
T: 020 7394 1788
F: 020 7394 1614
E: info@expressmedicals.co.uk
W: www.expressmedicals.co.uk

Express Rail Alliance
W: www.expressrailalliance.com

Eye for Solutions
See EFS

Faber Maunsell
Enterprise House, 160 Croydon Rd, Beckenham, Kent BR3 4DE
T: 0870 905 0906
F: 020 8663 6723
E: malcolm.taylor@fabermaunsell.com
W: www.fabermaunsell.com

Factair Ltd
49 Boss Hall Rd, Ipswich, Suffolk IP1 5BN
T: 01473 746400
F: 01473 747123
E: enquiries@factair.co.uk
W: www.factair.co.uk

Faithful & Gould
Euston Tower, 286, Euston Rd, London NW1 3AT
T: 020 7121 2121
F: 020 7121 2020
E: info@fgould.com
W: www.fgould.com

Faiveley Transport Birkenhead
Morpeth Wharf, Twelve Quays, Birkenhead, Wirral CH41 1LW
T: 0151 649 5000
F: 0151 649 5001
E: Kevin.smith@faiveleytransport.com
W: www.faiveleytransport.com

Falcon Electrical Engineering Ltd
Falcon House, Main St, Fallin, Stirlingshire FK7 7HT
T: 01786 819920
F: 01786 814381
E: sales@falconelectrical.com
W: www.falconelectrical.com

Fantuzzi Noell (UK) Ltd
Units 3&4, Oldham West Business Centre, Watts Green, Chadderton, Manchester OL9 9LH
T: 0161 785 7870
F: 0161 670 6582
E: info@fantuzzi.co.uk
W: www.fantuzzi.co.uk

Fastrack (Expamet Security Products)
PO Box 14, Longhill Ind. Est.(North), Hartlepool TS25 1PR
T: 01429 867366
F: 01429 867355
E: michellet@exmesh.co.uk
W: www.expandedmetalfencing.com

Federal Mogul Friction Products (Ferodo)
Chapel-en-le-Frith, Derbys SK23 0JP
T: 01298 811689
F: 01298 811580
E: mark.doughty@federalmogul.com
W: www.federal.mogul.com

Fencing & Lighting Contractors Ltd
Unit 21, Amber Drive, Bailey Brook Ind Est, Langley Mill, Derbys NG16 4BE
T: 01773 531383
F: 01773 531921
E: info@fencingandlighting.co.uk

The Fenning Lovatt Partnership Ltd
Davina House, 137-149 Goswell Rd, London EC1V 7ET
T: 020 7251 6802
F: 020 7490 8127
E: ian@fenninglovatt.com
W: www.fenninglovatt.com

Ferrabyrne Ltd
Fort Rd Ind. Est, Littlehampton BN17 7QU
T: 01903 721317
F: 01903430452
E: sales@ferrabyrne.co.uk
W: www.ferrabyrne.co.uk

Ferrograph Ltd
Unit 1, New York Way, New York Ind Park, Newcastle Upon Tyne NE27 0QF
T: 0191 280 8800
F: 0191 280 8810
E: info@ferrograph.com
W: www.ferrograph.com

Fibergrate Composite Structures Ltd
Wass Way, Durham Lane Ind Park, Eaglescliffe, Stockton on Tees TS16 0RG
T: 01642 784747
F: 01642 784748
E: info@fibergrate.com
W: www.fibergrate.com

Fibreglass Grating Ltd
Unit 14, Telford Rd, Gorse Lane Ind. Est, Clacton on Sea, Essex CO15 4LP
T: 01255 423601
F: 01255 436428
E: info@fibreglassgrating.co.uk
W: www.fibreglassgrating.co.uk

Fifth Dimension Associates
Hamilton House, Mabledon Place, London WC1H 9BB
T: 020 7953 0250
E: london@fdal.co.uk
W: www.fdal.co.uk

Findlay Irvine Ltd
Bog Rd, Penicuik, Midlothian EH26 9BU
T: 01968 671200
F: 01968 671237
E: sales@findlayirvine.com
W: www.findlayirvine.com

Finning (UK) Ltd
Geldard Road, Gildersome, Morley, Leeds LS27 7JS
T: 0113 201 2064
F: 0113 238 1871
E: oillab@finning.co.uk
W: www.finning.co.uk

Fircroft
Trinity House, 114 Northenden Rd, Sale, Cheshire M33 3FZ
T: 0161 905 2020
F: 0161 969 1743
E: hq@fircroft.co.uk
W: www.fircroft.co.uk

First Capital Connect
Freepost RRBR-REEJ-KTKY, PO Box 443, Plymouth PL4 6WP
T: 0845 026 4700
F: 0845 676 9904
E: customer.relations.fcc@firstgroup.com
W: www.firstcapitalconnect.co.uk

First Choice Protection
See Portwest

First Class Partnerships provides strategic, commercial, operations, engineering and infrastructure rail consultancy and advice to leading rail companies, investors in rail, governments and regulators around the globe.
First Class Partnerships
148 Lawrence St, York, YO10 3EB
T: 01904 870792
F: 01904424499
E: info@firstclasspartnerships.com
W: www.firstclasspartnerships.com
fcp
First Class Partnerships
Rail Consultants

First Class Partnership
148 Lawrence St, York YO10 3EB
T: 01904 870792
F: 01904 424499
E: info@firstclasspartnerships.com
W: www.firstclasspartnerships.com

Firstco Ltd
4 Celbridge Mews, London W2 6EU
T: 020 7034 0833
F: 020 7229 8002
E: info@firstco.uk.com
W: www.firstco.uk.com

First Engineering Ltd
See Babcock Rail

First Great Western
Milford House, 1 Milford St, Swindon SN1 1HL
T: 08457 000125
E: fgwfeedback@firstgroup.com
W: www.firstgreatwestern.co.uk

First Group Plc
395 King St, Aberdeen AB24 5RP
T: 01224 650100
F: 01224 650140
W: www.firstgroup.com/corporate

First Procurement Associates (FPA Consulting)
1, St Andrews House, Vernon Gate, Derby DE1 1UJ
T: 01332 604321
F: 01332 604322
E: johnb@fpaconsulting.co.uk
W: www.fpaconsulting.co.uk

First Scotrail
Customer Relations, PO Box 7030, Fort William PH33 6WX
T: 0845 601 5929
E: scotrailcustomer.relations@firstgroup.com
W: www.firstgroup.com/scotrail

First Trans Pennine Express
Bridgewater House, 60 Whitworth St, Manchester M1 6LT
T: 08700 005 151
F: 0161 228 8120
E: tpecustomer.relations@firstgroup.com
W: www.tpexpress.co.uk

Fitzpatrick Contractors Ltd - Rail Division
19 St Christopher's Way, Patriot Way, Pride Park, Derby DE24 8JY
T: 01332 242270
F: 01332 367519
E: enquiries@fitzpatrick.co.uk
W: www.fitzpatrick.co.uk

FKI Switchgear
See Hawker Siddley

Flamboyant Trains
E: customer.relations@flamboyanttrains.co.uk
W: www.donnypsb.myby.co.uk/flamboyant

Flexible & Specialist (FS) Cables
Alban Point, Alban Park, Hatfield Rd, St Albans AL4 6JX
T: 01727 840841
F: 01727 840842
E: sales@fscables.com
W: www.fscables.com

Flexicon Ltd
Roman Way, Coleshill, Birmingham B46 1HG
T: 01675 466900
F: 01675 466901
E: steve.cheek@flexicon.uk.com
W: www.flexicon.uk.com

Flint Bishop Solicitors
St Michaels Court, St Michaels Lane, Derby DE1 3HQ
T: 01332 340211
E: info@flintbishop.co.uk
W: www.flintbishop.co.uk

Flir Systems Ltd (UK)
2 Kings Hill Ave, West Malling, Kent ME19 4AQ
T: 01732 220011
F: 01732 220014
E: sales@flir.uk.com
W: www.flir.uk.com

FLI Structures
Waterwells Drive, Waterwells Business Park, Gloucester GL2 2AA
T: 01452 722200
F: 01452 722244
E: j.johnson@fli.co.uk
W: www.fli.co.uk

Fluke UK Ltd (Tracklink)
52 Hurricane Way, Norwich NR6 6JB
T: 020 7942 0700
F: 020 7942 0701
E: industrial@uk.fluke.nl
W: www.fluke.co.uk

Foremost Rail
Kersey Hall, Tannery Rd, Combs, Stowmarket, Suffolk
T: 01449 742450
F: 01449 771207
E: info@foremostrail.com
W: www.foremostrail.com

ForgeTrack Ltd
Thistle House, St Andrew St, Hertford SG14 1JA
T: 01992 500900
F: 01992 589495
E: sales@forgetrack.co.uk
W: www.forgetrack.co.uk

Forward Chemicals Ltd
PO Box 12, Tanhouse Lane, Widnes, Cheshire WA8 0RD
T: 0151 422 1000
F: 0151 422 1011
E: salesandservice@forwardchem.com
W: www.forwardchem.com

Fourway Communications Ltd
Delamere Rd, Cheshunt, Herts EN8 9SH
T: 01992 629182
F: 01992 639227
E: enquiries@fourway.co.uk
W: www.fourway.co.uk

FPA Consulting Ltd
1 St Andrew's House, Vernon Gate, Derby DE1 1UJ
T: 01332 604321
F: 01332 604322
E: johnb@fpaconsulting.co.uk
W: www.fpaconsulting.co.uk

Franklin Andrews
Sea Containers House, 20 Upper Ground, London SE1 9LZ
T: 020 7633 9966
E: enquiries@franklinandrews.com
W: www.franklinandrews.com

Fraser Eagle Management
Pendle Court, 4 Mead Way, Shuttleworth Mead Bus. Park, Padiham, Lancs BB12 7NG
T: 08700 842710
F: 08700 842726
E: fems@frasereagle.com
W: www.frasereagle.com

Frazer Nash Consultancy Ltd
Stonebridge House, Dorking Business Park, Station Rd, Dorking, Surrey RH4 1JH
T: 01306 885050
F: 01306 886464
E: info@fnc.co.uk
W: www.fnc.co.uk

Freeman Williams
College Business Centre, Uttoxeter New Rd, Derby DE22 3WZ
T: 01332 869342
F: 01332 869344
E: abi@freemanwilliams.co.uk
W: www.freemanwillams.co.uk

Freeth Cartwright LLP
2nd Floor, West Point, Cardinal Square, 10 Nottingham Rd, Derby DE1 3QT
T: 01332 361000
F: 0845 634 9804
E: mike.copestake@freethcartwright.co.uk
W: www.fretthcartwright.co.uk

Freight Europe (UK) Ltd
Asra House, 4th Floor, 1 Long Lane, London SE1 4PG
T: 020 7939 1900
F: 020 7939 1901
E: info@freighteurope.co.uk
W: www.freighteurope.co.uk

Freightliner Group Ltd
3rd Floor, The Podium, 1 Eversholt St, London NW1 2FL
T: 020 7200 3900
F: 020 7200 3975
E: pressoffice@freightliner.co.uk
W: www.freightliner.co.uk

Fresh Approach Solutions Ltd
Ground Floor, Norfolk House, Smallbrook Queensway, Birmingham B5 4LJ
T: 0121 633 5035
F: 0871 431 6083
E: jbanks@freshapproachsolutions.com
W: www.freshapproachsolutions.com

Frequentis UK Ltd
Gainsborough Business Centre, 2 Sheen Rd, Richmond upon Thames TW9 1AE
T: 020 8973 2616
E: marketing@frequentis.com
W: www.frequentis.com

CB Frost & Co Ltd
Green St, Digbeth, Birmingham B12 0NE
T: 0121 773 8494
F: 0121 772 3584
E: info@cbfrost-rubber.com
W: www.cbfrost-rubber.com

FS Cables
See Flexible & Specialist

Fuchs Lubricants (UK) Plc
New Century St, Hanley, Stoke on Trent ST1 5HU
T: 08701 200400
F: 01782 202072
E: peter.baker@fuchs-oil.com
W: www.fuchslubricants.com

Fugro Aperio
Focal Point, Newmarket Rd, Bottisham, Cambridge CB5 9BD
T: 0870 600 8050
F: 0870 800 8040
E: rail@fugro-aperio.com
W: www.fugro-aperio.com

Funkwerk Information Technologies York Ltd
Jervaulx House, 6 St Mary's Court, Blossom St, York YO24 1AH
T: 01904 639091
F: 01904 639092
E: Richard.hammerton@funkwerk-it.com
W: www.funkwerk-it.com/fs_cms/en/index.html

Furneaux Riddall & Co Ltd
Alchorne Place, Portsmouth, Hants PO3 5PA
T: 02392 668624
F: 02392 668625
E: info@furneauxriddall.com
W: www.furneauxriddall.com

Furrer + Frey
Thunstrasse 35, PO Box 182, CH-3000 Berne 6, Switzerland
T: 0041 31357 6111
F: 0041 31357 6100
E: adm@furrerfrey.ch
W: www.furrerfrey.ch

Furtex
See Camira Fabrics

Fusion People Ltd
2nd/3rd Floor, Aldermary House, 10-15 Queen St, London EC4N 1TX
T: 020 7653 1070
F: 020 7653 1071
E: rail@fusionpeople.com
W: www.fusionpeople.com

Future Welding Ltd
Unit 1, Cinderhill Ind Est, Weston Coyney Rd, Stoke on Trent ST3 5LB
T: 01782 333555
F: 01782 333332
E: futurewelding@futurewelding.com
W: www.futurewelding.com

Gabriel & Co Ltd
Abro Works, 10 Hay Hall Rd, Tyseley, Birmingham B11 2AU
T: 0121 248 3333
F: 0121 248 3330
E: jan.price@gabrielco.com
W: www.gabrielco.com

GAI Tronics (Hubbel Ltd)
Brunel Dr., Stretton Business Park, Burton upon Trent DE13 0BZ
T: 01283 500500
F: 01283 500400
E: sales@gai-tronics.co.uk
W: www.gai-tronics.co.uk

Galliford Try Water and Rail
Crab Lane, Fearnhead, Warrington WA2 0XR
T: 01925 822821
F: 01925 812323
E: ron.stevenson@gallifordtry.co.uk
W: www.gallifordtry.co.uk

Gamble Rail
Meadow Rd Ind. Est., Worthing BN11 2RY
T: 01903 234727
F: 01903 820311
E: info@gamblegroup.co.uk
W: www.gamblegroup.co.uk

Ganymede Solutions Ltd
26 Hershel St, Slough SL1 1PA
T: 01753 820810
F: 0870 890 1894
E: gary.hewett@ganymedesolutions.co.uk
W: www.ganymedesolutions.co.uk

Gardiner & Theobald
32, Bedford Square, London WC1B 3JT
T: 020 7209 3000
F: 020 7209 3359
E: p.armstrong@gardiner.com
W: www.gardiner.com

Garrandale Group
Alfreton Rd, Derby DE21 4AP
T: 01332 291676
F: 01332 291677
E: sales@garrandale.co.uk
W: www.garrandale.co.uk

Gates Power Transmission
Tinwald Downs Rd, Heath Hall, Dumfries DG1 1TS
T: 01387 242000
F: 01387 242010
E: mediaeurope@gates.com
W: www.gates.com

Gatwick Express
52 Grosvenor Gardens, London SW1W 0AU
T: 020 7973 5000
F: 020 7973 5048
E: sales@airportexpressalliance.com
W: www.gatwickexpress.co.uk

Gatwick Plant Ltd
Woodside Works, The Close, Horley, Surrey RH6 9EB
T: 01293 824777
F: 01293 824077
E: transport@gatwickgroup.com
W: www.gatwickgroup.com

GB Railfreight Ltd
15-25 Artillery Lane, London E1 7HA
T: 020 7983 5177
F: 020 7983 5170
E: info@firstgroup.com
W: www.gbrailfreight.com

Geatech S.r.l
Via Del Plazzino 6/b, 40051 Altedo (BO) Italy
T: 0039 051 6601514
F: 0039 051 6601309
E: info@geatech.it
W: www.geatech.it

Geismar UK Ltd
Salthouse Rd, Brackmills Ind. Est., Northampton NN4 7EX
T: 01604 769191
F: 01604 763154
E: sales@geismar.co.uk
W: www.geismar.com

Directory

Geldards LLP
Number One, Pride Place, Pride Park, Derby DE24 8QR
T: 01332 331631
F: 01332 294295
E: roman.surma@geldards.co.uk
W: www.geldards.co.uk

Geodesign Barriers Ltd
3 Fore St, Topsham, Exeter EX3 0HF
T: 01392 876100
F: 01392 874407
E: britt.warg@palletbarrier.com
W: www.geodesignbarriers.com

Geoff Brown Signalling Ltd
The Cottage, Old Lodge, Minchinhampton, Stroud GL6 9AQ
T: 07977 265721
F: 01453 836754
E: geoffbrownsignalling@supanet.com

Geosynthetics Ltd
Fleming Rd, Harrowbrook Ind.Est., Hinckley, Leics LE10 3DU
T: 0870 850 1018
F: 0870 850 6572
E: sales@geosyn.co.uk
W: www.geosyn.co.uk

Geotechnical Engineering Ltd
Centurion House, Olympus Park, Quedgeley, Glos GL2 4NF
T: 01452 527743
E: geotech@geoeng.co.uk
W: www.geoeng.co.uk

GE Transportation Systems
Inspira House, Martinfield, Welwyn Garden City, Herts AL7 1GW
T: 01707 383700
F: 01707 383701
E: jon.raymond@ge.com
W: www.getransportation.com

Getzner Werkstoffe GmbH
Herrenaus, A-6706 Burs, Austria
T: 0043 5552 2010
F: 0043 5552 201899
E: sylomer@getzner.at
W: www.getzner.at

GGB UK
Wellington House, Starley Way, Birmingham Int. Park, Birmingham B37 7HB
T: 0845 230 0442
F: 0121 781 7313
W: greatbritain@ggbearings.com

GGS Engineering (Derby) ltd
Atlas Works, Litchurch Lane, Derby DE24 8AQ
T: 01332 299345
F: 01332 299678
E: enquiries@ggseng.com
W: www.ggseng.com

Gifford
Carlton House, Ringwood Rd, Woodlands, Southampton SO40 7HT
T: 02380 817500
F: 02380 817600
E: info@gifford.uk.com
W: www.gifford.uk.com

Giken Europe BV
Room 302, Burnhill Bus. Centre, Kingfisher House, Elmfield Rd, Bromley, Kent BR1 1LT
T: 0845 260 8001
F: 0845 260 8002
E: info@giken.co.uk
W: www.giken.com

Gilbarco Veeder-Root
Crompton Close, Basildon, Essex SS14 3BA
T: 0870 010 1136
F: 0870 010 1137
E: uksales@gilbarco.com
W: www.gilbarco.com

Glenair UK Ltd
40 Lower Oakham Way, Oakham Business Park, Mansfield, Notts NG18 5BY
T: 01623 638100
F: 01623 638111
E: cbaker@glenair.com
W: www.glenair.com

Global Crossing (UK) Telecommunications Ltd
1 London Bridge, 4th Floor, London SE1 9BG
T: 020 7904 2607
E: chris.dawes@globalcrossing.com
W: www.globalcrossing.com

Globalforce UK Ltd
The Willows, College Avenue, Grays, Essex RM17 5UN
T: 01375 380629
F: 01375 381995
E: graham@globalforceuk.co.uk
W: www.globalforceuk.co.uk

Global House Training Services Ltd
35a Astbury Rd, London SE15 2NL
T: 020 7639 3322
E: contact@globalhousegroup.com
W: www.globalhouse.co.uk

Global Rail Support
8 Curzon Lane, Alvaston, Derby DE24 8QS
T: 01332 601596
F: 01332 727494
E: ask@globalrailsupport.com
W: www.globalrailsupport.com

GME Springs
Boston Lpace, Foleshill, Coventry CV6 5NN
T: 02476 664911
F: 02476 663020
E: sales@gmesprings.co.uk
W: www.gmesprings.co.uk

GMPTE
2 Piccadilly Place, Manchester M1 3BG
T: 0871 200 2233
E: publicity@gmpte.gov.uk
W: www.gmpte.com

GM Rail Services Ltd
65 Somers Rd, Rugby, Warks CV22 7DG
T: 01788 573777
F: 01788 551138
E: info@gmrail.co.uk
W: www.gmrail.co.uk

GMT Manufacturing Ltd
Old Gorsey Lane, Wallasey CH44 4AH
T: 0151 630 1545
F: 0151 630 8555
E: sales@gmtman.co.uk
W: www.gmt.co.uk

GMT Rubber-Metal-Technic Ltd
The Sidings, Station Rd, Guiseley, Leeds LS20 8BX
T: 01943 870670
F: 01943 870631
E: sales@gmt.gb.com
W: www.gmt-gb.com

Goldline Bearings Ltd
Stafford Park 17, Telford, Shropshire TF3 3DG
T: 01952 292401
F: 01952 292403
E: alanhancock@goldlinebearings.co.uk
W: www.goldlinebearings.com

Gordon Services Ltd
Unit 8, Daws Farm, Ivy Barn Lane, Ingatestone, Essex CM4 0PX
T: 01277 352895
F: 01277 356115
E: enquiries@gordonservicesltd.co.uk
W: www.gordonservicesltd.co.uk

Goskills
Concorde House, Trinity Park, Solihull, West Midlands B37 7UQ
T: 0121 635 5520
F: 0121 635 5521
E: info@goskills.org
W: www.goskills.org

Go-Tel Communications Ltd
See Samsung Electronics

Govia
Go-ahead Group Rail, Go-ahead House, 26-28 Addiscombe Rd, Croydon, Surrey CR9 5GA
E: contact@go-ahead-rail.com
W: www.govia.info

Grammer Seating Systems Ltd
Willenhall Lane Ind. Est., Bloxwich, Walsall WS3 2XN
T: 01922 407035
F: 01922 710552
E: david.bignell@grammer.com
W: www.grammer.com

Gramm Interlink
17-19 High St, Ditchling, East Sussex BN6 8SY
T: 07827 947086
F: 01275 846397
E: enquiries@gramminterlinkrail.co.uk
W: www.gramminerlinkrail.co.uk

Gramos Applied Ltd
Spring Rd, Smethwick, West Midlands B66 1PT
T: 0121 525 4000
F: 0121 525 4950
E: info@gramos-applied.com
W: www.gramos-applied.com

Grampian Railtours
T: 01358 789513
E: info@caledonian-heritage-tours.co.uk
W: www.caledonian-heritage-tours.co.uk

Grand Central Railway Co. Ltd.
River House, 17 Museum Street York YO1 7DJ
T: 01904 633307
F: 01904 466066
E: info@grandcentralrail.com
W: www.grandcentralrail.co.uk

Grand Union Railway Company Ltd
River House, 17 Museum St, York YO1 7DJ
T: 01904 633307
F: 01904 466066
E: info@grandcentralrail.com
W: www.grandcentralrail.com/grand_central

Grant Rail Group
Carolina Court, Lakeside, Doncaster DN4 5RA
T: 01302 791100
F: 01302 791200
E: marketing@grantrail.co.uk
W: www.grantrail.co.uk

Graybar Ltd
10 Fleming Close, Park Farm Ind. Est, Wellingborough, Northants NN8 6QF
T: 01933 676700
F: 01933 676800
E: sales@graybar.co.uk
W: www.graybar.co.uk

Greenleader Ltd
21 Foxmoor Close, Oakley, Basingstoke, Hants RG23 7BQ
T: 01256 781739
E: enquiries@greenleader.co.uk
W: www.greenleader.co.uk

Greenbrier Europe/ Wagony Swidnica SA
Ul Strzelinska 35, 58-199 Swidnica, Poland
T: 0048 74 856 2000
F: 0048 74 856 2035
E: europeansales@gbrx.com
W: www.gbrx.com

Green Express Railtours
66 Stoneygate, Hunmanby, Filey YO14 0PP
T: 01723 891400
E: info@greenexpressrailtours.co.uk
W: www.greenexpressrailtours.co.uk

GreenMech Ltd
Mill Ind. Park, Kings Coughton, Alcester, Warks B49 5QG
T: 01789 400044
F: 01789 400167
E: sales@greenmech.co.uk
W: www.greenmech.co.uk

Groundwise Searches Ltd
Suite 8, Chichester House, 45 Chichester Rd, Southend on Sea SS1 2JU
T: 01702 615566
F: 01702 460239
E: mail@groundwise.com
W: www.groundwise.com

Gunnebo UK Ltd
PO Box 61, Woden Rd, Wolverhampton WV10 0BY
T: 01902 455111
F: 01902 351961
E: marketing@gunnebo.com
W: www.gunnebo.com

Hadleigh Castings Ltd
Pond Hall Rd, Hadleigh, Ipswich, Suffolk IP7 5PW
T: 01473 827281
F: 01473 827879
E: RFQ: nm@hadleighcastings.com
E: Cad: data@hadleighcastings.com
W: www.hadleighcastings.com

Hako Machines Ltd
Eldon Close, Crick, Northants NN6 7SL
T: 01788 825600
F: 01788 823969
E: sales@hako.co.uk
W: www.hako.co.uk

Halcrow
Excellence in Rail Engineering
- Turnkey Project Management Services in Traction and Rolling Stock
- Rail Commercial
- Rail Approvals
- Operations Planning
- Electrification

Halcrow Group Ltd
44 Brook Green
Hammersmith
London
W6 7BY
T: 01332 222620
E: hansonc@halcrow.com
W: www.halcrow.com

Sustaining and improving the quality of people's lives

Halcrow Group Ltd
44 Brook Green, London W6 7BY
T: 01332 222620
E: hansonc@halcrow.com
W: www.halcrow.com

Halfen Ltd
Humphrys Rd, Woodside Est., Dunstable, Beds LU5 4TP
T: 0870 531 6300
F: 0870 531 6304
E: info@halfen.co.uk
W: www.halfen.co.uk

HALO RAIL
Livery Solutions
Tel: 023 8024 0777
www.HaloRail.com

KJ Hall
30 Church Rd, Highbridge, Somerset TA9 3RN
T: 01278 794600
F: 01278 785562
E: admin@kjhsurvey.co.uk
W: www.kjhsurvey.co.uk

Hallrail Ltd
Lyons Ind Est, Hetton le Hole, Tyne & Wear DH5 0RF
T: 0191 526 2114
F: 0191 517 0112
E: enquiries@hallrail.co.uk
W: www.hallrail.co.uk

Halo Rail
Trafalgar Close, Chandlers Ford Ind. Est, Eastleigh, Hants SO53 4BW
T: 023 8024 0777
F: 023 8025 5620
E: paul.mcglone@halorail.com
W: www.halorail.com

Harmill Systems Ltd
Harmill Ind. Est., Grovebury Rd, Leighton Buzzard, Beds LU7 4FF
T: 01525 851133
F: 01525 851531
E: sales@harmill.co.uk
W: www.harmill.co.uk

Harp Visual Communications Solutions
Unit 7, Swanwick Business Centre, Bridge Rd, Lower Swanwick, Southampton SO31 7GB
T: 01489 580011
F: 01489 580022
E: sales@harpvisual.co.uk
W: www.passengerinformation.com

Harrington Generators International
Ravenstor Rd, Wirksworth, Matlock, Derbys DE4 4FY
T: 01629 824284
F: 01629 824613
E: sales@harringtongen.co.uk
W: www.harrington-international.co.uk

E C Harris
Lynton House, 7-12 Tavistock Square, London WC1H 9LX
T: 020 7387 8431
F: 020 7380 0493
E: information@echarris.com
W: www.echarris.com

Harry Fairclough Construction
Howley Lane, Howley, Warrington WA1 2JT
T: 01925 628300
F: 01925 628301
E: post@harryfairclough.co.uk
W: www.harryfairclough.co.uk

Harry Needle
PO Box 60, St Helens WA11 8GD
T: 01744 883141
F: 01744 883665
E: harrycneedle@aol.com

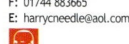

Harsco Track Technologies
Harsco House, Regent Park, 299 Kingston Rd, Leatherhead, Surrey KT22 7SG
T: 01372 381400
F: 01372 381420
E: httuk@harscotrack.com
W: www.permaquip.com

Harting Limited
Caswell Rd, Brackmills Ind. Est, Northampton NN4 7PW
T: 01604 827500
F: 01604 706777
E: gb@harting.com
W: www.harting.com

The Haste Partnership
10 The Croft, Sheriff Hutton, York YO60 6SQ
T: 01347 878034
F: 01347 878034
E: richardhaste@aol.com

Hawart UK
Hawart GmbH, Handweksweg 8, 2777 Ganderskesse, Germany
T: 01854 622321
E: billhilton@achiltibuie.fsnet.co.uk
W: www.hawart.com

Hawker Siddley Switchgear Ltd
Newport Rd, Blackwood, S.Wales NP12 2XH
T: 01495 223001
F: 01495 225674
E: sales@hss-ltd.com
W: www.hss-ltd.com

Hawkgrove Ltd
2 The Business Courtyard, Trudoxhill, Somerset BA11 5DL
T: 01373 837900
F: 08700 518155
E: info@hawkgrove.co.uk
W: www.hawkgrove.co.uk

Hayley Rail
48-50 Westbrook Rd, Trafford Park, Manchester M17 1AY
T: 0161 877 3005
F: 0161 755 3425
E: phil.mccabe@hayley-group.co.uk
W: www.hayley-group.co.uk

John Headon Ltd
6 Holland Rd, Bramhall, Stockport, Cheshire SK7 2PQ
T: 0161 439 8557
E: info@johnheadonltd.co.uk
W: www.johnheadonltd.co.uk

Health, Safety & Engineering Consultants Ltd (HSEC)
70 Tamworth Rd, Ashby de La Zouch, Leics LE65 2PR
T: 01530 412777
F: 01530 415592
E: hsec@hsec.co.uk
W: www.hsec.co.uk

Heath Lambert Group
Transportation Division, 133 Houndsditch, London EC3A 7AW
T: 020 7560 3819
F: 020 7560 3294
E: mhawkes@heathlambert.com
W: www.heathlambert.com/projects

Heathrow Connect
50 Eastbourne Terrace, Paddington, London W2 6LX
T: 020 8750 6600
E: andrew_mcconnell@airportexpressalliance.com
W: www.heathrowconnect.com

Heathrow Express
50 Eastbourne Terrace, Paddington, London W2 6LX
T: 020 8750 6600
E: andrew_mcconnell@airportexpressalliance.com
W: www.heathrowexpress.com

Heavy Haul Power Ltd
Fore St, Castle Cary, Somerset BA7 7BG
T: 01963 350101
E: richard.painter@hhpi.org
W: www.hhpi.org

Hedra
See Mouchel

Hegenscheidt MFD GmbH & CO KG
Hegenscheidt Platz, D-41812 Erkelenz, Germany
T: 0049 2431 86279
F: 0049 2431 86480
E: k.panek@de.heg.nshgroup.com
W: www.hegenscheidt-mfd.de

Hellermann Tyton
Wharf Approach, Aldridge, Walsall WS9 8BX
T: 01922 458151
F: 01922 743053
W: www.hellermanntyton.co.uk

Henkel Loctite
Technologies House, Wood Lane End, Hemel Hempstead, Herts HP2 4RQ
T: 01442 278100
F: 01442 278293
E: keely.tate@uk-henkel.com
W: www.loctite.com

Henry Williams Ltd
Dodsworth St, Darlington, Co. Durham DL1 2NJ
T: 01325 462722
F: 01325 245220
E: info@hwilliams.co.uk
W: www.hwilliams.co.uk

Hepworth Rail International
4 Merse Rd, North Moons Moat, Redditch, Worcs B98 9HL
T: 01527 60146
F: 01527 66836
E: markjones@b-hepworth.com
W: www.b-hepworth.com

Hertford Controls Ltd
14 Ermine Point, Gentlemens Field, Westmill Rd, Ware, Herts SG12 0EF
T: 01920 467578
F: 01920 487037
E: info@hertfordcontrols.co.uk
W: www.hertfordcontrols.co.uk

Hexagon Metrology Ltd
Halesfield 13, Telford, Shropshire TF7 4PL
T: 01908 246252
F: 0870 446 2668
E: enquiry.uk@hexagonmetrology.com
W: www.hexagonmetrology.com/uk

Hiflex Fluidpower
Howley Park Rd, Morley, Leeds LS27 0BN
T: 0113 281 0031
F: 0113 307 5918
E: sales@hiflex-europe.com
W: www.dunlophiflex.com

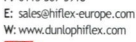

The Highgate Partnership
Joel House, 19 Garrick St, London WC2E 9AX
T: 020 7010 7750
F: 020 7010 7751
E: lucy@highgatepartners.com
W: www.highgatepartners.com

High Point Rendel
61 Southwark St, London SE1 1SA
T: 020 7654 0400
F: 020 7654 0401
E: j.zeffert@highpointrendel.com
W: www.highpointrendel.com

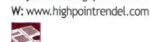

High Speed 1
73 Collier St, London N1 9BE
T: 020 7014 2700
W: www.highspeed1.com

Hill Cannon (UK) LLP
Royal Chambers, Station Parade, Harrogate HG1 1EP
T: 01423 562571
F: 01423 530018
E: harrogate@hillcannon.com
W: www.hillcannon.com

Hillfort Communications Ltd
3 Campion Way, Lymington, Hants SO41 9LS
T: 01590 670912
F: 01590 688341
E: hillfort@doc2prod.demon.co.uk

Hill McGlynn
Prospect House, Meridians Cross, Ocean Way, Ocean Village, Southampton SO14 3TJ
T: 02380 221177
F: 02380 221133
W: www.hillmcglynn.com

Hilti (GB) Ltd
1 Trafford Wharf Rd, Trafford Park, Manchester M17 1BY
T: 0800 886 100
F: 0800 886 200
E: gbsales@hilti.com
W: www.hilti.co.uk

HSBC

In association with railalliance

HIMA-SELLA
SAFETY CONTROL & AUTOMATION SYSTEMS

Hima-Sella has over 30 years experience in providing innovative, cost-effective and reliable safety, control and automation systems to the rail industry, including -

Train Control • CIS • PIS
GSM-R • SCADA • CCTV
Selective Door Opening (SDO)
Sensors • Displays • Loggers

Link-Up ID 3633

Hima-Sella Ltd
Carrington Field Street
Stockport Cheshire SK1 3JN
Tel +44 (0)161 429 4500
Fax +44 (0)161 476 3095
Web www.hima-sella.co.uk
Email sales@hima-sella.co.uk

your safety... our future

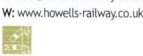

HSBC Rail (UK) Limited provides a comprehensive range of services including asset finance and related services that are geared to the changing needs of the railway industry.

A: PO Box 29499,
1 Eversholt Street,
London, NW1 2ZF

T: 020 7380 5040
F: 020 7380 5148

E: wendyfiler@hsbc.com

HSBC

Hima-Sella Ltd
Carrington Field St,
Stockport SK1 3JN
T: 0161 429 4500
F: 0161 476 3095
E: sales@hima-sella.co.uk
W: www.hima-sella.co.uk

Hiremasters
Imperial House, 1 Factory Rd,
Silvertown, London E16 2EL
T: 020 7473 2712
F: 020 7476 2713
E: hire@hiremasters.co.uk
W: www.hiremasters.co.uk

Hiremee Ltd
York Way, Royston, Herts SG8 5HJ
T: 01763 247111
F: 01763 247222
E: warren@hiremee.co.uk
W: www.hiremee.co.uk

Holdfast Level Crossings Ltd
Brockenhurst, Cheap St,
Chedworth, Cheltenham,
Glos GL54 4AA
T: 01242 578801
F: 01285 720748
E: request@railcrossings.co.uk
W: www.railcrossings.co.uk

Holdsworth
See Camira

Holland Company
1000 Holland Drive, Crete,
Illinois 60417 USA
T: 001 708 672 2300
F: 001 708 672 2417
E: cewing@hollandco.com
W: www.hollandco.com

Hitachi is railway system supplier including rolling stock, signalling systems, maintenance and turnkey projects. Hitachi is delivering Class 395 High Speed trains.

16 Upper Woburn Place
London WC1H 0AF

Tel: 0207 970 2700
Fax: 0207 970 2799

hirofumi.ojima@hitachi-eu.com
www.hitachi-rail.com

HITACHI
Inspire the Next

Hitachi Europe Ltd - Rail Group
4th Floor, 16 Upper Woburn Place,
London WC1H 0AF
T: 020 7970 2700
F: 020 7970 2799
E: Hirofumi.ojima@hitachi-eu.com
W: www.hitachi-rail.com

HOCHTIEF (UK) Construction Ltd
Epsilon, Windmill Hill Business
Park, Whitehill Way,
Swindon SN5 6NX
T: 01793 755555
F: 01793 755556
E: enquiries@hochtief.co.uk
W: www.hochtief.co.uk

Hodge Clemco Ltd
Orgreave Drive, Sheffield S13 9NR
T: 0114 254 8811
F: 0114 254 0250
E: sales@hodgeclemco.co.uk
W: www.hdgeclemco.co.uk

M Holleran Ltd
23-27 Goodwood Rd, New Cross,
London SE14 6BL
T: 020 8692 4442
F: 020 8691 5160
E: steve.webber@holleran.co.uk
W: www.holleran.co.uk

Hosiden Besson Ltd
11 St Josephs Close, Hove,
East Sussex BN3 7EZ
T: 01273 861166
F: 01273 777501
E: info@hbl.co.uk
W: www.hbl.co.uk

Howells Railway Products Ltd
Longley Lane, Sharston Ind. Est.,
Wythenshawe, Manchester
M22 4SS
T: 0161 945 5567
F: 0161 945 5597
E: info@howells-railway.co.uk
W: www.howells-railway.co.uk

HSBC Rail (UK)
PO Box 29499, 1 Eversholt St,
London NW1 2ZF
T: 020 7380 5040
F: 020 7380 5148
E: wendyfiler@hsbc.com

Huber + Suhner (UK) Ltd
Telford Rd, Bicester,
Oxon OX26 4LA
T: 01869 364101
F: 01869 249046
E: info.uk@hubersuhner.com
W: www.hubersuhner.co.uk

Hull Trains
Europa House, 184 Ferensway,
Hull HU1 3UT
T: 01482 215746
E: customer.services@hulltrains.co.uk
W: www.hulltrains.co.uk

Human Engineering Ltd
Shore House, 68, Westbury Hill,
Westbury-on -Trym, Bristol
BS9 3AA
T: 0117 962 0888
F: 0117 962 9888
E: barry.davies@humaneng.co.uk
W: www.humaneng.net

Human Reliability
1 School House, Higher Lane,
Dalton, Lancs WN8 7RP
T: 01257 463121
F: 01257 463810
E: stevecross@humanreliability.com
W: www.humanreliability.com

Hunslet Barclay
See Brush Barclay

Hunslet Engine Co
See LH Group Services

Husqvarna Construction Products
Unit 1, Millennium Way, Park 2000,
Westland Rd, Leeds LS11 5AL
T: 0870 850 1394
F: 0113 395 6851
W: www.husqvarna.co.uk

Hutchinson Team Telecom Ltd
Field House, Uttoxeter Old Rd,
Derby DE1 1NH
T: 0845 121 8326
F: 0845 126 8326
E: info@httltd.com
W: www.teamtele.com

Hyder Consulting (UK) Ltd
29 Bressenden Place, Victoria,
London SW1E 5DZ
T: 0870 000 3006
F: 0870 000 3908
E: mahmoud.alghita@hyderconsulting.com
W: www.hyderconsulting.com

Hydrex Equipment UK Ltd
Hydrex House, Serbert Way,
Portishead, Bristol BS20 7GD
T: 01275 399400
F: 01275 399500
E: alec.davis@hydrex.co.uk
W: www.hydrex.co.uk

Hydro Aluminium Extrusions Ltd
Pantglas Ind. Est., Bedwas,
Caerphilly CF83 8DR
T: 0870 777 2262
F: 02920 863728
E: sales.haeuk@hydro.com
W: www.hydro.com/extrusion/uk

Hydrotech Europe Ltd
Beaufort Court, 11 Roebuck Way,
Knowlhill, Milton Keynes MK5 8HL
T: 01908 675244
F: 01908 397513
E: Celina.lyn@hydro-usl.com
W: www.hydro-usl.com

Hydrotechnik UK Ltd
Unit 10, Easter Lane, Lenton,
Nottingham NG7 2PX
T: 01159 003550
F: 01159 705597
E: sales@hydrotechnik.co.uk
W: www.hydrotechnik.co.uk

Hypertac UK
36-38 Waterloo Rd,
London NW2 7UH
T: 020 8450 8033
F: 020 8208 3455
E: info@hypertac.co.uk
W: www.hypertac.co.uk

IAD Rail Systems
63-64 Gazelle Rd, Weston Super
Mare, Somerset BS24 9ES
T: 01934 427000
F: 01934 427020
E: mick.ledger@iadrailsystems.com
W: www.iadrailsystems.com

Ian Catling Consultancy
Ash Meadow, Bridge Way,
Chipstead CR5 3PX
T: 01737 552225
F: 01737 556669
E: info@catling.com
W: www.catling.com

Ian Riley
See Riley & Son

I C Consultants Ltd
47 Prince's Gate, Exhibition Rd,
London SW7 2QA
T: 020 7594 6565
F: 020 7594 6570
E: consultants@imperial.ac.uk
W: www.imperial-consultants.co.uk

Icomera UK
1092 Galley Drive, Kent Science
Park, Sittingbourne, Kent ME9 8GA
T: 01884 860 799
E: information@icomera.com
W: www.icomera.com

Icon Silentbloc UK Ltd
Wellington Rd, Burton upon Trent,
Staffs DE14 2AP
T: 01283 741700
F: 01283 741742
E: info@iconpolymer.com
W: www.iconpolymer.com

Icore International Ltd
220 Bedford Ave, Slough,
Bucks SL1 4RY
T: 01753 896600
F: 01753 896601
E: salesdept@icore.zodiac.com
W: www.icoregroup.com

ID Computing Ltd
73 Montague way, Chellaston,
Derby DE73 5AJ
E: info@idcomputing.co.uk
W: www.idcomputing.co.uk

IETG Ltd
Cross Green Way, Cross Green Ind.
Est., Leeds LS9 0SE
T: 0113 201 9700
F: 0113 201 9701
W: www.ietg.co.uk

Inbis Ltd
Club St, Bamber Bridge,
Preston, Lancs PR5 6FN
T: 01772 645000
F: 01772 645001
W: www.inbis.com

Inchmere Design
Inchmere Studios, Grange Park,
Chacombe, Banbury, Oxon
OX17 2EL
T: 01295 711801
E: mark@inchmere.co.uk
W: www.inchmere.co.uk

Independent Glass Co Ltd
540-550 Lawmoor St, Dixons Blazes
Ind. Est, Glasgow G5 0UA
T: 0141 429 8700
F: 0141 429 8524
E: toughened@ig-glass.co.uk
W: www.independentglass.co.uk

Independent Rail Consultancy Group (IRCG)
E: info@ircg.co.uk
W: www.ircg.co.uk

Industrial Flow Control Ltd
Unit 1, Askews Farm Lane,
Grays, Essex RM17 5XR
T: 01375 387155
F: 01375 387420
E: sales@inflow.co.uk
W: www.inflow.co.uk

Inflow
See Industrial Flow Control Ltd

Infodev
1995 Rue Frank-Carrel, Suite 202,
Quebec G1R 5AY Canada
T: 001 418 681 3529
F: 001 418 681 1209
E: info@infodev.ca
W: www.infodev.ca

Infor
Infor House, 1 Lakeside Rd,
Farnborough, Hants GU14 6XP
T: 01252 356000
E: ukmarketing@infor.com
W: www.hansen.com

Informatiq
Gresham House, 53 Clarendon Rd,
Watford WD17 1LA
T: 01923 224481
F: 01923 224493
E: permanent@informatiq.co.uk
W: www.informatiq.co.uk

Infotec Ltd
The Maltings, Tamworth Rd, Ashby
De La Zouch, Leics LE65 2PS
T: 01530 560600
F: 01530 560111
E: sales@infotec.co.uk
W: www.infotec.co.uk

Infra Safety Services
6 Cotton Brook Rd, off Shaftesbury
St, Sir Francis Ley Ind. Park South,
Derby DE23 8YJ
T: 01332 542800
F: 01332 542829
E: m.forrest@infrasafetyservices.co.uk
W: www.infrasafetyservices.co.uk

Initial Transport Services
4th Floor, Alexander House, 94/96
Talbot Rd, Old Trafford,
Manchester M16 0PG
T: 0161 868 6200
F: 0161 898 6280
E: contactus@ri-facilities.co.uk
W: www.initial.co.uk

Inline Track Welding Ltd
Ashmill Business Park, Ashford Rd,
Lenham, Maidstone ME17 2GQ
T: 01622 854730
F: 01622 854731
E: david.thomson@fsmail.net

Innotrans
Messe Berlin GmbH, Messedamm
22, D-14055 Berlin, Germany
0049 303038 0
T: 0049 303038 2190
E: innotrans@messe-berlin.de
W: www1.messe-berlin.de

Insituform Technologies Ltd
Roundwood Ind. Est., Ossett,
West Yorks WF5 9SQ
T: 01924 277076
F: 01924 265107
E: jbeech@insituform.com
W: www.insituform.co.uk

Installation Project Services
53 Ullswater Cres., Coulsdon,
Surrey CR5 2HR
T: 020 8655 6060
F: 020 8655 6070
E: sales@ips-ltd.co.uk
W: www.ips-ltd.co.uk

Institute of Rail Welding
Granta Park, Great Abingdon,
Cambridge CB1 6AL
T: 01223 899000
F: 01223 894219
E: twi@twi.co.uk
W: www.twi.co.uk

Institution of Civil Engineers (ICE)
One Great George St, Westminster,
London SW1P 3AA
T: 020 7222 7722
E: communications@ice.org.uk
W: www.ice.org.uk

Institution of Engineering & Technology
Michael Faraday House, Six Hills
Way, Stevenage SG1 2AY
T: 01438 767359
F: 01438 767305
E: ccrump@theiet.org
W: www.theiet.org

Institution of Mechanical Engineers (I Mech E)
1 Birdcage Walk, Westminster,
London SW1H 9JJ
T: 020 7222 7899
F: 020 7222 4557
E: railway@imeche.org.uk
W: www.imeche.org.uk

Institution of Railway Operators
PO Box 128, Burgess Hill,
West Sussex RH15 0UZ
T: 01444 248931
F: 01444 246392
E: admin@railwayoperators.org
W: www.railwayoperators.org

Institution of Railway Signal Engineers (IRSE)
4th Floor, 1 Birdcage Walk,
Westminster, London SW1H 9JJ
T: 020 7808 1180
F: 020 7808 1196
E: hq@irse.org
W: www.irse.org

Intec (UK) Ltd
York House, 76-78 Lancaster Rd,
Morecambe, Lancs LA4 5QN
T: 01524 426777
F: 01524 426888
E: intec@inteconline.co.uk
W: www.inteconline.co.uk

Integrated Transport Planning Ltd
50 North Thirtieth St,
Milton Keynes MK9 3PP
T: 01908 259718
F: 01908 605747
E: wheway@itpworld.net
W: www.itpworld.net

Integrated Utility Services
16 Toft Green, York YO1 6JT
T: 01904 685678
E: railenquiries@ius.biz
W: www.ius.biz

Intelligent Locking Systems
Bordesley Hall, Alvechurch,
Birmingham B48 7QA
T: 01527 68885
F: 01527 66681
E: info@ilslocks.co.uk
W: www.ilslocks.co.uk

Interfleet Technology

Interfleet provides consulting services across the railway system, working throughout the asset lifecycle. Our services range from Strategy & Policy advice through to engineering & technology services.

Interfleet House, Pride Parkway, Derby, DE24 8HX

Tel: 01332 223000
Fax: 01332 223001

info@interfleet.co.uk

www.interfleet-technology.com

Interfleet Technology Ltd
Interfleet House,
Pride Parkway,
Derby DE24 8HX
T: 01332 223 000
F: 01332 223 001
E: info@interfleet.co.uk
W: www.interfleet.co.uk

Intermodality LLP
6 Belmont Business Centre,
East Hoathly, Lewes,
East Sussex BN8 6QL
T: 0845 130 4388
F: 01825 841049
E: info@intermodality.com
W: www.intermodality.com

Intermodal Logistics
The Old Brewery House, 74 High
St, Marlow, Bucks SL7 1AH
T: 01234 822821
F: 01628 486800
E: derekbliss@intermodallogistics.co.uk
W: www.intermodallogistics.co.uk

Intertrain (UK) Ltd
Intertrain House, Union St,
Doncaster DN1 3AE
T: 01302 815530
F: 01302 815531
E: intertraininfo@intertrain.biz
W: www.intertrain.biz

Invensys Rail Systems
See Westinghouse

Ionbond Ltd
Unit 36, Number One Ind Est,
Medomsley Rd, Consett DH7 6TS
T: 01207 500823
F: 01207 590254
E: maria.beadle@ionbond.com
W: www.ionbond.com

Iosis
34 Strathmore Rd, Bristol BS7 9QT
T: 0117 951 4755
E: info@iosis.co.uk
W: www.iosis.co.uk

IQPC
Anchor House, 15-19 Bitten St,
London SW3 3QL
T: 020 7368 2363
F: 020 7368 9301
E: enquire@iqpc.co.uk
W: www.iqpc.co.uk

Irish Traction Group
31 Hayfield Rd, Bredbury,
Stockport SK6 1DE
T: 07713 159869
E: info@irishtractiongroup.com
W: www.irishtractiongroup.com

IRL Group Ltd
Unit C1, Swingbridge Rd,
Loughborough, Leics LE11 5JD
T: 01509 217101
F: 01509 611004
E: info@irlgroup.com
W: www.irlgroup.com

Ischebeck Titan
John Dean House, Wellington Rd,
Burton upon Trent DE14 2TG
T: 01283 515677
F: 01283 516126
E: sales@ischebeck-titan.co.uk
W: www.ischebeck-titan.co.uk

IS-Rayfast Ltd
Unit 2, Westmead,
Swindon SN5 7SY
T: 01793 616700
F: 01793 644304
E: sales@israyfast.com
W: www.israyfast.com

Directory

ITSO Ltd
4th Floor, Quayside Tower, 252-260 Broad St, Birmingham B1 2HF
T: 0121 634 3700
F: 0121 634 3737
E: info@itso.org.uk
W: www.itso.org.uk

ITT Flygt Ltd
Colwick, Nottingham NG4 2AN
T: 0115 940 0111
F: 0115 940 0444
E: sales@flygt.com
W: www.flygt.co.uk

Jacksons Security Fencing
54 Stowting Common, Ashford, Kent TN25 6BN
T: 01233 750393
F: 01233 750403
E: security@jacksons-fencing.co.uk
W: www.jacksons-fencing.co.uk

Jacobs Consultancy UK Ltd
16 Connaught Place, London W2 2ES
T: 020 7087 8700
F: 020 7706 7147
E: jacobsconsultancy.transport@jacobs.com
W: www.jacobsconsultancy.co.uk

JACOBS Consultancy
Experience That Matters

Jacobs Consultancy has worked extensively on rail franchise transactions, service specification, and planning studies for public and private sector clients.

We have expertise in strategy, operations, commercial planning and economic advice provision within the UK rail industry.

David Bradshaw
Director Rail
E: david.bradshaw@jacobs.com
Tel: +44 (0)20 7087 8744

Jacobs UK Ltd
95 Bothwell St, Glasgow G2 7HX
T: 0141 204 2511
F: 0141 226 3109
E: katie.watson@jacobs.com
W: www.jacobsbabtie.com

Jafco Tools Ltd
Access House, Great Western St, Wednesbury, West Midlands WS10 7LE
T: 0121 556 7700
F: 0121 556 7788
E: info@jafcotools.com
W: www.jafcotools.com

Jarvis Rail and Fastline Ltd
Meridian House, The Crescent, York YO24 1AW
T: 01904 712712
F: 01904 697532
E: enquiries@jarvisrail.com
info@fastline-group.com
W: www.fastline-group.com

JCB
World Headquarters, Rocester, Staffs ST14 5JP
T: 0'889 590312
F: 0'889 593455
W: www.jcb.co.uk

Jefferson Sheard Architects
Fulcrum, 2 Sidney St, Sheffield S1 4RH
T: 0'14 276 1651
F: 0'14 279 9191
E: philippa.debono@jeffersonsheard.com
W: www.jeffersonsheard.com

Jim Hailstone Ltd
Broadfield, Church Lane, Coldwaltham, RH20 1LW
T: 07860 478197
F: 01798 872892
E: jimhailstone@bluebottle.com
W: www.icrg.co.uk

JMJ Laboratories
Geveny Court, Brecon Rd, Abergavenny, Monmouthshire NP7 7RX
T: 01873 856688
F: 01873 585982
E: Samantha.mapley@jmjlabs.co.uk
W: www.jmjlabs.co.uk

JMP Consulting
Audrey House, 16-20 Ely Place, London EC1N 6SN
T: 020 7405 2800
F: 020 7430 9049
E: david.gooden@jmp.co.uk
W: www.jmp.co.uk

John Fishwick & Sons
Golden Hill Lane, Leyland, Lancs PR25 3LE
T: 01772 421207
F: 01772 622407
E: enquiries@fishwicks.co.uk
W: www.fishwicks.co.uk

John Headon Ltd
www.johnheadonltd.co.uk

- Business Analysis (Passenger and Freight)
- Demand Forecasting
- Timetable Planning and Diagramming
- Resource Planning
- Economic Benefit Assessment
- Stakeholder Consultation

Contact: John Headon
Tel: 0161 439 8557
Email: info@johnheadonltd.co.uk

John Prodger Recruitment
The Courtyard, Alban Park, Hatfield Rd, St Albans, Herts AL4 0LA
T: 01727 841101
F: 01727 838272
E: jobs@jprecruit.com
W: www.jprecruit.com

Johnson Rail
Orchard Ind Est, Toddington, Glos GL54 5EB
T: 01242 621362
F: 01242 621554
E: Stephen.Phillips@johnson-security.co.uk

Jonathan Lee Recruitment
3 Sylvan Court, Southfield Business Park, Basildon, Essex SS15 6TU
T: 01268 455520
F: 01268 455521
E: southfields@jonlee.co.uk
W: www.jonlee.co.uk

Jones Garrard Move
31, Morland Ave, Leicester LE2 2PF
T: 0116 270 1118
F: 0116 270 2995
E: michael-rodber@jonesgarrardmove.com
W: www.jonesgarrardmove.com

JourneyPlan
12 Abbey Park Place, Dunfermline, Scotland KY12 7PD
T: 01383 731048
F: 01383 731788
W: www.journeyplan.co.uk

Kaba Door Systems Ltd
Door Automation, Halesfield 17, Telford, Shropshire TF7 4AP
T: 0870 000 5252
F: 0870 000 5253
E: info@kaba.co.uk
W: www.kabadoorsystems.co.uk

Kelly Rail
Kelly House, Headstone Rd, Harrow, Middx HA1 1PD
T: 020 8424 0909
F: 020 8424 0509
E: info@kelly.co.uk
W: www.kelly.co.uk

Kelman Ltd
Bermuda Innovation Centre, Bermuda Park, Nuneaton CV10 7SD
T: 02476 320100
F: 02476 641172
E: mail@kelman.co.uk
W: www.kelman.co.uk

Kent Modular Electronics Ltd (KME)
621 Maidstone Rd, Rochester, Kent ME1 3QJ
T: 01634 835407
F: 01634 830619
E: kcoleman@kme.co.uk
W: www.kme.co.uk

Kiel Seating UK Ltd
Regents Pavillion, 4 Summerhouse Road, Moulton Park, Northampton NN3 6BJ
T: 01604 641147
F: 01604 641149
E: p.scott@kiel-seating.co.uk
W: www.kiel-sitze.de

Kier Rail
Tempsford Hall, Sandy Beds SG19 2BD
T: 01767 640111
F: 01767 641710
E: info@kier.co.uk
W: www.kier.co.uk

Kilborn Consulting Ltd
Kilborn House, 1 St Johns St, Wellingborough, Northants NN8 4LG
T: 01933 279909
F: 01933 276629
E: pmcsharry@kilborn.co.uk
W: www.kilborn.co.uk

Kinetic Rail
2nd Floor, 4 St James Court, Friargate, Derby DE1 1BT
T: 01332 362698
F: 01332 381977
E: info@kinetic-rail.co.uk
W: www.kinetic-jobs.co.uk/rail

Kingfisher Railtours
Felmersham, Mills Rd, Osmington Mills, Weymouth, Dorset DT3 6HE
T: 0845 053 3462
E: roger@kingfisher-prods.demon.co.uk
W: www.railwayvideo.com

King Rail
King Trailers Ltd, Riverside, Market Harborough, Leics LE16 7PX
T: 01858 467361
F: 01858 467161
E: info@kingtrailers.co.uk
W: www.kingtrailers.co.uk

Klaxon Signals Ltd
Wrigley St, Oldham OL4 1HW
T: 0161 287 5555
F: 0161 287 5511
E: sales@klaxonsignals.com
W: www.klaxonsignals.com

Kluber Lubrication GB Ltd
Hough Mills, Halifax HX3 7BN
T: 01422 319149
F: 01422 206073
E: info@uk.klueber.com
W: www.kluber.com

KMC International
7 Old Park Lane, London W1K 1QR
T: 020 7317 4600
F: 020 7317 4620
E: london@kmcinternational.com
W: www.kmcinternational.com

KM&T Ltd
The Techno Centre, Coventry University Technology Park, Puma Way, Coventry CV1 2TT
T: 02476 248406
E: andrea.harrison@kmandt.com
W: www.kmandt.com

KME
See Kent Modular

Knights Rail Services Ltd (KRS)
The Bakery, 23 Church St, Coggeshall, Essex CO6 1TX
T: 01376 561194
F: 01376 563992
E: bruce@knightsrail.fsnet.co.uk
W: www.rail-services.net

KNORR-BREMSE
Knorr-Bremse Rail Systems (UK) Limited operate their OE and *rail*services service and maintenance business divisions, serving the UK and Ireland, from their new, purpose built and equipped facility located at:

Westinghouse Way, Hampton Park East, Melksham, Wiltshire, SN12 6TL.

Tel: 01225 898700
Fax: 01225 898705

Enquiries via e-mail to:
ian.palmer@westbrake.com

www.knorr-bremse.co.uk

railservices

Knorr Bremse Rail Systems (UK) Ltd
Westinghouse Way, Hampton Park East, Melksham, Wilts SN12 6TL
T: 01225 898700
F: 01225 898705
E: ian.palmer@westbrake.com
W: www.knorr-bremse.co.uk

Kone UK
Global House, Station Place, Chertsey, Surrey KT16 9HW
T: 0870 770 1122
F: 0870 770 1144
W: marketing@kone.uk.com
W: www.kone.com

Korec Group
Bludellsands House, 34-44, Mersey View, Waterloo, Liverpool L22 6QB
T: 0845 603 1214
F: 0151 931 5559
E: info@korecgroup.com
W: www.korecgroup.com

Kroy (Europe) Ltd
Unit 2, 14 Commercial Rd, Reading, Berks RG2 0QJ
T: 0118 986 5200
F: 0118 986 5205
E: sales@kroyeurope.com
W: www.kroyeurope.com

KME

KME are a leading designer and manufacturer of LCD – TFT monitors for the rail industry. Standard, custom built and replacement displays are used worldwide in control rooms, train cabs and digital signage.

621 Maidstone Road, Rochester, Kent ME1 3QJ
T: +44 (0)1634 830123
F: +44 (0)1634 830619
E: railsales@kme.co.uk
W: www.kme.co.uk

KV Mobile Systems Division
Presley Way, Crownhill, Milton Keynes MK8 0HB
T: 01908 561515
F: 01908 561227
E: sales@kvautomation.co.uk
W: www.kvglobal.com

Kwik Step Ltd
Unit 5, Albion Dockside, Hanover Place, Bristol BS1 6UT
T: 0117 929 1400
F: 0117 929 1404
E: info@kwik-step.com
W: www.kwik-step.com

Laboursite Group Ltd (Rail)
See Wyse Rail

Lafarge Aggregates (UK) Ltd
Granite House, PO Box 7388, Watermead Business Park, Syston, Leicester LE7 1WA
T: 0870 336 8250
F: 0870 336 8650
E: generalenquiries@lafarge.com
W: www.lafarge.co.uk

Laing O'Rourke Infrastructure
Bridge Place, Anchor Blvd., Admirals Park, Crossways, Dartford, Kent DA2 6SN
T: 01322 296200
F: 01322 296262
E: info@laingorourke.com
W: www.laingorourke.com

Laing Rail
Western House, 14 Rickfords Hill, Aylesbury, Bucks HP20 2RX
T: 01296 332108
F: 01296 332126
W: www.laingrail.co.uk

Lanes For Drains/ Lanes Engineering & Construction
17 Parkside Ind. Est, Leeds LS11 5TD
T: 0113 385 8400
F: 0113 385 8401
E: sales@lanesfordrains.co.uk
W: www.lanesfordrains.co.uk

Lankelma
The Old Dairy, Wittersham Rd, Iden, East Sussex TN31 7UY
T: 01797 280050
F: 01797 280195
E: darrenward@lankelma.co.uk
W: www.lankelma.co.uk

Lantern Engineering Ltd
Hamilton Rd, Maltby, Rotherham S66 7NE
T: 01709 813636
F: 01709 817130
E: info@lantern.co.uk
W: www.lantern.co.uk

Laser Rail
Fitology House, Smedley St. East, Matlock, Derbys DE4 3GH
T: 01629 760750
F: 01629 760751
E: info@laser-rail.co.uk
W: www.laser-rail.co.uk

Laserthor
30 Leamington Crescent, Lea on Solent, Hants PO13 9HN
T: 07788 582244
F: 02392 551440
E: enquiries@laserthor.com
W: www.laserthor.com

Leda Recruitment
Leda House, 46-48 New York St, Leeds LS2 7DY
T: 0113 242 0940
F: 0113 243 8739
E: david.adams@leda-recruitment.co.uk
W: www.leda-recruitment.co.uk

Legion
22-26 Albert Embankment, Vauxhall, London SE1 7TJ
T: 020 7793 0200
F: 020 7793 8948
E: info@legion.com
W: www.legion.com

Leica Geosystems Ltd
Davy Ave., Knowlhill, Milton Keynes MK5 8LB
T: 01908 256500
F: 01908 246259
E: uk.sales@leica-geosystems.com
W: www.leica-geosystems.com

Leighs Paints
Tower Works, Kestor St, Bolton, Lancs BL2 2AL
T: 01204 521771
F: 01204 382115
E: enquiries@leighspaints.co.uk
W: www.leighspaints.co.uk

Lemon Consulting
221 St John St, Clerkenwell, London EC1V 4LY
T: 020 7688 2561
F: 020 7688 2562
E: enquiries@lemon-consulting.com
W: www.lemon-consulting.com

Lesmac (Fasteners) Ltd
73 Dykehead St, Queenslie Ind. Est, Queenslie, Glasgow KA7 4SN
T: 0141 774 0004
F: 0141 774 2229
E: sales@lesmac.co.uk
W: www.lesmac.co.uk

LH Group Services
Graycar Business Park, Barton-under-Needwood, Burton Upon Trent DE13 8EN
T: 01283 722600
F: 01283 722622
E: lh@lh-group.co.uk
W: www.lh-group.co.uk

LH Safety Footwear
Greenbridge, Rawtenstall, Rossendale, Lancs BB4 7NX
T: 01706 235100
F: 01706 235150
E: john.mcwicker@lhsafety.co.uk
W: www.lhsafety.co.uk

Liebherr-Group Great Britain Ltd
Normandy Lane, Stratton Business Park, Biggleswade, Beds SG18 8QP
T: 01767 602100
F: 01767 602110
E: info.lgb@liebherr.com
W: www.liebherr.com

Liebherr - Sunderland Works Transportation Systems
Ayres Quay, Deptford Terrace, Sunderland SR4 6DD
T: 0191 515 4930
F: 0191 515 4936
E: alan.lepatourel@liebherr.com
W: www.liebherr.com

Light Rail Transit Association (LRTA)
Haslams, 133 Lichfield St, Walsall WS1 1SL
T: 01179 517785
E: office@lrta.org
W: www.lrta.org

Lindapter International
Lindsay House, Brackenbeck Rd, Bradford BD7 2NF
T: 01274 521444
F: 01274 521130
E: enquiries@lindapter.com
W: www.lindapter.com

Link Associates International
Trent House, RTC Business Park, London Rd, Derby DE24 8UP
T: 01332 222299
F: 01332 222298
E: info@linkassociates.com
W: www.linkassociates.com

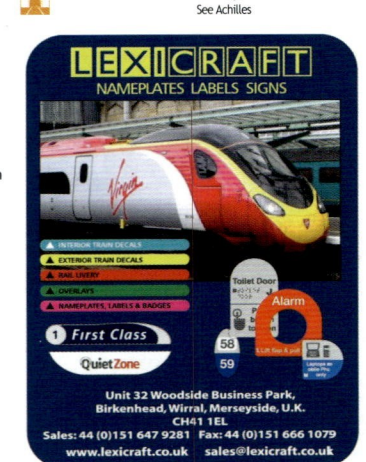

Link-up
See Achilles

Lexicraft Ltd
Unit 32, Woodside Business Park, Birkenhead, Wirral CH41 1EL
T: 0151 647 9281
F: 0151 666 1079
E: sales@lexicraft.co.uk
W: www.lexicraft.co.uk

Lionverge Civils Ltd
Unit 5, Ransome Rd, Far Cotton, Northampton NN4 8AA
T: 01604 677227
F: 01604 677218
E: enquiries@lionverge.com
W: www.lionverge.co.uk

LEXICRAFT
NAMEPLATES LABELS SIGNS

Unit 32 Woodside Business Park, Birkenhead, Wirral, Merseyside, U.K. CH41 1EL
Sales: 44 (0)151 647 9281 Fax: 44 (0)151 666 1079
www.lexicraft.co.uk sales@lexicraft.co.uk

In association with **railalliance**

Managing change for train operators

mouchel

Mouchel is a consulting and business services group that works in the public and private sectors and regulated industry.

To find out how we can support your business, please contact Andy Norris on:

T +44 (0)20 7227 6800
E consult@mouchel.com

www.mouchel.com

EAST LANCASHIRE RAILWAY

BOLTON STREET STATION, BURY, BL9 0EY. Telephone: 0161 764 7790. Fax: 0161 763 4408

The rail industry uses the ELR

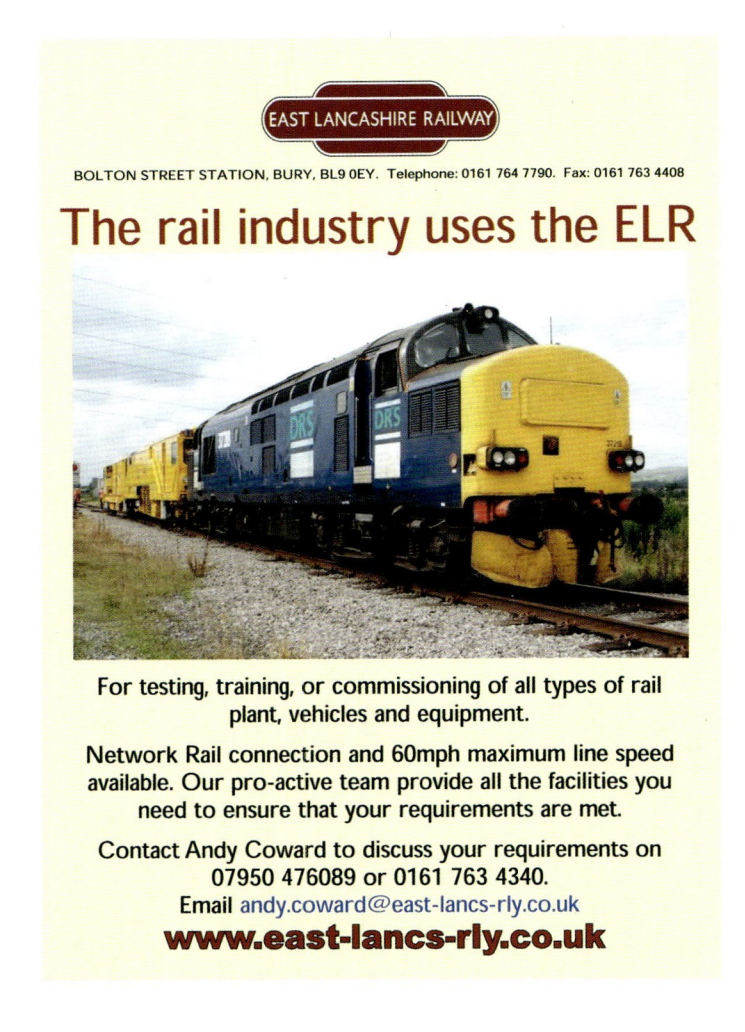

For testing, training, or commissioning of all types of rail plant, vehicles and equipment.

Network Rail connection and 60mph maximum line speed available. Our pro-active team provide all the facilities you need to ensure that your requirements are met.

Contact Andy Coward to discuss your requirements on 07950 476089 or 0161 763 4340.
Email andy.coward@east-lancs-rly.co.uk

www.east-lancs-rly.co.uk

ACORP
Association of Community Rail Partnerships

new life for local lines

Tel: 01484 847 790
Fax: 01484 847 877
Email: info@acorp.uk.com
www.acorp.com

Rail and River Centre, Civic Hall, 15a New Street, Slaithwaite, Huddersfield HD7 5AB

Plant & Transport Solutions
www.fastline-group.com

fastline

JARVIS

Rail Infrastructure Specialists
www.jarvisrail.com

Meridian House, The Crescent, York YO24 1AW
T +44 (0)1904 712712

HSBC

Directory

jobs-in-rail.co.uk

Join the 1st Class Service

National Rail Recruitment From

modern railways

Register now at the national rail recruitment site **Jobs-in-Rail.co.uk** to start receiving weekly or daily job alerts tailored to **your specialism...**

LINK Associates provide crisis, emergency, BC & safety training and consultancy services to a wide range of industries. Our experience includes working with a number of TOCs.

LINK Associates International
(A SEACOR Company)
Trent House, RTC Business Park,
London Road, Derby, DE24 8UP, UK

T: +44 (0) 1332 222299
F: +44 (0) 1332 222298
E: info@linkassociates.com
W: www.linkassociates.com

Lloyd's Register Rail supports the safety, functional and business performance of rail systems covering strategic development, infrastructure, systems, rolling-stock, signaling, telecommunications, operations and safety management.

Strutt House, Bridge Foot,
Belper, Derbyshire DE56 1XG
T 01773 828 359
F 01773 881 448
E sarah.bullock@lrrail.com

www.lr.org

Lloyds Register
Gervase House, 111 Friar Gate,
Derby DE1 1EX
T: 01332 375257
F: 01332 349747
E: martin.hayhoe@lrrail.com
W: www.lrrail.com

Llumar Anti-Grafitti Coating
See CP Films

LMG Project Services
Eastfield Depot, Carron Cres.,
Springburn, Glasgow G22 6HY
T: 0141 335 2965
F: 0141 335 3756
E: enquiries@LMGprojects.com
W: www.lmgprojects.co.uk

LML Products Ltd
13 Portemarsh Rd, Calne, Wilts
SN11 9BN
T: 01249 814271
F: 01249 812182
E: sales@lmlproducts.co.uk
W: www.lmlproducts.co.uk

LNWR Co Ltd
PO Box 111, Crewe,
Cheshire CW1 2FB
T: 01270 251467
F: 01270 251468
E: m.knowles@lnwr.com
W: www.lnwr.com

Logica CMG
Stephenson House, 75 Hampstead
Rd, London NW1 2PL
T: 020 7637 9111
F: 020 7468 7006
E: info@.logica.com
W: www.logicacmg.com

Logikal Programme Management Consultancy
4th Floor, 50 Eastbourne Terrace,
Paddington, London W2 6LX
T: 020 7725 2530
F: 020 7725 2535
E: enquiry@logikalplan.com
W: www.logikalplan.com

Logic Engagements Ltd
45-47 High St, Cobham,
Surrey KT11 3DP
T: 01932 869869
F: 01932 864455
E: sandrabullock@logicrec.com
W: www.logicrec.com

London & Continental Railways Ltd (LCR)
3rd Floor, 183 Eversholt St,
London NW1 1AY
T: 020 7391 4369
F: 020 7391 4400
E: bruse@lcrhq.co.uk
W: www.lcrhq.co.uk

London Midland
PO Box 4323, Birmingham B3 4JB
T: 0121 634 2040
F: 0121 654 1234
E: comments@londonmidland.com
W: www.londonmidland.com

London Overground Rail Operations Ltd (LOROL)
Customer Services Centre,
Overground House, 125 Finchley
Rd, London NW3 6HY
T: 0845 601 4867
E: overgroundinfo@tfl.gov.uk
W: www.lorol.co.uk

London Underground
Customer Service Centre,
55 Broadway, London SW1W 0BD
T: 0845 330 9880
W: www.tfl.gov.uk/tube

London Rail
See Transport for London

Look CCTV
Unit 4, Wyrefields, Poulton le
Fylde, Lancs FY6 8JX
T: 01253 891222
F: 01253 891221
E: enquiries@lookcctv.com
W: www.lookcctv.com

LPA Long Life Reliability does not cost the earth

LPA Channel Electric, Bath Road,
Thatcham, West Berkshire,
RG18 3ST England
Tel: +44 (0)1635 864 866
Fax: +44 (0)1635 869 178
e-mail: enquiries@lpa-channel.com

LPA Excil Electronics, Ripley Drive, Normanton,
West Yorkshire,
WF6 1QT England
Tel: +44 (0)1924 224 100
Fax: +44 (0)1924 224 111
e-mail: enquiries@lpa-excil.com

LPA Niphan Systems, Tudor Works,
Debden Road, Saffron Walden, Essex,
CB11 4AN England
Tel: +44 (0)1799 512 800
Fax: +44 (0)1799 512 828
e-mail: enquiries@lpa-niphan.com

www.lpa-group.com

LPA Group
Todor Works, Debden Way, Saffron
Walden, Essex CB11 4AN
T: 01799 512800
F: 01799 512828
E: enquiries@lpa-niphan.com
W: www.lpa-group.com

Lucchini UK Ltd
Wheel Forge Way, Trafford Park,
Manchester M17 1EH
T: 0161 886 0300
F: 0161 872 2895
E: salesuk@lucchini.co.uk
W: www.lucchinisiderrmeccanica.com

Mace Ltd
Atelier House, 64 Pratt St,
London NW1 0LF
T: 020 7554 8000
E: mace@mace.co.uk
W: www.mace.co.uk

Macemain + Amstad Ltd
Boyle Rd, Willowbrook Ind. Est.,
Corby, Northants NN17 5XU
T: 01536 401331
F: 01536 401298
E: sales@macemainamstad.com
W: www.macemainamstad.com

MacRail
T: 01934 319810
F: 01934 424139
E: info@macrail.co.uk
W: www.macrail.co.uk reporting

Maddox Consulting Ltd
44 Wardour St. London W1D 6QZ
T: 020 7664 0499
E: info@madcoxconsulting.com
W: www.madcoxconsulting.com

Maestro Cleaning & Facilities Ltd
Maestro House, Project Park,
North Crescert, Cody Rd,
London E16 4TQ
T: 020 7474 1133
F: 020 7474 1134
E: sales@maestrocleaning.co.uk
W: www.maestrocleaning.co.uk

Mainframe Communications Ltd
Network House, Journeymans Way,
Temple Farm Ind Est, Southend on
Sea, Essex SS2 5TF
T: 01702 443800
F: 01702 443801
E: info@mainframecomms.co.uk
W: www.mainframecomms.co.uk

MACK BROOKS exhibitions

Organising exhibitions for the rail industry in the UK:
Railtex and Infrarail

As well as in France, Italy,
Russia and India

**Mack Brooks Exhibitions Ltd,
Romeland House,
Romeland Hill,
St Albans AL3 4ET**

Tel: +44 (0) 1727 814400
Fax: +44 (0) 1727 814401

railtex@mackbrooks.co.uk

www.mackbrooks.co.uk

Mack Brooks Exhibitions Ltd
Romelands House, Romelands Hill,
St Albans AL3 4ET
T: 01727 814400
F: 01727 814401
E: railtex@mackbrooks.co.uk
W: www.mackbrooks.co.uk

Mainline Staffing
1st Floor, Suite 38-40, 35-37
Grosvener Gardens, Victoria,
London SW1W 0BS
T: 0845 083 0245
F: 020 7821 8185
E: info@mainlinestaffing.com
W: www.mainlinestaffing.com

MAN Diesel Ltd
Bramhall Moor lane, Hazel Grove, Stockport SK7 5AQ
T: 0161 483 1000
F: 0161 487 1465
E: primeserv-uk@mandiesel.com
W: www.mandiesel.com

M&M Rail Services Ltd
First Floor, Unit 7, Portland House, 1-7 Portland Place, Doncaster DN1 3DF
T: 01302 349888
F: 01302 349899
W: www.mmrailservices.co.uk

Mane Rail
UCB House, 3 St George St, Watford WD18 0UH
T: 01923 470720
E: rail@mane.co.uk
W: www.mane.co.uk

Mansell Recruitment Group
Mansell House, Priestley Way, Crawley, West Sussex RH10 9RU
T: 01293 404050
F: 01293 404122
E: jharrison@mansell.co.uk
W: www.mansell.co.uk

Marcroft Engineering Services
Whieldon Rd, Stoke-on-Trent ST4 4HP
T: 01782 844075
F: 01782 843578
E: r.mcneil@marcroft.co.uk
W: www.marcroft.co.uk

Maritime and Rail
E-Business Centre, Consett Business Park, Villa Real, Consett DH8 6BP
T: 01207 693616
F: 01207 693917
E: mail@maritimeandrail.com
W: www.maritimeandrail.com

Marl International
Marl Business Park, Ulverston, Cumbria LA12 9BN
T: 01229 582430
F: 01229 585155
E: sales@marl.co.uk
W: www.marlrail.com

Martek Powertron Ltd
Glebe Farm Technical Campus Knapwell, Cambridge CB23 4GG
T: 01954 267726
F: 01954 267626
E: sales@powertron.co.uk
W: www.powertron.co.uk

Martin Higginson Transport Research & Consultancy
5 The Avenue, Clifton, York YO30 6AS
T: 01904 636704
E: mhrc@waitrose.com
W: www.martinhigginson.co.uk

Martineau Johnson
No.1 Colmore, Birmingham B4 6AA
T: 0870 763 1552
F: 0870 763 1952
E: lawyers@martjohn.com
W: www.martineau-johnson.co.uk

Matisa (UK) Ltd
PO Box 202, Scunthorpe, N.Lincs DN15 6XR
T: 01724 877000
F: 01724 877001
E: melissa.carne@matisa.co.uk
W: www.matisa.ch

Matchtech Group
1450 Park Way, Solent Business Park, Whiteley, Fareham, Hants PO15 7AF
T: 01489 898989
F: 01489 898290
E: info@matchtech.com
W: www.matchtech.com

Maxim Power Tools (Scotland) Ltd
40 Couper St, Glasgow G4 0DL
T: 0141 552 5591
F: 0141 552 5064
E: enquiries@maximpower.co.uk
W: www.maxim-power.com

Maxmax Ltd
Beech Grove, Wootton, Eccleshall, Staffs ST21 6HU
T: 01785 859106
E: sales@maxmaxltd.com
W: www.maxmaxltd.com

May Gurney Rail Services
Haden House, Argyle Way, Stevenage SG1 2AD
T: 01438 363333
F: 01438 363945
E: marketing@maygurney.co.uk
W: www.maygurney.co.uk

MBM
MODERN BUILDING MATERIALS
Precast concrete parts such as manholes, cable troughs, platform edges and pavement coatings for rail infrastructure as well as for airports, energy supply, telecommunication, industry, water and sewage.
MBM Trade Ltd.
Endeavour House, Coopers End Road
London Stansted, Essex, CM24 1SJ
Tel: 01279 669443 Fax : 01279 669444
info@MBM-trade.co.uk
www.MBM-trade.co.uk

MBM Trade Ltd
Endeavour House, Coopers End Road, Stansted, Essex CM24 1SJ
T: 01279 669 443
F: 01279 669 444
E: info@mbm-trade.co.uk
W: www.mbm-trade.co.uk

W & D McCULLOCH
RAIL DIVISION
W & D McCulloch Rail Division are the number one rail installer and scrap recovery company in the UK.
For more information please visit our web site on www.wdmccullochrail.co.uk

W&D Mc Culloch Rail Division
Craigiemains, Main St, Ballantrae, Girvan, S. Ayrshire KA26 0NB
T: 01465 831350
F: 01465 831350
E: wdmcculloch@btinternet.com
W: www.mccullochrail.co.uk

MC Electronics
61, Grimsdyke Rd, Hatch End, Middx HA5 4PP
T: 020 8428 2027
F: 020 8428 2027
E: mcelectron@aol.com
W: www.mcelectronics.co.uk

Mc Ginley Specialist Recruitment
Rainbow House, 24 Water Lane, Watford, Herts WD17 2HB
T: 01923 725645
F: 01923 725651
E: warren.kingham@mcginley.co.uk
W: www.mcginley.co.uk

McKenzie Martin Partnership Ltd
182-186 Above Bar, Southampton SO14 7DW
T: 01489 784183
F: 01489 790562
E: info@mmpartnership.co.uk
W: www.mmpartnership.co.uk

MCL (Martin Childs Ltd)
Wimbledon Ave, Brandon, Suffolk IP27 0NZ
T: 01842 812882
F: 01842 812002
E: tracyedwards@martinchilds.com
W: www.martinchilds.com

Mc Lellan & Partners
Sheer House, West Byfleet, Surrey KT14 6NL
T: 01932 343271
F: 01932 348037
E: hq@mclellan.co.uk
W: www.mclellan.co.uk

Mc Nicholas Rail
1st Floor, Consort House, Waterdale, Doncaster DN1 3HR
T: 01302 380551
F: 01302 380591
E: mark.bugg@mcnicholas.co.uk
W: www.mcnicholas.co.uk

MCT Brattberg Ltd
Commerce St, Carrs Ind. Est, Haslingden, Lancs BB4 5JT
T: 01706 244890
F: 01706 244891
E: info@mctbrattberg.co.uk
W: www.brattberg.com

MDM Transportation
Walkmill Lane, Bridgetown, Cannock, Staffs

MDS Transmodal Ltd
5-6 Hunters Walk, Canal St, Chester CH1 4EB
T: 01244 348301
F: 01244 348471
E: enquiries@mdst.co.uk
W: www.mdst.co.uk

Mechan Ltd/Mechan Technology Ltd
Thorncliffe Park, Newton Chambers Rd, Chapeltown, Sheffield S35 2PH
T: 0114 257 0563
F: 0114 245 1124
E: richardc@mechan.co.uk
W: www.mechan.co.uk

MEDC Ltd
Colliery Rd, Pinxton, Nottingham NG16 6FF
T: 01773 864100
F: 01773 582800
E: sales@medc.com
W: www.medc.com

Medicals Direct
Buckingham House East, The Broadway, Stanmore HA7 4EB
T: 020 8416 1401
F: 0871 900 2861
E: sales@medicalsdirect.com
W: www.medicalsdirect.com

Medscreen
Harbour Quay, 100 Prestons Rd, London E14 9PH
T: 020 7712 8000
F: 020 7712 8001
E: sales@medscreen.com
W: www.medscreen.com

Melford Electronics Ltd
Cressex Business Park, Blenheim Rd, High Wycombe HP12 3RS
T: 01494 638069
F: 01494 463358
E: info@melford-elec.co.uk
W: www.melford-elec.co.uk

Mendip Rail Ltd
Merehead, East Cranmore, Shepton Mallet, Somerset BA4 4RA
T: 01749 881202
F: 01749 880141
E: karen.taylor@mendip-rail.co.uk
W: www.fosteryeoman.co.uk

Mennekes Electrical Ltd
Unit 4, Crayfields Ind. Park, Main Rd, St Pauls Cray, Orpington, Kent BR5 3HP
T: 01689 833522
F: 01689 833378
E: sales@mennekes.co.uk
W: www.mennekes.co.uk

Merc Engineering UK Ltd
Lower Clough Hill, Pendle St, Barrowford, Lancs BB9 8PH
T: 01282 694290
F: 01282 613390
E: sales@merceng.co.uk
W: www.merceng.co.uk

Mercia Charters
PO Box 1926, Coventry CV3 6ZL
T: 01926 887499
E: team@merciacharters.co.uk
W: www.merciacharters.co.uk

Merseyrail
Rail House, lord Nelson St, Liverpool L1 1JF
T: 0151 702 2534
F: 0151 702 3074
E: comment@merseyrail.org
W: www.merseyrail.org

Meteo Group UK Ltd
292 Vauxhall Bridge Rd, London SW1V 1AE
T: 020 7963 7534
F: 020 7963 7599
E: Jeremy.fidlin@meteogroup.com
W: www.meteogroup.com

Metcalfe Railway Products Ltd
Tolletts Farm, Leek Old Rd, Sutton, Macclesfield, Cheshire SK11 0HZ
T: 01260 252329
F: 01260 253413
E: info@metcalferailprodltd.co.uk
W: www.metcalferailprodltd.co.uk

Mettex Electronic Co Ltd
Beaumont Close, Banbury, Oxon OX16 1TG
T: 01295 250826
F: 01295 268643
E: sales@mettex.com
W: www.mettex.com

Metrolink (Manchester)
Serco Metrolink, Metrolink House, Queens Rd, Manchester M8 0RY
T: 0161 205 8665
W: www.metrolink.co.uk

Metronet Rail
Templar House, 81-87 High Holborn, London WC1V 6NU
T: 020 7038 5000
F: 020 7038 4981
E: jane.leaker@metronetrail.com
W: www.metronetrail.com

Metronet Rail Trains Group
130 Bollo Lane, Acton, London W3 8BZ
T: 020 7918 6555
F: 020 7918 6599
E: ian.ferguson@metronetrail.com
W: www.metronetrail.com

Metronet Rail REW
130 Bollo Lane, Acton, London W3 8BZ
T: 020 7918 6555
F: 020 7918 6599
E: richard.turner@metronetrail.com
W: www.metronetrail.com

MGB Signalling (Magnate Grey Box)
Tamar Science Park, 9 Research Way, Derriford, Plymouth PL6 8BT
T: 0845 070 2490
F: 0845 070 2495
E: enquiries@mgbl.co.uk
W: www.mgbl.co.uk

Micro-Epsilon UK Ltd
Dorset House, West Derby Rd, Liverpool L6 4BR
T: 0151 260 9800
F: 0151 261 2480
E: info@micro-epsilon.co.uk
W: www.micro-epsilon.co.uk

Micro-Mesh Filtration
60 Basford Rd, Old Basford, Nottingham NG6 0JL
T: 01159 786348
F: 01159 422688
E: enquiries@micro-mesh.co.uk
W: www.micro-mesh.co.uk

Micromotive
38 Coney Green Business Centre, Wingfield View, Clay Cross, Derbys S45 9JW
T: 01246 252360
F: 01246 252361
E: a1micromotive@btopenworld.com
W: www.micromotive.co.uk

Midland Metro
Travel Midland Metro, Metro Centre, Potters Lane, Wednesbury, West Midlands WS10 0AR
T: 0121 502 2006
F: 0121 556 6299
W: www.travelmetro.co.uk

Mike Worbey Survey Consultancy
37 Ramblers Way, Welwyn Garden City, Herts AL7 2JU
T: 01707 333677
F: 01707 333677
E: land_data@msn.com
W: www.mikewarbysurveyconsulting.co.uk

Mirror Technology Ltd
Redwood House, Orchard Ind Est, Toddington, Glos GL54 5EB
T: 01242 621534
F: 01242 621529
E: enquiries@mirrortechnology.co.uk
W: www.mirrortechnology.co.uk

Mita (UK) Ltd
Manor Ind. Est., Bagillt, Flint CH6 5UY
T: 01352 792300
F: 01352 792314
E: marketing@mita.co.uk
W: www.mita.co.uk

Mono Design
4 St Andrews House, Vernon gate, Derby DE1 1UJ
T: 01332 361616
E: lynne@monodesign.co.uk
W: www.monodesign.co.uk

Morgan Electrical Carbon Ltd
Upper Fforest Way, Swansea SA6 8PP
T: 01792 763000
F: 01792 763167
E: sales@mecl.co.uk
W: www.morgancarbon.com

Morgan Est Plc
Morgan Est House, Corporation St, Rugby, Warks CV21 2DW
T: 01788 534500
F: 01788 534579
E: info@morganest.com
W: www.morganest.com

Morris Material Handling
PO Box 7, North Rd, Loughborough, Leics LE11 1RL
T: 01509 643200
F: 01509 610666
E: info@morriscranes.co.uk
W: www.morriscranes.co.uk

Morson International
Stableford Hall, Monton, Eccles, Manchester M30 8AP
T: 0161 707 1516
F: 0161 788 8372
E: rail@morson.com
W: www.morson.com

Morson Projects
Darwen House, Liverpool Rd, Irlam, Manchester M44 6TB
T: 0161 777 4000
F: 0161 777 4001
E: andy.hassall@morson-projects.co.uk
W: www.morsonprojects.co.uk

Motorail Logistics
The Control Tower, Long Marston Storage Site, Long Marston, Stratford upon Avon, Warks CV37 8QR
T: 01789 721995
F: 01789 721396
E: ruth.dunmore@motorail.co.uk
W: www.motorail.co.uk

Mott MacDonald Group
St Anne House Wellesley Rd, Croydon CR9 2UL
T: 020 8774 2000
F: 020 8681 5706
E: railways@mottmac.com
W: www.mottmac.com

mouchel
Managing change for train operators
Mouchel's management consulting business - providing specialist expertise to train operating companies
See our full page display advertisement for more information
T 020 7227 6800
E andy.norris@mouchel.com
www.mouchel.com

Mouchel
4 Matthew Parker Street, London SW1H 9NP
T: 020 7227 6800
F: 020 7277 6801
E: consult@mouchel.com
W: www.mouchel.com

Movares
Mireille Ros, Leidseveer 10, 3511 SB Utrecht, Netherlands
T: 0031 30265 3101
F: 0031 30265 3111
E: info@movares.nl
W: www.movares.com

Moveright International Ltd
Dunton Park, Dunton Lane, Wishaw, Sutton Coldfield B76 9QA
T: 01675 475590
F: 01675 475591
E: Andrew@moverightinternational.com
W: www.moverightinternational.com

MPEC Technology Ltd
Wyvern House, Railway Terrace, Derby DE1 2RU
T: 01332 363979
F: 08701 363958
E: andrew.whawell@mpec.co.uk
W: www.mpec.co.uk

MRO Software
Now part of IBM UK Ltd.
PO Box 41, North Harbour, Portsmouth, PO6 3AU
T: 0870 542 6426
E: maximo@uk.ibm.com
W: www.maximo.com

MSD Services Ltd
20/22 Lower Stanton Rd, Ilkeston, Derby DE7 5FW
T: 0115 932 3555
F: 0115 932 3666
E: msd@msdservices.co.uk
W: www.msdservices.co.uk

MTR Corporation
Finland House, 56 Haymarket, London SW1Y 4RN
T: 020 7766 3500
F: 020 7839 6217
E: europe@mtr.com.hk
W: www.mtr.com.hk

MTR Training Ltd
Hydrex House, Serbert Way, Portishead, Bristol BS20 7GD
T: 01275 399401
F: 01275 399459
E: sales@mtrgroup.co.uk
W: www.mtrgroup.co.uk

MTU UK Ltd
Unit 29, The Birches Ind. Est, East Grinstead, West Sussex RH19 1XZ
T: 01342 335450
F: 01342 335475
E: firstname.lastname@mtu-online.com
W: www.mtu-online.com

Multicell
Swannington Rd, Broughton Astley, Leicester LE9 6TU
T: 01455 283443
F: 01455 284250
E: help@multicell.co.uk
W: www.multicell.co.uk

J Murphy & Sons Ltd
81 Highgate Rd, London NW5 1TN
T: 020 7267 4366
F: 020 7482 3107
E: info@murphygroup.co.uk
W: www.murphygroup.co.uk

MVA Consultancy
17 Hanover Square, London W1S 1HU
T: 0207 529 6500
F: 020 7529 6556
E: info@mvaconsultancy.com
W: www.mvaconsultancy.com

National Car Parks Ltd (NCP)
6th Floor, Centre Tower, Croydon CR0 1LP
T: 0845 050 7080
E: richard.talbot@ncp.co.uk
W: www.ncp.co.uk

National Express East Anglia
Olivers Yard, 55 City Rd, London EC1Y 1HQ
T: 020 7549 5900
F: 020 7549 5999
W: www.nationalexpresseastanglia.com

National Express East Coast
East Coast House, Skeldergate, York YO1 6HD
T: 0845 059 3155
F: 01904 524532
W: www.nationalexpresseastcoast.co.uk

National Express Group Plc
75, Davies St, London W1K 5HT
T: 020 7529 2000
F: 020 7529 2100
E: info@natex.co.uk
W: www.nationalexpressgroup.com

National Rail Enquiries
T: 08457 484950
W: www.nationalrail.co.uk

National Railway Museum
Leeman Rd, York YO26 4XJ
T: 0844 815 3139
E: nrm@nrm.org.uk
W: www.nrm.org.uk

The Nationwide Accreditation Bureau Ltd
The Olympic Office Centre, 8 Fulton Rd, Wembley HA9 0NU
T: 08458 902902
F: 08458 903903
E: enquiries@thenab.co.uk
W: www.thenab.co.uk

Directory

SEVERN VALLEY RAILWAY

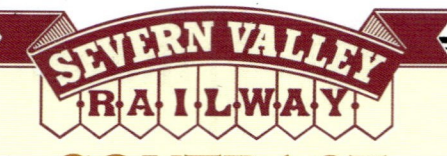

CONTRACT ENGINEERING

It may surprise you but at the SVR we can supply components and services for the following:

- Overhaul and repair of vacuum brake cylinders
- Tyre turning • Remetalling
- Unfinished and finished machined castings
- Valve and piston rings, heads and liners
- Washout plugs
- Boiler water treatment chemicals

Contact **01299 403816**
with your requirements or write to
The Railway Station, Bewdley, Worcs DY12 1BG

MC Electronics
Railway Safety Equipment

See our full range of Railway Safety Products for Depot and Trackside use on our new website

www.mcelectronics.co.uk

Or call us for a catalogue on
020 8428 2027

"Highly commended at the National Rail Awards 2005 for "Innovation of the year"

New LED EROS Equipment
NOT TO BE MOVED Signs
Possession Limit & Marker Boards

MC Electronics Ltd, 61 Grimsdyke Road, Hatch End, Middx, HA5 4PP
T: 020 8428 2027   F: 020 8428 2027   E: mcelectron@aol.com

EDUCATION AND RESEARCH FOR THE RAILWAY INDUSTRY AT THE UNIVERSITY OF BIRMINGHAM

Continuous Educational Development for Railway Professionals

RAILWAY SYSTEMS ENGINEERING AND INTEGRATION:
The University of Birmingham's Masters and Diploma programmes for experienced railway staff and new recruits to the industry have helped to enhance the skills and knowledge of some 300 individuals. Many have achieved promotion or moved to challenging new posts. Although most participants have been from the UK, graduates of the programmes work in Australia, China, Germany, Greece, Holland, India, Ireland, Malaysia, Singapore, Spain and Switzerland.

For further information on the MSc programmes and the conditions for admission, contact
Mrs. Joy Grey, Administrator RSEI, Railway Research and Education Centre, University of Birmingham, Gisbert Kapp Building, Pritchatts Road, Birmingham, B15 2TT.
tel: 0121 414 4342 and e-mail: rsei-eng@contacts.bham.ac.uk

Information and Interviews for September 2009 entry: Prospectus, Module List and Course Dates for Full and Part-Time Study in 2009/10 are now available. Open days and interviews for both the MSc and Diploma programmes are held in Birmingham, London and Manchester. Please contact the course team on 0121 414 4342 or 0121 414 5138 to request an information pack about the degree programmes and continuous professional development opportunities. Interviews can be arranged by getting in touch with Charles Watson on 0121 414 5138 or c.watson.1@bham.ac.uk.

Information on railway research at the University of Birmingham is available from the research co-ordinator on 0121 414 5063 or rsei-eng@contacts.bham.ac.uk

The University of Birmingham encourages equality of opportunity for all and offers railway engineering studies as part of its provision of higher education in a research-led environment.

UNIVERSITY OF BIRMINGHAM

HSBC

Nationwide Healthcare Connect
Connections House, 105 Bellingdon Rd, Chesham, Bucks HP5 2HQ
T: 01494 773007
F: 01494 773008
E: sales@hccnationwide.com
W: www.healthcare-connections.com

Nazeing Glass Works
Nazeing New Rd, Broxbourne, Herts EN10 6SU
T: 01992 464485
E: r.briden@nazeing-glass.co.uk
W: www.nazeing-glass.com

NCH (UK) Ltd - Chemsearch
Landchard House, Victoria St, West Bromwich B70 8ER
T: 0121 524 7300
F: 0121 500 5386
W: www.chemsearch.co.uk

NDT Services Ltd
5 Side Ley, Kegworth, Derby DE74 2FJ
T: 01509 680087
F: 01509 680080
E: sales@ndtservices.co.uk
W: www.ndtservices.co.uk

Neale Consulting Engineers Ltd
Highfield, Pilcot Hill, Dogmersfield, Fleet, Hants RG27 8SX
T: 01252 629199
F: 01252 815625
E: ncel@tribology.co.uk
W: www.tribology.co.uk

Neary Rail
Mort Lane, Tyldesley, Manchester M29 8PF
T: 0161 790 3060
F: 0161 790 3036
E: info@neary.co.uk
W: www.neary.co.uk

Nedtrain BV
Kantorencentrum Katereine 9, Stationshal 17, 3511 ED Utrecht
T: 0031 30 300 4929
F: 0031 30 300 4647
W: www.nedtrain.nl

Nelsons Solicitors
Pennine House, 8 Stanford St, Nottingham NG1 7BQ
T: 0115 958 6262
E: enquiries@nelsonslaw.co.uk
W: www.nelsonslaw.co.uk

Nenta Traintours
Railtour House, 10 Buxton Rd, North Walsham, Norfolk NR28 0ED
T: 01692 406152
F: 01692 406152
E: ray.davies@nenta traintours.co.uk
W: www.nentatraintours.co.uk

NES International Ltd (NEStrack)
Station House, Stamford New Rd, Altrincham, Cheshire WA14 1EP
T: 0161 942 4016
F: 0161 942 7969
E: nestrack.manchester@nes.co.uk
W: www.nestrack.co.uk

Network Construction
34 Mortimer St, London W1W 7JS
T: 020 7580 1947
F: 020 7580 1951
E: jobs@network construction.co.uk
W: www.network construction.co.uk

Network Rail Infrastructure Ltd
Kings Place, 90 York Way, London N1 9AG
T: 020 3356 9595
W: www.networkrail.co.uk

Neway Training Solutions Ltd
Kelvin House, RTC Business Park, London Rd, Derby DE24 8UP
T: 01332 360033
F: 01332 366367
E: enquiries@neway-training.com
W: www.neway-training.com

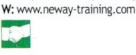

Newburn Consultancy
1 Wood St, Old Town, Swindon, Wilts SN1 4AN
T: 01793 435000
E: info@newburn.co.uk
W: www.newburn.co.uk

Newbury Data Recording Ltd
T: 0870 224 8110
F: 0870 224 8177
E: ndsales@newburydata.co.uk
W: www.newburydata.co.uk

NEW infrastructure Services Group
Coliseum Business Centre, Riverside Way, Camberley, Surrey GU15 3YL
T: 01276 676966
F: 01276 673115
E: n.palmer@new-isg.com
W: www.new-isg.com

Nexans

Nexans manufacture power, signalling and telecommunications cables and components, specifically designed for evolving rail networks. Nexans' cables meet the highest technological performance for signal integrity and fire safety.

Nexans, Nexans House, Chesney Wold, Bleak Hall, Milton Keynes MK6 1LA

Tel: 01908 250840
Fax: 01908 250841
Email: steve.robbins@nexans.com
Web: www.nexans.co.uk

Newtown Fleet Services
See NVR

Nexans
Nexans House, Chesney Wold, Bleak Hall, Milton Keynes MK6 1LF
T: 01908 250840
F: 01908 250841
E: steve.robbins@nexans.com
W: www.nexans.com

Nextiraone (UK) Ltd
Aldershawe Hall, Claypit Lane, Wall, Lichfield WS14 0AQ
T: 01543 414751
F: 01543 250159
E: enquiries@nextiraone.co.uk
W: www.nextiraone.co.uk

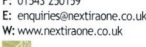

Nexus (Tyne & Wear Metro)
Nexus House, 33 St James Blvd, Newcastle upon Tyne NE1 4AX
T: 0191 203 3333
F: 0191 203 3180
E: metro.communications @nexus.org.uk
W: www.tyneandwearmetro.co.uk

Nexus Training
277 Stockport Rd, Guide Bridge, Ashton under Lyne, Lancs OL7 0NT
T: 0161 339 2160
F: 0161 339 2190
E: info@nexustraining.org.uk
W: www.nexustraining.org.uk

Nichols Group Ltd
2 Savile Row, London W1S 3PA
T: 020 7292 7000
F: 020 7292 5200
E: operations@nichols.uk.com
W: www.nicholsgroup.co.uk

Nigel Nixon Consulting
Suite 1, AD Business Centre, Hithercroft Rd, Wallingford, Oxon OX10 9EZ
T: 01491 824030
F: 01491 824078
E: nigel@nigelnixon.com
W: www.nigelnixon.com

Nightsearcher Ltd
Unit 4, Applied House, Fitzherbert Spur, Farlington, Portsmouth PO6 1TT
T: 023 9238 9774
F: 023 9238 9788
E: sales@nightsearcher.co.uk
W: www.nightsearcher.co.uk

Nitech Ltd
4-6 Highfield Business Park, St Leonards on Sea TN38 9UB
T: 01424 852788
F: 01424 851008
E: accounts@nitech.co.uk
W: www.nitech.co.uk

NMB Minebea
Doddington Rd, Lincoln LN6 3RA
T: 01522 500933
W: www.nmb-minebea.co.uk

No1 Scaffolding Service
Swinbourne Rd, Burnt Mills Ind.Est., Basildon, Essex SS13 1EF
T: 01268 724793
F: 01268 725606
E: enquiries@no1scaffolding.co.uk
W: www.essexscaffolders.co.uk

Nomad Rail
First Floor, Baltic Chambers, 3 Broad Chere, Newcastle NE1 3DQ
T: 020 7096 6966
F: 0191 221 1339
E: enquiries@uknomad.com
W: www.nomadrail.com

Nomix Enviro Ltd a division of Frontier Agriculture Ltd
The Grain Silos, Weyhill Rd, Andover, Hants SP10 3NT
T: 01264 388000
F: 01264 337642
E: nomixenviro@frontierag.co.uk
W: www.nomix.co.uk

Nord-Lock (UK) Ltd
Office 4a, Aspire Business Centre, Ordnance Rd, Tidworth, Wilts SP9 7QD
T: 01980 847129
F: 01980 847674
E: enquiries@nord-lock.co.uk
W: www.nord-lock.com

Norgren Ltd
Eastern Ave, Lichfield, Staffs WS13 6SB
T: 01543 265000
F: 01543 265811
E: mtodd@norgren.com
W: www.norgren.com

Norman Butcher & Jones (NBJ)
52 Lime St, London EC3M 7AF
T: 020 7337 4060
F: 020 7337 4061
E: julianberry@nbj.co.uk
W: www.nbj.co.uk

Northern Ireland Railways (Translink)
Central Station, East Bridge St, Belfast BT1 3PB
T: 02890 899400
E: feedback@translink.co.uk
W: www.translink.co.uk

Northern Rail Ltd
Northern House, 9 Rougier St, York YO1 6HZ
T: 0870 000 5151
E: firstname.lastname@northernrail.org
W: www.northernrail.org

North Star Consultancy Ltd
78 York St, London W1H 1DP
T: 020 7692 0936
F: 020 7692 0937
E: enquiries@northstar consultancy.com
W: www.northstarconsultancy.com

Norton & Associates
32a, High St, Pinner, Middx HA5 5PW
T: 020 8869 9237
F: 07005 964635
E: mail@nortonweb.co.uk
W: www.nortonweb.co.uk

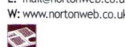

Norton Rose
Kempson House, Camomile St, London EC3A 7AN
T: 020 7283 6000
F: 020 7283 6500
E: deirdre.walker@nortonrose.com
W: www.nortonrose.com

Norwest Holst Construction
Astral House, Imperial Way, Watford WD24 4WW
T: 01923 470435
F: 01923 240594
E: information@vinci.plc.uk
W: www.norwest-holst.co.uk

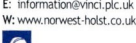

Nottingham Express Transit
Wilkinson St, Nottingham NG7 7NW
T: 0115 942 7777
E: tram@nottinghamcity.gov.uk
W: www.nottingham expresstransit.com

Novacroft
Harvest Barn, Spring Hill, Harborough Rd, Pitsford, Northants NN6 9AA
T: 0845 330 0601
F: 0845 330 0745
E: projects@novacroft.com
W: www.novacroft.com

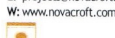

Novus Rail Ltd
Solaris Centre, New South Prom, Blackpool FY4 1RW
T: 01253 478027
F: 01253 478037
E: mmcm@novusrail.com
W: www.novusrail.com

Nu Star Material Handling
Unit C, Ednaston Business Centre, Ednaston, Derby DE6 3AE
T: 0870 443 5646
F: 0870 443 5647
E: matt@nu-starmhl.com
W: www.nu-starmhl.com

Nuttall Finchpalm
St James House, Knoll Rd, Camberley, Surrey GU15 3XW
T: 01276 63484
F: 01276 66060
E: info@bamnuttall.co.uk
W: www.bamnuttall.co.uk

NVR Fleet UK
Newtown House, Tanworth Lane, Alcester Rd, Redditch, Worcs B98 9EJ
T: 01564 741100
F: 01564 741130
E: nvr.sales@newtown.co.uk
W: www.newtown.co.uk

Odgers Ray & Berndtson
11 Hanover Square, London W1S 1JJ
T: 020 7529 1111
F: 020 7529 1000
E: info@rayberndtson.co.uk
W: www.odgers.com

Office of Rail Regulation (ORR)
One Kemble St, London WC2B 4AN
T: 020 7282 2000
F: 020 7282 2040
E: firstname.lastname@orr.gsi.gov.uk
W: www.rail-reg.gov.uk

Oil Analysis Services Ltd
Unit 6/7, Blue Chalet Ind. Park, London Rd, West Kingsdown, Kent TN15 6BQ
T: 01474 854450
F: 01474 854408
E: lhbrown@oas-online.co.uk
W: www.oas-online.co.uk

Oleo International
Grovelands, Longford Rd, Exhall, Coventry CV7 9ND
T: 02476 645555
F: 02476 664287
E: royh@oleo.co.uk
W: www.oleo.co.uk

Omega Reed Group
Dabell Ave, Blenheim Ind.Est., Bulwell, Nottingham NG6 8WA
T: 0115 877 6666
F: 0115 876 7766
E: enquiries@omegaredgroup.com
W: www.omegaredgroup.com

Omnicom Engineering Ltd
292 Tadcaster Rd, York YO24 1ET
T: 01904 778100
F: 01904 778200
E: sales@omnieng.co.uk
W: www.omnieng.co.uk

O'Neill Transport Consultancy
87, Neville Rd, Darlington, Co.Durham DL3 8NQ
T: 01325 482193
F: 01325 256053
E: rita.oneill@talk21.com
W: www.icrg.co.uk

One-On Railway Engineering Ltd
Walton House, Park Rd, Sutton Coldfield, West Midlands B73 6BT
T: 0845 260 5585
F: 0845 260 5595
E: info@one-on.co.uk
W: www.one-on.co.uk

On Track Design Solutions Ltd
1st Floor Suite, 11 Pride Point Drive, Pride Park, Derby DE24 8BX
T: 01332 204450
F: 01332 204458
E: brianchadwick@ontrackdesign.co.uk
W: www.ontrackdesign.co.uk

On Track Flooring Ltd
Unit E18, Laws Lane, Stanton by Dale, Derbys DE7 4RT
T: 01159 321691
E: t.carter@ontrackflooring.co.uk

On Track Training
2 Walmsley Drive, Upton, West Yorks WF9 1JW
T: 01977 658639
E: ontracktraining@fsmail.net
W: www.ontracktraining.net

Optelecom-NKF Ltd
Endeavour House, 98 Waters Meeting Rd, Navigation Business Park, The Valley, Bolton BL1 8SW
T: 01204 546635
F: 01204 546636
E: faston@optelecom-nkf.com
W: www.nkfelectronics.com

Optilan Communication Systems
Sibree Rd, Stonebridge Ind. Est, Coventry CV3 4FD
T: 01926 864999
F: 01926 851818
E: sales@optilan.com
W: www.optilan.com

Optimum Consultancy
Spencer House, Millgreen Rd, Haywards Heath, West Sussex RH16 1XQ
T: 01444 443551
F: 01444 448071
E: mail@orchard-consulting.co.uk
W: www.orchard-consulting.co.uk

Orchard Consulting
See Optimum

Oracle Recruitment
Rivington House, 82 Great Eastern St, London EC2A 3JF
T: 0871 200 0005
F: 0871 200 0006
E: info@oracleglobal.com
W: www.oracleglobal.com

Ordnance Survey
Romsey Rd, Southampton SO16 4GU
T: 02380 305030
F: 02380 792615
E: customerservice@ordnancesurvey.co.uk
W: www.ordnancesurvey.co.uk

Orient Express
T: 020 7921 4028
F: 020 7805 5908
E: oesales.uk@orient-express.com
W: www.orient-express.com

Orion Electrotech
4 Danehill, Lower Earley, Reading RG6 4UT
T: 0118 923 9239
F: 0118 975 3332
E: reading@orionelectrotech.com
W: www.orionelectrotech.com

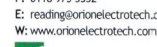

Orion Rail Services Ltd
29-31 Lister Road, Hillington Park, Glasgow G52 4BH
T: 0141 892 6666
F: 0141 892 6662
E: sales@orioneng.com
W: www.orioneng.com

Oscar Associates
Grove House, 744/780 Wilmslow Rd, Didsbury, Manchester M20 2DR
T: 0161 445 0445
F: 0161 438 8438
E: enquiries@oscar-associates.com
W: www.oscar-associates.com

Osborne Rail
Raven House, 29 Linkfield Lane, Redhill, Surrey RH1 1JP
T: 01737 378200
F: 01737 378295
E: paul.williams@osborne.co.uk
W: www.osborne.co.uk

Owen Williams - Part of AMEY Plc
SBQ3, Hagley Rd, Edgbaston, West Midlands B16 8NH
T: 0121 456 1568
E: office-sbq3bham@amey.co.uk
W: www.owenwilliams.co.uk

Pandrol UK Ltd
Gateford Rd, Worksop, Notts S81 7AX
T: 01909 476101
F: 01909 500004
E: info@pandrol.com
W: www.pandrol.com

Panolin
Ripon Way, Harrogate, N Yorks HG1 2AU
T: 01423 522911
F: 01423 530043
E: admin@cardev.com
W: www.cardev.com

Pantrak Transportation Ltd
G&S Building, 5, Sholto Cresc., Righead Ind. Est., Bellshill, Lanarkshire ML4 3LX
T: 01698 840465
F: 01698 749672
E: gavinroser@pantrak.com
W: www.pantrak.com

Parc Group
22 Queen Anne's Gate, St James, London SW1H 9AA
T: 020 7960 7600
F: 020 7960 7634
E: london@parc-group.com
W: www.parc-group.com

Parkeon Ltd
10 Willis Way, Fleets Ind Est, Poole, Dorset BH15 3SS
T: 01202 339494
F: 01202 667293
E: sales_uk@parkeon.com
W: www.parkeon.com

PS
Park Signalling Limited

PSL supplies novel and conventional signalling equipment and provides design, development, repair and consultancy services for UK signalling, including re-engineering and support for legacy systems.

Address: Houldsworth Mill Business Centre, Houldsworth Street, Reddish, Stockport SK5 6DA

Telephone: 0161 975 6161
Fax: 0161 975 6160

Email: info@park-signalling.co.uk
Website: www.park-signalling.co.uk

Park Signalling Ltd
Houldsworth Mill Business Centre, Houldsworth St, Reddish, Stockport SK5 6DA
T: 0161 975 6161
F: 0161 975 6160
E: info@park-signalling.co.uk
W: www.park-signalling.co.uk

Parker Hannifin (UK) Ltd
Brunel Way, Thetford, Norfolk IP24 1HP
T: 01842 763299
F: 01842 756300
E: filtrationinfo@parker.com
W: www.parker.com

JPM Parry & Associates Ltd
Overend Rd, Cradley Heath, West Midlands B64 7DD
T: 01384 569171
F: 01384 637753
E: info@parryassociates.com
W: www.parryassociates.com/transport

Parry People Movers Ltd
Overend Rd, Cradley Heath, West Midlands B64 7DD
T: 01384 569553
F: 01384 637753
E: info@parrypeoplemovers.com
W: www.parrypeoplemovers.com

Parsons Brinckerhoff Ltd
Westbrook Mills, Godalming, Surrey GU7 2AZ
T: 01483 528400
F: 01483 528989
E: morrisj@pbworld.com
W: www.pbworld.com/pbltc

Parsons Transport Group
4 Grosvenor Place, London SW1X 7PG
T: 020 7823 0700
F: 020 7823 8178
E: enquiries.pgil@parsons.com
W: www.parsons.com

Partsmaster Ltd (NCH Europe)
Landchard House, Victoria St, West Bromwich B70 8ER
T: 0121 525 8939
F: 0121 524 7379
E: victoria.summerfield@nch.com
W: www.partsmaster.com

Passcomm Ltd
Unit 24, Tatton Court, Kingsland Garage, Warrington WA1 4RR
T: 01925 821333
F: 01925 821321
E: info@passcomm.co.uk
W: www.passcomm.co.uk

Passenger Focus
Whittles House, 14 Pentonville Rd, London N1 9HF
T: 0870 336 6000
F: 0207 713 2729
E: contact@passengerfocus.org.uk
W: www.passengerfocus.org.uk

Passenger Transport Networks
49, Stonegate, York YO1 8AW
T: 01904 611 87
E: ptn@btconnect.com

Past-Time Rail
116 Trent Valley Rd, Lichfield, Staffs WS13 6EU
T: 01543 419971
F: 01543 417531
E: pasttimerail.ltd@btconnect.com
W: www.past-timerail.co.uk

Pathfinder Systems UK PTY Ltd
Unit 6, Bighams Park Farm, Waterend, Hemel Hempstead HP1 3BN
T: 07711 139366
F: 020 7328 8818
E: cel@pathfindersystems.com.au
W: www.pathfindersystems.com.au

Directory

Pathfinder Tours
Stag House, Gydynap Lane, Inchbrook, Woodchester, Glos GL5 5EZ
T: 01453 835414
F: 01453 836538
E: office@pathfindertours.co.uk
W: www.pathfindertours.co.uk

Paul Fabrications Ltd
Unit 10a, Sills Rd, Willow Farm Business Park, Castle Donington DE74 2US
T: 01332 818000
F: 01332 818089
E: sales@paulfabs.co.uk
W: www.paulfabs.co.uk

Paul John Plant
Telford Way, Stephenson Ind. Est, Coalville, Leics LE67 3HE
T: 01530 513444
F: 01530 513446
E: coalvilleplant@pauljohngroup.com
W: www.pauljohngroup.com

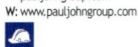

PB Design & Development
Unit 9/10, Hither Green Ind. Est., Clevedon, Bristol BS21 6ZT
T: 01275 874411
E: sales@pbdesign.co.uk
W: www.pbdesign.co.uk

Peacock Salt Ltd
North Harbour, Ayr KA8 8AE
T: 01292 292000
F: 01292 292001
E: info@peacocksalt.co.uk
W: www.peacocksalt.co.uk

A S Peck Engineering
116 Whitby Rd, Ruislip, Middx HA4 9DR
T: 01895 621398
F: 01895 613761
E: markjones@aspeckeng.co.uk
W: www.aspeckeng.co.uk

Peeping Ltd
14 Lovelstaithe, Norwich NR1 1LW
T: 01603 625604
E: kmpeeping@btinternet.com

Pegasus Transconsult Ltd
17 North Court, Hassocks, West Sussex BN6 8JS
T: 01273 845 583
F: 01273 845 645
E: marketing@pegasustransconsult.com
W: www.pegasustransconsult.com

Peli Products (UK) Ltd
Peli House, Peakdale Rd, Brookfield, Glossop, Derbys SK13 6LQ
T: 01457 869999
F: 01457 569966
E: sales@peliproducts.co.uk
W: www.peliproducts.co.uk

Pell Frischmann
5 Manchester Square, London W1A 1AU
T: 020 7486 3661
F: 020 7487 4153
E: pflondon@pellfrischmann.com
W: www.pellfrischmann.com

Pennant Consulting Ltd
1 Sopwith Cres., Wickford Business Park, Wickford, Essex SS11 8YU
T: 01268 493495
E: enquiries@pennant-recruit.com
W: www.pennant-consult.com

Pennant information Services Ltd
Renold House, Heald Green, Manchester M22 5WZ
T: 0161 493 1600
F: 0161 499 0102
E: john.churchman@pennantplc.co.uk
W: www.pennantplc.co.uk

Pennant International Group Plc
Pennant Court, Staverton Technology Park, Cheltenham GL51 6TL
T: 01452 714881
F: 01452 715196
E: sales@pennantplc.co.uk
W: www.pennantplc.co.uk

Perco Engineering Services
Cornhill Close, Lodge Farm Ind. Est., Northampton NN5 7UB
T: 01604 590200
F: 01604 590201
E: nick.sheehan@perco.co.uk
W: www.perco.co.uk

Permali Gloucester Ltd
Permali Park, Bristol Rd, Gloucester GL1 5TT
T: 01452 528282
F: 01452 507409
E: fraser.rankin@permali.co.uk
W: www.permali.co.uk

Permanent Way Institution
8 Douglas Road, Bingham, Notts NG13 8EL
T: 01949 837 067
F: 01949 838 826
E: colin.cowie@talk21.com
W: www.permanentwayinstitution.com

Petards Joyce-Loebl Ltd
390, Princesway North, Team Valley Est., Gateshead, Tyne & Wear NE11 0TU
T: 0191 423 3608
F: 0191 423 3604
E: sales@petards.com
W: www.petards.com

Peter Brett Associates
Caversham Bridge House, Waterman Place, Reading RG1 8DN
T: 0118 950 0761
F: 0118 959 7498
E: reading@pba.co.uk
W: www.pba.co.uk

Peter Davidson Consultancy
Brownlow House, Rowens Lane, Berkhamsted, Herts HP4 2DX
T: 01442 879075
F: 01442 879776
E: mail@peter-davidson.com
W: www.peter-davidson.com

Peter Staveley Ltd
247 Davidson Rd, Croydon CR0 6DQ
T: 07973 168742
E: peter@peterstaveley.co.uk
www.ircg.co.uk

Pfleiderer
See RailOne

PFS Ltd
Unit 1, Parker House Est., Manor Rd, West Thurrock, Essex RM20 4EH
T: 01708 252960
F: 01708 864140
E: trevor.mason@pfsfueltec.com
W: www.pfsfueltec.com

Pharos Modtech Solutions Ltd
13 Cornwall Business Centre, Cornwall Rd, Wigston, Leicester LE18 4XH
T: 0116 222 2000
F: 0116 277 9369
E: mick.heron@pharosmodtech.co.uk
W: www.pharosengineering.co.uk

Phi Group Ltd
Harcourt House, Royal Crescent, Cheltenham, Glos GL50 3DA
T: 0870 333 4126
F: 0870 333 4127
E: marketing@phigroup.co.uk
W: www.phigroup.co.uk

Philmor Rail Services Ltd
Heritage Court Rd, Gilchrist Thomas Ind Est, Blaenavon, Torfaen NP4 9RL
T: 01495 792030
F: 01495 792757
E: sales@philmor.com
W: www.philmor.com

Phoenix Contact Ltd
Halesfield 13, Telford, Shropshire TF7 4PG
T: 01952 681700
F: 01952 681799
E: info@phoenixcontact.co.uk
W: www.phoenixcontact.co.uk

PHS Besafe incorporating Hiviz Laundries Ltd
Western Ind. Est., Caerphilly CF83 1XH
T: 02920 851000
F: 02920 863288
E: enquiries@phs.co.uk
W: www.phs.co.uk/hiviz

Pipeline Drillers Ltd
10 Kirkford, Stewarton, Kilmarnock KA3 5HZ
T: 01560 482021
F: 01560 484809
E: info@pipelinedrillers.co.uk

Pilkington Glass ltd
Prescot Rd, St Helens, Merseyside WA10 3TT
T: 01744 28882
F: 01744 692660
W: www.pilkington.com

Pinsent Masons
City Point, One Ropemaker St, London EC2Y 9AH
T: 020 7418 7000
F: 020 7418 7050
E: annie.kilvington@pinsentmasons.com
W: www.pinsentmasons.com

Pirtek (UK) Ltd
35 Acton Park Estate, The Vale, Acton, London W3 7QE
T: 020 8749 8444
F: 020 8749 8333
E: info@pirtek.co.uk
W: www.pirtekuk.com

Pitchmastic PMB
Royd's Works, Attercliffe Rd, Sheffield S9 4WZ
T: 0114 270 0100
F: 0114 276 8782
E: info@pitchmasticpmb.co.uk
W: www.pitchmasticpmb.co.uk

Planet Platforms Ltd
146 Wakefield Rd, Ossett, Wakefield, West Yorks WF5 9AR
T: 0800 0854 161
F: 01924 267090
E: info@planetplatforms.co.uk
W: www.planetplatforms.co.uk

Plan Me
PO Box 281, Malvern WR14 9EP
T: 07906 439055
F: 0800 471 5332
E: info@plan.me.uk
W: www.plan.me.uk

Plasser Machinery, Parts & Services Ltd
Manor Rd, West Ealing, London W13 0PP
T: 020 8998 4781
F: 020 8997 8206
E: info@plasser.co.uk
W: www.plasser.co.uk

Platipus Anchors Ltd
Unit Q, Philanthropic Rd, Kingsfield Business Centre, Redhill RH1 4DP
T: 01737 762300
F: 01737 773395
E: info@platipus-anchors.com
W: www.platipus-anchors.com

Plowman Craven & Associates
141 Lower Luton Rd, Harpenden, Herts AL5 5EQ
T: 01582 765566
F: 01582 765370
E: webenquiry@plowmancraven.co.uk
W: www.plowmancraven.co.uk

PMA UK Ltd
Unit 4, Imperial Court, Magellan Close, Walworth Ind. Est., Andover, Hants SP10 5NT
T: 01264 333527
F: 01264 333643
E: sales@pma-uk.com
W: www.pma-uk.com

PMProfessional Learning
Bourne End Business Park, Cores End Rd, Bourne End, Bucks SL8 5AS
T: 0870 242 6097
F: 0870 242 6098
E: learning@pmprofessional.com
W: www.pmprofessional.co.uk

PM Safety Consultants Ltd
Suite D, 3rd Floor, Saturn Facilities, 101 Lockhurst Lane, Coventry CV6 5SF
T: 02476 665770
F: 02476 582401
E: info@pmsafety.com
W: www.pmsafety.com

Pohl, Llewellyn Davies & Co
The Barn, Church Walks, Chester CH3 7AF
T: 01244 332393
F: 0870 7065536
E: info@pld.cc
W: www.pld.cc

Polyamp AB
Box 229, Atvidaberg, 597 25 Sweden
T: 0046 120 85410
F: 0046 120 85405
E: info@polyamp.se
W: www.polyamp.com

Polydeck Ltd
Unit 14, Burnett Ind Est, Cox's Green, Bristol BS40 5QS
T: 01934 863678
F: 01934 863683
E: sales@gripfast.co.uk
W: www.gripfast.co.uk

Polypipe Civils Ltd
Union Works, Bishop Meadow Rd, Loughborough, Leics LE11 5RE
T: 01509 615100
F: 01509 610215
E: civilssales@polypipe.com
W: www.polypipe.com

Polysafe Level Crossings
King St. Ind. Est., Langtoft, Peterborough PE6 9NF
T: 01778 560555
F: 01778 560773
E: sales@polysafe.co.uk
W: www.polysafe.co.uk

Portec Rail Products (UK) Ltd.
Stamford Street, Sheffield S9 2TL
T: 0114 256 7598
F: 0114 261 7826
E: info@coronetrail.co.uk
W: www.portecrail.com

Porterbrook Leasing Company Ltd
Burdett House, Becket St, Derby DE1 1JP
T: 01332 262405
F: 01332 262045
E: enquiries@porterbrook.co.uk
W: www.porterbrook.co.uk

Portwest Clothing Ltd
Commercial Rd, Goldthorpe Ind. Est., Goldthorpe, S.Yorks S63 9BL
T: 01709 894575
F: 01709 880830
E: info@portwest.com
W: www.portwest.com

Postfield Systems
53, Ullswater Cres.,Coulsdon, Surrey CR5 2HR
T: 020 8645 9760
F: 020 8660 1804
E: sales@postfield.co.uk
W: www.postfield.co.uk

Potensis Ltd
7th Floor, Froomsgate House, Rupert St, Bristol BS1 2QJ
T: 0117 910 7999
F: 0117 927 2722
E: office@potensis.com
W: www.potensis.com

The Potter Group Ltd
Rail Freight Terminal, Barlby Rd, Selby, N yorks YO8 5DZ
T: 01757 702303
F: 01757 210834
E: enquiries@pottergroup.co.uk
W: www.pottergroup.co.uk

The Potter Group Ltd
Road and Rail Distribution Centre, Queen Adelaide Way, Ely, Cambs CB7 4UB
T: 01353 646703
F: 01353 662764
E: enquiries@pottergroup.co.uk
W: www.pottergroup.co.uk

The Potter Group Ltd
Rail Freight Terminal, Woodward Rd, Knowsley Ind Park, Knowsley, Merseyside L33 7UZ
T: 0151 290 0671
F: 0151 289 1310
E: enquiries@pottergroup.co.uk
W: www.pottergroup.co.uk

Power 4 from Fox & Cooper
Lancaster Approach, North Killingholme, Immingham, NE Lincs DN40 3TZ
T: 0870 414 1400
F: 0870 414 1440
E: power4@foxandcooper.co.uk
W: www.power4.biz

Power Electronics (PE Systems Ltd)
Victoria St, Leigh, Lancs WN7 5SE
T: 01942 260330
F: 01942 261835
E: sales@pe-systems.co.uk
W: www.power-electronics.co.uk

Powernetics International Ltd
Power House, Jason Works, Clarence St, Loughborough, Leics LE11 1DX
T: 01509 214153
F: 01509 262460
E: sales@powernetics.co.uk
W: www.powernetics.co.uk

Powertron Convertors Ltd
Glebe Farm Technical Campus, Knapwell, Cambridge CB3 8GG
T: 01954 267726
F: 01954 267626
E: sales@powertron.co.uk
W: www.powertron.co.uk

Praxis High Integrity Systems Ltd
20 Manvers St, Bath BA1 1PX
T: 01225 466991
F: 01225 469006
E: info@praxis-his.com
W: www.praxis-his.com

Praybourne Ltd
Unit 11 Dunlop Road, Hunt End Ind. Est, Redditch B97 5XP
T: 0870 242 0004
F: 01527 543 752
E: enquiries@praybourne.co.uk
W: www.praybourne.co.uk

PRC Rail Consulting
10 Park Lane, Sutton Bonington, Loughborough LE12 5NH
T: 01509 670679
F: 01509 670679
E: piers.connor@railway-technical.com
W: www.railway-technical.com

Premier Calibrations
Unit 31, Lake Enterprise Park, Sandall Stores Rd, Kirk Sandall, Doncaster DN3 1QR
T: 01302 888448
F: 01302 881197
E: enquiries.premcal@btconnect.com
W: www.premier-calibration.co.uk

Premier Stampings
Station St, Cradley Heath, West Midlands B64 6AJ
T: 01384 353100
F: 01384 353101
E: ashleyh@premierstampings.co.uk
W: www.premierstampings.co.uk

Premier Train Catering
T: 01255 556222
E: graham@ptcatering.com
W: www.ptcatering.com

PremTech Solutions Ltd
9 Saffron Meadow, Harrogate, North Yorks HG3 2NU
T: 07778 981641
E: david@premtech.net
W: www.premtech.net

Price Tool Sales Ltd
90 Summer Lane, Newtown, Birmingham B19 3ND
T: 0121 689 2000
F: 0121 689 2100
E: sales@pricetools.co.uk
W: www.pricetools.co.uk

Price Waterhouse Coopers
1 Embankment Place, London WC2N 6NN
T: 020 7583 5000
F: 020 7822 4652
E: julian.smith@uk.pwc.com
W: www.pwcglobal.com

Primarius UK Ltd
12b, Earlstrees Rd, Earlstrees Ind Est, Corby, Northants NN17 4AZ
T: 01536 263691
E: sales@primariusuk.com
W: www.primariusuk.com

Primat Recruitment
William Press House, Haughton Rd, Darlington DL1 2ED
T: 01325 376200
F: 01325 358111
W: www.primatrecruitment.com

Probst
Wem Ind. Est., Soulton Rd, Wem, Shrewsbury SY4 5SD
T: 01939 235325
F: 01939 235562
E: pbolland@probst-handling.co.uk
W: www.probst-handling.co.uk

Progress Rail Services
See Caterpillar

Prolec Ltd
25 Benson Rd, Nuffield Ind. Est., Poole, Dorset BH17 0GB
T: 01202 681190
F: 01202 677709
E: info@prolec.co.uk
W: www.prolec.co.uk

Prostaff Rail Recruitment
172, Buckingham Ave, Slough, Bucks SL1 4RD
T: 01753 575888
W: www.prostaff.com

Proteq
96, High St, Epworth, Doncaster DN9 1JJ
T: 01427 872572
E: info@proteq.co.uk
W: www.proteq.co.uk

Prysmian Cables & Systems
Chickenhall Lane, Bishopstoke, Hants SO50 6YU
T: 023 8029 5029
F: 023 8060 8769
E: marketing.telecom@prysmian.com
W: www.prysmian.com

Prysm Rail
See Archer Signs

Psion Teklogix
Unit Q, Bourne End Business Centre, Cores End Rd, Bourne End, Bucks SL8 5AS
T: 01628 648800
F: 01628 648810
E: hannah.jefferys@psionteklogix.com
W: www.psionteklogix.co.uk

PSV GLASS
BUS-COACH-RAIL
PSV Glass supply and fit windscreens and body sideglass to main line trains, light rail trams and underground systems - round the clock, 7 days a week, nationwide.
Hillbottom Road, High Wycombe, Bucks HP12 4HJ
Tel: 01494 533131
Fax: 01494 462675
steve.pitwood-brown@psvglass.co.uk
www.psvglass.com

PSV Glass
Hillbottom Rd, High Wycombe, Bucks HP12 4HJ
T: 01494 533131
F: 01494 462675
E: steve.pitwood-brown@psvglass.co.uk
W: www.psvglass.com

Ptarmigan Transport Solutions Ltd
Arran House, Arran Rd, Perth PH1 3DZ
T: 01738 459268
E: info@ptarmigansolutions.co.uk
W: www.ptarmigansolutions.co.uk

PTM Design Ltd
Unit B2, Sovereign Park Ind Est, Lathkill St, Market Harborough LE16 9EG
T: 01858 463777
F: 01858 463777
E: ptmdesign@aol.com

Pullman Group
Train Maintenance Depot, Leckwith Rd, Cardiff CF11 8HP
T: 02920 368866
F: 02920 368874
E: colin@pullmans.net
W: www.pullmans.net

Pulsarail
See Praybourne Ltd

Pyeroy Group
Kirkstone House, St Omers Rd, Western Riverside Route, Gateshead NE11 9EZ
T: 0191 493 2600
F: 0191 493 2601
E: mail@pyeroy.co.uk
W: www.pyeroy.co.uk

Pym & Wildsmith
Bramshall Ond Est, Bramshall, Uttoxeter, Staffs ST14 8TD
T: 01889 565653
F: 01889 567064
E: enquiries@pymandwildsmith.co.uk
W: www.pymandwildsmith.co.uk

QC Data Ltd
Park House, 14 Kirtley Drive, Castle Marina, Nottingham NG7 1LD
T: 0115 941 5806
F: 0115 947 2901
E: cbaker@qcdata.com
W: www.qcdata.com

QHI Rail
Talisman House, Allied Business Centre, Coldharbour Lane, Harpenden, Herts AL5 4UT
T: 01582 461123
F: 01582 461117
E: sales@qhigroup.com
W: www.qhirail.com

QinetiQ
Cody Technology Park, Building A7, Room 2008, Iveley Road, Farnborough, Hants GU14 0LX
T: 01252 394 786
F: 01252 397 298
E: jldavies@QinetiQ.com
W: www.QinetiQ.com

The QSS Group Ltd
2 St Georges House, Vernon Gate, Derby DE1 1UQ
T: 01332 221400
F: 01332 221401
E: claire.mulholland@theqssgroup.co.uk
W: www.theqssgroup.co.uk

Q'straint
Unit 72-76, John Wilson Business Park, Whitstable, Kent CT5 3QT
T: 01277 773035
F: 01277 770035
E: info@qstraint.co.uk
W: www.qstraint.com

QTS Plant
QTS Group, Rench Farm, Drumclog, Strathaven, S. Lanarks ML10 6QJ
T: 01357 440222
F: 01357 440364
E: enquiries@qtsgroup.com
W: www.qtsgroup.com

HSBC

Qualter Hall & Co Ltd
PO Box 8, Johnson St, Barnsley S75 2BY
T: 01226 205761
F: 01226 286269
E: admin@qualterhall.co.uk
W: www.qualterhall.co.uk

Quasar Associates
8 Flitcroft St, London WC2H 8DJ
T: 020 7010 7700
F: 020 7010 7701
E: jonathan@quasarassociates.co.uk
W: www.quasarassociates.co.uk

Quattro Plant Ltd
Greenway Court, Canning Rd, Stratford, London E15 3ND
T: 020 8519 6165
F: 020 8503 0505
W: www.quattroplant.co.uk

Quest Diagnostics
Unit B1, Parkway West, Cranford Lane, Heston, Middx TW5 9QA
T: 020 8377 3378
F: 020 8377 3350
E: uksales@questdiagnostics.com
W: www.questdiagnostics.com

Ra'alloy Trading Company
B8 Hortonwood 10, Telford, Shropshire TF1 7ES
T: 01952 677877
F: 01952 677833
E: enquiries@raalloy.co.uk
W: www.raalloy.co.uk

Radio-Tech Ltd
U1/U2, The London Road Campus, London Road, Harlow, Essex CM17 9NA
T: 01279 635 849
F: 01279 442 261
E: sales@radio-tech.co.uk
W: www.radio-tech.co.uk

Rail-Ability Ltd
Tilcon Ave, Baswich, Stafford ST18 0YJ
T: 01785 214747
F: 01785 214717
E: skelly@railability.co.uk
W: www.railability.co.uk

Rail Accident Investigation Branch
The Wharf, Stores Rd, Derby DE21 4BA
T: 01332 253300
F: 01332 253301
E: enquiries@raib.gov.uk
W: www.raib.gov.uk

Rail Air Engineering
See Sigma Coachair

Rail Alliance
The Control Tower, Long Marston Storage, Campden Rd, Long Marston, Stratford upon Avon, Warks CV37 8QR
T: 01789 720026
E: info@railalliance.co.uk
W: www.railalliance.co.uk

Rail-Blue Charters
32 Sydney rd, Haywards Heath, West Sussex RH16 1QA
T: 01444 450011
F: 01444 450011
E: Ingrid.sluis@rail-bluecharters.co.uk
W: www.rail-bluecharters.co.uk

Railcare Ltd
Wolverton Works, Stratford Rd, Wolverton, Milton Keynes MK12 5NT
T: 08000 741122
E: info@railcare.com
W: www.railcare.com

railalliance

The Rail Alliance provides a forum where members can network and collaborate to maintain and grow their business. Membership spans all aspects of the railway and supporting industries, suppliers and customers, public and private sector, all united in the goal of trading and working with each other.

Rail Alliance, Long Marston Storage, Campden Road, Long Marston, Stratford-on-Avon, Warwickshire. CV37 8QR
T: 01789 720026
E: info@railalliance.co.uk
www.railalliance.co.uk

Rail Domain Ltd
Greenway Court, 502 The White House, 9 Belvedere Rd, London SE1 8YT
T: 020 7928 8995
F: 020 7928 9121
E: info@raildomain.com
W: www.raildomain.com

Rail Door Solutions Ltd
Blackhill Drive, Wolverton Mill, Milton Keynes MK12 5TS
T: 01908 224140
F: 01908 224149
E: sales@raildoorsolutions.co.uk
W: www.raildoorsolutions.co.uk

Railex Aluminium Ltd
12/26 Dry Drayton Ind. Est., Dry Drayton, Cambridge CB3 8AT
T: 01954 211905
F: 01954 210352
E: info@railex.net
W: www.railex.net

Rail Freight Group
Monticello House, 45 Russell Square, WC1 4JS
T: 020 7907 4641
F: 020 7907 4884
E: tony@rfg.org.uk
W: www.rfg.org.uk

Railfuture
29 Granby Hill, Bristol BS8 4LT
T: 07759 557389
E: iae001@netgates.co.uk
W: www.railfuture.org.uk

Rail Gourmet Group
Mac Millan House, Paddington Station, London W2 1FT
T: 020 7313 0720
F: 020 7922 6596
E: jfleet@railgourmetuk.com
W: www.railgourmet.com

Rail Images
5 Sandhurst Cres., Leigh on Sea, Essex SS9 4AL
T: 01702 525059
F: 01702 525059
E: info@railimages.co.uk
W: www.railimages.net

Rail Industry First Aid Association (RIFAA)
Room 103, Denison House South, Hexthorpe Road, Doncaster DN4 0BF
T: 01302 329 729
F: 01302 320 590
E: bookings@rifaa.com
W: www.rifaa.com

Railko Ltd
See Tenmat

Rail Link Engineering (RLE)
11 Pilgrim St, London EC4V 6RN
T: 020 7651 7708
E: rle@rle-online.co.uk
W: www.rle-online.co.uk

Rail Operations Developments Ltd
Electra House, Electra Way, Crewe Business Park, Crewe CW1 6GL
T: 01270 588500
F: 01270 588500
E: enquiries@rodl.co.uk
W: www.railoperationsdevelopment.co.uk

Rail Order
Unit 2, Anglia Way, Mansfield, Notts NG18 4LP
T: 01623 627208
F: 01623 633914
E: sales@rail-order.co.uk
W: www.rail-order.co.uk

Rail Personnel International Ltd
Knaresborough, North Yorks HG5 0NA
T: 07875 099964
E: colina@railpersonnel.com
W: www.railpersonnel.com

RMF

RMF is a leading provider of railway reservation based international settlement and clearing services, providing sophisticated revenue and cost allocation, including business critical management information.

Rail Manche Finance EEIG
Suite 1a, Floor 3, Eurostar House, Waterloo Station, London, SE1 8SE
T: 00 44 (0) 20 7202 8451
F: 00 44 (0) 20 7633 0224
E: david.hiscock@rmf.co.uk
www.rmf.co.uk

Rail Manche Finance EEIG
Suite 1a, Eurostar House, Waterloo Station, London SE1 8SE
T: 020 7202 8451
F: 020 7633 0224
E: david.hiscock@rmf.co.uk
W: www.rmf.co.uk

RAIL.ONE GmbH
Ingolstaedter Strasse 51, 92318 Neumarkt, Germany
T: 0049 9181 28-693
F: 0049 9181 28-646
E: hedwig.blomeier@railone.com
W: www.railone.com

Rail Operations Competence Solutions Ltd
40 Weston Lane, Shavington, Crewe, Cheshire CW2 5AN
T: 07796 548651
E: info@rail-operations-competence-solutions.co.uk
W: www.rail-operations-competence-solutions.co.uk

Rail Op UK Ltd
Unit D1, The Maltings, Station Rd, Sawbridgeworth, Herts CM21 9JX
T: 0845 450 5332
E: info@railop.co.uk
W: www.railop.co.uk

Rail Photo Library
T: 0116 259 2068
E: studio@railphotolibrary.com
W: www.railphotolibrary.com

railphotolibrary.com
Search and Buy Railway Photographs On-line
Picture Library & Photographers to the Railway Industry
0116 2592068 studio@railphotolibrary.com
Link-Up registered

Rail Operations Development Ltd is a dynamic railway management consultancy company in the UK, offering a choice of innovative solutions to the railway industry.

Contact Details:
T: 01270 588500
F: 01270 588500
E: enquiries@rodl.co.uk
W: www.railoperationsdevelopment.co.uk

Rail Operations Development Ltd
MacdonaldO'Connor

Verba mea auribus

Rail Positive Relations

Rail Positive Relations is the UK's leading specialist communications consultancy for the railway industry. Services include Stakeholder & Government Relations, Lobbying and Media Management.

A: The Bothy, 18 Holloway Road Duffield, Derbyshire DE56 4FE
T: +44 (0) 7973 950 923
F: +44 (0) 8712 429 613
E: rupert@railpr.com
W: www.railpr.com

Rail Positive Relations
The Bothy, 18 Holloway Rd, Duffield, Derbys DE56 4FE
T: 07973 950923
F: 08712 429613
E: Rupert@railpr.com
W: www.railpr.com

Rail Professional Development
2 Cornhouse Buildings, Arterial Rd, Rayleigh Weir, Rayleigh, Essex SS6 7UL
T: 01268 747222
F: 01268 747221
E: info@rpd.co.uk
W: www.rpd.co.uk

Rail Recruit
39 Mitchell Point, Ensign Way, Southampton SO31 4RF
T: 02380 744454
F: 02380 458135
E: info@railrecruit.com
W: www.railrecruit.com

Rail Safety & Standards Board
Evergreen House, 160 Euston Rd, London NW1 2DX
T: 020 7904 7518
F: 020 7557 9072
E: enquirydesk@rssb.co.uk
W: www.rssb.co.uk

Railscape Ltd
Graphic House, 11 Totman Close, Brook Rd Ind Est, Rayleigh, Essex SS6 7UZ
T: 01268 777795
F: 01268 777762
E: info@railscape.com
W: www.railscape.com

Rail Tech Group (Railway & Signalling Engineering) Ltd
91 Dales Rd, Ipswich IP1 4JR
T: 01473 242330
F: 01473 242379
E: reception@railtech.co.uk
W: www.railtech.co.uk

Rail Technology Ltd
T: 01283 790012
F: 01283 792371
E: info@railtechnologyltd.com
W: www.railtechnologyltd.com

Railtourer Ltd
42 Kingston Rd, Willerby, Hull HU10 6BH
T: 01482 659082
E: davetyler@fsmail.net
W: www.railtourer.co.uk

Rail Training International Ltd
North Suite, Parsonage Offices, Church Lane, Canterbury, Kent CT4 7AD
T: 01227 769096
F: 01227 479435
E: rtiuk@rti.co.uk
W: www.rti.co.uk

Rail Vision
410 Park Rd, Loughborough, Leics LE11 2HN
T: 01509 635748
F: 01509 635749
E: enquiries@rail-vision.com
W: www.rail-vision.com

Rail Waiting Structures Ltd
Dyffryn Business Park, Llantwit Major Rd, Llandow, Vale of Glamorgan
T: 01446 795444
F: 01446 793344
E: sarah.galton@shelters.demon.co.uk
W: www.shelters.demon.co.uk

Railway & Industrial Safety Consultants Ltd
See RISC Ltd

Railway Approvals Ltd
31, Brunel Parkway, Pride Park, Derby DE24 9JN
T: 0870 140 7639
F: 01332 201764
E: info@railwayapprovals.co.uk
W: www.railwayapprovals.co.uk

Railway Civil Engineers Association
One Great George St, Westminster, London SW1P 3AA
T: 020 7665 2233
F: 020 7799 1325
E: gavin-bowyer@ice.org.uk
W: www.rcea.co.uk

The Railway Consultancy Ltd
1st Floor, South Tower, Crystal Palace Station, London SE19 2AZ
T: 020 8676 0395
F: 020 8778 7439
E: info@railcons.com
W: www.railcons.com

Railway Convalescent Home (RCH)
Bridge House, 2 Church St, Dawlish, Devon EX7 9AU
T: 01626 863303
F: 01626 866676
E: annette@rch.org.uk
W: www.rch.org.uk

Railway Engineering Associates Ltd
68 Boden St, Glasgow G40 3PX
T: 0141 554 3868
F: 0141 556 5091
E: postmaster@rea.uk.com
W: www.rea.uk.com

The Railway Engineering Company
The Old Church, Church Rd, Heywood, Westbury, Wilts BA13 4LP
T: 01373 823737
F: 01373 823838
E: info@theraileng.co.uk
W: www.theraileng.co.uk

Railway Finance Ltd
Barrow Rd, Wincobank, Sheffield S9 1JZ
T: 01223 891300
F: 01223 891900
E: nick.preston@railwayfinance.co.uk
W: www.railwayfinance.co.uk

The Railway Forum
12 Grosvenor Place, London SW1X 7HH
T: 020 7259 6543
F: 020 7259 6544
E: railinfo@railwayforum.com
W: www.railwayforum.com

Railway Friendly Society
MacMillan House, Paddington Station, London W2 1FT
T: 0800 032 4326
E: enquiries@railwayfs.co.uk
W: www.railwayfs.co.uk

Railway Industry Association
22 Headfort Place, London SW1X 7RY
T: 020 7201 0777
F: 020 7235 5777
E: ria@riagb.org.uk
W: www.riagb.org.uk

Railway Management Services Ltd
Nutmeg House, 3rd Floor, 60 Gainsford St, London SE1 2NY
T: 020 7403 8966
F: 020 7403 8869
E: peter.coysten@railwayms.com
W: www.railwayms.com

Railway Mission
PO Box 495, Bedford MK41 9WQ
T: 01234 214790
F: 01124 214790
E: dickicrane@aol.com
W: www.railwaymission.org

Railway Projects Ltd
Lisbon House, 5-7 St Marys Gate, Derby DE1 3JA
T: 01332 349255
F: 01332 349261
E: enquiries@railwayprojects.co.uk
W: www.railwayprojects.co.uk

Railway Research UK - Centre North
University of Birmingham, Edgbaston, Birmingham B15 2TT
T: 0121 414 5067
F: 0121 414 3145
E: enquiries@railresearchuk.org.uk
W: www.railway.bham.ac.uk

Railway Research UK - Centre South
University of Southampton, Highfield, Southampton SO17 1BJ
T: 023 8063 3214
F: 023 8067 7519
E: enquiries@rruk.soton.ac.uk
W: www.railresearch.org.uk

Railway Study Association (RSA)
37 Charlwood Rd, Burgess Hill RH15 0RJ
T: 01444 246379
E: info@railwaystudyassociation.org
W: www.railwaystudyassociation.org

Railway Systems Engineering & Integration Group
School of Engineering, University of Birmingham, Edgbaston, Birmingham B15 2TT
T: 0121 414 4191
F: 0121 414 5150
E: f.schmid@bham.ac.uk
W: www.eng.bham.ac.uk/civil/pg/railway

Railway Touring Company
14a Tuesday Market Place, Kings Lynn, Norfolk PE30 1JN
T: 01553 661500
F: 01553 661800
E: louise@btconnect.com
W: www.railwaytouring.co.uk

Railway Vehicle Engineering Ltd (RVEL)
RTC Business Park, London Rd, Derby DE24 8UO
T: 01332 293035
F: 01332 331210
E: enquiries@rvel.co.uk
W: www.rvel.co.uk

Railweight
Foundry Lane, Smethwick, Birmingham B66 2LP
T: 0121 568 1708
F: 0121 697 5655
E: sales@railweight.co.uk
W: www.averyweight-tronix.com/railweight

Railwork (UK) Ltd
Railtrain Yard, Rolling Mill St, Walsall WS2 9EG
T: 01922 698012
F: 01922 639571
E: info@railwork.co.uk
W: www.railwork.co.uk

Ransome Engineering Services Ltd
Clopton Commercial Park, Clopton, Woodbridge, Suffolk IP13 6QT
T: 01473 737731
F: 01473 737398
E: info@ransomeengineering.co.uk
W: www.ransomeengineering.co.uk

Ratcliff Palfinger
Bessemer Rd, Welwyn Garden City, Herts AL7 1ET
T: 01707 325571
F: 01707 327752
E: info@ratcliffpalfinger.co.uk
W: www.ratcliffpalfinger.com

Rayleigh Instruments
Raytel House, Brook Rd, Rayleigh, Essex SS6 7XH
T: 01268 749300
F: 01268 749309
E: sales@rayleigh.co.uk
W: www.rayleigh.co.uk

REACT by Autoclenz
Stanhope Rd, Swadlincote, Derbys DE11 9BE
T: 08707 510422
F: 08707 510417
E: react@autoclenz.co.uk
W: www.react-decon.co.uk

HSBC
113

Ransome Engineering Services Ltd

Supply and installation of air conditioning to signal equipment buildings in compliance with NR/SP/ELP/40083. All works including building fabric repair/alteration. Link-up no 21717

Clopton Commercial Park, Clopton, Woodbridge, Suffolk, IP13 6QT

T: 0147 373 7731
F: 0147 373 7398
E: info@ransomeengineering.co.uk
W: www.ransomeengineering.co.uk

RESCO EUROPE

Importer, supplier and maintainer of freight vehicles, mainly sourced from China, in partnership with CSRE Limited.

Tony Mosley, Managing Director
Suite 3D, North Mill,
Belper, DE56 1YD
Tel: +44-1773-828666
Fax: +44-1773-828414
tony.mosley@resco.co.uk
Web: www.rescoeurope.co.uk

React Engineering Ltd
Fleswick Court, Westlakes Science & Technology Park, Moor Row, Whitehaven, Cumbria CA24 3HZ
T: 01946 590511
F: 01946 591044
E: mail@react-engineering.co.uk
W: www.reactengineering.co.uk

Readypower
Readypower House, Molly Millars Bridge, Wokingham, Berks RG41 2WY
T: 01189 774901
F: 01189 774902
E: info@readypower.co.uk
W: www.readypower.co.uk

Real Time Consultants Plc
118-120, Warwick St, Royal Leamington Spa, Warks CV32 4QY
T: 01926 313133
F: 01926 422165
E: contract@rtc.co.uk
W: www.rtc.co.uk

Recruitrail (Recruit Engineers)
Bank Chambers, 36 Mount Pleasant Rd, Tunbridge Wells, Kent TN1 1RA
T: 01909 540825
F: 0870 443 0453
W: www.recruitrail.com

Redex Rail Services Ltd
Unit 7, Abbey Way, North Anston Trading Est, Sheffield S25 4JL
T: 01909 552070
F: 01909 569893
E: info@redexrail.co.uk
W: www.redexrail.co.uk

Rehau Ltd
Units 5J&K, Langley Business Centre, Station Rd, Langley, Slough SL3 8DS
T: 01753 588500
F: 01753 588501
E: jason.chapman@rehau.com
W: www.rehau.co.uk

REHAU
Unlimited Polymer Solutions

INNOVATION IN MOTION...
...AND MORE

- Cutting edge polymer developments
- Cost reducing live rail insulators
- High-tech protective boarding and shrouds
- Installation friendly cable management
- Innovative solutions to meet your needs

Challenge us on:
Tel: 01753 588500
Email: rachel.board@rehau.com
www.rehau.co.uk

Reid Lifting Ltd
Unit 3, Bulwark Business Park, Bulwark Rd, Chepstow, Monmouthshire NP16 5JG
T: 01291 620796
F: 01292 626490
E: enquiries@reidlifting.com
W: www.reidlifting.com

Relec Electronics Ltd
Animal House, Justin Bus. Park, Sandford Lane, Wareham, Dorset BH20 4DY
T: 01929 555700
E: sales@relec.co.uk
W: www.relec.co.uk

Renaissance Trains Ltd
4 Spinneyfield, Ellington, Cambs PE28 0AT
T: 07977 917148
E: peter.wilkinson@renaissancetrains.com
W: www.renaissancetrains.com

Renown Consultants
Brookside House, Brookside Bus. Park, Cold Meece, Staffs ST15 0EZ
T: 01785 764476
F: 01785 760896
E: enquiries@renownrailway.com
W: www.renownrailway.co.uk

Replin Fabrics
March St Mills, Peebles EH45 8ER
T: 01721 724311
F: 01721 721893
E: enquiries@replin-fabrics.co.uk
W: www.replin-fabrics.co.uk

Resco Railways
Suite 30, North Mill, Belper DE56 1YD
T: 01773 828666
F: 01773 828414
E: tony.mosley@resco.co.uk
W: www.resco.co.uk

Resourcing Solutions
Vector House, 5 Ruscombe Park, Ruscombe, Berks RG10 9JW
T: 0118 932 0100
F: 0118 932 1818
E: ge@resourcing-solutions.com
W: www.resourcing-solutions.com

Retro Railtours Ltd
2 Brookfield Grove, Ashton-under-Lyne, Lancashire OL6 6TL
T: 0870 312 1066
E: info@retrorailtours.co.uk
W: www.retrorailtours.co.uk

Rexquote
Broadgauge Business Park, Bishops Lydeard, Taunton, Somerset TA4 3BU
T: 01823 433398
F: 01823 433725
E: sales@rexquote.co.uk
W: www.rexquote.co.uk

RGS Rail
Lathkill House, rtc Business Park, London Rd, Derby DE24 8UP
T: 01332 258891
F: 01332 258823
E: mail@rgsrail.co.uk
W: www.rgsrail.co.uk

RIB Software (UK) Ltd
79 Clerkenwell Rd, London EC1R 5AR
T: 020 7400 5400
F: 020 7400 5409
E: brs@rib-software.co.uk
W: www.rib-software.co.uk

Riello UPS Ltd
Unit 68, Clywedog Rd North, Wrexham Ind.Est., Wrexham LL13 9XN
T: 01978 729297
F: 01978 729290
E: marketing@riello-ups.co.uk
W: www.riello-ups.co.uk

Riker Ltd
13 Portemarsh Rd, Portemarsh Ind Est, Calne, Wilts SN11 9BN
T: 01249 814271
F: 01249 812182
E: sales@lmlproducts.co.uk
W: www.lmlproducts.co.uk

Riley & Son (E) Ltd
Baron St, Bury, Lancs BL9 0TY
F: 0161 764 2892
F: 0161 763 5191
E: ian.riley@btconnect.com

RIQC Ltd
2 St Geoges House, Vernon Gate, Derby DE1 1UQ
T: 01332 221421
F: 01332 221401
E: enquiries@riqc.co.uk
W: www.riqc.co.uk

RISC
Railway & Industrial Safety Consultants

Specialists in Technical and Operational fields, and across the interfaces

We help you with:
- Developing your SMS, QMS, EMS or IMS;
- Risk assessment;
- Auditing;
- Reliability engineering;
- Technical and Operational Approvals, Assurance and Safety Cases;
- T&RS Engineering and Operations Management
- New train introduction for heavy and light rail;
- ROGS and other railway Regulations compliance:
- Independent Competent Person assessments.

Contact: David Greenway, RISC Ltd, 3 Doveridge Rd, Burton on Trent, DE15 9GB
Telephone/Fax: 0870 350 9420 / 9421
Email: enquiries@railwaysafety.co.uk
Web: www.railwaysafety.co.uk

RISC Ltd
Harlyn House, 3 Doveridge Rd, Stapenhill, Burton Upon Trent DE15 9GB
T: 0870 350 9420
F: 0870 350 9421
E: enquiries@railwaysafety.co.uk
W: www.railwaysafety.co.uk

Risk Solutions
59-60 Russell Square, London WC1B 4HP
T: 0870 850 4889
F: 0870 850 4895
E: enquiries@risksol.co.uk
W: www.risksol.co.uk

Ritchies
Glasgow Rd, Kilsyth, Glasgow G65 9BL
T: 01236 467000
F: 01236 467030
E: ritchies@edmund-nuttall.co.uk
W: www.ritchies.org

Ritelite Systems Ltd
Meadow Park, Bourne Rd, Essendine, Stamford, Lincs PE9 4LT
T: 01780 765600
F: 01780 765700
E: sales@ritelite.co.uk
W: www.ritelite.co.uk

Rittal Ltd
Braithwell Way, Hellaby Ind Est, Hellaby, Rotherham S66 8QY
T: 01709 704000
F: 01709 701217
E: information@rittal.co.uk
W: www.rittal.co.uk

Riviera Trains
116, Ladbroke Grove, London W10 5NE
T: 020 7727 4036
F: 020 7727 2083
E: enquiries@riviera-trains.co.uk
W: www.riviera-trains.co.uk

RM Consultants Ltd
Suite 7, Hitching Court, Abingdon Business Park, Abingdon, Oxon OX14 1RA
T: 01235 555755
F: 01235 525143
E: rmc@rm-consultants.co.uk
W: www.rmconsultants.co.uk

RMS Locotec
Unit 1, Greens Ind. Park, Calder Vale Road, Wakefield WF1 5PF
T: 01924 234440
F: 01924 234441
E: sales@rmslocotec.com
W: www.rmslocotec.com

RMT
National Union of Rail, Maritime & Transport Workers, Unity House, 39 Chalton St, London NW1 1JD
T: 020 7387 4771
F: 020 7387 4123
E: info@rmt.org.uk
W: www.rmt.org.uk

RMT Solutions Ltd
ID Centre, Laithkill House, RTC Business Park, London Rd, Derby DE24 8UP
T: 0845 602 4151
E: sales@rmtsolutions.co.uk
W: www.rmtsolutions.co.uk

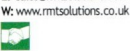

Robel Bahnbaumaschmen GmbH
Industriestrasse 31, D 83395, Freilassing, Germany
T: 0049 8654 6090
F: 0049 8654 609100
E: info@robel.info
W: www.robel.info

Robert West Consulting
West House, 46 High St, Orpington, Kent BR6 0JQ
T: 01689 820216
F: 01689 831582
E: orpington@robertwest.co.uk
W: www.robertwest.co.uk

Rock Mechanics Technology Ltd
Bretby Business Park, Ashby Rd, Stanhope Bretby, Burton on Trent DE15 0QP
T: 01283 522201
F: 01283 522279
E: rmt@rmtltd.com
W: www.rmtltd.com

ROCOL Acme Panels
Rocol House, Wakefield Rd, Swillington, Leeds LS26 8BS
T: 0113 232 2800
F: 0113 232 2850
E: customer-service.safety@rocol.com
W: www.rocol.com

ROCOL Site Safety Systems
Rocol House, Wakefield Rd, Swillington, Leeds LS26 8BS
T: 0113 232 2800
F: 0113 232 2850
E: customer-service.safety@rocol.com
W: www.rocol.com

Roechling Engineering Plastics (UK) Ltd
Waterwells Business Park, Waterwells Drive, Quedgeley, Glos GL2 2AA
T: 01452 727905
F: 01452 728056
E: david.ward@roechling-plastics.co.uk
W: www.roechling-plastics.co.uk

Roevin Management Services Ltd
4th Floor, Clydesdale Bank House, 33 Lower Regent St, Piccadilly, London WC1Y 4NB
T: 0845 643 0471
F: 08707 598381
E: rail@roevin.co.uk
W: www.roevin.co.uk

Rollalong Ltd
Woolsbridge Ind. Park, Three Legged Cross, Wimborne, Dorset BH21 6SF
T: 01202 824541
F: 01202 826525
E: enquiries@rollalong.co.uk
W: www.rollalong.co.uk

Romac Technical Services Ltd
Clements House, Mount Ave, Mount Farm, Bletchley, Milton Keynes MK1 1LS
T: 01908 375845
F: 01908 270524
E: tom.appleton@romac.co.uk
W: www.romac.co.uk

Romag
Leadgate Ind. Est., Leadgate, Consett, Co Durham DH8 7RS
T: 01207 500000
F: 01207 591979
W: www.romag.co.uk

Romic House
A1/M1 Business Centre, Kettering, Northants NN16 8TD
T: 01536 414244
F: 01536 414245
E: sales@romic.co.uk
W: www.romic.co.uk

Rosehill Polymers
Rose Hill Mills, Beech Rd, Sowerby Bridge, West Yorks HX6 2JT
T: 01422 839456
F: 01422 316952
E: stuart@rosehillpolymers.com
W: www.rosehillpolymers.com

Rosenqvist Rail AB
Box 334, 82427 Hudiksvall, Sweden
T: 0046 650 16505
F: 0046 650 16501
E: info@rosenqvist-group.se
W: www.rosenqvistrail.se

Rossmore Group
Cornwall House, Blythe Valley Park, Solihull B90 8AF
T: 0121 213 3456
F: 0121 213 3455
E: jo.williams@rossmore.co.uk
W: www.rossmore.co.uk

Rotabroach Ltd
Imperial Works,Sheffield Rd, Tinsley, Sheffield S9 2YL
T: 0114 221 2510
F: 0114 221 2563
E: sales@rotabroach.co.uk
W: www.rotabroach.co.uk

Rotamag Rail
41, Catley Rd, Darnall, Sheffield S9 5JF
T: 0114 291 1020
F: 0114 261 8186
E: sales@bryar.co.uk
W: www.rotamag.co.uk

Rowe Hankins Components Ltd
Parker St, Bury, Lancs BL9 0RJ
T: 0161 765 3000
F: 0161 763 1421
E: elizabeth@rowehankins.com
W: www.rowehankins.com

Roxtec Ltd
Unit 3, Leigh St, Walshaw, Bury, Lancs BL8 3AL
T: 0161 761 5280
F: 0161 763 6065
E: info@uk.roxtec.com
W: www.roxtec.com

Royal British Legion Industries (RBLI)
Royal British Legion Village, Hall Rd, Aylesford, Kent ME20 7NL
T: 01622 795938
F: 01622 795978
E: signs@rbli.co.uk
W: www.rbli-railsigns.co.uk

Royal Haskoning Ltd
Rightwell House, Bretton, Peterborough PE3 8DW
T: 01733 334455
F: 01733 262243
E: info@peterborough.royalhaskoning.com
W: www.royalhaskoning.com

RSIS
See Wyse Rail

RSK Health & Safety Services
Spring Lodge, 172 Chester Rd, Helsby, Cheshire WA6 0AR
T: 01928 726006
F: 01928 725633
E: communications@rsk.com
W: www.rsk.com

RSM Robson Rhodes LLP
30 Finsbury Square, London EC2P 2YU
T: 020 7184 4300
F: 020 7184 4301
W: www.rsmi.co.uk

RTI UK
35 Old Queen St, London SW1H 9JD
T: 020 7340 0900
F: 020 7233 3411
E: rtiuk@rti.co.uk
W: www.rti.co.uk

Rullion Engineering Personnel
2nd Floor, Unit 5, Bath Court, Islington Row, Edgbaston, Birmingham B15 1NE
T: 0121 622 7720
F: 0121 622 7721
E: james.millward@rullion.co.uk
W: www.rullion.co.uk/rep

RVEL Ltd
See Railway Vehicle Engineering Ltd

RWA Rail Ltd
Loughborough Technology Centre, Loughborough University, Epinal Way, Loughborough LE11 3GE
T: 01509 210110
F: 01509 210110
E: robert.watson@rwa-rail.co.uk
W: www.rwa-rail.co.uk

RWD Technologies UK Ltd
Furzeground Way, First Floor, Stockley Park, Uxbridge UB11 1AJ
T: 020 8569 2787
F: 020 8756 3625
W: www.rwd.com

Rydon Signs
Unit 3, Peek House, Pinhoe Trading Est, Exeter, Devon EX4 8JN
T: 01392 466653
F: 01392 466671
E: sales@rydonsigns.com
W: www.rydonsigns.com

Sabre Rail Services Ltd
Grindon Way, Heighington Lane Business Park, Newton Aycliffe, Co Durham DL5 6SH
T: 01325 300505
F: 01325 300485
E: sales@sabre-rail.co.uk
W: www.sabre-rail.co.uk

Safeglass (Europe) Ltd
Nasmyth Building, Nasmyth Ave, East Kilbride G75 0QR
T: 01355 272828
F: 01355 272788
E: sales@safeglass.co.uk
W: www.safeglass.co.uk

Safeguard Ltd
6 Churchill Bus. Park, The Flyers Way, Westerham, Kent TN16 1BT
T: 0800 195 7766
F: 01959 565888
E: info@safeguardpestcontrol.co.uk
W: www.safeguardpestcontrol.co.uk

Safestyle Security Services
Exe. Suite 1, Cardiff International Arena, Mary Ann St, Cardiff CF10 2FQ
T: 02920 221711
F: 02920 234592
E: office@safestylesecurity.co.uk
W: www.safestylesecurity.co.uk

RVEL
RAILWAY-VEHICLE-ENGINEERING-LIMITED

Railway Vehicle Engineering Limited (RVEL) is based at the Railway Technical Centre in Derby and specialises in rolling stock heavy overhaul, repair, refurbishment and maintenance.

Railway Vehicle Engineering Ltd
RTC Business Park, London Road
Derby DE24 8UP
Phone: 01332 293035
Fax: 01332 331210
Email: enquiries@rvel.co.uk
www.rvel.co.uk

Safetech Environmental Care
4 Upton St, Hull HU8 7DA
T: 01482 224155
F: 01482 214522
E: info@safetechenv.com
W: www.safetechenv.com

Safetell Ltd
Unit 46, Fawkes Ave, Dartford Trade Park, Dartford DA1 1JQ
T: 01322 223233
F: 01322 277751
E: sales@safetell.co.uk
W: www.safetell.co.uk

HSBC

SAFETELL

Safetell Limited, Unit 46, Fawkes Avenue, Dartford, Kent DA1 1JQ

T: 01322 223 233
E: sales@safetell.co.uk
W: www.safetell.co.uk

Safetell's Eye2Eye counter is featured in the latest Department for Transport Code of Practice for Accessible Train and Station Design.

It is widely accepted by TOCs as the cost effective solution to provide equal access to ticket offices for all passengers irrespective of ability or stature.

Safetrack Baavhammar AB
1 Moleberga, S-245 93 Staffanstorp, Sweden
T: 0046 4044 5300
F: 0046 4044 5553
E: sales@safetrack.se
W: www.safetrack.se

SAFT Ltd
1st Floor, Unit 5, Astra Centre, Edinburgh Way, Harlow CM20 2BN
T: 01279 772550
F: 01279 420909
E: sarah.carter@saftbatteries.com
W: www.saftbatteries.com

SAFT Power Systems Ltd - See AEG

Saint Gobain Abrasives Ltd
Doxey Rd, Stafford ST16 1EA
T: 01785 279550
F: 01785 213487
E: sonia.uppal@saint-gobain.com
W: www.saint-gobain.com

Saltburn Railtours
16 Bristol Ave, Saltburn TS12 1BW
T: 01287 626572
E: r.dallara@btinternet.com
W: www.saltburnrailtours.com

Samsung Electronics Hainan Fibreoptics
C/O Go Tel Communications Ltd, 4 Hicks Close, Wroughton, Swindon SN4 9AY
T: 01793 813600
F: 01793 529380
E: robindash@gtcom.co.uk
W: www.samsungfiberoptics.com

Santon Switchgear Ltd
Unit 9, Waterside Court, Newport NP20 5NT
T: 01633 854411
F: 01633 854999
E: sales@santonswitchgear.com
W: www.santonswitchgear.com

SBC Rail Ltd
Littlewell Lane, Stanton by Dale, Ilkeston, Derbys DE7 4QW
T: 0115 944 1448
F: 0115 944 1466
E: sbc@stanton-bonna.co.uk
W: www.stanton-bonna.co.uk

Scanmoor Rail (Scanmoor Ltd)
Scanmoor House, 56-60 Northolt Rd, Harrow, Middx HA2 0DW
T: 020 8515 0900
F: 020 8515 0901
E: info@scanmoor.com
W: www.scanmoor.com

Schaeffler (UK) Ltd
Forge Lane, Minworth, Sutton Coldfield, West Midlands B76 1AP
T: 0121 351 3833
F: 0121 351 7686
E: info.uk@schaeffler.com
W: www.schaeffler.co.uk

Scheidt & Bachmann (UK) Ltd
7 Silverglade Business Park, Leatherhead Rd, Chessington, Surrey KT9 2QJ
T: 01372 230400
F: 01372 722053
E: info@scheidt-bachmann.de
W: www.scheidt-bachmann.de

Schenck Process Systems
Emery Court, Embankment Business Park, Heaton Mersey, Stockport SK4 3GL
T: 0161 975 1800
F: 0161 443 2645
E: transport@schenckprocess.com
W: www.schenck.co.uk

Schneider Electric Ltd
Stafford Park 5, Telford, Shropshire TF3 3BL
T: 01952 209226
F: 01952 292238
W: www.schneider-electric.co.uk

Schofield Lothian
Temple Chambers, 3-7 Temple Ave, London EC4Y 0DT
T: 020 7842 0920
F: 020 7842 0921
E: enquiries@schofieldlothian.com
W: www.schofieldlothian.com

Schweerbau GmbH & Co KG
Branch Office UK, 53 Kinburn Street, London SE16 6DW
T: 07725 888933
F: 020 7681 3971
E: verheijen@schweerbau.de
W: www.schweerbau.de

Schweizer Electronic AG
Industriestrasse 3, CH-6260 Reiden, Switzerland
T: 0041 6274 90707
F: 0041 6274 90700
E: info@schweizer-electronic.ch
W: www.schweizer-electronic.ch

Schwihag AG
Trach Technology, Lebernstrasse 3, CH8274 Tagerwilen
T: 0041 71666 8800
E: info@schwihag.com
W: www.schwihag.com

Scientifics Ltd
500, London Rd, Derby DE24 8BQ
T: 0800 5288852
F: 01332 268495
E: sales@scientifics.com
W: www.scientifics.com

Scisys
Methuen Park, Chippenham, Wilts SN14 0GB
T: 01249 466466
F: 01249 466666
E: marketing@scisys.co.uk
W: www.scisys.co.uk

Scott White & Hookings
Fountain House, 26 St Johns St, Bedford MK42 0AQ
T: 01234 213111
F: 01234 213333
E: bed@swh.co.uk
W: www.swh.co.uk

Scott Wilson Railways
Tricentre 3, Newbridge Square, Swindon SN1 1BY
T: 01793 508560
F: 01793 508501
E: rail.marketing@scottwilson.com
W: www.scottwilson.com

Scotweld Employment Services
270 Peters Hill Rd, Glasgow G21 4AY
T: 0141 557 6133
F: 0141 557 6143
E: admin@scotweld.com
W: www.scotweld.com

Screwfast Foundations Ltd
7c Smallford Works, Smallford Way, St. Albans, Herts AL4 0SA
T: 01727 821282
F: 01727 828098
E: info@screwfast.com
W: www.screwfast.com

SCT Europe Ltd
Evans Business Centre, Mitcheldson Ind Est, Kirkcaldy KY1 3UF
T: 01592 657523
F: 01592 657524
E: jlongton@stdcar.com
W: www.sctco.com

SEA (Group) Ltd
SEA House, PO Box 800, Bristol BS16 1SU
T: 01373 852000
F: 01373 831133
E: info@sea.co.uk
W: www.sea.co.uk

SebaKMT UK Ltd
19 Harris Rd, Portemarsh Ind Est, Calne, Wilts SN11 9PT
T: 01249 816181
F: 01249 816186
E: sales@sebakmtuk.com
W: www.sebakmt.com

Secheron SA
Route les Moulieres 5, 1217 Meyrin-Geneva, Switzerland
T: 0041 22 739 4111
F: 0041 22 739 4811
E: info@secheron.com
W: www.secheron.com

Seco-Rail
Trafalgar House, 11 Waterloo Place, London SW1Y 4AU
T: 020 7863 8815
F: 020 7930 3176
E: info@seco-rail.com
W: www.seco-rail.com

Sefac UK Ltd
Unit R8, Barton Rd, Water Eaton, Bletchley MK2 3HU
T: 01908 821274
F: 01908 821275
E: info@sefac-lift.co.uk
W: www.sefac-lift.co.uk

Selectequip Ltd
Unit 7, Britannia Way, Britannia Enterprise Park, Lichfield, Staffs WS14 9UY
T: 01543 416641
F: 01543 416083
E: sales@selectequip.co.uk
W: www.selectequip.co.uk

Semikron Ltd
John Tate Rd, Foxholes Business Park, Hertford SG13 7NW
T: 01992 584677
F: 01992 503847
E: sales.skuk@semikron.com
W: www.semikron.com

Semmco
16, Wintonlea Ind. Est, Monument Way West, Woking, Surrey GU21 5EN
T: 01483 757200
F: 01483 740795
E: sales@semmco.com
W: www.semmco.com

Semperit Industrial Products
25 Cottesbrooke Park, Heartlands, Daventry, Northants NN11 8YL
T: 01327 313144
F: 01327 313149
E: ian.rowlinson@semperit.co.uk
W: www.semperit.at

Semple Plc
Drumhead Place, Sullerton Court, Cambuslang, Glasgow G32 8EY
T: 0141 646 5252
F: 0141 646 5250
W: www.semple.co.uk

Sentripod Company Ltd
Honeystone, 13 The Hamlet, Chippenham, Wilts SN15 1BY
T: 01249 462039
F: 01249 462039
E: info@sentripod.co.uk
W: www.sentripod.com

Serco Integrated Transport
Serco House, 16 Bartley Wood Bus. Park, Bartley Way, Hook, Hants RG27 9XB
T: 01256 745900
F: 01256 744111
E: generalenquiries@serco.com
W: www.serco.com/markets/transport

Serco Rail Operations
Derwent House, RTC Business Park, London Rd, Derby DE24 8UP
T: 01332 263340
F: 01332 262964
E: generalenquiries@serco.com
W: www.serco.com/sit/

Serco NedRailways
1 Ely Place, 2nd Floor, London EC1N 6RY
T: 020 7430 8270
E: anton.valk@serconedrailways.com
W: www.serconedrailways.com

Serco Technical & Assurance Services
Derwent House, RTC Business Park, Derby DE24 8UP
T: 01332 262975
F: 01332 262405
E: john.benyon@serco.com
W: www.serco.com/assurance

Sersa (UK) Ltd
Sersa House, Auster Rd, Clifton Moor, York YO30 4XA
T: 01904 479968
F: 01904 479970
E: sersa.UK@sersa-group.com
W: www.sersa.ch

The Severn Partnership Ltd
The Maltings, 59 Lythwood Rd, Bayston Hill, Shrewsbury SY3 0NA
T: 01743 874135
F: 01743 874716
E: mark.combes@severn-partnership.co.uk
W: www.severn-partnership.co.uk

Severn Valley Railway
The Railway Station, Bewdley, Worcs DY12 1BG
T: 01299 403816
F: 01299 400839
E: svrholdingsplc@btconnect.com
W: www.svr.co.uk

SGA (Stuart Gray Associates)
88 Spring Hill, Arley, Warks CV7 8FE
T: 01676 541040
E: info@stuartgrayassociates.co.uk
W: www.stuartgrayassociates.co.uk

SGS Engineering
Unit 2, Coburn Place, Newland St, Derby DE1 1JT
T: 0845 880 1255
F: 01332 366232
E: sales@sgs-engineering.com
W: www.sgs-engineering.com

Sheerspeed Shelters Ltd
Unit 3, Diamond House, Reme Drive, Heath Park, Honiton, Devon EX14 1SE
T: 01404 46006
F: 01404 45520
E: sales@sheerspeedshelters.com
W: www.sheerspeed.com

Shere Ltd
10 Deacon Field, Guildford, Surrey GU2 8YT
T: 01483 557400
F: 01483 557401
E: enquiries@shere.com
W: www.shere.com

Sheridan Maine
Regus House, George Curl Way, Southampton SO18 2RZ
T: 02380 302500
F: 02380 302300
E: southampton@sheridanmaine.com
W: www.sheridanmaine.com

Shorterm Rail
Station House, High St, West Drayton, Middx UB7 7DJ
T: 0845 241 0448
F: 0845 241 4641
E: rail@shorterm.co.uk
W: www.shorterm.co.uk

Siegrist-Orel Ltd
Pysons Rd Ind. Est., Broadstairs, Kent CT10 2LQ
T: 01843 865241
F: 01843 867180
E: sersa.UK@sersa-group.com
W: www.siegrist-orel.co.uk

Siemens Mobilty is at the forefront of rail technology, designing, manufacturing and maintaining rolling stock, signalling, electrification and rail communications systems across the globe.

Ashby Park, Ashby de la Zouch, Leicestershire, LE65 1JD

Telephone: 01530 258000
Fax: 01530 258008

uk.mobility@siemens.com
www.siemens.co.uk/mobility

SIEMENS

Siemens Mobility Division
Ashby Park, Ashby de la Zouch, Leics LE65 1JD
T: 01530 258000
F: 01530 258008
E: uk.mobility@siemens.com
W: www.siemens.co.uk/mobility

SGS Engineering - see SGS

Sigma Coachair Group UK Ltd
Unit 1, Queens Drive, Newhall, Swadlincore, Derbys DE11 0EG
T: 01283 559140
F: 01283 225253
E: hsingh@sigmacoachair.com
W: www.sigmacoachair.com

Signal House Ltd
Cherrycourt Way, Stanbridge Rd, Leighton Buzzard, Beds LU7 8UH
T: 01525 377477
F: 01525 850999
E: sales@signalhouse.com
W: www.signalhousegroup.co.uk

Signalling Solutions Ltd
Borehamwood Ind Park, Rowley Lane, Borehamwood, Herts WD6 5PZ
T: 020 8953 9922
E: southampton@sheridanmaine.com
W: www.signallingsolutions.com

Signet Solutions
Kelvin House, RTC Business Park, London Rd, Derby DE24 8UP
T: 01332 343585
F: 01332 367132
E: enquiries@signet-solutions.com
W: www.signet-solutions.com

Sill Lighting UK
3 Thame Park Bus. Centre, Wenman Rd, Thame, Oxon OX9 3XA
T: 01844 260005
E: sales@sill-uk.com
W: www.sill-uk.com

Simmons & Simmons
City Point, One Ropemaker St, London EC2Y 9SS
T: 020 7628 2020
F: 020 7628 2070
E: juliet.reingolo@simmons-simmons.com
W: www.simmons-simmons.com

Sinclair Knight Merz
Victoria House, Southampton Row, London WC1B 4EA
T: 020 7759 2600
F: 020 7759 2601
E: scurnick@skm.co.uk
W: www.skmconsulting.com

Sitec T&C Ltd
11-12 Villiers House, Lansdowne Court, Bumpers Farm, Chippenham, Wilts SN14 6RZ
T: 01249 464150
F: 01249 464160
E: office@sitec.uk.com
W: www.sitec.uk.com

Site Vision Surveys
Suite 11, The Locks, Hillmorton, Rugby, Warks CV21 4PP
T: 01788 575036
F: 01788 576208
W: www.svsltd.net

Skanska UK
Maple Cross House, Denham Way, Maple Cross, Rickmansworth, Herts WD3 9SW
T: 01923 423100
F: 01923 423111
E: skanska@skanska.co.uk
W: www.cementation foundations.skandka.co.uk

HJ Skelton & Co Ltd
9 The Broadway, Thatcham, Berks RG19 3JA
T: 01635 865256
F: 01635 865710
E: info@hjskelton.com
W: www.hjskelton.com

SKF UK Ltd
Railway Sales Unit, Sundon Park Rd, Luton LU3 3BL
T: 01582 496490
F: 01582 496327
E: stewart.mclellan@skf.com
W: www.skf.com

Skymasts Antennas
Unit 2, Clayfield Close, Moulton Park Ind. Est, Northampton NN3 6QF
T: 01604 494132
F: 01604 494133
E: info@skymasts.com
W: www.skymasts.com

Slender Winter Partnership
The Old School, London Rd, Westerham, Kent TN11 1DN
T: 01959 564777
F: 01959 562802
E: swp@swpltd.co.uk
W: www.swpltd.co.uk

S M Consult Ltd
3 High St, Stanford in the Vale, Faringdon, Oxon SN7 8LH
T: 01367 710152
F: 01367 710152
E: info@smconsult.co.uk
W: www.smconsult.co.uk

SMI Conferences
SMi Group Ltd, Unit 122, Great Guildford Business Square, 30 Great Guildford St, London SE1 0HS
T: 020 7827 6000
F: 020 7827 6001
W: www.smi-online.com

Smith Bros & Webb Ltd
Britannia House, Arden Forest Ind. Est, Kinwarton, Alcester, Warks B49 6EX
T: 01789 400096
F: 01789 400231
E: mark.prockter@vehicle-ashing-systems.co.uk
W: www.vehicle-washing-systems.co.uk

Directory

Sigma Coachair Group
are global leaders in the design and supply of state-of-the-art rolling stock air conditioning equipment. Our "Sigma" range of air conditioning systems are purpose built total climate control systems which provide the best in passenger comfort and safety for metro, intercity, light rail and locomotive applications.

Unit 1, Queens Drive, Newhall, Swadlincote, Derbyshire, UK, DE11 0EG

Contact Harjit Singh
Phone: +44 (0) 1283 559140
Mobile: +44 (0) 7967 302420
Fax: +44 (0) 1283 225253
Email: hsingh@sigmacoachair.com

Sigma Coachair Group

www.sigmacoachair.com

SML Resourcing
201 Great Guildford Business Square, 30 Great Guildford St, London SE1 0HS
T: 020 7928 0060
F: 07092 810920
E: lisa@sml-resourcing.com
W: www.sml-resourcing.com

SMP Electronics
Unit 6, Border Farm, Station Rd, Chobham, Surrey GU24 8AS
T: 01276 855166
F: 01276 855115
E: sales@smpelectronics.com
W: www.smpelectronics.com

Snap-On Rail Solutions
Distribution Centre, Telford Way, Kettering, Northants NN16 8SN
T: 01536 413904
F: 01536 413874
E: rail@snapon.com
W: www.snapon.com/industrialuk

Society of Operations Engineers (SOE)
22 Greencoat Place, London SW1P 1PR
T: 020 7630 1111
F: 020 7630 6677
E: soe@soe.org.uk
W: www.soe.org.uk

Softech Global Ltd
Softech House, London Rd, Albourne, West Sussex 3N6 9BN
T: 01273 833844
F: 01273 833044
E: rail@softechglobal.com
W: www.softechglobal.com

Solo Fabrications
Landor St, Saltley, Birmingham B8 1AE
T: 0121 327 3378
F: 0121 327 3757
W: www.solofabs.com

Solution Rail
T: 07951 361723
E: enquiries@solutionrail.co.uk
W: www.solutionrail.co.uk

Somers Totalkare
15 Forge Trading Est., Mucklow Hill, Halesowen B62 8TR
T: 0121 585 2700
F: 0121 501 1458
E: sales@somerstotalkare.co.uk
W: www.somerstotalkare.co.uk

Sonic Rail Service Ltd (SRS)
Unit 15, Springfield Ind. Est, Springfield Rd, Burnham-on-Crouch, Essex CM0 8UA
T: 01621 784688
F: 01621 786594
E: stewart.robinson@sonicrail.co.uk
W: www.sonicrail.co.uk

Sonic Windows Ltd
Unit 14/15, Beeching Park Ind.Est., Wainwright Rd, Bexhill on Sea, E Sussex TN39 3UR
T: 01424 223864
F: 01424 215859
E: enquiries@sonicwindows.co.uk
W: www.sonicwindows.co.uk

Sortimo International Ltd
Old Sarum Park, Salisbury, Wilts SP4 6EB
T: 01722 411585
F: 01722 320831
E: vanrack1@sortimo.co.uk
W: www.sortimo.co.uk

Sotera Risk Management Ltd
22 Glanville Rd, Bromley BR2 9LW
T: 07946 638 424
F: 01737 551203
E: chris.chapman@sotera.co.uk
W: www.sotera.co.uk

Southeastern
Friars Bridge Court, 41-45 Blackfriars Rd, London SE1 8PG
T: 020 7620 5000
W: www.southeasternrailway.co.uk

Southern
Go-Ahead House, 26-28 Addiscombe Rd, Croydon CR9 5GA
T: 020 8929 8600
F: 020 8929 8638
E: communications@southernrailway.com
W: www.southernrailway.com

M H Southern & Co Ltd
Church Bank Sawmills, Jarrow, Tyne & Wear NE32 3EB
T: 0191 489 8231
F: 0191 428 0146
E: timber@mhsouthern.co.uk
W: www.mhsouthern.co.uk

Southern Electric Contracting
55 Vastern Rd, Reading RG1 8BU
T: 0118 953 4081
F: 0118 953 4755
E: marketing@sec.eu.com
W: www.sec.eu.com

South West Trains
Friars Bridge Court, 41-45 Blackfriars Rd, London SE1 8NZ
T: 0870 000 5151
E: customerrelations@swtrains.co.uk
W: www.southwesttrains.co.uk

South Yorkshire PTE
11 Broad St West, Sheffield S1 2BQ
T: 0114 276 7575
F: 0114 275 9908
E: comments@sypte.co.uk
W: www.sypte.co.uk

Sovereign Planned Services On Line Ltd
Unit 3d, Forge Way, Brown Lees Ind Est, Biddulph, Stoke on Trent ST8 7DN
T: 01782 510600
F: 01782 510700
E: sales@sovonline.co.uk
W: www.soveonline.com

Sovereign Trains Ltd
Unit 3, Lower Ledge Farm, Dyrham, Bristol SN14 8DY
T: 01279 778999
F: 01279 778084
E: david.shipley@sovereigntrains.com
W: www.sovereigntrains.com

Spartan Safety Ltd
Unit 3, Waltham Park Way, Walthamstow, London E17 5DU
T: 020 8527 5888
F: 020 8527 5999
E: post@spartansafety.co.uk
W: www.spartansafety.co.uk

Specialist Engineering Services Ltd (SES)
Wright Business Park, Carr Hill, Doncaster DN4 8DE
T: 01302 733693
F: 01302 733693
E: info@ses-holdings.com
W: www.ses-holdings.com

Speedy Hire Plc
Chase House, 16 The Parks, Newton le Willows, Merseyside WA12 0JQ
T: 01942 720000
F: 01942 720077
E: admin@speedyhire.co.uk
W: www.speedyhire.co.uk

Speno International SA
26 Parc Chateau-Banquet POB 16, 1211 Geneva 21, Switzerland
T: 0041 22906 4600
F: 0041 22906 4601
E: info@speno.ch
W: www.speno.ch

C Spencer
Mill Lane, Barrow upon Humber DN19 7DB
T: 01469 532266
F: 01469 532233
E: mailbox@cspencerltd.co.uk
W: www.cspencerltd.co.uk

Sperry Rail International is the only rail testing company totally focused on rail flaw detection. It currently has the rail testing contract for the whole of the UK network as well as Metronet on the London Underground.

TRENT HOUSE, RTC BUSINESS PARK, LONDON ROAD, DERBY DE24 8UP

Tel: +44 (0)1332 262 565
Fax: +44 (0)1332 262 541

sales@sperryint.com

www.sperryrail.com

SPERRY RAIL INTERNATIONAL LTD.
a Rockwood Company

Sperry Rail International Ltd
Trent House, RTC Business Park, London Rd, Derby DE24 8UP
T: 01332 262565
F: 01332 262541
E: sales@sperryint.com
W: www.sperryrail.com

Spescom Software Ltd
Woolbrook House, Crabtree Office Village, Eversley Way, Thorpe, Surrey TW20 8RY
T: 0870 890 8000
F: 0870 890 9000
E: info-uk@spescom.com
W: www.spescomsoftware.com

Spitfire Tours
PO Box 824, Taunton TA1 9ET
T: 0870 879 3675
E: info@spitfirerailtours.co.uk
W: www.spitfirerailtours.co.uk

Spring Personnel
1 Canal Arm, Festival Park, Stoke on Trent ST1 5UR
T: 01782 221500
F: 01782 221600
E: personnel@spring.com
W: www.spring.com

SPX Rail Systems
Unit 7, Thames Gateway Park, Choats Rd, Dagenham, Essex RM9 6RH
T: 020 8526 7100
F: 020 8526 7151
E: brian.cannon@spx.com
W: www.spx.com

SRPS Tours
T: 01698 263814
E: society@srps.org.uk
W: www.srps.org.uk

SRS Rail Systems
Unit 3, Riverside Way, Gateway Business Park, Bolsover, Chesterfield S44 6GA
T: 0870 050 9244
E: info@srsrailuk.co.uk
W: www.srsrailuk.co.uk

SSDM
Freemantle Rd, Lowestoft, Suffolk NR33 0EA
T: 0845 052 5241
F: 01502 501234
E: talk2me@ssdm.co.uk
W: www.ssdm.co.uk

SSP
169, Euston Rd, London NW1 2AE
T: 020 7543 3300
F: 020 7543 3389
E: nerissa.potter@ssp.uk.com
W: www.ssp-intl.com

Stagecoach Supertram
Nunnery Depot, Woodbourn Rd, Sheffield S9 3LS
T: 0114 275 9888
F: 0114 279 8120
E: enquiries@supertram.com
W: www.supertram.com

Stagecoach Group
10 Dunkeld Rd, Perth PH1 5TW
T: 01738 442111
F: 012738 643648
E: info@stagecoachgroup.com
W: www.stagecoachgroup.com

Stanley Tools
Sheffield Business Park, Sheffield City Airport, Europa Link, Sheffield S3 9PD
T: 0114 244 8883
F: 0114 273 9038

Stansted Express
Enterprise House, Stansted Airport, Essex CM20 1QW
E: eleni.jordan@nationalexpres.com
W: www.stanstedexpress.com

Stanton Bonna Concrete Ltd
Littlewell Lane, Stanton by Dale, Ilkeston, Derbys DE7 4QW
T: 0115 944 1448
F: 0115 944 1466
E: sbc@stanton-bonna.co.uk
W: www.stanton-bonna.co.uk

STATS
Porterswood House, Porters Wood, St Albans AL3 6PQ
T: 01727 833261
F: 01727 811528
E: info@stats.co.uk
W: www.stats.co.uk

Stauff UK Ltd
500 Carlisle St East, Sheffield S48 BS5
T: 01142 518518
E: sales@stauff.co.uk
W: www.stauff.co.uk

Staytite Ltd
Staytite House, Coronation Rd, Cressex Bus.Park, High Wycombe, Bucks HP12 3RP
T: 01494 462322
F: 01494 464747
E: fasteners@staytite.com
W: www.staytite.com

Steel Team Construction
46 Goods Station Rd, Tunbridge Wells, Kent TN1 2DD
T: 01892 533677
F: 01892 511535
E: sales@steelteamconstruction.co.uk
W: www.steelteamconstruction.co.uk

Steer Davies Gleave
28-32 Upper Ground, London SE1 9PD
T: +44 (0)20 7910 5000
F: +44 (0)20 7910 5001
E: sdginfo@sdgworld.net
W: www.steerdaviesgleave.com

Stent
Pavilion C2, Ashwood Park, Ashwood Way, Basingstoke, Hants RG23 8BG
T: 01256 400200
F: 01256 400201
E: foundations@stent.co.uk
W: www.stent.co.uk

Stewart Signs
See Halo Rail

Stirling Maynard
Construction Consultants, Stirling House, Rightwell, Bretton, Peterborough PE3 8DJ
T: 01733 262319
F: 01733 331527
E: enquiries@stirlingmaynard.com
W: www.stirlingmaynard.com

Stobart Rail
Brunthill Rd, Kingstown Ind. Est, Carlisle, Cumbria CA3 0EH
T: 01228 822500
F: 01228 530384
E: enquiries@eddiestobart.co.uk
W: www.eddiestobart.co.uk

Stobart Railtours
Pullman House, RTC Business Park, London Rd, Derby DE24 8UP
T: 01332 374517
E: reservations@stobartrailtours.co.uk

Stock Redler Ltd
Redler House, Dudbridge, Stroud, Glos GL3 3EY
T: 01423 819461
F: 0049 6151 321043
E: r.illsley@schenckprocess.com
W: www.schenckprocess.com

Stocksigns Ltd
43,Ormside Way, Holmethorpe Ind Est, Redhill, Surrey RH1 2LG
T: 01737 764764
F: 01737 763763
E: jgodden@stocksigns.co.uk
W: www.stocksigns.co.uk

Stored Energy Technology Ltd
Atlas Works, Litchurch Lane, Derby DE24 8AQ
T: 01332 346035
F: 01332 346494
E: sales@set.gb.com
W: www.set.gb.com

Story Rail
Burgh Rd Ind Est, Carlisle CA2 7NA
T: 01228 640880
F: 01228 640881
E: info@storyrail.co.uk
W: www.storyrail.co.uk

STRAIL (UK) Ltd
Room 3, First Floor, 3 Tannery House, Tannery Lane, Send, Woking, Surrey GU23 7EF
T: 01483 222090
F: 01483 222095
E: richard@srsrailuk.co.uk
W: www.strail.com

Strainstall UK Ltd
9-10, Mariners way, Cowes, IOW PO31 8PD
T: 01983 203600
F: 01983 201335
E: enquiries@strainstall.com
W: www.strainstall.co.uk

Strataform
Unit C, Henfaes Lane, Welshpool, Powys SY21 7BE
T: 01562 515183
F: 01562 742648
E: sales@strataform.co.uk
W: www.strataform.co.uk

Strathclyde Partnership for Transport
Consort House, 12 West George St, Glasgow G2 1HN
T: 0141 332 6811
E: enquiry@spt.co.uk
W: www.spt.co.uk

STS Signals
Doulton Rd, Cradley Heath, West Midlands B64 5QB
T: 01384 567755
F: 01384 567710
E: martin.rubrey@sts-international.co.uk
W: www.sts-signals.com

Stuart Maher Ltd (SML)
Unit 3.07, New Loom House, 101 Back Church Lane, London SE1 1LU
T: 020 7423 4390
F: 07092 810 920
E: nick.stuart@stuart-maher.co.uk
W: www.stuart-maher.co.uk

Superform Aluminium
Cosgrove Close, Worcester WR3 8UA
T: 01905 874300
F: 01905 874301
E: sales@superform-aluminium.com
W: www.superform-aluminium.com

Superjet London
Unit 1, Park Road Ind. Est., Park Rd, Swanley, Kent BR8 8AH
T: 01322 666040
F: 01322 668060
E: superjetlondon@tiscali.co.uk
W: www.jetchem.com

Survey Systems Ltd
Willow Bank House, Old Road, Handforth, Wilmslow SK9 3AZ
T: 01625 533444
F: 01625 526815
E: enquiries@survsys.co.uk
W: www.survsys.co.uk/rail

Survey Inspection Systems Ltd (SIS)
Eaglescliffe Logistics Centre, Durham Lane, Stockton-on-Tees TS16 0RW
T: 01642 787839
F: 01642 785005
E: sales@survey-inspection.com
W: www.survey-inspection.com

Synectic Systems Group Ltd
32 Alexandra Way, Tewkesbury, Glos GL20 8NB
T: 01684 295807
F: 01684 850011
E: sales@synx.com
W: www.synecticsystems.com

Syntax Recruitment
1 College Place, Derby DE1 3DY
T: 01332 287720
F: 01332 296128
E: carl.veselis@syntaxnet.com
W: www.syntaxnet.com

SYSTRA

SYSTRA – International Consulting Engineers for Rail and Urban Transport.

Now with UK offices:
SYSTRA
1st Floor, Dukes Court
Duke Street
Woking
Surrey GU21 5BH
+44 (0)1483 742937
www.systra.com

Systra UK
First Floor, Dukes Court, Duke St, Woking, Surrey GU21 5BH
T: 01483 742937
E: aboagey@systra.com
W: www.systra.com

TAC Europe
Matrix House, Basing View, Basingstoke, Hants
T: 08700 600822
F: 01256 356371
E: enquiries@taceurope.com
W: www.taceurope.com

Tanfield Engineering Systems
Tanfield Lea Ind. Est. North, Stanley, Co Durham DH9 9NX
T: 01207 521111
F: 01207 523318
E: enquiries@tanfieldgroup.co.uk
W: www.tanfieldgroup.co.uk

Tarmac Precast Concrete
Tallington, Stamford, Lincs PE9 4RL
T: 01778 381000
E: enquiries@tarmac.co.uk
W: www.tarmac.co.uk/precast

The TAS Partnership Ltd.
Guildhall House, Guildhall St, Preston PR1 3NU
T: 01772 204988
F: 01772 562070
E: info@taspartnership.co.uk
W: www.tas.uk.net

Tasty Plant Sales
Chipstead Farm, Amersham Rd, Chalfont St Giles, Bucks HP8 4RT
T: 0845 677 4444
E: info@tastyplant.co.uk
W: www.tastyplant.co.uk

Taylor Woodrow
41 Clarendon Rd, Watford WD17 1TR
T: 01923 478400
F: 01923 478401
E: tim.fitch@taylorwoodrow.com
W: www.taylorwoodrow.com

TEAL Consulting Ltd
Deangate, Tuesley Lane, Godalming, Surrey GU7 1SG
T: 01483 420550
F: 01483 415705
E: info@tealconsulting.co.uk
W: www.tealconsulting.co.uk

Team Construction Ltd
Kings House, Home Park Estate, Station Rd, Kings Langley, Herts WD4 8LH
T: 0845 620 9268
F: 0845 620 9269
E: info@buildcis.com
W: www.buildcis.com

Team Surveys Ltd
Team House, St Austell Bay Bus.Park, Par Moor Rd, St Austell PL25 3RF
T: 01726 816069
F: 01726 814611
E: email@teamsurveys.com
W: www.teamsurveys.co.uk

Tecalemit Garage Equipment Co Ltd
Eagle Rd, Langage Business Park, Plymouth PL7 5JY
T: 01752 219111
T: 01752 219128
E: sales@tecalemit.co.uk
W: www.tecalemit.co.uk

Tecforce
Litchurch Lane, Derby DE24 8AA
T: 01332 268000
F: 01332 268030
E: sales@tecforce.co.uk
W: www.tecforce.co.uk

Technology Project Services Ltd
Warwick Row, London SW1E 5LR
T: 020 7963 1234
F: 020 7963 1299
E: mail@tps.co.uk
W: www.tps.co.uk

HSBC

Technology Resourcing Ltd
The Technology Centre, Surrey Research Park, Guildford GU2 7YG
T: 01483 302211
F: 01483 301222
E: railways@tech-res.co.uk
W: www.railway engineeringjobs.co.uk

Techno Rail (Technocover)
Henfaes Lane, Welshpool, Powys SY21 7BE
T: 01938 555511
F: 01938 555527
E: terry.batten@technorail.co.uk
W: www.technorail.co.uk

TEK Personnel Consultants Ltd
Norwich House, Irongate, Derby DE1 3GA
T: 01332 360055
F: 01332 363345
E: derby@tekpersonnel.co.uk
W: www.tekpersonnel.co.uk

Telent - Rail
Point 3, Haywood Rd, Warwick CV34 5AH
T: 01926 693569
F: 01926 693023
E: services@telent.com
W: www.telent.com

Telerail Ltd
9a New St, Carnforth, Lancs LA5 9BX
T: 01524 735774
F: 01524 736386
E: steve@telerail.co.uk
W: www.telerail.co.uk

Ten 47 Ltd
Unit 2B, Frances Ind. Park, Wemyss Rd, Dysart, Kirkcaldy KY1 2XZ
T: 01592 655725
F: 01592 651079
E: admin@ten47.com
W: www.ten47.com

Tenmat Ltd (Railko Ltd)
Ashburton Road West, Trafford Park, Manchester M70 1RU
T: 0161 872 2181
F: 0161 872 7596
E: info@tenmat.com
W: www.tenmst.com

Tensar International Ltd
Lions Drive, Shadsworth Business Park, Shadsworth, Blackburn BB1 2QX
T: 01254 262431
F: 01254 266867
E: info@tensar.co.uk
W: www.tensar-international.com

Tension Control Bolts
Whitchurch Business Park, Shakespeare Way, Whitchurch, Shropshire SY13 1LJ
T: 01948 667700
F: 01948 667744
E: info@tcbolts.co.uk
W: www.tcbolts.co.uk

Terram Ltd
Mamhilad Park Estate, Pontypool, Gwent NP4 0YR
T: 01495 757722
F: 01495 762383
E: info@terram.com
W: www.terram.com

Tew Engineering Ltd
Crocus St, Nottingham NG2 3DR
T: 0115 935 4354
F: 0115 935 4355
E: sales@tew.co.uk
W: www.tew.co.uk

TFR
4 Forestgrove Business Park, Nowtownbreda Rd, Belfast BT8 6AW
T: 02890 642800
F: 02890 648400
E: rebeccaharvey@tfrgroup.co.uk
W: www.tfrgroup.co.uk

Thales
Ground Floor, Unit 4b, Kenavon Drive, Forbury Park, Reading RG1 3DH
T: 0118 908 6000
F: 0118 908 7732
E: uk.enquiries@thalesgroup.com
W: www.thalesgroup.com

Thermit Welding (GB) Ltd
87 Ferry Lane, Rainham, Essex RM13 9YH
T: 01708 522626
F: 01708 553806
E: rsj@thermitwelding.co.uk
W: www.thermitwelding.co.uk

Thomas & Betts Holdings UK
Wilford Rd, Nottingham NG2 7EB
T: 0115 964 3700
F: 0115 986 0538
E: enquiry@furse.com
W: www.tnb-europe.com

T J Thomson & Sons Ltd
Millfield Works, Grangefield Rd, Stockton on Tees TS18 4AE
T: 01642 672551
F: 01642 672556
E: postbox@tjthomson.co.uk
W: www.tjthomson.co.uk

Thomson Rail Equipment Ltd
Valley Rd, Cinderford, Glos GL14 2NZ
T: 01594 826611
F: 01594 825560
E: thomson.rail@btconnect.com
W: www.thomson-rail.com

Thurlow Countryside Management Ltd
2 Charterhouse Trading Est, Sturmer Rd, Haverhill, Suffolk CB9 7UU
T: 01440 760170
F: 01440 760171
E: info@t-c-m.co.uk
W: www.t-c-m.co.uk

Thurrock Engineering Supplies Ltd
Unit 1 Motherwell Way, West Thurrock, Essex RM20 3XD
T: 01708 861178
F: 01708 861158
E: david@thurrockengineering.com
W: www.thurrockengineering.com

Thursfield Smith Consultancy
25 Grange Rd, Shrewsbury SY3 9DG
T: 01743 246407
E: david@thursfieldsmith.co.uk
W: www.thursfieldsmith.co.uk

Thurston Building Systems
Quarry Hill Estate, Horbury, Wakefield, West Yorkshire WF4 6AJ
T: 01924 265461
F: 01924 280246
E: david.bailiff@thurstongroup.co.uk
W: www.thurstongroup.co.uk

Thyssenkrupp GFT Gleistechnik GmbH
Altendorfstrasse 120, 45143 Essen, Germany
T: 0049 201 188 3710
F: 0049 201 188 3714
E: gleistechnik@thyssenkrupp.com
W: www.tkgftgleistechnik.de

TICS Ltd
Oxford House, Sixth Avenue, Robin Hood Airport, Doncaster DN9 3GG
T: 01302 623074
F: 01302 623075
E: info@tics-ltd.co.uk
W: www.tics-ltd.co.uk

tie Ltd (Transport Initiatives Edinburgh)
Citypoint, 65 Haymarket Terrace, Edinburgh EH12 5HD
T: 0131 622 8300
F: 0131 622 8301
E: comms@tie.ltd.uk
W: www.tie.ltd.uk

Tie & Track Systems Inc.
12300 South New Ave, Lemont IL 60439, USA
T: 001 630 985 1864
E: information@ttsties.com
W: www.ttsties.com

Tiflex Ltd
Tiflex House, Liskeard, Cornwall PL14 4NB
T: 01579 320808
F: 01579 320802
E: tsmith@tiflex.co.uk
W: www.tiflex.co.uk

Time 24 Ltd
Unit 69, Victoria Rd, Burgess Hill, West Sussex RH15 9TR
T: 01444 257655
F: 01444 259000
E: sales@time24.co.uk
W: www.time24ltd.co.uk

TI Protective Coatings
Unit 6, Lodge Bank, Crown Lane, Horwich, Bolton, Lancs BL6 5HY
T: 01204 468080
F: 01204 695188
E: sales@ticoatings.co.uk
W: www.ticoatings.co.uk

TMD Friction UK Ltd
PO Box 18 Hunsworth Lane, Cleckheaton, West Yorks BD19 3UJ
T: 01274 854000
F: 01274 854001
E: info@tmdfriction.com
W: www.tmdfriction.com

TMP Worldwide
Chancery House, Chancery Lane, London WC2A 1QS
T: 020 7406 5075
E: paul.turner@tmpw.co.uk
W: www.tmpw.co.uk

Tony Gee & Partners (TGP)
TGP House, 45-47 High St, Cobham, Surrey KT11 3DP
T: 01932 868277
F: 01932 866003
E: tgp@tgp.co.uk
W: www.tgp.co.uk

Torrent Trackside Ltd
Network House, Europa Way, Britannia Enterprise Park, Lichfield, Staffs WS14 9TZ
T: 01543 421900
F: 01543 421931
E: richard.donald@torrent.co.uk
W: www.torrent.co.uk

Totectors (UK) Ltd
1 Diamonds Business Centre, Nene Park, Attley Way, Irthlingborough, Wellingborough NN9 5GF
T: 0870 600 5055
F: 0870 600 5056
E: sales@totectors.net
W: www.totectors.net

Touchstone Renard
Lynton House, Station Approach, Woking, Surrey GU22 7PY
T: 01483 763123
F: 01483 757699
E: jmendleton@touchstonerenard.co.uk
W: www.touchstonerenard.co.uk

Tower Surveys Ltd
Vivian House, Vivian Lane, Nottingham NG5 1AF
T: 0115 960 1212
F: 0115 962 1200
E: Beverley.chiang@opusjoynespike.co.uk
W: www.towersurveys.co.uk

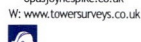

TPA Ltd
T: 0870 240 2381
F: 0870 240 2382
E: enquiries@tpa-ltd.co.uk
W: www.tpa-ltd.co.uk

TPK Consulting Ltd (RPS Group)
Centurion Court, 85, Milton Park, Abingdon, Oxon OX14 4RY
T: 01235 438151
F: 01235 438188
E: rpsab@rpsgroup.com
W: www.rpsplc.com

TRAC
Unit 14, Chesterfield Busines Centre, Pottery Lane West, Chesterfield S41 9BN
T: 01246 238400
F: 01246 238411
E: mail@tracinternational.com
W: www.tracinternational.com

Track Maintenance Equipment Ltd
Witham Wood, Marley Lane, Haslemere, Surrey GU27 3PZ
T: 01428 651114
F: 01428 644475
E: info@tmeltd.co.uk
W: www.tmeltd.co.uk

Track Safe Telecom (TST)
Unit 4, South Point Ind. Est, Foreshore Rd, Cardiff CF10 4SP
T: 0845 120 4571
F: 02920 461426
E: enquiries@tstservices.co.uk
W: www.tstservices.co.uk

Tracksure Ltd
8 Woburn St, Ampthill, Beds MK45 2HP
T: 01525 840557
F: 01525 403918
E: sales@tracksure.co.uk
W: www.ytracksure.co.uk

Trackwork Ltd
PO Box 139, Kirk Sandall Lane, Kirk Sandall Ind., Est.,Doncaster DN3 1WX
T: 01302 888666
F: 01302 888717
E: sales@trackwork.co.uk
W: www.trackwork.co.uk

Tractel UK Ltd
Old Lane, Halfway, Sheffield S20 3GA
T: 0114 248 2266
F: 0114 247 3350
E: tracteluk.info@tractel.com
W: www.tractel.com

TracTruc Bi-modal
See TruckTrain

Train'd Up
Elmbank Mill, Menstrie Bus. Centre, Mestrie, Clackmannanshire FK11 7BU
T: 0870 850 4525
F: 0870 850 3397
E: enquiries@traindup.org
W: www.traindup.org

The Trainline
Trainline Holdings Ltd, 498 Gorgie Rd, Edinburgh EH11 3AF
T: 08704 111111
W: www.thetrainline.com

Tramlink (Croydon)
Suffolk House, George St, Croydon CR0 1PE
T: 0845 748 4950
E: feedback@tramlink.info
W: www.tfl.gov.uk/trams

Tram Power Ltd
Unit 2/3, Appleby Business Centre, Blackburn BB1 3BL
T: 01254 583002
F: 01254 667024
E: info@trampower.co.uk
W: www.trampower.co.uk

Tranect Ltd
Unit 4, Carraway Rd, Gilmoss Ind. Est, Liverpool L11 0EE
T: 0151 548 7040
F: 0151 546 6066
E: sales@tranect.co.uk
W: www.tranect.co.uk

Transaction Systems Ltd
See Transys

Transdev Plc
Garrick House, Stamford Brook Garage, 74 Chiswick High Rd, London W4 1SY
T: 020 8400 6052
F: 020 8400 6053
E: information@transdevplc.co.uk
W: www.transdevplc.co.uk

Transeo
Lakeside Business Park, Carolina Way, Doncaster DN4 5PN
T: 0870 140 5000
F: 0870 140 5600
E: david.taylor@transeoalliance.com
W: www.transeoalliance.com

Translec Ltd
Saddleworth Business Centre, Huddersfield Rd, Delph, Oldham OL3 5DD
T: 01457 878888
F: 01457 878887
E: kparker@translec.co.uk
W: www.translec.co.uk

Transmitton
See Siemens

Trans Pennine Express (TPE)
See First Trans Pennine

Transport 2000
See Campaign for Better Transport

Transport & Travel Research Ltd (TTR)
Minster House, Minster Pool Walk, Lichfield, Staffs
T: 01543 416416
F: 01543 416681
E: enquiries@ttr-ltd.com
W: www.ttr-ltd.com

Transport Benevolent Fund
87a, Leonard St, London EC2A 4QS
T: 08450 100500
F: 0870 831 2882
E: help@tbf.org.uk
W: www.tbf.org.uk

Transport for London
1 Butler Place, London SW1H 0PT
T: 0845 748 4950
E: enquire@tfl.gov.uk
W: www.tfl.gov.uk/rail

Transport Interchange Consultants Ltd
1 Lochaline St, London W6 9ST
T: 020 8563 0555
F: 020 8563 0555
E: mw@ticonsultants.co.uk
W: www.ticonsultants.co.uk

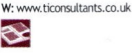

Transport Planning International
London House, 243-253 Lower Mortlake Rd, Richmond, Surrey TW9 2LL
T: 020 8948 9599
F: 020 8948 9685
E: info@tpi-london.com
W: www.tpi-online.com

Transport Research Laboratory (TRL) Ltd
Old Wokingham Rd, Crowthorne, Berks RG45 6AU
T: 01344 773131
F: 01344 770356
E: enquiries@trl.co.uk
W: www.trl.co.uk

Transport Scotland
Buchanan House, 58 Port Dundas Rd, Glasgow G4 0HF
T: 0141 272 7100
E: info@transportscotland.gsi.gov.uk
W: www.transportscotland.gov.uk

Transsol Ltd
32 Buxton Rd West, Disley, Cheshire SK12 2LY
T: 07775 893620
F: 0870 052 5838
E: enquiries@transsol.net
W: www.transsol.net

TranSys (Transaction Systems Ltd)
49 Pelham St, London SW7 2NJ
T: 020 7918 5929
F: 020 7918 5938
E: contact@transys.com
W: www.transys.com

Transys Projects Ltd
2 Priestley Wharf, Holt St, Aston, Birmingham B7 4BN
T: 0121 359 7777
F: 0121 359 1811
E: klane@transysprojects.ltd.uk
W: www.transysprojects.ltd.uk

Travel Info. Systems
Suite 1, Grand Union House, 20 Kentish Town Rd, London NW1 9NX
T: 020 7428 1288
F: 020 7267 2745
E: enquiries@travelinfosystems.com
W: www.travelinfosystems.com

Traxsydes Training
80-86 St Mary Rd, Walthamstow, London E17 9RE
T: 020 8223 1257
F: 020 8223 1258
E: mary.roberts@traxsydes.co.uk
W: www.tracksydes.co.uk

Trelleborg Industrial AVS
1 Hoods Close, Leicester LE4 2BN
T: 0116 267 0300
F: 0116 267 0510
E: rail@trelleborg.com
W: www.trelleborg.com

Tremco Illbruck Limited
Coupland Rd, Hindley Green, Wigan WN2 4HT
T: 01942 251400
F: 01942 251410
E: masterdeck@tremco-illbruck.co.uk
W: www.tremco-illbruck.com

TRANSYS PROJECTS LTD

- Rail Vehicle Refurbishment
- Maintenance
- Equipment Installation
- Design Consultancy
- Turnkey Service
- Labour Provision

2 Priestley Wharf, Holt Street, Aston, Birmingham B7 4BN
T: 0121 359 7777
E: 0121 359 1811
E: klane@transysprojects.ltd.uk
W: www.transysprojects.ltd.uk

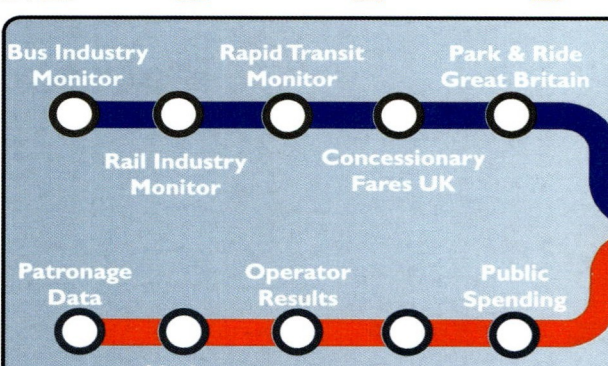

Your route to the passenger transport industry's vital statistics

- Bus Industry Monitor
- Rapid Transit Monitor
- Park & Ride Great Britain
- Rail Industry Monitor
- Concessionary Fares UK
- Patronage Data
- Operator Results
- Public Spending
- Market Analysis
- Capital Investment

www.tas.uk.net

Visit our web site for details or buy on-line.
Digital download now available for many products, giving instant access to data.
Leaflets and sample pages

TAS
TAS Publications & Events Limited
Ross Holme, West End, Long Preston, Skipton, North Yorkshire BD23 4QL.
Tel: 0870 900 1440. Fax: 0870 900 1470
info@tas-passtrans.co.uk

Trimble UK
Trimble House, Meridian Office Park, Osborn Way, Hook, Hants RG27 9HX
T: 01256 760150
F: 01256 760148
W: www.trimble.com

Tritech Rail Ltd
Wigan Investment Centre, Waterside Drive, Wigan, Lancs WN3 5BA
T: 01942 322333
F: 01942 248005
E: antony.kearns@tritechrail.com
W: www.tritechrail.com

Tritech Rail/Tritech Rail Training
Enterprise House,Enterprise Park, Seaman Way, Ince, Wigan WN2 2LE
T: 01942 322333
F: 01942 248005
E: antony.kearns@tritechrail.com
W: www.tritechrail.com

TRS Staffing Solutions
8th Floor, York House, Kingsway, London WC2B 6UJ
T: 020 7419 5800
F: 020 7419 5801
E: info-uk@trsstaffing.com
W: www.trsstaffing.com

Truck Train Developments Ltd (and TracTruc Bi-Modal)
4 Elfin Grove, Bognor Regis, W.Sussex PO21 2RX
T: 01243 869118
E: pmtrucktrain@tiscali.co.uk

Truflame Welding
Truflame House, 56 Newhall Rd, Sheffield S9 2QL
T: 0114 243 3020
F: 0114 243 5297
E: sales@truflame.co.uk
W: www.truflame.co.uk

TSSA (Transport Salaried Staff's Association)
Walkden House, 10 Melton St, London NW1 2EJ
T: 020 7387 2101
F: 0141 332 9879
E: enquiries@tssa.org.uk
W: www.tssa.org.uk

TTCI UK
13 Fitzroy St, London, W1T 4BQ
T: 020 7755 4080
F: 020 7755 4203
E: firdausi_irani@aar.com
W: www.ttciuk.com

TTR
See Transport & Travel Research

Tubelines
15 Westferry Circus, Canary Wharf, London E14 4HD
T: 0845 660 5466
E: enquiries@tubelines.com
W: www.tubelines.com

Tufcoat
Fox House, 8-10 Whimple St, Plymouth PL1 2DH
T: 01752 227333
F: 0871 264 5801
E: info@tufcoat.co.uk
W: www.tufcoat.co.uk

Tufnol Composites Ltd
Wellhead Lane, Perry Barr, Birmingham B42 2TB
T: 0121 356 9351
F: 0121 331 4235
E: sales@tufnol.co.uk
W: www.tufnol.com

Turbo Power Systems Ltd
Unit 2 Nest Rd, Felling, Gateshead, Tyne & Wear NE10 0ES
T: 0191 495 4850
F: 0191 495 4851
E: sales@turbopowersystems.com
W: www.turbopowersystems.com

Turkington Precast
James Park, Mahon Rd, Portadown, Co. Armagh, N.Ireland BT62 3EH
T: 028 38 332807
F: 028 38 361770
E: gary@turkington-precast.com
W: www.turkington-precast.com

Turner & Townsend
Low Hall, Calverley Lane, Horsforth, Leeds LS18 4GH
T: 0113 258 4400
F: 0113 258 2911
E: lee@turntown.com
W: www.turnerandtownsend.com

Turner Diesel Ltd
Unit 1A, Dyce Ind. Park, Dyce, Aberdeen AB21 7EZ
T: 01224 214200
F: 01224 723927
E: diesel.sales@turner.co.uk
W: www.turner-diesel.co.uk

Turner Recruitment
Caswell Rd, Sydenham Ind. Est, Leamington Spa, Warks CV31 1QF
T: 01926 612266
F: 01926 885590
E: mail@turnerrecruitment.co.uk
W: www.turnerrecruitment.co.uk

Turton Springs Ltd
Burton Rd, Sheffield S3 8DA
T: 0114 270 1577
F: 0114 275 6947
E: sales@turtonsprings.com
W: www.turtonsprings.com

TUV Product Service Ltd
Octagon House, Concorde Way, Segensworth, North Fareham, Hants PO15 5RL
T: 01489 558100
E: 01489 558101
F: info@tuvps.co.uk
W: www.tuvps.co.uk

TUV-SUD Rail GmbH
Ridlerstrasse 65, D-80339, Munich, Germany
T: 0049 89519 03537
F: 0049 89519 02933
E: michaela.mengel@tuevsued.de
W: www.tuv-sued.com

TXM Recruit Ltd
Blackhill Drive, Wolverton Mill, Milton Keynes, Bucks MK12 5TS
T: 0845 2263454
F: 0845 2262453
E: info@txmrecruit.co.uk
W: www.txmrecruit.co.uk

Tyne & Wear Metro
See Nexus

Tyrone Fabrication Ltd
Goland Rd, Ballygawley, Co Tyrone BT70 2LA
T: 028 8556 7200
F: 028 8556 7089
E: sales@tfl.eu.com
W: www.tfl.eu.com

UK Accreditation Service (UKAS)
21-47 High St, Feltham, Middx TW13 4UN
T: 020 8917 8400
E: info@ukas.com
W: www.ukas.com

UK Railtours
T: 01438 715050
E: john@ukrailtours.com
W: www.ukrailtours.com

UK Trade & Investment
Kingsgate House, 66-74 Victoria St, London SW1E 6SW
T: 020 7215 4951
F: 020 7828 1281
E: enquiries@uktradeinvest.gov.uk
W: www.uktradeinvest.gov.uk

UK Ultraspeed
Warksburn House, Wark, Hexham, Northumberland NE48 3LS
T: 020 7861 2497
F: 020 7861 2497
E: ncameron@bell-pottinger.co.uk
W: www.500kmh.com

Ultra Electronics-Electrics
Kingsditch Lane, Cheltenham, Glos GL51 9PG
T: 01242 221166
F: 01242 221167
E: peter.rogers@ultra-electrics.com
W: www.ultra-electrics.com

Ultra Electronics PMES Ltd
Armitage Rd, Rugeley, Staffs WS15 1DR
T: 01889 503300
F: 01889 572913
E: trevor.boston@ultra-pmes.com
W: www.ultra-pmes.com

Underground Pipeline Services Ltd
Park Lane West, Tipton, Dudley DY4 8LH
T: 0121 520 1006
F: 0121 521 2811
E: solution@upls.co.uk
W: www.upls.co.uk

Unic Cranes Europe
Units 8-10, Ridgeway, Drakes Drive, Long Crendon Ind Est, Bucks HP18 9BF
T: 01844 202071
F: 01844 202075
E: info@ggrglass.co.uk
W: www.unic-cranes.co.uk

UNIFE
Avenue Louise 221, B-1050 Brussels, Belgium
T: 0032 2642 2328
F: 0032 2626 1261
E: niall.doheny@unife.org
W: www.unife.org

UIC
The Universal Improvement Company

With offices in the UK and Australia, the UIC specialises in organisational improvement providing training, facilitation and consultancy in strategy development, project management, performance improvement, leadership and data.

A: 17 Knowl Avenue, Belper, Derbyshire, DE56 2TL.
T: 01773 826659
F: 01773 826659
E: info@theuic.com
W: www.theuic.com

Unipart Dorman
See Dorman

Unipart Rail (UK) Ltd
Jupiter Building, Firstpoint, Balby Carr Bank, Doncaster DN4 5JQ
T 01302 731400
F: 01302 731401
E: trsenquiries@unipartrail.com
W www.unipartrail.com

Unipart Rail (infrastructure)
Gresty Rd, Crewe CW2 6EH
T: 01270 847600
F: 01270 847601
E: enquiries@unipartrail.com
W: www.unipartrail.com

Unipart Rail (infrastructure)
Leeman Rd, York YO26 4ZD
T: 01904 544020
F: 01904 544021
E: enquiries@unipartrail.com
W: www.unipartrail.com

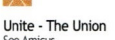

Unite - The Union
See Amicus

Universal Heat Transfer Ltd
Well Spring Rd, Carlyon Rd, Atherstone, Warks CV9 1QZ
T: 01827 722171
F: 01827 722174
E: nina@uhtltd.com
W: www.universalheattransfer.co.uk

UNIPART RAIL

Unipart Rail is the UK's largest partner in infrastructure and T&RS materials supply & management, and lean business solutions

Unipart Rail (T&RS):
Jupiter House, First Point
Balby Carr Bank, Doncaster
DN4 5JQ

T: +44 (0) 1302 731 400
F: +44 (0) 1302 731 401
trsenquiries@unipartrail.com

Unipart Rail (Infrastructure):
Gresty Road, Crewe,
Cheshire CW2 6EH

Tel: +44 (0) 1270 847 600
Fax: +44 (0) 1270 847 601

Unipart Rail (Infrastructure):
Leeman Road, York
Yorkshire YO26 4ZD

T: +44 (0) 1904 544 020
F: +44 (0) 1904 544 021

enquiries@unipartrail.com

www.unipartrail.com

UNIPART RAIL

The Universal Improvement Company
17 Knowl Ave, Belper, Derbys DE56 2TL
T: 01773 826659
F: 01773 826659
E: info@theuic.com
W: www.theuic.com

Up & Cuming Consultancy Ltd (UCCL)
74 Chenies Mews, London WC1E 6HU
T: 020 7388 2232
F: 020 7388 3730
E: info@uccl.net
W: www.uccl.net

Urban Hygiene Ltd
Sky Business Park, Robin Hood Airport, Doncaster DN9 3GA
T: 01302 623193
E: enquiries@urbanhygiene.com
W: www.urbanhygiene.co.uk

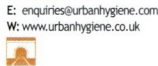

Urbis Lighting Ltd
Telford Rd, Houndmills, Basingstoke, Hants RG21 6YW
T: 01256 354446
F: 01256 841314
E: sales@urbislighting.com
W: www.urbislighting.com

URS Corporation Ltd
URS House, Horne Lane, Bedford MK40 1TS
T: 01234 349641
E: tony_wakeman@urscorp.com
W: www.urscorp.eu

Albashaw ltd (t/a Vacuum Reflex Ltd)
Unit 2, Gamma Terrace, West Rd, Ransomes Euro Park, Ipswich IP3 9SX
T: 01473 725176
F: 01473 271941
E: info@vacuum-reflex.com
W: www.vacuum-reflex.com

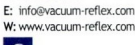

VAE UK Ltd
Sir Harry Lauder Rd, Portobello, Edinburgh EH15 1DJ
T: 0131 550 2297
F: 0131 550 2660
E: jim.gemmell@vae.co.uk
W: www.voestalpine.com/vae

Vaisala Ltd
349, Bristol Rd, Birmingham B5 7SW
T: 0121 683 1200
F: 0121 683 1269
E: liz.green@vaisala.com
W: www.vaisala.com

Van Der Vlist
The Deep Business Centre, Kingston upon Hull HU1 4BG
T: 01482 382004
F: 01482 382005
E: info@vandervlist.co.uk
W: www.vandervlist.co.uk

Variable Message Signs Ltd (VMS)
Unit 1, Monkton Business Park North, Mill Lane, Hebburn, Tyne & Wear NE31 2JZ
T: 0191 423 7070
F: 0191 423 7071
E: aisaacs@vmslimited.co.uk
W: www.vmslimited.co.uk

Vector Management Ltd
Strathclyde House, Green Man Lane, London Heathrow Airport, Feltham, Middx TW14 0NZ
T: 020 8844 0444
F: 020 8844 0666
E: ju-liang.trigg@vecman.com
W: www.vecman.com

Vectra Group Ltd
Europa House, 310 Europa Blvd., Gemini Business Park, Westbrook, Warrington WA5 7YG
T: 01925 402100
F: 01925 444701
E: rail@vectragroup.co.uk
W: www.vectragroup.co.uk

Verint Systems
241 Brooklands Rd, Weybridge, Surrey KT13 0RH
T: 01932 839500
F: 01932 839501
E: marketing.emea@verint.com
W: www.verint.com

Veritec Sonomatic Ltd
Ashton House, The Village, Birchwood Bus.Park, Warrington WA3 6FZ
T: 01925 414000
E: 01925 655595
F: jl@vsonomatic.com
W: www.veritecltd.co.uk

Veryards Opus
See Opus International

Video 125 Ltd
Glade House, High St, Sunninghill, Berks SL5 9NP
T: 01344 299551
F: 01344 628565
E: clive@video125.co.uk
W: www.video125.co.uk

SA Viewcom (now Axion Technologies)
Lokesvej 7-9, 3400 Hilleroed, Denmark
T: 0045 721 93500
F: 0045 721 93501
E: info@axiontech.dk
W: www.axiontech.dk

Vintage Trains Ltd
670 Warwick Rd, Tyseley, Birmingham B11 2HL
T: 0121 708 4960
F: 0121 708 4963
E: vintagetrains@btconnect.com
W: www.vintagetrains.co.uk

Virgin Trains (West Coast)
North Wing Offices. Euston Station, London NW1 2HS
T: 0845 000333
E: firstname.lastname@virgintrains.co.uk
W: www.virgin.com/trains

Vision Fire & Security
Vision House, Focus 31, Mark Rd, Hemel Hempstead, Herts HP2 7BW
T: 01442 242330
F: 01442 249327
E: helpme@vision-fs.com
W: www.vision-fs.com

Vision Infrastructure Services
Intertrain House, Union St, Doncaster DN1 3AE
T: 01302 815530
F: 01302 815531
E: ianraeburn@hotmail.com
W: www.visioninfrastructureservices.com

Vistorm Ltd
3200 Daresbury Park, Daresbury, Warrington WA4 4BU
T: 01925 665500
F: 01925 667200
E: info@vistorm.com
W: www.vistorm.com

Vita Safety Ltd
1 Gillingham Rd, Eccles, Manchester M30 8NA
T: 0161 789 1400
F: 0161 280 2528
E: ian.hutchings@vitasafety.com
W: www.vitasafety.com

Vital Resources Ltd
The Mill, South Hall St, Ordsall Lane, Salford M5 4TP
T: 0161 836 7000
F: 0161 836 7048
E: linda.davison@vital-solutions.biz
W: www.vital-solutions.biz

Vitec Webber Lenihan
Innovation Centre, Technology Drive, Bridgend Science Park, Bridgend CF31 3NA
T: 01656 654060
F: 01656 767361
E: mail@vitecwebberlenihan.com
W: www.vitecwebberlenihan.com

VMS
See Variable Message Systems

Voest-Alpine Group
Voestalpine-Strasse 1, 4020 Linz, Austria
T: 0043 732 65850
F: 0043 732 65859311
E: martin.platzer@voestalpine.com
W: www.voestalpine.com

Voith Turbo GmbH & Co.KG
Alexanderstrasse 2, 89522 Heidenheim, Germany
T: 0044 7321 37 4069
F: 0044 7321 37 7616
E: rail-division@voith.com
W: www.voith.com

Voith Turbo Ltd
Regent House, Pump Lane, Hayes, Middx UB3 3NB
T: 020 8561 2131
F: 020 8569 1726
E: turbo.uk@voith.com
W: www.voith.co.uk

Volo TV
83 Victoria St, London SW1H 0HW
T: 020 3008 7894
F: 020 7078 6030
E: yeshpaul.soor@volo.tv
W: www.volo.tv

Vortok International
Units 6-8, Haxter Close, Belliver Ind. Est, Roborough, Plymouth PL6 7DD
T: 01752 700601
F: 01752 702353
E: sales@vortok.co.uk
W: www.vortok.co.uk

Vossloh Fastening Systems GmbH
Am Schimmersfeld 7a, D-40880 Ratingen, Germany
T: 0049 2102 49090
F: 0049 2102 49094
W: www.vossloh-fastening-systems.de

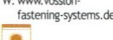

VTG Rail UK Ltd
Sir Stanley Clare House, 7 Ridgeway, Quinton Business Park, Birmingham B32 1AF
T: 0121 421 9180
F: 0121 421 9192
E: salesuk@vtg.com
W: www.vtg.com

Vulcascot
Gatwick Gate Estate, Lowfield Heath, Crawley, W Sussex RH11 0TG
T: 01293 560130
F: 01293 537743
E: crawley@vulcascot.co.uk
W: www.vulcascot.co.uk

Vultron International Ltd
Unit 2, Stadium Way, Elland Rd, Leeds LS11 0EW
T: 0113 387 7310
F: 0113 387 7317
E: sales@vultron.co.uk
W: www.vultron.co.uk

Wabtec Rail Ltd
PO Box 400, Doncaster Works, Hexthorpe Rd, Doncaster DN1 1SL
T: 01302 340700
F: 01302 790058
E: wabtecrail@wabtec.com
W: www.wabtecrail.co.uk

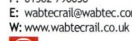

Wacker Neuson (GB) Ltd
Lea Rd, Waltham Cross, Herts EN9 1AW
T: 01992 707228
F: 01992 707201
E: chris.pearce@eu.wackergroup.com
W: www.wackerneuson.com

W A Developments Ltd
See Stobart Rail

Walker Rail Consult
Wellington Building, 28-32 Wellington Rd, St Johns Wood, London NW8 9SP
T: 020 7483 9355
F: 020 7483 9356
W: www.wrconsult.co.uk

Washroom Joinery Ltd
The Loughton Seedbed Centre, Langston Rd, Loughton, Essex IG10 3TQ
T: 0700 492 7476
F: 08700 111860
E: info@washroomjoinery.co.uk
W: www.washroomjoinery.co.uk

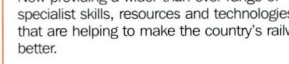

Wabtec
RAIL LIMITED

- Vehicles
- Wheelsets and Bogies
- Air Conditioning
- Door Systems
- Components

Now providing a wider than ever range of specialist skills, resources and technologies that are helping to make the country's railways better.

Wabtec Rail Ltd
PO Box 400, Doncaster DN1 1SL
T: 01302 340700
F: 01302 790058
E: wabtecrail@wabtec.com
W: www.wabtecrail.co.uk

HSBC

Waterman

Waterman is an international engineering and environmental consultancy.

We are a Link Up and Network Rail approved framework consultant and LUL accredited.

Waterman provides a total engineering solution, including specialist asset management with our Autorail™ software.

Contact Paul Worrall
t: 020 7928 7888
e: p.r.worrall@waterman-group.co.uk
www.watermangroup.com

WESTINGHOUSE platform screen doors

Westinghouse Platform Screen Doors, a business division of Knorr-Bremse, is a world leader in the design, manufacture and installation of platform screen systems.

To find out more contact:
Colin Fullalove on 01225 898835.
e-mail: colin.fullalove@westbrake.com

www.platformscreendoors.com

KNORR-BREMSE

Washtec UK Ltd
Unit 14A, Oak Ind. Park, Great Dunmow, Essex CM9 1XN
T: 01371 878800
F: 01371 878810
E: dawn.fraser@washtec-uk.com
W: www.washtec-uk.com

Waterman Civils Ltd
Pickfords Wharf, Clink St, London SE1 9DG
T: 020 7928 7888
F: 020 7902 0992
E: p.r.worrall@waterman-group.co.uk
W: www.waterman-group.co.uk

Waverley Rail Project
Communications Office, Weber Shandwick, 9 York Place, Edinburgh EH1 3EB
T: 0800 652 3406
E: info@waverleyrailwayproject.co.uk
W: www.waverleyrailwayproject.co.uk

Wavesight Ltd
Talon House, Presley Way, Crownhill, Milton Keynes MK8 0ES
T: 01908 265223
F: 01908 265143
E: sales@wavesight.com
W: www.wavesight.com

Webasto AG
Kraillinger Strasse 5
82131 Stockdorf
Germany
T: 0049 89 857 94 433
F: 0049 89 899 217 433
E: tac3@webasto.it
W: www.webasto.com

AP Webb Plant Hire Ltd
Common Rd, Stafford ST16 3DQ
T: 01785 241335
F: 01785 255178
E: mail@apwebbplanthire.com
W: www.apwebbplanthire.com

Webro Cable & Connectors
Vision House, Meadow Brooks Business Park, Meadow Lane, Long Eaton, Notts NG10 2GD
T: 0115 972 4483
F: 0115 946 1230
E: sales@webro.com
W: www.webro.com

Weedfree
Holly Tree Farm, Park Lane, Balne, Goole DN14 0EP
T: 01405 860022
F: 01405 862283
E: sales@weedfree.net
W: www.weedfree.net

Weidmuller Ltd
1, Abbey Wood Rd, Kings Hill, West Malling, Kent ME19 4YT
T: 0845 0942006
F: 01732 874296
E: roger.buckley@weidmuller.co.uk
W: www.weidmuller.co.uk

Weightmans
High Holborn House, 52-54 High Holborn, London WC1V 6RL
T: 020 7822 1900
F: 020 7822 1901
E: sarah.seddon@weightmans.com
W: www.weightmans.com

Weighwell Ltd
23 Orgreave Place, Sheffield S13 9LU
T: 0114 269 9955
F: 0114 269 9256
E: rwood@weighwell.co.uk
W: www.weighwell.co.uk

Weld-A-Rail Ltd
Lockwood Close, Top Valley, Nottingham NG5 9JM
T: 0115 926 8797
F: 0115 926 4818
E: info@weldarail.com
W: www.weldarail.com

A J Wells & Sons Vitreous Enamellers
Bishop's Way, Newport, IOW PO30 5WS
T: 01983 537766
F: 01983 537788
E: enamel@ajwells.co.uk
W: www.ajwells.com

Westbury White & Nunn
10 Waterfront Business Park, Fleet, Hants GU51 3TX
T: 01252 620091
F: 01252 627034
E: info@wwnrecruitment.com
W: www.wwnrecruitment.com

Weston Williamson
43, Tannner St, London SE1 3PL
T: 020 7403 2665
F: 020 7403 2667
E: chris@westonwilliamson.com
W: www.westonwilliamson.com

West Coast Railway Co.
Jesson Way, Carnforth, Lancs LA5 9UR
T: 01524 732100
F: 01524 735518
E: info@wcrc.co.uk
W: www.wcrc.co.uk

Westcode Semiconductors
Langley Park Way, Langley Park, Chippenham, Wilts SN15 1GE
T: 01249 444524
F: 01249 659448
E: customer.services@westcode.com
W: www.westcode.com

Westcode (UK) Ltd
Unit 1, Carnegie Rd, Calne, Wilts SN11 9PS
T: 01249 822823
F: 01249 822284
E: tonypark@westcodeuk.com
W: www.westcodeus.com

Westermo Data Comms Ltd
Talisman Business Centre, Duncan Rd, Park Gate, Southampton SO31 7GA
T: 01489 580585
F: 01489 580586
E: sales@westermo.co.uk
W: www.westermo.co.uk

Westinghouse Rail Systems
PO Box 79, Pew Hill, Chippenham, Wilts SN15 1JD
T: 01249 441441
F: 01249 441442
E: wrsl.marketing@wrsl.com
W: www.wrsl.com

Westinghouse Platform Screen Doors
Westinghouse Way, Hampton Park East, Melksham, Wilts SN12 6TL
T: 01225 898835
E: colin.fullalove@westbrake.com
W: www.platformscreendoors.com

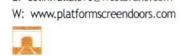

West Midlands PTE
See Centro

Westquay Trading Co. Ltd
3F, Lyncastle Way, Appleton Thorn Trading Est, Warrington WA4 4ST
T: 01925 214 105
F: 01925 211700
E: garry@westquaytrading.com
W: www.westquaytrading.co.uk

Westshield Ltd
Waldron House, Drury Lane, Chadderton, Oldham OL9 8LU
T: 0161 682 6222
F: 0161 682 6333
E: mail@westshield.co.uk

West Yorkshire PTE (Metro)
Wellington House, 40-50 Wellington St, Leeds LS1 2DE
T: 0113 251 7272
W: www.wypte.gov.uk

---

invensys rail group WESTINGHOUSE rail systems

Westinghouse Rail Systems (WRSL) is a world leader in advanced signalling and integrated control systems for main line and mass transit railways.

Westinghouse Rail Systems
PO Box 79,
Pew Hill,
Chippenham,
Swindon SN15 1JD

Tel: 01249 441441
Fax: 01249 441442

marketing@wrsl.com
www.westinghouserail.com

William Bain Fencing Ltd
Lochin Works, 7 Limekilns Rd, Blairtirin Ind. Est., Cumbernauld G67 2RN
T: 01236 457333
F: 01236 451166
E: sales@lochrin-bain.co.uk
W: www.lochrin-bain.co.uk

William Cook Rail
Cross Green, Leeds LS9 0SG
T: 0113 249 6363
F: 0113 249 1376
E: sales@cook-rail.co.uk
W: www.william-cook.co.uk

Windhoff Bahn und Anlagentechnik GmbH
Hovestrasse 10, D-48431 Rheine, Germany
T: 0049 5971 58347
F: 0049 5971 58445
E: aka@windhoff.de
W: www.windhoff.de

Wind River UK Ltd
Oakwood House, Grove Business Park, White Waltham, Maidenhead, Berks SL6 3HY
T: 01793 831831
F: 01793 831808
E: peter.mylchreest@windriver.com
W: www.windriver.com

Wheelsets UK
Carr Hill, Balby, Doncaster DN4 8DH
T: 01302 322266
F: 01302 322299
E: martin@wheelsets.co.uk
W: www.wheelsets.co.uk

White & Case LLP
5 Old Broad St, London EC2N 1DW
T: 020 7532 2310
F: 020 7532 1001
E: twinsor@whitecase.com
W: www.whitecase.com

Whiteley Electronics Ltd
Victoria St, Mansfield, Notts NG18 5RW
T: 01623 415601
F: 01623 420484
E: email@whiteleyelectronics.com
W: www.whiteleyelectronics.com

White Young Green
Arndale Court, Headingley, Leeds LS6 2UJ
T: 0113 278 7111
W: www.wyg.com

Wicek Sosna Architects
Unit 15, 21 Plumbers Row, London E1 1EQ
T: 020 7655 4430
E: wicek@sosnaarchitects.co.uk
W: www.sosnaarchitects.co.uk

Wilkinson Star Ltd
Shield Drive, Wardsley Ind Est, Manchester M28 2WD
T: 0161 793 8127
F: 0161 727 8538
E: steve.ross@wilkinsonstar.com
W: www.wilkinsonstar.com

Winn & Coales (Denso) Ltd
Denso House, Chapel Rd, London SE27 0TR
T: 020 8670 7511
F: 020 8761 2456
E: mail@denso.net
W: www.denso.net

Winsted Ltd
Units 7/8, Lovett Rd, Hampton Lovett Ind Est, Droitwich, Worcs WR9 0QG
T: 01905 770276
F: 01905 779791
E: alan@winsted.co.uk
W: www.winsted.com

Wintersgill
110 Bolsover St, London W1W 5NU
T: 020 7580 4499
F: 020 7436 8191
E: info@wintersgill.net
W: www.wintersgill.net

Woking Homes
Oriental Rd, Woking, Surrey GU22 7BE
T: 01483 763558
F: 01483 721048
E: info@uknursinghomes.org/wokinghomes

HV Wooding Ltd
Range Rd, Hythe, Kent CT21 6HG
T: 01303 264471
F: 01303 262408
E: sales@hwwooding.co.uk
W: www.hwwooding.com

Workthing
Beamont House, Kensington Village, Avonmore Rd, London W14 8TS
T: 0870 898 0022
F: 0870 898 0033
E: info@workthing.com
W: www.workthing.com

Works Infrastructure Ltd
Mallard House, 75 The Mount, York YO24 1AX
T: 01904 672233
F: 01904 672244
E: steve.horn@works.co.uk
W: www.works.co.uk

Wor-Rail (Wor-lifts Ltd)
90 Roebuck Lane, West Bromwich B70 6QX
T: 0121 525 1011
F: 0121 525 1022
E: sales@worlifts.co.uk
W: www.worlifts.com

The Wrexham, Shropshire & Marylebone Railway Company
Great Central House, Marylebone Place, London NW1 6JJ
T: 0845 260 5233
E: info@wrexhamandshropshire.co.uk
W: www.wrexhamandshropshire.co.uk

WSP Civils
Mountbatten House, Basing View, Basingstoke, Hants RG21 4HJ
T: 01256 318802
F: 01256 318700
E: nicky.bushnell@wspgroup.com
W: www.wspgroup.com

WTB Geotechnics
Earl Russell Way, Lawrence Hill, Bristol BS5 0WT
T: 0845 600 5505
F: 0845 609 2525
E: geotechnics@wtbgroup.com
W: www.geotechnics-uk.com

WWP Consultants
5-15 Cromer St, London WC1H 8LS
T: 020 7833 5767
F: 020 7833 5766
E: admin@wwp-london.com
W: www.wwp-london.com

Wynnwith Rail
Wynnwith House, Church St, Woking, Surrey GU21 6DJ
T: 01483 748206
E: rail@wynnwith.com
W: www.wynnwith.com

Wyse Rail Ltd
Cressex Business Park, Lancaster Rd, Bucks HP12 3QP
T: 0870 145 0552
F: 01494 560929
E: wyserail@wysegroup.com
W: www.wysegroup.com

WyvernRail Plc
Wirksworth Station, Station Rd, Coldwell st, Wirksworth, Derbys DE4 4FB
T: 01629 821828
E: wirksworth_station@wyvernrail.co.uk
W: www.mytestrack.com

XiTRACK Ltd
Station Rd, Birch Vale, High Peak, Derbys SK22 1BR
T: 01663 746518
F: 01663 746605
E: DMFrost@dow.com
W: www.hyperlast.com

XL Lubricants
PO Box 2, Summerbridge, Harrogate HG3 4XN
T: 01423 781010
F: 01423 781279
E: info@xl-lubricants.com
W: www.xl-lubricants.com

Yardene Engineering 2000 Ltd
Daux Rd, Billingshurst, West Sussex RH14 9SJ
T: 01403 783558
F: 01403 783104
E: sales@yardene.co.uk
W: www.yardene.co.uk

YJL Infrastructure Ltd
39 Cornhill, London EC3V 3ND
T: 020 7650 2234
F: 020 7522 3261
E: mccabepl@yjli.co.uk
W: www.yjli.co.uk

York EMC Services Ltd
Market Square, University of York, Heslington, York YO10 5DD
T: 01904 434440
F: 01904 434434
E: enquiry@yorkemc.co.uk
W: www.yorkemc.co.uk

Yorkshire Rail Academy
National Railway Museum, Leeman Rd, York YO26 4XJ
T: 01904 770780
E: reception@yra.ac.uk
W: www.yorkshirerailacademy.com

Z+F UK Ltd
Unit 9, Derwent House, Clarence Ave, Trafford Park, Manchester M17 1Q
T: 0161 869 0450
F: 0161 869 0451
E: info@zf-uk.com
W: www.zf-uk.com

Zetica
Holdan House, 26 Bridge St, Witney, Oxon OX28 1HY
T: 01993 706767
F: 01993 773040
E: info@zetica.com
W: www.zetica.com

ZF Great Britain Ltd
Abbeyfield Rd, Lenton, Nottingham NG7 2SX
T: 0115 935 5445
F: 0115 851 5508
E: glenn.ayres@zf.com
W: www.zf-group.co.uk

Zircon Software Ltd
Avon Court, Castle St, Trowbridge, Wilts BA14 8AR
T: 01225 764444
F: 01225 753087
E: Phil.cooper@zirconsoftware.co.uk
W: www.zirconsoftware.co.uk

Zollner UK Ltd
Clayton Business Ctr, Midland Rd, Leeds LS10 2RJ
T: 0113 270 3008
F: 0113 277 1007
E: frank.peters@zollner-uk.co.uk
W: www.zollner-uk.co.uk

Zuppinger & Co Ltd
42 Macclesfield Rd, Hazel Grove, Stockport SK7 6BE
T: 01625 877277
F: 01625 850242
W: www.erlau.com

Zwicky Track Tools
Intamech Ltd, Bridge Trading Centre, Corngreaves Rd, Cradley Heath, West Midlands B64 7BT
T: 01384 413413
F: 01384 412853
E: info@zwicky.co.uk
W: www.zwicky.co.uk

ADDENDUM

APT Skidata Ltd
The Power House, Chantry Place, Headstone Lane, Harrow, Middlesex HA3 6NY
T: 020 8421 2211
F: 020 8428 6622
E: d.murphy@aptskidata.co.uk
W: www.aptcontrols-group.co.uk

Comech Metrology Ltd
Castings Rd, Derby DE23 8YL.
T: 01332 867700
F: 01332 867707
E: sales@comech.co.uk
W: www.comech.com

The Train Chartering Company Ltd
Monleaze Farm, Braydon, Wilts SN5 0AZ
T: 01666 860172
E: info@trainchartering.com
W: www.trainchartering.com

York EMC Services Ltd

Railway System EMC Consultancy, Testing and CPD Training for:

- Signalling and Telecommunications
- Rolling Stock
- Power Supply
- Substations and Switchgear
- Trackside Equipment

York EMC Services
Market Square, University of York,
York, YO10 5DD
Tel: +44 (0) 1904 434440
Fax: +44 (0) 1904 434434
enquiry@yorkemc.co.uk
www.yorkemc.co.uk

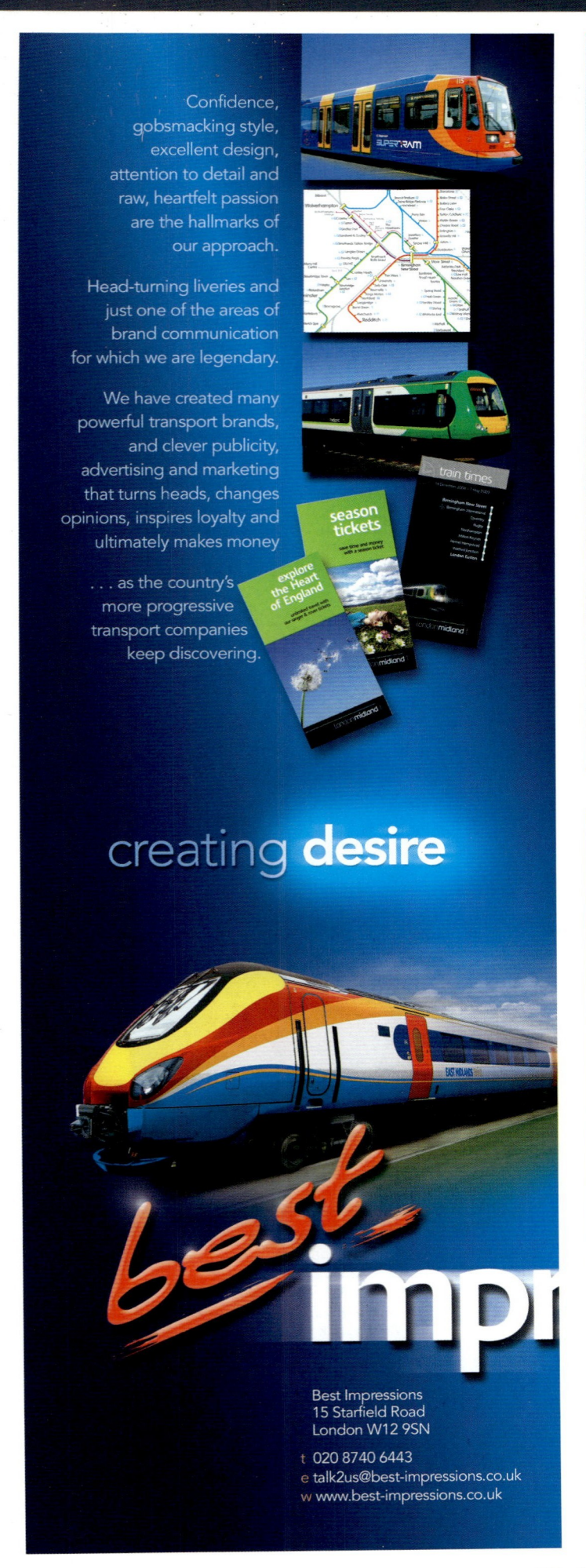

Directory

Best Impressions

Confidence, gobsmacking style, excellent design, attention to detail and raw, heartfelt passion are the hallmarks of our approach.

Head-turning liveries and just one of the areas of brand communication for which we are legendary.

We have created many powerful transport brands, and clever publicity, advertising and marketing that turns heads, changes opinions, inspires loyalty and ultimately makes money

... as the country's more progressive transport companies keep discovering.

creating desire

best impr

Best Impressions
15 Starfield Road
London W12 9SN

t 020 8740 6443
e talk2us@best-impressions.co.uk
w www.best-impressions.co.uk

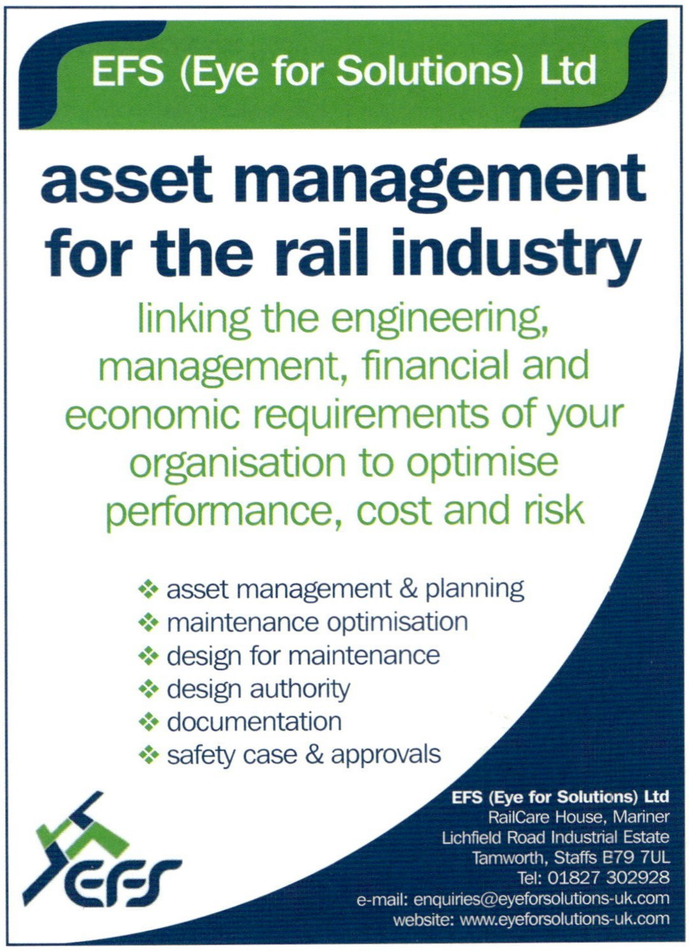

EFS (Eye for Solutions) Ltd

asset management for the rail industry

linking the engineering, management, financial and economic requirements of your organisation to optimise performance, cost and risk

- asset management & planning
- maintenance optimisation
- design for maintenance
- design authority
- documentation
- safety case & approvals

EFS (Eye for Solutions) Ltd
RailCare House, Mariner
Lichfield Road Industrial Estate
Tamworth, Staffs B79 7UL
Tel: 01827 302928
e-mail: enquiries@eyeforsolutions-uk.com
website: www.eyeforsolutions-uk.com

RISC
Railway & Industrial Safety Consultants

Specialists in Technical and Operational fields, and across the interfaces

We help you with:
- Developing your certificated SMS, QMS, EMS or IMS;
- Risk assessment;
- Auditing;
- Reliability engineering;
- Technical and Operational Approvals, Assurance and Safety Cases;
- T&RS Engineering and Operations Management
- New train introduction for heavy and light rail;
- ROGS and other railway Regulations compliance:
- Independent Competent Person assessments.

Contact: David Greenway, RISC Ltd,
3 Doveridge Rd, Burton on Trent, DE15 9GB
Telephone/Fax: 0870 350 9420 / 9421
Email: enquiries@railwaysafety.co.uk
Web: www.railwaysafety.co.uk

Freight & Haulage

In association with

CSRE

Freight & Haulage

A rosy future for railfreight?
The Modern Railway looks behind the headlines of the freight business

EWS's Class 66 No 66173 passes Cholsey as it travels east towards Reading with an intermodal working on 4 May 2007. Paul Bigland

It would be difficult to paint a more upbeat picture about freight in the UK than the headlines have given us in 2008: English, Welsh & Scottish Railway (EWS) and Freightliner sold to new owners for sums that could only be dreamt of at the time of privatisation, substantial orders for new wagons, a new high-tech freight loco for the UK from GE, and infrastructure enhancements to create additional capacity and capability on key freight routes.

And yet. The statistics for 2007 show an uncomfortable reality of year-on-year volume decline (Table 1), and in 2008 the worldwide financial crisis has clearly hit import container and construction volumes hard. The highly cyclical metals business seems destined to follow. Further pain seems certain, as the world talks itself into an economic recession, if not 1930s-style Depression. So, are we deluding ourselves about the rosy future for railfreight?

Well, no, but the angle of the growth trajectory may need to be reassessed and, crucially, the less-than-inspiring market development performance of the major freight operating companies (FOCs) will need a big improvement. We are progressively putting in place a physical infrastructure in terms of track and trains which is well-geared to future requirements and, recession notwithstanding, customers are keener than ever to use rail (and water) to reduce their carbon footprint and the reliance on road haulage. Environmental pressures may take more of a back seat for a while, but they will not go away. The big question is, will the FOCs step up to the plate and take advantage of this?

First the positives. There can be little question that investors see UK railfreight as a good place to be for the long term. The past year has seen remarkable prices paid for both EWS and Freightliner. Shareholders in the former, in particular, must have offered a prayer of thanks for the arrival of Deutsche Bahn AG with their fat (state-guaranteed) chequebook. Certainly, a price rumoured to be in the region of £330m, or even perhaps £500m if debt is included, could be virtually double what a normal business valuation, based on profit generation, would give - so producing handsome returns for the original investors.

Whatever one's views of large profits heading back to New Zealand and the US for UK taxpayers' assets sold cheaply by the government (where are you now, all-knowing Treasury experts?), we should at least be glad that the EWS staff, who bought shares through a company savings scheme, saw some benefit - which might well not have been the case if Dr Medhorn (DB Chairman) had chosen to enter France in a different way. (Euro Cargo Rail, EWS's nascent French open access operation, is widely believed to have been the main reason for the DB acquisition, rather than the barely-profitable UK operation). Similarly, the original management buy-out and venture capital investors in Freightliner were handsomely rewarded when the company was sold to the

In association with **CSRE**

sovereign wealth of Bahrain, in the guise of Arcapita, for a sum rumoured to be in the region of £350m.

New entrants
In addition, new entrants continue to surface and claim a share of the freight action. Fastline Freight, having enjoyed mixed fortunes with intermodal services from Thamesport, has moved into the bulk market with a contract from E.ON to transport coal to Ratcliffe power station. Advenza Freight, part of the Cotswold Rail stable which had previously focused on a variety of passenger work, has been operating scrap trains to the Celsa steelworks at Cardiff and outbound finished steel thence to Barking for the Olympics. Clearly, there is a view that money can be made from running freight trains.

More prosaic, but ultimately more important, investment in hardware has also been running at a high level. Orders for new wagons across Europe have outstripped the capacity of the builders to produce the required vehicles. Exacerbated by shortages of steel, and particularly wheelsets, delivery dates have gone out from under a year to two years or more in some cases. The recession may have a small silver lining in returning the availability and price of key raw materials to more acceptable levels.

For all the impressive increase in wagon capacity, the most important technical development in the world of wagons is undoubtedly the WH Davis 'Super Lowliner', currently undergoing acceptance trials. Its ability to convey 9ft 6in high, 45ft long 'palletwide' containers and swap bodies within W8 gauge is unique, and a major step forward in intermodal capability in the UK. ('Palletwide' containers allow two pallets to be loaded side by side.)

Small wheel technology makes the wagon more expensive, both at first cost and in ongoing maintenance, but it allows hi-cube boxes to be moved on non-gauge enhanced routes – a critical factor for parts of the country where lower volumes of such containers make it difficult to justify expensive infrastructure changes.

On the locomotive front, we are about to see the first new freight loco type for the UK market since the advent of the EMD Class 66 ten years ago and, arguably, since the Class 59 progenitor of the 66 was introduced 23 (yes, twenty three!) years ago. The new GE Genesis design, rated at 3,700hp, should be introduced during 2009 and is testament to Freightliner's commitment to future revenue growth. It also marks GE's entry to the UK market, and is doubly welcome in providing a more fuel-efficient machine and an alternative supplier to Electro-Motive Diesel, which had been virtually the only game in town.

While GBRf and Fastline Freight have continued to order additional Class 66s for the UK, EWS purchases have been targeted on Euro Cargo Rail in France - where growth has been rapid as customers switch from the troubled SNCF Fret. Indeed, such has been the speed and extent of growth that ECR now employs over 80 locos and is bigger than each of the EWS bulk businesses - minerals, construction and Industrial. The arrival of the new continental-gauge machines would allow EWS to transfer some of the UK-gauge locos back through the Channel Tunnel if necessary. Meanwhile, EWS is set to refurbish over half the Brush-built Class 60s, now some 20 years old but preferred to the Class 66 for the real heavy-haul drags in construction, metals and petroleum.

Infrastructure
Route improvement to W10 gauge (allowing 9ft 6in high containers on standard height container flats) has already been achieved - without fanfare - from Felixstowe to Peterborough, and work on the extensions to Yorkshire via the ECML and to the WCML via Leicester and Nuneaton continued apace in late 2008. Contrary to expectations, the Peterborough to Leicester section, with its tunnel under Stamford, has proved less problematic than the stretch onward to Nuneaton. One wonders how many more 'no hoper' structures could actually be enhanced at quite reasonable cost?

The route from Southampton to the West Midlands and the WCML should be cleared in 2010, with the branch to Birch Coppice ready in late 2009. W10 clearance of the Tottenham & Hampstead (Gospel Oak-Barking) route - relieving the North London Line - is also forging ahead, none too soon, with the Olympics

Freight & Haulage

Coal haulage is still a dominant feature of the railfreight scene. Freightliner's No 66552 waits as its train is loaded at Hull Bulk Terminal. Network Rail has carried out a £14.5million project to more than double capacity on the line into Hull docks. Network Rail

approaching rapidly and the likelihood of much extra container traffic from the recently authorised London Gateway port at Thameshaven.

Private sector infrastructure investment is also coming through in large measure. Across the UK there are now 35 proposals for rail-related distribution parks, not all of which will come to fruition, but the signs are good for several large facilities in key locations. Planning permission remains a hurdle, and Helioslough's plans for a major distribution facility at Radlett were rejected on appeal, although Prologis was successful in gaining permission for a facility at Howbury Park near Dartford, adjacent to Slade Green depot.

It is evident that the big commercial property developers now realise that rail is an essential component of a major logistics facility, and are prepared to fund the often substantial cost of connecting a site to the national network, along with an on-site intermodal terminal and rail-connected warehouses. The wisdom of this can be seen from the (then) Secretary of State's decision letter on Radlett, in which she indicates that, had Helioslough conducted a more rigorous site search to demonstrate that Radlett was the only suitable site to the north of London, she would have been prepared to grant permission, in spite of its location in very sensitive Green Belt - such is the importance now attached to rail-related logistics developments by government.

Potential for growth

Seeing all these innovations, a newcomer might ask why rail carryings are not increasing rapidly. First, in response, much of the foregoing has yet to be delivered – the time lapse from authorisation through construction to implementation is as long, if not longer, than ever. Secondly, we ought to remind our new friend that, for the foreseeable future, a relatively small reduction in coal will dwarf the small but encouraging growth in domestic intermodal traffic – as was indeed the case in 2007. Elsewhere in bulk, loss of long-distance semi-finished steel volumes from Lackenby to South Wales offset growth in finished steel, construction and petroleum. In one sense, the rail freight industry has done well to offset much of the decline due to factors outwith its control.

Accepting that overall carryings have held up better than they would have done in the 'give us the bulk and to hell with rest' days of Trainload Freight, one is still left with the feeling that more ought to be happening in the newer sectors, such as supply chain logistics, to provide a stronger overall upward trend. Granted there has been growth in the new markets. There are now six trains a day (all hauled by Direct Rail Services - DRS) in each direction between Daventry and Central Scotland, carrying retail goods and manufactured products. Some 2,000 lorry journeys each week are thereby kept off the M6/M74. Further north, Tesco is launching a daily service from Central Scotland to Inverness to supply its Highland stores, again using DRS for the rail haul and Stobart for the

Table 1 - Freight moved, Great Britain (billion net tonne km)

Year	Coal	Metals	Construction	Oil & petroleum	International*	Domestic intermodal*	Other	Total
2002-03	5.66	2.64	2.51	1.15	0.46	3.38	2.72	18.52
2006-07	8.56	2.04	2.70	1.53	0.44	4.72	1.89	21.88
2007-08	7.73	1.83	2.79	1.58	0.37	5.15	1.73	21.18
% change 2007-08 on 2006-07	-9.7	-9.9	3.3	3.5	-16.8	9.1	-8.5	-3.2

Notes to table: * 'International traffic' comprises trains travelling through the Channel Tunnel; 'domestic intermodal' includes goods that have arrived by sea at ports.
Source - ORR National Rail Trends; Network Rail

Freight operator finances

The UK's rail freight operators managed to arrest the decline in profit levels in 2006/07, according to analysis undertaken by consultants TAS in 'Rail Industry Monitor'. This reversed a trend of falling profits which had lasted for several years. Operating profits rose by 12.8%, partially reversing the previous year's 15.5% fall. Margins recovered to 5.3% during the year, but still remaining at not much more than half the 9% earned in 2003/04.

Combined turnover was 1.6% up in 2006/07 to £817.9m, whilst the rise in operating costs was constrained to 1.1%, taking them up to £774.5m. Thus, operating profits recovered from the previous year's £38.5m to £43.4m.

TAS also reports on market share, as measured by turnover. EWS retained the lion's share of the business, with just over 60% (down from over 80% in the late 1990s). Freightliner was next with 31.2%. The two post privatisation new entrants, Direct Rail Services and FirstGroup's GB Railfreight subsidiary, have each built up a market share of just under 4.5% each from a standing start less than a decade ago.

Freight Operators

GB Railfreight

The company increased its turnover by more than a quarter during the year, thanks to the commencement of new contracts for infrastructure trains for Metronet and other clients, whilst future expansion was guaranteed by the capture of new contracts for the haulage of coal which started during 2007/08.

However, the rise in operating costs was slightly greater than in revenue, so that - though operating and pre-tax profits rose in cash terms - margins were slightly lower.

Period to:	31 Mar 07	31 Mar 06
	£000	£000
Turnover	35,289	27,855
Operating Costs:	33,144	25,924
Operating Profit:	2,145	1,931
Operating Margin:	6.1%	6.9%
Turnover per Employee	£142,870	£135,878
Rolling stock lease	4,317	3,784

Direct Rail Services

The company - a subsidiary of the state-owned Nuclear Decommissioning Authority - grew substantially again during the year, and also improved operating margins, as the rise in turnover outstripped increases in operating costs.

Period to:	31 Mar 07	31 Mar 06
	£000	£000
Turnover	34,954	27,877
Operating Costs:	33,149	26,503
Operating Profit:	1,805	1,374
Operating Margin:	5.2%	4.9%
Turnover per Employee	£138,158	£120,159
Revenue Grant	1,203	1,193

English Welsh & Scottish Railway

The company - since acquired by the German state-owned railway giant Deutsche Bahn - increased its operating and pre-tax profits during the year, improving its profit margins in the process, but turnover fell again. During the year, the company reorganised itself into four railfreight business units - construction, energy, industrial and network (covering infrastructure operations).

Period to:	31 Mar 07	31 Mar 06
	£000	£000
Turnover	463,900	485,300
Operating Costs:	435,400	457,600
Operating Profit:	28,500	27,700
Operating Margin:	6.1%	5.7%
Turnover per Employee	£106,546	£103,365

EWS International

The company recorded reduced operating and pre-tax losses during the year. The original agreement for access to the Channel Tunnel expired in November 2006, leading to a series of changes in access charging, continuing into the following year.

Period to:	31 Mar 07	31 Mar 06
	£000	£000
Turnover	24,000	21,900
Operating Costs:	36,900	36,900
Operating Profit:	(12,900)	(15,000)
Operating Margin:	-53.8%	-68.5%
Turnover per Employee	£76,923	£58,245
Revenue Grant	100	0

Freightliner

The company achieved a small cash increase in operating profits, but at a slightly lower margin. Turnover growth was maintained as demand for container shipments from the deep water ports continued to grow. Increases in operating costs depressed margins slightly, though this was offset by reduced net interest charges.

Period to:	31 Mar 07	25 Mar 06
	£000	£000
Turnover	163,768	155,736
Operating Costs:	152,528	144,541
Operating Profit:	11,240	11,195
Operating Margin:	6.9%	7.2%
Turnover per Employee	£146,746	£138,802
Track Access	16,583	15,178

Freightliner Heavy Haul

The company, which specialises in heavy haul of coal and other trainload commodities, continued the strong growth it has maintained since being founded in 1999. However, it traded at slightly lower margins during the year as increases in operating costs took their toll.

Period to:	31 Mar 07	25 Mar 06
	£000	£000
Turnover	91,441	80,568
Operating Costs:	79,968	69,611
Operating Profit:	11,473	10,957
Operating Margin:	12.5%	13.6%
Turnover per Employee	£169,649	£165,437
Track Access	14,033	11,838

road legs. The service will closely replicate the ground-breaking service for Safeway launched in the early days of EWS, which ceased as a result of the Competition Commission-enforced disposal of Safeway's Highland stores on the takeover by Morrisons.

Elsewhere, Tesco is said to be close to starting a Northwest England to South Wales intermodal service, and Asda is running a daily service from Tilbury to Wakefield (hauled by EWS) to convey imported fruit in refrigerated containers. Also on North Thamesside, JG Russell has taken over the former Freightliner terminal at Barking and is using it to load Tate & Lyle bulk sugar containers to Scotland. The service starts back at Tilbury to provide a link for Daventry and Scotland with short sea container services, operated by P&O and Samskip.

Nevertheless, for all these - very welcome - standard bearers, there is a sense that much more could be happening. The retailers, in particular, are very keen to see more of their enormous volumes on rail but, other than the flows above and deep sea containers moved on Freightliner and EWS services, have failed to find a service/price offer that suits their needs. Not that they are looking for a reduction on the road rate - if rail can offer the same price (or even a little higher) they will switch if the service is comparable in terms of transit and reliability.

Sad to report, this has not, and is not, happening. The co-operative approach between retailers we mentioned last year ultimately came to nought. Only one FOC apparently came up with an acceptable offer and, for reasons unconnected with the project, was subsequently unable to take matters forward to contract stage. The missing factor is that, in general, the big FOCs seem - for whatever reason - not to be using the new found scope to grow the market and take advantage of the best climate for rail for decades. Potential customers in the logistics and supply chain sectors are frustrated that they can get neither the response nor the type of service they require to substitute for road, even on long distance legs of several hundred miles where rail should be well-suited.

Freight & Haulage

This North Downs location, hidden by lineside trees in recent years, has been opened up again. On 6 May 2008, a line-up of First GBRf locos passes Polhill, between Knockholt and Dunton Green, heading to Tonbridge yard, following Bank Holiday weekend engineering work. Class 66/7 No 66707 leads No 66701 and Class 73/2s Nos 73208, 73209 and 73206. Brian Morrison

It is significant that those routes which do exist have been developed by enlightened road hauliers, notably WH Malcolm (winners of the 2008 Rail Freight Group award) and JG Russell. In both cases, DRS simply provides locos and hauls the customer's block train from terminal to terminal. While there is nothing wrong with hauliers and logistics companies making the running – indeed Malcolm and Russell deserve considerable praise for their efforts – the railfreight industry cannot afford to rely on others to bring traffic to them. Why do the big FOCs, who make it their business to understand their customers' requirements in the bulk markets, seemingly often fail to do the same with the newer logistics business?

Perhaps it is the perceived profitability of logistics versus bulk. FOCs may be happier to knock lumps out of each other competing for the same business in traditional markets than to go out and grow the overall market. With fierce competition for every piece of bulk traffic tendered by customers, the traditional railfreight business can be a zero sum game. Organic growth in bulk is limited at the best of times and, going into a recession, relying on it would seem to be a somewhat flawed business strategy. So, as well as trumpeting the latest contract wins in bulk, infrastructure and haulage of passenger stock, which do nothing to grow the overall railfreight market, the FOCs should actively pursue some substantial new business from the retailers and logistics companies – they are ready to talk!

Rail Freight Group opinion

2008 has seen the final stages of the Periodic Review of Network Rail's Access charges. At the time of writing, no final decision has been made, but strong expectations are that this will lead to a further reduction in access charges for freight, coupled win a requirement from the Office for Rail Regulation for Network Rail to move quickly towards a seven day a week railway.

In the autumn, a government reshuffle appointed Geoff Hoon as Secretary of State for Transport and Lord Adonis as the minister for railways. They will have to move fast to match the recently announced Conservative and Lib-Dem policies to construct a high-speed passenger line to relieve congestion on existing lines and cater for growth.

This is becoming an urgent issue. New forecasts of demand for rail freight to 2015 and 2030, published by the Rail Freight Group and Freight Transport Association, show a 30% increase in tonne km from 2006 to 2015, with demand more than doubling by 2030. However, the growth in intermodal traffic is forecast to be very much higher: more than doubling by 2015 and a five-fold increase by 2030. This reflects continuing expansion of trade from continental Europe and further afield, plus a significant use of rail to and from new rail-connected warehouses.

By 2030, there is forecast to be shortfall in capacity of between 100 and 200 trains a day on many routes, even assuming no increase in passenger train numbers. The greatest shortfalls are, perhaps unsurprisingly, on the West Coast and East Coast main lines, as well as on the Midland main line and on the routes to the Channel Tunnel and London Gateway.

Following the second serious truck fire in the Channel Tunnel since it opened, it will be essential for the UK and French governments to review the safety rules to reduce the risk of a repeat and, at the same time, recognise the high level of safety achieved in the rail operation there.

Equally important will be the provision of terminals around the country to transfer the cargoes to and from rail; it is essential that the planning process for these becomes easier (we hope that this will be achieved with the Planning Bill currently, in late 2008, before Parliament) - and that most new freight distribution centres will be built with rail connections as a matter of course. That would reduce not only the cost of the road leg but greatly improve the carbon footprint of the logistics flows concerned.

So the challenge for 2009 is to plan for growth and start delivering the infrastructure necessary to allow this to happen.

Tony Berkeley
Chairman, Rail Freight Group
www.rfg.org.uk

In association with CSRE

Chinese built wagons for Europe

A new alliance supported by UK specialists offers high quality and affordable wagons

Grain hopper wagon for export to Australia.

Little more than a decade ago, eyebrows would have been raised at the prospect of Eastern European plants becoming major suppliers of freight wagons to the UK – but these products are now an everyday sight across Britain's rail network.

Now a similar challenge to expectations has been raised by an alliance involving major manufacturers in China, supported by British engineering and certification specialists. Their aim is to provide high quality and affordable wagons for the UK and continental Europe.

China's producers have already won international contracts to export passenger and freight rolling stock - to Australia, as well as several Asian and African countries. In China itself, manufacturers are working in joint ventures with big international names such as GE, Bombardier, Siemens and Alstom.

Production and support

The newcomer to the freight wagon markets in Britain and other European countries is an alliance between CSRE Limited and rail vehicle engineering consultants Resco Europe.

CSRE was established in 2006, to promote the introduction of Chinese rolling stock to Europe. David Shipley, Managing Director of CSRE, has represented CSR (China South Locomotive & Rolling Stock Corporation) since 2004, and the CSRE company now works together with four CSR and CNR factories, with the combined ability to produce, each year:
- 350 diesel / electric locomotives;
- 10,000 freight wagons; and
- 650 passenger cars (electric and diesel multiple-units and hauled coaches).

The capabilities of CSRE cover all stages of a rolling stock project. These include procuring not just the vehicles and components from China, but also services from Europe to support the manufacturers, and then maintenance services on behalf of the end-user.

Other key CSRE capabilities take in:
- project management;
- arrangement of lease finance;
- delivery into service; and
- after-sales support.

Comprehensive range

In 2007, CSR's export contracts were valued at nearly 600 million US dollars. Current workload of Chinese plants, and available designs, cover a wide range of rolling stock and traction:
- Potenta heavy freight locomotive (3,750hp, MTU engined, aimed at the same markets as the EMD Class 66, GE Powerhaul, or Voith Maxima).
- Polaris Inter-City Express Train (200 km/h train set, with diesel, electric and electro-diesel motive power options and 'power source future-proofing' built-in).
- Pacemaker DMU concept (a natural Pacer / Sprinter replacement).
- Pacemaker LT Light Train concept (lightweight DMU, offering 7 tonne axle loads in tare).
- Various freight wagon projects (coal and aggregate hoppers, petroleum tanks, container flats and steel carriers).
- A range of component supply projects (Y25 bogies and wheel sets).

Freight wagon designs and production

Freight wagon and component supply projects are typically fulfilled by the major specialist plant of CNR Jinan. The plant's advanced steel structure production line has recently been complemented by investment in the installation of a semi-automated production line dedicated to the production of type Y25 bogies for the European market. Facilities at Jinan also include computer-controlled machining and milling machines, robotic welding workstations and steel pre-treatment.

Recent production has included a variety of aluminium and steel bodied coal hopper wagons, steel coil wagons with retractable canopies, double-deck car transporter wagons, container flat wagons, insulated and standard tank wagons, ballast discharge wagons, and (for export to Australia) grain hopper wagons.

CSRE has developed designs for a new range of wagons for the UK and continental Europe markets, including:
- 102-tonne coal hopper wagons,
- 100-tonne side-discharge hopper wagons,
- 60ft container flat wagons,
- 100 tonne steel carriers, and
- petroleum tank wagons.

Professional support, certification and testing

CSRE and Resco Europe established a relationship in 2007, under which CSRE acts for the manufacturer (the 'Authorised Representative' under the Interoperability Regulations) while Resco Europe acts as importer and supplier.

CSRE provides documentation, spare parts and warranty support for the manufacturer, while Resco Europe provides project management and engineering support for the end user.

Lloyds Register Rail in general provides most certification and Notified Body services to CSRE, with a detailed 'Route to Conformance' being developed for each project.

A testing plan is developed for each project, in support of Notified Body submissions. Some elements (such as wheel sets, bogies) can be certified as 'Interoperability Constituents'.

Material testing (including thorough metallurgy) is part of the CSRE programmes, to confirm that Chinese sourced materials meet European standards and that heat treatment (applied, for example, to wheels) has been effective. Static testing (mainly strain gauge testing with applied loads) is carried out to validate finite element analysis (FEA) modelling.

Dynamic testing is also carried out (on a 52km high-speed test track in China) to validate ride performance and prove that wagons will operate within noise limits.

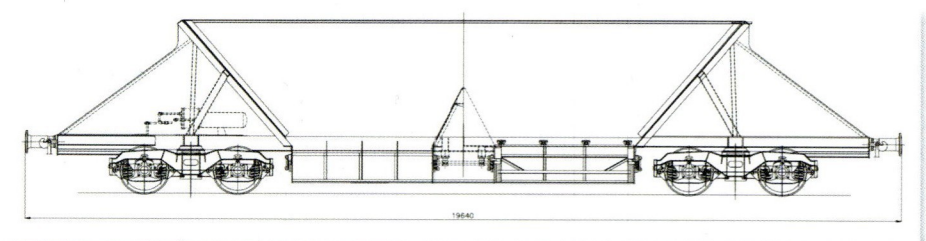

CSRE drawing of 102 tonne coal hopper wagon for the UK market.

Freight & Haulage

At Cardiff on 9 June 2008, EWS's Class 66 No 66152 heads west with a Corby-Margam empty steel train, while on the left No 158950 leaves for Portsmouth Harbour. Paul Bigland

DB-owned, diversified freight operator

English, Welsh & Scottish Railway (EWS), the largest rail freight operator in Britain, is now part of DB Schenker, after a 2007 takeover by Deutsche Bahn (DB - German Rail).

DB Schenker combines all transport and logistics activities of DB, employing over 88,000 staff in around 2,000 locations in 130 countries, with turnover of about 18billion Euros.

The Spanish company Transfesa was also taken over, and these and other transactions have extended DB's reach in Western Europe, with EWS represented in France by its subsidiary Euro Cargo Rail.

EWS was launched in February 1996 after the company acquired four divisions of British Rail's freight operations - Rail Express Systems, Loadhaul, Transrail Freight and Mainline Freight. This was followed by the purchase of National Power's rail unit and British Rail's European division, Railfreight Distribution.

With a workforce of around 5,000, EWS provides a range of rail freight haulage, passenger, engineering support and hire services nationwide in addition to its rail freight operations.

The previous majority shareholder was Canadian National, which in 2001 bought Wisconsin Central Railroad - the US company that originally led the formation of EWS.

Companies within the EWS group include EWS International (operator of freight trains via the Channel Tunnel), Euro Cargo Rail (supplier of rail freight services in France, Germany and Spain), Engineering Support Group (traction and rolling stock engineering consultancy), Railway Approvals (specialising in enabling approval of new locomotives and wagons for operation on Network Rail infrastructure), and Marcroft Engineering (rolling stock construction and maintenance). Axiom Rail is a supplier of maintenance, refurbishment, leasing solutions and suspension systems, developed after EWS took over Probotec.

Transeo is an EWS alliance with IT services provider Thales, which provides information technology services to the transport sector. It operates the National Rail Communication Centre, providing live information to National Rail Enquiries and media companies.

A four-division business structure was introduced in 2006/07:

* EWS Energy moves coal and other fuels for the energy sector, accounting for about a quarter of EWS revenue. It is based at Knottingley, close to power station generators and suppliers.

* EWS Industrial, based at Doncaster, moves heavy industrial materials, such as metals and petroleum products.

* EWS Construction, based at Toton, near Nottingham, moves products for the construction and waste industries.

* EWS Network, based at Doncaster, provides services for Network Rail, the logistics sector and the rail industry. This includes trains for Network Rail's infrastructure engineering work, as well as locomotive and driver hire. EWS Network also markets passenger rail services including specialist trains for sporting occasions. It offers intermodal, automotive, chemicals and express parcels services for the logistics sector.

Soon after its launch in 1996, EWS began a £500million investment programme, including the development with Electro-Motive Diesel of the Class 66 diesel locomotive, now used by all Britain's main freight operators. EWS ordered 250 of the '66s' which form the backbone of the company's fleet.

50 of the Class 66s have been modified for use in continental Europe by Euro Cargo Rail (ECR), and a further 60 of the class were ordered for ECR in 2007. Vossloh diesel locomotives and Bombardier TRAXX multi-voltage electric locomotives have also been added to ECR's fleet. Engineering Support Group (ESG) has also expanded into France.

EWS also worked with Electro-Motive to develop a new high-speed freight locomotive, the Class 67. Primarily intended for Royal Mail trains,. EWS purchased 30 of these 125mph locomotives, but EWS ceased operation of mail trains in 2004, losing around 8% of its overall revenue. The Class 67s are now used on ScotRail sleeper trains; Wrexham, Shropshire & Marylebone Railway trains; and special passenger trains; as well as on general duties.

EWS initially invested £200million in wagons, placing a major order for 2,500 new wagons from US wagon builder Thrall. More than half were new high capacity coal wagons.

An economy drive led by Chief Executive, Keith Heller, who moved in 2004 from Canadian

National, saw much tighter utilisation of resources, and a decline in the number of former British Rail locomotives in use. About half of the 100 heavy-haulage Class 60 locomotives were in use in 2008, and many of the class were expected to undergo overhaul or improvement.

Every week, 8,000 rail freight services are operated by EWS. While there has been some retrenchment since the early days of the company, it held a market share of 57% by turnover in 2006-07 (60% including EWS International).

New services

EWS launched new European intermodal rail freight services from January 2008, operated by its subsidiary Euro Cargo Rail. A network of services was announced to connect Belgium, Germany, Italy, France, Spain and Switzerland with Scotland and the Midlands and North West of England. Initial services planned included Duisburg and Milan to Manchester, with connecting services to Grangemouth - EWS acquired logistics firm TDG's intermodal rail freight terminal at Grangemouth in late 2007.

Since autumn 2007, EWS Energy has announced new contracts with British Energy, Drax Power Limited, E.ON UK, EDF Energy, RWE npower, Scottish & Southern Energy, and ScottishPower.

In April 2008, ScottishPower awarded EWS Energy a new contract for the delivery of coal by rail to Longannet and Cockenzie power stations. In October 2007, Drax Power and EWS Energy agreed on a new contract and commercial approach.

EWS Energy has also introduced regular trains of gypsum from Drax power station to Gascoigne Wood, for onward delivery by road to its customer British Gypsum's plant at Sherburn. Gypsum is a by-product of flue-gas desulphurisation process used at Drax.

A new long term, £50million contract from EDF Energy was also awarded in October 2007, to deliver coal to power stations at Cottam and West Burton. RWE npower awarded a contract to EWS Energy in the same month, for coal trains to power stations at Aberthaw and Didcot.

ZIM Integrated Shipping Services awarded a contract to EWS Network in June 2008 to move intermodal containers by rail from Felixstowe or Tilbury to Wakefield – initially 100 containers a week. This is ZIM's first major use of rail freight in the UK.

EWS runs regular trains of deep sea containers from Southampton and Felixstowe. In September 2006, it introduced a new daily high-cube-container service between the Port of Southampton and the new Birmingham Intermodal Freight Terminal (BIFT). After expansion work on the Southampton terminal, capacity was increased from four to 10 trains a day.

The Ministry of Defence awarded a new Strategic Rail Capability and Mainline Rail Freight Services haulage contract to EWS Network in October 2007. MoD awarded the £28million contract following competitive tender. The four-year deal also covers wagon maintenance.

In September 2007, Imerys and EWS Network agreed a new five-year contract for the haulage of china clay by rail from production sites in Cornwall.

In 2008, more than 100 low-sided box wagons were ordered by EWS Network to support its seven year infrastructure haulage contract with Network Rail. These 90 tonne wagons are manufactured in Poland by Greenbrier.

Building materials company Cemex UK awarded a six-year contract to EWS Construction in June 2007 for its entire rail freight haulage requirements for aggregates and coal, using new, high capacity, track-friendly wagons owned by EWS and painted in Cemex livery. The first of 34 Greenbrier-built wagons (code-IIA) for Cemex traffic were delivered in August 2008.

Senior personnel

Chief Executive Keith Heller (left)
Commercial Director David Kerr
Planning Director Graham Smith
MD, EWS Energy Paul Bates
MD, EWS Industrial Neil McDonald
MD, EWS Construction Nigel Smith
MD, EWS Network Stuart Boner
MD, Axiom Rail Paul McKeown

EWS's high-profile contract with Mendip Rail, renewed in 2005, covers operation of trains carrying up to 3,000 tonnes of stone from the Mendips quarries of Foster Yeoman (Merehead) and Hanson (Whatley).

EWS Industrial in March 2007 introduced heavier steel-slab-carrying freight trains, operating from Port Talbot to Llanwern in Wales. They haul 33% more product than before, thanks to a modification programme.

A new train maintenance facility was opened by Axiom Rail at Cambridge in November 2007 to service trains for the new CrossCountry franchise - Axiom's first long-term contract direct with a passenger franchise operator. Axiom has extensive experience in servicing Voyager trains through its continuing contract with Bombardier for Virgin Trains.

Axiom Rail launched a new freight suspension system in 2006 - the TF25E. Axiom says it exerts low track forces resulting in low bogie wear and lower maintenance requirements, produces a low level of noise, and is also 'freight friendly' with low vertical acceleration.

A Calvert to Northolt 'Binliner' waste train approaches West Ruislip on 28 April 2008, hauled by EWS Class 60 No 60063 'James Murray' whose paintwork is in faded condition. Many of the former British Rail Class 60s are set for overhaul or improvement. Brian Morrison

Freight & Haulage

First GBRf

Turnover at record levels

First GBRf, now the largest British-owned rail freight company, was formed as GB Railfreight in 1999. It has been part of FirstGroup plc since its takeover of GB Railways in 2003. A new track access contract gives access to the network until December 2016. First GBRf employs some 320 people.

Turnover in 2007-08 was the highest since the company began and more than 37% higher than 2007. Average annual growth stood at over 40% in 2008.

First GBRf locomotive drivers are called Train Managers, reflecting enhanced responsibility. They work flexible hours to help services run non-stop, utilise trains productively, and avoid disruptions.

The company now has a 12% share of the coal haulage market, building rapidly after its first coal train in March 2007 for Drax Power. A new contract with British Energy saw haulage commence in April 2008 from Immingham to Eggborough power station in the Aire Valley, and an agreement with Alcan includes haulage of both imported coal from the Port of Tyne and indigenous coal from UK Coal, Widdrington to Lynemouth power station near Ashington.

Additional contracts were secured with coal trading companies who import coal into Immingham, Hull, Redcar and Port of Tyne, hauling to both Aire and Trent valley power stations. First GBRf also has a significant coal contract with EDF Energy, and an expanded contract was agreed with Drax Power in 2007. A mid 2008 order for new HYA coal hoppers, built by IRS in Romania, took First GBRf's fleet to over 150 wagons.

In June 2008, a new five-year deal was signed with British Gypsum, First GBRf's first bulk haulage customer, after an initial contract, including movement of desulphogypsum from West Burton power station from 2003.

Bulk transportation also extends to a contract with PetroChem Carless, agreed in 2005, to transport large quantities of gas condensate from its depot in East Anglia to Harwich. A separate service takes mud oil from Harwich to Aberdeen.

The company first established itself with an eight-year contract to haul rail infrastructure materials, and operates trains for Network Rail across East Anglia, the East Midlands and south of England. It also manages all operations at Network Rail's Whitemoor yard, Cambridgeshire.

August 2006 saw a new ten-year, £80million service contract to provide infrastructure haulage services for London Underground. First GBRf's new Wellingborough depot was opened in June 2007 to stable and load materials for the work. In January 2008, a new contract was won from the Balfour Beatty Carillion Joint Venture to transport construction materials for the East London Line project.

First GBRf's No 66716 on an intermodal train at Felixstowe. First GBRf

In the intermodal container business, a five-year contract with MSC, signed in 2002, made First GBRf the first freight operator other than Freightliner to serve the Port of Felixstowe. In 2003 First GBRf began operating services to Hams Hall and Selby on behalf of MSC, and its own 'turn up and go' service to Hams Hall. In 2006 a 'turn up and go' multimodal service to Doncaster began.

Rail Industry Services activities cover test runs and deliveries for train manufacturers, train and production planning, route conductor hire, and provision of standby locomotives. Recent customers include Bombardier, Angel Trains, HSBC Rail and Porterbrook. First GBRf in September 2008 won new contracts with Wabtec Rail and Railcare Limited for movement of trains to works for refurbishment or maintenance.

Under agreements with Serco Rail Operations and Eurailscout, First GBRf supplies conductor drivers to provide route knowledge on specialist infrastructure trains.

First GBRf brought mail back to the rail network after a successful 2004 trial. A new three-year contract from 2007 took carryings to more than a million items a day between North London, Warrington and Wishaw terminals, using Royal Mail's own Class 325 trains. In early 2008, postal train journeys were increased from two to five a day, and an extension of services to link London, Doncaster and Newcastle has been under development.

27 Class-66 locomotives leased from HSBC Rail are the backbone of GBRf's fleet, and a further five, leased from Porterbrook, were delivered in March 2008. Further fleet expansion is likely.

GBRf also has five Class 73 electro-diesels and hires others as required, while a Class 86 electric hired from the AC Locomotive Group's company Electric Traction Ltd is used as a standby for mail trains.

Senior personnel

Managing Director
John Smith

Deputy Managing Director
Ralph Goldney

Finance Director
David Simons

Operations Director
Kevin Walker

Business Development Director
Neil Crossland

Head of Business Development & Marketing
Ashley Stower

In association with CSRE

Direct Rail Services Limited
Safe Secure Reliable

Intermodal work increases

Direct Rail Services Limited (DRS) was established in 1995 to provide British Nuclear Fuels Limited with a strategic rail transport service, and became a wholly owned subsidiary of the Nuclear Decommissioning Authority (NDA) in 2005.

In support of its core business, DRS has set out to provide a safe, secure and reliable service to an expanding general freight market, providing intermodal services, railhead treatment trains, and hire of locomotives and train crew.

Third party distribution work began in 2000, when DRS started running Grangemouth-Daventry trains for logistics company W.H. Malcolm, followed by a daily Mossend-Daventry container train. Another Malcolm service is an intermodal train from Grangemouth to Elderslie, introduced in 2004. A Grangemouth-Aberdeen train is run for Asda by DRS.

In June 2006, DRS began an intermodal service for Scotland-based logistics company John G. Russell, a twice-a-day Daventry-Coatbridge return trip, which increased to three per day from October 2008. A service from Tilbury to Daventry began in July 2008, carrying 18 containers five days a week.

DRS launched a new dedicated service for Eddie Stobart Limited in September 2006, to transport Tesco containers between Daventry and Grangemouth. Stobart deliver goods from Tesco sites to Daventry International Rail Freight Terminal (DIRFT) for loading for early morning departure. Arriving at Grangemouth in late afternoon, the goods go by road to Tesco's Livingston distribution centre.

26 specially designed 45ft curtain-sided containers, directly transferable between lorries and trains, are used on each train. 8ft 6in in height, they can be accommodated within any British rail loading gauge. The Scottish Executive awarded a Freight Facilities Grant of £200,000 to Eddie Stobart Ltd to contribute to the capital cost of 90 containers. The Department for Transport also provided Company Neutral Revenue Support of £235,130 to Stobart - this scheme provides revenue support for the transport of intermodal containers by rail rather than road. The service replaces more than 13,000 lorry journeys each year, estimated to reduce carbon dioxide emissions by around 6,000 tonnes a year. Environmental benefits are valued at nearly £3m over the three-year contract. A move to six-days-per-week operation was announced in 2008.

A second service for Stobart and Tesco - from Grangemouth to Inverness - was announced in mid 2008, with the Scottish Government awarding Eddie Stobart Ltd £525,000 of Freight Facilities Grant funding for 70 new curtain sided intermodal units, and £457,000 of Rail Environmental Benefit Procurement Scheme funding to help with the running costs.

Under a five-year contract, the service will run six days a week, removing an estimated 13,000 lorry journeys each year - equivalent to a saving of 2,610 tonnes of CO_2 per year.

In August 2007, in partnership with W.H. Malcolm and British Gypsum, DRS began a new five-days-a-week service between Kirby Thore in Cumbria and Elderslie in Scotland, transporting 24 British Gypsum containers specifically designed and built for the contract.

DRS is to provide transport for large volumes of aggregates for the Low Level Waste Repository development at Drigg near Sellafield. It is estimated that over 100 rail deliveries will be made for the 130,531 tonnes of construction materials.

Under a two-year contract, haulage of railhead treatment trains for Network Rail (to mitigate autumn adhesion problems for trains) increased to 13 trains - requiring 26 locomotives - in autumn 2007 and 15 in autumn 2008. DRS also provides traction for Serco Rail Technologies' track assessment trains.

Complementing its HQ and depot at Carlisle Kingmoor, DRS also has its own Crewe depot facilites at Gresty Bridge, officially opened in March 2007.

DRS ran the first special passenger train operated entirely with its own resources in conjunction with the company's open day in July 2007. Charter operations were further developed throughout 2008, though a Stobart Railtours venture is not being continued.

DRS began operations with refurbished Class 20, 37 and 47 locomotives but has now built up a fleet of modern Class 66s. A fleet of 24 of the later design, low-emission Class 66s, leased through HBOS, was due to be completed with the delivery of four new locomotives in late 2008. Ten earlier-design Porterbrook-owned Class 66s were being taken off lease. The Class 66s are generally used on long distance intermodal services.

DRS has also now acquired 10 Class-57s (ex-Freightliner), most of them leased from Porterbrook. Further Class 37s and 47s were acquired in 2007 and 2008, bringing the DRS fleet to nine Class-47s and 31 Class-37s. The Class 20 fleet now numbers 15. In October 2008, DRS acquired Class 55 'Deltic' No 55016 (D9016) 'Gordon Highlander', and planned eventually to return it to main line service.

Above: DRS Class 66 No.66408 returns to its Crewe depot light engine. Paul Bigland

Senior personnel

Managing Director
Neil McNicholas

Commercial Director
Chris Connelly

Freight & Haulage

Above: A Freightliner Heavy Haul train heads south through Doncaster on 25 September 2007 behind No 66619. Brian Morrison

Freightliner

New design locomotives on order

Now an international operation, Freightliner Group's core business at privatisation was the movement of deep-sea containers (carried on by Freightliner Ltd), and it has since entered the bulk rail freight market, establishing Freightliner Heavy Haul (FHH) in 1999. The group has continued its success by establishing a further two subsidiaries - Freightliner Poland Ltd and Freightliner Maintenance Ltd.

Freightliner Group announced in June 2008 that it had been acquired by Arcapita, an international investment firm based in Bahrain, from its previous owners 3i, Electra Private Equity and Freightliner management and staff. 3i and Electra were the founder majority shareholders of Freightliner at privatisation in 1996.

In November 2007, Freightliner placed an order for 30 diesel locomotives of a brand new design, giving greater hauling capacity than currently seen on the UK network, with a significant improvement in fuel economy. Developed in partnership with GE Transportation, the loco will enable Freightliner to increase payload per train, leading to a reduction of CO_2 emissions per tonne.

Other state-of-the-art features include AC traction technology and dynamic braking - which helps generate a 10% fuel efficiency when compared to previous diesel locos - as well as an ergonomic cab. The 30 locomotives are due to be delivered late 2009. This is Freightliner largest single order of locomotives to date, and will compliment its existing fleet of over 160 locos and 3,000 wagons.

Industry bodies have awarded the group several accolades, including train operator of the year at the HSBC Rail Awards, and the International Freighting Weekly rail freight award for four years running, and seven times in total. In 2008, Freightliner Heavy Haul was awarded the Coal UK logistics provider of the year award.

Freightliner Limited

Freightliner Ltd is the largest haulier of maritime containers in the UK with services operating from the five key deep-sea ports of Felixstowe, Southampton, Thamesport, Tilbury and Seaforth. In addition it has a network of strategically located rail freight interchanges with secure container storage facilities and an available road fleet of over 300 vehicles enabling a port to door, door to port, around the clock, seven days a week service. Moving up to 3,000 containers every day, it has over 20% of the UK container market and over 80% of the rail container market.

In March 2004 Freightliner launched 'Logico', operated independently, to encourage a more diverse group of freight movers to use its intermodal transport services - including manufacturers, importers, exporters, freight forwarders, shippers and road transport operators. Logico provides regular rail-service space without the need to make a long-term commitment. Since its inception, Logico has grown the volume of boxes moved by 70%, removing in excess of 130million lorry miles from UK roads annually.

Freightliner maintains relationships with a number of the world's leading shipping lines including Hamburg Sud, Evergreen and Hapag-Lloyd, and has the largest intermodal contract in the UK with Maersk, the container arm of the Danish conglomerate A.P. Moller-Maersk. There are 100 daily services across the network, with 32 direct routes.

Freightliner operates services to 14 inland terminals, of which it owns and operate eight. 65% of all deep-sea boxes transported by rail are transported through one of Freightliner's terminals for onward distribution. Collectively handling over 500,000 containers per year, they serve all the UK rail freight operators, and handle over 1,600 lorries daily. Last year Freightliner added to its network of inland terminals by acquiring the operating lease of Doncaster Railport. Previously operated by DHL Exel Supply Chain, Doncaster is ideally situated to encourage more freight to be transported by rail, serving the major conurbations in the Yorkshire area and facilitate the growth of the deep-sea container market in the northeast.

Freightliner has made substantial investments at other sites. Two new rail gantry cranes have been replaced at the Birmingham site in 2008, with a further two on order for Manchester. Representing an investment of over £8million, the new cranes can accommodate 10 lifts per hour more than previous equipment. Working 24 hours, 5.5 days per week, this investment will help maximise efficiency, and reduce the time taken to load containers.

- Ports: Felixstowe, Southampton, Thamesport (Isle of Grain), Tilbury and Seaforth (Liverpool).
- Inland terminals: Birmingham, Cardiff, Cleveland, Coatbridge, Doncaster, Leeds, Liverpool and Manchester.
- Independent terminals include Birmingham International Freight Terminal, Daventry,

Barton Dock (Manchester), Hams Hall (West Midlands), and Widnes.

Freightliner Heavy Haul
Established in 1999, Freightliner Heavy Haul (FHH) has grown to a turnover of over £100million, with over 600 employees, a fleet of 80 locomotives and over 1,300 wagons – a capital investment of over £180m.

FHH sets out to offer a service-led approach, operating a 'line of route' service which means customers have dedicated trains to pick up and deliver with no stops in between. High levels of reliability are achieved through its team based management system, priority is given to punctuality, and dedicated control offices operate 24/7 from two UK locations.

Using these resources FHH has branched out into all sectors of the industry, including aggregates, cement, petroleum, waste and infrastructure services. It has secured approximately 30% of the bulk rail freight market.

In December 2001, FHH entered the coal sector, now its largest market in the bulk freight industry. FHH serves most of the UK's coal fired power stations from opencast sites and collieries in Britain, and import terminals. It has steadily increased capacity, investing in extra locomotives and wagons.

In 2007 FHH started a new service from the reopened Hatfield colliery in Stainforth, part of a long-term deal between FHH and E.ON to move significant volumes of coal to Ratcliffe and Ironbridge power stations. To support this and recent contract renewals, the company increased haulage capacity by some 38% in 2007 when it took delivery of another 110 HXA coal hopper wagons from Greenbrier in Poland, and a further five Class 66 locomotives purely for coal operations. This represents an investment of nearly £17m in the coal industry and takes FHH's coal fleet to over 650 hoppers. Although tonnages have increased somewhat, what is more significant is an increase in distance, and therefore workload, as the average FHH coal trainload now travels some 90 miles to its destination, unlike traditional shorter merry-go-round operation from mine to local power station.

Since it started moving aggregates materials in 2004, FHH has increased tonnages nine-fold. 2008 saw new flows from Cricklewood to Trowse, Northampton and Chesterton, Middlesbrough to Eastleigh, and from Cottam to Ferrybridge for the major UK construction companies.

Lafarge opened a new rail, river and distribution hub at West Thurrock, Essex, in 2008, allowing raw materials to be delivered more sustainably to construction projects across the City of London, including the Thames Gateway and the 2012 Olympic and Paralympic games. FHH has been transporting marine sourced sand and gravel from Thurrock to these facilities by rail for processing and/or onward distribution, with payloads of up to 1,500 tonnes per train.

FHH also works in partnership with Aggregate Industries, hauling significant tonnages from Bardon Hill and Croft quarries, with several new flows of recycled aggregates and stone to Bow East Logistics Centre.

FHH is active in other business sectors. Already operating waste services from Bristol, Bath, Dagenham and Cricklewood to Calvert, FHH expanded its portfolio by securing a deal with Greater Manchester Waste Authority and Viridor for the movement of municipal waste from four sites in the Greater Manchester area to a landfill at Roxby Gullet, Scunthorpe. To support this, FHH set up a new driver depot at Guide Bridge. FHH has also established various fuel points in strategic locations across the UK, including one at Bardon Hill, to increase efficiency by minimising empty running, so reducing the carbon footprint.

Freightliner PL
The Polish subsidiary, Freightliner Poland (FPL) commenced operations in 2007, operating services to Kozeince power station. Freightliner has invested £30million in new rolling stock, including seven Class-66 locomotives and 432 wagons - the first such investment the Polish rail freight industry in two decades. Freightliner is also one of the first private freight companies in Poland to use reliable and efficient Class 66 locos, which are set up for cross border operations into Germany. New state-of-the-art wagons have brought innovation and economies of scale. The wagons are specifically designed to carry coal or aggregates, and have a carrying capacity of almost 70 tonnes despite a shorter length than traditional wagons. On some routes FPL can therefore carry some 17% more payload than a standard train. This investment combined provides the largest single investment into Poland by a private operator. Since the initial coal contract, FPL has quickly diversified, offering cross-border aggregates services, transporting aggregates within a comprehensive network spanning Germany and Poland.

Freightliner Maintenance Limited
The group established a new subsidiary, Freightliner Maintenance Ltd (FML), in April 2006, which took over the assets and staff of LNWR's former Leeds Midland Road depot, together with field engineering support in Scotland and southeast England. FML operates as a separate entity dedicated to the repair and maintenance of traction and rolling stock.

Initially FML was responsible for scheduled maintenance and repairs on the FHH fleet of locomotives, but has now taken over the maintenance of the fleet of HHA and HXA coal wagons and the newly acquired Lafarge cement wagons, along with the entire Freightliner fleet of diesel locomotives.

Freightliner's locomotive fleet totals 126 Class-66 diesels, with electric locomotives of Class 86 (16 locos), and Class 90 (10 locos), plus diesel shunting locomotives.

Impression of the Freightliner PowerHaul locomotive, due to be delivered by GE Transportation during 2009.
GE Transportation

Senior personnel
Chief Executive, Freightliner Group
Eddie Fitzsimons
Finance Director, Freightliner Group
Russell Mears
Corporate Development Director, Freightliner Group
Adam Cunliffe
Managing Director, Freightliner Ltd
Peter Maybury
Managing Director, Freightliner Heavy Haul
Paul Smart
Engineering Director, Freightliner Group
Tim Shakerley
Managing Director, Freightliner PL
Rafal Milczarski

Freight & Haulage

Freight, haulage and rolling stock providers

Fastline Freight

Fastline Freight, part of Jarvis plc, entered the container freight market in June 2006 and has now become active in the bulk haulage sector with a major contract hauling coal for E.ON UK plc. The five-year contract commenced in May 2008 and Fastline Freight now supplies a dedicated service hauling coal by rail to power stations at Ratcliffe-on-Soar and Ironbridge from ports at Immingham, Bristol and Liverpool.

The first of five new Class 66 locomotives arrived at Newport docks in June 2008. The full fleet including 94 new hoppers was soon fully operational, running primarily between Daw Mill and Hatfield collieries and Ratcliffe-on-Soar power station.

For its intermodal services, Fastline Freight operates three Class 56 locomotives and a fleet of container flat wagons. It has established two depots, one at Rugby and the other at Roberts Road Freight Delivery Centre, Doncaster. The first intermodal services were introduced in June 2006 between Hutchinson Ports' Thamesport, on the Isle of Grain in Kent, and Doncaster Railport. The company targeted its offering at users of road haulage, benefiting from good road access to Doncaster via the M18, A1 and M1.

A second service was introduced in August 2006 between Thamesport and the new Birmingham Intermodal Freight Terminal at Birch Coppice Business Park, alongside Junction 10 of the M42 motorway near Tamworth. In 2008, a service linking Manchester (Barton Dock) with the Isle of Grain terminal began.

Colas Rail

Colas Rail (formerly Amec Spie Rail) began operation of timber trains for timber products company Kronospan in January 2007 under a five-year contract. Class 57 locomotives hired from Virgin Trains are used.

Colas's haulage of timber was boosted in 2008 by a £250,000 grant for a flow originating at Rannoch. The Scottish Government grant is for a rail facility to improve timber traffic handling, removing 180,000 lorry miles per year from roads. The Freight Facilities grant was jointly awarded to UPM Tilhill and CSP Forestry to allow for the movement of 120,000 tonnes of timber by rail from Rannoch to Irvine over the next eight years. The timber will be delivered to Scotland's newest combined heat and power plant at Caledonian Paper.

The award covers mobile and handling equipment for the movement and loading of timber on to the train, and a lineside loading facility.

Colas has its own small fleet of Class 47 locomotives principally for infrastructure work: these also employed in haulage work for other companies.

The company sees third party freight as an opportunity to exploit its railway and commercial skills, alongside infrastructure and projects work.

Colas has also been active in developing proposals for the use of lightweight multi-purpose vehicles (the self powered rail vehicles primarily used in infrastructure work) for freight traffic.

Cotswold Rail and Advenza

Cotswold Rail is a locomotive and rolling stock spot-hire and contract-hire company based in Gloucester, with a depot facility next to Gloucester station.

Through its Advenza Freight subsidiary it operates a number of freight services and is concentrating most of its efforts on expanding in this area of the marketplace, although it remains able to run charter trains if contracted to do so. The company operates mainly in the southwest of England, East Anglia and the Midlands and has fitters and engineering staff based at Norwich and Gloucester.

Major contracts include the provision of Class 47 locomotives to National Express East Anglia for 'Thunderbird' standby and summer Saturday duties, and to First Great Western on standby duties for its sleeper service and the haulage of Class 43 power cars as part of the MTU engine fitment programme.

Other contracts have included the delivery of refurbished Mk3 coaching stock for both NXEA and FGW and other regular short-term and ad-hoc contracts with a number of major UK railway businesses.

Advenza Freight Ltd is a Freight and Train Operating Company wholly owned by Cotswold Rail Engineering Ltd. It provides the company with a UK-wide safety case which includes the carriage of dangerous goods. Its operational fleet of Class 47 and 57 locomotives carry the Advenza livery and brand rather than that of Cotswold Rail, and these have been supplemented by hired in traction, such as a Class 20 locomotive, when additional resources have been required. During 2008 Advenza

Riviera Trains loco No 47812 takes the Swindon line at Standish Junction near Gloucester, with a Riviera Trains coaching stock move between Cardiff Canton and Old Oak Common on 10 September 2006. Martin Loader

Great for Freight

NEW from Knorr-Bremse . . .
. . . EP1001 - Wheel Flat Protection

Self-powered, anti-lock brake system technology developed especially for Freight Wagons

This innovative new system provides a solution to the potentially dangerous, disruptive and expensive problem of wheel tread damage, such as "flats" caused by locking wheels as well as rail damage and its consequences.

Small, light and simple to install, EP1001 can be integrated into new build freight wagons and in most cases is easily retro-fitted.

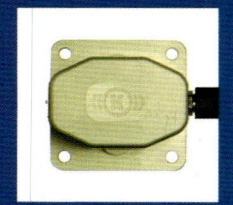

www.knorr-bremse.com

KNORR-BREMSE

DBC — DISTRIBUTED BRAKE CONTROL

Freight & Haulage

Freight began operating scrap metal trains from T.J. Thomson & Son Ltd in Stockton on Tees to Cardiff using leased bogie box wagons. Since then the company has won a number of other contracts, including one for Tyne Dock scrap metal flows, and Advenza Freight also provides locomotives, and crew for stock moves for Grand Central and National Express East Coast. These include the movement of Class 43 power cars and Mk3 coaches.

The possibility of winning a number of new contracts could see the Advenza locomotive fleet expanded in 2009 with a number of additional locomotives being restored to main line standards.

Cotswold operates a rake of Mk2 coaches which carry the Blue Pullman livery and these are available to work charter trains or corporate specials, which can be operated under Advenza's charter licence.

Riviera Trains

Riviera Trains Ltd was formed in 1996, with the intention of creating a charter train set of Mk1 coaching stock. The company has subsequently grown to become the leading independent charter train provider in the UK. The company operates from its main base at the LNWR depot at Crewe, with a fleet of 30 coaches, and another 130 vehicles are out-based at Old Oak Common.

Riviera Trains operates with EWS as part of the Charter Alliance, which was launched in April 2007, and prides itself on being the leading 'one stop shop' for the provision of coaching stock for franchised train operating companies and charter trains.

Riviera is the leading provider of charter trains to the railtour industry, working closely with the leading charter train operating companies. Principal railtour customers have included the Branch Line Society, Compass Tours, Past-Time Rail, Pathfinder SRPS, The Railway Touring Company and UK Railtours, as well as Pathfinder Tours which is a wholly owned subsidiary of Riviera Trains.

Charter rakes can be anything from sets to work railtours for enthusiasts, often using a variety of heritage traction, through mixed rakes of First and Standard Class coaches for 'days out' railtours, to full rakes of First Class vehicles with at-seat dining for luxury VIP charters.

During 2008 Riviera reached agreement with Virgin Trains for the use of the 'Royal Scot' train name by Riviera Trains on its programme of premier steam-hauled excursions, which will be operated in conjunction with the Railway Touring Company as part of a five year contract. This has also seen an investment of half a million pounds in refurbishing a fleet of 13 Mk1 coaches for use on the trains, which is expected be the last major investment in Mk1 vehicles.

The company's highest level of accommodation is provided by the Great Briton which was launched in 2006 and carries the Riviera Livery of Oxford blue and cream. This is a dining car train of Mk2 vehicles which offers up to 336 premier First Class dining seats for day excursion, land cruise and special event trains.

These two trains will enable Riviera to serve the growing market for premium quality trains to sporting events such as Royal Ascot, the Cheltenham Gold Cup and major golf tournaments as well as for corporate clients.

One of Riviera's specialities is the ability to provide rolling stock at very short notice to train operating companies, whether to cover for fleet shortfalls or to provide additional capacity for special events such as sports fixtures. Riviera has supplied locomotives on short term hire to First Great Western, Arriva Trains Wales, Direct Rail Services, First GB Railfreight, First ScotRail, EWS, Freightliner, Grand Central and Serco Rail, and in the summer of 2008 resourced and operated 62 locomotive hauled trains for First Great Western in conjunction with EWS.

As well as its fleet of 160 Mk1 and Mk2 coaches, which includes catering vehicles and a generator car, the company has nine operational Class 47 diesel locomotives and two more in reserve, should these be required.

Cargo-D

Cargo-D Ltd was established in February 2006 and offers a range of rolling stock for use by charter operators and to other train operators on a 'spot hire' basis. The fleet of coaches has undergone an internal makeover, and externally all operational vehicles have been repainted in the British Rail blue and grey livery which makes them a distinctive sight on the national network.

Within its fleet Cargo-D operates 17 Mk3 and 20 Mk2 vehicles in a fleet which includes

A Cargo D restaurant car forms part of a Wrexham & Shropshire train at Wrexham on 18 September 2008. Tony Miles

In association with CSRE

First and Standard Class coaches and three restaurant cars.

This versatile fleet enables a wide variety of formations to be created, including mixed trains, part dining, full dining, corporate trains and 'people movers' for big events. Rakes can accommodate from 240 to 700 seats.

High profile work in the last year has included the hiring of a Mk3 trainset to Hull Trains to cover for a damaged Pioneer train, and the provision of 12 Mk3 vehicles to Wrexham & Shropshire to enable the open access operator to begin services while its own fleet of vehicles was refurbished.

Cargo-D prides itself on offering high quality coaching stock maintained internally and externally to a high standard.

The company has also started its own charter subsidiary, Rail Blue Charters, which will operate a number of charters under its own name as well as providing services to external clients.

Cargo-D is also able to provide freight wagons and resource traction to work with its coaching stock. In particular Class 86 electric locomotives are available for charter and 'spot hire' work through a partnership with the AC Locomotive Group's company Electric Traction Ltd.

The company states: 'We are dedicated to improving the current offer available in both the rail freight and charter industry. We want to offer something that is unique, flexible and different. Attention to detail is extremely important to us. We take the delivery and quality of our rolling stock seriously.'

The West Coast Railway Company

The West Coast Railway Company has been a licensed train operating company since 1998, when it became the first privately owned company to obtain a licence, under rail privatisation, allowing the company to co-ordinate and run its own trains without third-party involvement. Based at Carnforth, Lancashire, WCRC is the UK market leader in operating regular, timetabled open access services and is a specialist operator of timetabled, steam-hauled services. West Coast also runs charter trains with steam, diesel or electric traction serving everything from enthusiast tours to sports fixtures and special events.

Probably the most well known services are the three steam-hauled trains; the Jacobite, which offers an 84 mile return journey between Fort William and Mallaig throughout the summer, the Scarborough Spa Express service between York and Scarborough and the Cambrian which works over the Machynlleth to Porthmadog and Pwllheli section of the Cambrian Coast line. WCRC operates the Shakespeare Experience between Birmingham and Stratford-upon-Avon on behalf of Vintage Trains, Steam Dreams services out of London, and has now operated the luxury Royal Scotsman train on behalf of Venice Simplon Orient Express for four years. In 2008 WCRC was selected to supply operational services to the new Rail Blue Charters business.

WCRC also operates a variety of charter trains in the north of England and supplies rolling stock and operational services to franchised TOCs. During the summer of 2008 the company resourced and operated a series of additional summer services between Nottingham and Skegness for East Midlands Trains.

WCRC supplies conductor drivers to a number of other operators and Network Rail, uses the company to haul and operate inspection saloon trains around the network. With a licence to operate Freight services, WCRC is actively seeking work in this field.

The company employs its own experienced train crew, with a broad experience of traction types and wide route knowledge. For its timetabled tourist services WCRC retails tickets directly to passengers, although it also works in conjunction with other TOCs for retailing, marketing and station facilities.

WCRC owns, maintains and operates a large fleet of diesel locomotives which includes classes 33, 37, 47 and 57 along with over 80 Mk1 and Mk2 passenger vehicles (including the last 10 Pullman carriages to be built, in 1965). Its fleet of three working steam locomotives, which will expand to four during 2009, includes GWR 'Hall' No 5972 'Olton Hall', which has assumed a specialist role in recent years by taking the role of the Hogwarts Express locomotive for the Harry Potter series of films. This has involved WCRC in working with the film producers to arrange the filming of a number of sequences anywhere from King's Cross station to the West Highland line.

Freight & Haulage

GE PowerHaul unveiled

GE Transportation introduced its new PowerHaul engine and locomotive at InnoTrans in Berlin in September 2008.

The PowerHaul engine represents GE Transportation's first entry to the UK and European marketplace. The UK's Freightliner Group placed an order for 30 PowerHaul locomotives in November 2007 - representing the largest order of freight locomotives in Freightliner's history. These first PowerHaul PH37ACmi locomotives are scheduled for delivery in late 2009.

GE Transportation says the PowerHaul engine is its most technologically advanced locomotive engine to-date. Combined with other technologies from GE, it is projected to reduce PowerHaul locomotive fuel use by up to 9% compared to current operating fleet averages. The 3,700 GHP engine is European Stage IIIA compliant.

'The new PowerHaul engine significantly increases fuel efficiency while lowering emissions,' said Lorenzo Simonelli, President and CEO of GE Transportation. 'PowerHaul Locomotives are designed for cost-effective long-haul operating range, high tractive effort and haulageability, long-term emissions compliance and reduced life-cycle cost.'

The PowerHaul locomotive is based on the company's global Evolution series locomotive platform introduced in 2005. More than 2,800 units are in use.

ELECTRO-MOTIVE

EMD '710' engine milestone

Electro-Motive Diesel announced in September 2008 that it had just produced its 7,500th '710' engine. The North American manufacturer had been granted 37 patents over the last 24 months on new 710 engine technologies aimed at reducing emissions and improving fuel efficiency.

After investment in development of the 710 engine family to meet US and European exhaust emissions standards, the 12-710G3B-T2 (as used in the Class 66 locomotive familiar in the UK) and 16-710G3B-T2 engines received type approval for the Stage IIIA limit values of Directive 97/68/EC in 2006, the first locomotive engine to do so. EMD also reports that, through management of accessory loads, it had in 2008 been able to improve locomotive fuel efficiency by a further 2%.

EMD expected to achieve Stage IIIB compliance and to meet the emissions limits without the need for urea aftertreatment to reduce nitrogen oxides emissions, so avoiding the expense a second fluid and installation of infrastructure to handle it. Confirmation testing to prove the feasibility of meeting Stage IIIB NOx limits was expected to be completed in late 2008.

EMD is developing a successor to the Class 66 locomotive design, adopting an AC traction system. This is planned to be built to a larger loading gauge and aimed only at the continental European market.

The continental version of GE Transportation's PowerHaul locomotive has a full-width body, instead of the narrow hood configuration of the UK locomotives as ordered by Freightliner. GE Transportation

---

INCREASE GLOBAL RAIL NETWORK CAPACITY

45ft container wagon increases UK rail capacity for high cube boxes by 21%

Barber Low Ride bogies enable transport of high cube containers on restricted loading gauge clearances

BLR14.25 577mm dia wheel 14.25t axle load

Evans Business Centre, Mitchelston Industrial Estate, Kirkcaldy, Fife, KY1 3UF, UK
Tel: +44 (0)1592 657 523 Fax: +44 (0)1592 657 524
www.sctco.com

SCT Europe Ltd

Innovation & Environment

Plan Design Enable

In association with

ATKINS

Innovation and Environment

Technical Review

Regen revolution cuts energy costs and emissions

Modern Railways Industry & Technology Editor, Roger Ford, examines a major factor in the continuing improvement in the railway's green credentials

Regenerative braking is a long established technology on electric railways. In the United Kingdom, the classic example was the 1,500V DC-electrified Woodhead line. With its steady flow of coal traffic over the spine of the Pennines, regenerated energy from a Class 76 locomotive braking on the falling gradient could be used by traction units climbing in the opposite direction.

Until the development of power electronics and three-phase alternating-current drives, direct-current electrification was the easiest form of regenerative braking to implement. The DC current in the overhead line or third rail was transmitted to DC traction motors, with control by resistors switched in and out by relays.

To initiate braking, the DC motors were simply switched to run as dynamos and the current they produced was returned to the power supply. While this was simple and effective, it depended on other trains being available to draw the regenerated current from the overhead wire or contact rail. The likelihood that another train will be able to accept the current is known as receptivity.

Up to the 1980s, AC electrification traction

By the end of 2008, it was expected that all the 750V DC-powered Electrostar fleets would have regenerative braking in use. Southeastern's Class 375 Electrostar No 375630 arrives at Canterbury West on 1 July 2008 working the 13.42 Ramsgate-Charing Cross. Tony Miles

Class 323 was the first 25kV AC electric train fleet with three-phase drive to enter service in Britain. Newly painted in Northern livery, No 323223 approaches Stockport on the 13.03 Manchester-Crewe on 18 February 2008. Tony Miles

units transformed the incoming 25kV AC current to a lower voltage and then converted it to DC in a rectifier for use by the traction motors. The rectifier was a one-way device, which meant that the DC current from regenerating traction motors could not be returned to the AC contact wire.

This limitation disappeared with the introduction of three-phase drive in the 1990s. From contact wire, via the transformer, converter and inverter, to the traction motor, the electrical system became reversible, as with DC. But AC electrification provided an even greater benefit – this reversibility extends back from the contact wire through the trackside sub-stations to the National Grid. In effect, regenerating AC electric traction units effectively enjoy unlimited receptivity.

By the end of 2008, Network Rail had completed an investment programme to make its entire AC electrified network capable of supporting regenerative braking. In fact, all the existing train fleets capable of regenerative braking had been able to use the facility from the start of the year.

To date, the savings from regeneration have been estimated from the difference in overall electricity consumption, before and after a fleet was switched over. The scale of the saving depends on service characteristics, with the benefit increasing with frequency of station stops.

In the case of the Hunslet TPL Class 323 fleet - the first 25 kV AC electric trains with three phase drive to enter service in Britain - the recorded savings from regeneration on the Birmingham CrossCity line when the trains were introduced some 15 years ago were up to 23%. In June 2007, c2c became the first operator of post-privatisation three-phase drive trains to exploit regenerative braking with its Class 357 25kV Electrostar EMU fleet in June 2007. Claimed savings are 21-22% - similar to the earlier experience in Birmingham.

On high speed services, only the Virgin West Coast Class 390 Pendolino fleet uses regenerative braking. With traction distributed along the train, the high proportion of motored axles means that a high proportion of the braking energy is recovered and disc brakes are rarely required in service braking. However, intercity operation, particularly with a tilting train, reduces the amount of braking and thus the potential savings from regeneration.

Under a joint research programme - supported by train operator Virgin West Coast, manufacturer and maintainer Alstom, and the Association of Train Operating Companies - electricity meters were fitted to Class 390 Pendolino No 390049 in August 2007. The aim was to analyse the train's power consumption 24 hours a day with the aim of indentifying potential savings during time on depot and in station layovers, as well as in service.

Table 1 shows the measured energy consumption during the first five months of the project. The meter measured both the total energy consumed and the regenerated energy returned to the grid. Given the nature of the duty, this is an impressive figure which matches Network Rail's previous blanket discount of 16.5% on the electricity tariff for trains equipped with regenerative braking.

In terms of cost savings, this equates to around £7,000 per month per train. Since 390049 ran on a representative range of Pendolino duties, this saving can be applied across the 52-strong fleet with confidence.

Energy saving also reads across into emissions reduction. Taking the average emissions from the current mix of power stations at 500g of CO_2 per kilowatt hour, using actual load factors, No 390049 achieved emissions of 35gm CO_2/passenger kilometre. In

Table 1 - Class 390 energy consumption and cost in 2007-08 research programme

Month	MWh Energy consumed	MWh Energy regenerated	Percent Regeneration	£ Saving
September	622.3	110.1	17.7	6826
October	725.6	128.9	17.8	7992
November	680.6	110.9	16.3	6876
December	634.6	99.2	15.6	6150
January	689.8	112.4	16.3	6969
Total	3352.9	561.5	16.7	34813

Innovation and Environment

On high speed services, only the Virgin West Coast Class 390 Pendolino fleet uses regenerative braking. No 390003 arrives at Crewe on 30 April 2008. Tony Miles

terms of per seat kilometre, which gives a better indication of rail's potential, the figure is 16.6gm CO2.

DC comeback

In June 2008, following an 18 month project managed by Booz Allen Hamilton and involving Network Rail, train operators Southern and Southeastern, and train makers Bombardier, the Class 375, 376 and 377 Electrostar fleets received safety approval to regenerate on the 750V DC network. By the end of 2008, it was expected that all the Electrostar fleets would have regenerative braking in use.

While all Electrostars are supplied with regenerative braking as standard, this was not implemented on DC electrified lines because of concerns about the effect on the infrastructure. At 750V, DC traction currents can exceed 3,000 Amps. It was feared that current being generated at this level could mask a short circuit in the supply system.

To prevent such masking, the protective systems on adjacent sub-stations would have to be linked, a technique known as 'inter-tripping'. However, with theoretical studies showing receptivities of around 6%, the energy savings from regenerative braking would not pay for the cost of modifying the protective systems.

But with the cost of electricity rising steeply, the financial case for regenerative braking was strengthened, leading to the 18 month joint study. This included running tests under possession to check that short circuits would be tripped.

In addition, every electrical section on the Southern network was analysed for fault masking, taking into account such variables as train length and age of the conductor rail. This analysis showed that the Southern fleet of 28 Class-377/3 units would produce between zero and four fault-masking events every 100 years – overcoming the final obstacle.

As a result, despite all the previous concerns, no physical modifications were needed to either infrastructure or trains before regenerative braking could be introduced. The only changes were to the software of the Electrostar's traction control system.

Another key finding from the test programme is that receptivity is not an issue. Even on less busy routes, such as the mid-Sussex line, a Class 377/3 proved capable of regenerating 20% of the energy consumed. This is attributed, in part, to the train compensating for supply system losses which would otherwise be met by the sub-stations.

Table 2 shows Network Rail's current proposals for discounts which will replace the single figure of 16.5% for any train equipped for regenerative braking. Translated into reductions in CO2 emissions, it also highlights the continuing improvement in the railway's green credentials.

Table 2 - Electricity tariff discounts for trains with regenerative braking

Type of infrastructure/service frequency	CP4 discount
AC, long distance (more than 10 miles between stations)	16%
AC, regional and outer suburban (less than or equal to 10 miles between stations)	18%
AC, local and commuter (less than or equal to 2.1 miles between stations)	20%
DC, Southern region Central ESTA*	15%
Rest of DC	5%

*Electricity Supply Traction Area

In association with **ATKINS**

Innovation: beating the resource crunch

Rail can learn from the approach to innovation shown by its travel competitors - innovation is an investment in being in business in the long term, says Atkins' Daniel Jonas. Network Rail

Daniel Jonas, Professional Head of Innovation – Atkins, says the rail industry needs to challenge, challenge and challenge again

After 20 years of under-investment, 'UK plc' is finally understanding the importance of public transport and rail in particular in addressing a pressing growth challenge. Demand for capacity has never been higher, whether in road, rail or air. The challenges of congestion, reliability and sustainability are being driven by ever-rising regulatory standards and societal expectations. There are higher expectations around the delivery of design for major events – like the Olympics being used not just as a sporting event, but as an opportunity to regenerate East London – but also around the ability to work across multiple design and engineering disciplines.

The trouble is that even in today's competitive environment, it is tough to recruit and retain key people and there is still a dearth of engineering graduates which cannot simply be filled from abroad – or filled fast enough. In short, we are facing a 'resource crunch' – so how do we meet this challenge? Can we do it by doing things the same way we've always done? No. That is why we need to innovate.

And what do we mean by innovate? We mean doing things better – and doing better things. Our travel competitors are innovating faster: aircraft are quieter, more fuel-efficient, cheaper at point of use, road vehicle emissions are dropping, safety, comfort and economy continue to improve and their timescales for innovation are measurably quicker than rail. So what do we need to learn?

We need to challenge, challenge and challenge again. To understand new technology platforms like ERTMS. To work with complementors, like they do in the aviation industry. To show leadership by collaborating to develop joint platforms rather than obtaining temporary cost advantages which stifle innovation and deliver less value for the industry. To inspire and reward innovation behaviours. To measure appropriately, avoiding passion killers like projections and budgetary minutiae and focus on value delivered. To cluster, recycle and filter ideas. To learn from failure: if you're not failing, you're not doing anything innovative.

Innovation is not for the faint-hearted and quiet-lived organisation. It is not a 'quick fix': don't expect to innovate on a Monday and put something into service on a Tuesday – unless it's a no-brainer that's definitely going to work! It is neither a 'nice-to-have', nor an overhead – it's an investment in being in business in the long term.

Green Giants

'Green Giants' is a recent environmental initiative from Atkins Rail. The Green Giants are members of staff who have volunteered and been tasked with the responsibility of reducing environmental impacts of their specific Atkins office. This is achieved through promoting environmental friendly practices, by communicating and influencing staff to adopt green initiatives relating to low energy and water use, waste recycling schemes, reduced travel as well as green procurement of materials and resources.

Atkins' Rail division has been compiling an environmental database and using carbon calculation tool for the collation of data on utility readings for electricity, gas and water as well as information on tonnages of wastes produced and recycled from the specific Rail offices. The information collated will be used for office carbon calculations with the aim of identifying areas of inefficiencies and best measures to be adopted to address this.

Sustainability project

A report on sustainability with the transport sector, researched by Atkins Rail in conjunction with a university MSc student, highlights key issues on sustainability within the Rail sector, along with a review of other transport systems both in the UK and overseas including best practice examples. The report is being used to benchmark Atkins against other transport systems and review best practices, and has enabled the enterprise to fully understand how design and procurement can practically influence projects.

Atkins has embarked on pilot work towards achieving 'Carbon Critical Design', looking at two projects to identify their embodied carbon from design through to construction, and identify ways of reducing the projects' carbon loads.

Rail Infrastructure Environment Forum

The Rail Infrastructure Environment Forum brings together a number of Network Rail's key contractors, working jointly with Network Rail to improve the environmental performance of projects on the rail infrastructure. Atkins Rail is one of the industry environmental ambassadors from each sector of the Infrastructure Investment Contractor base, who work with Network Rail towards environmental improvements of the rail network, striving to get the best out of project working relationships, and continuing to review operating procedures and best practice.

RIEF has an established a number of key environmental objectives attained through regular meetings and associated working groups aimed at minimising environmental impact.

A continuing forum, RIEF records success based on the successful completion of working group projects, and intends to implement improvements and influence upon the railway environment for many years.

Innovation and Environment

RAILTEX 2009

Earls Court to host next Railtex show

London's Earls Court Two is to be the venue for Railtex 2009. Taking place from 10 to 12 March 2009, this will be the ninth event in a now familiar series that over some 15 years has grown to become the leading showcase in the UK for railway technology, equipment and services.

The choice again of a London venue for the show was strongly influenced by the scale of rail development under way or planned in the capital. The impressive list of projects is dominated by the Crossrail and Thameslink schemes, but also includes ongoing modernisation of the London Underground system, work connected with establishment of the London Overground network and Docklands Light Railway extensions.

At Railtex 2009 there will be an increased focus on the show's role as an interactive, live marketing event for the UK rail industry. Organiser Mack Brooks Exhibitions is working with various partner organisations to repeat several features successfully introduced at its Infrarail 2008 exhibition in Birmingham, as well as adding new ones.

Michael Wilton, Exhibition Manager for the show explains: 'In introducing new activities at Railtex we aim to provide visitors with additional opportunities to learn much more about the direction the UK rail industry is taking. We are setting up two lecture theatres in the main exhibition hall as seminar venues. One will be used by the rail engineer magazine for its programme "The Rail Engineer Seminars at Railtex 2009", which will cover innovations in railway technology. The other will be used for a series of exhibitor presentations as well as for daily sessions by the monthly industry newspaper Railnews covering training and recruitment. Access to all these will be free for visitors.'

On the first two days of the show there will also be a co-located high-level conference addressing one of the key issues currently facing the rail industry – capacity. Entitled 'Growth and the capacity challenge – an international perspective', this event is being devised by our contemporary, Railway Gazette International.

And following a well received initiative taken at the Birmingham show, sections of track are again to be installed in the exhibition hall, offering an authentic setting for the display of items of rail-mounted equipment and providing a setting for on-track demonstrations.

Among other familiar features of Railtex 2009 will be Meet the Buyers sessions for UK exporters and an informal networking reception to provide a further opportunity for all sides of the industry to meet.

The response from the railway industry to Railtex 2009 has been characteristically positive, with the majority of key suppliers to the UK market early to add their names to the list of exhibitors. The latest list of companies taking part can be accessed on the show website (www.railtex.co.uk).

The show is again benefiting from the participation and support of many of the industry's leading organisations, with most of these taking a stand. They include the Department for Transport, Network Rail, Transport for London subsidiary Crossrail, and the Railway Industry Association. Also providing support are the Institution of Railway Signal Engineers, the Permanent Way Institution and the Rail Freight Group.

The last Railtex, held at ExCel in London's Docklands in February 2007, drew an ABC-audited figure of 9,214 industry professionals from 49 countries. While most of those attending were from the UK, the majority of manager level or above, this worldwide attendance by foreign visitors underlines another key role of Railtex – helping to promote the UK's railway supply industry abroad.

Access to Railtex 2009 will be free of charge for pre-registered visitors but an entrance fee at the door will apply to those not registered. Registration will be available in the weeks leading up to the show at the show website (www.railtex.co.uk). Visitor leaflets with registration forms will also be distributed with industry journals.

The show's Central London location at Earls Court Two is well placed for visitors, with good rail connections by London Underground, London Overground and Southern. The venue offers high levels of on-site facilities, while off-site it is served by the best in accommodation, eating and entertainment that London has to offer. More information on getting to Earls Court Two can be found at: www.eco.co.uk

Railtex covers all aspects of the rail industry, embracing rolling stock and infrastructure, as well as the many diverse products and services needed to operate safe and efficient networks. The next of Mack Brooks' Infrarail railway infrastructure shows takes place at Birmingham's NEC in April 2010. More information is available at: www.infrarail.com

Railtex covers all aspects of the rail industry, embracing rolling stock and infrastructure.

In association with **ATKINS**

HS1 recognised at 2008 Innovation Awards

The achievement of realising High Speed 1 was recognised by several of the 2008 Railway Industry Innovation awards. The 15.07 Eurostar from Paris Nord to St Pancras International is seen on 28 June 2008, approaching Ebbsfleet International station on HS1 in north Kent, Class 373 powercar No 3215 leading with No 3216 on the rear. Brian Morrison

The railway industry celebrated the innovations that are essential for Britain's railway to deliver the safety, efficiency and reliability rightly demanded by its customers at the 2008 annual Railway Forum/Modern Railways Rail Innovation Awards.

The 2008 Innovator of the Year Award, sponsored by Atkins, was presented to Rob Holden, Chief Executive of London & Continental Railways (LCR).

Reading the citation, Dr Mike Mitchell - Director-General of Rail and National Networks at the Department for Transport - said that Rob Holden's story on High Speed 1 is one of real innovation and a tribute to planning, risk-sharing and making sure that the right partnerships were in place and working in total harmony to get the £5.8billion job done.

LCR built and operates the high speed Channel Tunnel Rail Link (High Speed 1), and owns and operates the UK arm of the Eurostar international train service.

On behalf of LCR, HS1 was designed and project managed by Rail Link Engineering (RLE), a consortium of Bechtel, Arup, Systra and Halcrow, all of whom are also shareholders in LCR. The other shareholders are National Express Group, SNCF, electricity supply company EDF, and UBS investment bank.

London & Continental Stations and Property (LCSP) is developing the new international stations on the CTRL and is the property division of LCR. LCSP has responsibility for the regeneration of land around the CTRL stations in partnership with developers and in co-ordination with government agencies, local authorities and communities - including for the London 2012 Olympics.

HS1 operation is the hands of Network Rail. CTRL (UK) Ltd, another subsidiary of LCR, acts as client for operation and maintenance.

Presentation of the latest awards was hosted by Graham Smith, Planning Director of rail freight operator EWS.

The winners in each of the other categories were as follows:

- **Engineering/Safety**
  sponsored by Bombardier
  Winner - Rail Link Engineering.
  London & Continental Railways/Union Railways, the company behind High Speed 1 (HS1) appointed Rail link Engineering - the joint venture between Arup, Bechtel, Halcrow and Systra - to manage the delivery of the project. On LCR's behalf, Rail Link Engineering has been responsible for supervising the design and construction of HS1, and it honoured the commitment to deliver on time and within budget – a major achievement for something of this scale. The judges commented that this was an overall outstanding entry spanning a lengthy process and many companies brought together in a massive engineering project

- **Environment**
  sponsored by ATOC
  Winner: First TransPennine Express/ Siemens Transportation Systems
  First TransPennine Express and Siemens Transportation Systems achieved proven fuel savings of up to 7% in phase one of their Eco-Initiative for the Class 185 fleet of 51 three-car units. This represented savings of more than 1.8m litres of fuel per year. This had been achieved through Eco-Mode, Eco-Driving, fuel messaging, and reduced engine running during the initial nine months of the project without requiring any capital investment or significant modification to the trains. Judges commented on the fact that this is really doing something that has been complained about for years - cutting out engines which idle at stations: 'a simple process with real results'.

HSBC

Innovation and Environment

The awards evening was hosted by Graham Smith, Planning Director of rail freight operator English, Welsh & Scottish Railway. Tony Miles

- **The John Armitt award for Innovation of the Year**
  Winner - Network Rail.
  Network Rail, in partnership with Transport for London and Mott MacDonald, have recently pioneered the first ever major passenger Track Access Option in the UK rail industry – The East London Line Access Option. This is a regulated contract that has been approved by the ORR and will enable TfL's significant investment in London railway infrastructure and the benefits that this will bring. First opened in 1869 as part of the East London Railway, it runs through the Thames Tunnel. TfL are now investing £1bn into the project to transform the route as an extension to the newly established London Overground network. The award was presented by John Armitt, Chairman of the Olympic Delivery Authority.

- **Marketing/Customer Experience sponsored by Modern Railways magazine**
  Winner -Eurostar.
  Eurostar had a huge challenge on its hands to communicate the launch of services from St Pancras on 14 November 2007. By working closely with focus groups it soon realised that different groups of people would respond to the move in different ways. The date of the new services was launched a year in advance giving Eurostar 12 months to build the narrative that would lead up to the move.

- **Performance and Operations sponsored by mace**
  Winner – Alstom.
  Alstom Transport has developed the innovative Fleet Console Tool (now known as Traintracer) that converts raw train data

Innovation file

High cube wagon development
At the inaugural Rail Freight Group awards event in September 2008, SCT Europe and W.H. Davis accepted the award for best Technical Development for a joint submission based on the development of a new wagon for transporting high cube containers on restricted loading gauge rail networks.

SCT Europe designed and developed the new bogie, the Barber Low Ride, which enabled W.H. Davis to design and build a wagon with a platform height of 720mm above rail. The wagon, named the SL45, can transport 45ft x 9ft 6in containers within W8 gauge - effectively increasing UK rail network capacity for high cube boxes by 21%. This increase in rail capacity will allow a major transfer of freight traffic from road to rail.

Jim Longton Managing Director of SCT Europe Ltd, said, 'I am delighted to receive this award on behalf of SCT Europe. It reflects the expertise, creativity and ingenuity of our team - this demonstrates what can be achieved by two companies with a vision working together from initial concept through to final delivery.' Ian Whelpton, Sales Director of W.H. Davis, added, 'We faced and resolved many problems during the development of the wagon. Today we have a superb product of which we are very proud.'

The Barber Low Ride bogie can be adapted to suit different rail gauge requirements and offer a solution to capacity problems of restricted loading gauge rail networks wherever they occur.

Greenbrier's 10 years in Europe
In 2008, Greenbrier celebrated ten years of doing business in Europe. Greenbrier Europe's manufacturing facility, WagonySwidnica SA, is located in Swidnica, Poland, and was purchased in 1998. Its sales support facility, Greenbrier Germany GmbH, is located in Leipzig, Germany.

The company comments that in those 10 years, the rail freight industry has experienced a transformation that few could have imagined - it has been exposed to forces of competition, which are driving fundamental change and restructuring the industry.

Greenbrier's largest customers include SBB Cargo AG (Swiss Railways), DB Cargo/Railion (German Railways), Green Cargo (Swedish Railways), as well as companies such as Freightliner, EWS and VTG.

Greenbrier has built many 90-tonne / 102-tonne open hopper wagons mainly used for of coal and aggregates haulage in Britain, and 90 cubic metre hydraulic side discharge wagons for the continent. In addition, Greenbrier builds a wide variety of general purpose box wagons mainly used for aggregate and scrap material.

The company constructed Freightliner's new design HXA wagons, introduced in 2007. The design features a new design of track-

Railway Forum Chairman and Eurostar UK Chief Executive Officer, Richard Brown, welcomed guests to the awards evening. Tony Miles

Standing behind a picture celebrating the 200th anniversary of Trevithick's steam locomotive demonstration in London, the man who oversaw construction of the UK's first very high speed line receives his trophy as Innovator of the Year. Left to right: Douglas McCormick, Trading Director of award sponsor Atkins; the award winner, LCR's Rob Holden; and Dr Mike Mitchell of the DfT. Tony Miles

into business information that drives maintenance activity and provides reports to the operator and infrastructure providers. An integrated regimented business process allows the business plan for today's failures tonight. Judges commented on this being a true way of capturing data and actually using it to drive availability and reliability improvements to benefit the train operator and its customers.

- **Small Scale Project**
sponsored by the Railway Industry Association
Winner - Kier Construction Ltd.
Kier Construction Ltd, who were the principal contractor on the huge project to replace a damaged bridge at Ely, worked to resolve the work in record time so that the Ely-Ipswich line could be used as a diversionary route over Christmas 2007. The project duration was shrunk to an estimated one sixth of the normal time. In total 54 organisations were involved in the project including Network Rail as facilitating client and the Environmental Agency as principal regulator.

- **Teamwork and Cross Industry Partnership**
sponsored by NedRailways
Winner - First TransPennine Express.
First TransPennine Express and Carlisle Cleaning and Support Services have worked together to ensure that rather than being 'just a 'contractor' to FTPE an integrated relationship has been developed based on shared values and goals of enhancing the complete customer experience. This 'One Team' approach offers joint training to employees in developing an NVQ in customer Service. Colleagues from both parties are made to feel involved in both businesses by the introduction of shared mess rooms and joint invitations to events held throughout the year. Carlisle act not only as a

friendly bogie and, despite being one metre shorter than its predecessor, can still carry the same volume of coal, increasing the payload per train by up to 10%.

Voith offers Intercity Express cooling systems
Following the Intercity Express Programme (IEP) launched by the British Department for Transport, Voith was among the bidders for the delivery of the cooling systems.

'We feel well equipped for the British rail market,' said Jürgen Knigge, Voith Sales Manager for Cooling Systems. When the new cooling systems for the previous HST vehicles were specified, Voith believes customers invariably regarded them as the best available technology.

As many as 134 Voith Turbo cooling systems have been in service in the Class 43 High-Speed Trains for several years. Up to 15,000 operating hours per vehicle are quite common.

Superior technical solutions are also required for the more than 400 power cars of the five and eight-car trains envisaged within the IEP, with electric and diesel-electric drives in different power cars on the same train. The project team around Jürgen Knigge is not discouraged by this prospect. 'Voith has already successfully implemented the cooling of such a hybrid structure' – the new Bitrac 3600 locomotive, from Spanish manufacturer CAF. The special feature of this vehicle is its drive concept: apart from two 1800 kW-diesel engines, traction is provided by a further 4450 kW-electric motor. Voith has developed a combined cooling system for this 'powerhouse among rail vehicles'.

Main supplier of wheels in UK and Ireland
Lucchini RS has become the first wheelset supplier to obtain International Railway Industry Standard (IRIS) certification.

In 2008 Lucchini UK's wheel and axle plant in Trafford Park, Manchester celebrated one hundred years in existence. Founded in 1908 as Taylor Brothers, this was the first plant in the world solely laid out for the mass production of railway tyres, centres and axles, self contained from the manufacture of steel by the open hearth process to the shipping of finished products, either as loose components or as assembled wheelsets.

In November 2000 it was purchased by Lucchini Sidermeccanica (now called Lucchini RS – RS for rolling stock). After nearly 10m Euros of investment and a refocusing on wheelset overhaul, the plant is working profitably, employs some 150 people and has a full order book for 2009. It is the main supplier of wheels to the UK and Irish markets, has a new axle line, a gearbox overhaul facility and supplies product to North America, Germany, Japan and South Africa.

The plant is well set up for the future, comments Lucchini RS – maybe even another hundred years?

Innovation and Environment

Simon Montague, Eurostar's Director of Corporate Communications, receives the Marketing/Customer Service award from Roger Ford (right), Industry & Technology Editor of Modern Railways magazine. Tony Miles

cleaning partner at stations across the FTPE network and on-board trains, but also uniquely as a dispatch partner at the key passenger stations of Leeds and Manchester Piccadilly.

Paul Martin, Director-General of The Railway Forum, said that the awards had recognised the 'innovations of today that show the continuing development of our industry': the innovation that has brought high-speed trains into the Neo-Gothic masterpiece at the rejuvenated St Pancras International, innovations on sustainability such as improved fuel efficiency on diesel multiple units, partnerships to deliver customer excellence, and innovations on data management and innovations across all engineering disciplines. 'I congratulate all of the winners and those highly commended. Judging of all of these entries was not easy. I thank all those who entered and we look forward to the Innovation Awards 2009!'

Golden Spanners focus on reliable trains
The sixth annual review of traction and rolling stock fleet reliability by Modern Railways magazine's Industry & Technology Editor, Roger Ford, is published in the January 2009 issue of the magazine.

The review is based on data collated by the National Fleet Reliability Improvement Programme (NFRIP) under the auspices of the Association of Train Operating Companies.

A little fun is added to the informal competition by awarding trophies to the best performers: the 'Golden Spanners' are handed out at a meeting of the Modern Railways / Railway Forum 'Fourth Friday Club'.

For 2007-08, Golden Spanners were awarded to c2c's Class 357 fleet, the Norwich Crown Point-based Class 170 fleet, South West Trains ' Class 159/0s, the Bounds Green-based Class 91 fleet, and the Bletchley-based Class 321s. Silver Spanners are also awarded for the most-improved trains in each category.

The Fourth Friday Club
The Modern Railways/Railway Forum Fourth Friday Club provides a unique networking forum for executives from all sectors in the railway industry. There are club meetings on five Fridays in each year, the season running from September to June.

Co-sponsors of the Fourth Friday Club are Modern Railways magazine, and The Railway Forum, the industry representative body. The club was the brainchild of Modern Railways Editor, James Abbott who is also Club Secretary.

Since the first meeting in 2003, the growing reputation of the Club for attracting senior policy makers and top railway managers as guest speakers has seen membership expand rapidly.

For more information see the website - 4thfriday.co.uk - or contact James Abbott (modern.railways@googlemail.com)

Low noise wheels: Lucchini solutions

Four different solutions to wheel noise as patented by Lucchini RS of Italy: (top row L to R) *Syope*, where a constrained viscoelastic layer is applied to both sides of a wheel, employed in axle-mounted disc-braked wheelsets for passenger coaches and high speed trains; *Galene*, a series of fins attached to the outer part of the wheel, suitable for resilient tram wheels or for freight wheels, where a web-mounted treatment is not possible; (bottom row L to R) *Syope Braw*, a solution for wheels with web-mounted disc brakes, in which the constrained viscoelastic layer is applied in a limited location just below the rim and *Hypno*, a treatment for tread-braked wheels, typically found on freight wagons, involving the application of two finned steel discs riveted together and held in place via an intermediate ring under tension. For further information please contact Lucchini UK (see advertisement on page 40).

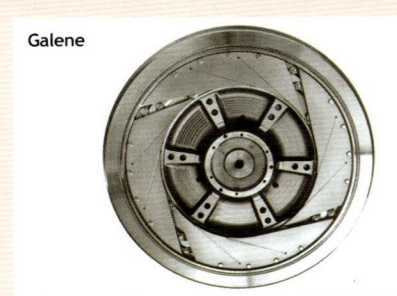

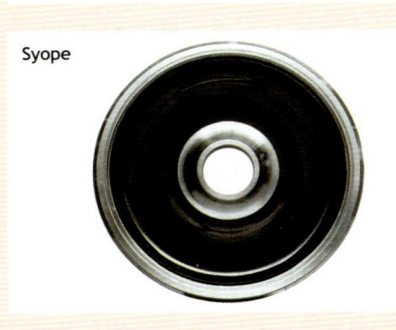

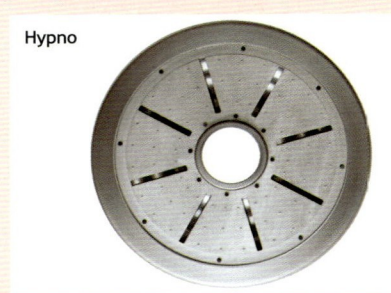

Galene

Hypno

Syope

Syope Braw

Key Projects

In association with

BOMBARDIER

Key Projects

Impression of the new Blackfriars station, part of the Thameslink Programme. Network Rail

Key projects

Thameslink Programme

The Thameslink Programme has been developed to improve the frequency and capacity of train services that operate north-south through central London via Farringdon and Blackfriars. The government has committed £5.5bn in a programme of work for rebuilt stations, platform extensions, new rolling stock, track and signalling realignment, power supply enhancement and gauge clearance work. It will enable new cross-London routes to be operated and new, longer and more frequent train services to be provided, with the express purpose of relieving overcrowding.

There will be a step change in capacity, allowing 12-car operations and 24 trains per hour in both directions through the centre of London. The enhanced route will serve a greater number of stations (51 to 172), providing significant relief both on national rail and London Underground, and offering capacity for future growth.

The broad timescale is as follows:
- December 2008:
  Services between St Pancras International and London Bridge suspended during weekday evenings and most weekends. Major works at Farringdon, Blackfriars and Borough begin.
- March 2009:
  Farringdon-Moorgate branch closed permanently.
  Blackfriars London Underground station closed for redevelopment.
  Six additional 4-car Class 319 units acquired from Southern by Thameslink train operating company, First Capital Connect, which also gains 23 four-car Class 377 Electrostars.
  Direct services introduced between Thameslink and destinations in Kent and southeast London.
- December 2011:
  12-car platform lengthening programme for main line completed.
  A 16 trains per hour service offered through central London at peak times.
  Major reconstruction works at Farringdon finished. Station redesigned with new footbridge and entrance, better Underground interchange.
  Blackfriars rebuilding complete with longer platforms, entrances both sides of the Thames, and new roof over entire platform length. London Underground station reopens.
  New viaduct at Borough (parallel to the existing) completed. Part of existing viaduct widened.
  New turnback facility at Herne Hill plus infrastructure work by Network Rail to increase service reliability.
  Services temporarily diverted via Tulse Hill to avoid London Bridge.
- During 2013:
  Public consultation on the routes to be served under the new franchise.
- December 2015:
  Major London Bridge station redevelopment and revised track layouts completed. This will remove key bottlenecks, increase the number of through platforms, improve passenger facilities and significantly improve passenger capacity.

In association with **BOMBARDIER**

New fleet of trains delivered.
Great Northern services become part of Thameslink network.
New service offers 24 trains per hour at peak times through central London.
New Thameslink franchise starts.

Network Rail's contractors for initial works are Balfour Beatty (Blackfriars); Skanska Construction (Borough); Costain/Laing O'Rourke (Farringdon).

In July 2008, the Department for Transport announced shortlisted applicants to build a new fleet of trains for Thameslink routes, valued at around £1.4bn: Alstom Transport, Bombardier Transportation, Hitachi Europe, and Siemens Transportation Systems. 1,100 new carriages are envisaged, increasing the current fleet size by around 380 carriages. The DfT intended that a manufacturer/maintainer would provide a financed solution, working with a financier who would provide a rental price.

Crossrail

The Crossrail Bill for a new cross-London railway became an Act on 22 July 2008. Following the Prime Minister's announcement in October 2007 that the £15.9bn funding package had been secured, the project is expected to be operational in 2017. The Act grants the necessary powers to acquire land and for the railway to be built and maintained.

The Crossrail project objectives are:
- To support a world class city, which is the financial centre of Europe;
- To support economic growth with transport capacity;
- To support regeneration with improved rail access.

Crossrail will run from Maidenhead and Heathrow in the west, through tunnels under central London (with new stations at Paddington, Bond Street, Tottenham Court Road, Farringdon, Liverpool Street, and Whitechapel) and on out to Shenfield north of the Thames, and Isle of Dogs / Canary Wharf, Woolwich and Abbey Wood to the south. With 24 trains an hour during peak times throughout the central section, and 12 an hour off-peak, an estimated 160,000 passengers will be carried in the morning rush hour. The total length of Crossrail is 118.5km, including 41.5km in tunnels. 38 stations will be served directly.

Crossrail will use trains of main line dimensions and a 21km tunnel under the centre of the city. Enabling works start in 2009, but main construction will begin in 2010. When it does, it will be the largest civil engineering project in Europe, designed specifically to cope with the growing population of the region. Up to 14,000 people will be employed in its construction.

The company structure of Cross London Rail Links Limited (CLRL) has changed from a planning and promotional organisation to that of delivery agent. London Underground has a similar role for some work at Tottenham Court Road and Bond Street stations. CLRL is owned 50/50 by the Secretary of State and Transport for London (TfL), but is to become wholly-owned by TfL.

The government is to provide about £5billion by means of a grant from the Department for Transport. Crossrail passengers will ultimately contribute about one third of the overall cost through fares, with revenue servicing debt raised during construction by Transport for London and by Network Rail.

London businesses will contribute the remaining third through:
- Direct contributions from the Canary Wharf Group, the City of London Corporation and BAA;
- A supplementary business rate of two pence per pound of rateable value across London from April 2010, with relief for smaller businesses;
- Contributions from property developers in the vicinity of Crossrail stations.

In November 2008, £230million of funding from airport company BAA was agreed in return for the guarantee of a fast four-train-per-hour service for most of the day for Heathrow airport.

Network Rail is responsible for the design, development and delivery of works outside the tunnel area, including platform extensions at over 20 stations, and rebuilds of stations including Abbey Wood, Ilford, Romford and Ealing Broadway. Electrification will be needed west of Airport Junction and substantial resignalling throughout. Network Rail will also manage about two million cubic metres of tunnel spoil. At Paddington, there will be a major reworking of platforms and interchange between the Crossrail station and main line platforms.

Timetables will also need to be remodelled and franchise requirements reworked. TfL has reached agreement with the DfT that a seven-year Crossrail train operating company (TOC) concession will be let by November 2013 in parallel with the award of the new East Anglia franchise. From 1 April 2014, Crossrail TOC will operate the existing Liverpool Street-Shenfield services and take on the Paddington-Heathrow/Maidenhead services when the new Great Western franchise is awarded in November 2015, to begin operations on 1 April 2016. Operations on the new central tunnel section and connections to the east and west sections will be phased.

TfL and Network Rail have agreed that Crossrail route control will be based at Liverpool Street in the first instance and later at a new centre at Romford.

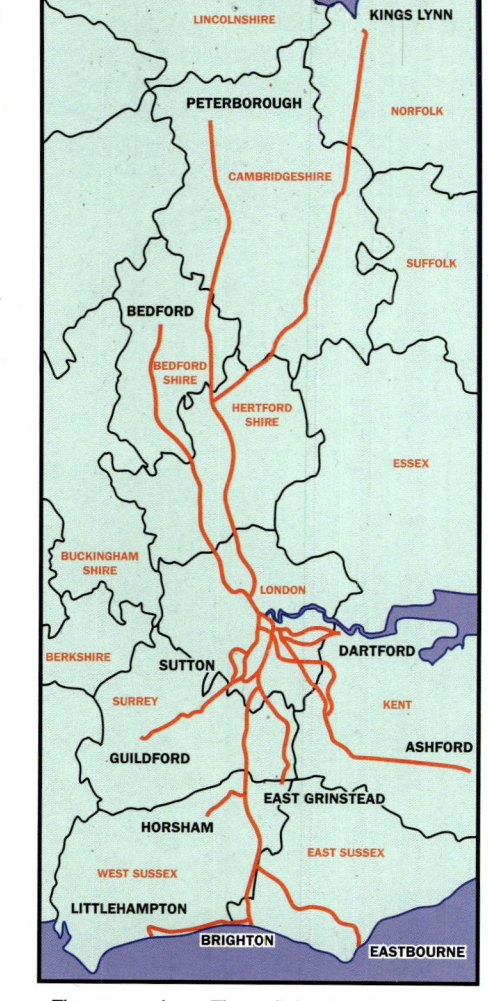

The proposed new Thameslink network

Impression of a Crossrail train. Crossrail

Key Projects

View eastwards over the main Olympics site at Stratford in mid 2008. Stratford International – the Channel Tunnel Rail Link station – is at the centre, with the new Docklands Light Railway station under construction to its left (north side). Olympic Delivery Authority

Some projected comparative journey times are as follows:

Journey	Crossrail	London Underground
Heathrow to Canary Wharf	43min	70min
Heathrow to Tottenham Court Road	31min	52min
Ealing Broadway to Liverpool Street	20min	37min
Abbey Wood to Tottenham Court Road	22min	45min*

* also using South Eastern trains

Outstanding issues include whether any extension west of Maidenhead or east of Abbey Wood is likely to come about, and how the relationships with existing rail services, including freight, will evolve.

London 2012 – The Olympics

An immovable date in the national calendar is the Olympic Games Opening Ceremony on 27 July 2012, at 19.30 in the Olympic Park at Stratford. The Games will then run until 13 August, followed by a short break. They will be followed by the opening of the Paralympics on 29 August, which will continue until 9 September. Over 200 nations will compete. The Olympics are the world's largest such event, but the Paralympics come second.

The main venue is the Olympic Park in the former railway lands at Stratford. Other venues (needing transport facilities) are activities at Broxbourne, Excel, Greenwich and Woolwich. Events will also be held in central London and further afield.

London 2012 Games will be delivered by the London Organising Committee of the Olympic Games and Paralympic Games (LOCOG), and the Olympic Delivery Authority (ODA). LOCOG is responsible for the preparation and the staging of the Games; the ODA is the public body responsible for developing and building the venues and the infrastructure.

Transport will be delivered through a partnership between the ODA, LOCOG and transport operators and authorities. A main aim is to achieve 100% of ticketed spectators travel to competition venues by public transport, walking or cycling.

Three stations will play a key part in delivering spectators and the workforce to the Olympic Park – the existing Stratford 'Regional', Stratford International and West Ham. Currently, 37,000 passengers pass through Stratford Regional in the morning peak and by 2012 this number is forecast to rise to 55,000. An additional 63,000 spectators are expected to use the station each morning during the Games, bringing the total to 118,000.

These will be big events, though it is not so much the numbers arriving, but the speed at which they depart that is likely to give the greatest challenge. Hence the ODA funding of a new westbound Central Line platform to help take the strain, accessed by a new station entrance at mezzanine level. A new bridge will allow those leaving the Olympic Park to go directly to the Central Line and Docklands Light Railway (DLR) platforms for services towards London.

Other ODA-funded improvements to Stratford Regional to be delivered by Network Rail and London Underground include nine new lifts and eight new staircases, reopening the disused subway, wider and longer platforms, new information services, a new northern entrance and ticket hall, and new platforms for London Overground services from Richmond. All station works should be finished by the end of 2010.

New DLR services will run at approximately 10 trains per hour from Stratford international to Stratford Domestic, and then via three new stations to West Ham and Canning Town. The DLR will provide an important link with three of the nearby competition venues. Trains generally will be increased from two-car to three-car articulated sets, as part of an investment plan already under way. The ODA is co-funding 22 of them.

Work on the North London line will allow the use of four-car trains (in place of three) and higher frequencies.

The high speed 'Javelin' shuttle using South Eastern's Hitachi-built Class 395s will

BOMBARDIER + eco⁴ = A new formula in energy savings

Bombardier Transportation already leads the way with close to zero-emission and almost fully recyclable trains. And now our revolutionary energy-saving *ECO4* technologies are again changing the equation – setting new standards in profitable, sustainable mobility. Built on the four cornerstones of energy, efficiency, ecology and economy, *ECO4* products are easily customized to any fleet, for optimized energy use and minimized energy waste. Which equals dramatic new benefits for operators, passengers and the whole planet.

More than ever,
The Climate is Right for Trains.

www.bombardier.com

ECO4 and *The Climate is Right for Trains* are trademarks of Bombardier Inc. or its subsidiaries.

BOMBARDIER
The Global Leader in Rail Technology

Key Projects

operate between St Pancras, Stratford and Ebbsfleet. Up to 10 trains an hour in 12-car sets will run from St Pancras, with a journey time to Stratford of 7min. Eurostar services will not call at Stratford during the Games; passengers will need to change to Javelin services at Ebbsfleet, which will also be a main location for park-and-ride.

Labour availability and training are clearly matters of major significance. This includes ensuring that there are enough people to run the enhanced services and deal with the crowds, with many visitors unfamiliar with London and the transport system.

Scotland

The Scottish government's High Level Output Statement of 2007 set out a large programme. The aim of the extensive infrastructure enhancements is to deliver reliability, capacity, attractiveness and journey time savings across the network generally. Major capital projects with legislation and funding in place are:

- Airdrie-Bathgate: The disused 14 mile line between these points is being reconstructed to double track standards and electrified. There will be two new stations at Caldercruix and Armadale, and existing stations at Bathgate and Drumgelloch are being resited. A four train-per-hour (tph) service is likely to be provided with a 74min throughout journey time. The estimated completion is late 2010.
- Glasgow Airport Rail Link (GARL): A 1.25-mile electrified line is being constructed between Paisley and Glasgow Airport, with a new platform at Glasgow Central. Most of the intervening line will become three track rather than two. A 4tph service is to be provided, with a 16min journey time, including a stop at Paisley Gilmour Street. Estimated completion is early in 2012.
- Waverley Railway. The project will re-establish a 35 mile rail link from Edinburgh through Midlothian to Tweedbank in the Scottish Borders, reinstating part of the Waverley route, closed in 1969. The line will join the existing network at Newcraighall and seven new stations will be constructed. This will be a mainly single track railway with three dynamic passing loops, each two to four miles long (so 15 route miles will in effect be double track). The likely service levels are two trains per hour, with an end to end time of around 55min. The project has now been handed to Transport Scotland to deliver in partnership with the rail industry, with the procurement process starting at the end of 2008. Work is expected to start on site in 2011, with completion around the end of 2013. The estimated cost is in the region of £235-£295 million.

The Edinburgh Airport Rail Link, now dropped, is to be substituted by a new station at Gogar, about 0.75 mile beyond South Gyle station on the line from Edinburgh towards the Forth Bridge. This would act as an interchange for the tram services to Edinburgh Airport. A new chord would be

Consultant files - Supporting rail developments

Atkins
Atkins sets out to help clients in the rail industry to realise their vision and achieve success from their capital investment programmes. Wide-ranging services include: feasibility and planning, design and engineering, implementation and support, and asset management.

Multifunctional, integrated, early stage design and systems integration is provided across signalling, telecoms, power and vehicles capabilities, allowing for capacity enhancement, service and environmental improvement. Recent UK projects range from developing Network Rail's business case for the Western Concourse at King's Cross station, and being appointed as a specialist geotechnical consultant to Eurotunnel.
www.atkinsglobal.com

Arup
Arup is a global firm of designers, engineers, planners and business consultants which provides a full range of professional consultancy services to the rail industry. The services offered by the Rail team range from advice on corporate structure and procurement methods; the initial planning of new routes; operational analysis and simulation; design of infrastructure and systems through to specialist research and development.

The team includes signalling, track, traction power, systems and civil engineers working with planners, environmental engineers, architects, acousticians, fire and other specialists to create holistic solutions in: high speed rail, heavy rail, metros, light rail, monorail, guided bus, and heavy haul freight.
www.arup.com

Bechtel
Founded in 1898, Bechtel is a major engineering, construction, and project management corporation, active around the world. Major UK projects in which Bechtel has been involved include the West Coast route modernisation, and the Jubilee Line Extension. It was part of the Rail Link Engineering consortium creating High Speed One, is part of the Tube Lines consortium modernising the Jubilee, Northern, and Piccadilly London Underground lines; and has also been appointed as development manager for Crossrail.
www.bechtel.com

DeltaRail
DeltaRail is a leading independent railway technology adviser, supplying advanced solutions, combining the delivery of hardware, software and specialist consultancy with engineering, consulting, operations and products capabilities to improve business performance for customers across the entire railway system.

It works in five main areas: signalling and signalling control, infrastructure support services and systems, operational planning and real time railway management, design and project management of rolling stock refurbishment and enhancement, and rolling stock maintenance solutions.
www.deltarail.com

Halcrow
Halcrow has multi-disciplinary capabilities for the provision of advice in the rail sector, covering all stages of development, procurement, implementation, and operation of rail services and infrastructure. Services include: technical and engineering development; project management; risk assessment and control; financial modelling; commercial management; and support for development of independent financing.

Halcrow's portfolio of schemes includes high-speed heavy-rail projects including High Speed 1, freight handling facilities, new light rail and tram schemes, and upgrades and enhancements of existing metro and heavy rail systems.
www.halcrow.com

Jacobs Consultancy
Jacobs Consultancy staff work extensively on railway business and operational planning assignments in the UK and across the world, on heavy rail, metros and light rail systems.

Governments are seeking to limit environmental damage caused by the private car and road freight and an integrated approach to asset provision, planning and operations is needed to provide a quality railway service to help achieve this aspiration. Ever-higher standards of performance are necessary for railways if they are to meet the needs of customers.

Expert services are provided to clients including governments, train operators, regulators, international funding agencies, concessionaires, banks, and infrastructure companies.
www.jacobsconsultancy.co.uk

Lloyd's Register Rail
Lloyd's Register Rail is a member of the Lloyd's Register Group and provides services to help manage the safety, functional and business performance of new and existing rail systems and projects. The Lloyd's Register Rail companies are multifunctional specialist rail

provided south of Dalmeny station, towards Linlithgow, to allow rerouteing of Edinburgh-Glasgow trains to call at Gogar.

Electrification is planned on the core route between Edinburgh and Glasgow Queen Street, plus two diversionary routes; with infill electrification to include Paisley Canal, Whifflet, Cumbernauld, Maryhill, Stirling/Dunblane and Alloa. Services would switch to cross-Glasgow 'low level' routes where appropriate, to free up capacity at Glasgow Central and Queen Street. Later, electrification is planned for East Kilbride and Barrhead/Kilmarnock.

West Coast route modernisation
The £7.6billion West Coast route modernisation project's latest phase was virtually complete by December 2008, when major service improvements were introduced. 95% of a planned 390 new services a day were scheduled, with the remaining 5% to come early in 2009.

The substantial gains of the new timetable are three intercity trains per hour to

West Coast Route Modernisation work in progress at Lichfield in September 2008, part of the Trent Valley 'four-tracking' project. Network Rail

consultancy companies operating in Europe, Asia and Australia. They specialise in rail systems integration and safety assurance founded on core rail skills in all of the key rail disciplines, including rolling stock, signalling, telecommunications, power systems and operations. Key areas of experience include business support, risk assessment, system assurance, safety case preparation and independent safety assessment in the railway sector.
www.lr.org

Mott MacDonald
Mott MacDonald provides rail engineering consultancy services through teams based in ten UK offices and internationally. Its technical engineering disciplines cover all aspects of railway systems (trackwork, signalling, telecommunications, rolling stock, operations, safety assurance systems, mechanical and electrical, traction power, ergonomics) and infrastructure (tunnels, bridges, earthworks, stations, intermodal depots, marshalling yards). It also specialises in applying advanced simulation techniques.

The project portfolio includes the Channel Tunnel, West Coast route modernisation, London Underground, the Channel Tunnel Rail Link, and light rapid transit in cities such as London, Birmingham, and Manchester.
www.mottmac.com

Mouchel
Mouchel provides a combination of consultancy, business and technological services for rail and public transport. Services include civil and structural engineering, customer information systems, permanent way design and feasibility work, rail structures examination and assessment, rail freight consultancy, rail property asset management, rolling-stock and train systems consultancy, rail signalling and telecommunications, and strategic asset management.

The established transport practice delivers consultancy services to a wide range of UK transport organisations, including strategic and delivery services across the full range of transport modes.
www.mouchel.com

Parsons Brinckerhoff
PB (Parsons Brinckerhoff) provides multidisciplinary planning, engineering and programme and construction management services for all types of transportation projects. It offers an integrated transport capability from in-house resources.

Transport capability in rail includes civil and structural engineering, permanent way, electrification, telecommunications and programme management.

For Edinburgh's new light rail scheme, Parsons Brinckerhoff has provided comprehensive system design services, and it is programme manager for the East London Line extension and for Greater Manchester Passenger Transport Executive's expansion of the Metrolink network. Programme management support for the West Coast route modernisation has also been provided.

PB has also been restructuring its rail business unit in the UK, aimed at boosting management flexibility and increasing customer focus, with the objective of securing a leading role in a wide range of contracts.
www.pbworld.co.uk

QinetiQ
QinetiQ provides technology, systems and services to enhance performance in the European rail industry.

Areas of activity in rail are:- business and technical support, systems engineering, project management, decision support, rail asset management, training, condition monitoring, and waste management for trains.

In 2007 QinetiQ Rail Limited, a subsidiary specialising in wireless broadband for the rail industry, was acquired by Nomad Digital.
www.qinetiq.com

Scott Wilson Railways
Scott Wilson provides multi-disciplinary services to the railway sector. Specialist multi-disciplinary railway engineering skills are backed by planning, environment and management expertise available within the group. Specialisms include light rail and metro rail sectors, asset maintenance, station development and freight materials handling.

Scott Wilson is a multi-disciplinary consultant for surface routes west and northeast under the London Crossrail programme, and in October 2008 won a contract with Network Rail to provide designs for the above ground sections of the Crossrail project.

In recognition of the growing urban railway market in the UK and overseas, Scott Wilson established a distinct multi-disciplinary Metro unit in October 2008, strengthened by the acquisitions in 2008 of the Benaim Group and Terence Lee Partnership.
www.scottwilson.com

Key Projects

Birmingham, three intercity trains per hour to Manchester, a 50% increase in Sunday services, new London Midland services to Liverpool and London, and cuts in journey time.

Changes to the way the project was being delivered were made following engineering overruns at New Year 2009, and since then the major pieces of work had been completed on time.

In 2003 the former Strategic Rail Authority refocused the West Coast route modernisation effort after costs soared. It resulted in pruning of some of the more ambitious elements. Top design speeds were reduced from 140mph to 125mph, while new, conventional signalling replaced a proposed advanced signalling and train control system.

Schemes completed include line speed improvements, with track renewals, resignalling and overhead line overhaul and renewals; and the installation of beacons to interface with the train-borne tilt and speed supervision system.

The Birmingham-Leicester route at Nuneaton was separated with a flyover and new platforms. Additional platforms have been provided at Milton Keynes Central, and a new layout at Rugby minimises the conflict between fast line and slow line traffic, passing between the Trent Valley or Birmingham routes to the north, and the main line and Northampton routes to the south. In the Trent Valley (the direct route between Rugby and Stafford), four tracks in place of two have been provided over most of the route.

For the future, work is proposed in the Stafford area to resolve capacity issues, arising from the junctions and resulting conflicts between trains on the Birmingham and Trent Valley lines.

King's Cross redevelopment

Network Rail is carrying out a major redevelopment of the London King's Cross terminus, valued at £400m, creating a new concourse on the west side of the main trainsheds, serving both the main intercity station and also suburban platforms 9-11. It will also improve links with St Pancras, the High Speed 1 terminus. The new King's Cross concourse will provide 8,000 square metres of circulating space (against 2,500 at present).

The London Underground station at King's Cross / St Pancras already has a new western ticket hall under the facade of the Midland Grand Hotel building at the front of St Pancras, and the concourse of the original tube station ticket hall has been modernised. A new northern ticket hall will serve King's Cross and the circulating area at the middle of St Pancras.

Designed by John McAslan & Partners with engineering support from Arup, the western concourse will be a dramatic structure with what is known as a 'dio grid' roof to give a light and airy feel to the interior.

All the works are planned to be finished by the end of 2011, well before operation of the 'Javelin' service from St Pancras to the Olympics site at Stratford.

Heathrow Airtrack

Heathrow Airtrack is a scheme to provide a rail link between Heathrow airport and the national rail network to the south and west of the airport.

AirTrack would use new tunnels from the Terminal 5 station - which already has platforms for Airtrack - to join the remains of the former West Drayton-Staines branch line, reaching the London Waterloo-Windsor line at Staines. Trains would serve a new station at Staines High Street and continue towards London Waterloo, or run via a reinstated link towards Egham and Woking/Guildford or Reading. Some Heathrow Express services are proposed to continue through Heathrow Terminal 5 to Staines.

In October 2008, a second stage of consultation on the scheme was launched by airport company BAA, which now includes a proposed new depot at Feltham. BAA planned an application for a Transport & Works Act order in early 2009.

Airtrack will operate in each direction from Heathrow Terminal 5 to London Waterloo, Guildford and Reading. These trains will be in addition to the services already operating on these lines. BAA says Airtrack would mean approximately 72% of Heathrow's current passengers would be living in areas within one rail interchange of the airport.

Intercity Express Programme

The Intercity Express Programme (IEP) is a Department for Transport initiative aimed at providing for the eventual replacement of the existing fleet of diesel High Speed Trains, and also providing the basis of a fleet of trains that can provide many of other long distance services on Britain's railways.

The DfT proposals are for procurement of a fleet of between 500 and 2,000 vehicles, to be provided for approximately 30 years by a single supplier, or consortium or Special Purpose Vehicle (SPV), under an availability and reliability agreement to future passenger rail franchisees. The scope requires the design, manufacture, financing, servicing and maintenance of the complete package, over the entire life of the fleet.

A small 'pre-series' batch of trains is envisaged, to test the trains in a customer and operational environment to identify and resolve any problems before full fleet production commences. It is likely that these trains will be deployed on the southern part of the ECML route which, after cross-industry assessment, appears to offer the best potential, including testing with self-powered operation and under 25kV electrification.

A strong business case was identified by the DfT for the introduction of a replacement and higher capacity fleets to a new design, and to replace existing fleets, on several long distance routes, including the East Coast and Great Western main lines. The design is to be capable of operating on: fully electrified routes; routes that are only partially electrified and would therefore benefit from dual power trains (electric and self power); and on routes without significant electrification. It may also be suitable, subject to price and value, for wider deployment.

A feature of the IEP is the concept of a 'family of trains' with a set of standard vehicles. IEP trains may be self-powered, electric or bi-mode and may be full, half or intermediate length.

Bidders returning tenders in June 2008 were:
- Express Rail Alliance (a consortium of Bombardier Transportation, Siemens, Angel Trains and Babcock & Brown);
- Agility Trains Ltd (a consortium of Hitachi (Japan) Ltd, Barclays Private Equity and John Laing Projects and Developments).

Impression of Express Rail Alliance electric train for Intercity Express Programme. Express Rail Alliance

Infrastructure Maintenance & Renewal

In association with

SPERRY RAIL INTERNATIONAL LTD.
a Rockwood Company

Infrastructure Maintenance & Renewal

Maintaining and renewing the infrastructure

Electrification work was carried out on the Mound tunnel, Edinburgh, at the turn of 2007/08, as part of preparations for electric trains to run between Edinburgh and Glasgow via the new Airdire-Bathgate line. Network Rail

Demand for rail continued to grow in all sectors into 2008, with the highest level of passenger journeys since 1946, on a railway that has not seen significant expansion for decades: so said Network Rail Chief Executive, Iain Coucher, in his annual review.

The challenge for the rail industry and, therefore, Network Rail is managing a further growth in demand – not just in the numbers of people wishing to travel by train or putting freight onto the rail system, but responding to changes in travel patterns, continued Mr Coucher. The railway of the future needed to provide services earlier in the morning, later at night, and more at weekends and at bank holidays, which had huge implications for Network Rail, he said.

The challenge for Network Rail is clear, said Mr Coucher: 'we need to provide a railway that is more available and more reliable. We need to manage annual, multi-billion pound investment programmes in a way that minimises the impact on those that wish to use the railway, and we need to continue to achieve further efficiencies, on top of the 23% we have delivered in the last four years. However, this is a challenge we relish. The whole of Network Rail is determined to meet our vision: one in which passengers and freight users rate rail as the best mode of transport for overall safety, reliability, accessibility, convenience and value for money; and where Britain's railway is recognised by taxpayers as being amongst the best in the world for safety, reliability and affordability.'

Renewals

In its October 2008 determination of Network Rail's outputs and funding for Control Period 4 (CP4 - April 2009 until March 2014), the Office of Rail Regulation (ORR) concludes overall that there is a 'considerable and persuasive body of evidence' that broadly supports the renewals activity volumes proposed by Network Rail. The track asset policy appears to reflect a soundly judged, evidence based approach to managing the track system, said the ORR's review, which concluded that it is one of Network Rail's most robust asset policies, founded on sound engineering principles, and differentiating well between asset management regimes and output requirements for different types of route.

ORR points out that there is a 'bow-wave' created by peaking of the renewals cycle, where track renewed in the 1970s/1980s requires replacement because it is becoming life-expired and an increasing performance risk on the primary routes. The increase in renewal volumes during CP3 has begun to address this, and although volumes in CP4 are somewhat less, ORR expects this age profile to remain a significant influence on activity levels for the next few years. The proposed rate of renewal (2.2% to 2.7% per annum) is in the range that ORR would expect to see during CP4, given that rates of renewal during the late 1970s and early 1980s are known to have run as high as 3% per annum.

Beyond CP4, ORR expects track renewal volumes to fall steadily, and has reflected this in long run average expenditure assessment.

However, ORR makes minor reductions to the volumes of plain line track renewals proposed by Network Rail because it believes that there are further opportunities to reduce the amount of plain line renewal by local engineers applying objective risk-based criteria to prioritise renewals. ORR also believes increased attention to drainage, better maintenance, improving standards of renewal, and more consistent application of policies in the specification of work to minimise whole life costs should all lead to better reliability and longer asset lives (although the principal asset life benefit is expected to be in subsequent control periods).

Forecasts in Network Rail's November 2007 Strategic Business Plan (which contained the company's proposals for CP4 and the funding required) reflect developments in track asset policies, particularly increased differentiation between route categories. Tertiary routes (rural and freight-only) were classified as either suitable for continuous maintenance through tactical rail and sleeper replacement where overall condition is satisfactory, or as requiring significant levels of renewal activity because component condition has deteriorated to the point where continuous maintenance will be insufficient. For some routes which have already been largely converted to continuously welded rail, further renewals are planned to complete the conversion when this is justified by asset condition.

There was specific provision for additional re-railing and switch & crossing renewal work as a result of the impact of new rolling stock on commuter routes south of London. Early experience of new fleets of heavier trains with stiffer suspension shows a significant increase in the level of rolling contact fatigue and other track defects.

For switch & crossing renewals, initial assessment of condition-renewal and enhancement volumes produced a level of complete renewals in excess of what can be delivered efficiently. It was therefore proposed to carry out a significantly higher level of refurbishment or partial renewal activity to extend unit life.

Network Rail's modular switches & crossing project is expected to steadily reduce unit costs and increase the overall delivery capability.

Renewals contractors

Network Rail in 2008 implemented a reduction in the number of track renewals contractors delivering work from six to four, bringing switch & crossing and plain-line track renewals under single local contractors - a change designed to improve the ability to plan and co-ordinate renewals work, which will also allow contractors to reduce the distance between depots and worksites.

Table 2 - Volumes of major track asset renewals 2009-14 (GB) - ORR assessment*

	Volume: Average annual	Indicative total (5 yr)
Rail	788km	3940km
Sleepers	659km	3295km
Ballast	744km	3721km
Switches & crossings:		
(full renewal)	359 units	1796 units
(partial renewal)	188 units	940 units

*October 2008 determination of Network Rail's outputs and funding

The four contractors are:
- Amey Colas;
- Balfour Beatty;
- Babcock Rail;
- Jarvis.

Under the terms of existing framework contracts, running from 2004 until 2009, the renewals deals can to be extended to 2014.

Balfour Beatty Rail said its renewals contracts were worth about £90million a year, while Amey Colas placed an annual value of £95million a year on it deals. First Engineering (now Babcock Rail) said the value of its contracts was expected to be up to £85million annually. Jarvis Rail expected a net increase in turnover of about £15million a year.

Route organisation

Network Rail's operation of the railway was organised by eight Routes under an organisation structure implemented in May 2004. Each train operating company has a single point of contact, the Route Director.

Areas (whose geography is similar to the areas covered by train operating companies) are responsible for day to day running, both operational delivery and asset stewardship.

Each area has a general manager, and an infrastructure maintenance manager.

Area engineering and maintenance activities are organised by Asset Management Territories which match the geography of the Routes - the South East Territory covers four Routes. Priorities for the routes, including maintenance, are set by Route Directors, liaising with Territory Maintenance Directors (TMDs).

In 2008 a ninth Route, Midland & Continental, was created, taking over the Midland main line from the London North Eastern route and adding maintenance and operation of the Channel Tunnel Rail Link, High Speed 1.

Maintenance

ORR's October 2008 determination broadly accepts Network Rail's forecasts of maintenance expenditure. ORR comments that Network Rail's infrastructure cost model provides visibility of maintenance activity levels by route segment, but it remains more difficult to assess and evaluate the justification for maintenance volumes (many of which are essentially reactive) than for renewal volumes generated by modelling of asset age, service lives and so on. Network Rail has developed significant efficiency proposals for maintenance expenditure, said ORR, many of which are based on expected changes in activity volumes as it improves productivity during CP4.

NR brought maintenance in-house in May 2004, replacing the previous arrangement of contracts with infrastructure maintenance companies. ORR does not take account of costs associated with Network Rail's intention to harmonise the terms and conditions of its maintenance employees, but says it understands that NR has around 75 different sets of terms and conditions, largely as an inheritance from bringing these employees in-house.

As the network becomes busier, access for scheduled maintenance will reduce and more activity is expected to move to nights and weekends. ORR acknowledges the general merits of moving to common terms and conditions and ensuring that these reflect the changing work patterns needed. ORR says it would expect this to enable greater and faster efficiency improvement than NR forecasts assumed.

Additional traffic growth has led to increased maintenance costs, particularly in the

Table 1 - Total renewals and maintenance expenditure in 2009-14 (GB) - ORR assessment**

£m (2006-07 prices) Renewals	Network Rail SBP update	ORR assessment
Track	3,992	3,869
Signalling	2,565	2,454
Civil engineering	2,198	1,895
Operational property	1,480	1,480
Electrification	684	673*
Telecoms	887	963*
Plant & machinery	402	418*
Information management	475	434
Corporate offices	90	90
Discretionary investment	74	84
Unallocated overheads	92	95
Total renewals	12,938	12,456
Maintenance	5,311	5,430
Total M&R	18,249	17,886

Notes to Table 1:
* Includes deferral from CP3: £9m electrification, £253m telecoms, £16m plant & machinery.
** October 2008 determination of Network Rail's outputs and funding.
SBP Network Rail's Strategic Business Plan (SBP) proposals for CP4 and the funding required, updated in April 2008.

Infrastructure Maintenance & Renewal

Table 3 - Track renewals contracts from 2008

Area	Territory	Contractor
Scotland East	Scotland	Babcock Rail
Scotland West	Scotland	Babcock Rail
North Eastern	London North Eastern	Jarvis
Great Northern	London North Eastern	Jarvis
East Midlands	Midland & Continental	Jarvis
Lancs & Cumbria	London North Western	Babcock Rail
Manchester	London North Western	Babcock Rail
Liverpool	London North Western	Babcock Rail
West Coast South	London North Western	Amey Colas
West Midlands	London North Western	Amey Colas
Wessex	South Eastern	Balfour Beatty
Kent	South Eastern	Balfour Beatty
Sussex	South Eastern	Balfour Beatty
Anglia	South Eastern	Balfour Beatty
Wales and Marches	Western	Amey Colas
West Country	Western	Amey Colas
Thames Valley	Western	Amey Colas

southeast, because of heavier new trains with stiffer suspensions.

Track machine orders

Network Rail ordered in 2008 a further new ballast cleaning system from Plasser & Theurer - its third such system. Valued at £41.7million, the 800 metre, 3,200 tonne cleaner cuts the time it takes to clean and replace track ballast, and is capable of cleaning around 600 hundred yards of track ballast during a typical midweek eight-hour night-shift.

The system will be used to clean ballast on the West Coast and East Coast main lines as well as in Scotland. The total system comprises of one ballast cleaner, two power wagons, 44 MFS wagons, one compaction machine and one consolidation machine. The other systems operate on the western and eastern routes.

Network Rail also planned to order another high output track relaying train to speed up the time it takes to carry out track renewals.

26 specialised 'tilting' wagons for points renewal have been ordered by Network Rail under a £10m contract with Kirow. The order forms part of the modular switches and crossings programme which will help engineers renew a set of points in overnight eight-hour possessions.

Inspection

Network Rail has developed improved infrastructure monitoring to improve the safety and value provided by the rail network using advanced technology. This is enabling a move from a 'find and fix faults' regime to 'predict and prevent' asset management.

As there are expected to be fewer, more expensive, skilled workers available to the industry in the future, Network Rail has also aimed to design every part of its system for low maintenance while improving reliability and safety integrity. Gathering performance data intelligently from remote condition monitoring of assets can give early visibility of equipment degradation and performance issues, helping a more proactive approach to maintenance and fault rectification.

A £10m project to boost rail freight along the Barnetby-Brigg-Gainsborough line was completed in June 2008, as part of a package to increase rail traffic from/to Associated British Ports' Humber ports - mostly coal to Cottam and West Burton, Ratcliffe and Rugeley power stations. The work included reconstruction of a railway embankment between the Old and New Ancholme rivers, and refurbishing the railway bridge over the New Ancholme. This was the first train to run over the improved line, on 23 June 2008. Network Rail

Understanding of current asset condition, the factors causing asset degradation and the nature of this degradation, has underpinned a move into train-based technology and remote condition monitoring to measure the infrastructure, supported by centralised systems to diagnose trends and patterns.

At the core of the train-based technology is the New Measurement Train (NMT), introduced in 2003 and now operating a two weekly measurement cycle on key parts of the network, monitoring 250,000 km of track annually at speeds of up to 125mph. The NMT provides a live platform to evaluate and develop advanced monitoring systems, including:

- track geometry;
- ultrasonic surveys;
- train passing clearances;
- video inspection;
- overhead line; and
- radio surveys.

Infrastructure contractors

While Network Rail took maintenance work in-house in 2004, it relies on contractors for track renewals and infrastructure projects work, and contractors continue to supply on-track plant such as tampers to Network Rail. Some of the main contractors are featured below.

Amey

Amey supplies services across the whole range of rail operations from engineering to project management for Network Rail, train operating companies and government agencies.

Working with partner Colas (formerly SECO), Amey brings together planning, design and operations skills and renews around 160 kilometres of track every year at over 150 sites.

The Amey group now includes professional support services provider, Owen Williams, which provides management and consultancy services for clients in strategic highways and transportation, railways, operational services and local government sectors. Drawing on this area of expertise, Amey Infrastructure Services was awarded a design contract for the Bletchley-Milton Keynes remodelling and resignalling project.

Amey also holds a Network Rail minor renewals contract for development, design, installation and commissioning of a variety of signalling renewals to the rail network in the Western Territory. Under an electrical minor plant renewals contract, Amey works with Network Rail in London North West, London North East and Western territories to deliver design and installation of a wide range of plant and electrical equipment.

Amey has provided turnkey telecommunication solutions to more than 450 stations - including customer information systems, CCTV, help points and public address.

During 2005 Amey consolidated a two thirds stake in London Underground infrastructure company Tube Lines after purchasing Jarvis's 33.3% stake. Since 2003, Amey has been part of Grupo Ferrovial, one of the largest services and construction groups in Europe.

Rail work falls within the Amey Infrastructure Services business which in the year to 31 December 2007 had an operating profit of £31.62m (2006: £32.74m), with revenue of £544.6m (2006: £490.8m).

Babcock Rail

Babcock Rail - formerly First Engineering - is a major track renewals contractor to Network Rail, delivering conventional and high output track renewals work. The high-output track renewals and plant joint venture, with partners Swietelsky of Austria, continues to operate under the name First Swietelsky.

Babcock Rail also delivers signalling and control systems, rail power solutions, plant, consultancy, training and multi-disciplinary projects for a wide range of customers.

A significant restructuring of the business was implemented in 2007-08 around three key national business units – track renewals, projects, and signalling and control systems. The business returned to profit in the second half and delivered a small profit for the full year with what was characterised as 'a more robust and stable platform from which to move forward'.

Babcock Rail was selected as one of the four main contractors to deliver track renewals for Network Rail, bringing additional work worth around £30million per annum in Scotland and the North West of England from 2008. Around 300 employees transferred to Babcock under TUPE regulations as a result of this process.

First Swietelsky won a further extension to the National Plant contract valued at £2.5million for the automated finishing machines, which Babcock described as the most productive advanced such systems available. Awarded the first operation and maintenance contract for high-output track-renewal systems by Network Rail in 2004, First Swietelsky won two high-output contracts until 2009, together estimated to be worth circa £50million per annum.

Significant recent project work has included capacity improvement works on the Settle-Carlisle line (£15million), a multi-disciplinary contract to reinstate Olive Mount chord to provide a freight link between the Port of Liverpool and the West Coast main line (£3million), and a contract to design, install and commission the replacement of 33kV switchgear in substations from South West London to Ramsgate (£4million).

The installation of customer information systems at stations throughout Scotland and other national telecoms projects for Network Rail are being successfully delivered through telecoms framework contracts. A further opportunity to become framework provider for level crossings was being pursued in partnership with GE Transportation Systems.

Balfour Beatty

Balfour Beatty's UK rail activity is undertaken by several separate organisations.

Balfour Beatty Rail Projects carries out rail engineering project management internationally, covering design, construction and commissioning of infrastructure projects in main line, mass transit and light rail. It has recently been working on high-profile UK rail projects including Heathrow Terminal 5 and the West Coast main line. It undertakes both the remodelling and upgrading of existing infrastructure and the construction of new systems, with specialisation in permanent way, overhead line electrification and power supply systems.

Balfour Beatty Rail Services is one of the UK's largest track renewals organisations and also offers maintenance service provision. Expertise within the plant businesses includes track maintenance, track support and engineering, and an innovations team provides solutions for safer and more productive working.

A track geometry service includes tamping, regulating, ballast cleaning and track stabilisation. A specialist services team provides a range of services including road rail vehicles, Kirow cranes, rail grinding, new track construction, and drain cleaning remediation.

Balfour Beatty Rail Systems & Solutions provides specialist input in the form of innovation, new technology, professional consultancy and special trackwork. Two distinct elements of the business cover design and manufacture of trackwork and technology-based products and services.

The track systems element specialises in the design, manufacture and supply of special trackwork, switches and crossings which can be delivered as a modular assembly with the advantage of minimum on-track installation time. The scope of capabilities was increased with the acquisition of Edgar Allen Ltd (who have specialised in cast manganese crossings) in 2006.

The technologies element provides innovative solutions to enhance railway infrastructure asset performance, and specialises in signalling, track inspection, track geometry and structure gauging, the latter of which were gained through the acquisition of Laser Rail Limited in 2007 and retain this branding. A research & development team continues to develop step change solutions such as embedded rail slab track and offers direct consultancy in value engineering, risk management and civil engineering sectors.

In September 2008, Network Rail awarded a £60m contract for the Airdrie to Bathgate rail link to Balfour Beatty Rail Projects, who will lay new track, double track an existing stretch, and electrify the entire route.

Carillion

Carillion provides services for network enhancements to Network Rail, Passenger Transport Executives and Transport for London. On High Speed 1's second section, Carillion was part of the consortium that installed track and overhead line, and it holds

Infrastructure Maintenance & Renewal

A First Capital Connect train passes track workers at East Croydon on 30 January 2008. Tony Miles

the maintenance contract for HS1's infrastructure.

Services provided include major and minor enhancements, life extension work and projects, maintenance, private finance schemes, trainborne inspection, welding and rail testing and consultancy services.

Carillion in joint venture with Balfour Beatty is fulfilling the £363million contract to create the new East London rail line between Dalston Junction in the north and West Croydon in the south, for Transport for London.

Carillion Rail carried out a £20m contract involving replacement of approximately 20 miles of track on the Manchester Metrolink Bury and Altrincham lines during 2007. Other recent projects to enhance the UK railway recently have included the reconstruction of Leven viaduct, Cumbria; and station upgrades and construction for Laing Rail.

Following Carillion's takeover of McAlpine, it worked with Network Rail on the £15m project at Manchester Airport to build a third platform. This is aimed at relieving congestion and improving operational flexibility, leading to better punctuality and reliability of trains.

For Aylesbury Vale Parkway, Chiltern Railways' new station 3km north of Aylesbury, Carillion Rail and Carillion Civil Engineering are the contractors, with Mott MacDonald (track and civil engineering design) and Delta Rail (signalling design support).

£280million of revenue was generated from Carillion's rail sector in 2007 (2006: £368 million). Track renewal work valued at about £80million of annual revenue was taken over by other contractors from January 2008.

Colas Rail

Colas Rail Ltd was created in May 2007 after Amec Spie Rail was taken over by the French infrastructure company Colas, part of the Bouygues group. An integrated management structure now embraces both Colas Rail Ltd and Seco Rail Ltd, another UK subsidiary of Colas.

Colas Rail Ltd combines the engineering skills of specialist businesses to provide total solutions in all aspects of railway infrastructure, from high speed rail systems to light and urban rail.

In January 2008, Colas Rail announced its purchase of Carillion's rail plant business, giving it the largest fleet of modern on-track plant in the UK. Associated contracts were also transferred.

Among the plant involved were 12 tampers, a 125-tonne Kirow Crane, and 16 switch handling units. Charles-Albert Giral, Chief Executive Officer, commented, 'We are delighted to have secured this contract and the acquisition ties in with our long-term strategy. Colas Rail Ltd will continue to deliver these contracts for Network Rail offering a quality service, delivered on time, on budget and most importantly safely.'

Colas begin its first commercial freight operations in the UK in 2007. Four Class 47 locomotives have been purchased to haul ballast cleaners, tampers and railhead treatment trains, and may also be used for freight operations. Colas has also extended its multi-purpose vehicle and railhead treatment contract with Network Rail and said it would continuing to invest in plant on a selective basis to meet the growing demands of the rail market.

Colas' project work has included extensions of the Docklands Light Railway (including the current extension to Woolwich), infrastructure installation for High Speed 1, the Edinburgh Waverley remodelling project, and electrification work for Network Rail.

As part of its restructuring, Amec in 2007 sold its remaining 50% interest in Amec Spie Rail Systems Limited to Colas for an undisclosed sum. In July 2006, Amec had sold the France-based Spie business and 50% of Amec Spie Rail to a new company controlled by PAI-Partners-managed funds, for approximately £707million. Colas also acquired this 50% of the rail business in 2007.

GrantRail

GrantRail is a UK-based group of companies, formed through a joint venture between Volker Wessels and Corus, providing a wide range of contracting services to the railway industry - including projects and specialised operations including signalling, welding, plant and overhead power supply.

Volker Wessels is one of the Netherlands' largest civil engineering companies with extensive experience in rail infrastructure construction, renewal and maintenance. Corus (now part of the Indian group, Tata) is a global industrial concern with a range of established rail-related businesses in the UK and France.

GrantRail has successfully undertaken work on projects including the West Anglia Route Modernisation, and track construction work for

In association with **SPERRY RAIL**

invensys rail group
WESTINGHOUSE rail systems

SPEEDING UP SCOTLAND
WE DELIVER

In Scotland, Westinghouse is helping to deliver a faster, more dependable and efficient rail service, with the highest safety standards.

After the success of Edinburgh Waverley's resignalling and new Integrated Electronic Control Centre (IECC), WRSL Regional Director Alistair McWhirter commented, "A major factor in the project's success was the smooth integration with Network Rail's multi-disciplinary team – we were all delighted when we got it right first time"

"Now it's the turn of Airdrie to Bathgate – with signalling and telecoms for the new double track. Plus we're busy installing a WESTLOCK interlocking to maximise capacity at Scotland's busiest station, Glasgow Central. We're committed to delivering safe, successful solutions."

We can help make your next project a success

Call us now on **+44 (0) 1249 441 441**
or email **marketing@wrsl.com**

www.wrsl.com

When Did YOU Last Get Your Head Examined?

SPERRY RAIL INTERNATIONAL LTD.
a Rockwood Company

Not your head exactly, but your rail head. You can't be too careful you know. It only takes one defect to cause a rail break. Don't panic - we can help you.

Sperry Rail is the world leader is ultrasonic rail flaw detection services. With our unique test system we can test your rails with ease. We test 98% of the entire rail head and even take dipped joints in our stride.

Whether using train-borne or pedestrian test systems, our team of ultrasonic specialists has a wealth of experience across the globe, in greatly differing environments. From the chills of Northern Europe to the heat in India, Sperry Rail tests it all.

To find out more about how you can get your head examined, call Sperry Rail now on +44 (0) 1332 262565. We're a cracking good company!

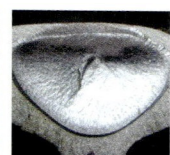

SPERRY RAIL – Trent House, RTC Business Park, London Road, Derby. DE24 8UP. UK.   Tel: +44 (0) 1332 262565   Fax: +44 (0) 1332

HSBC

Infrastructure Maintenance & Renewal

Trackbed consolidation under way in June 2008 for the new Down Fast line, as part of remodelling work to improve track capacity at Milton Keynes. Network Rail

mass transit schemes including metro programmes for Sunderland, the West Midlands, Manchester and Nottingham.

In October 2007, GrantRail was awarded a £9.5million contract by Network Rail to undertake the Hull Docks Branch Enhancement project, including permanent way, civil, power supply, signaling & telecommunications elements. GrantRail Projects Division, as the Principal Contractor, was supported by GrantRail Signalling and Fitzpatrick Contractors Limited (part of Volker Wessels) to offer an integrated technical solution.

GrantRail Projects, as part of the M-Pact Thales consortium, has been awarded the construction and maintenance contract on the Manchester Metrolink Phase 3a extension project. A joint venture of GrantRail and Skanska has won two contracts - including the £67m main construction contract - for the Docklands Light Railway's Stratford International extension.

VCV (Modular) Ltd - a joint venture between GrantRail and Corus Cogifer (the UK rail infrastructure businesses of Vossloh, Corus and Volker Wessels) - has secured a key partnership role with Network Rail to develop modular systems and processes for switch & crossing replacement, in line with Network Rail's drive to pioneer switch & crossing renewal in 8hr possessions.

In June 2006, Network Rail awarded GrantRail a £16million West Coast main line contract for the design and implementation of the Nuneaton Area Remodelling.

GrantRail and Volker Stevin have joined forces in a project to introduce the prefabricated concrete Harmelen level crossings, designed for heavy duty use, to the UK.

GrantRail lifted its turnover to £120m in 2007 and pre-tax profit to £3.1m, compared to a 2006 pre-tax profit of £2.1m and turnover of £110m.

Jarvis

Jarvis plc is an infrastructure support services group which is focused on its core competencies in rail, plant and freight.

Jarvis Rail is the rail engineering arm of the business which undertakes rail enhancement projects, signalling and telecommunications, overhead line and track renewals across the UK. Fastline, the company's plant division, provides on-track machinery, specialist plant and small plant equipment as well as an extensive fleet of commercial vehicles. The final element of the business is Fastline Freight (see 'Freight and Haulage' section).

In the 2007-08 financial year, Jarvis Rail reported a 45% increase in revenue. This was predominantly due to increased work on a number of high profile enhancement projects including Rugby station remodelling, Airdrie-Bathgate, Glasgow Airport Rail Link and Thameslink.

Jarvis Rail secured substantial new Network Rail contract work, including four-tracking on Trent Valley, several stages of the West Coast Line Speed Enhancement project, and the Ipswich to Ely gauge enhancement. The rationalisation of track renewals contractors by Network Rail also saw Jarvis Rail extend its London North Eastern (LNE) territory significantly to include the Midlands region, and the switch & crossing framework contract in Scotland transferred to another contractor in early 2008.

The division's Electrical Projects Group has also been very active with continued signalling and multidisciplinary infrastructure renewals including high profile projects such as the Brough East signalling and level crossing renewal and the Durham Coast interlocking renewal.

Fastline offers an innovative and integrated approach supplying the rail industry with a wide range of on track machines, specialist and small plant. By incorporating small plant, on-track machines and transport within one business, Fastline is able to create solutions for projects that both improve efficiency and reduce costs.

Fastline also operates and maintains a total of 64 machines owned by Network Rail, including six multi-purpose vehicles which undertake seasonal railhead treatments and weed killing.

Fastline continues to operate a fleet of four Stoneblowers for Network Rail, and a contract for 2008-09 was secured for the operation of Network Rail's High Output System 1 including two Medium Output Ballast Cleaners.

An innovation developed in house is an automatic lifting beam for use with Fastline's track renewal system, Slinger. This has been designed to reduce the necessity for the workforce to work at height when loading panel lengths of track on to wagons, providing a safe and efficient handling solution.

In the year to 31 March 2008, Jarvis's Rail business reported an operating profit of £9.5m (previous year £2.6m) on revenue of £206.3m (2007: £142.3m). Plant - which includes the Fastline Freight business for reporting purposes - delivered an operating profit of £4.5m (2007: £4m) on £88.5m revenue (2007: £103.8m). Both these figures are reported after the deduction of central recharges.

Signalling & Control

In association with

invensys rail group
WESTINGHOUSE rail systems

Signalling & Control

Invensys WESTINGHOUSE rail systems

New Modular Signalling solution offers cost-effective performance

Westinghouse Rail Systems Limited (WRSL), part of Invensys Rail Group, is a world leader in advanced signalling and integrated control systems for mainline and mass transit railways. The company has been signalling railways for over 140 years, with products and systems at the heart of many of the world's major rail networks - from simple, single lines to heavy haul freight, inter-city, suburban and urban mass transit systems.

With a commitment to research and development and an absolute focus on safety, combined with unrivalled engineering expertise and a determination to meet the evolving needs of its customers, Westinghouse has consistently delivered significant technological advancements to the market. Today, the company is at the leading edge of providing safer, more efficient transport services, delivering exceptional systems for world class railway operators.

The company's advanced range of products, integrated systems and services combine to provide fully integrated, tailored solutions - from initial system design right through to manufacture, installation, testing, commissioning, training and maintenance.

With a portfolio that ranges from colour light signals to fully integrated control systems, and from safety relays and complete level crossing solutions to computer-based interlockings, solutions may be configured to meet specific project needs – whether that is for a routine system upgrade or a completely new signalling and control scheme.

At the heart of many schemes lies the WESTRACE vital logic system, which has now been installed in over 1,200 operational applications worldwide. The system's versatile modules deliver almost any vital functionality - including interlockings, radio block systems, trackside and on-board Automatic Train Protection, level crossing control and safe data transmission for centralised traffic control systems.

WESTRACE is a key component in the company's new Modular Signalling solution, which has been developed to meet a wide range of applications - particularly secondary routes or rural lines where it is becoming increasingly difficult for railway operators to build a business case for resignalling schemes.

Operational railways not only require control systems to be available 24 hours a day, 7 days a week, but also need those systems to be commissioned and maintained with a minimum of disruption. WRSL's Modular Signalling approach enables any signalling scheme to be implemented from a small range of core components, providing railway operators with the means of achieving cost-effective performance and reducing whole life costs - including both capital and operational expenditure. The system provides value for money, is future proof, fully ETCS compatible and is capable of being delivered in the minimum time.

The development of new Modular Signalling techniques complements WRSL's existing services, further extending its capability and, as part of its commitment to continuous improvement, the company aims to introduce additional Modular Signalling techniques and practices across a range of conventional projects.

A time-sensitive project at Edinburgh Waverley replaced the old geographical interlocking with four new Westinghouse Solid State Interlockings (SSIs). They were commissioned in 53 hours, significantly improving signalling availability with minimal changes to track layout and railway operation. Three new SSIs for the Airdrie-Bathgate project will be controlled from Edinburgh.

UK projects

Westinghouse has delivered solutions across the world – with both mainline and metro systems operating in Asia, Mainland Europe, Scandinavia, North America and the UK.

Against the background of its core business, which includes Network Rail Type A and Type E framework agreements, WRSL is involved in major mainline and metro infrastructure projects across the UK. This includes the Reading Redevelopment, Thameslink, Airdrie to Bathgate, Glasgow Central and London Underground Victoria Line programmes, with the company providing high quality solutions together with expert support, advice and service based on proven project management skills.

In September 2008, Westinghouse began work at Reading, having been awarded a £20million contract by Network Rail to undertake the signalling enabling works which represent the first stage of the £425m Reading Redevelopment Project. One of the major hubs in the UK rail network, the current configuration of Reading station means that traffic is often delayed – a situation which could only be addressed by a re-modelling of the tracks and station layout, with new and extended platforms and an elevated track to untangle the lines.

The 30 month programme of enabling works includes a series of 12 commissionings, which will see Westinghouse re-lock the existing Reading station and Spur interlockings to three new WESTLOCK units, re-control the remaining 18 relay interlockings and move signalling and telecommunications control from Reading station to the new Thames Valley Signalling Centre at Didcot.

Westinghouse Rail Systems commissioned a WESTeX GCP3000 Level Crossing Predictor (LCP) system for a pilot trial with the Finnish Rail Administration Ratahallintokeskus in 2008. The LCP is also being introduced on Network Rail and offers a significant reduction in both the amount of equipment required and the overall project cost, as well as specific performance and operational benefits which considerably improve the efficiency of the crossing.

Critical to the selection of WESTLOCK was Network Rail's requirement for the enabling works to be non-disruptive and for the chosen technology to allow future migration to ERTMS signalling solutions. WESTLOCK is a high capacity, ERTMS-ready interlocking solution with proven performance both in the UK and mainland Europe. Each unit typically provides four times more capacity than a Solid State Interlocking, providing headroom for future expansion and delivering significant cost savings compared to conventional technology.

In Scotland, the company was awarded the contract to design, install and commission the signalling and telecommunications infrastructure for the Airdrie-Bathgate (A2B) Rail Link.

This line, which is being re-opened to passengers after over 50 years, brings considerable benefits for communities along the route by improving transport links for West Lothian and North Lanarkshire with Glasgow and Edinburgh. On completion, the line will be double-tracked and electrified from Edinburgh to Glasgow, providing a fourth passenger route between the two cities. The first phase of this £300million project, funded by Transport Scotland, saw the commissioning of the new double-tracked line between Bathgate and Edinburgh in October 2008.

The key elements of WRSL's work on the A2B project include modifications to the two existing Integrated Electronic Control Centres. The route will be controlled from Edinburgh Signalling Centre (fringing with Yoker Signalling Centre), where there have been signalling alterations to support the operation of the new double-track line and the new and altered stations. In addition, the installation of three new Solid State Interlockings - to be controlled from one of the new IECC workstations at Edinburgh - and the installation of full telecommunications systems for the stations complete this broad ranging project.

These are just a few examples of the many projects that Westinghouse is engaged in across the world – as it continues to deliver high-performing, cost-effective solutions to the world's railway operators.

One hundred SSI Interlockings have been successfully commissioned in Portugal by the Dimetronic/Westinghouse consortium and Portuguese Railways (REFER), including 300km of main line to the south and west of Lisbon supervised from two High Integrity CTC Centres, and the main line from the Lisbon Coast to the Algarve.

Signalling & Control

A total of almost £2.5bn of signalling renewals expenditure is expected from 2009 until March 2014. Tony Miles

Signalling and control

Plans for implementing the European Rail Traffic Management System have shaped the scope and timing of signalling renewals

A total of almost £2,500m of expenditure on signalling renewals is allowed for on signalling in Control Period 4 (CP4 - April 2009 until March 2014), in the Office of Rail Regulation's (ORR's) final determination of Network Rail funding, published in October 2008.

Just over half the expenditure is for the planned renewal of 5,300 signalling equivalent units (SEUs - a unit cost measure) - this represents a reduction in ORR's determination from NR's proposed 5,971 SEUs.

Most of this is for complete renewal of interlockings, but it includes some partial equipment renewals. This volume of work is close to the total likely to have been delivered by the end of CP3 in March 2009, but the CP4 workload is expected to avoid the peaks and troughs that ORR says have characterised the 2004-09 period.

The plans are based on roll-out of the full European Rail Traffic Management System (ERTMS) over the long term. The system includes automatic train protection and in-cab signalling, providing movement authority directly and continuously to the train driver. The long-run unit rate for ERTMS infrastructure fitment has been estimated at around 60% of the cost for conventional resignalling - but as trial and migration schemes carry a significant premium, the effective unit rate for ERTMS infrastructure fitment in CP4 was expected to be higher, on average, than the cost for conventional resignalling.

After study by the industry, a realistic and affordable ERTMS roll-out was thought possible if close integration with the signalling and rolling stock renewals programmes is achieved. Migration towards ERTMS technology is expected during CP4, and the roll-out plan has been further integrated with the conventional signalling plan, including alignment with other discipline's renewals, and major enhancement programmes such as Thameslink.

What ORR describes as the 'emerging proposals' for implementing ERTMS have strongly shaped the scope and timing of the condition-led conventional signalling renewals programme, to the extent that Network Rail reduced its forecast SEU volumes from almost 9,500 in earlier plans. At the same time it has increased the scope of the minor works and life extension programme to provide effective migration towards ERTMS implementation.

Renewals only represent part of the overall signalling workload in CP4, as there will be significant work associated with enhancement.

In association with **Invensys rail group WESTINGHOUSE rail systems**

Invensys rail group
WESTINGHOUSE rail systems

COMPLETE SOLUTIONS?
WE DELIVER

With innovative signalling and control solutions, effective management and the support of the worldwide Invensys Rail group, Westinghouse will bring superior performance to your railway.

Find out how we can help your business

Call us now on **+44 (0) 1249 441 441**
or email **marketing@wrsl.com**
www.wrsl.com

---

nelsons
www.nelsonslaw.co.uk

one source of solutions

Rail projects can be complex and demanding, making informed advice one of the highest priorities for success.

One place the industry can rely on for effective solutions is Nelsons Solicitors.

Our specialist experience advising on high speed, underground and light rail projects embraces manufacturing, renovation, service and parts supply functions as well as regulatory matters including depot management, leases and licences.

We can also advise you on all business-to-business endeavours including contract drafting and negotiation, agency and distribution agreements, franchising, know-how agreements, supply and purchase contracts, intellectual property, business trading, data protection and UK and EU competition.

Talk to the one firm who really can clear the track for your project – call Michelle Craven on 0800 0241 976.

Nelsons Solicitors LLP
Derby • Leicester • Nottingham

Signalling & Control

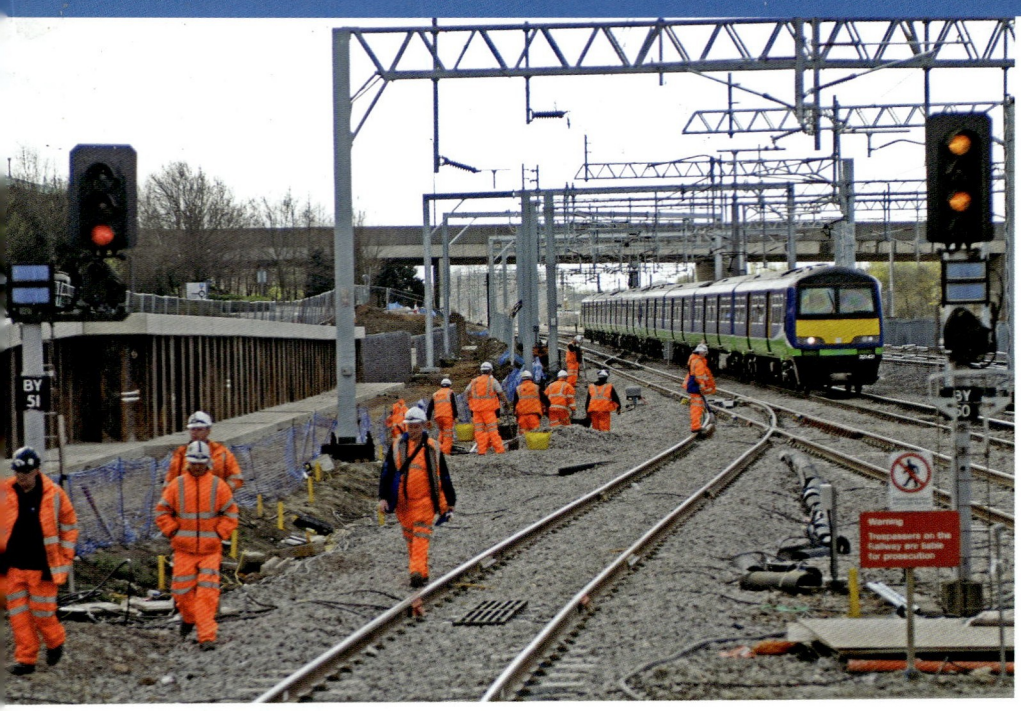

Resignalling at Milton Keynes as part of the area's capacity improvement project was due for final commissioning at the turn of 2008-09. Tony Miles

Taking renewals and enhancements together, the volume of work in CP4 is estimated to be 9,680 SEUs, with annual levels between 1,600 and 2,400 SEUs, peaking in 2011-12. A key issue for CP4 is the deliverability challenge that this poses to Network Rail and its suppliers, says ORR.

Unlike other asset types, forecasting of signalling renewal volumes is not reliant upon statistical modelling, comments ORR, as Network Rail's SICA (Signalling Infrastructure Condition Assessment) tool is a well established procedure for assessing the condition and estimating the remaining life of its signalling installations. This means that it is able to generate a future work plan with robust information about the scope, timing and priorities of resignalling activities based on the condition and performance of individual interlockings.

Network Rail has also improved its knowledge about the condition of level crossings on the network and how it applies that knowledge to forecast level crossing renewals. Its plans for CP4 represent a doubling of current activity levels to an average of 40 crossings a year.

ORR considers it likely that Network Rail will need to make further deferrals of signalling renewals during CP4, not least as it implements the lessons learned about avoiding over-extending its resources following recent project overruns.

Forecast expenditure in 2008/09 was reduced substantially, as a result of reprioritisation of commissioning of signalling schemes to support the West Coast route modernisation project. The major schemes deferred were Colchester-Clacton, South Erewash, Newport and Oxley.

Signal developments

Hitachi ETCS trial
Hitachi Europe is running a trial alongside Network Rail to test and introduce a signalling system compatible with the European Train Control System (ETCS). The system is based on an Automatic Train Protection (ATP) system used in Tokyo, as well as on the Shinkansen high-speed train.

Hitachi and Network Rail plan to have a demonstration train running by 2010/2011 and the results of the tests will be shared with the appropriate UK and European technical bodies.

Alistair Dormer, general manager, Rail Systems Group at Hitachi Europe, said: 'We are delighted to have the opportunity to work with Network Rail on a project to bring our highly reliable signalling service to the UK market. Through the launch of our ETCS-compatible signalling system, we hope to make major contributions to the UK ERTMS National Implementation plan that will ultimately help to improve overall conditions on the rail infrastructure across Europe.'

Ansaldo ERTMS contract
Network Rail awarded Ansaldo the contract for the first, design stage of the £60million project for the implementation of the European Rail Traffic Management System (ERTMS) in the UK. The project team includes Ansaldo's French sister company CSEE, French consultancy Systra and Ansaldo Signal UK.

NR said it was awarded to Ansaldo because of its significant experience in designing and implementing ERTMS systems in Italy, Spain and France.

Thales Tube contracts
Tube Lines has awarded contracts to Thales's rail signalling solutions business (formerly of Alcatel) to provide new signalling systems on the London Underground Piccadilly Line by 2014, the Jubilee Line in 2009 and Northern Line in 2011. The new Seltrac system will be similar to that in place on the Docklands Light Railway to enable trains to safely run faster and more frequently. On the Piccadilly Line, together with a new fleet of trains, it is expected to result in a 20% increase in capacity and improved reliability.

Thales has also won a resignalling contract worth £10.4million to provide the London Underground's Neasden depot with its modular interlocking system, LockTrac 6172 PMI, to improve the expanded depot's signalling control functionality. Thales is also to supply telecommunication services for Transport for London's extended East London Railway, and tis providing an integrated communication and supervision system for the Tyne & Wear Metro. Thales will also deliver the entire electromechanical systems for the extension of Metrolink in Manchester.

Signalling Solutions' new interlocking
Signalling Solutions Ltd, the 50-50 joint venture company formed by Alstom Transport Information Solutions and Balfour Beatty Rail Projects, is now the UK and Ireland's sole channel for signalling products and systems previously supplied by the parent companies.

Table 1 - ORR conclusions - signalling renewal expenditure 2009-14 £m (2006-07 prices) before efficiency savings

	Network Rail SBP (April 08)	ORR determination (Oct 08)
Conventional resignalling (full & partial)	1,282	1,217
Minor works & life extension	468	444
Level crossing renewals	220	209
ERTMS	350	350
Mechanical locking refurbishment	50	47
Other (safety and central costs)	195	187
Total	2,565	2,454

SBP - Strategic Business Plan, containing Network Rail's proposals for 2009-14.

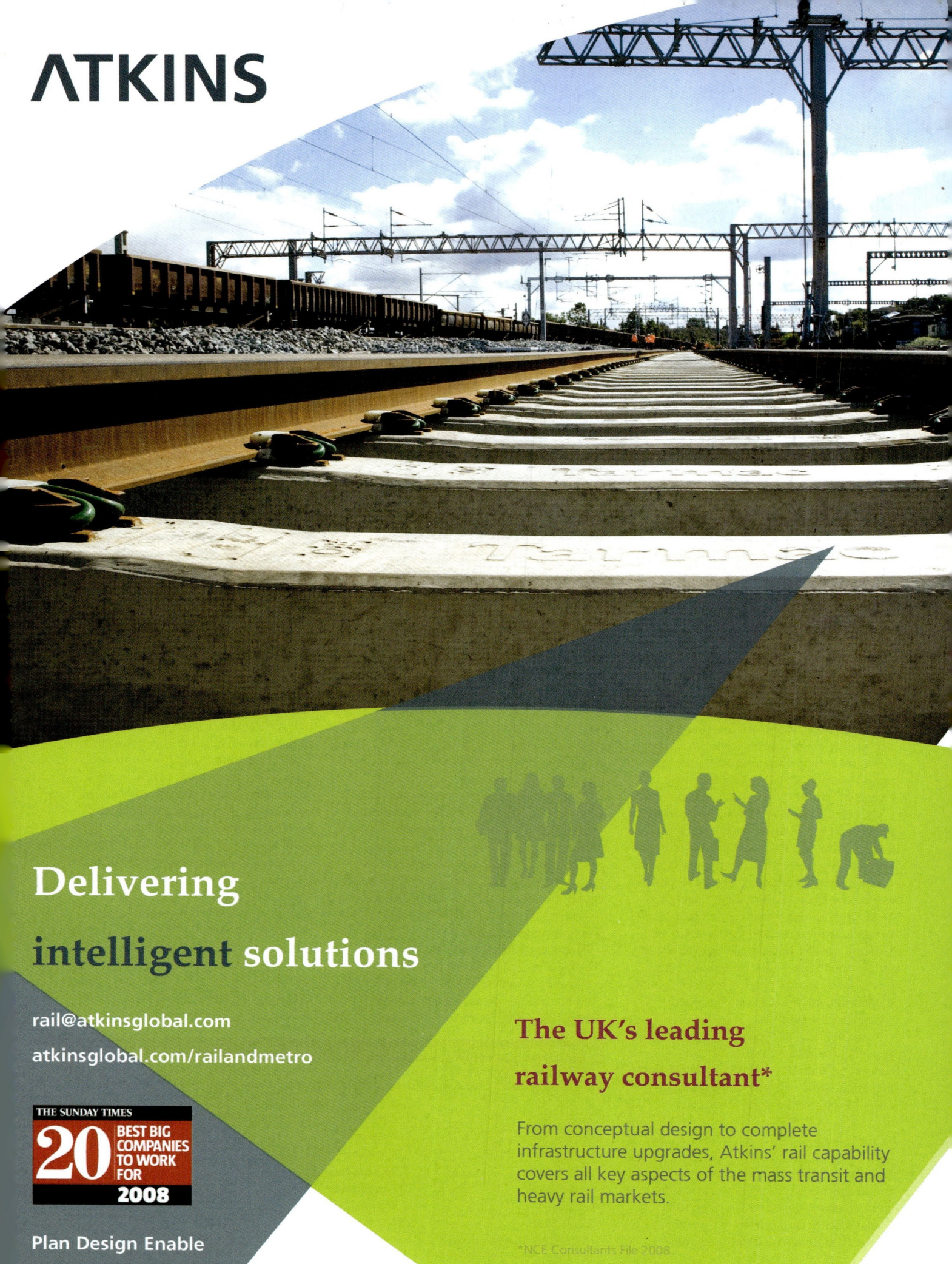

ATKINS

Delivering

intelligent solutions

rail@atkinsglobal.com

atkinsglobal.com/railandmetro

THE SUNDAY TIMES
20 BEST BIG COMPANIES TO WORK FOR **2008**

Plan Design Enable

The UK's leading railway consultant*

From conceptual design to complete infrastructure upgrades, Atkins' rail capability covers all key aspects of the mass transit and heavy rail markets.

*NCE Consultants File 2008

Signalling & Control

Arlesford level crossing, following its successful commissioning by Signalling Solutions Ltd as part of the Colchester to Clacton resignalling project in October 2008. Signalling Solutions Ltd

Signalling Solutions' collective in-house expertise offers a complete range of capabilities including planning, design, product supply, installation, testing and commissioning for all types of railways.

The company has been heavily involved in work on the infrastructure upgrade on West Coast main line. In August 2008, the company continued stage commissionings for the Milton Keynes project, including installation of points and forming of a temporary fringe to Bletchley power signalbox. The main commissioning of this project was take place over the Christmas period. The major, final commissioning of the Trent Valley four tracking project also took place in August 2008, bringing increased capacity in terms of frequency and speed.

For the Gretna to Annan project, which has reinstated eight miles of double track railway, SSL commissioned the signalling and telecoms work on behalf of Balfour Beatty Rail Projects.

Alstom's Smartlock 400T interlocking system was commissioned by Signalling Solutions at Three Bridges Area Signalling Centre in October 2008, controlling the Horsham area. This new system replaces the three existing Alstom Solid State Interlockings (SSI) with a single, high capacity central interlocking, new support system and trackside interface communications cubicle.

Smartlock 400T is capable of controlling an area equivalent to eight SSIs, utilising a new concept of 'virtual' interlockings within the processor, significantly reducing the time taken to set routes across interlocking boundaries.

Arup

Arup has extensive experience in the design and specification of signalling systems up to and including detailed design stage (GRIP 5).

As designers, Arup's team has also supported the Test and Commissioning Stages (GRIP 5).

This experience has been gained on re-signalling projects, Switch and Crossing renewals work and major scheme developments ranging from the feasibility work to complex scheme signalling plans. Such projects include: Network Rail S&C renewals, including major S&C renewals project such as Shields Junction; substantial remodelling projects such as Edinburgh Waverley; general infrastructure re-instatement projects such as East London Line (ELL); and major re-signalling schemes such as Sheerness and Montrose.

Atkins signalling

Atkins has been associated with virtually every major UK rail industry and infrastructure renewal and upgrade project over the past 10 years, and so lays claim to a strong record of implementing and delivering major infrastructure projects.

With 240 signalling design engineers, the company has one of the largest railway design capabilities in the country, with teams working on a series of technically challenging signalling renewals projects in the UK.

Recent projects include West Coast RuN (Rugby-Nuneaton), a key element of the programme to deliver improved West Coast main line journey times, valued at about £350m, and delivering remodelled station areas at both Rugby and Nuneaton, new train control and indication at Rugby signalling control centre, and 16 new solid state interlockings, alongside upgraded overhead line electrification, telecoms and power systems.

Atkins Rail's contract covers the design, construct, testing and commissioning of 16 interlockings and modification of five adjacent interlockings. The project is one of four major projects migrating control to Rugby, and Atkins was appointed as design authority to help manage the logistics and design requirements of the large number of commissionings.

For the Basingstoke Area Infrastructure Upgrade Project, Atkins was awarded a £65million contract for signalling design, installation, testing and commissioning, together with all associated civil and electrical design and installation. The project - involving eight solid state interlockings and a new signalling control centre - is an early application of the Hub and Spoke Management and Procurement model developed by Network Rail, which is the Hub Manager and Client for the project.

Atkins consultants have also been advising on the development and implementation of Network Rail's £1billion programme of resignalling for the Midland main line.

Major resignalling frameworks

Network Rail's current signalling 'framework' agreements for major resignalling schemes were awarded in 2006. Estimated values for works in the first three years of the agreements were:

Area	Contractor	Est value for 3 years
North Thames	Alstom *	£50m
South Thames	Siemens	£48m
East Midlands	Westinghouse	£73m
West Midlands	Westinghouse	£105m
Glasgow	Westinghouse	£42m
South Wales	Atkins	£95m
(*Now Signalling Solutions)		

Light Rail & Metro

In association with **Transit**

Light Rail & Metro

An impression of new CAF-built trams in Princes Street, Edinburgh. TIE

Light Rail and Metro

Growth continues on most light rail and metro systems as new technologies step forward

Growth was experienced on most of Britain's light rail systems in 2007-08, and construction has got under way on the new Edinburgh tram system. New technologies are being adopted in the change to Parry People Mover operation of the Stourbridge Town branch line, and the decision to explore the possibilities of Tram-Trains, with trials starting on the Penistone line. These trials are proposed to continue with through running to Rotherham using both Sheffield Supertram and Network Rail lines.

Manchester Metrolink is moving forward with big changes, as new operator Stagecoach and Greater Manchester Passenger Transport Executive work together to renew the existing system and deliver the Phase 3a extensions. Despite line closures for refurbishment in the summer, growth on the system resumed in 2007/08, after a small decline in 2006/07. Work is under way on the extensions, with tram services scheduled to start running to Chorlton and Central Park in spring 2011, Oldham in autumn 2011, and to Rochdale and Droylsden in spring 2012. The first of 40 new Bombardier trams will arrive in the city in 2009.

Centro continues to prepare the ground for the proposed extension of the Midland Metro's original Snow Hill-Wolverhampton line into Birmingham city centre, but meanwhile patronage on that original line continues to be stuck at around the 4.8m to 5million range, falling back to the bottom end in 2007-08.

Nottingham faced a reopened public inquiry into its proposals for lines 2 and 3 of the Nottingham Express Transit system, extending it southwards to Clifton and Beeston/Chilwell. The decision of the inquiry was expected in 2009, after which the competition to let a new contract could begin. Meanwhile, the original lines from Station Street to Phoenix Park and Hucknall continued to do well, with patronage growing by another 2.0% in 2007-08.

A 5.7% increase in passenger numbers in 2007-08 meant another record-breaking year for the Sheffield Supertram system, as developments continued, with such innovations as a dedicated feeder bus service from the Stocksbridge and Oughtibridge areas to the Middlewood tram stop.

Growth was recorded on the Tyne & Wear Metro system for the second year in succession, welcome news after a difficult few years. Passenger numbers rose by 5.7% in 2007-08, taking the total to a level not seen for more than a decade. Meanwhile, the Passenger Transport Executive is proceeding with its £350million modernisation programme. Market testing is also being planned for letting an operating franchise from April 2010.

After Transport for London's takeover of the Croydon Tramlink system in 2008, work was forging ahead to upgrade the system and expand services to cope with growing demand. Tramlink saw the largest growth of any UK light rail system in 2007-08, with a 10.6% increase in patronage. Plans to extend the system, which TfL had been working on, have been put on ice by the Mayor of London, Boris Johnson.

As London's Docklands Light Railway makes preparations for the opening of its latest extension, under the Thames to Woolwich Arsenal, early in 2009, the system continues to grow, although its immediate future must be clouded by fears over job losses in the City and at Canary Wharf following the credit crunch. Meanwhile, patronage was 4.2% up in 2007-08, with passenger kilometres rising by over 8% - implying longer journeys on the lines.

Construction work on the project to double capacity by 2010 is also well under way, while the system will reach Stratford International from Canning Town well in time for the Olympics in 2012. The Mayor Of London, Boris Johnson, has decided to suspend the project for an eastward DLR extension to Dagenham Dock, for which funding had not yet been identified.

Light rail and metro networks

Blackpool Tramway

Key statistics 2007/08:
Passenger journeys (millions)	2.9
Passenger km (millions)	8.7
Route km open for passengers	18
Stops served	121
Passenger revenue (£m)	3.9

The Blackpool Tramway's 17.8km route runs along the seafront between Starr Gate in the south and Fleetwood in the north. The last 1.8km section to Fleetwood is a traditional on-street operation; the rest is segregated. System usage has been in slow but long term decline.

The infrastructure is owned by the local authority and operation is by Blackpool Transport Services Ltd. A mixed fleet of 75 cars dates back to 1901, though the newest were built between 1984 and 1993. They comprise single and double deckers and include open, illuminated and vintage vehicles. Electrification is at 550V DC.

In February 2008, government funding of £60.3m, matched by £12.5m from each of Blackpool Council and Lancashire County Council, was agreed for upgrading the system. This will also see the construction of 16 new modern trams, though the best of the older vehicles will be retained for summer season extras. In July 2005, government provided a grant of £11.8m to assist in emergency repairs to the infrastructure.

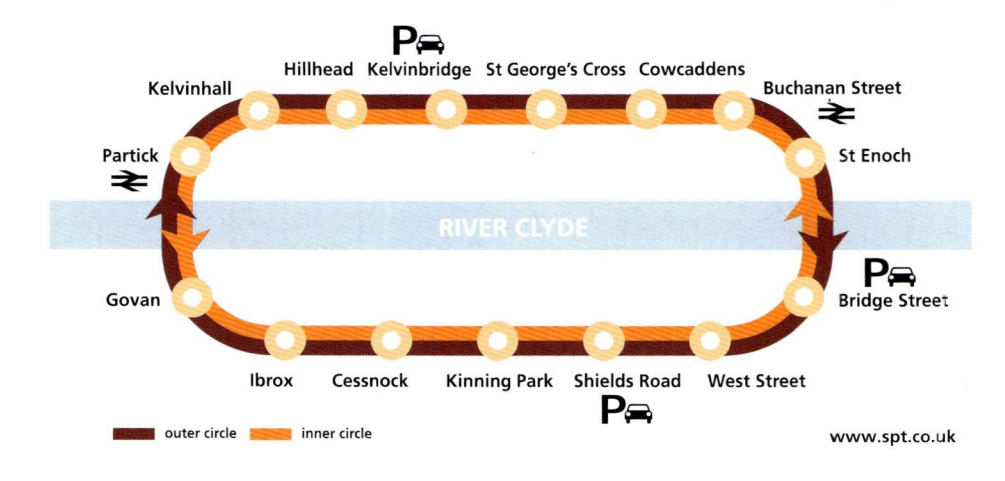

The English Concessionary Fares Scheme for the Elderly has resulted in a diversion of customers to broadly parallel bus services.

Edinburgh Tram (under construction)

The new tram route under construction is a central spine running Edinburgh Airport-Edinburgh Park-Haymarket-St Andrew's Square (for Waverley)-Newhaven.

Project management is by the city-council-owned Transport Initiatives Edinburgh (TIE), and the construction consortium consists of Bilfinger Berger, Siemens and CAF. This group is responsible for civil engineering, including earthworks, structures and roads, tracklaying, tram stop construction, electrification equipment, and communications. It will also provide the 27 CAF-built trams which, at over 40 metres, will be the longest in Great Britain.

Preparatory utility diversions are being carried out by Carillion, and the system operator will be Transdev, also responsible for technical advice.

The final price of the current phase of work (known as Phase 1a) was fixed at £512m when contracts were signed in May 2008, within a total of £545m of funding available, including £500m from the Scottish Government.

The tram depot at Gogar is due for completion in Spring 2010. That will enable the vehicles to be accepted from the manufacturers, followed by route testing and crew training before service operation commences, anticipated for July 2011.

Subsequent construction envisaged, though still to be funded, is for Phase 1b, Haymarket-Granton; Phase 2, Newhaven-Granton, completing a loop; and Phase 3, Ingliston-Newbridge North.

Glasgow Subway

Key statistics 2007/08:
Passenger journeys (millions)	14.45
Passenger km (millions)	46.3
Route km open for passengers	10
Stations served	15
Passenger revenue (£m)	13.7

The number of passengers using the Glasgow Subway - 14.45m journeys in the year to the end of March 2008 - was the highest recorded in seven years.

Operator Strathclyde Partnership for Transport announced plans in 2008 to spend more than £8m as part of an overall modernisation, including £2.6m on a digital radio system on trains, £900,000 for trailer car refurbishment, £750,000 on tunnel reinforcement, £500,000 on a new Subway

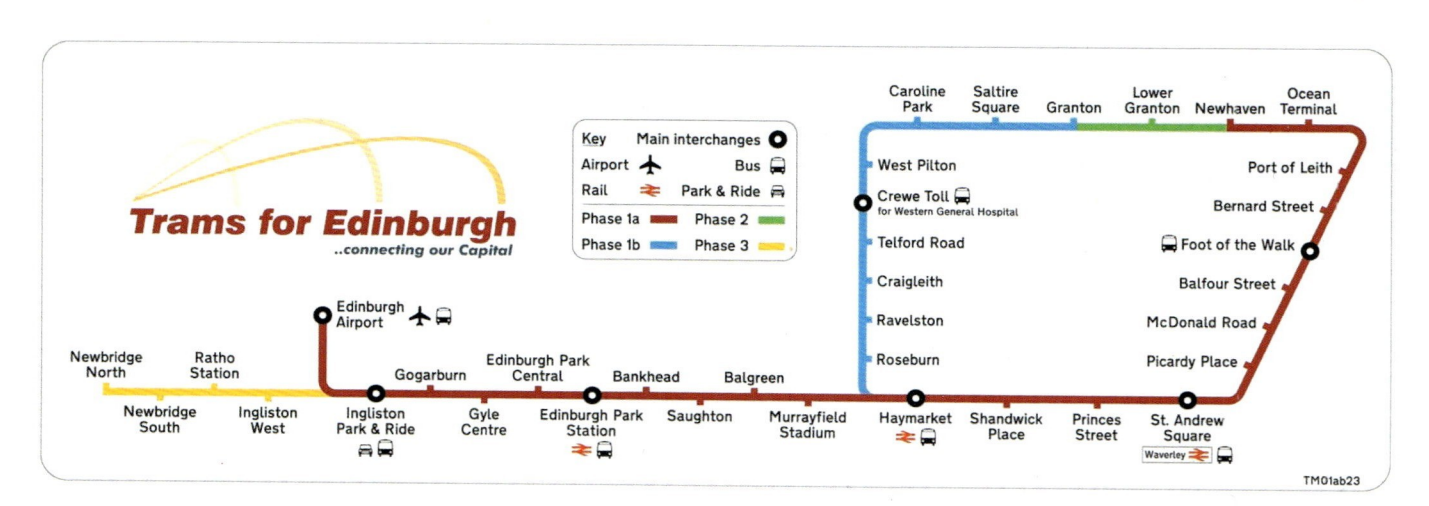

Light Rail & Metro

Large scale reconstruction and renewal work was completed in 1980. Metro-Cammell built a series of 33 power cars to run as 2-car trains, and a further eight trailers by Hunslet TPL entered service in 1992. Cars are a diminutive 12 metres in length and a three car set has 112 seats and space for about 165 standing. Automatic Train Operation is used.

The option of an additional Eastern Subway at a cost of about £2.3billion has been rejected. A more affordable scheme, using light rail vehicles and with extensive use of abandoned infrastructure, was being considered, to serve the Clyde Gateway regeneration area and Celtic Park, a key venue for the city's 2014 Commonwealth Games.

Manchester Metrolink

Key statistics 2007/08:

Passenger journeys (millions)	20.0
Passenger km (millions)	210.0
Route km open for passengers	42
Stops served	37
Passenger revenue (£m)	22.6

The genesis of Manchester Metrolink was the suburban railways to Bury and Altrincham, connected using street running in the city centre. This 31km network with a branch to Manchester Piccadilly constituted Phase 1, completed in 1992. Phase 2 saw new construction of 6km from Cornbrook to Eccles (2000).

31km of new lines are due to start opening in Greater Manchester from Spring 2011, and Greater Manchester Passenger Transport Executive (GMPTE) has appointed M-Pact Thales to design, build and maintain them as part of a £575million project. This 'Phase 3a' has received a funding package, mostly from the government, with the balance from the Passenger Transport Authority sourced from revenue over 30 years. M-Pact Thales is made up of Laing O'Rourke, GrantRail and Thales UK. The team will work closely with GMPTE staff and the Metrolink delivery partner, Parsons Brinckerhoff.

The network additions are:

- Oldham and Rochdale: 22.5km extension following an abandoned railway corridor, then taking over the existing line between Manchester, Oldham and Rochdale, with six additional stops. Northern Rail trains will cease to operate in October 2009, with bus service replacement. The direct Manchester-Rochdale rail services will not be affected.

- East Manchester: 6.3km extension to Droylsden, with eight new stops.

- South Manchester: 2.7km extension to St Werburgh's Road along abandoned railway

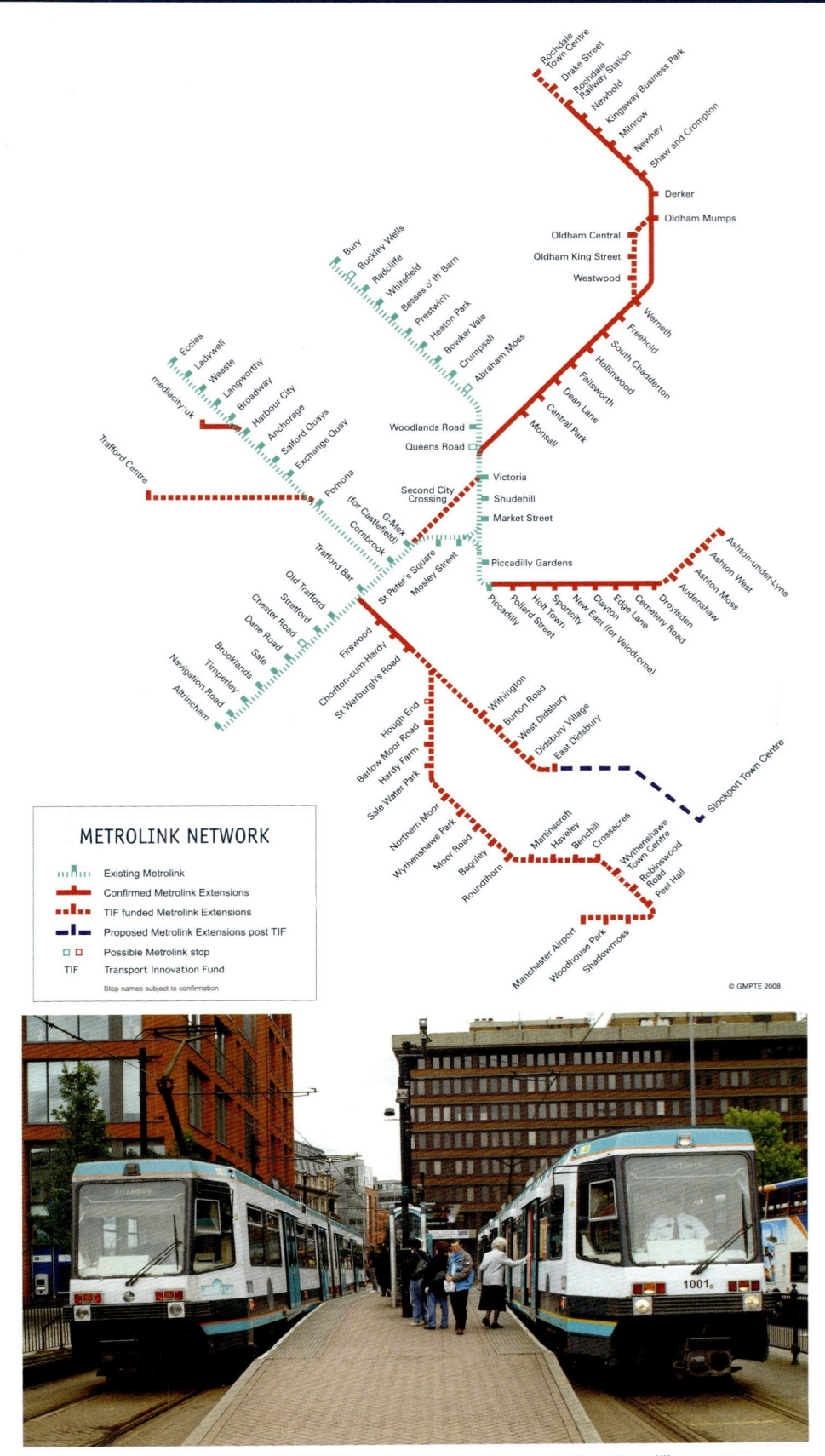

Manchester Metrolink trams pass at Piccadilly Gardens while working to and from Piccadilly – a route now to be extended to Droylsden and possibly Ashton-under-Lyne. Tony Miles

ticketing system; and £500,000 on passenger platform screens at Ibrox and Hillhead.

The Subway opened in 1896 as a cable-powered operation. It runs for 10.4km in a complete circle, with 15 stations. It is entirely underground, apart from Broomloan depot on the surface. Two separate running tunnels are to a restricted diameter of 3.35 metres and track gauge is set at the decidedly unusual 1,220mm (4ft 0in). The Subway was converted to electric operation in 1935.

corridor, with three new stops, and a new depot built at Trafford Bar.

A separate 0.4km extension to the MediaCity:UK development is related to the BBC's big move north in 2011. This £8m line, leaving the Eccles route near the Broadway stop, is funded jointly by the North West Regional Development Agency and Salford City Council.

The initial fleet of 26 two-section 29m-long cars for this 750V DC overhead-powered system was built by Firema, and increased by six built by Ansaldo for the Eccles extension. There is a single depot at Queen's Road, north of the city centre.

40 new trams (to a new design) have been ordered for the latest extensions and to relieve overcrowding. They will be delivered by Bombardier in partnership with Vossloh Kiepe.

A further Phase, 3b, would see routes to Oldham and Rochdale town centres, Ashton-under-Lyne, East Didsbury, and Manchester Airport via Wythenshawe, funded primarily from the government's Transport Innovation Fund, and from a loan supported by the introduction of a limited, peak-time only, congestion charge. There would also be a new line to Trafford Park and the Trafford Centre.

70million journeys are anticipated per year if all the new lines are built, taking the total length of the network to 103km.

Tram-Train at Stourbridge

The Network Rail branch between Stourbridge Junction and Stourbridge Town is a mere 1km in length, and has been operated as a shuttle by a single diesel unit for many years. The present London Midland franchise, which includes this operation, is run by Govia.

As an experiment, a prototype Parry People Movers railcar operated by licensed train operator Pre-Metro Operations Ltd, ran on this route between December 2005 and December 2006. With over 4,000 trips operated in passenger service, reliability and punctuality stood at 99%.

Govia's introduction of lightweight Parry People Movers railcars to operate all services on the branch was due in December 2008. They use energy stored by a flywheel, which is charged by electricity from a shore supply when the vehicle is stationary. Two new PPM 60 railcars have been built by a British industrial supply chain which includes Clayton Equipment, East Lancashire Coachbuilders, Power Torque Engineering, Linde Hydraulics and Brecknell Willis Composites. They are based in a new Stourbridge Junction facility, eliminating the need for empty stock operation to and from Tyseley.

Midland Metro

Key statistics 2007/08:

Passenger journeys (millions)	4.8
Passenger km (millions)	50.0
Route km open for passengers	20
Stops served	23
Passenger revenue (£m)	4.5

Midland Metro Line 1 was built almost entirely on the formation previously used by the Great Western line between Birmingham Snow Hill and Wolverhampton. On this 20.4km route, only the last 2.3km to Wolverhampton St George's are on-street. Trams have priority on the road section of the route.

Promoted by the West Midlands Passenger Transport Authority and its Executive, now known as Centro, Line 1 opened in 1999 and is operated by Travel Metro, part of the UK Bus Division of the National Express Group. The system cost £145m, £31m of which was a European Grant.

A fleet of 16 two-section articulated cars, 24m in length, was built by Ansaldo. Electrification is at 750V DC overhead, and the depot is at Wednesbury. There are 23 tram stops along the route, each of which has CCTV linked to the Metro Centre in Wednesbury.

Proposed extensions are based on regeneration, accessibility and mobility in the areas to be served. Routes 'ready for implementation' are:

- Birmingham Snow Hill to Five Ways via Corporation Street, New Street station and Broad Street; and
- Wednesbury to Brierley Hill via Dudley town centre and Merry Hill. Westfield, owners of the major shopping centre at Merry Hill, have committed £36.5million towards the estimated £268m cost of this scheme.

Other routes still being developed are Birmingham city centre to the Airport and Great Barr; Five Ways to Quinton; and Wolverhampton to Wednesbury via Walsall.

Centro is also looking at enhancing the case for future Metro lines through shared use of rail lines using tram-trains. Possibilities include the Wednesbury-Brierley Hill and Coventry-Nuneaton corridors.

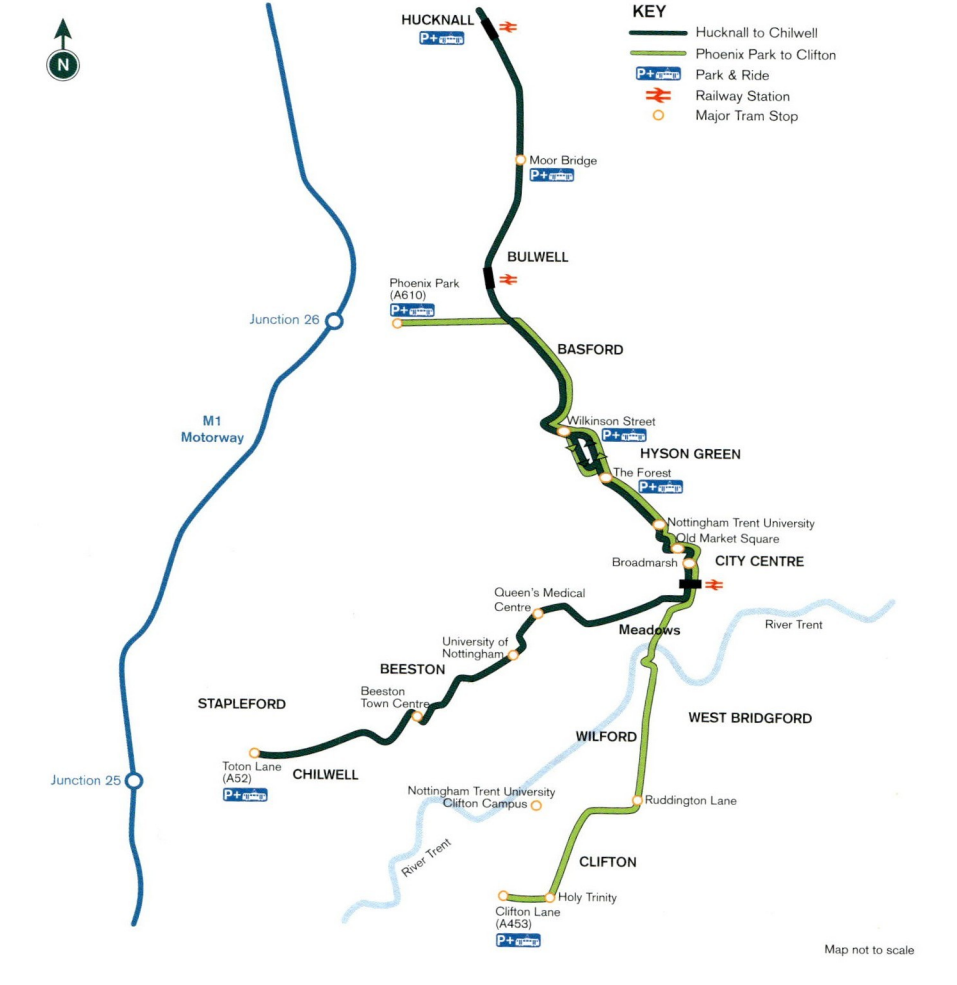

Nottingham Express Transit

Key statistics 2007/08:

Passenger journeys (millions)	10.2
Passenger km (millions)	44.0
Route km open for passengers	14
Stops served	23
Passenger revenue (£m)	7.5

Nottingham Express Transit's Line 1 runs from a site adjacent to Nottingham main-line station,

Light Rail & Metro

via the city centre on-street, and then alongside the reinstated Network Rail line which runs north towards Mansfield. From Bulwell, NET becomes single track with passing places, running parallel with the railway, also single track, to the terminus at Hucknall. A short branch leads to Phoenix Park. The system's depot is at Wilkinson Street.

The line is 14km in length, of which roundly 4km are on street and 10km beside the railway. Services commenced in 2004. The fleet consists of 15 articulated cars of 22m built by Bombardier in Derby. Electrification is at 750V DC and each car has 58 seats. Something like a quarter of all passenger journeys are to or from one of five Park & Ride sites.

Nottingham City and Nottinghamshire County councils awarded a private finance initiative (PFI) concession to Arrow Light Rail Ltd for a period of 30.5 years - the largest local authority PFI deal ever completed. Arrow is a special purpose company owned by six partners.

Arrow let a 3.5 year fixed price turnkey contract to the Bombardier Carillion consortium for the design and construction of the tram system. Bombardier provided the trams, power, signalling and communications systems, and Carillion the civil engineering, track and tram stops.

Arrow also let a contract to the Nottingham Tram Consortium (NTC), comprising Transdev and Nottingham City Transport, who are to operate and maintain the system for 27 years.

The two councils are seeking powers under the Transport & Works Act procedures to construct two further lines, for which government has announced a grant of £480m. These will continue beyond the present Nottingham station terminus. Line 2 will run 7.6km southwards to Clifton via Wilford, partly over the former Great Central Railway. Line 3 will run 9.8km southwestwards to Chilwell via Beeston.

The length of the system thus created at around 31km will be slightly more than double that of the original Line 1. A further 15 trams will be required. Assuming the application for the Transport & Works Act order is successful, construction might start in 2010, with operation from 2013.

Sheffield Supertram
Key statistics 2007/08:

Passenger journeys (millions)	14.8
Passenger km (millions)	44.4
Route km open for passengers	29
Stops served	48
Passenger revenue (£m)	11.3

Sheffield Supertram opened in eight stages in 1994/95 over a 29km network. Roundly half of this is fully segregated. The route incorporates some tight geometry, with a minimum horizontal curve radius of 25m and vertical curve of 100m. Maximum gradients are 10%.

Revenue grew by around 10% in the 12 months to April 2008, but despite the system's much improved commercial performance, plans to extend it remain on hold, forcing the PTE to propose bus-based systems instead.

The prospect of diesel tram-trains running onto the Supertram network has been raised by the planned trials of such vehicles, starting on the Sheffield-Penistone-Huddersfield line. The proposed Phase 2 of the trials would include an extension of Supertram's Meadowhall route to Rotherham via a new link in the Tinsley area onto Network Rail infrastructure.

The Supertram fleet of three-section cars of 34.8m is 25 strong; they were built by Siemens/Duewag. A £3m, three-year project to refresh the livery and interiors of the tram fleet is due for completion by early 2009. The work is also helping to maintain the fleet's high standard of reliability and has included detailed consideration of the needs of the mobility handicapped in the interiors, and some reseating. Each refreshed vehicle has 80 ordinary and six tip-up seats, with space for a nominal 164 standing. The work has been carried out by Stagecoach Supertram Maintenance Ltd in a dedicated facility at the Nunnery depot in Sheffield, helping to do more within the available budget.

Tyne & Wear Metro
Key statistics 2007/08:

Passenger journeys (millions)	39.8
Passenger km (millions)	312.8
Route km open for passengers	78
Stations served	60
Passenger revenue (£m)	34.7

The Tyne & Wear Metro was the earliest of the modern light rail systems in Britain. The initial 55km system opened in stages between 1980 and 1984; subsequent extensions have taken the Metro 4km to Newcastle Airport (1991) and Sunderland/South Hylton, 19km in 2002. This last involves running over Network Rail tracks beyond Pelaw.

The Metro was created from the former British Rail lines radiating from Newcastle on both the north and south sides of the Tyne, coupled with the building of two new underground sections of line in the central area. These cross at an interchange station at Monument.

The system is operated by a 90-strong fleet of six-axle articulated Metrocars built by Metro-Cammell. Each seats 68 in its refurbished form, and they usually run in pairs. Each unit is 27.4m long. The system is electrified at 1,500V DC overhead, and the single depot is at Gosforth. Tyne & Wear Passenger Transport Executive, Nexus, both owns and operates the system.

Metro usage grew as the system expanded reaching a high of 59.1m passenger journeys in 1985, and then suffered a serious decline to reach a low of 32.5m journeys in 2000/01. Subsequently, recovery has reached nearly 40million.

A system now approaching 30 years of age needs serious refreshing, and substantial changes are under way. Nexus has secured a commitment from central government of over £320m to invest in the infrastructure from April 2010. To secure this, Metro is being split into two parts, ending its complete ownership and operation within the public sector:

■ Nexus Rail (about 200 staff) will be concerned with rail infrastructure, engineering, buildings and facilities, and projects/renewals. Nexus Rail will be retained as a wholly owned subsidiary of the PTE, letting contracts within the £350m modernisation programme. This includes new communications systems, a comprehensive improvement plan for 45 stations and a wide-ranging overhaul of overhead lines, track and structures.

■ Metro Operations (about 450 staff) will comprise commercial, operational and Metro service engineering functions, and will be franchised competitively, including an in-house bid. The key functions are train maintenance, depot operation and some station maintenance; service operation of about 450 trains per day, including stations; three-quarter-life fleet refurbishment; marketing, revenue protection, and the generation of non-fare income on stations.

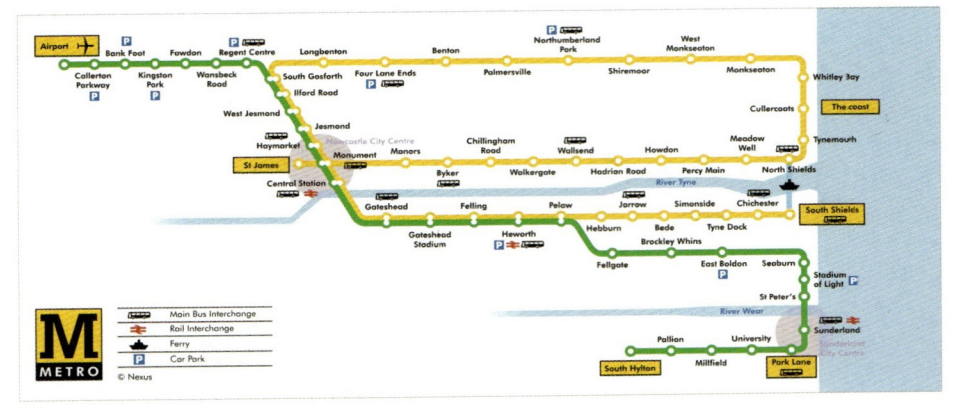

In association with **Transit**

SHERE | FAST™ Self-Service Systems.

We're more than just the ticket

Shere processes in excess of £1.5 billion worth of transactions a year in the travel and hospitality business through integrated web and self-service kiosk channels

Chiltern Railways
Virgin Trains · Southern
First Capital Connect
First Great Western
one · c2c
national express
DLR · OVERGROUND
KLM · Premier Inn

Call Shere to find out more

01483 557400

email info@shere.com
www.shere.com

Interfleet Technology

We're with you all the way

From strategy to implementation, we help our clients throughout the world to achieve maximum impact from their investment programmes. Our wide range of business solutions and other consultancy services helps clients including governmental authorities, asset owners, operators, manufacturers and financial institutions. Our clients come back time and again, because they trust us to find innovative, cost-effective and targeted total rail solutions.

We can make your journey easier. Contact us today:
T +44 (0)1332 223000
E grace.m@interfleet.co.uk

T +44 (0)131 220 8375
E conn.m@interfleet.co.uk

www.interfleet.co.uk

citibase Edinburgh, Suite 25, One St Colme Street, Edinburgh EH3 6AA

HSBC

modern railways

NEWS, VIEWS AND ANALYSIS ON TODAY'S RAILWAY

SUBSCRIBE TODAY!

...AND RECEIVE TWO FREE ISSUES! (14 ISSUES FOR THE PRICE OF 12)

Published for over 45 years, *Modern Railways* has earned its reputation in the industry as an established and highly respected railway journal. It is essential reading for professionals in the railway industry as well as individuals with a general interest in the state and developments of the British railway network.

Providing in-depth coverage for all aspects of the industry, from traction and rolling stock to signalling and infrastructure management, *Modern Railways* carries not only the latest news but also analysis of why those events are happening.

Modern Railways keeps its readers fully informed with detailed articles, informative features, and special issues throughout the year.

UK - £45.60   EUROPE - £55.00   ROW - £60.40

CALL 01932 266622
OR SUBSCRIBE ONLINE
WWW.MODERN-RAILWAYS.COM
ONLY OPEN TO NEW SUBSCRIBERS -
QUOTE CODE **TMR09**

Offer ends 31/12/09

Magazine cover: NEWS, VIEWS AND ANALYSIS ON TODAY'S RAILWAY — modern railways — London Rail expansion • New trains • Extra capacity • Line extensions — Reading remodelling explained — Money off this book! — BOMBARDIER — NOVEMBER 2008 £3.80

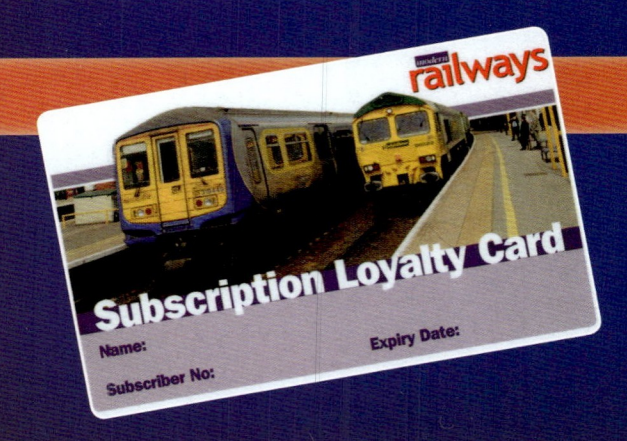

INCLUDES FREE MEMBERSHIP...

Plus **ALL** new subscribers receive **FREE** membership to the Ian Allan Publishing Subs Club. Each subscriber receives a personalised Loyalty Card, and quarterly newsletter with great subscriber benefits, discounts, offers and competitions!

The franchise is to be tendered in April 2009, with bids due by the autumn. The new contractor will start operations in April 2010. The value of the concession over the nine years to 2019 is estimated at £200m to £300m.

London Cross River Tram

This wholly street-running proposal would see trams running along a north-south Euston to Waterloo axis, with two termini on separate branches at each end. In the north the destinations would be Camden Town and King's Cross St Pancras; in the south Brixton and Peckham Rye. One of the objectives is to offer relief to sections of the Northern, Piccadilly and Victoria lines.

Priced at about £1.3bn, this is one of a number of projects put on ice under the revised transport strategy of the new London mayor, Boris Johnson.

The proposed West London Tram scheme was abandoned by the previous mayor, Ken Livingstone, in August 2007.

Croydon Tramlink

Key statistics 2007/08:

Passenger journeys (millions)	27.2
Passenger km (millions)	141.4
Route km open for passengers	28
Stops served	38
Passenger revenue (£m)	16.6

Croydon Tramlink had its origins in the need to improve access to Croydon town centre and the availability of four underused or disused railway lines in the area. Apart from the on-street one-way loop around Croydon centre and the 1km extension to Sandilands in the east, virtually the whole construction is on railway formations. The system became fully operational in May 2000.

On the three lines feeding central Croydon, there is double track on the whole of the line from New Addington, but both of the others have sections of single track, with loops at stations, and on the line to Wimbledon also between stations. The fleet consists of 24 pairs of articulated cars 30.1m long.

Tramtrack Croydon Ltd held a 99-year design, build, operate and maintain concession agreement dating from 1996, but this has been bought out and since 30 June 2008 Tramlink has been owned and managed by Transport for London. This brings an end to compensation payments for changes to the fares and ticketing policy.

Four possible Tramlink extensions were under consideration, only one of which had received funding to be taken to development stage, but work has been suspended by Mayor Boris Johnson.

The extension from the Beckenham branch was planned to run west along the route of the now lifted second track of the Network Rail line with new stops at Penge West and Anerley Road, continuing to Crystal Palace rail and bus stations.

The other three schemes had only proposal status (Sutton-Wimbledon, Sutton-Tooting and Streatham-Purley).

Docklands Light Railway

Key statistics 2007/08:

Passenger journeys (millions)	66.6
Passenger km (millions)	326.4
Route km open for passengers	55
Stations served	39
Passenger revenue (£m)	62.0

The original section of the London Docklands Light Railway opened in 1987. It has been extended progressively. Most recently this was to King George V via London City Airport (2005), and the further 2.5km beneath the Thames to Woolwich Arsenal opens in February 2009. This is a 750V DC third rail electrified system, with underside contact.

The DLR is now double track throughout, apart from the short Bow Church-Stratford section. A series of grade separated junctions in the Poplar area keeps the principal services apart. The original and very congested single platform at Stratford has now been rebuilt on a new site. All line termini now have two platforms.

Under way is the conversion to DLR standards of the North London Line from Canning Town to Stratford, and its extension to Stratford International station for opening in 2010. There will be three new intermediate stations.

The annual passenger usage of the DLR was expected to rise 50% above 2007/08 levels to 100m by 2011. The most effective way of coping with this is the lengthening of the trains themselves. Presently formed of a pair of articulated units each 28.8m long, platform extensions and other works will allow sets of three articulated cars to be accommodated. South Quay station is having to be reconstructed on a new site 200m eastwards.

Bank/Tower Gateway to Lewisham trains will have an extra car from 2010, with the rest of the network getting extra cars shortly afterwards. The main Beckton depot is being extended to accommodate a fleet which will grow from 94 vehicles to 149.

Serco Docklands was awarded a new seven-year operations franchise in May 2006 following a competitive tender process.

DLR is supported by concessionaires who have designed, financed built and maintained the most recent extensions. City Greenwich Lewisham (CGL) Rail manage the Lewisham extension, while City Airport Rail Enterprises (CARE) is responsible for the London City Airport extension. Woolwich Arsenal Rail Enterprises (WARE) is managing the new DLR Woolwich Arsenal extension.

The DLR has been built on the basis of its capability for encouraging economic regeneration, and this is still the case. A further extension under consideration is for 6km from Gallions Reach on the Beckton branch to Dagenham Dock c2c station. With perhaps four intermediate stations, there is considerable opportunity in this area for major housing growth and employment. In late 2008, DLR asked the Department for Transport to delay the start of a public inquiry under the Transport and Works Act into the proposed extension. The extension was then dropped from TfL's latest 10-year plan.

A Sheffield Supertram, in 'refreshed' livery, calls at the stop which serves Sheffield main-line station on 23 June 2008. Tony Miles

Light Rail & Metro

A Central Line train of '1992' stock approaches Leyton on 24 June 2008, forming a service for Epping. Driving Motor No 91227 leads. Brian Morrison

Transport for London

Passenger numbers break records as TfL modernises

Transport for London (TfL) was created in 2000 under Section 154 of the Greater London Authority Act 1999. Directly accountable to the Mayor, TfL is a functional body of the Authority, responsible for implementing the Mayor's transport strategy and managing transport services across the capital. Following the election of the new Mayor, Boris Johnson in 2008, a new draft Transport Strategy is to be consulted upon in early 2009, with final publication due in the autumn.

TfL is not just a public transport organisation. It is also responsible for a 580km network of main roads and all London's 4,600 traffic lights. In addition, TfL manages the central London Congestion Charging scheme and regulates the city's taxis and private hire trade. TfL also promote a range of walking and cycling initiatives across the capital. To ensure greater accessibility, TfL co-ordinates schemes for transport users with impaired mobility, as well as running the Dial-a-Ride scheme in conjunction with the Taxicard of London boroughs.

Projections of population growth are that, compared with 2000, there will be 700,000 additional people living and working in London by 2016, with the population of around 7.3m in 2000 rising to 8.1m. That in itself offers a considerable challenge in accommodating the additional travel demands. In the 2007/08 financial year, the Underground carried a new record of 1,073million passengers. Projections suggest that this could rise by another 15% by 2016, which would equate to 3.4million passengers each and every day.

There are several principal TfL companies with public transport responsibilities related to rail. London Underground Ltd is responsible for operating the London Underground network and owns (in whole or in part) over 250 London Underground stations. Docklands Light Railway Company Ltd owns the land on which the Docklands Light Railway is built and is responsible for the operation of the railway.

Transport Trading Ltd is the holding company for all TfL's operating transport companies, and receives revenues from the sales of Travelcards and similar in connection with all forms of transport operated by TfL. By law, TfL can only carry out certain activities through a limited liability company which is a TfL subsidiary, or which TfL formed alone or with others. Thus Rail for London Ltd is a wholly owned subsidiary of Transport Trading Ltd, which carries out the infrastructure upgrade for the North London line and entered into the agreement for the London Rail Concession. Transport Trading Ltd also runs the London Transport Museum.

London Rail is a division of TfL which deals with the National Rail network in London (overseeing London Overground - also Croydon Tramlink) and has these main responsibilities:
■ to implement the rail objectives in the Mayor's transport strategy;
■ to develop a Rail Plan for London;
■ to work with the DfT and the rail industry to improve national rail services in London;
■ to ensure progress on major new rail projects; and
■ to develop National Rail's contribution to an integrated public transport system for London. Cross London Rail Links Ltd (CLRL) (see Key Projects section) is mainly responsible for the Crossrail line between Maidenhead and Heathrow in the west, via central London, and

Shenfield and Abbey Wood in the east: it also has a second proposed Crossrail project between Northeast London and Southwest London in its portfolio.

London Underground

London Underground's (LU's) operational structure is based on the lines of route. The Chief Operating Officer leads a team of two service directors. The line general managers concentrate on the day-to-day running of the services, and report to the service directors who look at long-term development and overall network performance. They assess the issues and complexities unique to each line and work on strategies to address them.

Both work closely with the Director of Strategy & Service Development, Head of Operational Upgrades and Head of Operational Support, who provide the planning, communications, information and other support.

The Chief Programmes Office also works with the operating team. Together, they manage the complex Public Private Partnership (PPP) and Private Finance Initiative (PFI) contracts to ensure the private sector infrastructure companies and PFI contractors deliver the promised improvements, and that LU gets maximum value.

LU's fundamental objective is to provide a reliable service. This means assets that consistently perform well, correctly trained staff, and the ability to recover swiftly from delays when they do occur.

This results in challenges:
- to deliver a safe service day-in, day-out, irrespective of the reliability of the ageing and often obsolete assets;
- to use the investment programme to make good deficiencies in asset quality and to build in sufficient new capacity to meet future demand expectations; and
- to maintain customer service during the biggest rebuilding programme that the Underground has ever seen.

To illustrate the scale of what London Underground achieves, Table 1 shows the 15 busiest stations on the system, in descending order. Compared with 2005/06, the same stations feature, but the 2007 total usage is 15% higher and some individual station patronage is more than 20% up. Of the 15, Canary Wharf is the only station with a single Underground line, the Jubilee (the DLR station of the same name is completely separate), and is also the only one of the 15 which is not in central fare zone 1.

Of course, there are some stations with relatively low usage, and 15 have an annual entry/exit count of less than one million passengers a year.

Table 2 sets out the length of each line in km, the maximum number of trains needed to maintain the service, the number of stations served, and the annual passenger total. In the case of the latter two, some stations serve more than one line, and passengers too may use more than one line in the course of their journeys. Thus neither of these figures tally to a system total.

It will be noted from Table 2 that the lines differ considerably in their characteristics and use of assets. An abbreviated table of this nature can only skim the surface; what it does not show is how the situation varies by time of day and day of week, nor can it take account of the length of the journeys made by passengers. Thus the 530 trains required in the morning peak reduce by about 100 during the midday period and on Saturdays, and another 20 fewer on Sundays. The Waterloo & City does not operate a Sunday service at all and there is only one possible journey length, while the relatively modest numbers of passengers on the Metropolitan Line travel on average much further than most.

Investment programme

Investment in progress on the Underground includes major upgrades to the Victoria, Northern, Central, District and Circle lines to increase capacity, improve reliability and modernise stations. New trains will be delivered as part of a programme for the complete replacement of all trains on the sub-surface lines. (These are the lines built to dimensions similar to, if slightly smaller than, the main line railways - as opposed to the 'tube' lines which are much smaller and have deep bored tube tunnels). The new 'S stock' trains, which will not be identical for each line, will be delivered to the Metropolitan from 2010, the Circle/Hammersmith & City/Edgware Road-Wimbledon lines from 2012, and the main District Line from 2013. Work already delivered includes:

- lengthening Jubilee Line trains from six cars to seven;
- capacity works at Wembley Park;
- King's Cross St Pancras new western ticket hall complete, northern ticket hall under way for completion in December 2009;
- Waterloo & City Line upgrade;
- lift replacement and station modernisation at Regent's Park, Bakerloo Line;
- total modernisation of White City sidings, Central Line;
- many stations renewed with more CCTV, improved accessibility and heritage features restored.

A new station (and connecting line) at Heathrow Terminal 5, Piccadilly Line was opened on 27 March 2008; and another at Wood Lane, Hammersmith & City Line, on 14 October 2008, providing access to the new Westfield London retail and leisure centre. The design combines the old viaduct arches

Table 1 - Underground station usage 2007 - million passengers

1	Victoria	76.41
2	Waterloo	74.84
3	Oxford Circus	72.05
4	King's Cross St Pancras	66.36
5	Liverpool Street	61.32
6	London Bridge	56.95
7	Bank & Monument	41.88
8	Canary Wharf	41.62
9	Leicester Square	38.69
10	Piccadilly Circus	38.09
11	Tottenham Court Road	37.29
12	Paddington	37.24
13	Bond Street	36.70
14	Holborn	31.11
15	Green Park	30.03
Total, 2007		740.58
Total, 2005/06		643.54
Increase		97.04

Note to Table 1: The station figures represent annual usage during 2007 - totals of entry and exit counts taken on Mondays to Fridays, Saturdays and Sundays during the year. Passengers interchanging between lines are not included.

Table 2 - London Underground line statistics

Line	Route km	Max trains required	Stations served	Annual passenger total (millions)
Bakerloo	23.2	33	25	96
Central	74.0	79	49	184
Circle	22.5	14	14	69
District	64.0	77	60	173
Hammersmith & City	26.5	17	19	46
Jubilee	36.2	51	27	128
Metropolitan	66.7	47	34	54
Northern	58.0	91	50	207
Piccadilly	71.0	78	52	177
Victoria	21.0	38	16	162
Waterloo & City	2.4	5	2	10

Light Rail & Metro

London Overground Class 313 No 313120 arrives at a crowded West Brompton station on 22 September 2008, forming the 18.05 Clapham Junction-Willesden Junction on the West London line. The platforms served by the London Underground District Line's Wimbledon route are to the left (east side). Tony Miles

with a modern stainless steel and glass structure.
Work in progress includes:
- Victoria Line major upgrade for new trains, new control systems;
- Central Line works at Stratford in preparation for London 2012;
- District Line track replacement, Earls Court-Whitechapel;
- Jubilee Line signalling upgrade to increase line capacity;
- Northern Line track replacement works.

Some London Underground services run on parts of Network Rail infrastructure, and some London Underground-operated sections of line are used also by trains on the national rail network, notably, operation by Chiltern Railways over the Metropolitan Line between Harrow-on-the-Hill and Amersham.

Infraco PPPs

Before the Underground was transferred to TfL, the government adopted the Public Private Partnership (PPP) model as its preferred solution for investment.

Under the 30-year PPP contracts, the infrastructure companies, or Infracos, were made responsible for the maintenance and renewal of LU's assets - its rolling stock, stations, track, signalling, tunnels and the infrastructure generally. The Infracos were required contractually to deliver a certain level of daily asset performance, and to upgrade the network to deliver improved capability in the longer term. They were made subject to financial incentives or penalties based on their delivery, against the performance levels set out in the contracts. The network was divided into three Infraco groupings.

Tube Lines' contract was signed in December 2002. The company is responsible for the Jubilee, Northern and Piccadilly lines (JNP). Metronet Rail's two contracts were signed in April 2003. These were for BCV (the Bakerloo, Central, Victoria and Waterloo & City lines), and SSL (Sub-Surface Lines - the Circle, District, East London, Hammersmith & City and Metropolitan lines). The 30-year contracts are due for review every seven and a half years.

Metronet Rail went into administration on 18 July 2007. In November that year the administrator confirmed that a bid from TfL was the only one to have been received for Metronet. TfL's bid was constructed on the basis that there should be no net additional cost to the organisation.

The Metronet businesses were transferred to TfL on 27 May 2008, with nominee companies responsible for maintenance and refurbishment on the BCV and SSL groups of lines. Tube Lines continues as previously.

Passengers

For many journeys, the Underground is fast, convenient and saves time. However, surveys show consistently that the quality of the journey is also important. The aim of London Underground is to provide visible and helpful staff, high-quality information and security systems, and to invest to make the network more open and accessible for all. It is intended that 25% of Underground stations will have step-free access by 2010.

The fares system on all TfL Underground, tram and bus services is now dominated by the Oyster smartcard. This card acts as a prepaid credit card which can be topped up as necessary with additional in-payments. Oysters can also accommodate Travelcards, or work on a pay-as-you-go basis on the Underground, Docklands Light Railway, Croydon Tramlink and buses ('pay as you go' is to be extended on National Rail within Greater London). Cash fares are still available, but are priced to discourage cash payments. Thus when using an Oyster card in Greater London, adult Underground fares vary between £1.50 and a maximum of £3.50. All

Senior personnel

Transport for London
Commissioner
Peter Hendy (left)
Managing Director, London Rail
Ian Brown
Managing Director, London Underground
Tim O'Toole

cash fares which include central Zone 1 are a flat rate of £4.00, or £3.00 if Zone 1 is not included. As a result, cash fares now account for only 3.5% of Underground journeys. Oyster pay-as-you-go (as opposed to period contracts) was responsible for 29.7% of Underground journeys in the 2007/08 financial year. Passengers are able to use Oyster and Travelcards on Transport for London's new London Overground service, following its transfer to TfL on 11 November 2007.

A new fares package applies from January 2009.

London Overground

The London Overground operation contract was let by Transport for London rather than the Department for Transport. It runs for seven years from 11 November 2007, with a possible two year extension.

The name has been applied to the lines operated formerly by the Metro part of Silverlink as a National Rail franchised train operating company, with the future addition of the revamped and extended East London line which closed for reconstruction on 22 December 2007. The letting of this franchise has been presented as a first step by Transport for London in relation to National Rail services around the capital generally. The routes are shown on the Underground map, and the intention is to offer a similar style of service frequency and quality.

The contract competition was won in June 2007 by a consortium of the Mass Transit Railway of Hong Kong and Laing, the parent company of the Chiltern Railways franchise, which was taken over by Deutsche Bahn in 2008.

The new joint venture company trades as London Overground Rail Operations Ltd (LOROL). Unlike a National Rail franchisee, the company is not responsible for setting fares, procuring rolling stock or deciding service levels. These functions are retained by TfL.

The initial routes of the London Overground network, collectively known as the North London Railway, and the services now operated, are:

■ London Euston to Watford Junction (the 'DC' local lines, 19 stations). From Queen's Park to Harrow & Wealdstone (10 stations), services are provided also by the Bakerloo Line.
■ Stratford to Richmond via Dalston Kingsland and Willesden Junction (the North London Line, 23 stations). This service has joint operation with the District Line between Gunnersbury and Richmond (three stations). Operation is by dual-voltage electric multiple-units (EMUs), as part of the line has overhead electrification and part third/fourth rail.
■ Willesden Junction to Clapham Junction via Kensington Olympia (the West London Line, five stations at present). This line too requires dual-voltage trains as it is part overhead and part third rail.
■ Gospel Oak-Barking (12 stations). This line is not electrified and is thus operated by diesel trains.

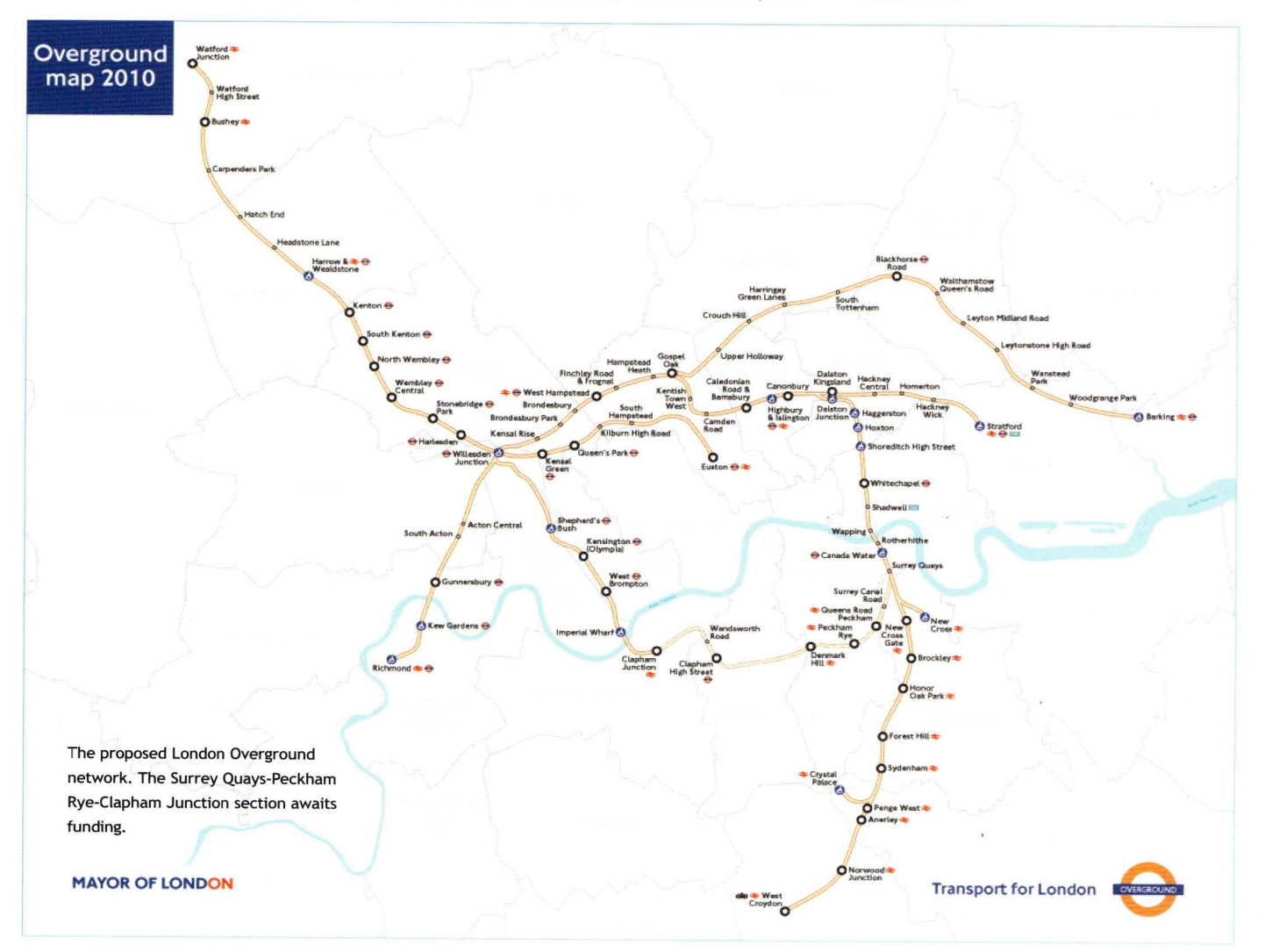

Senior personnel

London Overground Rail Operations Ltd
Managing Director
Steve Murphy (left)
Deputy Managing Director
Rob Brighouse
Fleet Director
Peter Daw
Finance Director
Peter Austin
Customer Services Director
Claire Brown
Operations Director
Perry Ramsey

Overground map 2010

The proposed London Overground network. The Surrey Quays-Peckham Rye-Clapham Junction section awaits funding.

Light Rail & Metro

Showing Heathrow T123/5 as its destination, a Piccadilly Line train from Cockfosters arrives at Heathrow Terminals 1,2,3, en route to Terminal 5 on its opening day, 27 March 2008. Brian Morrison

The basic off peak services operated in trains per hour (tph) are, respectively, 3tph, 4tph, 2tph, and 2tph, though this will change over time.

LOROL has promised to achieve a step change in passengers' experience, including punctuality, security, quality of trains and stations, and customer service.

The existing electric rolling stock consists of a fleet of Class 313 dual-voltage EMUs, plus some very similar Class 508 units which are restricted to the third-rail electrified Euston-Watford service only.

All existing EMUs will be replaced by a fleet of Class 378 Electrostar units presently under construction by Bombardier at Derby, to be leased via the QW Rail Leasing consortium. Operation of the first trains is due to start early in 2009. The original £223m contract in 2006 provided for 24 dual-voltage 3-car units for the North London Lines and 20 DC-only 4-car units for the extended East London Railway when that is operational in 2010.

A subsequent order for 36 additional vehicles, costing £36m and placed in summer 2007, will extend the three-car North London sets to four-cars (with platform lengthening to be carried out), and provide an additional three 4-car trains for the East London Railway.

Seven more 4-car dual-voltage Class 378s, costing £23m, were ordered in April 2008. They will allow an 8tph frequency on the core route between Camden Road and Stratford, as required by London's Olympic and Paralympics Games Transport Plan and for future growth. The total fleet will therefore number 54 four-car trains.

A new station opened at Shepherd's Bush on the West London line on 28 September 2008, and a further station is presently under construction at Imperial Wharf. It is expected to open at the end of 2009.

Track upgrading and gauge widening have made the Gospel Oak-Barking line suitable for higher gauge containers so that the line can act as an alternative route to the North London for some freight traffic. £18.5m from the government's Transport Innovation Fund is being complemented by £16.5m from Network Rail.

The signalling system will also be renewed. TfL intends to double the number of trains presently running and eight new air-conditioned 2-car trains of Class 172 Turbostar diesel stock have been ordered. Leased from Angel Trains, these are expected to enter service in 2009.

TfL is investing £1bn in extending the former Underground East London Line southwards from New Cross Gate to West Croydon and Crystal Palace, and north over the old Broad Street viaduct to Dalston Junction and then to Highbury & Islington. That will complete Phase 1 of the East London Railway scheme. The main part serving 21 stations is due to be completed and operational in June 2010, the remaining short section beyond Dalston Junction in 2011.

Operating plans are that a 12tph service will run south from Dalston Junction, with 4tph to New Cross, 4tph to Crystal Palace, and 4tph to West Croydon.

Work by Taylor Woodrow in a £30m contract involved replacing and refurbishing 22 bridges along the disused viaduct structures on the Broad Street section, and track bed preparation.

The main construction work was awarded to Balfour Beatty and Carillion in a £363m contract. This includes the replacement of 7.4km of track and signalling equipment on the former Underground route, the construction of four new accessible stations at Dalston Junction, Haggerston, Hoxton and Shoreditch High Street, installation of a flyover north of New Cross as part of the connection with Network Rail, and the building of a new train maintenance depot at New Cross.

An event which caused a near 24hr closure of the Great Eastern line of Network Rail occurred on 28 May 2008, when new bridge GE19, which is to carry the East London Extension across the Great Eastern, slipped off its temporary supports. Debris fell on the tracks beneath.

Station works on the Southern section will include gating of all stations, and Crystal Palace will be restored to showpiece standard.

Eventually, TfL plans for the Overground service to form an orbital route right around London. Phase 2 of the East London Railway scheme, presently unfunded, will provide another link from Surrey Quays to Peckham Rye and thence to Clapham Junction over existing Network Rail lines. Service levels over the core section will rise to 16tph when Phase 2 is complete.

A total of £1.4bn is being invested in the London Overground network, of which £1bn is being spent on building the East London Railway.

Croxley proposals

The long-standing Croxley rail link proposal aims to re-route the Watford branch of the Metropolitan Line via a new viaduct and a station at Ascot Road to join the now defunct Croxley Green branch line, with a station at Watford West. On reaching the existing Euston-Watford 'DC' local line, trains would call at Watford High Street (for the town centre) and terminate at Watford Junction. This project is wholly within Hertfordshire. Despite some earlier encouragement, the proposals have made slow progress.

Funding is planned in partnership between Hertfordshire county council, TfL and the Department for Transport. The total cost is expected to be over £145million, with the council seeking a £119.5million grant from the DfT via the regional transport funding allocation. In late 2008, the DfT was considering the council's latest business plan for the link.

London Travelwatch

This statutory consumer body (formal title, London Transport Users Committee) covers the whole of London Underground, Docklands Light Railway, Croydon Tramlink, bus services, taxis and river services within Greater London, plus National Rail services within an area roundly 25 miles from Charing Cross.

The committee has four principal spheres of activity: dialogue with planners and operators, monitoring service quality, investigating user complaints where the user is dissatisfied with the operator response, and taking part in wider public debate.

Members are appointed by the London Assembly, which funds the committee.

Into Europe

In association with

Halcrow

Into Europe

Caption: Halcrow's Traction and Rolling Stock division recently acted as Iarnród Éireann's (Irish Rail's) technical and safety adviser during the design, manufacture and introduction into service of the Class 22000 InterCity DMU. Halcrow

Halcrow

A major part of Halcrow's focus for future growth is Europe

Europe represents a large, complex and challenging market for providers of railway services. The rail networks of member countries range from some of the most advanced in the world, to those that have weathered years of neglect and which now require massive investment to realise their full potential for providing a sustainable means of public transportation for local commuters, intercity and inter-country travellers and freight hauliers.

Halcrow Group Limited is a worldwide organisation with over 70 offices in all corners of the globe. A major part of the Group's focus for future growth is Europe. At present, Halcrow's activities in the region are focused on new European Union Member States, EU candidates and acceding countries. In addition, Halcrow is well placed to work within the private sector or on Public Private Partnership (PPP) projects as these develop in the region.

Halcrow aims to focus on a few current target countries, including Romania, Latvia, Poland and Ireland and has established offices in these countries. The objective is to build a sustainable business, with local engineers, scientists and business support staff employed by a national Halcrow company.

In most cases, business in the acceding countries is built up from involvement in the Instrument for Structural Policies for Pre-Accession (ISPA) projects, which often tend to be water and sanitation or power supply projects, followed by transportation infrastructure projects (usually roads first, railways second). Following these, railway projects will move to the procurement or refurbishment of rolling stock.

In Romania for example, the first ISPA covering water and sanitation projects in Satu Mare and Braila, for which Halcrow has provided a supervisory role, has recently been completed. Halcrow's success in this project has led to a major road design and supervision contract (Road Rehabilitation Lot C). In rail transport Halcrow has recently completed a comprehensive strategy plan to enable CFR Calatori (CFRC - the national passenger rail operator in Romania) to reverse a long-term trend of falling market share and lost traffic in order to ensure a financially viable future. Halcrow developed a new marketing strategy and strategic plan for CFRC, making 25 recommendations for improvement measures to enhance their competitive position.

In Poland, in addition to the many and varied contracts won in the water, highways and environmental sectors, Halcrow has reached the initial milestone approval stage on the E65 rail design project and the team is actively tendering for more - even larger - rail projects.

In Ireland, building on recent experience of specialist rail projects undertaken on behalf of Irish Rail, Crossrail and London's Tottenham Court Road redevelopment, Halcrow has recently won the Dublin Interconnector project, the city's equivalent to London's Crossrail scheme. The project involves the planning of a new five-station, 5km-long rail link beneath the centre of Dublin, and will provide a key component of the Dublin Area Rapid Transport (DART) system. The project was won in a joint venture with Arup. Halcrow's Traction and Rolling Stock division has a long and successful history of providing technical support to Iarnród Éireann, most recently acting as the authority's technical and safety adviser during the design, manufacture and introduction into service of the Class 22000 InterCity DMU.

In addition to projects won in target countries, Halcrow has undertaken work on behalf of MÁV Cargo, the state-owned freight operator in Hungary and ZSR and ZSSK cargo, the state-owned infrastructure operator and freight operator respectively, in Slovakia.

Throughout Europe, a broad range of clients has made Halcrow a consultancy of choice, including governments, developers, contractors and funding agencies. They have come to rely on Halcrow's ability to understand their needs and to deliver timely and successful outcomes, whatever the challenge.

www.halcrow.com

In association with **Halcrow**

Into Europe

Ken Harris reviews significant developments in the European railway industry

The prospect of true competition on the growing high-speed network, continuing seismic shifts in the freight sector, and a buoyant market for rolling stock builders and lessors all point to more significant progress in the development of Europe's railway industry.

France again claimed the high-speed headlines in 2008 with the February unveiling of Alstom's AGV (Automotrice à Grande Vitesse) 360km/h demonstrator. Developed entirely as a commercial venture, the train represents a significant departure from its TGV forerunners in the adoption of distributed power rather a power cars-plus-trailers configuration. One factor driving this move is the resulting increase in passenger capacity within the train length. Articulation is retained, with standard formations of seven, 11 and 14 cars on offer. These are to be formed of combinations of 3-car modules carrying traction equipment, dubbed 'triplettes', and single key cars incorporating auxiliaries. Using insulated-gate bipolar transistor (IGBT) traction converters and Alstom's latest synchronous traction motors, the 7-car prototype is rated at 6,000kW, while the 14-car version will develop 12,000kW. The train is designed to take current from all four main European supply systems and is ERTMS-equipped.

Alstom is keen to position itself well to respond to future SNCF orders, which will be needed both to equip planned expansion of the LGV network and to replace its oldest TGV sets. It will also be proposing AGV for other future high-speed contracts both in Europe and beyond. Remarkably, it secured an order for 25 examples of the 11-car version of the train even before the prototype was launched. Italian open access operator Nuovo Trasporto Viaggiatori (NTV) awarded Alstom a 650million Euro contract for a fleet of AGVs to equip it to challenge FS Trenitalia on domestic high-speed lines from December 2011. A separate contract covers maintenance of the trains for 30 years, and there is an option on 10 more sets.

Established in 2006, NTV is funded by Italian business and banking interests and is headed by the former General Manager of FS, Giuseppe Sciarrone. It plans to run services on three routes, all using the core Bologna-Florence-Rome section of Italy's high-speed network: Turin-Milan-Bologna-Florence-Rome-Naples-Salerno; Venice-Bologna-Florence-Rome; and Rome-Bari. The company aims to carry 10million passengers annually once full operating capacity is achieved.

International competition?

While this assault by NTV on Trenitalia's market in Italy has been made possible by domestic legislation, there are initial indications that incumbent operators of international services are likely to face competition from 2010 as a result their liberalisation under the EU's Third Railway Package, discussed in last year's edition of The Modern Railway. Rumours that Air France-KLM was considering replacing some short-haul flights with high-speed rail services were confirmed in 2008 when the company said it was in discussion with Veolia Transport concerning their possible operation. Paris to Amsterdam, Brussels, London and German were cited as routes being studied, with AGV again the likely rolling stock candidate.

And it is not only passenger services that are set to make greater use of the high-speed rail network. For some time a group of organisations operating out of Paris Roissy-CDG airport have been exploring the possibilities of using rail for air cargo movements to reduce road haulage and short-haul flights, the so-called Carex project. In July 2008 the group's partners, which include Air France KLM Cargo, Aéroports de Paris, La Poste, FedEx and Worldwide Flight Services, as well as public and institutional members, confirmed their intention to develop Euro-Carex, a network of high-speed cargo services linking major European airports. It is planned to launch services in March 2012, provisionally using a fleet of eight TGV-derived trainsets comprising two power cars and nine specially designed trailers. In its first phase, the planned Euro-Carex network is to link Roissy-CDG with Amsterdam, Liège/Cologne, Lille/London and Lyons. A second phase,

Timetabling test runs on the Rotterdam-Hoofddorp section of the HSL-Zuid high-speed line in the Netherlands commenced in September 2008 using Bombardier TRAXX Class 186 electric locomotives and Prio coaching stock, which were to be employed pending commissioning of Ansaldobreda-built 'Albatros' trainsets. Quintus Vosman

Into Europe

necessitating up to 12 more trains, would add Bordeaux, Frankfurt and Strasbourg to the network, with the eventual prospect of additional destinations in Germany, Italy and Spain being served.

Among the latest additions to Europe's growing high-speed network is the 630km high-speed line linking Madrid Atocha and Barcelona Sants, finally commissioned throughout in February 2008 at a cost of 10billion Euro. Operated mainly using Siemens-built Class S103 trainsets similar to DB's ICE3, the fastest services now connect the two cities in a little over two and a half hours. And there is no let-up in the rapid development of Spain's high-speed network. Work is now in progress on the Barcelona-Figueres-Perpignan section that will eventually connect with France's planned LGV Languedoc-Roussillon, and on the Madrid-Cuenca-Valencia line, due to be commissioned in 2010. Construction was also underway in 2008 on the first section of the high-speed line between Madrid and the border with Portugal via Extremadura. Tendering for a 40-year PPP concession to construct the Portuguese portion from Lisbon to the border was initiated in 2008.

The French government has confirmed its ongoing commitment to high-speed rail with an announcement in 2008 that it was sanctioning construction of 2,000km of lines by 2020, with a further 2,500km to be built after that. Early priorities include the Nîmes/Montpellier bypass (2013), LGV Bretagne-Pays de la Loire (2013), the second phase of LGV Est from Baudrecourt to Strasbourg (2015) and Tours-Bordeaux (2016). Already under construction are Perpignan-Figueras, Spain, due to open in February 2009, and the eastern branch of LGV Rhin-Rhône, with commissioning expected in 2011.

Work continues on Germany's high-speed route between Berlin and Munich, a combination of new and upgraded infrastructure. However, this is a long-term project, now unlikely to see completion before 2017, when the journey time between the two cities should be cut to less than 4hr. The same date has been quoted for completion of the 85km Neubaustrecke between Frankfurt and Mannheim.

In Italy the 182km Milan-Bologna AV/AC (high-speed/high-capacity) line was due to be commissioned in December 2008, to be followed a year later by the 78.5km section from Bologna to Florence. This will complete the key north-south 'trunk' of Italy's planned T-shaped network. At peak periods Trenitalia plans to run four services per hour between Milan and the capital, but as outlined above, it will soon face competition from NTV. The 39km Novara-Turin section should also be commissioned in 2009 to complete the high-speed line from Milan.

There was less encouraging news from the Netherlands and Belgium, where in 2008 passengers were still waiting for high-speed services to begin on the Dutch HSL-Zuid line and on to Antwerp and Brussels. Limited operations over part of HSL-Zuid using Class 186 electric locomotives and hauled stock were expected to start in October of that year but May 2009 at least was being quoted as the earliest date for a commencement of fleet service using the much-delayed V250 Albatros trainsets from Ansaldobreda.

Freight access

Europe's rail freight scene continues to be dominated by the impact of open access, despite frustrating challenges still presented by widely varying technical standards and bureaucratic obstacles. Newer private sector entrants to the market have been strengthening their cross-border capabilities through alliances and mergers. Among examples of this trend are the takeover by France's Veolia Cargo of rail4chem and the acquisition of Dillen & Le Jeune Cargo in Belgium by Babcock & Brown-owned Swiss operator Crossrail.

In Germany, which sees more open access activity than any other European country, it was reported by the independent operators' trade association VDV that in 2007 as much as 20% of traffic was handled by carriers other than DB. The extent to which such operators can continue to win and retain a significant market share remains to be seen but further consolidation seems inevitable if they are to remain competitive with state-owned rail freight companies.

For their part, established national operators have been taking their own strategic steps to consolidate their positions internationally, recognising that the neighbours with which they used to cooperate are now often their competitors. Facing strong competition in its domestic market, especially from DB-owned EWS subsidiary Euro Cargo Rail, Fret SNCF moved to establish a foothold in Germany with the 2008 acquisition of a 75% stake in open access operator ITL Eisenbahn. In the same year it also took full ownership of road transport and logistics company Geodis to broaden its role in the freight market.

However, this seems unlikely to unduly concern DB, which has been progressively establishing itself as a very formidable force in European rail freight. Having completed its purchases of EWS in the UK and Transfesa in Spain, DB has since increased its shareholding in BLS Cargo in Switzerland from 20% to 45% and in April 2008 established Railion Scandinavia, a joint venture with Swedish national rail freight company Green Cargo to handle traffic between the Nordic countries and central Europe. DB owns 51% of the shares in the new company. These moves follow DB's earlier takeover of the national freight operators in Denmark and the Netherlands and the establishment through acquisitions of Italian and Swiss subsidiaries Railion Italia and Railion Schweiz.

DB further consolidated its position in Italy in September 2008 when through its Railion Italia subsidiary it acquired a 49% stake in the country's second largest rail freight company,

Class 285 Bombardier TRAXX 140 DE diesel-electric locomotive leased from CB Rail by German freight operator ITL Eisenbahn, in which Fret SNCF acquired a 75% stake in 2008. Philip Wormald

A Siemens employee in the in Krefeld-Uerdingen factory working on the nose cone of the Velaro RUS. Eight of these new high-speed trains were ordered by the Russian railway company RZD for the Moscow-St Petersburg line, with an operating speed of 250 km/h. Siemens

NordCargo – previously reported as an acquisition target for Fret SNCF. At the same time, DB has been busily forming links with counterparts to the east with an eye on freight traffic opportunities between Europe and Asia.

Elsewhere in Europe it has been a story of mergers of equals – or at least near-equals. ÖBB subsidiary Rail Cargo Austria was named in 2008 as the successful bidder in the Hungarian government's sell-off of national rail freight company MÁV Cargo. And the governments of the Czech Republic and Slovakia agreed in principle to the merger of national operators CD Cargo and ZSSK Cargo.

Unsurprisingly, these profound changes in Europe's rail freight market are making their mark on locomotive procurement, with manufacturers and leasing companies enjoying something of a boom, albeit a highly competitive one. Although most trunk rail routes in Europe are electrified, diesel traction is still finding favour among many freight operators, especially private companies taking advantage of cross-border opportunities. With only a few adjoining Western European networks employing similar power supply systems, operating with electric traction implies the use of expensive and complex multi-current locomotives or time-consuming motive power changes at frontier yards. And diesel handling is still needed at non-electrified terminals and sidings.

Diesel innovations

Using diesel traction for long hauls under the wires may not seem sound from an environmental viewpoint, nor possibly from an economic one, given the high cost of fuel and uncertainty over prices in the long term. Nevertheless, this is the route being followed by many operators in Europe and locomotive builders are lining up to meet their needs.

So far a large slice of the market in the upper power range has been won by EMD, with its 2,420kW JT42CWR model – familiar in the UK and widely known abroad as Class 66. Including those supplied to British operators, EMD has now delivered nearly 600 examples of the type for use in Europe, where it is certified for use in 11 countries, with more approvals expected soon. The latest variant, the JT42CWRM, conforms to European Stage IIIA exhaust emissions requirements and TSI noise limits.

EMD is now developing a successor to this successful design with interoperability very much in mind. The Class 66EU is aimed only at the continental market, taking advantage of less restrictive loading gauge constraints to create a slightly longer and higher machine than the existing design. The Stage IIIA-compliant 12N-710G3B-T2 engine is to be retained – and this can be retrofitted to meet the more stringent future Stage IIIB requirements. The big change is in the adoption of an all-AC traction system. Improvements are also promised in the design of the driver's cab, a feature of the existing Class 66 which has attracted some criticism.

However, EMD will by no means have the field to itself. Its North American rival GE Transportation – not previously a significant traction supplier this side of the Atlantic – used the InnoTrans 2008 exhibition in Berlin as a launch pad for its proposed contender for the European market, the PowerHaul Series. This 2,750kW six-axle all-AC design is a development of the PH37ACmi model ordered in 2007 by Freightliner in the UK. The continental version of PowerHaul also takes advantage of the UIC 505-1 loading gauge, adopting a full-width body instead of the narrow hood configuration of the UK locomotives and offering a generous 9,000-litre fuel capacity compared to 6,000 litres for the Freightliner machines. With a 22 tonne axleload, the continental version will also be slightly heavier than its Freightliner counterpart, which comes in at 21.5 tonnes.

The P616 V16 engine to be used in PowerHaul locomotives is new to high-power rail traction applications. Its origins are with GE Energy's Austrian subsidiary Jenbacher, which specialises in engines for power generation. GE Transportation claims that by using this unit together its other traction control technologies, reductions in fuel use of up to 9% compared to current fleet averages can be achieved.

Into Europe

European designs include Bombardier's TRAXX 140 DE, a derivative of its highly successful TRAXX electric locomotive family, which has become one of Europe's standard designs. A modular concept means that some 70% of the content is common to both diesel and electric versions, enabling Bombardier to respond quickly to new orders. Powered by a 2,200kW MTU 16 V 4000 engine, the four-axle locomotive is a relatively new entrant to the market, with orders so far limited to 10 for leasing company CB Rail, although the first of the type to be built were eight examples of a 160 DE passenger version for use in northern Germany by regional operator metronom. Among CB Rail's first freight customers, leasing three of the machines, was ITL Eisenbahn, the German open access operator in which SNCF took a 75% stake in April 2008. Other examples have been leased to Havelländische Eisenbahn.

Siemens has also picked up orders for its contender in this power range, the four-axle 2,000kW ER20 'EuroRunner', supplied in large numbers to ÖBB as Class 2016 as well as to various private operators. A batch of 34 examples of a six-axle ER20 CF version was being supplied to Lithuania in 2008.

Also pitching for a share of Europe's high-power diesel-electric market is the Euro 4000 from Vossloh Transportation Systems, which operates from the former Alstom plant in Valencia, Spain. Powered by an EMD 710 Series 3,178kW engine with AC-DC transmission, the Euro 4000 is Co-Co machine. Since its 2006 launch Vossloh has secured orders for 45 examples for the type, the largest of these for 30 from Angel Trains Cargo.

Meanwhile, diesel-hydraulic traction continues to find favour with some rail freight companies. In the higher power range Angel Trains Cargo lists in its portfolio 56 of the 2,240kW Caterpillar-engined G 2000 BB model manufactured at Vossloh Locomotives' Kiel plant. But it is Voith's 2006 entry into the locomotive market that has been making the headlines, notably with its 3,600kW Maxima 40 CC, claimed to be the world's most powerful single-engined diesel-hydraulic. Examples have been ordered by Ox-traction, a joint venture leasing company set up by Voith Turbo, Stephenson Capital and the former head of Angel Trains Cargo, André Bloemen.

A driving trailer of Railjet, the new 230m/h push-pull train being built by Siemens for Austrian Federal Railways, on show at Innotrans 2008. Siemens

Havelländische Eisenbahn was named as one of the first users of the type. A 2,750kW 30 CC version of the Maxima is also offered by Voith.

Leasing opportunities

It will have been evident from this coverage of diesel traction developments in Europe that rolling stock leasing companies have been quick to recognise opportunities, especially in the provision of locomotives for the freight sector. This was underlined in September 2008 when Railpool, founded just two months earlier as a joint venture by HSH Nordbank and the KfW-IPEX Bank, placed an order with Bombardier for 58 TRAXX locomotives, with an option on 80 more. Deliveries start in August 2009. Ox-traction, mentioned above, is also a new venture.

Other leading participants in the leasing market, playing a key role in enabling operators to respond quickly to traffic opportunities, include Angel Trains, sold in June 2008 by Royal Bank of Scotland to a consortium led by Babcock & Brown; CB Rail, formerly Porterbrook's non-UK business and also part-owned by Babcock & Brown; and MRCE Dispolok, owned by Mitsui and incorporating the former Siemens Dispolok locomotive leasing business. Also active is BTMU Capital Corporation, which in May 2008 acquired the European rail leasing business of Allco Finance Group.

However, it is back to Germany for perhaps the next biggest structural change in Europe's railways – the part privatisation of DB. In 2008 DB AG was restructured, with its train operating businesses grouped together as DB Mobility Logistics AG. It is this company, incorporating DB's passenger, freight/logistics and services activities, which was planned to see 24.9% of its shares floated on the Frankfurt Stock Exchange in a move which the German government expects to raise between 5billion and 8billion Euro. Remaining parts of DB AG, notably infrastructure owner DB Netz, traction power supply subsidiary DB Energie and DB Stations & Service, are to stay under state ownership.

At the time this year's 'Into Europe' was written, it was unclear whether the financial crises affecting banking systems globally would lead to a postponement of the flotation of DB Mobility Logistics, which at one point was scheduled for late 2008. There is certainly expected to be great interest in the sale of this expanding and growing business – even Russian Railways expressed its keenness to acquire a stake in the company.

Model of Alstom's AGV for Italian open access high-speed operator Nuovo Trasporto Viaggiatori. Alstom

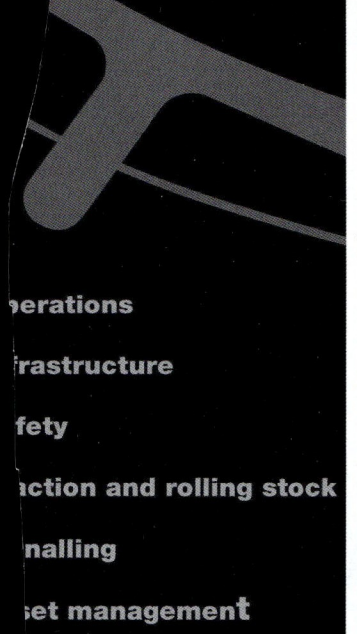

Traction and rolling stock:
turnkey project management services

- perations
- frastructure
- fety
- ction and rolling stock
- nalling
- set management

Successful traction and rolling stock projects often demand cross-disciplinary project management skills to deal with the many different requirements of the vehicle design, approvals, operation and maintenance processes within the modern railway industry.

Halcrow's traction and rolling stock team stands out from the industry norm due to its ability and expertise to assume complete turnkey project management responsibility for a variety of projects.

Projects can vary in size and complexity from complete vehicle refurbishments through to documentation management, but they all have one thing in common. Each one has a requirement for the management of diverse tasks that are not simply of a technical nature.

Our team has a breadth of management experience gained not only across all aspects of the railway rolling stock industry but also from major rail and non-rail construction projects.

Our ability to utilise resources across Halcrow to bring together the right combination of experience and expertise for each project is second to none.

Key experience

- procurement of new rolling stock; from development of specifications to selection of manufacturers, project management, approvals, testing and commissioning

- maintenance system and documentation management for rolling stock owners

- design, supply, installation, certification and approval of equipment for vehicle modification and refurbishment

- combining technical expertise with commercial and project management know-how

To find out more about how we can help you meet your business objectives, call Andrew Witkowski (witkowskia@halcrow.com) or Chris Hanson (hansonc@halcrow.com) on +44 (0)1332 222620

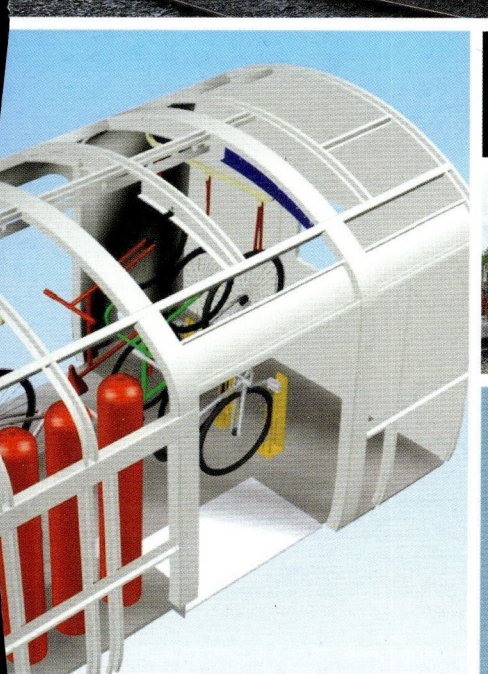

Image courtesy of Transplant

INVESTOR IN PEOPLE

halcrow.com

Halcrow

Advertisers Index

Class 66, 66615, approaches Barnetby on November 12 2008. Mike Wild

Company	Page
Acorp	97,107
AEG	97
Alstom Transport	23,98
Angel Trains	33,98
Arthur D Little	98
Atkins	97,171
ATOC	89,98
Basic Solutions	99
Best Impressions	120
Bombardier	99,153
CILT	100
Corus Cogifer	101
CSR Europe	38,101
David Brice	101
Delta Rail	37,101
Direct Link North	102
Dorman	102
East Lancashire Railway	107
Eldapoint	102
Eye for Solutions	120
First Class Partnerships	103
Halcrow	104,193
Halo Rail	104
Hima Sella	105
Hitachi	105
HSBC Rail	19,105
Institution of Railway Operators	11
Interfleet	105,179
Jacobs	106
Jarvis/Fastline	107
jobs-in-rail.com	108
John Headon	106
KME	106
Knorr Bremse Rail Systems	106,135
Lexicraft	106
Link Associates	108
Lloyds Register	108
LPA Group	108
Lucchini UK	49
Mack Brooks Exhibitions	71,108
MBM Trade	109
W&D McCulloch	109
MC Electronics	110
Mouchel	107,109
Moveright	37
Modern Railways	180
MTU	2
Nexans	111
Nelsons	169
Park Signalling	111
Passenger Focus	8
PSV Glass	112
Rail Alliance	87,113
Rail Manche Finance	113
Railphotolibrary.com	113
Rail Positive Relations	113
Rail Research UK	110
Ransome Engineering Services	114
Rehau	114
Resco Europe	114
RISC	114
RODL	113
RVEL	114
Safetell	115
SAFT Batteries	43
SCT Europe	138
Shere	179
Severn Valley Railway	110
Siemens Transportation	41,115
Sigma	116
Sperry	116,163
SSDM	195
Systra	116
TAS Publications	117
Transys Projects	117
Unipart Rail	118
Universal Improvement Company	118
Voith Turbo	15
Wabtec Rail	118,196
Waterman Civils	119
Westinghouse Platform Screen Doors	119
Westinghouse Rail Systems	119,163,169
York EMC Services	119

To be sure that your company features in the next edition of The Modern Railway Directory please contact Chris Shilling for an entry form on 01778 421550 or email chris@shillingmedia.co.uk